The Palgrave Handbook of Research Design in Business and Management

The Palgrave Handbook of Research Design in Business and Management

Edited by

Kenneth D. Strang

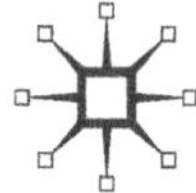

Softcover reprint of the hardcover 1st edition 2015 978-1-137-37992-4

First published in 2015 by
PALGRAVE MACMILLAN®
in the United States—a division of St. Martin's Press LLC,
175 Fifth Avenue, New York, NY 10010.

Where this book is distributed in the UK, Europe and the rest of the world, this is by Palgrave Macmillan, a division of Macmillan Publishers Limited, registered in England, company number 785998, of Houndmills, Basingstoke, Hampshire RG21 6XS.

Palgrave Macmillan is the global academic imprint of the above companies and has companies and representatives throughout the world.

ISBN 978-1-349-47906-1 ISBN 978-1-137-48495-6 (eBook)
DOI 10.1007/978-1-137-48495-6

Library of Congress Cataloging-in-Publication Data

The Palgrave handbook of research design in business and management / edited by Kenneth D. Strang.
pages cm
Summary: "Any research study needs a solid design before data collection or analysis can begin. This design ensures that any experimental evidence obtained by a researcher serves its purpose in making the researcher's argument more robust. Just as an architect prepares a blueprint before he approves a construction project, a researcher needs to prepare a plan their own before they start their research. The Palgrave Handbook of Research Design in Business and Management uses a new state-of-the-art research design typology model to guide researchers in creating the blueprints for their experiments. By focusing on theory and cutting-edge empirical best-practices, this handbook utilizes visual techniques to appease all learning styles. "— Provided by publisher.
Includes bibliographical references and index.

1. Business—Research. 2. Management—Research. I. Strang, Kenneth D.

HD30.4.P35 2015
650.072—dc23 2014037214

A catalogue record of the book is available from the British Library.

Design by Newgen Knowledge Works (P) Ltd., Chennai, India.

First edition: March 2015

10 9 8 7 6 5 4 3 2 1

Contents

Part II Positivist Applications

Part III Pragmatistic Applications

Part IV Constructivist Applications

Part V Final Generalizations and Descriptive Characteristics

Figures and Tables

Figures

Tables

Foreword: Vision and Reality

When Ken Strang initially contacted me about his interest in preparing a new book on research design I was quite excited, but also knew it would be a very challenging task. While scholars have been writing about research design for many years in an effort to clarify its principles and improve research outcomes, there is still a lot of work to be done in this area. An effective research design should enable researchers to address and obtain evidence that answers the research questions as unambiguously as possible. This is true whether the approach is qualitative or quantitative. Indeed, perhaps the most daunting challenge in compiling a book like this is the need to adequately cover in a nonbiased way the many considerations in deciding whether a qualitative or quantitative, or perhaps even a mixed, design is the most appropriate roadmap to obtain an answer to the research questions. I am pleased to say that the *Palgrave Handbook of Research Design in Business and Management* has achieved that goal.

This compilation of research design concepts and recommendations encompasses 28 chapters (most from different teams of authors). The topics are diverse, with extensive supporting references, and unique insights are shared that make this volume worthwhile reading. The ideas presented will benefit not only scholars and budding scholars in the social sciences, but also practitioners wishing to improve their approaches to gathering information for decision making. The contributing authors are building upon a foundation of many years of success in their research endeavors as well as learning from failures in their pursuit of new knowledge. The book includes topics about the philosophy of social sciences research design, conducting fieldwork, specific research tasks such as the design of surveys, and the analysis of statistical data. It also includes guidelines on how to pose questions and to develop scholarly research that facilitates both causal and descriptive inferences. Therefore, it is positioned in the middle ground between abstract and often ambiguous philosophical debates and "how to" guidelines for researchers. In sum, it addresses the underlying logic across a broad spectrum of issues currently facing scientific social sciences researchers.

This is a remarkable book, a bibliography, and a valuable resource rolled into one. It is a single, bright light shining across the often esoteric and obscure pages of research design compilations in the social sciences, which provides an overview of what we know at this point in time about the status of social sciences research. I wish I had had access to a book like this, not only in my masters and doctoral programs but also throughout my journey through the maze of conducting research and attempting to publish in peer-reviewed journals. It is not light reading, but it is straightforward and compelling for those who are looking for a single source of current social sciences research design knowledge.

Joseph F. Hair Jr.
Founder and Senior Scholar, DBA Program
Kennesaw State University
Director Emeritus
Louisiana State University
Entrepreneurship Institute and
Alvin C. Copeland Endowed Chair of Entrepreneurship

Preliminary Introductions

Preface: What's Unique for Practitioners

To build on and extend Dr. Hair's foreword, this preface will briefly identify the unique features of the handbook and then outline what may be expected to facilitate access by researchers.

I should first point out the interesting rationality underpinning these preliminary materials. Not surprisingly, during the management of this handbook project I received many inquiries about its structure. Publishers and editors across the sociocultural disciplines structure textbooks differently, according to practitioner norms. I rely primarily on the *American Psychological Association Style Guide* and secondarily on the *Chicago Manual of Style* to explain these terms.

The foreword is traditionally written by someone other than the author, usually by an expert in the field, a writer of a similar book, or a well-known practitioner. Dr. Hair fits all three of these descriptions. Strategically, the foreword helps the publisher design the marketing promotions. An opening statement by an eminent well-published scholar-practitioner subject-matter expert lends a high degree of credibility in pitching the handbook to bookstores, universities, government institutions, and research associations. In this sense, the foreword places a stamp of approval on the contributors' work.

A preface is generally written by the primary author(s), or in this case the editor, to introduce the structure and nature of the material. Interestingly, if you research the etymology of preface you may find it means an apology or explanation—I choose the latter definition here.

The preface is also of strategic value to the publisher for promoting the handbook, and also to marketing channel distributors for mass as well as direct selling. The latter, direct selling, in the research field, is often a pull force by consumers—researchers. Therefore, the preface assists these consumers in understanding the content and making selection decisions. In many cases, a preface explains briefly why the book was written and perhaps offers some acknowledgments. I admit I am marketing oriented so I wrote this preface to help the consumer (not to thank people—because I feel gratefulness will be in the consumption level of this product; so my role as editor and project manager is to make this a success in design and in reality).

Unique features

Dr. Hair let the cat out of the bag so to speak when he stated, "the topics are diverse, with extensive supporting references, and unique insights... it is a bibliography, and a valuable resource rolled into one."

All 26 handbook authors and contributors wrote their chapters using visual techniques—tables and diagrams—to appease all learning styles. The handbook contains 74 figures, 22 research design typology maps, and 57 tables along with several in-text illustrations and bulleted lists distributed over approximately 600 pages. A concise keyword index is included, and since each chapter features a customized reference section those citations are not duplicated in the index. An electronic version of the handbook is available from Palgrave that provides full-text search capability. Hence, this format is highly recommended for doctoral students and their committee members. The tables and diagrams were created to stand alone, and so was the text—they were not integrated. This was to allow those with textual learning styles to ignore the visual styles, and likewise, those preferring visual techniques could, to varying degrees, focus on the diagrams to obtain a better understanding of the concepts.

Additionally, all authors integrated examples into their chapters. Some authors also included a separate section illustrating an applied example from a recent study. As the editor, I wrote the introductory chapters (using a few example statements), and I also wrote two independent chapters with applied examples cited from empirical studies published in reputable journals.

Handbook structure

Figure 2.1 (in chapter 2) is a visual map of this handbook. The handbook is grouped into four core sections (beyond the preliminary and summary materials): Research Design Guidelines, Positivist Applications, Pragmatistic Applications, and Constructivist Pragmatistic Applications. This is the preliminary section and the handbook concludes with a forward-looking: Final Generalizations and Descriptive Characteristics. Occasionally the term *pragmativistic* is used in this handbook as an alternative spelling to *pragmatistic*.

The three core applied sections—Positivist, Pragmatistic, and Constructivist Applications—are groupings for the main research design ideologies as explained in the first core component: Research Design Guidelines section. A typology model is created in the first guidelines section and this becomes the structure for the handbook. Although I wrote the first few handbook chapters in the guidelines section, other authors supplemented and built on these with unique perspectives, including multicultural issues and best practices. I included a visual chapter map in the first guidelines section so as to act as a reader checklist of the research typology components discussed (ideology, strategy, method, technique). Since this first guidelines section was intended to be philosophically neutral I did not indicate the author's ideology in the chapter map.

Each chapter author within the three core applied sections chose their topic, research ideology, strategy, method, and technique. A visual map shows a thumbnail diagram to illustrate where each chapter is positioned on the research ideology continuum (positivism pragmatism, constructivism) and which of the typology layers are discussed (ideology, strategy, method, technique). Every author included at least one applied example. Most examples were from empirical studies published in reputable peer-reviewed journals or edited books. Some authors included examples from their own dissertations (published by Proquest Information and Learning or equivalent institution).

The concluding chapter was written by several handbook authors (including myself) because we were most aware of the limitations and gaps that needed to be closed in future research design work. This will serve as the rationale for other authors to write another handbook or for ourselves to extend this one. I included the bibliographies of the authors as my own way to share the qualitative descriptive characteristics of our sample, and to gain credibility for this handbook.

Chapter summaries

Chapter 1, "Why Practitioner-Scholars Need a Research Design Typology," opens the handbook, its scholarly rationale, and the protocol used to develop the content. It introduces the research design typology as a four-layer top-down process-oriented model. Each layer is introduced. Two diagrams are supplied: the first is a scaled-down version and the second the full model.

Chapter 2, "Articulating a Research Design Ideology," explains the first top layer of the research design typology model—ideology—using examples. Considerable discussion is offered on the underlying components: axiology, epistemology, ontology, and how these define the general ideologies on the continuum from positivism to constructivism.

Chapter 3, "Developing a Goal-Driven Research Strategy," defines and then discusses how research strategy must be aligned with ideology (and methods). In research strategy, the purpose (deductive to inductive), research questions, and hypotheses are formed based on the unit, level of analysis, and generalization goal.

Chapter 4, "Matching Research Method with Ideology and Strategy," reviews the more common formal research methods and how these are selected based on research strategy.

Chapter 5, "Selecting Research Techniques for a Method and Strategy," charts new territory by showing how techniques are selected based on method and research strategy (specifically the unit of analysis, with a between-group or within-group focus).

Chapter 6, "Design Issues in Cross-Cultural Research: Suggestions for Researchers," builds on the above five chapters, by exploring research design issues in cross-cultural situations. This chapter concentrates on how to integrate specific components of the typology, regardless of which ideology the researcher holds on the continuum (positivist, post-positivist, pragmatistic, interpretivist, or constructivist).

Chapter 7, "Establishing Rationale and Significance of Research," also builds on the above chapters by explaining how to establish the rationale and significance of a scholarly study.

Chapter 8, "Organizing and Conducting Scholarly Literature Reviews," extends the above seven chapters by discussing how to organize and conduct a scholarly literature review.

Chapter 9, "Interpreting Findings and Discussing Implications for all Ideologies," supplements the above nine chapters, by elaborating on how to end a study. This chapter explains how practitioner-scholars ought to interpret findings and discuss implications, in the research technique layer, regardless of which ideology the researcher holds (positivist, post-positivist, pragmatistic, interpretivist, or constructivist). This concludes the "guidelines" core section.

Chapter 10, "Implications of Experimental versus Quasi-Experimental Designs," begins the positivist section. In this chapter the author explains the rationale for using either the true experiment or a quasi-experiment method in a research design based on several of his studies. He clearly holds a positivist ideology. The unit of analysis in his research strategy was the treatment or preexisting condition for the nonequivalent groups. The level of analysis was group in these designs and the focus was between-groups rather than within-group. The heavy use of a priori factors from his literature review would suggest a deductive purpose with a generalization target to similar groups in business and management.

Chapter 11, "Structural Equation Modeling: Principles, Processes, and Practices," continues in the positivist core section. The authors clearly hold a positivist ideology. In this chapter they explain how to design study for a within-group factor comparison unit of analysis research strategy. This is an excellent discussion of the best practices for applying structural equation modeling (SEM). SEM is usually inductive in principle, although confirmatory factor analysis (the first phase of SEM) is deductive since it measures the reliability of an a priori construct using the sample data. They use applied examples drawn from their own studies.

In chapter 12 too, "Correlation to Logistic Regression Illustrated with a Victimization-Sexual Orientation Study," the authors hold a positivist ideology. They explain a common positivist technique: correlation. They go on to discuss regression and a specialty technique: logistic regression. Correlation and regression are generally deductive within-group unit of analysis strategies, since factors of interest are measured as predictors of the dependent variable. The factors and dependent variable of interest in the unit of analysis are established through a scholarly literature review. As with all true positivistic ideologies, hypotheses are developed to test the unit of analysis. A unique aspect of their example was the ex post facto use of logistic regression on existing data. Using correlation and regression is not considered mixed methods or multi-methods because researchers with a positivist ideology generally use correlation first to show evidence of the hypothesized relations between factors or between factors and the dependent variable, otherwise it may not be feasible to continue the analysis. Logistic regression has specific assumptions that must be met in order to be applied, and they discuss this.

Chapter 13, "Survey Method versus Longitudinal Surveys and Observation for Data Collection," is more of an interesting critical discussion rather than an applied example. In this chapter the author applies the positivist ideology using the critical analysis research method. This method applies the literature review and general analytic techniques (including pair wise *t*-tests and other parametric statistics). The unit of analysis in the research strategy was the "inconsistent" use of semantics across the years and journals for the survey, observation, and experiment methods versus the incorrect use of these terms for data collection techniques, using a deductive between-groups focus. The level of analysis was the social science literature. The generalization target was all practitioner-scholars intending to use these methods in their research design. Since the unit of analysis was qualitative and complex, very few positivistic techniques were applicable. However, the ideology remains positivist rather than pragmatistic due to evidence cited and due to the lack of interpretation on the data content done by the researcher.

In chapter 14, "Cross-Sectional Survey and Correspondence Analysis of Financial Manager Behavior," the author (myself) holds a post-positivist ideology although this is formally positioned in the positivistic section. The chapter explains how a cross-sectional survey technique was used with a questionnaire to collect data from human participants. Correspondence analysis was used for the data analysis. This is one of the better chapters to illustrate an applied research design typology from ideology through technique. The applied example was based on an article published in the *Journal of Asset Management*. This was a relevant article to illustrate how various qualitative and quantitative techniques were integrated in the general analytics method, and especially how to collect qualitative data representing self-reports of professional behavior (financial portfolio asset managers were sampled from New York Stock Exchange listed companies).

Chapter 15, "Control Variables: Problematic Issues and Best Practices," was written by two authors holding a positivist ideology. They discuss an important aspect of the unit of analysis strategy in a research design: how to account for or control factors that the researcher is aware of in the model but which is beyond the focus of a within-groups or between-groups comparison. In other words, control factors are confounding, moderating, or mediating variables. It is important to identify and control (or account for) these factors so that the researcher can generalize these to other populations, that is, by identifying the confounding factors that are present but are beyond the unit of analysis interest. When participants are samples for a between-group unit of analysis comparison, individual attributes in each participant often differ.

In chapter 16, "Monte Carlo Simulation Using Excel: Case Study in Financial Forecasting," the author holds a post-positivist ideology since data are constructed based on empirical foundations, such as previous samples or known distribution shapes. Simulations are generally based on known parameters or on probability distributions. Simulations are often used in operations research. The unit of analysis in the research strategy for simulations will often be a within-group focus, such as whether a simulation could produce a resulting model that is a good fit with an a priori distribution shape. Thus, a deductive approach is normally adopted, though there are also ways to design simulation research as inductive. In either case, the goal is usually to generalize the findings to an industry where the results would be applied within the ongoing operations.

Chapter 17, "Critical Analysis Using Four Case Studies across Industries," is the first chapter in the pragmatistic core section. In this chapter the author discusses how she applied the pragmatistic ideology using an integrated critical analysis with multiple case studies. This method applies the critical analysis literature review and interpretive critical thinking techniques (from the perspective of the researcher), as a multiple case study ($N = 4$). The cases were drawn from business, engineering, health-care, and higher education industries. The unit of analysis in the research strategy was the "creative use of critical thinking skills in critical analysis across four case studies," an inductive within-group focus (since there was an overall analysis and not a comparison between cases). The level of analysis was the organization. The generalization target was to all practitioner-scholars in academia and in organizations intending to use these methods.

In chapter 18, "Integrating Multiple Case Studies with a Merger and Acquisition Example," the author holds a post-positivist philosophy, which he nicely integrates into the pragmatistic research design ideology. He does a thorough job at explaining the single and multiple case study methods. More so, he explains how multiple cases are integrated in the latter method. This relates the ideology to the unit of analysis within-group versus between-group focus in the research design strategy. In the multiple case study method researchers ought to use the within-case (within-group) and cross-case analysis (between-groups) nomenclature as explained in the first chapter. When researchers follow the post-positivist ideology, a single case study may be conducted like an experiment, observation, or field study method, using deductive theory-driven research questions (or hypotheses). In contrast, when the researcher takes a pragmatic ideology, they are more likely to use multiple case studies, with either a deductive or inductive unit of analysis, with a goal to generalize the findings to other populations.

Chapter 19, "Iterative-Pragmatic Case Study Method and Comparisons with Other Case Study Method Ideologies," is an innovative chapter as it discusses theory and proposes a new model. In this chapter the author succinctly explains the differences in research ideology and strategy (deductive vs. inductive-driven) case study research methods. The post-positivist ideology form of case study method uses a deductive a priori theory-driven and strategy for the unit of analysis that has been popularized by thought leader Robert Yin (1994). The pragmatic ideology form of case study method (further right on the continuum, close to constructivist) uses an inductive-oriented, theory-grounded unit of analysis research strategy. This latter interpretivist form of case study follows the work of thought leaders Glaser and Strauss (2007) as well as Locke (1996). The author clearly has a pragmatistic ideology that he labels as towards the Straussian and Glaserian school of grounded theory. After reviewing and contrasting the post-positivist versus interpretative-pragmatic forms of case study approaches in the literature, he introduces a new research methodology (with relevant techniques) to implement his approach: interactive-pragmatic case study method.

Chapter 20, "Action Research Applied with Two Single Case Studies," is a well-written pragmatistic research ideology application. The authors expose many of the controversies in classifying the action research method, and then they apply it with two case studies (in Singapore and South Korea). As they cite from the literature, some writers position action research method under the pragmatistic ideology but, as advocated in chapter 1, as a pragmatic method falling under either the pragmatistic or constructivistic ideologies, according to the nature of how it is applied because it requires the researcher to involve the participants in the process of the problem and phenomena that they are trying to solve. There is agreement in the literature that action research uses an organizational problem as the unit of analysis to develop a solution for, which is a deductive-inductive theory-building purpose. It starts as deductive so as to review any a priori best practices that may exist, but usually existing procedures require modification (inductively developing a new process model). Otherwise why would an action research project be needed? The generalization is often organization specific although the implications apply to the industry or more broadly. As the authors of this chapter clarify, action research requires the researcher to participate with and within the target community. This is similar to the continuous improvement paradigm of total quality management in the post-positivist ideology where operations research methods are applied.

In chapter 21, "Transportation Queue Action Research at an Australian Titanium Dioxide Mining Refinery," I take on the pragmatistic ideology, just to illustrate that a research philosophy is not carved in stone. In this chapter I discuss an applied example of an empirical study featuring a combination of operations research (general analytics) with the action research method. An outline of the manuscript is provided to demonstrate the normative structure of a peer-reviewed article in business and management. Subsequent sections explain how each topic relates to the research design typology layers. Two example studies are used, but the majority of the chapter discusses the operations research article. That main article was taken from the *European Journal of Operational Research,* where queue theory was utilized to develop a model for a sand refinery plant in Western Australia. A contrast article was added from the *International Journal of Internet and Enterprise Management* to demonstrate that rationale of using grounded theory instead of action research or ethnography. The second study was designed using a far-right pragmatic ideology (close to constructivist), with a unit of analysis focused on discovering how a new product development team at a multinational company in Australia used creativity to develop cellular phone products.

Chapter 22, "Participant Observation as Ethnography or Ethnography as Participant Observation in Organizational Research," was written from a pragmatistic ideology. The author notes there is a strong tradition of observational research in most areas of the social sciences, especially in Anthropology and Sociology. However, in business and management research observation is often seen as a poor relative to questionnaire surveys and qualitative interviewing. This chapter discusses the use of observational techniques especially for less experienced researchers planning their first major investigation, exploring the difference between participant and nonparticipant approaches, different techniques of data collection, recording, and analysis. Rather than seeking to provide a full guide to conducting participant observation, an impractical task in a single chapter, this offering discusses some of the key issues facing researchers in Business and Management who choose to conduct this sort of research, exploring different approaches to participant observation and some of the ethical and practical challenges associated with the collection and analysis of observational data. The chapter draws on the author's experience of conducting participant observation in organizations with examples of both employee (Sandiford & Seymour, 2002; Seymour & Sandiford, 2013) and customer perspectives (Sandiford & Divers, 2011). It also draws from "classic" observational studies such as Mars and Nicod (1984) and more recent examples such as Watson and Watson (2012).

Chapter 23, "Constructivist Grounded Theory Applied to a Culture Study," begins the third constructivist core section with an excellent example of how to structure a dissertation study that could also be published in a peer-reviewed journal (it was actually). A constructivist grounded theory is an empirical form of qualitative inquiry grounded in individual experiences and interpretations of the world. Similar to phenomenological research, constructivist grounded theory also focuses on how individuals experience a phenomenon rather than why the individuals experience the phenomenon. The focus of this chapter is on how constructivist-grounded theories are constructed by researchers rather than why constructive grounded theory research is used. Hence, this chapter adopts a unique approach in integrating a constructivist grounded theory within a case study, describing the instances when a constructivist grounded theory is suitable. This chapter explores constructivist grounded theory in the context of knowledge creation and sharing using the Nvivo software for exploring the different phases in a constructivist grounded theory, including coding, working with nodes, demographic data, summarizing the data, identifying main and subthemes, querying the data, creating reports, and creating visual models as well as graphs. A case study of knowledge creation and sharing forms the basis for exploring the phenomenological research process. This chapter concludes with a description of the variants of phenomenological research.

Chapter 24, "Phenomenology Variations from Traditional Approaches to Eidetic and Hermeneutic Applications," discusses two method variations. As the author states, the unit of analysis when using a phenomenology method is usually the "lived experience" of a human participant and the level of analysis is individual (within-group). As she explains, eidetic phenomenology is interpretative, which means the research is at the left of a constructivist ideology, by comparison to hermeneutic phenomenology, which is fully constructivist.

In a follow up to the above, chapter 25, "Hermeneutic and Eidetic Phenomenology Applied to a Clinical Health-Care Study," the author goes through two examples from a constructivist research ideology perspective using two phenomenology method variations. She illustrates two positions on this continuum, an interpretive one with the eidetic phenomenology and the hermeneutic descriptive method. The unit of analysis in the research strategy for the first study was "the lived experience of telephone follow-up appointments for physicians and patients," and "the lived experience of health care managers" for the second, both having an inductive within-group focus. The level of analysis was individual and the generalization target was to scholars in the health-care discipline (as an inductive model).

Chapter 26, "Structure of a Dissertation for a Participatory Phenomenology Design," was written from the constructivist ideology but it could easily be done from the pragmatistic standpoint. The interesting aspect of this chapter is that the author integrates action research as a technique to become the participatory-phenomenology method. Action research is both a technique and a method that can be used in interpretative or constructivist ideologies. The author discusses how a researcher with a constructivist ideology would articulate and then apply the participatory-phenomenology method on a health-care nurse's experience as an inductive within-group unit of analysis with a group level of analysis (the nurses at a particular hospital).

Finally, in chapter 27, "Emancipatory Phenomenology Applied to a Child Sex Offender Study," the author demonstrates how to apply the emancipatory-phenomenology method with the Van Kaam technique using a constructivist research ideology. As discussed in chapter 4 (research method) the emancipatory research method has been titled advocacy, social advocacy, or participant advocacy, and it is similar to action research except that the focus is purely on less advantaged individuals (as a group), which could present additional challenges for doctoral students and organizational researchers because the participants will often be drawn from protected groups. The unit of analysis when using this phenomenology method is usually the "socially advocated problem" or the "extent of social advocacy for the problem." This is generalized to other people in the community (generally practitioners) although it could also be generalized to researchers so as to motivate them to continue to investigate the phenomenon. The level of analysis is usually group or community (within-group) although it could be an individual (such as exploring the perceptions of rape victims so as to improve social policies). With the emancipatory or social advocacy approach in a constructivist ideology, the researcher draws the meaning of the data or phenomena from the community.

This concludes the three core applied sections of the handbook. As noted earlier, the remaining chapter proposes future research topics based on limitations uncovered during the writing of this handbook. This is followed by the index. Three of the contributing authors joined me to write this final chapter. We took the dry-humor approach to illustrate why there is not a single right solution for a research design and formal method-technique match. We anticipate readers will understand the theoretical and practical message underlying the concluding chapter. We also hope readers will give us the requested feedback so we may improve the next handbook.

I would like to thank the 26 authors for their contributions and peer-reviews as well as the 14 subject matter experts for their independent peer reviews and advice. Special thanks to my wife Ellen for helping me with this large project. My sincere thank you goes out to case study methods global icon Dr. Robert K. Yin (COSMOS Corporation) and to Dr. Debra Dosemagen (Mount Mary College) for their insightful constructive feedback and for the support they extended to my handbook idea. A warm thank you to foreword editor Professor Joe E. Hair Jr. (Kennesaw State University) who remains a world-wide authority on multivariate design and methods. Thank you Palgrave Macmillan staff for believing in my ideas for producing this handbook. Thank you Newgen Knowledge Works staff for typesetting and helping to proof this.

In concluding this preface, I request the readers to please complete this brief online survey to allow us to improve future handbooks for you.

http://unitydiversity.multinations.org/handbooksurvey.php

If you provide your name and email address we will thank you in future editions and invite you to participate in upcoming projects.

KENNETH D. STRANG, Professor,
State University of New York,
Plattsburgh at Queensbury

Contributor Biographies

Torgeir Aleti is a lecturer in Marketing at Victoria University in Melbourne, Australia. Torgeir teaches marketing subjects to postgraduate and undergraduate students and supervises postgraduate research students. His research interests are consumer socialization with a specific focus on how consumers learn new behavior and pass it on to others.

Rodney Alexander (Rod) is a project officer for the Department of Defense (DOD) Joint Interoperability Test Command (JITC). The department's mission is to verify that the DOD computer and communications equipment are interoperable throughout the four US Armed Forces (Army, Navy, Air Force, and Marines).

He has been a DOD civilian employee for the last 12 years, completing the vast majority of his service with the army in Germany. He recently received his masters degree in Information Systems/Management from the University of Phoenix. He received his bachelor's degree 20 years ago in Criminal Justice from the University of Washington in Seattle. After completing his degree, he became an army officer in the military police corps, where he served for nine years.

His hobbies include listening to jazz music and taking long, quiet walks. He is single (never married). He currently lives in Tucson, Arizona, and works at the army base Ft Huachuca, AZ. He aims to significantly improve his knowledge of information system organizations and increase his analytical skills by taking up a PhD program.

Mark Beaulieu is an assistant professor at the State University of New York College at Plattsburgh. He is particularly interested in issues surrounding segregation, concentrated disadvantage, and violent crime. He is currently continuing his work on the effects of long-term segregation on crime.

Linda Brennan is a professor in the School of Media and Communication at RMIT in Melbourne. Her research interests are social and government marketing and, especially, the influence of marketing communications and advertising on behavior.

Dae Seok Chai is a doctoral candidate at Texas A&M University. Before joining the doctoral program, Dae Seok was involved in designing and conducting leadership and cultural training programs for employees in a large Korean conglomerate; and as a doctoral candidate, he had also worked with a professor to design and develop a diversity training program for other Korean companies. Dae Seok's research interests include research methods, culture, diversity, learning organization, and expatriate training and management.

Creaig A. Dunton is an assistant professor of Criminal Justice at the State University of New York College at Plattsburgh. He received his PhD in Criminal Justice at SUNY Albany. His research focuses mostly on sex offending and social deviance.

Richard Fuller is an associate professor and currently serves as the head of the Education Department in the School of Education and Social Sciences at Robert Morris University. Dr. Fuller teaches graduate and doctoral courses in instructional leadership, instructional design for traditional and distance education, and educational technology. He has over 35 years of experience in education and business as administrator, instructor, and trainer. He received his doctorate of Education from the Penn State University. His research interests center on leadership and motivation, creating interaction in distance education pedagogies, and how the use of technology can enhance learning.

John F. Gaski is an associate professor of Marketing at the University of Notre Dame. His degrees include a BBA and MBA from Notre Dame, and an MS and PhD from the University of Wisconsin at Madison. He is the author of over 135 published articles, papers, and monographs that have appeared in the *Journal of Marketing, Journal of Marketing Research, Journal of Consumer Research, Journal of the Academy of Marketing Science, Journal of Business Ethics, Journal of Public Policy & Marketing, Journal of Consumer Policy, European Journal of Marketing, International Journal of Market Research, Review of Marketing, Research in Marketing, Industrial Marketing Management, International Journal of Physical Distribution & Logistics Management, Advances in Distribution Channel Research, Advances in Financial Economics, Business Horizons, Psychology & Marketing, International Journal of Management, Business and Society Review, Social Behavior and Personality, Sociological Spectrum, Society, Psychological Reports, Perceptual and Motor Skills, Sporting Traditions, The Journal of European Economic History, The Geographical Bulletin,* the *Journal of Educational Psychology,* the *International Journal on World Peace, Defence Studies, Indiana Policy Review,* and the *Journal of Neuroscience, Psychology, and Economics,* as well as proceedings of leading professional associations. His primary research interests are related to power in distribution channels and the societal impact of marketing activity. The courses he taught include Marketing Management, Marketing Strategy and Planning, Marketing Research, and Distribution Management, at both the graduate and undergraduate levels.

Professor Gaski serves or has served on the editorial review boards of the *Journal of Marketing, Journal of the Academy of Marketing Science, Journal of Marketing Channels,* and *Journal of Education for Business.* He is a member of the

Beta Gamma Sigma, Mu Kappa Tau, and Alpha Mu Alpha honorary societies, and was selected as one of the "100 Best Researchers in Marketing" by a peer-review study (published in *Marketing Educator,* 1997). Dr. Gaski's recent books include *Frugal Cool: How to Get Rich—Without Making Very Much Money* (2009) and *The Language of Branding* (2010). He has had his commentary published in the *Chicago Tribune, Chicago Sun-Times, Indianapolis Star, The Washington Times, Investor's Business Daily, The Center Magazine, The American, Human Events,* and *Contemporary Review,* and he is recognized in various Who's Who lists.

Jeremy W. Grabbe is an assistant professor of psychology at the State University of New York Plattsburgh. His research focuses on vision and attention as well as on improving cognition among the aging population. He is the author of many scientific papers and recently became the father of triplets. He earned his PhD in Applied Cognitive Aging Psychology at the University of Akron.

Linnaya Graf received her PhD in Public Health from Walden University in 2011. She has worked across the social science, human service, and public health arenas for the last 15 years, serving at both individual and community health levels. Professionally, she is a faculty member and instructional mentor with the MPH program at Liberty University Online, located out of Lynchburg, Virginia. She also teaches doctoral courses in research and evaluation for the University of Phoenix, School of Advanced Studies, as well as undergraduate courses in Social Sciences and Natural Sciences for the University of Phoenix, Harrisburg Campus. Outside of her passion for teaching, Dr. Graf is the owner of a small research company, PrePEAR, LLC. PrePEAR was founded in 2009 and became an LLC in 2012. PrePEAR, LLC focuses on providing research support to community organizations, schools, and graduate students in the form of support, trainings, design, implementation, and consultation. PrePEAR, LCC focuses on addressing challenges by bringing together practice, evaluation, academics, and research to address complex problems in the area of social sciences and public health.

Her personal research interests are related to vulnerable populations, violence prevention, community action-research, resilience, built communities, best practices in front-line prevention programming, and application of research to practice. In 2013, she founded the SMALL fund, which is a small nonprofit providing emergency aid for individuals and families experiencing unexpected tragedies. Deeply vested in community activism, Dr. Graf has been a Girl Scout leader since 2002 and is a member of Rotary International since 2010, where she has held a variety of leadership positions, including president of her West York Club.

During her doctoral studies she lived abroad in Germany. But, she currently resides in a rural area of York, PA, with her husband, four children, and small homestead. She continues to enjoy international travel as part of her work and enjoys camping with her family, training her animals, hiking, reading, traveling, theater, finding a good movie, and photography.

Judith Hahn resides in Cudahy, Wisconsin, with her husband, Bill, who is a long-haul truck driver, and other family members. Judith is adamant that her name is Jude, which she jokingly claims was "named after the Beatles song Hey Jude." Her daughter is an accountant, while Jude is a registered nurse working in the humanitarian field.

Jude is currently working as a liaison social worker for the State Social Service Department. Her current portfolio is focused on helping the newly immigrated Congolese population from the Rwanda refugee camp to relocate to Milwaukee, WI. Prior to this she worked for a large medical center for five years, until she received her BSN. In 1998, she got an interesting opportunity to do volunteer work in Prague-Repy, Czechoslovakia, at the Hein Des HL. Karl Barromaus Hospice. This was a convent that had been confiscated by the Nazi regime in 1970, and after the fall of the "Iron curtain," the German government returned the convent to the nuns in 1996.

Jude is completing her doctorate, purely for self-actualization. She taught psychology in one of the technical colleges in her area. She revealed that one of her motivations for contributing to this handbook was because she felt that nursing students needed to improve their ability to communicate with patients, especially to develop a trusting relationship with inpatients in a minimal amount of time. She felt that nursing students needed to enhance their education to learn the theories and practices for this, which would come through conducting better scholarly research. In fact, this motivation and her experience were instrumental in developing her own doctoral dissertation.

Joseph F. Hair is the founder and a senior scholar of the DBA Program in the Coles College of Business at Kennesaw State University, Georgia. He previously held the Copeland Endowed Chair of Entrepreneurship and was director, Entrepreneurship Institute, Ourso College of Business Administration, Louisiana State University. He was a United States Steel Foundation Fellow at the University of Florida, Gainesville, where he earned his PhD in Marketing in 1971. He has authored over 50 books, including *Marketing* (2013); *Marketing Essentials* (2010); *Essentials of Business Research Methods* (2011); *Research Methods for Business* (2007); *Marketing Research* (2009); *Essentials of Marketing Research* (2013); *A Primer on Partial Least Squares Structural Equations Modeling* (2014), and *Sales Management: Building Partnerships* (2009). He also has published numerous articles in scholarly journals such as the *Journal of Marketing Research, Journal of Academy of Marketing Science, Journal of Business/Chicago, Organizational Research Methods, Journal of Advertising Research, Journal of Business Research, Journal of Long Range Planning, Management Decision, Journal of Marketing Theory and Practice,*

European Business Review, International Marketing Review, Journal of Personal Selling and Sales Management, Industrial Marketing Management, Journal of Experimental Education, Business Horizons, Journal of Retailing, Marketing Education Review, Journal of Marketing Education, Multivariate Behavioral Research, and others. His research has been cited more than 144,000 times (Google Scholar citations).

He is a Distinguished Fellow of the Academy of Marketing Sciences, the Society for Marketing Advances, and Southwestern Marketing Association. He also has served as president of the Academy of Marketing Sciences, the Society for Marketing Advances, the Southern Marketing Association, the Association for Healthcare Research, the Southwestern Marketing Association, and the American Institute for Decision Sciences, Southeast Section, and has been program chairperson and proceedings editor for several scholarly associations. He currently serves as chair of the Board of Governors of the Academy of Marketing Sciences and the Society for Marketing Advances.

He was recognized as the 2011 Academy of Marketing Science Marketing Educator of the year, the 2009 Academy of Marketing Science/Harold Berkman Lifetime Service Award recipient, the KSU Coles College Foundation Distinguished Professor in 2009, the Aronoff Distinguished Professor in 2008, and the Innovative Marketer of the Year in 2007 by the Marketing Management Association. In 2004 he received the Academy of Marketing Science Outstanding Marketing Teaching Excellence Award. The Louisiana State University Entrepreneurship Institute under his leadership was recognized nationally by *Entrepreneurship Magazine* in 2003 as one of the top 12 programs in the United States, and also was ranked number 3 in the United States in 2004 and 2005 by *Forbes Magazine/Princeton Review.* He has been retained as a consultant for numerous companies in a wide variety of industries, as well as by the US Department of Agriculture and the US Department of Interior. He also has provided expert testimony, most often in the areas of marketing, entrepreneurship, and economic analysis, and has planned/presented executive development and management training programs. Finally, he is often invited to give keynote presentations on research techniques, data analysis, and marketing issues for organizations in Europe, Australia, Asia, and other locations outside the United States.

Seifedine Kadry is a published author of 12 books, in prestigious publishers like IGI, Elsevier, Springer, and Bentham. Some of them are related to mathematical sciences, system simulation, system prognostics, and reliability engineering. He has also published more than 90 articles and organized numerous conference tracks and workshops. Professor Kadry is the editor-in-chief of *ARPN Journal of Systems and Software* and *Maxwell Journal of Mathematics and Statistics.* He is an IEEE senior member. He is an associate professor and department head at the American University of the Middle East, Kuwait. His specialized areas of research include computing, simulation, software engineering, and systems reliability and safety.

Eun Sook Kim is an assistant professor of educational and psychological studies at the University of South Florida. She has a broad interest in research methodology and psychometrics. Her focal research interests include measurement invariance testing for multilevel and longitudinal data using structural equation modeling. She has conducted simulation studies to investigate the behaviors of widely used statistical methods under various research settings and has been involved in research groups studying propensity score analysis, multilevel SEM, Bayesian estimation, and ANOVA. Her recent articles appear in *Structural Equation Modeling, Multivariate Behavioral Research*, and *Educational and Psychological Measurement*, among others.

Sewon Kim is an assistant professor of organization behavior and human resources at the State University of New York (SUNY) Empire State. He received his PhD from Texas A&M University. His research and teaching interests include research methods, organization behavior and change, strategic human capital, and global management and leadership development. He is a former recipient of dissertation awards from the American Society for Training and Development (ASTD), Academy of Human Resource Development (AHRD), and Emerald/European Foundation for Management Development (EFMD).

Angeline Lim is a senior research consultant at Organisation Solutions and is based in Singapore. Angeline manages research initiatives and provides research and consulting support to OS clients. Angeline has nine years of experience conducting basic and applied research in the areas of HR and organizational behavior. Educated mainly in Singapore, Angeline holds a PhD in Management and Organisation and a Bachelor of Business Administration (with Honors) from the National University of Singapore, where she was awarded the Apollo Enterprises Gold Medal. In addition to her role at Organisation Solutions, she also serves as an associate tutor at the Department of Psychology in UNISIM. Angeline's research interests include diversity, culture, interpersonal relationships, growth, and leadership.

Jillian McCarthy is a senior lecturer within the Business School at the University of Manchester. Based in the Health Management Group, Jill's expertise lies in health management and leadership, and related topics. An experienced academic, Jill has been involved in teaching and researching into management and leadership for over 20 years.

A registered nurse by profession, Jill previously worked in management within health-care settings and is now committed to enhancing patient experience through the leadership education of healthcare professionals. Her research and teaching interests lie in management, leadership, and patient experience;

ethical issues in leadership; and technology-enhanced learning in education, and she has presented and published internationally in these areas.

Dang Nguyen is an emerging scholar in the Centre for Commerce and Management at RMIT University, Vietnam. She conducts research into social marketing with an interest in social change communications and public policy communications.

Lukas Parker is an assistant professor in the Centre for Commerce and Management at RMIT University, Vietnam. He lectures in marketing and advertising to undergraduate students and supervises postgraduate research students. His research interests are in social marketing and marketing communications.

Mary Ann Rafoth, PhD is dean of the School of Education and Social Sciences at Robert Morris University. A frequent consultant to schools and agencies, her research interests involve strengthening independent learning skills in students, alternatives to retaining students, school readiness issues, and program and student learning outcomes evaluation. Dr. Rafoth has authored several chapters in the frequently referenced *Best Practices in School Psychology and Children's Needs* volumes published by the National Association of School Psychologists. She is the first author of *Strategies for Learning and Remembering: Study Skills across the Curriculum* (1993) and the author of *Inspiring Independent Learning: Successful Classroom Strategies* (1999). Dr. Rafoth has published over 30 publications and made over 50 presentations at state, national, and international conferences.

Peter John Sandiford is an organizational ethnographer with a particular interest in the sociology of work. He worked in the hospitality iIndustry prior to his academic career and much of his research reflects this, often focusing on employment in and the hospitality offered by public houses (pubs). His specific research interests include emotion at work, occupational community, third place and hospitality, the role of intoxicants in society, learning in the workplace and internship, and volunteering.

He researched for an MPhil (Tourism Planning) at the Hong Kong Polytechnic University obtained his PhD (Emotion in Organisations) from Oxford Brookes University.

He has researched and lectured in Hong Kong, China, the United Kingdom, Australia, and Singapore. His has lectured in a number of subject areas including Organizational Behavior, International/Cross-Cultural Management, Employee Resourcing, Management for Marketing/Public Relations, Personal and Professional Development and Research Methods. He is closely involved with research training at postgraduate level and his program management roles (past and present) include: Honours and Master of Business Research coordinator (University of Adelaide), Master of Research coordinator and

Masters Dissertation coordinator for HRM and OB (Manchester Metropolitan University), and Faculty Masters Dissertation coordinator (Leeds Metropolitan University).

Krittaya Sangboon is a faculty member in the accounting department at Mahasarakham Business School, Mahasarakham University, Thailand. Her research interest is in the area of accounting. Krittaya has authored three accounting textbooks and seven other publications including articles in journals, such as *Journal of International Finance and Economics*. Her research has also been presented at academic conferences, such as the conferences for the International Academy of Business and Economics and International Academy of Management and Business. Krittaya earned her graduate degrees from Illinois State University and Thammasat University.

Leon Schjoedt is a member of the management faculty in the Judd Leighton School of Business and Economics, Indiana University South Bend, Indiana. His research interest is in the area of entrepreneurship. Leon has authored more than 30 journal articles and book chapters, including journals such as *Entrepreneurship Theory and Practice*. His research has been presented at more than 45 academic conferences, including conferences such as the Annual Meeting for the Academy of Management and Babson College Entrepreneurship Research Conference. Leon serves on the editorial review boards of *Entrepreneurship Theory and Practice, Journal of Business Venturing, Journal of Small Business Management*, and *Journal of Management Studies*. He earned his graduates degrees from University of Wisconsin-Oshkosh and University of Colorado-Boulder.

Lars Schweizer holds the UBS-Endowed Chair of Strategic Management at Goethe University Frankfurt since December 2007. Prior to that he was an associate professor (tenured) for Organizational Behavior and Management at the Grenoble Graduate School of Business in France. In addition, he was dean of Goethe Business School (GBS) and the academic director of the Goethe Full-Time MBA Program. His research interests are strategic management, mergers and acquisitions, and entrepreneurship. He holds a doctoral degree and the habilitation from the University of Bamberg, Germany. His publications appeared among others in journals such as the *Academy of Management Journal*, the *Journal of Management, Industrial and Corporate Change, the Journal of Engineering and Technology Management*, and the *Scandinavian Journal of Management*. Prof. Schweizer has been honored several times for his scientific contribution and his teaching.

George Semich is the director of the Instructional Management/Leadership doctoral program at Robert Morris University and a professor of education in the School of Education and Social Sciences. He was the former chair of the Communications Department at RMU and the former chair of the Secondary

Education and Graduate Studies Department. George also serves as editor for two publishers and publishes primarily in the area of impact of technology on learning, curriculum, learning theory, leadership theory, and qualitative methods. In his spare time, he enjoys traveling, reading, and writing.

Harm-Jan Steenhuis is a professor of Management at Eastern Washington University. He received his MSc in Industrial Engineering and Management and his PhD in International Technology Transfer from the University of Twente, the Netherlands. Most of his research is based on the case study method. His main research areas include international operations and technology transfer in combination with technological and economic development, university-industry technology transfer in combination with innovation, and instructor-student knowledge transfer in combination with methods. He also has a special interest in aerospace.

Kenneth D. Strang is a senior scholar and professor at the State University of New York, Plattsburgh at Queensbury campus, New York. Dr. Strang has over 31 years of combined industry with research experience, several degrees and certifications along with numerous published studies. He is the coordinator and a professor in the Bachelor of Science Business Administration program at his campus. He is also a doctoral supervisor for students at several universities in the United States, Australia, and other countries. He has over 150 publications (since 1981) across several disciplines and industries. Prior to becoming a professor, he worked for Blue Cross, IBM, and then as a project management consultant at other large corporations around the world. Dr. Strang created organizations and he still serves as a CEO/president or a board of director executive on a few. He has won corporate grants and managed large teams of people in projects with million-dollar budgets. In 2011, he founded and now serves as editor-in-chief of the *International Journal of Risk and Contingency Management (IJRCM)*. *IJRCM* is indexed by numerous reputable organizations and it is listed by the highly respected Cabell's institution (a benchmark used for accredited school of business performance evaluations and promotions). He is also an area editor/associate editor for six other respected global journals. Dr. Strang continues to be involved in local communities, volunteering whenever possible to help people.

Edward Sturman is an associate professor of psychology at SUNY Plattsburgh. He has been the co-coordinator of the psychology program at the Queensbury branch campus since 2007, where he has regularly taught courses related to research methods and statistics, including experimental design, psychological statistics, and psychological assessment. He has authored a number of studies relating to statistics and assessment in peer-reviewed journals and is the coauthor of a textbook, *Psychological Testing and Assessment*, 8th edition, with

Dr. Ron Cohen and Dr. Mark Swerdlik. He received his doctorate in social-personality psychology from York University in Toronto.

Narasimha Rao Vajjhala is an assistant professor at the University of New York Tirana and has a doctorate in management from the University of Phoenix, Arizona. He has an MCA from Osmania University in India as well as an MBA from IUKB, Switzerland. He is a senior member of the Association of Computer Machinery (ACM). His research interests include knowledge management, knowledge sharing in transition economies, cross-cultural management, e-commerce, and e-business. He holds several professional certifications including Certified E-Commerce Consultant, Microsoft Office Specialist (MOS), Oracle Certified SQL Expert, Oracle Certified Associate (OCA), Microsoft Certified Trainer (MCT), Sun Certified Java Professional (SJCP), Microsoft Certified Solution Developer (MCSD), Microsoft Certified Application Developer (MCAD), and Cisco Certified Network Associate (CCNA).

Part I

Research Design Guidelines

1
Why Practitioner-Scholars Need a Research Design Typology

Kenneth D. Strang

Introduction

The *Palgrave Handbook of Research Design in Business and Management* is a scholarly peer-reviewed, edited book. The book's scope was designed-in through team selection and review processes. Experienced practitioner-scholars and subject-matter experts were selected from accredited universities and respected organizations around the world. Edited and peer-reviewed involved at least two scholars reviewing each chapter through a double-blind methodology, plus the editor also reviewing each chapter. All chapters were double-blind peer reviewed including those written by the editor. The assistant editor, associate editor, and the staff at Palgrave Macmillan as well as Newgen Knowledge Works also reviewed the content for grammar, format and writing-style suitability.

Purpose and conceptual model

The main objective for writing this handbook was to bring together experienced practitioner-scholars from across the business and management disciplines to develop a research design guidebook featuring visual models with applied examples. A secondary goal was to provide a simple scientific research design paradigm for practitioners. A model was developed as a four-layer top-down typology rather than as a framework or methodology. A conceptual model of the research design typology is illustrated in figure 1.1 and it is explained in subsequent chapters.

The typology in figure 1.1 is a top-down process-oriented model. As a process-oriented typology, the workflow can be in any direction, but it normally starts at the top with ideology. All layers should be considered, but there is not an exact correlation between topics down the layers (otherwise I could have used a table matrix). Some layers may require multiple processes in the same study, such as with techniques, while an ideology is generally a specific philosophical position on the continuum for the duration of the research project. In addition

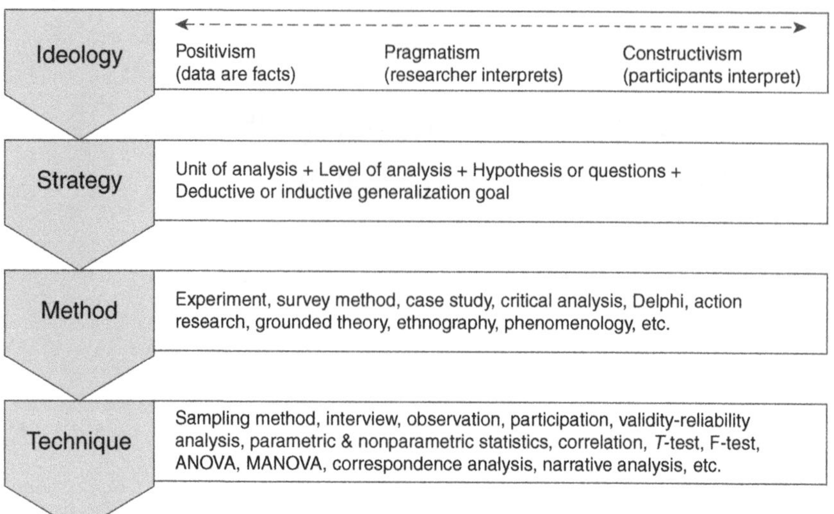

Figure 1.1 Research design typology conceptual overview.

to being a process-oriented workflow, the typology is a construct for communicating between researchers and stakeholders. This model has been tested in practice by a sample of doctoral students and myself.

Research ideology

All research is driven by the researchers' ideology in combination with the strategy. The ideology is a continuum with evidence driven from the left through pragmatism and interpretivism in the middle toward social-constructivism on the right. Not all ideologies are listed (e.g., missing are post-positivism, interpretivism, social constructivism, and so on).

The continuum in figure 1.1 is not linked directly in a left versus right section with any of the other levels. This is what makes it unique. For example, a researcher using the case study method could have a post-positivistic ideology, with hypotheses, and use nonparametric statistical techniques. At the other extreme, a researcher with a constructivist ideology may use a multiple case study method, along with a survey technique to collect qualitative data, and then use thematic text analysis to summarize, compare, and contrast the results in tables.

Research strategy

Research strategy is the focal point driven by the researcher's ideology. Strategy refers to the unit and level of analysis, along with research questions or hypotheses, and a deductive or inductive goal. According to this typology, a study cannot proceed until the researcher adapts an ideology, and then develops a strategy (which includes the goal). The reader should note that this model applies to business and management disciplines, so philosophy and terminology may differ from that of other fields (e.g., education, engineering, history, psychology, sociology, etc.).

Research method

Research methods are formal methodologies. These are the topics with a large number of textbooks published. Common methodologies include the survey method, experiment, grounded theory, multiple case study, ethnography, phenomenology, action research, and others. There is no mandatory link between strategy, method, and technique, but there are customary combinations. For example, a positivistic researcher with a hypothesis will likely chose a well-known method, perhaps an experiment, along with parametric statistical techniques. When researchers combine several methods, especially when collecting different data types at interrupted points in time, they may describe them as using mixed methods.

Research technique

Research techniques are the scientific procedures and tools used to carry out the above, such as sampling, data collection, interviewing, correlation, correspondence analysis, regression, and so on. Research ideologies and strategies are linked (e.g., a positivistic researcher often formulates specific quantitative hypotheses to test, while an interpretative researcher will likely start with research questions or a theoretical lens). Methods are commonly associated with techniques, such as interviews as data collection for case studies, grounded theory, and others.

The remainder of this introductory chapter develops the scholarly rationale for the handbook, that is, the rest of this chapter demonstrates the gap in the existing body of knowledge that warrants this new contribution to the community of practice. Readers interested in exploring the details of the research design typology may skip to the next chapter.

Practitioner problems and rationale

The problem was clear. "This field has many different individuals with different perspectives who are on their own looms creating the fabric of qualitative research" (Creswell, 2012, p. 42). Credible experts have called for better quantitative and qualitative research method documentation across the disciplines. Business and management practitioner-scholars recognized the need for a clearer research design paradigm in this field (Hallebone & Priest, 2009; Wahyuni, 2012).

Researchers and students need holistic research design guidelines with applied examples that accommodate multiple learning styles and sociocultural diversity (Strang, 2008b, 2009d, 2010e, 2012k, 2009g). Research practitioners need a single comprehensive resource of alternative approaches for designing research, formulating strategies, as well as selecting appropriate method and technique combination designs (Goodwin & Strang, 2012).

Stakeholders in universities, organizations, and communities of practice need a contemporary high-quality, peer-reviewed, cross-disciplinary, and multicultural edited research design book to serve as a foundation to help faculty, staff, and clients navigate the complex paradigms of applied research (Creswell, 2012; Gill, Johnson & Clark, 2010; Gomes, Moshkovich & Torres, 2010; Mero-Jaffe, 2011; Silverman, 2010; Vogt, Gardner & Haeffele, 2012; Yin, 2009).

In fact, industry practitioners were in need of better research design guidance. I concluded this from many of my own studies on project managers and business analysts (Goodwin & Strang, 2012; Strang, 2003, 2005a, 2006, 2008a, 2009a, 2010a, 2010b, 2010h, 2011a, 2011b, 2011f, 2011g, 2011h, 2012a, 2012b, 2012c, 2012d, 2012e, 2012f, 2012g, 2012h, 2012i, 2013; Strang & Chan, 2010; Strang & Symonds, 2012).

Research methodology thought leaders acknowledge that current textbooks provide overwhelming, sometimes conflicting information due to the numerous approaches and terminology differences across disciplines (Babbie, 2007; Charmaz, 2006; Creswell, 2009, 2012; Creswell & Tashakkori, 2007; Ellingson, 2009; Freedman, 2006; Gill et al., 2010; Greene, 2008; Guba & Lincoln, 2005; Hammersley, 2006; Kline, 2004; Maxwell, 2005; Neuman, 2000; Onwuegbuzie & Leech, 2005; Richards, 2009; Yin, 2009). A modern cross-disciplinary multiple-method research design handbook was needed for the business and management disciplines, which needed to focus on design rather than on methods or techniques.

Additionally, being a supervisor of business and management doctoral students, I wanted to help them navigate the complex landscape of research design. The premise was that a fatally flawed study with an invalid or obscure design has very little chance of being published even if it is well written. On the other hand, a well-designed study that reveals innovative practices or new models but with a few grammatical errors can be easily revised to make a significant contribution to the global community of practice. Ironically, as a triangulation of this hypothesis, several of our authors read portions of this handbook and specifically commented that doctoral students, researchers and industry practitioners need a better research design guidebook.

There was a demonstrated scientific need for better research guidelines from the practitioner community of practice. I published a recursive regression technique manuscript several years ago in the peer-reviewed *Journal of*

Practical Assessment, Research and Evaluation [PARE] (Strang, 2009f). The article critically discussed quantitative research methods and techniques with an applied example of recursive regression and cluster analysis applied to a multicultural education study (Strang, 2008b). As I understood it, that article was reprinted as a supplement in a higher education textbook by Pearson due to practitioner interest (Strang, 2010j). The PARE Internet site tracks manuscript access, so when I checked the statistics I was curious why this particular article received so much attention (more than 14,000 downloads at the time of writing). Another peer manuscript in the same issue (Randolph, 2009) garnered 13 times more interest (over 180,000 downloads at the time of writing). I believe his article was popular due to the topic of providing guidance for doctorate students to write a dissertation proposal. In fact Randolph's manuscript was the most popular in the entire journal at least at the time of writing (which started publishing ca. 1996).

I discovered that English-second-language doctorate students preferred diagrammatic frameworks with action research examples due to their predominately visual and sequential learning styles (Strang, 2009c, 2009e). As supplemental evidence that international university students needed visual and sequenced pedagogy, I had completed numerous learning-style-related studies with diverse multicultural samples in Australia, New Zealand, Europe, and North America (Strang, 2005b, 2007, 2008b, 2009b, 2010c, 2010d, 2010e, 2010f, 2010g, 2011c, 2011d, 2011e, 2012j, 2012k, 2010i).

Approach to develop the research design typology

I conducted a pilot study to prepare for this handbook. I interviewed 11 doctoral students across several disciplines, namely: management, education, health care/nursing, and business. I used a simple open-ended question to have them describe how research method guidelines could be improved. I then developed a draft framework for organizing risk management research studies. I reviewed this framework with a dozen participants at the International Disaster Conference after which I published it as a pilot study in a peer-reviewed journal (Strang, 2013a, 2013b) to raise an awareness of the need and to motivate other practitioners to support this cause.

I then collected perceptional feedback data from 33 organizational and academic researchers on their research design needs using the Delphi technique through email. I asked questions to help refine the research design framework, and I included a draft of this handbook chapter. I used the feedback, observations of doctoral students, along with an extensive literature review to develop the typology as a paradigm, which informed the structure and content of this handbook.

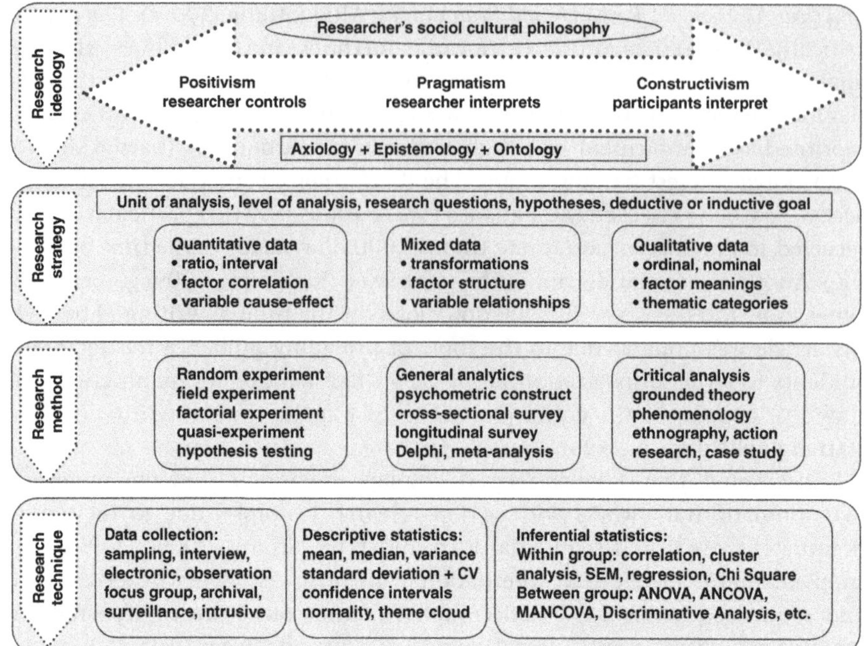

Figure 1.2 Research design typology full model.

The research design used for developing this typology was grounded in pragmatic ideology. The strategy consisted of research questions focused on the problem explained above, with a process improvement unit of analysis and a community of practice level of analysis. I used mixed methods (Delphi with critical analysis). My techniques included thematic analysis, literature reviews, and operations research general analytics (workflow process analysis).

The full research design typology model developed through the above processes is shown below in figure 1.2—this model will be fully explained in the following chapters.

Significance and generalizations

This handbook makes a significant contribution to the qualitative and quantitative research design body of knowledge because it addresses the problems outlined earlier. The significance is that it attempts to close the gap in current literature by offering a simplistic research design typology, accompanied by applied visual-oriented examples, written by subject-matter experts and practitioner-scholars from across the business and management disciplines.

One of our authors, Dr. Peter Sandiford, made an excellent point that exemplifies the significance of this handbook. "I do think the difference between this text and other broad based and often simplistic research methods textbooks is that they [latter] are authored by a smaller number of academics" (Sandiford, 2014, June 2, personal communication). This handbook shares the collective work of over 40 practitioner-scholars or subject-matter experts, from their respective discipline, located in different regions or countries (socialized in distinct cultures).

We have provided high-quality signposts as references from recognized thought leaders cited within the past ten years. This introductory chapter contains many relevant thought-leader citations (APA, 2010; Babbie, 2007; Cohen, Cohen, West & Aiken, 2003; Creswell, 2012; Gill et al., 2010; Glaser & Holton, 2005; Greenacre & Blasius, 2006; Guba & Lincoln, 2005; Hammersley, 2006; Keppel & Wickens, 2004; Maxwell, 2005; Neuman, 2000; Patton, 2002; Whitley, 2002; Yin, 2009; Zechmeister, Zechmeister & Shaughnessy, 2001). Furthermore, I am a multidisciplinary practitioner-scholar with many publications and have applied most of the generally accepted methods and techniques. This experience is the competitive advantage that I leveraged in order to develop the typology.

This handbook also highlights the contemporary state of the art in research design literature from the last ten years, with emphasis on the current best practices from scholars. These references should be useful for other researchers to cite in the methods section of their study or in grant proposals.

Therefore, this handbook should generalize, and thus be valuable, to organizational researcher-practitioners, academic scholars, and university students in terms of a research design framework and for the references of exemplary method thought leaders. Additionally, this handbook will be of interest to dissertation committee chairs and members. Furthermore, the concepts will be helpful to emerging researchers, to faculty seeking scholarly publications for performance evaluations, and to journal review board members in any discipline or industry.

However, this handbook is not a replacement for a specific methods textbook; rather, it is a guide to assist in mapping the complex topology of scholarly research design planning. Handbook contributor Dr. Rao Vajjhala commented on this from the perspective of being a recent doctoral student (Vajjhala, 2014, April 24, personal communication):

> The handbook should benefit students, especially doctoral students intending to take up qualitative research as they get an exposure to the various qualitative research techniques. Although several books on qualitative techniques are available, this book is rather comprehensive in terms of the techniques described and also presents an applied perspective.

I agree that there is much more out there, in terms of research guidelines. I recommend that emerging organizational researchers and doctoral students should have at least three books:

- this handbook (or any other research design-oriented book they prefer);
- a method-specific book with relevant techniques and examples for the method; and
- a format style guide to aid in writing, communicating, and publishing the study.

Limitations

The major limitation with this handbook is that we had only a small sample of subject-matter experts and practitioner-scholars available to participate in the making of this book. Small in this sense is relative to the millions of experts and scholars in the business and management disciplines around the world.

This handbook is written in English and most of the body of knowledge is in English. Although English is the language of science and one of the most common languages in the world, we do hope to offer translations of this to other popular languages such as Mandarin and Spanish, the other two top languages of the world based on population (www.ciafacts.gov).

Furthermore, we have certainly not covered all of the subdisciplines or industries within the field of business and management. We hope to improve upon this limitation through additional editions and new handbooks, which will be focused on specific fields and industries.

Additionally, not all combinations of methods and techniques are covered in this edition of the handbook. Only select methods are included here, based on the interest and experience of the contributing authors. For example, several well-known methods are not included in this edition, such as topics on operations research or business intelligence/data mining analytics. As with the methods covered in the handbook, since only select techniques were applied as necessary for the chapter author's examples, other important techniques were not covered, including correspondence analysis, narrative analysis, along with many others. Future handbooks will expand upon these shortcomings by adding additional methods and techniques with new applied examples across more disciplines.

Conclusions

In closing this chapter, I want to emphasize the collective philosophy of our team, which includes all contributing authors and the Palgrave Macmillan employees: "We want to help."

We felt that we as researcher-practitioners and practitioner-scholars needed to take the responsibility to provide better research documentation for emerging scholars. Therefore, we collaborated to write this descriptive edited handbook to help emerging researchers design studies in a way such that their work would more likely be published in scholarly journals or become highly respected in organizations. We wanted this to be a global handbook so we—as geographically dispersed scholars from different cultures—employed a broad array of visual styles with applied examples.

The research design typology is intended to serve as a guide for organizing a study. It consists of four major layers: research ideology, research strategy, formal research method, and the techniques that are used to analyze the data. The graphical research design typology is supplemented with a discussion on how the layers integrate, and how the techniques are customarily applied across the methods, strategies, and ideologies.

The techniques cover sampling, data collection, descriptive statistics, inferential parametric and nonparametric statistics, ethics, validity, and reliability—according to the needs of the applied example. In some chapters, the techniques go further into general analytical procedures. However, the focus of the handbook is on research design not methods or techniques, so practitioners will require a methods-specific book or article to provide the relevant details on how to execute a study.

The following chapters in this section explain the research design typology. Subsequent sections delve into specific designs, methods, and techniques using applied examples. Those chapters are organized into three sections according to the ideology from the typology in figure 1.1, namely: positivistic, pragmatistic, and constructivistic. Each chapter contains a visual map indicating where in the research design typology ideology the author is grounded with check marks to let the reader know which elements are discussed.

References

APA. (2010). *Publication manual of the American Psychological Association* (6th ed.). Washington, DC: American Psychological Association (APA).

Babbie, E. (2007). *The practice of social research* (11th ed.). Belmont, CA: Wadsworth /Thompson.

Charmaz, K. (2006). *Constructing grounded theory: A practical guide* (2nd ed.). London: Sage.

Cohen, J., Cohen, P., West, S. G., & Aiken, L. S. (2003). *Applied multiple regression/correlation analysis for the behavioral sciences* (3rd ed.). Mahwah, NJ: Lawrence Erlbaum Associates.

Creswell, J. W. (2009). *Research design: Qualitative, quantitative, and mixed methods approaches* (3rd ed.). New York: Sage.

Creswell, J. W. (2012). *Designing qualitative studies*. New York: Sage.

Creswell, J. W., & Tashakkori, A. (2007). Differing perspectives on mixed methods research. *Journal of Mixed Methods Research, 1*(4), 303–308.

Ellingson, L. L. (2009). *Engaging crystallization in qualitative research*. Thousand Oaks, CA: Sage.

Freedman, D. M. (2006). Reflections on the research process: Emancipatory research or emancipatory zeal? *Reflective Practice, 7*(1), 87–99.

Gill, J., Johnson, P., & Clark, M. (2010). *Research methods for managers* (4th ed.). London: Sage.

Glaser, B. G., & Holton, J. (2005). Basic social processes, the grounded theory review. *International Journal of Grounded Theory Review, 4*(3), 1–27.

Gomes, L. F. A. M., Moshkovich, H., & Torres, A. (2010). Marketing decisions in small businesses: How verbal decision analysis can help. *International Journal of Management and Decision Making, 11*(1), 19–36.

Goodwin, Y., & Strang, K. D. (2012). Socio-cultural and multi-disciplinary perceptions of risk. *International Journal of Risk and Contingency Management, 1*(1), 1–11. Retrieved from http://www.igi-global.com/article/international-journal-risk-contingency-management/65728.

Greenacre, M., & Blasius, J. (2006). *Multiple correspondence analysis and related methods*. Boca Raton, FL: Taylor & Francis, p. 40. Retrieved from http://books.google.com/books?id=ZvYV1lfU5zIC&printsec=frontcover&source=gbs_ge_summary_r&cad=0#v=onepage&q&f=false.

Greene, J. C. (2008). Is mixed methods social inquiry a distinctive methodology? *Journal of Mixed Methods Research, 2*(1), 7–22.

Guba, E. G., & Lincoln, Y. S. (2005). Paradigmatic controversies, contradictions, and emerging confluences. In N. K. Denszin & Y. S. Lincoln (Eds.), *Handbook of qualitative research* (pp. 191–215). Thousand Oaks, CA: Sage.

Hammersley, M. (2006). Ethnography: Problems and prospects. *Ethnography & Education, 1*(1), 3–14. Retrieved from http://journalsonline.tandf.co.uk/openurl.asp?genre=article&id=doi:10.1080/17457820500512697

Keppel, G., & Wickens, T. D. (2004). *Design and analysis: A researcher's handbook* (4th ed.). Upper Saddle River, NJ: Pearson Prentice-Hall.

Kline, R. B. (2004). *Beyond significance testing: Reforming data analysis methods in behavioral research*. Washington, DC: American Psychological Association.

Maxwell, J. (2005). *Qualitative research design: An interactive approach* (2nd ed.). Thousand Oaks, CA: Sage.

Mero-Jaffe, I. (2011). Is that what I said? Interview transcript approval by participants: An aspect of ethics in qualitative research. *International Journal of Qualitative Methods, 10*(3), 231–247.

Neuman, W. L. (2000). *Social research methods: Qualitative and quantitative approaches*. Boston: Allyn & Bacon.

Onwuegbuzie, A. J., & Leech, N. L. (2005). On becoming a pragmatic researcher: The importance of combining quantitative and qualitative research methodologies. *International Journal of Social Research Methodology, 8*(5), 375–387.

Patton, M. Q. (2002). *Qualitative research and evaluation methods* (3rd ed.). Thousand Oaks, CA: Sage.

Randolph, J. (2009). A guide to writing the dissertation literature review. *Practical Assessment, Research & Evaluation, 14*(13), 1–13.

Richards, L. (2009). *Handling qualitative data: A practical guide* (2nd ed.). Thousand Oaks, CA: Sage.

Silverman, D. (2010). *Doing qualitative research* (3rd ed.). London: Sage.

Strang, K. D. (2003, Sep 19–26). *Achieving organizational learning across projects*. Paper presented at the Proceedings of the Project Management North America Global Congress, Baltimore, MD. Retrieved from http://marketplace.pmi.org/Pages/ProductDetail.aspx?GMProduct=00100740900.

Strang, K. D. (2005a). Examining effective and ineffective transformational project leadership. *Team Performance Management Journal, 11*(3/4), 68–103. Retrieved from http://dx.doi.org/10.1108/13527590510606299.

Strang, K. D. (2005b, May 28-Jun 13). *Teaching multicultural professionals online: Andragogical design and instruction approaches*. Paper presented at the Congress of the Humanities and Social Sciences, London.

Strang, K. D. (2006). *Advancing project management by applying learning theories for designing and delivering professional education online*. Ann Arbor, MI: ProQuest Information and Learning. Retrieved from http://books.google.com/books?id=iCchNQAACAAJ&dq=kenneth+david+strang.

Strang, K. D. (2007, 14–16 February). *Building quality and interaction into elearning: Applying andragogy theory to synchronous and asynchronous online course design*. Paper presented at the Innovation, Education, Technology, and You: Online Conference for Teaching & Learning, Chicago, IL. Retrieved from www.learningtimes.net/media/IOC2007/strang_72.pdf.

Strang, K. D. (2008a, November 6). *Interdisciplinary theories and statistical techniques underlying the collaborative-synergy-leadership-ebusiness model*. Paper presented at the Proceedings of Studying Electronic Collaboration: Research, Theories and Methods, Tenton, NJ. Retrieved from http://kstrang.wordpress.com/files/2008/12/leadershipecollaborationebusiness2008nov06–08.pdf.

Strang, K. D. (2008b). Quantitative online student profiling to forecast academic outcome from learning styles using dendrogram decision models. *Multicultural Education & Technology Journal, 2*(4), 215–244. Retrieved from http://dx.doi.org/10.1108/17504970810911043.

Strang, K. D. (2009a). Assessing team member interpersonal competencies in new product development e-projects. *International Journal of Project & Organisation Management, 1*(4), 335–357. Retrieved from http://dx.doi.org/10.1504/IJPOM.2009.029105.

Strang, K. D. (2009b). How multicultural learning approach impacts grade for international university students in a business course. *Asian English Foreign Language Journal Quarterly, 11*(4), 271–292. Retrieved from http://www.asian-efl-journal.com/December_2009_ks.php.

Strang, K. D. (2009c). Improving supervision of cross-cultural post graduate university students. *International Journal of Learning and Change, 4*(2), 181–202. Retrieved from http://www.inderscience.com/search/index.php?action=record&rec_id=32711.

Strang, K. D. (2009d, December). *International university student diaspora: Finding culture and learning style to improve online pedagogy*. Paper presented at the Conference on Culture in Higher Education, Singapore.

Strang, K. D. (2009e). Measuring online learning approach and mentoring preferences of international doctorate students. *International Journal of Educational Research, 48*(4), 245–257. Retrieved from http://dx.doi.org/10.1016/j.ijer.2009.11.002.

Strang, K. D. (2009f). Using recursive regression to explore nonlinear relationships and interactions: A tutorial applied to a multicultural education study. *Practical Assessment, Research & Evaluation, 14*(3), 1–13. Retrieved from http://pareonline.net/getvn.asp?v=14&n=3.

Strang, K. D. (2009g). Multicultural e-education: Student learning styles, culture and performance. In H. Song & T. Kidd (Eds.), *Handbook of research on human performance and instructional technology* (pp. 392–412). Houston, TX: Information Science Reference. Retrieved from http://www.igi-global.com/Bookstore/Chapter.aspx?TitleId=38299.

Strang, K. D. (Ed.). (2010a). *Articulating tacit knowledge in multinational e-collaboration on new product designs*. Hershey, PA: IGI-GLOBAL Global. Retrieved from http://www.biggerbooks.com/bk_detail.aspx?isbn=9781615208418.

Strang, K. D. (2010b). Comparing learning and knowledge management theories in an Australian telecommunications practice. *Asian Journal of Management Cases, 7*(1), 33–54. Retrieved from http://ajc.sagepub.com/content/7/1/33.short.

Strang, K. D. (2010c). Education balanced scorecard for online courses: Australia and USA best-practices. *Journal of Cases on Information Technology, 12*(3), 46–51. Retrieved from http://www.irma-international.org/teaching-case/education-balanced-scorecard-online-courses/46038/.

Strang, K. D. (2010d). *Effectively teach professionals online: Explaining and testing educational psychology theories* (2nd ed.). Saarbrücken, Germany: VDM Publishing. Retrieved from http://www.amazon.com/Effectively-Teach-Professionals-Online-Educational/dp/3639230841/ref=pd_rhf_p_t_1.

Strang, K. D. (2010e). Global culture, learning style and outcome: An interdisciplinary empirical study of international students. *Journal of Intercultural Education, 21*(6), 519–533. Retrieved from http://www.tandfonline.com/doi/abs/10.1080/14675986.2010.533034#preview.

Strang, K. D. (2010f). Knowledge articulation dialog increases online university science course outcomes. *Journal of Education and Information Technology, 16*(2), 123–137. Retrieved from http://www.springerlink.com/content/bw72346331140342/.

Strang, K. D. (2010g). Measuring self-regulated e-feedback, study approach and academic outcome of multicultural university students. *International Journal of Continuing Engineering Education and Life-Long Learning, 20*(2), 239–255. Retrieved from http://www.inderscience.com/search/index.php?action=record&rec_id=36818.

Strang, K. D. (2010h). Radiology manufacturing projects and politics: Scientist and politician normalized risk decision processes. *International Journal of Management and Decision Making, 11*(3/4), 231–248. Retrieved from http://www.inderscience.com/search/index.php?action=record&rec_id=40701.

Strang, K. D. (2010i). Balanced assessment of flexible e-learning versus face-to-face campus delivery at an Australian university. In S. Mukerji & P. Tripathi (Eds.), *Cases on technological adaptability and transnational learning: Issues and challenges* (pp. 42–68). London: Information Sciences International. Retrieved from http://www.igi-global.com/bookstore/chapter.aspx?titleid=42426.

Strang, K. D. (2010j). Using recursive regression to explore nonlinear relationships and interactions: Applied multicultural education study [textbook supplement]. In W. Lee (Ed.), *Assessment and evaluation in higher education* (3rd ed., pp. 206–238). Upper Saddle River, NJ: Pearson and Association for Study of Higher Education. Retrieved from http://vig.pearsoned.com/store/product/1,1207,store-18100_isbn-055857579X,00. html.

Strang, K. D. (2011a). Applying multidisciplinary logistic techniques to improve operations productivity at a mine. *Logistics Research Journal, 3*(4), 207–219. Retrieved from http://dx.doi.org/10.1007/s12159-011-0058-5.

Strang, K. D. (2011b). Articulating knowledge sharing processes in multinational e-business product designing. *International Journal of Collaborative Enterprise, 2*(2/3), 203–224. Retrieved from http://www.inderscience.com/browse/index.php?journalID=82&year=2011&vol=2&issue=2/3.

Strang, K. D. (2011c). Asynchronous knowledge sharing and conversation interaction impact on grade in an online business course. *Journal of Education for Business, 86*(4), 223–233. Retrieved from http://www.tandfonline.com/doi/abs/10.1080/08832323.2010.510153#preview.

Strang, K. D. (2011d). Constructivism in synchronous and asynchronous virtual learning environments for a research methods course. *International Journal of Virtual and Personal Learning Environments, 2*(3), 50–63. Retrieved from http://www.igi-global.com/viewtitlesample.aspx?id=55936.

Strang, K. D. (2011e). E-learning effectiveness in a quantitative course: Theoretical versus industry-related discussion and exam questions. *International Journal of Information Communication and Technology Education, 7*(2), 26–39. Retrieved from http://www.igi-global.com/bookstore/article.aspx?titleid=53212.

Strang, K. D. (2011f). A grounded theory study of cellular phone new product development. *International Journal of Internet and Enterprise Management, 7*(4), 366–387.

Retrieved from http://www.inderscience.com/browse/index.php?journalID=39&year=2011&vol=7&issue=4.

Strang, K. D. (2011g). Leadership substitutes and personality impact on time and quality in virtual new product development. *Project Management Journal, 42*(1), 73–90. Retrieved from http://www3.interscience.wiley.com/journal/114291333/issueyear?year=2010.

Strang, K. D. (2011h). Portfolio selection methodology for a nuclear project. *Project Management Journal, 42*(2), 81–93. Retrieved from http://onlinelibrary.wiley.com/doi/10.1002/pmj.20212/abstract.

Strang, K. D. (2012a). Applied financial nonlinear programming models for decision making. *International Journal of Applied Decision Sciences, 5*(4), 370–395. Retrieved from http://www.inderscience.com/info/inarticletoc.php?jcode=ijads&year=2012&vol=5&issue=4.

Strang, K. D. (2012b). Case study: Risk mitigation for hurricanes near Texas coast oil refineries. *International Journal of Risk and Contingency Management, 1*(2), 43–53. Retrieved from http://www.igi-global.com/article/case-study-risk-mitigation-hurricanes/67374.

Strang, K. D. (2012c, January 26). *Evaluating marketing investment projects in the uranium mining industry.* Paper presented at the System of Systems Conference, El Paso, TX. Retrieved from http://personal.plattsburgh.edu/kstra003/itea.pdf.

Strang, K. D. (2012d). Group cohesion, personality and leadership effect on networked marketing staff performance. *International Journal of Networking and Virtual Organisations, 10*(2), 187–209. Retrieved from http://www.inderscience.com/browse/index.php?journalID=22&year=2012&vol=10&issue=2.

Strang, K. D. (2012e). Importance of verifying queue model assumptions before planning with simulation software. *European Journal of Operational Research, 218*(2), 493–504. Retrieved from http://www.sciencedirect.com/science/article/pii/S0377221711010319.

Strang, K. D. (2012f). Investment selection in complex multinational projects. *International Journal of Information Technology Project Management, 3*(2), 1–13. Retrieved from http://www.igi-global.com/journal/international-journal-information-technology-project/1103.

Strang, K. D. (2012g). Man versus math: Behaviorist exploration of post-crisis non-banking asset management. *Journal of Asset Management, 13*(5), 348–467. Retrieved from http://www.palgrave-journals.com/jam/journal/v13/n5/index.html.

Strang, K. D. (2012h). Nonparametric correspondence analysis of global risk management techniques. *International Journal of Risk and Contingency Management, 1*(3), 1–24. Retrieved from http://www.igi-global.com/journal-contents/international-journal-risk-contingency-management/53135.

Strang, K. D. (2012i). Prioritization and supply chain logistics as a marketing function in a mining company. *Journal of Marketing Channels, 19*(2), 141–155. Retrieved from http://www.tandfonline.com/doi/abs/10.1080/1046669X.2012.667763.

Strang, K. D. (2012j). Skype synchronous interaction effectiveness in a quantitative management science course. *Decision Sciences Journal of Innovative Education, 10*(1), 3–23. Retrieved from http://authorservices.wiley.com/bauthor/onlineLibraryTPS.asp?DOI=10.1111/j.1540-4609.2011.00333.x&ArticleID=916161.

Strang, K. D. (2012k). Student diaspora and learning style impact on group performance. *International Journal of Online Pedagogy and Course Design, 2*(3), 1–19. Retrieved from http://www.igi-global.com/article/student-diaspora-learning-style-impact/68410.

Strang, K. D. (2013). Planning for Hurricane Isaac using probability theory in a linear programming model. *International Journal of Risk and Contingency Management, 2*(1), 51–65. Retrieved from http://www.igi-global.com/article/planning-hurricane-isaac-using-probability/76657.

Strang, K. D., & Chan, C. E. L. (2010). Simulating e-business innovation process improvement with virtual teams across Europe and Asia. *International Journal of*

E-Entrepreneurship and Innovation, 1(1), 22–41. Retrieved from http://www.igi-global.com/bookstore/article.aspx?titleid=40921.

Strang, K. D., & Symonds, R. J. (2012). Analyzing research activity duration and uncertainty in business doctorate degrees. *International Journal of Risk and Contingency Management, 1*(1), 29–48. Retrieved from http://www.igi-global.com/article/international-journal-risk-contingency-management/65730.

Vogt, P. W., Gardner, D. C., & Haeffele, L. M. (2012). *When to use what research design.* New York: Guilford.

Whitley, B. E. Jr. (2002). *Principles of research in behavioral science* (2nd ed.). New York: McGraw-Hill.

Yin, R. K. (2009). *Case study research: Design and methods* (4th ed.). London: Sage.

Zechmeister, J. S., Zechmeister, E. B., & Shaughnessy, J. J. (2001). *Essentials of research methods in psychology.* New York: McGraw-Hill.

2
Articulating a Research Design Ideology

Kenneth D. Strang

Research design typology overview and intended uses

A simplified conceptual diagram was introduced in the previous chapter. Figure 2.1 illustrates the research design typology model, with ideology highlighted for discussion in this chapter.

This model may also be used by a single researcher or an entire research team. Coauthors or coresearchers should examine their philosophical alignment with ideology carefully, because if the research team members differ substantially at the first layer, they are unlikely to be effective, efficient, or satisfied working with one another. On the other hand, if all team members are similar in their ideology, then it is a very healthy process for scholars to cooperatively develop their research strategy along with choice of method and techniques. This is probably one of the most powerful generalizations of the typology model.

The topics in this chapter will theoretically explain the research ideology layer, grounded in the literature. Subsequent chapters will present the other three layers (again grounded in the literature). A final chapter will discuss how to use the research design typology and in doing so I will present several applied examples drawn from my research or from my students'.

As shown at the top of figure 2.1, positivism is arbitrarily positioned on the left, constructivism (participant's interpret) on the right, with everything else located in between these two polarized continuum extremes. Most business and management researchers rarely consider themselves positivists; instead fact-driven scholars are post-positivists (as explained later).

Interpretivism was not used for this model although it is a recognized research philosophy. The reason for this is that in this typology, the degree of interpretivism, and who performs it, discriminates between pragmatism and constructivism. Constructivism in this model means that the participants interpret the meaning of the data as compared to pragmatism whereby the

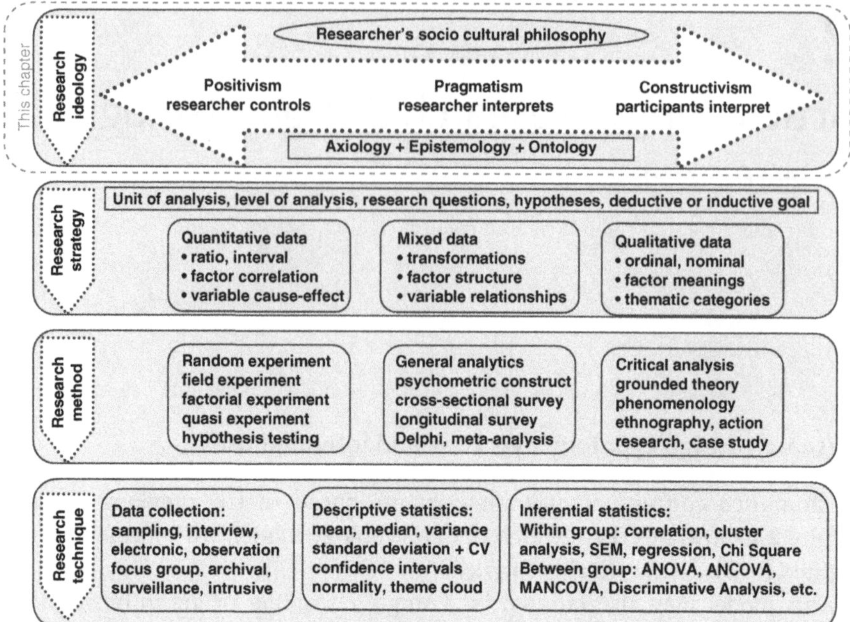

Figure 2.1 Research design typology—ideology focus.

researcher would perform the data interpretation. Only three labels were utilized because the goal was to produce a simple visual model to help researchers (as explained in the previous chapter).

Research ideology factors

Terminology differs across cultures, disciplines, industries, and individuals (Adekola & Sergi, 2007). Research ideology refers to how the researcher thinks about knowledge claims, as being on a continuum based on explicit evidence structured from theories to the other extreme of authentic qualitative tacit meanings expressed by participants. This is driven by the researchers' sociocultural philosophy, meaning that knowledge, experience, learning, and socialization develop a scholar's ideology in conjunction with their basic personality and attitude (Strang, 2013, 2014).

Ideologies can be decomposed into sociocultural philosophical attitudes or preference factors. A business and management scholar's philosophical attitudes are generally categorized on the basis of axiology, epistemology, and ontology. These categories of within the ideology are merely for relative comparison between scholars so that they may understand one another's terminology and priorities—there is no incorrect ideology. Note that some thought leaders in the literature describe ethics as an additional component within philosophy (e.g., Creswell, 2009), but in this research design typology ethical preferences are addressed within axiology. As mentioned earlier there will be variances in terminology across the disciplines, industries, and global cultures.

The purpose of the ideology layer in the typology is two-fold. First it forces researchers to articulate their philosophical view or belief system that in turn strongly influences how they design, execute, and report a scholarly study. Second, it serves as a common baseline for researchers to communicate and understand one another's publications. In fact, knowing another researcher's ideology will assist in understanding their conceptual diagrams and models, even if those are not published. Ideology may be analyzed as a criterion for selecting research team membership. Ideology is a sociocultural philosophy, and since it is socialized, it may change over time, in comparison to basic personality, which generally does not significantly vary.

Axiology factor

Axiology in general refers to the theory of beliefs, such as religious influences, cultural, or aesthetic values. In business and management, axiology refers to the priority of values conditioned by organizational and global culture socialization. Axiology also includes moral beliefs and how these impact ethics. An ethical dilemma is one that has multiple acceptable outcomes that differ according to axiological beliefs (often driven by cultural values). Thus, in business and management, axiology does not question the existence but rather the importance of values in the mind of the researcher. Religion is often an influence to be considered and then integrated into global culture. All scholars understand that cultures and religions may differ between researchers. Many organizations train and expect their employees to uphold specific missions, values, and beliefs.

Axiology is socialized through culture. A researcher may have been culturally socialized to value and perhaps practice a specific religion, which will likely impact his or her ideology for designing a study. According to the old axiom that beauty is in the eye of the beholder, the meaning of beauty differs across cultures and time (Strang, 2003). Some cultures believe certain colors (e.g., red, gold) and words (e.g., spirit, euthanasia) are either fundamentally good or bad—beyond linguistic differences (Strang, 2012b; Strang & Chan, 2010).

Some cultures believe it is incorrect to conduct experiments with humans or specific animals, while others refrain from comparing genders or sexual orientations. Socioculturally driven axiology values impact the research design and literature selection. Since axiology includes ethics, researchers will differ on what they believe is fair, according to a teleological (consequences of outcome) versus deontological (process leading to outcome) orientation. These types of axiological differences have an impact on the researcher's ideology.

Epistemology factor

Epistemology can be defined as the theory of knowledge. In business and management, this encompasses the disciplinary terminology for communicating knowledge between scholars. There are many differences in terminology between disciplines, such as what an assessment scale is, one in which quantitative ordinals range from 1 to 5 where 5 is high, versus what a qualitative competency scale is, where the range is from just learning to highly developed learning. Different notational systems are used across disciplines, such as Newtonian in physics and operations research, while algebraic expressions are commonly used in the social sciences and statistics.

In business and management, industry and disciplinary socialization govern the nomenclature of the practitioners: the terminology and words we choose to use. These differences usually surface as qualitative versus quantitative approaches (not my term), which actually means the preference for specific techniques for collecting and analyzing either quantitative data (e.g., response scales from experiments, surveys, or observation outcomes) versus qualitative data (e.g., interview narratives, pictures, or observation comments). Epistemology differences often impact the choice of statistical technique: in engineering or math, vector analysis may be used to analyze participant response data agreement, while in economics or psychology, correlation or exploratory factor analysis would be de facto. These differences influence ideology.

Another way in which epistemological differences impact the researcher's ideology is by the choice of validity and reliability processes along with standard benchmarks. Certain formal methods call for specific validity and reliability checking techniques. Average inter-item correlation is generally expected to be performed after a confirmatory factor analysis (CFA) and then compared to a priori Cronbach alpha coefficients to judge validity. Participant verification of interview comments is an accepted form of validity in phenomenology. Notice the difference in where the standards were derived from: positivistic CFA from a priori literature benchmarks versus constructivistic phenomenology from the sample participant authentication process.

Finally, in business and management, triangulation is a common epistemological difference impacting ideology. Triangulation generally means to get three sources of confirmation, but how and why that is done could constitute validity or reliability. If a researcher uses three different techniques (e.g., method triangulation) on the data, such as asking participants to verify interview or observations transcripts, along with researcher assistant verifications, this would constitute validity checking. If a researcher collected interview comments, along with personnel file reports and observations of behavior, this would constitute data triangulation, but it would still be validity. If the researcher were to repeat the entire process with either the same individual (at different times) or with other individuals in different contexts, that would be reliability.

Triangulation of data, method, or both of them impact the researcher's ideology. A researcher may be focusing the scope of a grounded theory study on understanding employee perceptions within a context that has not been examined and perhaps would be difficult to repeat (e.g., sexual assault at a specific organization). Reliability may not be highly valued due to the credibility and authenticity of the data established by using transparency and descriptive techniques. By comparison, surveying victims about their perceptions of sexual assault using logistic regression on a quantitative scale data would require validity and reliability checks. Thus, epistemology of the disciplinary practice impacts research ideology along with the choice of method.

Ontology factor

Ontology is known as the theory of being, meaning the degree to which we think a phenomenon is real or not real. Is a dream a cognitive process? Does an organism in an antibiotic pill have a form of memory schema to identify and destroy specific bacteria? Is there intelligent life beyond Earth? Is there an after-life?

In business and management, we generally refer to this as our ontological understanding about how things exist as tangible versus intangible, tacit versus explicit, attitude versus behavioral intent, all of which are influenced by sociocultural values (axiology). Another way this has been expressed is by now retired Harvard University professors Chris Arygris and David Schön as espoused theories versus theories in use (Argyris & Schön, 1996).

Thus, in business and management, ontology impacts where a researcher looks for data and then what the researcher considers real versus imagined, true versus false, or conscious versus unconscious (this is not an exhaustive list). A positivistic-oriented researcher will often look for facts such as ex facto numbers or outcomes of behavior that agree or disagree with a priori scales. A pragmatic researcher usually interprets numbers and behaviors into facts having degrees of agreement with a priori scales, thus creating new construct scales or combinations. A constructivist engages participants to interpret their numbers and behaviors into a consensus of meaning, thus going beyond a priori scales (little or no agreement) to create new construct scales. These are merely examples illustrating how ontology impacts the researcher's potential extreme positions on the ideological continuum.

Ontology also influences the researcher's choice of data types to be collected. Is 0 a part number, lower than 1, freezing (0°C), or exactly nothing (nominal, ordinal, integer, continuous variable)? Is there an equal unit difference between an A versus A– or are they merely relative (e.g., in an integer scale an A– value multiplied by a positive constant will equal an A value). Ontology preferences contribute to the ideology of the researcher.

Philosophical positions within research ideology

The ideology term used in figure 2.1 is equivalent to worldview (Creswell, 2012), inquiry strategy (Creswell, 2009), philosophy (Neuman, 2000), design strategy (Patton, 2002), paradigm (Guba & Lincoln, 2005), epistemological framework (Babbie, 2007), theoretical orientation (Crotty, 1998), archetype (Gill, Johnson & Clark, 2010), and philosophical belief (Yin, 2009).

The consensus is that research ideology is a continuum of sociocultural philosophical knowledge beliefs and values held by the researcher, starting from positivism (fact based), toward pragmatic in the center with participant-constructed realities at the extreme left (opinion based). The following subsections define the commonly accepted philosophical positions within the research ideology continuum (only three are shown in figure 2.1 to simplify the model).

Positivism

Positivism is the oldest and best-known researcher philosophy, which refers to being evidence and theory driven (Crotty, 1998). I use the word "researcher" because this is individual; other researchers may have a very different ideology, which is the reason a scholar must state his or her epistemological basis (their terminology or theories in use). In this philosophy, the world is viewed as being systematic and deductive, relying on theories to explain most behaviors and processes (Babbie, 2007). Knowledge is tangible to the degree that tacit and complex information can be represented with language or diagrams.

Positivistic researchers first review a priori theory (laws, facts), then develop hypothesis to be tested (Keppel & Wickens, 2004). The purpose is to determine if a situation or participants follow a theory, which can supposedly be used to improve future operations, for example, if processes are out of alignment or if behaviors are atypical according to benchmarks. The researcher does not "interpret" the data but rather controls factors and uses techniques to describe or explain relationships based on what the "data" mean.

Pure positivism is rarely used except in highly controlled situations (such as behavioral experiments or process testing). Post-positivism is more frequently used by fact-driven researchers, otherwise the constraints imposed by positivist research designs would severely limit the contributions to the literature. Positivists apply the "scientific method"; they develop a rigorous protocol, they collect quantitative or mixed data, and they typically apply descriptive as well as inferential statistical techniques to test a priori hypothesis formed by reviewing theories. In this sense, a priori means theory driven, deductive rather than theory building, inductive.

Post-positivism, post-structuralism, postmodernism, and logical positivism are emergent terms that have arisen on the realization that it is difficult to have one "factual truth" as a theory and because it is almost impossible to know what exists in a human brain schemata (Phillips & Burbules, 2000; Polanyi, 1997). Plato, Aristotle, and other ancient philosophers pointed out that knowledge is "the justified truth of what individuals believe at a point in time, which can change over time and from one context to another" (Strang, 2003, p. 3).

"Postpositivists hold a deterministic philosophy in which causes probably determine effects or outcomes" (Creswell, 2009, p. 7). Deterministic means that the unit of analysis research factors are "practically limited" to what can be identified and controlled, rather than attempting to quantify uncertainty or articulate the unknowns (Goodwin & Strang, 2012; Strang, 2012a). Therefore, researchers will try to control experiments to account for all factors as best as possible, and allow flexibility in the determination of truth, while applying rigorous techniques and ensuring validity. Cohen has provided effect sizes (Cohen, 1992; Cohen, Cohen, West & Aiken, 2003) and advocated using these as relative benchmarks rather than a yes or no absolute claim from a hypothesis test.

Pragmatism

Although the label pragmatism appears in the center of figure 2.1, this position is not necessarily drawn to scale. Most other method writers consider positivist as quantitative, and everything else as qualitative—a version of the interpretative. Interpretative is relative, and if viewed as being purely researcher determined, this would be close to post-positivism.

Scholars may not be aware that a "pragmatic philosophy" is a credible research ideology (Creswell, 2009; Onwuegbuzie & Leech, 2005), developed by Rorty (1983) and advanced by Patton (2002) as well as others. Not surprisingly (given the title), this is the research ideology applied here. I describe this philosophy as on a continuum between the extreme positions of positivist (deductive theory driven, fact oriented) and interpretative (inductive qualitative, meaning focused). Thought leader John Creswell considers pragmatism a "worldview philosophical basis for research," having pluralistic assumptions for mixed quantitative and qualitative data, giving practitioners "freedom of choice" for "methods, techniques and procedures of research that best meet their needs and purpose" (Creswell, 2009, pp. 10–11).

Research philosophy scholars Emirbayer and Maynard (2011) provided a unique definition for pragmatism that contains three dimensions, which in their view aligns with Rorty (1983):

> First, their turn to experience means eschewing analyses that depend on inert background and other abstractions and bringing social life as it is lived in its member-produced practices to the forefront of sociological inquiry. Second, a focus on creative problem-solving—always a prime concern of the pragmatists and recently analyzed as situated creativity to be found in the full spectrum of human action rather than in a narrow swath (as in artistic endeavors)—leads to a theoretical approach that is non-teleological in character, comprehends embodied activity and language use, and captures actors' pre-reflective competencies. Such considerations point toward ethno-methodological and conversation-analytic research because there are few other theoretically informed empirical endeavors that fit Joas' criteria so well. Finally, language is a venerable pragmatist topic, as in Dewey's formulations about its eventful as well as eventual character in use and Mead's preoccupation with significant symbols. Ethno-methodology and conversation analysis are cognate with pragmatism insofar as they are concerned with understanding utterances both as context dependent in a local and temporally developing sense and as a site for social action and interaction—and in so far as they are intent on analyzing them in a way that captures their pragmatically cooperative (or, in ethno-methodological terms, collaborative or co-produced) character. (Emirbayer & Maynard, 2011, p. 256)

The first part of their (Emirbayer & Maynard, 2011) definition of pragmatism could be interpreted as that the researcher needs to be open-minded in considering the ontological position of his or her ideology to understand the meaning of the data (whether that be lived experiences using phenomenology or through surveys). Second, a point that I strongly advocate, they emphasize that the researcher must be creatively flexible in the overall approaches (methods and techniques) needed to achieve the research strategy. Finally, they identify the epistemological requirement of the ideology, one that I have not yet mentioned, which is to consider how verbal utterances and conversations could modify the data content or its interpretation.

Pragmatic researchers often use theories to guide the analysis rather than apply a single, generally accepted formal method. They may validate or refine theories after gathering mixed (quantitative and qualitative) data types, and then by using pluralistic combinations of techniques. The axiom "beauty is in the eye of the beholder" seems appropriate to describe this philosophy, because the research may use very quantitative-oriented data collection, methods, and techniques, but they may have values or ethical standards that focus more on having the participants or community validate the data meanings. Generally, the researcher ultimately interprets everything, even participant meanings. A deductive or inductive viewpoint may be taken (or a pluralistic combination).

Several other ideologies are grouped under pragmatism. Researchers taking a critical theory view use critical thinking and self-reflection. Critical theorists accept mixed data but they question interpretations of knowledge and processes, by searching for historical insights, as well as by comparing and contrasting theories (Crotty, 1998; Guba & Lincoln, 2005). Therefore, this is primarily deductive rather than inductive. An interesting premise underlying critical theory ideologies is that people cannot be free until they realize that they not free, meaning the researchers reality may be constrained and biased toward the "acceptable"; therefore, researchers must deconstruct and reconstruct social norms and practices (Kemmis & Wilkinson, 1998; McNiff & Whitehead, 2000). Critical theorists rely on participants taking control of their futures; constructivists desire participants to become active. Note though that the emphasis here on the researcher doing this, which is the differentiator from constructivism where participants are involved in the reflection.

In critical thinking modes of inquiry, researchers generally question their own reality and that of all participants; questions are more important than answers, so researchers raise questions about the ontology and epistemology of what is studied and the data collected (Mezirow, 2000). Critical thinking theory involves self-reflection and understanding one's own practice to make it explicit; practitioners confront a particular phenomenon and their own response to it (McNiff & Whitehead, 2000). Many thought leaders refer to case studies (Yin, 2009) or action research methods (Schön, 1983) when describing critical theory ideologies.

Constructivism

Constructivism emerged to overcome perceived inadequacies of cognitive educational psychology, "to establish meaning as the central concept of psychology" (Bruner, 1990, p. 2). Writers borrowed principles from psychology, anthropology, sociology, philosophy, and the humanities to do so. It means that reality is constructed in the mind of the participants or researcher, or both (Strang, 2010). At the extreme end of the research design typology continuum, it will be the participant or participants who determine the meaning of the data.

This label of constructivism toward the right in figure 2.1 is not necessarily drawn to scale either, as there seem to be more variations of this ideology than any other. Other writers will categorize constructivism as qualitative, mixed, interpretive, participatory, or emancipatory. The distinguishing characteristic of constructivism from other ideologies is that the participant or social community ultimately determines the meaning of the data and the processes, with or without the researcher contributing axiological, ontological, and epistemological influences.

Applying axiology (study of being, values, and esthetics) is a great way to explain the difference between constructivism and the other ideologies. As a contrast of values, the reason positivists and post-postivists reject interpretivism, social advocacy, or participatory ideologies is that they view researcher participation within a study as a form of contamination of the data, skewing the results. In addition, positivists believe participants should not interpret the data or results. Positivists would reject pragmatic ideologies because methods cannot be altered and data cannot be transformed in meaning or form without contaminating the evidence, except for experiments where factors are deliberately manipulated as treatments versus placebos.

Constructivism is similar to social-learning theory as advanced by Vygotsky who asserted that "mental functioning occurs first between people in social interaction and then within the child on the psychological plane," and "the very structure of individual functioning derives from and reflects the structure of social functioning" (Vygotsky, 1978, pp. 1–2).

Social constructivism is another term used in the industry, owing to the fact that "participants can construct the meaning of the situation typically forged in discussions or interactions...these subjective meanings are negotiated socially and historically" (Creswell, 2009, p. 8). As a research ideology, constructivism is a continuum in itself, starting from the reality being perceived by the researcher, by both researcher and participants, or by multiple participants (as a community consensus) without the researcher.

Qualitative or interpretive are the more popular terms used in the industry for this ideology. Interpretivism developed from the "hermeneutics" research method of studying ancient scripts, and it was advocated when using phenomenology as a method for searching for meanings (Crotty, 1998; Neuman, 2000). As with critical theory, the concluding phase for pragmatic interpretivism ideologies is that the researcher constructs the authentic lifeworld truth based a combination of theories and on the factual evidence collected from the participants (Crotty, 1998).

Ultimately, the researcher, the participants, or both will "interpret" their realities. This raises the axiological issues of ethics and values for the presentation and validation when a researcher does the writing. For this reason, researchers should quote the participant-authentic meanings in their studies. As a research ideology, interpretivism generally refers to the researcher recording (interpreting) the participants' behaviors or responses, perhaps from qualitative data collection, then by using coding and theme analysis. However, participants are generally consulted to review and revise both the data collected as well as the interpreted themes (Mero-Jaffe, 2011). Sometimes participants generate the data and interpret them together, as with using the nominal brainstorming or focus group methodologies. This ideology is often used for storytelling narrative analysis, grounded theory, phenomenology, and action research studies.

Participatory and emancipatory ideologies are variations of constructivism insofar as the researcher is active in the research but participants construct a shared understanding of their meaning (Creswell, 2009; Mezirow, 1991). The researcher is generally not an active participant when applying a purely interpretive ideology, although the researcher may interpret what the participant says or does; or instead the participants may provide their own perceptions. This is the "gray" area of interpretivism, which is why researchers should be clear about their ideology.

Emancipatory research refers to relaxing, freeing, or liberating the tacit-cognitive and mechanistic-tangible constraints for all data collection and interpretation. In other words, the taxonomical framework proposed in this handbook may be too restrictive for interpretive-emancipatory ideologies; so readers should consult expert literature (see: Ellingson, 2009; Mezirow, 1991).

Emancipatory variations of constructivist ideologies have been called transformational and "mode 2 knowledge conception" (Gummerson, 2000; Phillips & Burbules, 2000). Writers taking this perspective are willing to transform their frame of reference and question their own assumptions. Contrasting or paradynamic assumptions are welcome, and data are collected in various non-numeric formats such as sociolinguistic meanings, social norms, themes, videos, recordings, or anthropological artifacts (Guba & Lincoln, 2005; Reason & Bradbury, 2006). Researchers may use multiple data collection techniques not necessarily for triangulation of data or methods, but as a way to capture multiple meanings of phenomena. Researchers will more likely be sensitive to the various diverse learning styles and cultural orientations of participants.

Social advocacy is a variation of constructivism, whereby the community participants collect data and interpret the meanings. Data include embedded voices and participants use reflexivity with consensus to build socially constructed meaning. Agreements about the truth of evidence may be reached through community-of-practice negotiations; or agreements may be reached only through a dialogue that moves arguments past the need for objectivity and relativity toward a communal test of validity through argumentation of the participants in a discourse (Rorty, 1983).

A scholarly researcher adapting the social advocacy ideology could apply a critical analysis by searching online blogs of popular opinion, analyzing the themes for patterns of agreement and disagreement, and produce a taxonomy of the results either supporting (advocating) or opposing a social policy, a political event, or a government process. The ideology underlying this study would amount to describing the most popular opinion in the social community, yet in a scholarly manner. What is right or wrong would be asserted based on popular opinion, either through the majority or "truth wins" social-choice decision-making scheme.

Conclusions

The ideology layer of the research design typology was explained using a few examples from the business and management discipline. The important point about ideology is that many specific variations exist in the mind of the researcher. The first layer in figure 2.1 depicts only the extreme polarized ends of the continuum from positivism to constructivism, with pragmatism in the middle. In reality, these may overlap and the interpetivism philosphy was considered part of pragmatism.

The typology may be generalized to any discipline and culture, because the scientific method underlying this model is universal. The typology be used by a team as well as a single researcher. This opens interesting possibilities for using the typology for research project initiation and program evaluation. The next chapter will address the strategy, the second layer of the typology.

References

Babbie, E. (2007). *The practice of social research* (11th ed.). Belmont, CA: Wadsworth /Thompson.

Bruner, J. (1990). *Acts of meaning*. Cambridge, MA: Harvard University Press.

Cohen, J. (1992). Statistics a power primer. *Psychology Bulletin, 112*(1), 115–159.

Cohen, J., Cohen, P., West, S. G., & Aiken, L. S. (2003). *Applied multiple regression/correlation analysis for the behavioral sciences* (3rd ed.). Mahwah, NJ: Lawrence Erlbaum Associates

Creswell, J. W. (2009). *Research design: Qualitative, quantitative, and mixed methods approaches* (3rd ed.). New York: Sage.

Creswell, J. W. (2012). *Designing qualitative studies*. New York: Sage.

Crotty, M. (1998). *The foundations of social research: Meaning and perspectives in the research process*. Thousand Oaks, CA: Sage.

Ellingson, L. L. (2009). *Engaging crystallization in qualitative research*. Thousand Oaks, CA: Sage.

Gill, J., Johnson, P., & Clark, M. (2010). *Research methods for managers* (4th ed.). London: Sage.

Goodwin, Y., & Strang, K. D. (2012). Socio-cultural and multi-disciplinary perceptions of risk. *International Journal of Risk and Contingency Management, 1*(1), 1–11. Retrieved from http://www.igi-global.com/article/international-journal-risk-contingency-management /65728.

Guba, E. G., & Lincoln, Y. S. (2005). Paradigmatic controversies, contradictions, and emerging confluences. In N. K. Denszin & Y. S. Lincoln (Eds.), *Handbook of qualitative research* (pp. 191–215). Thousand Oaks, CA: Sage

Gummerson, E. (2000). *Qualitative methods in management research* (2nd ed.). Thousand Oaks, CA: Sage

Kemmis, S., & Wilkinson, M. (1998). Participatory action research and the study of practice. In B. Atweh & S. Kemmis (Eds.), *Action research in practice: Partnerships for social justice in education* (pp. 21–36). New York: Routledge.

Keppel, G., & Wickens, T. D. (2004). *Design and analysis: A researcher's handbook* (4th ed.). Upper Saddle River, NJ: Pearson Prentice-Hall.

McNiff, J., & Whitehead, J. (2000). *Action research in organisations*. London: Routledge.

Mero-Jaffe, I. (2011). Is that what I said? Interview transcript approval by participants: An aspect of ethics in qualitative research. *International Journal of Qualitative Methods, 10*(3), 231–247.

Mezirow, J. (1991). *Transformative dimensions of adult learning*. New York: Jossey-Bass.

Mezirow, J. (2000). *Learning as transformation: Critical perspectives on a theory in progress*. New York: Jossey-Bass.

Neuman, W. L. (2000). *Social research methods: Qualitative and quantitative approaches*. Boston: Allyn & Bacon.

Onwuegbuzie, A. J., & Leech, N. L. (2005). On becoming a pragmatic researcher: The importance of combining quantitative and qualitative research methodologies. *International Journal of Social Research Methodology, 8*(5), 375–387.

Patton, M. Q. (2002). *Qualitative research and evaluation methods* (3rd ed.). Thousand Oaks, CA: Sage.

Phillips, D. C., & Burbules, N. C. (2000). *Postpositivism and educational research*. Lanham, MD: Rowman & Littlefield.

Polanyi, M. (Ed.). (1997). *Tacit knowledge*. Oxford: Butterworth-Heinemann.

Reason, P., & Bradbury, H. (2006). Introduction: Inquiry and participation in search of a world worthy of human aspiration. In P. Reason & H. Bradbury (Eds.), *Handbook of action research*. London: Sage.

Rorty, R. (1983). *Consequences of pragmatism*. Minneapolis, MN: University of Minneapolis.

Schön, D. A. (1983). *The reflective practitioner—how professionals think in action*. Aldershot, UK: BasiAshgate ARENA.

Strang, K. D. (2003, Sep. 19–26). *Achieving organizational learning across projects*. Paper presented at the Proceedings of the Project Management North America Global Congress, Baltimore, MD. Retrieved from http://marketplace.pmi.org/Pages/ProductDetail.aspx?GMProduct=00100740900.

Strang, K. D. (2010). *Effectively teach professionals online: Explaining and testing educational psychology theories* (2nd ed.). Saarbruecken, Germany: VDM Publishing. Retrieved from http://www.amazon.com/Effectively-Teach-Professionals-Online-Educational/dp/3639230841/ref=pd_rhf_p_t_1.

Strang, K. D. (2012a). Man versus math: Behaviorist exploration of post-crisis non-banking asset management. *Journal of Asset Management, 13*(5), 348–467. Retrieved from http://www.palgrave-journals.com/jam/journal/v13/n5/index.html.

Strang, K. D. (2012b). Multicultural face of organizations. In M. A. Sarlak (Ed.), *The new faces of organizations in the 21st century* (Vol. 5, pp. 1–21). Toronto, ON: North American Institute of Science and Information Technology (NAISIT). Retrieved from http://naisit.org/book/detail/id/6.

Strang, K. D. (2013). Homeowner behavioral intent to evacuate after flood warnings. *International Journal of Risk and Contingency Management, 2*(3), 1–28. Retrieved from http://www.igi-global.com/article/homeowner-behavioral-intent-to-evacuate-after-flood-risk-warnings/80017.

Strang, K. D. (2014). Exploring marketing theories to model business web service procurement behavior. In J. Goodyear & Z. Sun (Eds.), *Demand-driven web services: Theory, technologies and applications* (Vol. 1, ch. 2, pp. 21–42). Hershey, PA: IGI-GLOBAL. Retrieved from http://www.igi-global.com/book/demand-driven-web-services/95218.

Strang, K. D., & Chan, C. E. L. (2010). Simulating e-business innovation process improvement with virtual teams across Europe and Asia. *International Journal of*

E-Entrepreneurship and Innovation, 1(1), 22–41. Retrieved from http://www.igi-global.com/bookstore/article.aspx?titleid=40921.
Vygotsky, L. S. (1978). *Mind in society* ([Translated from original material published in 1930, 1933, and 1935] ed. Vol. 15). Cambridge, MA: Harvard University Press.
Yin, R. K. (2009). *Case study research: Design and methods* (4th ed.). London: Sage.

3
Developing a Goal-Driven Research Strategy

Kenneth D. Strang

Research design typology: strategy focus

The research design typology model was introduced in chapter 1, and the ideology layer was explained in chapter 2. The strategy layer of the research design typology will be discussed in this chapter (as highlighted in figure 3.1).

Research strategy

Research design begins with a grounding in a research ideology (worldview philosophy or epistemology) followed by the unit(s) of analysis. This is the foundation of all designs. This component of the research design is straightforward, yet essential before continuing on to the selection of methods and techniques. Researchers can avoid articulating a specific ideology, but they cannot design or complete a high-quality scholarly study without a clear strategy.

While ideology identifies the researcher's way of thinking about the study, it is strategy wherein goals, research questions, or hypotheses are formed based on the unit(s), level(s) of analysis and generalization goal. Figure 3.2 visually depicts how the level(s) of analysis relates to the unit(s) of analysis. A sample generalization goal and research questions or hypotheses must be integrated with the level and unit of analysis. Usually the research design hierarchy is first the unit, then level of analysis, followed by generalization goal, and then purpose questions or hypotheses.

On the other hand, it is equally possible—and useful—to do this in reverse direction, by first writing draft research questions or hypotheses, to inform the development of the generalization goal, which helps to determine the unit of analysis, and finally the level of analysis. Any order is possible during the development of the research strategy, but note that this is a pragmatic ideology. A pure positivist would likely reject this notion and start with writing the

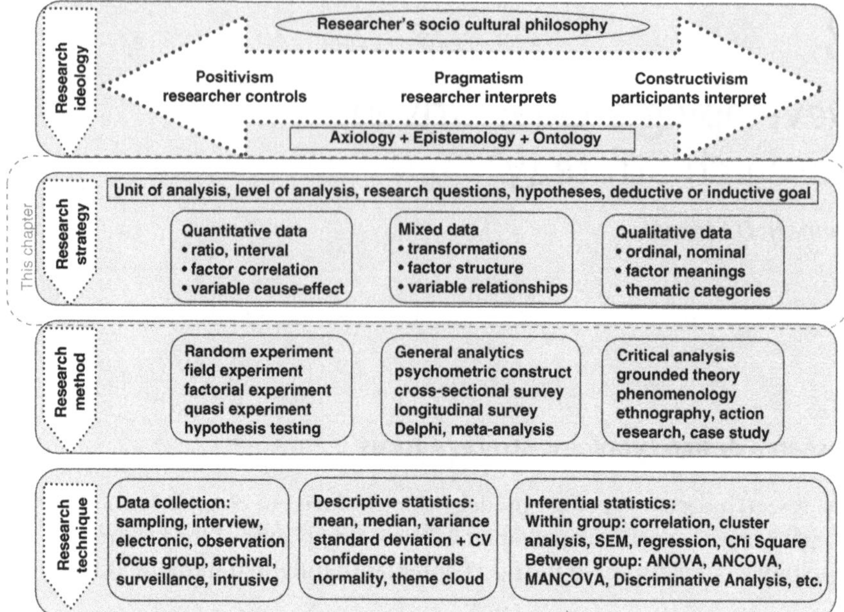

Figure 3.1 Research design typology model—strategy focus.

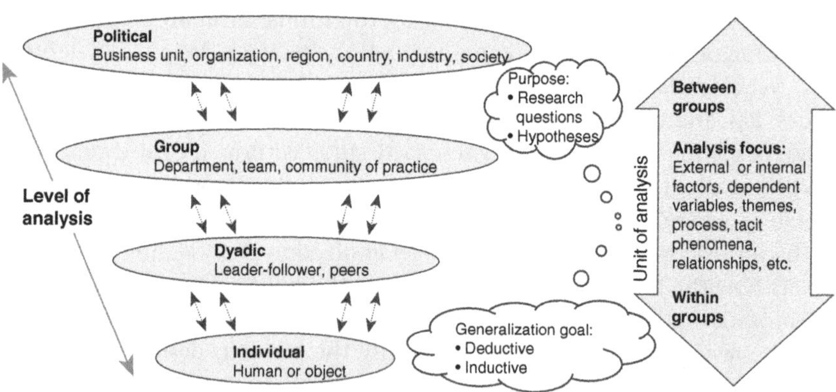

Figure 3.2 Level of analysis, unit of analysis with research questions or hypotheses.

hypothesis, while a constructivistic social advocate would start with a research question or level of analysis.

The important point is that all of these elements must be considered when developing the strategy, and overall the strategy must be practical to carry out. In many cases I have seen the level of analysis and unit of analysis modified to fit the practical feasibility of the researcher's ability or availability of the data. In fact, this is the point where many doctoral student proposals fail, because they are not specific or they are not feasible to execute within a specified timeframe.

Level of analysis

The levels of analysis are attributes referring to where the scholarly focus of the study is, such as the individual, the group, or a larger partition. I stopped at the political level in this diagram because the possibilities are infinite, especially in molecular science and astronomy (e.g., how would we define another galaxy as a level of analysis?).

Level of analysis conceptually relates to the goal for the sampling method. This is because the level of analysis defines where the researcher intends to generalize the findings to, assuming they are reliable and significant (positivism) or credible and inductive (constructivism). Later on in the research design process, the sampling technique ought to be selected in such a way as to ensure that the participant(s) or object(s) in the level of analysis will be generalizable to the intended population(s); otherwise who would find the implications credible?

Level of analysis is where the analysis of the data as a whole is performed. An interview of different people is individual. An interview of a team (together) is a group although it could be individual if the strategy was to understand (describe), compare, or evaluate people with an attribute of being on a specific team rather than evaluating the data by team. Surveys of teams would be a group level of analysis while surveys of employees would be individual. It is rare to find more than a single level of analysis in a study, although multiple levels of analysis may be found in pragmatic ideologies that are often accompanied by mixed methods.

The more common level of analysis ranges from individual, to dyadic (two people, such as a leader and a follower, an employee and his or her supervisor, husband and wife, etc.), group, and then everything beyond a group, such as region, country, industry, association, society, etc. It is more common to see the organizational level of analysis used with case studies. However, several empirical researchers have collected survey data and performed parametric statistical analysis on participants of a political region or country to measure culture (Hofstede, 2009; Strang, 2008a, 2009a, 2009b, 2009c, 2010a, 2010b, 2012j, 2012k; Vajjhala & Strang, 2014).

It may not seem obvious but the organizational level of analysis as viewed in this model includes associations and multiple companies in the industry. These could be broken into more detailed levels, so the model is intended to be conceptual and relative. Although I have implied that humans could be participants in the level of analysis, it is not mandatory. Animals or objects could be in the level of analysis.

The level of analysis could be one of more business processes, government policy, decision making, equipment, software programs, land, water, air, or any inanimate object with similar attributes that could be considered of theoretical interest for practitioners or researchers to study (Strang, 2012a, 2012b, 2012e, 2012g, 2012h, 2012j, 2013, 2014a, 2014b; Strang & Nersesian, 2014; Strang & Symonds, 2012). In operations research, it is common to examine queues using waiting line theory (Strang, 2012d, 2012f, 2012i), whereby the level of analysis could be competitive fleets of cargo ships (arriving at a dock to be unloaded) or different train systems transporting people and freight arriving at terminals for processing.

Unit of analysis

The unit of analysis refers to the factor, variable, process, relationship, tacit phenomena, or plural combination thereof, which is at the focus of the study. This is the "what" and "how" explanation of the units to be analyzed within the levels of analysis. Units are generally decided first, because there are generally multiple levels of analysis that one could describe, evaluate, explain, or explore. The unit of analysis must also be integrated with the generalization goal. Once the level of analysis, unit of analysis, and generalization goals are determined, then the research questions or hypotheses may be written.

There is a logical relationship between the unit of analysis and the level of analysis. The level of analysis defines where the unit of analysis originates, or is created by, and whether it is grouped or not. Levels of analysis are individual humans or objects (e.g., company process, product, etc.), dyadic (two-person unit), group, or political (country, international, etc.), as illustrated in figure 3.2. At the individual level, objects could refer to company products or processes. Dyadic is a professionally designated or workplace-mandated paired-group level of analysis often used for leadership, apprenticeships, clinical counseling, or medical practitioner studies (Strang, 1983, 2005, 2007, 2011, 2012c).

The unit of analysis along with the generalization goal impacts the level of analysis, because a group or higher level of analysis is often required for contrasts and comparisons between teams or departments within a defined entity such as a company or a school to be credible. At the highest level of analysis, the focus could be on a company, a community, a state, a country, or the world. Although most designs include a particular level of analysis, some research such as multiple case studies and historical or critical analysis may cover several levels of analysis.

Units of analysis may be variables of any data type, nominal, ordinal, integer, continuous, or a relationship. Examples include grades, satisfaction, tacit feelings, social meanings, narratives, business processes, or thematic categories (Richardson, 2000). There may be several variables, or relationship(s) between them. The unit of analysis may be inclusive of the relationship between variables (such as within-group correlation or regression). We must also specify what we wish to know about or test the unit of analysis. The what, in combination with the level of analysis, helps us identify where the findings could be generalized to.

The level of analysis also infers the scope of how the unit of analysis will be studied. For example, if the unit of analysis was the number of sales, and the level of analysis was the design team, then it seems likely that the researcher is planning to collect quantitative data (sales) from the team as a whole, so as to compare team performance. It is possible that there may be multiple units and levels of analysis, or that the units of analysis could exist at different levels of analysis, where for example an individual project leader performance may be examined based on perceptions gathered from a team as well as from organizational outcomes such as business product/service return on investment (Strang, 2009d).

A fundamental decision point when deciding the unit of analysis is whether the research will be examining differences (or similarities) between or within-groups. This decision will determine later parts of the research design, such as choice of formal method and techniques. For example, you cannot perform correlation on the results of a personality interview for one individual unless one we are interested in knowing how the factors within that person were related (which is an interesting possibility). On the other hand, when an individual is the unit and level of analysis, it is common to use phenomenological or ethnographical formal methods to analyze the data.

Within-group analysis refers to examining the unit of analysis in a sample as a whole. The sample could be from one person or object (e.g., a machine in a business or a process at a hospital). A within-group analysis could be directed at one or many individuals or objects. The unit of analysis here is the relationship among all the items in the sample as a whole, such as the descriptive statistics or characteristics of the nurses, or the x-ray machines, in a particular shift at a hospital. A within-group could also be at the organization or a higher level of analysis such as organization (hospital) or region (all hospitals in a state or country). Within-group organization analyses are often done using single case studies or grounded theory. An event during a hospital shift or project or any other natural context could be defined as the within-group unit of analysis. In that situation, the within-group unit of analysis would likely focus on describing the consensus of perceptions about the event, using thematic analysis or nonparametric descriptive statistics.

For example, if the unit of analysis were comparing perceptions of customer satisfaction based on the education level of the waitress, the unit of analysis would be the relationship of satisfaction with education. If the researcher wanted to know the direction and strength of this relationship, as would likely be the case for a positivist, a correlation technique could be used.

Correlation is generally a within-group technique, but the study could be designed to use it as a between-group comparison. This is often done by applying the Analysis of Variance (ANOVA) in conjunction with the regression technique. For example, if the positivistic researcher was interested in examining the predictive relationship between waitress education on customer satisfaction, regression would be a useful technique (considering that the assumptions of this parametric technique were met by the sample data). The reason this is a between-group unit of analysis design is that waitress education cannot be easily manipulated, so different waitresses would be used and the data regarding their education level would be collected.

It is a fact that regression can also be used as a within-group unit of analysis. If a constructivist researcher was interested in examining the predictive relationship between waitress education and customer satisfaction, the data would likely include waitress education statistics along with interview transcripts from the customer, followed by keyword analysis sorted frequency to uncover patterns to gain a better understanding of the relationship between the factors in the mind of the customer.

Between-group unit of analysis instead refers to comparing independent individuals or groups in the sample (according to level of analysis) or a dependent temporal perspective such as repeated testing of the same participants or objects at two or more independent points in time. Between-group analysis seems identical to within-group approaches, but the research methods and techniques differ. Sample size may not be a criterion for within- versus between-group unit of analysis, nor is level of analysis a factor, unless specific parametric techniques are used, such as multiple regression, factor analysis, or structural equation modeling.

If the unit of analysis in the previous example were to compare service capability between different waitresses or between teams of waitresses (at different companies, or regions), this would be a between-group design. Positivists would likely select parametric statistical techniques, such as *t*-tests or analysis of variance, to examine or compare quantitative responses from customer opinion surveys. Constructivists would likely select case studies or phenomenology to structure and analyze qualitative data (e.g., feedback comments from surveys or interviews). Interestingly, the pragmatist researcher may simply observe the waitresses and customers at multiple restaurants, make notes, and ask the owner for additional information, such as customer revisits or length of stay to triangulate the data, using ethnography, a multiple case study, or perhaps perform a nonparametric correspondence analysis technique on the data to identify underlying patterns.

Again looking at the above example, a positivist researcher might develop a true or quasi-experiment to analyze this between-group study by manipulating the waitress service quality, using control and test (treatment) customer groups, to test the satisfaction of customers. Furthermore, instead of groups, a positivist could design a between-group experiment with two individuals, a waitress, and a customer, and manipulate the treatments in different combinations (as the between-groups factor), each time measuring the customer reaction.

The above example requires mentioning another form of between-group experiment, the between-times (or pre-tests vs. post-tests, before and after tests), where the dependent variable is one person, one group, or multiple groups (as per the level of analysis). Of course with such a small sample size, this experiment would lack credibility to be generalized to other populations (most restaurants have more than one customer). Such a between-group experiment could be strengthened by adding a control group comprising a waitress with a business-as-usual treatment condition (no manipulation) and a customer (the same one or an additional client). The more the combinations of treatments and individuals (or groups), the more the power of the experiment. Nonetheless, it would still be considered a between-group unit of analysis. This could be redesigned as a within-group experiment if the customer or customers were surveyed for their average preferences after being served once, so as to perhaps identify attitude relationships with other factors.

Unit of analysis, level of analysis, research goal, and methods are commonly related. Additionally, there may be an inverse relationship between these components, insofar as lower levels of analysis (e.g., individual) are often paired with a between-group unit of analysis, and vice-versa (large groups using within-groups unit of analysis) at least in positivistic ideology designs. In pragmatic and constructivistic research designs, a between-group unit of analysis is often done through multiple case studies, while a within-group analysis could use a single case study, ethnography, phenomenology, or grounded theory methods.

Data type in unit of analysis

The unit of analysis data type is important since it impacts the choice of research technique to be used (e.g., *Pearson Product Moment* correlation is applicable only for metric data types, Spearman's *Rho* for ordinals, Kendall's *Tau* for unordered or binary). Tangible variables have a data type, and sometimes they are transformed from one type to another or combined as mixed (such as part numbers in operations research). Some data types are so complex that only the human brain can analyze them, such as cultural art, pictures, and voice recordings, although computer software routines are available to analyze the frequency and patterns of some content (e.g., words or bit patterns).

Data type means that the information can be stored and shared with other researchers because defining the type allows other researchers to know how to read the content. Is the data 0123 a number or a label—the definition has a significant impact on what a researcher can do. The fundamental tangible data types are: nominal (alphanumeric), ordinal (alphanumeric in order), interval (numeric integers but with no true zero point), ratio (continuous real numbers), images (including geography, pictures, and art), recording, and mixed (Strang, 2009d).

Qualitative data are considered nominal, ordinal, image, recording, mixed, or intangible content (such as meanings or feelings), which cannot necessarily be transformed to integer or continuous ratio data formats (Babbie, 2007). Nominal includes narratives, codes, words, and mixed types. Quantitative data type are generally numeric, such as an interval or a continuous ratio data type (Strang, 2009d). One type may look like another. For example a product code is nominal but may seem to be interval—the type depends on the situation; based on constructivism principles, data type is based on the interpretation or the research, participants, or both (Onwuegbuzie, Leech & Collins, 2010). Nominal data types are often called categorical variables in the literature.

As mentioned earlier, the unit of analysis data type is important to consider in the research design strategy because, when combined with the research ideology, this determines the permissible research methods and techniques that could be used. For example, if the purpose were to explore the tacit satisfaction of teaching performance at the university faculty level of analysis, if the data were qualitative (assuming it contained only textual or audio feedback), interpretative methods and techniques would be needed (e.g., grounded theory or case study method with keyword or theme analysis). Alternatively, if the satisfaction data were collected in ordinal format (1, 2, 3... 10) or continuous scales (0%, 10.0%, 20.0%... 100%), statistical techniques could be used within a number of formal methods (case study, survey, experiment, etc.).

Categorical or nominal data can be used as quantitative variables when endorsing positivist or pragmatic ideologies by counting the occurrences of each category type. Then descriptive statistics or nonparametric inferential statistics could be applied, such as in an experiment or in a case study. Furthermore, categorical or nominal data could be converted to quantitative format. Referring to the example above, if the satisfaction data were nominal (low, medium, high) but with an implied ordinal scale, these values could be transformed to an ordinal or ration data type so that statistical techniques could be applied (e.g., within the experiment or survey method). On the other hand, nominal data could be analyzed using frequency techniques, such as narrative analysis or chi-square contingency analysis (both are typically used in the algorithms of qualitative analysis software).

Generalization goal and purpose

Research generalization goal, deductive versus inductive, is perhaps the most confusing information in the literature. A generalization goal contains two things: a deductive or inductive goal and the generalization target population. Deductive refers to testing a priori theories, concepts, constructs, or instruments to replicate findings or to discover nuances when the context changes. Inductive refers to building theories, concepts, constructs, or instruments from the sample data. In some cases, inductive refers to significantly modifying a priori models. A generalization target refers to the place, the population, or the subpopulation to which the findings and implications of the research outcome(s) apply. On the one hand, some researchers do not have a generalization goal, that is, they are interested in only discovering and documenting the business processes used within their own company; this is still a generalization goal: The organization is the target, and it would be inductive because they would be creating a model that does not yet exist and may not be generalized outside the company.

On the other hand, if the researcher wishes to be able to generalize his or her findings to another company or to a multinational organization in another country, this would require two very different sampling techniques. The former—generalizing to another company (in the same national political region, e.g., country)—would require selecting a sample of one or more companies that are comparable to the company being examined in the unit of analysis. Comparable in this sense means that all but the unit of analysis would be similar, or the differences should be either controlled or accounted for. Researchers in general select companies to match their generalization goals, and they list the characteristics of each sampled company to establish credibility by allowing other researchers to clearly see that the sampled units are similar enough to the generalization goal. In this example, to generalize a goal to another multinational organization, it is likely that several companies with offices located in the same defined countries would be selected, with a generalization goal to these countries. Another variation is to attempt to generalize to the industry and account for differences between the other contextual factors. All of the above applies to the individual and group levels of analysis.

The research goal also can be deductive or inductive. Deductive simply refers to a researcher applying an existing theory or construct and showing how it can describe, explain, or evaluate the unit of analysis in the sample data within- or between-groups, according to the level of analysis, for example, using the transformational leadership theory and a survey instrument (Strang, 2008b) to compare the leading ability of female versus male project managers in the same industry. Inductive is the reverse, referring to the researcher trying to develop or modify a theory or construct from the sample data, for example, developing a new learning style instrument using the literature as a theoretical lens, piloting and replicating this with a representative sample of project managers, conducting exploratory factor analysis with validity and reliability estimates, and publishing the explanation of the factors (with reliabilities) along with the survey questions. In keeping with the pragmatic ideology, there are likely combinations of deductive-inductive research purposes.

A deductive generalization goal could specify that the results of a study would form implications that would likely be found to be applicable to another (similar) target population if another researcher were to repeat the study there. The same concept applies to an inductive goals, in that if the study were repeated by another researcher on a sample in the generalized target population, it is likely that the researcher would come up with similar findings of the new/modified theory or construct. This is because the concept of a generalization goal is itself inductive—all scholarly studies are inductive insofar as the researcher is trying to produce new findings, whereby the implications are a confirmation of an a priori theory or construct or the development of a new theory or construct, which ought to apply to another population.

If the researcher is aligning with post-positivism or pragmatism, and analyzing qualitative data types, then a hypothesis statement could be developed to deductively test a theory, perhaps by using narrative analysis or a chi-square goodness of fit on frequency counts of important keywords identified from the sample data. If a constructivistic researcher were conducting this same study, he or she would likely deductively test a theory by summarizing the qualitative data as a taxonomy, provide explanations created by the participants, and then compare those to the a priori model in the form of a point-by-point narrative discussion.

By comparison, inductive generalization goals are more common with constructivistic ideologies. However, positivists inductively create new theories and models by using experiments, surveys, and observation (collecting factual, usually quantitative data), by applying principal component analysis, exploratory factor analysis, or correspondence analysis techniques along with validity checking and reliability analysis.

For example, a constructivistic researcher wishes to know what successful CEOs think are team leadership competencies for project managers (PMs) in the US automobile manufacturing industry, in order to develop a guideline for hiring new PMs. The generalization goal is to inductively generalize to the US manufacturing industry. The level of analysis is individual and the unit of analysis is the CEOs since they are being sampled about their perceptions (what they think) of what are the best competencies for team leadership in a project context. A phenomenology method using the interview technique with a thematic analysis of the transcripts would be ideal to examine the meaning of the CEOs' cognitive experience. A sample size might start at 10% or 5% of the company (whichever is lower) and continue until the saturation point is reached (when an interview with a CEO does not reveal any new competency themes). The outcome of this analysis would likely be a mind map or a visual model of the themes. The study could also be undertaken with several other methods and technique combinations to meet the research goal.

Integrating research questions or hypotheses into strategy

Research questions or hypotheses should be aligned with the other components of a research strategy, namely the generalization goal (deductive or inductive, target population), unit of analysis, and level of analysis. The unit and level of analysis should be expressed within the research question or hypothesis (plural as necessary). The generalization goal and purpose require separate statements in the design, but they impact the wording of research questions and hypotheses. Thus the generalization goal should be determined (at least in draft form) before the researcher finalizes the research questions or hypotheses.

Some thought leaders suggest it is mandatory to first form research questions and then develop hypothesis statements from these. That is fine but not absolutely necessary in pragmatic or constructivistic ideologies. I will take that approach here. In fact I recommend it is a best practice to start with a research question and transform that into one or more hypotheses, when taking a positivistic ideology. Since I am a post-positivist, I also specify testable hypotheses where possible, even when conducting studies using qualitative data types (e.g., when using the multiple case study or action research method).

I should acknowledge that there is a huge amount of confusing literature under the topic "research inquiry" or "research strategy" (often going by other captions). This is an added layer of complexity imposed on inexperienced organizational researchers and academic scholars. The epistemology uses terms such as descriptive, exploratory, and explanatory, often summarized in tables, and it suggests they are a research method or strategy—but they are not. While there is absolutely nothing wrong with considering these taxonomies, a proper research strategy must specify the goal (where the findings and implications may be generalized to), the purpose (deductive theory testing or inductive theory building), the level of analysis, and the unit of analysis (including data types along with research questions and/or hypotheses). Nonetheless, the literature contains some excellent approaches for helping researchers create research questions and hypotheses. Actually if you change the phrase from research inquiry or research strategy to "research question," then I have found that the existing literature works well for doctoral students.

A researcher may form a research question by stating that he or she is interested in exploring or discovering and then describing hidden relationships or characteristics in the unit of analysis. Often the researcher is focused on finding a true meaning for the unit of analysis (e.g., when using the phenomenology method). Alternatively, the researcher may write a research question stating that he or she wishes to compare factors or relationships in the unit of analysis. Explanatory-type research questions generally point toward correlation to explain relationships or regression techniques to estimate the predictive ability of factors and variables within the unit of analysis.

A research question should follow the "W5" principle starting with, who, what, when, where, as well as how (Richardson, 2000). As explained earlier, the level of analysis may be individual, dyadic, group, or of a larger scope such as a company, association, or the entire industry. The unit of analysis could be to describe variables or to explain the relationships among the variables. A within-group or between-group comparison could be used. A deductive purpose mentions a theory or construct while an inductive purpose provides a theoretical lens intended to assist in building a new theory or construct.

Going back to the previous CEO example, the research question could be: What do successful CEOs think are the most important team leadership competencies for project managers (PMs) to succeed in the US automobile manufacturing industry? A hypothesis for that research question might be: a two-third of the total number of CEOs will agree on one particular competency to be considered important. If the literature had identified several important competencies for PMs, then a research question could be formed using this theoretical lens and a hypothesis could be developed to statistically test the agreement between the a priori competencies and those identified as important by the CEOs, through a nonparametric technique such as Kendall's Tau.

For a positivistic research design, research questions and hypotheses are usually easier to build. In the CEO example, the research question would likely reference an a priori construct and use either a structured interview (with the instrument) or a survey. The research question would be the same as before, but the hypothesis might be: CEOs rate communication skills as more important than math ability. This could be determined using a parametric *t*-test as long as the sample response data met the assumptions of a normal distribution. A pragmatic researcher might use an a priori instrument to guide the interpretation of the thematic analysis when using the grounded theory method, which might conclude with a taxonomy of competencies (a type of structured table).

Research questions differ from hypotheses in that the former includes an elaboration of the unit of analysis and indirectly the level of analysis. A hypothesis need only be used for positivist- or pragmatic-oriented ideologies that test a theory using quantitative data types, although as shown above, they can be formed for any research strategy. Scientific hypothesis statements start with the default null condition along with alternative propositions using <, >, or = combinations. For example, H1: the mean grades of students in the treatment condition will be higher than those in the control group. Inferential statistical techniques are needed to test hypothesis. Going back to the CEO example, the scientific hypothesis statement would be:

- H0: CEOs will not rate communication skills more important than math ability.
- H1: CEOs will rate communication skills as more important than math ability.

Conclusions

The strategy layer of the research design typology was explained using several examples from business and management. Defining strategy is essential and mandatory in the *scientific method* in comparison to ideology, which can be loosely articulated.

The strategy defines the generalization goal, stating where the findings and implications could be applied. It also articulates the purpose in the form of research questions or hypotheses. These are based on the level of analysis and unit of analysis (factors and relationships of interest). A key element of the unit of analysis is to identify the within-groups or between-groups analysis focus. The next chapter will discuss research method, the third layer of the typology.

References

Babbie, E. (2007). *The practice of social research* (11th ed.). Belmont, CA: Wadsworth /Thompson.

Hofstede, G. J. (2009). Research on cultures: How to use it in training. *European Journal of Cross-Cultural Competence and Management, 1*(1), 14–21.

Onwuegbuzie, A., Leech, N. L., & Collins, K. M. T. (2010). Innovative data collection strategies in qualitative research. *Qualitative Report Journal, 15*(3), 696–726. Retrieved from http://www.nova.edu/ssss/QR/QR15-3/onwuegbuzie.pdf.

Richardson, L. (2000). Writing: A method of inquiry. In N. K. Denzin & Y. S. Lincoln (Eds.), *Handbook of qualitative research* (2nd ed.). New York: Sage.

Strang, K. D. (1983). *Client/financial management system development.*Unpublished manuscript, Belmont, CA.

Strang, K. D. (2005). Examining effective and ineffective transformational project leadership. *Team Performance Management Journal, 11*(3/4), 68–103. Retrieved from http://dx.doi.org/10.1108/13527590510606299.

Strang, K. D. (2007). Examining effective technology project leadership traits and behaviours. *Computers in Human Behaviour, 23*(2), 424–462. Retrieved from http://www.amazon.com/Examining-effective-technology-leadership-behaviors/dp/B000P6OSN4.

Strang, K. D. (2008a). Quantitative online student profiling to forecast academic outcome from learning styles using dendrogram decision models. *Multicultural Education & Technology Journal, 2*(4), 215–244. Retrieved from http://dx.doi.org/10.1108/17504970810911043.

Strang, K. D. (2008b). Collaborative synergy and leadership in e-business. In J. Salmons & L. Wilson (Eds.), *Handbook of research on electronic collaboration and organizational synergy* (pp. 409–429). Hershey, PA: IGI-GLOBAL Global. Retrieved from http://www.igi-global.com/bookstore/chapter.aspx?titleid=20189.

Strang, K. D. (2009a). How multicultural learning approach impacts grade for international university students in a business course. *Asian English Foreign Language Journal Quarterly, 11*(4), 271–292. Retrieved from http://www.asian-efl-journal.com/December_2009_ks.php.

Strang, K. D. (2009b). Improving supervision of cross-cultural post graduate university students. *International Journal of Learning and Change, 4*(2), 181–202. Retrieved from http://www.inderscience.com/search/index.php?action=record&rec_id=32711.

Strang, K. D. (2009c). Measuring online learning approach and mentoring preferences of international doctorate students. *International Journal of Educational Research, 48*(4), 245–257. Retrieved from http://dx.doi.org/10.1016/j.ijer.2009.11.002.

Strang, K. D. (2009d). Using recursive regression to explore nonlinear relationships and interactions: A tutorial applied to a multicultural education study. *Practical Assessment, Research & Evaluation, 14*(3), 1–13. Retrieved from http://pareonline.net/getvn.asp?v=14&n=3.

Strang, K. D. (2010a). Global culture, learning style and outcome: An interdisciplinary empirical study of international students. *Journal of Intercultural Education, 21*(6), 519–533. Retrieved from http://www.tandfonline.com/doi/abs/10.1080/14675986.2010.533034#preview.

Strang, K. D. (2010b). Measuring self-regulated e-feedback, study approach and academic outcome of multicultural university students. *International Journal of Continuing Engineering Education and Life-Long Learning, 20*(2), 239–255. Retrieved from http://www.inderscience.com/search/index.php?action=record&rec_id=36818.

Strang, K. D. (2011). Leadership substitutes and personality impact on time and quality in virtual new product development. *Project Management Journal, 42*(1), 73–90. Retrieved from http://www3.interscience.wiley.com/journal/114291333/issueyear?year=2010.

Strang, K. D. (2012a). Applied financial nonlinear programming models for decision making. *International Journal of Applied Decision Sciences, 5*(4), 370–395. Retrieved from http://www.inderscience.com/info/inarticletoc.php?jcode=ijads&year=2012&vol=5&issue=4.

Strang, K. D. (2012b). Case study: Risk mitigation for hurricanes near Texas coast oil refineries. *International Journal of Risk and Contingency Management, 1*(2), 43–53. Retrieved from http://www.igi-global.com/article/case-study-risk-mitigation-hurricanes/67374.

Strang, K. D. (2012c). Group cohesion, personality and leadership effect on networked marketing staff performance. *International Journal of Networking and Virtual Organisations, 10*(2), 187–209. Retrieved from http://www.inderscience.com/browse/index.php?journalID=22&year=2012&vol=10&issue=2.

Strang, K. D. (2012d). Importance of verifying queue model assumptions before planning with simulation software. *European Journal of Operational Research, 218*(2), 493–504. Retrieved from http://www.sciencedirect.com/science/article/pii/S0377221711010319.

Strang, K. D. (2012e). Investment selection in complex multinational projects. *International Journal of Information Technology Project Management, 3*(2), 1–13. Retrieved from http://www.igi-global.com/journal/international-journal-information-technology-project/1103.

Strang, K. D. (2012f). Logistic planning with nonlinear goal programming models in spreadsheets. *International Journal of Applied Logistics, 2*(4), 1–14. Retrieved from http://www.igi-global.com/article/logistic-planning-nonlinear-goal-programming/74728.

Strang, K. D. (2012g). Man versus math: Behaviorist exploration of post-crisis non-banking asset management. *Journal of Asset Management, 13*(5), 348–467. Retrieved from http://www.palgrave-journals.com/jam/journal/v13/n5/index.html.

Strang, K. D. (2012h). Nonparametric correspondence analysis of global risk management techniques. *International Journal of Risk and Contingency Management, 1*(3), 1–24.

Retrieved from http://www.igi-global.com/journal-contents/international-journal-risk-contingency-management/53135.

Strang, K. D. (2012i). Prioritization and supply chain logistics as a marketing function in a mining company. *Journal of Marketing Channels, 19*(2), 141–155. Retrieved from http://www.tandfonline.com/doi/abs/10.1080/1046669X.2012.667763.

Strang, K. D. (2012j). Student diaspora and learning style impact on group performance. *International Journal of Online Pedagogy and Course Design, 2*(3), 1–19. Retrieved from http://www.igi-global.com/article/student-diaspora-learning-style-impact/68410.

Strang, K. D. (2012k). Multicultural face of organizations. In M. A. Sarlak (Ed.), *The new faces of organizations in the 21st century* (Vol. 5, pp. 1–21). Toronto, ON: North American Institute of Science and Information Technology (NAISIT). Retrieved from http://naisit.org/book/detail/id/6.

Strang, K. D. (2013). Homeowner behavioral intent to evacuate after flood warnings. *International Journal of Risk and Contingency Management, 2*(3), 1–28. Retrieved from http://www.igi-global.com/article/homeowner-behavioral-intent-to-evacuate-after-flood-risk-warnings/80017.

Strang, K. D. (2014a). Cognitive learning strategy as a partial effect on major field test in business results. *Journal of Education for Business, 89*(3), 142–148. Retrieved from http://www.tandfonline.com/doi/full/10.1080/08832323.2013.781988.

Strang, K. D. (2014b). Exploring marketing theories to model business web service procurement behavior. In J. Goodyear & Z. Sun (Eds.), *Demand-driven web services: Theory, technologies and applications* (Vol. 1, ch. 2, pp. 21–42). Hershey, PA: IGI-GLOBAL. Retrieved from http://www.igi-global.com/book/demand-driven-web-services/95218.

Strang, K. D., & Nersesian, R. (2014). Nonparametric estimation of petroleum accident risk to improve environmental protection. *Journal of Environment, Systems and Decisions, 34*(1), 150–159. Retrieved from http://link.springer.com/article/10.1007%2Fs10669-013-9476-z.

Strang, K. D., & Symonds, R. J. (2012). Analyzing research activity duration and uncertainty in business doctorate degrees. *International Journal of Risk and Contingency Management, 1*(1), 29–48. Retrieved from http://www.igi-global.com/article/international-journal-risk-contingency-management/65730.

Vajjhala, N. R., & Strang, K. D. (2014). Collaboration strategies for a transition economy: Measuring culture in Albania. *International Journal of Cross Cultural Management, 21*(1), 78–103. Retrieved from http://www.emeraldinsight.com/journals.htm?articleid=17105155&show=abstract.

4

Matching Research Method with Ideology and Strategy

Kenneth D. Strang

Research design typology method focus

The research design typology model was introduced in chapter 1. The ideology and strategy layers were explained in chapter 2 and chapter 3, respectively. The method layer of the research design typology, as highlighted in figure 4.1, will be examined in this chapter.

Matching research method with ideology and strategy

Figure 4.1 does not list all the methods or techniques simply because there are too many to fit into the diagram, and new approaches are periodically emerging in practice. This chapter does not explain all the methods, nor does it sufficiently explain any method to substitute for a methods-specific text. Each method listed in the third layer of figure 4.1 often has hundreds of books published, so this chapter merely provides an overview to assist in completing the research design. Thus, researchers must also utilize a methods-specific text book or article.

Research methods consist of formally recognized methodologies along with de facto methodologies for conducting defined types of studies. Subject-matter experts in specific fields have agreed upon the major formal research methods, and as stated above there are generally many textbooks written for each one. Emerging or hybrid research methods also exist. Researchers may develop their own de jure methods if following a pragmatic ideology.

The *scientific method* is not a methodology per se but rather it is a high-quality standard meaning to clearly approach a problem, articulate the research design, and carefully, ethically, execute the study, and then accurately, honestly communicate the findings. The *scientific methodology* recommends documenting the formal method applied and citing a thought leader.

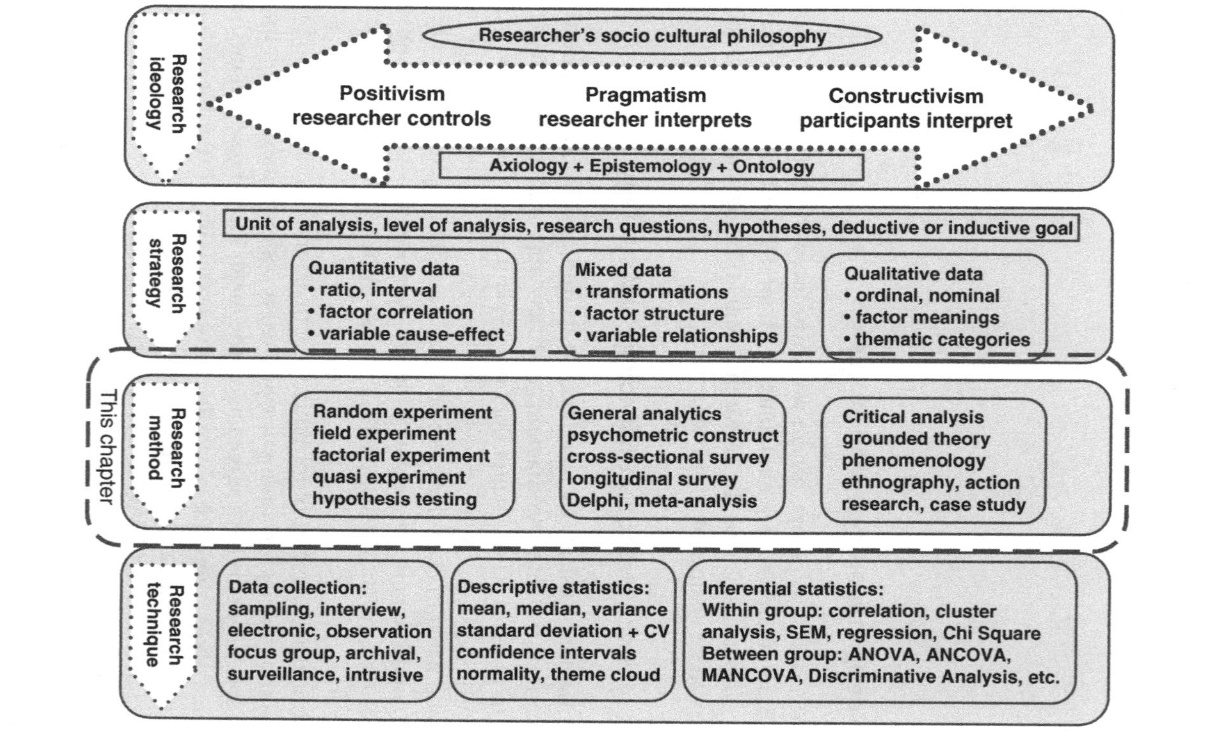

Figure 4.1 Research design typology model—method focus.

Methodologies are complete systems of processes that include recommended techniques. In this handbook, research methods are methodologies that cite the required or recommended techniques. Thus, it is difficult to separate techniques from methods in a discussion about either. Techniques are specific procedures to assist in answering the research questions and hypotheses. Most techniques are automated with software programs.

Techniques are often logically grouped together in a family of related procedures, such as sampling method or parametric statistics. Additionally, some techniques are called methods, but it is asserted here that they are techniques since they do not contain a methodological application explanation published by a thought leader or a disciplinary community of practice. ANOVA is a good example since it is a technique that can be applied in several de facto methods where between- and within-group means are compared to estimate their statistical similarity, such as the survey and experiment methods. On the other hand, case study and correspondence analysis are examples of de facto methodologies. The survey method should not be confused with a survey or a questionnaire since the latter are instruments used within data collection techniques.

There are several common technique categories used in all business and management research methods since the nature of a scholarly study is to find and communicate useful inductions or deductions of theory for generalizing to a population (or to several populations). Note that the term "population" in this context is not limited to human participants (as discussed earlier)—populations may include animals, plants, machinery, land, processes, policies, or any system of objects. Samples are drawn from populations.

These common cross-method technique categories include sampling, data collection, data analysis, validity-reliability analysis, and ethics. These are briefly discussed in this chapter and they are elaborated upon in the following chapter. Some practitioners include writing, formatting, citation, and referencing style as part of the methodology. Ethics is such an important component in all recognized methods that it warrants a discussion first.

Ethics and quality assurance in methods

Ethics are embedded in all formal business and management research methodologies that follow the *scientific method,* which sets methods apart from techniques. Other terms used for ethics are quality assurance, validity, reliability, and ethical standards. The principles of ethics are accuracy and honesty in the research method. Reliability, credibility, and validity are techniques although they fall under the auspices of ethics.

The researcher must use appropriate techniques to match research ideology with unit and level of analysis (including research questions, hypothesis, and analysis strategy). This is because when an incorrect method or technique is used on a data type, it may produce an incorrect answer to a research question or hypothesis. Furthermore, participants must be told about the study and all risks must be declared to them. Most studies do not put participants at risk, but some do, such as medical procedures and drug tests in experiments. Participants must have the right to withdraw from any study at any time. Ethics also applies to nonhuman objects, including animals and organizational assets. Creswell is an excellent authority on research ethics.

Ethical issues in research also reflect important moral concerns about the practice of responsible behavior in society. Careful consideration must be given to those research situations in which there is a possibility of physical or psychological harm, exploitation, invasion of privacy, risk of disclosure of confidentiality/trade secrets, and/or loss of dignity (Gill, Johnson & Clark, 2010, p. 14). Additionally, certain groups in society are considered vulnerable due to their status, such as children, mentally impaired, prisoners, and pregnant women (Creswell, 2012). Ethics relates to strategy because a researcher may not be aware of the expectations for some participants due to sociocultural differences, which as explained earlier also impacts the researcher's ideology. Rather than try to go through all variations, I suggest consulting the insightful chapter in this handbook written by Brennan, Parker, Nguyen, and Watne that discusses the essential multicultural issues to consider in a research design.

The researcher needs to develop a protocol to describe the processes for upholding ethics, and in many cases obtain approval from an independent committee before conducting the study (and they must rigorously apply the protocol during the study). This committee is generally the internal review board in a university, or the chief information officer in an organization (although titles and roles differ—e.g., in one company I worked with the VP of Human Resources who was the responsible authority). The techniques for ensuring validity and reliability are discussed in the next section (they are not methods).

How to identify a method for an ideology and strategy

Methods tend to fall in line with ideology and strategy. In particular, formal methods commonly are associated with the unit of analysis in the research strategy. Recall from the strategy chapter that the unit of analysis specifies the factors and/or relationships of interest, a between-group or within-group focus, the data types, and the research questions or hypotheses.

The hypothesis is the best component to examine first when selecting the applicable methods. If the hypothesis was not stated, the research question may be used. The between-group or within-group focus and data types are critical since there are often specific de facto methods that ought to be followed (and specific techniques that ought to be applied to each data type). Figure 4.2 is a conceptual diagram illustrating the most common methods relevant for

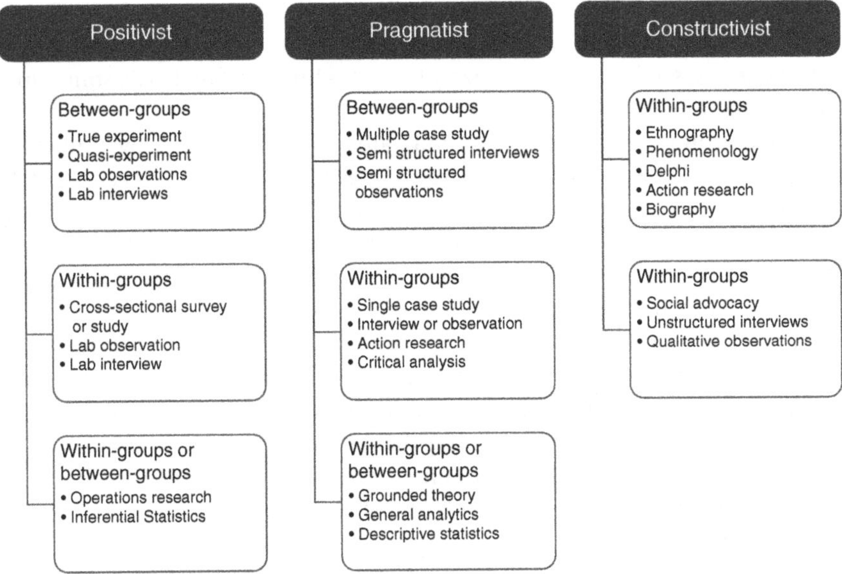

Figure 4.2 Typical methods used for each research ideology.

each research ideology position on the continuum (this is not an exhaustive list and some may be used by a research holding any ideology, such as action research and case studies).

The methods described under the next topics are not necessarily limited to positivistic ideologies, but rather, they are most commonly employed by positivistic researchers. Rather than attempt to list all possible methods, I will focus on how to select a method that is in correspondence with an ideology and strategy.

Aligning method and strategy with positivistic ideologies

The true random experiment method (labeled as experiment in figure 4.1) is done with a high level of control (often in a lab) and is considered to be the most robust, positivistic, of all methods. The data collection from an experiment could be done using observation, an interview, a survey, or an intrusive method (e.g., a blood draw in clinical health care). Quasi- or field-experiment methods use intact convenience groups. Factorial experiment methods vary the treatments (manipulated factors) across several participants or groups. Hypothesis testing is the formal scientific approach used for all experimental research methods.

Psychometric construct testing is nonexperimental. This involves testing the factor reliability of a survey. The cross-sectional survey method collects data from participants at one point in time while longitudinal surveys use two or more intervals of data collection to determine if there are any changes over time. Meta-analysis methods consist of a review of the literature to determine factorial models and their effect sizes. In fact, a literature review is sometimes called a "method."

The experiment and survey methods are well-documented by numerous expert sources (see: Babbie, 2007; Creswell, 2009; Keppel & Wickens, 2004). Experiments may be done in the field or in a laboratory, the latter of which has more control to reduce threats to validity (discussed later). The unit of analysis would be to manipulate an independent factor to determine how this changes the dependent variable.

The cross-sectional field study or survey method employs questions to collect responses from participants, through interviews, mail, or electronic techniques. The term cross-sectional is often applied in the literature to indicate a within-group, unit-of-analysis focus, meaning that no specific groups or sections are allocated; otherwise it would become an experiment or quasi-experiment. Some researchers in the literature use the term "observation field study" to mean a cross-sectional study.

The word "field" in figure 4.2 refers to conducting the observation or interview method in situ, on location, with the participants. Paradoxically, when an experiment is conducted in the field, it becomes a quasi-experiment since there is less control. The survey method is rarely conducted in the field (it would be inefficient), so we don't prefix it with field, but it is definitely a positivistic formal method. The survey method is often done through email (or sometimes mail). Survey instruments are not to be confused with the survey method, because survey instruments or questionnaires are used to collect data in many methods.

Surveys and experiments are typically employed when using the positivist ideology. However, surveys can also be used with pragmatist and constructivist philosophies, which illustrate that research methods are not necessarily constrained to ideology. Nonetheless, it would be rare to see a positivist use methods that explore qualitative variables such as feelings, geography, or images. Correlation study method is another term often used in practice to refer to the survey method, when the research strategy unit of analysis seeks to identify significant within-group relationships.

Factor analysis methods, as the term implies, are positivistic, but they could also be pragmatic-focused research methods. The factor analysis method requires a literature review to develop the factors and to develop question items for a survey instrument that is used to collect data. Factor analysis includes or specifies techniques for exploring or explaining "variable distinction" or "relationships" in the unit of analysis. Common techniques such as parametric correlation, principal component analysis, multidimensional scaling, structural equation modeling, canonical correlation, or confirmatory factor analysis are used to "prove" that quantitative unit of analysis data type structure is statistically significant (Strang, 2009). Less common techniques include distribution analysis comparisons (Nersesian & Strang, 2013; Strang & Nersesian, 2014) and recursive regression (Strang, 2009). When the data collected for the unit of analysis are qualitative, nonparametric statistical techniques can be used, such as Spearman correlation, correspondence analysis, cluster analysis, and ordinal factor analysis (Strang, 2009). The family of general analytical techniques may also be applied on qualitative data, notably scatter plots, line charts, theme analysis matrices, and tables, etc.

Operations research is a large de facto family of statistically oriented methods frequently applied in positivist ideologies on data collected from organizational processes or production equipment. They are also applied with pragmatist ideologies. Operations research strategies are likely to generalize to the organization or industry, focus on a between-groups unit of analysis, and use the individual level of analysis, although other combinations are possible. The operations research hypotheses often refer to testing the means from process measurement data for significance against standards or in comparison to groups in the sample frame. Common operations research methods include statistical process control, economic inventory order level analysis, waiting-line queue analysis, and process optimization (Strang, 2012a, 2012b, 2012c, 2012d, 2013).

Aligning method and strategy with pragmatist ideologies

There is an important distinction about the pragmatist. While a positivist would be unlikely to apply the phenomenology method from figure 4.2, and a constructivist would not choose a true experiment method in their research design, a pragmatist could utilize any method. This is the distinguishing characteristic of the pragmatism ideology. A pragmatist adopting a post-positivism philosophy, a position on the ideological continuum in figure 4.1, close but not exactly at positivism, might select a quasi-experiment. On the other hand, a pragmatist adopting an interpretivistic philosophy (a position on the figure 4.1 ideology continuum approaching constructivism), intending to interpret the findings rather than allow participants to supply the true meaning of the data, could employ grounded theory or ethnology.

Pragmatists have a larger suite of formal research methods than positivists or constructivists, despite the appearance of figure 4.2 layer two. Another point should be made about pragmatic ideology. Many practitioner-scholars create their own labels to describe how their methods are adapted for a particular ideology, such as participatory-phenomenology, interpretative-phenomenology, and constructed-grounded theory. In fact this is how the quasi-experiment method came to be formally recognized.

Critical analysis is a method similar to a literature review, but since it requires the researcher to make interpretive deductions or inductions it can be properly classified as a pragmatist ideology. When using this method, the researcher first performs a structured literature review, organized and guided by thematic topics or factors. A factor could be an event, a process, or any relevant object in the level and unit of analysis. The researcher then analyzes the credibility and contemporary relevance of important studies in the literature review. In the analysis the researcher typically compares and contrasts relevant studies and then forms a recommendation about the most accurate, credible, or relevant interpretation for each major theme or factor. This follows a deductively driven purpose, but it could be considered inductive if a new taxonomy were being created as a result of the study. Critical analysis is the method used (or least advocated) for this handbook.

As noted earlier, general analytics are a large de facto family of research methods relying on mathematical and grouping approaches, somewhat similar to operations research. General analytics as a method is frequently applied in both positivist and pragmatic ideologies on data collected from archives. Many researchers refer to the case study method and include general analytics or vice-versa (Denscombe, 2003; Macquarie, 2006; Yin, 2009). General analytic methods consist of approaches (and recommended techniques) for evaluating the unit of analysis, namely, "pattern-matching, explanation-building, time-series analysis, and program logic models" (Yin, 2009, p. 106).

General analytic methods may also contain nonstatistical techniques such as workflow analysis, database entity relationship diagrams, system analysis flowcharts, mind maps, Pareto charts, along with comparison matrices and graphing contrasts. The distinction between general analytics and operations research is that the former tends to utilize descriptive along with inferential statistical techniques for both qualitative and quantitative data. Additionally, general analytic methods leave more interpretation to the researcher, such as with pattern recognition, rather than using distribution comparisons as would be done in operations research. Another distinction between the two is that general analytics are usually inductive (create new theories or constructs) whereas operations research are deductive (prove or disprove hypotheses). Common general analytic methods include data mining and social network analysis. Operations research techniques rely heavily on mathematical concepts, so quantitative data are usually involved.

Grounded theory follows an interpretivistic ideology (this is not listed in the figure 4.1 research design typology). However, it falls under the pragmatist ideology insofar as far as he researcher interprets the data. Some practitioner-scholars consider grounded theory to be a part of a constructivist ideology and it is often termed "constructed grounded theory."

Grounded theory starts with a proposition for a theory as the unit of analysis. As with all empirical scientific research methods, the literature must be reviewed to ensure the study has not previously been conducted and to articulate the gap in the current body of knowledge. An additional reason for reviewing the literature in the grounded theory method is to discuss the current state of the art for the a priori theory being modified.

Grounded theory starts by collecting qualitative data from participants, and then the researcher attempts to organize the data into a categorical taxonomy of themes or factors (Glaser & Holton, 2005). The researcher then compares the data to the literature review to determine if the taxonomy is equivalent to existing theories or constructs, and if so, cites these (Charmaz, 2006). This phase may require reviewing additional literature especially when working across disciplines or cultures where the epistemology differs. If this is a new finding then it is proposed as a theory grounded for the data with a recommendation that positivists, pragmatists, and constructivists further study this to support or refute the findings (Glaser & Holton, 2005).

Content analysis is very similar to the grounded theory method except that linguistic qualitative data type narratives are collected from participants (Franzosi, 2010). The techniques used for content analysis focus on grammar constructs and keywords (such as nouns and verbs) to identify frequency patterns. Therefore content analysis research methods primarily are deductive and pragmatic, because "the categories are determined based on the investigator's theoretical and/or substantive interests" (Franzosi, 2010). General analytic techniques are used to count, in a diagram, or to summarize qualitative nominal keywords, which are the units of analysis.

Quantitative narrative analysis (QNA) is a method similar to, and sometimes used with, the content analysis method. In QNA, the relationships and frequencies of specific grammatical linguistic properties are examined, namely, subject-action-object or pro/noun-verb/infinitive-noun/adverb (Franzosi, 2010). The researcher then constructs a taxonomy of the resulting construct and reviews the literature for similarities citing anything relevant, or if this is a unique finding, a new theory is proposed to be tested. The reason this method is constructivist is because participants supply the meanings.

The case study research method is used across all ideologies, and some researchers employ a pluralistic mixture of philosophical orientations, although case studies are best suited for pragmatists. Case studies are used to investigate the unit of analysis "within its real-life context, especially when the boundaries between phenomenon and context are not clearly evident" (Yin, 2009, p. 13). The epistemology differs across the pragmatist (post-positivist) through constructivist ideologies when using the case study method. The unit of analysis for single cases is usually within-group but this is called a within-case unit of analysis. Obviously the generalization is more limited as it is generally toward the studies of organization or context. Multiple case studies are cross-case units of analysis in pragmatist and constructivist ideologies as compared with the between-groups analysis focus.

The level of analysis in case studies is often the organization (regardless of the unit of analysis), which distinguishes it from grounded theory and other methods that focus on qualitative data type collection that is usually at the individual level of analysis. Any type of data could be collected; yet it is often mixed with quantitative and qualitative evidence from multiple sources (Eisenhardt, 1989). All techniques may be used in a case study including quantitative (descriptive or inferential statistics) as well as qualitative data-oriented approaches (such as general analytic procedures or thematic diagramming). Interestingly, case studies have been described as using action research, and vice-versa, action research may use case studies as discussed in the chapter by Lim and Seok-Chai. On the one hand, as implied in this topic, the ideology of the researcher conducting an individual or multiple case study is usually pragmatism. On the other hand, as will be discussed below, the philosophy could be beyond the interpretivist side of pragmatism into constructivism, as with action research.

However, case studies should not be confused with experiments, surveys, or constructivist methods since the same techniques may be employed. Some experts use synonyms such as mixed methods, bibliographies, or business research (Gill et al., 2010). The following are the distinguishing attributes of the case study method:

- It can cope with a technically distinctive situation in which are present many more variables of interest than data points, and as one result (many factors, one unit of analysis—which would not likely pass positivistic validity or reliability tests).
- It relies on multiple sources of evidence (several levels of analysis), with data needing to converge in a triangulating fashion, and as another result.
- It benefits from the prior development of theoretical propositions to guide data collection and analysis (similar to grounded theory) (Yin, 2009, p. 13).

Aligning method and strategy with constructivist ideologies

Constructivists (like pragmatists) have a larger suite of formal research methods than positivists, should they wish to choose them (but usually does not happen). For example, a researcher could perform a controlled experiment on participants, observe them, survey them, and interview them to arrive at a deep rich understanding of the how the participants perceived the treatment (and placebo control). However, in practice this is rarely done for two reasons. The first is that a constructivist may ask the participants to interpret the meaning of the data but since statistical interpretation of the data is required, it generally confines the level of analysis to the scholar. Second, constructivists generally examine complex previously unstudied phenomena and they ask participants to provide the meaning of the data. Thus, constructivist methods do not work well for studying no-human objects, namely, animals, equipment, land, policies, decision making, and so on. This is perhaps why constructivist methods have taken so long to emerge and become respected in the social science literature. This also provides insight when designing a study because if a researcher wishes to analyze objects in the unit of analysis, he or she ought to consider a pragmatic ideology.

Some methods are used by both pragmatists and constructivists when the data require a great degree of interpretation by the researcher. The first layer in the typology in figure 4.1 does not distinguish between these levels of pragmatism or constructivism, so the reader must bear in mind that all methods listed in this section can be used under both ideologies except for those that require participant-only data meaning interpretation. For the purposes of this handbook, the accuracy of ideology is not as important as the correct alignment between strategy and method.

Constructivist methods generally begin with theory deduction to guide the analysis, even if the purpose is to answer a research question about discovering a new meaning to generalize to another population. This is called establishing the theoretical lens for the study. All constructivist methods require this literature-review step because otherwise a researcher could conduct a study without realizing that the findings had already been published (thus wasting time and effort, not to mention feeling embarrassed). Another purpose of the literature review is to determine whether the research strategy contains a unique goal and purpose (gap in current theories). The literature review is also done to identify the extent to which other researchers have explored the unit and level of analysis. It may be possible that studies exist for the same unit of analysis but the level of analysis may have been group, whereas a researcher might be planning to generalize the individual level to a population; thus, there would be a gap in the literature.

As explained earlier, social-constructed research methods will include everything else beyond experimental, nonexperimental surveys, general analytics, factor analysis, grounded theory, content analysis, and case studies. This discussion will start with research methods that are pragmatic oriented and end with those where the research holds a "pure" strong social-constructivist ideology.

Autobiographies and biographies are a type of research method insofar as the literature may be reviewed in addition to the scientific method being followed for data collection and reporting (Richardson, 2000). Meta-analysis and narrative research are also in this category where the researcher reviews the literature archives and summarizes what has been said, based on his or her interpretation of the evidence (Gill et al., 2010). The reason this is constructivist and not pragmatic is that here, in the meta-analysis of an autobiography, the researcher is constructing the meaning as a researcher-participant. Note though that other thought leaders may classify meta-analysis as a post-positivist method.

Several similar research methods focus on data collection and exploration/explanation of participant meanings as jointly or primarily interpreted by the researcher: hermeneutics, discourse analysis, anthropology, and ethnography. The difference between these methods concerns the unit and level of analysis, along with the data collection techniques.

Hermeneutics is focused on the descriptive or exploratory analysis of meanings in the data, using a variety of collection as well as analysis techniques (Babbie, 2007). When using hermeneutics, generally the data type collected is in the qualitative nominal narrative format such as transcripts from interviews or written passages (Franzosi, 2010). Another term for hermeneutics is narrative analysis (sometimes listed as a technique), which is differentiated from content analysis since the goal is to describe (count) rather than explore the relationships. While narrative analysis is focused on describing statements as the unit of analysis, discourse analysis is a similar technique used in hermeneutics methods to analyze conversations or linguistic interactions (Alvesson, Kärreman & Swan, 2002). Conversations are usually collected in qualitative data audio format, and then transcribed into narratives (nominal data type) so that software can be employed to automate the analysis. When content or QNA are used in conjunction with hermeneutic phenomenology, they are considered constructivist. McCarthy explains a further variation known as eidetic phenomenology, which is interpretativistic because the researcher interprets the data.

Action research is similar to the case study method, except that the researcher is an active participant in the project and thereby contributes his or her perspective to the meaning of the data collected. Action research is a problem-solving research methodology that seeks to introduce improvements having positive social values, where the level of analysis is an organization and the unit of analysis is any problem along with the feasibility of a worked-out solution (Kemmis & Wilkinson, 1998; McNiff & Whitehead, 2000; Zuber-Skerritt, 1993). Baskerville pointed out that "the researcher is actively involved, with expected benefit for both researcher and organization; the knowledge obtained can be immediately applied...; the research is a cyclical process linking theory and practice" (Baskerville, 2001, p. 239).

The researcher typically employs a pragmatic or constructive ideology (the meaning perspective remains grounded in the participants of the organization). I could have placed this under the pragmatist ideology but I placed it as a constructivist-oriented approach since the participants are involved in understanding the problem to be solved, and they are actively involved in the study itself. Readers may wish to consult the chapter by Lim and Seok-Chai to gain a better understanding of the action research method and how it integrates with the single case study method.

The action research method starts by the researcher reviewing the literature either before or after the analysis, so as to validate or improve upon existing theories (Checkland, 1999). However, a unique aspect of action research that differentiates it from all other research methods is that a recommended intervention for the unit of analysis may be implemented within the organization level of analysis; this results in changes within the institution (Kemmis & Wilkinson, 1998; McNiff & Whitehead, 2000).

General analytic techniques are most often employed in action research. Tabular lists and graphic sense-making diagrams or flowcharts are most often employed. A researcher begins the method by planning with organizational participants what action to take, carries on the intervention with the action, observes the effects of that intervention, and finally reflects upon the observations in order to learn how better to plan and execute the next cycle (Schön, 1983). The reflections are done by all participants including the researchers, which is why it is classified here as constructivist. However, it is similar to grounded theory because if the intervention is successful, the researcher could claim that an improved process was achieved in the form of a theory.

A criticism of action research is that it may not generalize to other entities (e.g., other organizations) since the goal is to advocate change. Therefore, action research method experts insist that the implications must go "beyond those required for action...in the domain of the project...it must be possible to envisage talking about the theories developed in relation to other situations" (Baskerville, 2001, p. 84). Thus, the strategy underlying action research is inductive, exploratory in nature, and if documented objectively, the findings should generalize externally to similar organizations.

Anthropology is a formal research method focused on describing the developmental culture of human beings. The unit of analysis is a combination of physical, cognitive, and emotional progression of the human species. Qualitative and quantitative (mixed) data types are collected from multiple sources of historical archives, geological traces, and from observations when specimens are available (Babbie, 2007; M. Hammersley & Atkinson, 1983). The unit of analysis is to describe the evolution of humans using narratives, pictures, tables, and diagrams.

Ethnography is a research method focused on observing and asking process questions to participants in a natural intact group about how their "experiences" change over time (M. Hammersley & Atkinson, 1983; Richards, 2009). Therefore, the level of analysis is generally the group, and the unit of analysis is a qualitative emotive data type such as feeling or perception (Martyn Hammersley, 2006). Techniques involve general analytics as well as narrative quotations to authentically describe the perceptions of the participants. Hence ethnography is considered here as socially constructed as compared to content analysis or grounded theory methods.

Phenomenology is similar to the ethnography research method, but the level of analysis is generally the individual, immersed in a small group, and the unit of analysis is the "lived experience" of each participant, as authentically articulated by each participant (Babbie, 2007; Neuman, 2000; Richards, 2009). Qualitative data such as narratives, images, and cultural artifacts may be collected from the participants during interviews. Most data are collected directly from participants using one-to-one interviews, along with phone, mail, or email correspondence. The researcher must take a strong social-constructivist ideology to correctly apply the phenomenology research method, to ensure she/he does not interpret the data collected (Richardson, 2000). If the participant observation technique is used to collect data (as would be the approach when using ethnography), care must be taken to have the participants review and reword the evidence (Ellingson, 2009; Richards, 2009). Narrative techniques are most frequently used to describe the data, and diagramming techniques such as mind mapping (from general analytics) are commonly employed to illustrate the themes.

The emancipatory research method has been titled advocacy, social advocacy, or participant advocacy (Freedman, 2006; Mezirow, 1991). The emancipatory method is similar to action research, except that the focus is purely on less advantaged individuals (as a group), rather than an organization, and the unit of analysis is generally on required social policy change rather than business process improvement (Freedman, 2006). For this reason, when emancipatory methods are proposed, they often involve sampling participants from protected groups, which requires more scrutiny from the internal review board or from a university or from the chief information officer of an organization. Some practitioner-scholars will add the term emancipatory to an existing constructivist method, namely phenomenology or grounded theory, to signal how they intend to apply the method.

The data collected and analysis techniques are also similar to the action research or the case study research methods. Additionally, newer qualitative data collection and analysis techniques are emerging such as crystallization (Ellingson, 2009), which uses focus groups along with other qualitative data types to create diagrams to describe the unit of analysis perspectives (Richards, 2009; Richardson, 2000).

Conclusions

The research method layer of the typology was discussed using several examples from the business and management discipline. It was mentioned that formal methodologies contain techniques, and there are numerous variations of methods in the literature. For this reason, only the most common were identified, to the extent necessary to facilitate explaining how to align method with strategy and ideology.

A key point in the chapter was that certain techniques can be found in all formal methods, namely, sampling technique, data collection, validity-reliability checking, and ethics. Ethics is considered pivotal to the *scientific method*; therefore, it was discussed in this chapter. There is a chapter in the handbook dedicated to discussing ethics and other issues in multicultural studies or that could be generalized to the researchers being from several distinct sociocultures. This interesting contribution by Brennan, Parker, Nguyen, and Aleti is located right after the techniques chapter (the last layer in the typology), which is discussed next.

References

Alvesson, M., Kärreman, D., & Swan, J. (2002). Departures from knowledge and management. *Management Communications Quarterly, 16*(2), 282–291.

Babbie, E. (2007). *The practice of social research* (11th ed.). Belmont, CA: Wadsworth /Thompson.

Baskerville, R. L. (Ed.). (2001). *Conducting action research: High risk and high reward in theory and practice*. Hershey, PA: Idea Group Publishing.

Charmaz, K. (2006). *Constructing grounded theory: A practical guide* (2nd ed.). London: Sage.

Checkland, P. (1999). *Systems thinking, systems practice*. Chichester: John Wiley & Sons Ltd.

Creswell, J. W. (2009). *Research design: Qualitative, quantitative, and mixed methods approaches* (3rd ed.). New York: Sage.

Creswell, J. W. (2012). *Designing qualitative studies*. New York: Sage.

Denscombe, M. (2003). *Good research guide for small-scale research projects* (2nd ed.). Berkshire: McGraw-Hill Education. Retrieved from http://site.ebrary.com/lib/utslibrary /docDetail.action 102375 pw=westpac.

Eisenhardt, K. M. (1989). Building theory from case study research. *Academy of Management Review, 14*(4), 488–511.

Ellingson, L. L. (2009). *Engaging crystallization in qualitative research*. Thousand Oaks, CA: Sage.

Franzosi, R. (2010). *Quantitative narrative analysis*. Thousand Oaks, CA: Sage.

Freedman, D. M. (2006). Reflections on the research process: Emancipatory research or emancipatory zeal? *Reflective Practice, 7*(1), 87–99.

Gill, J., Johnson, P., & Clark, M. (2010). *Research methods for managers* (4th ed.). London: Sage.

Glaser, B. G., & Holton, J. (2005). Basic social processes, the grounded theory review. *International Journal of Grounded Theory Review, 4*(3), 1–27.

Hammersley, M. (2006). Ethnography: Problems and prospects. *Ethnography & Education, 1*(1), 3–14. Retrieved from http://journalsonline.tandf.co.uk/openurl.asp?genre=article&id=doi:10.1080/17457820500512697.

Hammersley, M., & Atkinson, P. (1983). *Ethnography principles in practice*. London: Routledge

Kemmis, S., & Wilkinson, M. (1998). Participatory action research and the study of practice. In B. Atweh & S. Kemmis (Eds.), *Action research in practice: Partnerships for social justice in education* (pp. 21–36). New York: Routledge

Keppel, G., & Wickens, T. D. (2004). *Design and analysis: A researcher's handbook* (4th ed.). Upper Saddle River, NJ: Pearson Prentice-Hall.

Macquarie, E. F. (2006). *The marketing research toolbox: A concise guide for beginners* (2nd ed.). London: Sage.

McNiff, J., & Whitehead, J. (2000). *Action research in organisations*. London: Routledge.

Mezirow, J. (1991). *Transformative dimensions of adult learning*. New York: Jossey-Bass.

Nersesian, R., & Strang, K. D. (2013). Risk planning with discrete distribution analysis applied to petroleum spills. *International Journal of Risk and Contingency Management, 2*(4), 61–78.

Neuman, W. L. (2000). *Social research methods: Qualitative and quantitative approaches*. Boston: Allyn & Bacon.

Richards, L. (2009). *Handling qualitative data: A practical guide* (2nd ed.). Thousand Oaks, CA: Sage.

Richardson, L. (2000). Writing: A method of inquiry. In N. K. Denzin & Y. S. Lincoln (Eds.), *Handbook of qualitative research* (2nd ed.). New York: Sage.

Schön, D. A. (1983). *The reflective practitioner—how professionals think in action*. Aldershot: BasiAshgate ARENA.

Strang, K. D. (2009). Using recursive regression to explore nonlinear relationships and interactions: A tutorial applied to a multicultural education study. *Practical Assessment, Research & Evaluation, 14*(3), 1–13. Retrieved from http://pareonline.net/getvn.asp?v=14&n=3.

Strang, K. D. (2012a). Importance of verifying queue model assumptions before planning with simulation software. *European Journal of Operational Research, 218*(2), 493–504. Retrieved from http://www.sciencedirect.com/science/article/pii/S0377221711010319.

Strang, K. D. (2012b). Investment selection in complex multinational projects. *International Journal of Information Technology Project Management, 3*(2), 1–13. Retrieved from http://www.igi-global.com/journal/international-journal-information-technology-project/1103.

Strang, K. D. (2012c). Logistic planning with nonlinear goal programming models in spreadsheets. *International Journal of Applied Logistics, 2*(4), 1–14. Retrieved from http://www.igi-global.com/article/logistic-planning-nonlinear-goal-programming/74728.

Strang, K. D. (2012d). Prioritization and supply chain logistics as a marketing function in a mining company. *Journal of Marketing Channels, 19*(2), 141–155. Retrieved from http://www.tandfonline.com/doi/abs/10.1080/1046669X.2012.667763.

Strang, K. D. (2013). Planning for Hurricane Isaac using probability theory in a linear programming model. *International Journal of Risk and Contingency Management, 2*(1), 51–65. Retrieved from http://www.igi-global.com/article/planning-hurricane-isaac-using-probability/76657.

Strang, K. D., & Nersesian, R. (2014). Nonparametric estimation of petroleum accident risk to improve environmental protection. *Journal of Environment, Systems and Decisions, 34*(1), 150–159. Retrieved from http://link.springer.com/article/10.1007%2Fs10669-013-9476-z.

Yin, R. K. (2009). *Case study research: Design and methods* (4th ed.). London: Sage.

Zuber-Skerritt, O. (1993). Improving learning and teaching through action learning and action research. *Higher Education Research and Development, 12*(1), 45–58.

5

Selecting Research Techniques for a Method and Strategy

Kenneth D. Strang

Research design typology technique focus

The research design typology model was introduced in chapter 1. The ideology, strategy, and method layers were explained in chapter 2, chapter 3, and chapter 4, respectively. The technique layer of the research design typology will be discussed in this chapter (highlighted in figure 5.1).

On the one hand, the good news is that if you select a formal method (a methodology) that adequately explains the required techniques, then you may not have to read this chapter. On the other hand, this chapter may provide insightful ideas about how to integrate unique techniques into a design. First the common cross-method techniques are explained, and then selected techniques are discussed from across the research ideologies and methods.

Common cross-method techniques

An empirical study starts with a literature review and includes data collection of some type without which there would be no scholarly research. The *scientific research* method requires a protocol for the data collection and appropriate techniques to analyze the data according to the documented research strategy and chosen method. Data do not always mean numbers—they could mean reviewing existing literature, listening to stories, observing behavior or art, and so on. I should also clarify the above assertion: a literature review is a form of archival data collection technique used in the critical analysis method.

Sampling technique

Sampling techniques are used for all research methods as the protocol for collecting the data. Sample techniques are often implied in published journal studies, but scholarly researchers ought to be transparent in articulating how

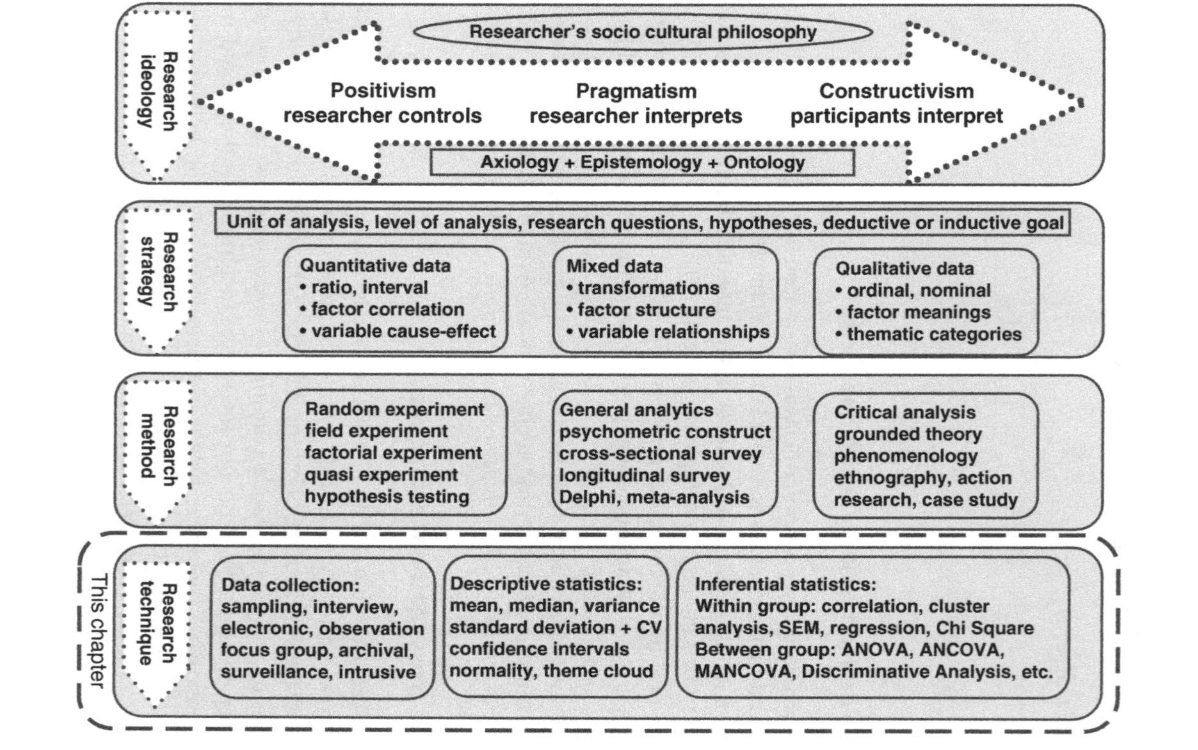

Figure 5.1 Research design typology model—technique focus.

they collected their data. Some authors call sampling techniques as "methods," but within the generally accepted methodology they are known as "techniques" (or "procedures") (Gill, Johnson & Clark, 2010). A sampling technique ought to include sample size estimation and the rationale for this before determining the data type and collection procedures. Sampling is linked to the research strategy, namely the proposed units of analysis, levels of analysis, and research questions or hypotheses.

Sampling is based on two fundamental principles: there is enough similarity among the artifacts, elements, or participants in a population such that a randomly selected few (the "sample") will adequately represent the characteristics of the total (the "population"); and although some samples may under- or overestimate a population parameter, these will balance out when large sample sizes are used, or if the study is replicated/repeated enough times (Keppel & Wickens, 2004).

When the unit of analysis is a quantitative data type, the research methods are usually experimental, survey, or case study, which require calculations to verify that an adequate sample size was obtained.

A researcher starts with identifying the target population and parameters of interest based on the unit and level of analysis, which will be articulated in the research questions or hypotheses. The sampling frame is a subset of the population, which is accessible (sometimes all of the population). Sampling techniques are scientific procedures to select a correct group of the required sample size from the sample frame, at a point in time or a defined range, to answer the research question or hypotheses.

Sampling techniques are classified by their representation basis and element selection procedure. Experimental, survey, factor analysis, and most general analytic methods recommend randomly drawn participants or objects from the sample frame, meaning that each has an equal chance of representation (Babbie, 2007). Element selection procedures for random representation include the following:

- randomized (often using random number generators, such as in experiments);
- systematic (every *n*th participant, often used with surveys);
- cluster (delimited by a political boundary or regional subgroup, often used with surveys); and
- stratified (random or systematic by political boundaries, often used with surveys or case studies) (Keppel & Wickens, 2004).

Non-random sample representation is called non-probability sampling. These are more often used for quasi-experiments, and all of the other pragmatic- as well as constructivist-oriented methods (such as case studies, grounded theory, and so on). Non-random selection procedures include the following:

- convenience (intact groups already formed, often used with quasi-experiments or ethnography);
- purposive (based on theoretical interest, such as good or bad performers, often used in phenomenology, grounded theory, and most constructivist oriented methods);
- judgment (based on the heuristics of the researcher, such as organizations in case studies);
- quota (arbitrary minimum or maximum defined by literature benchmarks or via unit of analysis strategy); and
- snowball (each participant suggests the next participant, common in phenomenology methods) (Gill et al., 2010; Guba & Lincoln, 2005; Neuman, 2000).

Data collection is done after the sampling method and size are determined. Data are collected by downloading archives, interviewing, electronic surveying, observation, focus group discussion, surveillance, or intrusive procedures (e.g., medical biopsy).

Mixed data may be collected from archives, through interviews, and as a participant-observer (Zuber-Skerritt, 1993), but usually the data types are qualitative and focused on business processes (Kemmis & Wilkinson, 1998).

Sample size

The required sample size varies according to the formal research method, confidence level, unit of analysis, and level of analysis. Experiments, surveys, and the general analytic method can use a sample-size estimate based on the *z*-score formula for standard confidence intervals of a normal distribution (Keppel & Wickens, 2004). The rule of thumb for survey sample sizes is to achieve at least 30 participants, but at least a 100 is recommended for regression, structural equation modeling, factor analysis, psychometric instrument development, and similar analysis techniques performed on "quantitative data" (Hair, Black, Babin, Anderson & Tatham, 2006; Keppel & Wickens, 2004).

Experiments rely on power and effect size to determine the required sample size that approximates a normal distribution, and this generally ranges from 5 to 30 participants (Cohen, Cohen, West & Aiken, 2003). There are several techniques to estimate the required sample size. One could cite a benchmark from the literature. Alternatively, one could deductively use a formula derived from the theory underlying the formal research method, such as assuming that the population of interest approximates a normal distribution. Strang (2012) applied equation (1) for calculating a sample size of 99 for data collection where he planned to use the ANOVA research method. He used a 95% level of confidence after a pilot study of standardized exams that produced a mean score of 155 with a population mean 152.4 and standard deviation 13.2:

$$z = \frac{\chi - \mu}{\sigma/\sqrt{n}}; \text{therefore} \rightarrow n = \left(\frac{\sigma * z}{\chi - \mu}\right)^2$$
$$= \left(\frac{13.2 * 1.96}{155 - 152.4}\right)^2 = 99.02 \qquad \text{(Eq.1)}$$

Case studies, meta-analysis, and narrative research that follow positivist or pragmatic ideologies, and those that collect data at the individual or group levels of analysis, to explore quantitative unit of analysis types may use the *z*-score deductive approach outlined above or cite benchmarks in the literature to estimate sample size. Most other research methods follow literature benchmarks or a theoretical saturation point to determine sample size. For example, when using case study, grounded theory, content analysis, hermeneutics, discourse analysis, anthropology, ethnography, and phenomenology methods, researchers generally select 4 to 15 samples but stop at theoretical saturation (Babbie, 2007; Charmaz, 2006; Hammersley & Atkinson, 1983; Neuman, 2000; Whitley, 2002; Yin, 2009). Other subjective techniques use the number of variables and proposed analysis technique to calculate the required sample size, such as specifying 10–20 samples per variable for between-group unit of analysis designs.

The saturation point is dynamic in the sense that the researcher starts with a goal to collect at least 1–4 samples, but stops when a theory emerges or no new theme patterns arise (or there are no more participants available). Action research and emancipatory and social advocacy research methods studies may use a single important sample or they may use up to 20 samples. Researchers with constructivist ideologies who have inquiry strategies that collect and explore qualitative data types generally do not go beyond 20 samples because having more would generate too much data, thus increasing the risk of losing rich details from each participant (Babbie, 2007; Hammersley & Atkinson, 1983).

Sample descriptive statistics

The purpose of calculating sample descriptive statistics is to communicate the characteristics of the sample to other researchers, so this is needed across all types of research methods. This is required for all ideologies in business and management, including constructivistic. However, the statistical procedures to be used for describing the sample data characteristics are specific to data types in the unit of analysis. Nonetheless, there are some general guidelines.

In all ideologies, the sample should be described, mentioning the sample frame, number of participants or objects, and the sampling technique used to select them. The context of the sample should be briefly described to share with other researchers and to establish the credibility of the sample for the generalization goal in the research strategy.

For positivist and pragmatist ideologies, all dependent variables in the unit of analysis strategy should be summarized, using the relevant parametric or nonparametric statistical procedures. For example, continuous and integer data types require means and standard deviations, while ordinals require the median and quartiles. Nominal data types should have frequency counts by type. Independent factors should also be summarized as above. When a between-groups analysis focus is specified in the unit of analysis, the factors and variables should also be summarized by group. This will help other researchers understand the sample and, as mentioned above for the sample context, it establishes credibility for generalization.

For constructivist and interpretivist ideologies, it is the same as above. For complex data types not mentioned above, such as art, images, recordings, and so on, there should be a rich description of these, organized by type, with counts of any categorization (e.g., by location or type). The literature review will have identified the theoretical lens and significant studies that serve as a guide for how to organize the descriptive characteristics for any complex data types. This should not be confused with the quotations from the participants, which come at a later point.

The generalization goal of the research strategy will indicate which contextual factors of the sample or situation would need to be described. This is also driven by the literature review so as to confirm to other leading studies on this topic in the business and management discipline. Usually this is done following the same approach as above, according to data type.

Selecting techniques for specific methods

In this section, only the commonly used techniques are mentioned. These will be required in formal methods, but it may not be clear in the methodology how to align them with the research questions or hypothesis, or with the unit of analysis, in the strategy layer of figure 5.1.

Validity and reliability in positivistic ideologies

Validity and reliability techniques in the positivist and pragmatist ideology are focused on illustrating that the findings were accurate, credible, and statistically significant. A positivist will start by defining the level of confidence for any statistical hypothesis testing, which is usually 95%, whereby the statistical complement 1–95% = 0.05% becomes the level of significance. Benchmarks are then used to determine if the results of any test are valid, reliable, and significant, according to the unit of analysis strategy. These benchmarks vary from technique to technique and also according to the cited thought leader. A few of the more important benchmarks are cited below where necessary.

The techniques for estimating validity and reliability across the research methods used by the positivist (and pragmatist) can be grouped into the following four briefly explained categories:

- internal validity (correct wording, content validity, relevant, experiment and survey items suitable to measure theory);
- construct validity (correct theoretical measures), for SEM psychometric measures, face, convergent, and discriminant validity also needed;
- reliability (instrument and study are repeatable); and
- external validity (generalized beyond study).

Instruments are often used to collect data from surveys or interviews. Internal validity for measuring instruments is the extent to which it provides adequate coverage and appropriate language of the unit of analysis in the research questions or hypothesis. If the instrument was designed as a representative sample of the universe of the subject matter of interest, then content validity is a priori (previously established). If a new instrument is created, the researcher must determine what factors are relevant and which items to use to represent the factors. The techniques to ascertain content validity is to use judgment, either by pilot testing the instrument, or having independent experts assess it, or by comparing responses in repeated (retests) of the instrument to ensure they are consistent to at least 70% across tests (Gill et al., 2010).

Another form of internal validity is criterion related, which means that it must correctly measure the factors. Any criterion measure must be judged in terms of four qualities: (1) relevance, (2) freedom from bias, (3) reliability, and (4) availability. A criterion is relevant if it is defined and scored in terms of what we judge to be the proper measures. Freedom from bias is attained when the criterion gives each participant an equal opportunity to score well. A reliable criterion is stable or reproducible. An erratic criterion cannot be considered a reliable standard by which to judge performance. Finally, the information specified by the criterion must be available to measure (Gill et al., 2010).

In attempting to evaluate construct validity, both the theory and the measuring instrument being used must be considered. If we were interested in measuring the effect of trust in teams, the way in which "trust" was operationally defined would have to correspond to an empirically grounded theory. If a known measure of trust was available, the results may be correlated using this measure with those derived from a newly designed instrument. Such an approach would provide preliminary indications of convergent validity (the degree to which scores on one scale correlate with scores on other scales designed to assess the same construct). If for example a newly designed instrument could contains factors that relate to one theory and do not relate to other theories, then the researcher has achieved discriminant validity (the degree to which scores on a scale do not correlate with scores from scales designed to measure different constructs).

Reliability refers to the degree to which an instrument supplies consistent results if repeated. Reliability is a necessary contributor to validity but is not a sufficient condition for validity. Reliability is concerned with estimates of the degree to which a measurement is free of random or unstable error. The relationship between reliability and validity can be simply illustrated with the use of a weight scale. If the scale measures your weight correctly (using a concurrent criterion of pounds, which are known to be accurate), then it is both reliable and valid. If it consistently overweighs you by a pound, then the scale is reliable but not valid. If the scale measures erratically from time to time, then it is not reliable and therefore cannot be valid. Thus, if a measurement is not valid, it cannot be reliable either.

A measure is considered stable if the instrument consistently produces the same results when repeated with the same participant. For example, an observation procedure is stable if it gives the same reading on a particular person when repeated one or more times. Stability measurement in surveys can be validated by doing a test-retest procedure, with a time delay, and then measuring the differences.

Another perspective on reliability is that error may be introduced by different investigators (in observation) or different samples of items being studied (in questioning items or scales). Thus, while stability is concerned with personal and situational variations from one time to another, equivalence is concerned with variations at one point in time among observers and samples of items. Furthermore, reliability can be controlled by the way the techniques are used during the study, which include sampling errors and bias associated with the participants, such as

- history (e.g., higher wages, illness, tutor);
- test effects or before-measure effects;
- selection bias (e.g., self-selection of keen or higher aptitude students);
- mortality (loss of test units during the experiment);
- maturation—changes in the test units over time (e.g., change to factory layout); or
- instrumentation effects from changes in instrument, observers, or scores.

Inter-rater correlations of the measures can be taken to ensure that different researchers or different samples of the same items are equivalent (Cohen,

1968; Cohen et al., 2003). The major interest with equivalence is typically not how respondents differ from item to item but how well a given set of items will categorize individuals or objects. In research terminology, an item on a survey instrument is a question designed to support the theoretical construct. There may be many differences in response between two retests of the same participant or items, but if a person is classified the same way by each test, then the measures are considered equivalent.

Internal consistency is another variation of a validity technique. This is needed to measure reliability by testing the homogeneity among the items in each factor. The split-half procedure can be used when the measuring tool has many similar questions or statements to which the participant can respond. The instrument is administered and the results are separated into randomly selected halves. A correlation is applied between the two halves of the sample and if the correlation estimate is above 0.70, then the instrument is considered to have internal consistency (Hair et al., 2006).

Confirmatory factor analysis can be used to measure internal consistency when there are at least six items per factor (benchmarks will differ) and the questions for each factor are different (Strang, 2009). As Kim, Sturman, and Kim point out later in this handbook (when discussing structural equation modeling), another benchmark is an item-to-data-point ratio of at least 1:5 (Babbie, 2007). While on this topic point, I should also note that thought-leader experts in the field will differ on benchmarks. For example Jöreskog (2006) recommends an item-to-factor ratio of 10 and a participant-to-data ratio of at least 1:100 when performing any type of factor analysis or structural equation modeling. This could be interpreted as one factor in a survey requiring 10 different questions along with 100 response sample records, and this is only one factor (most surveys have several factors each with many items).

External validity refers to the ability of the instrument, and the unit of analysis in the study, to generalize into other situations outside the particular research context. This is achieved by correctly designing the study, documenting the research ideology, methods, and techniques, as well as by showing the characteristics for the unit of analysis sample data (Babbie, 2007). The sample characteristics can be summarized for quantitative data types by utilizing descriptive statistics. This allows readers to compare the homogeneity of the sample other contexts in terms of generalizing the findings.

Validity and reliability in pragmatist and constructivist ideologies

Validity and reliability techniques are focused on illustrating that the findings are sufficiently accurate, believable, credible, and authentic. Any of the positivistic validity or reliability techniques may be used in the pragmatist ideology. Additionally, triangulation is often done to improve accuracy and credibility of the data for a pragmatic ideology.

Triangulation of data and method are common techniques used with the case study method (Yin, 2009) and other interpretive research methods. Triangulation of data involves collecting evidence for the unit of analysis from different sources (e.g., interviews and archival records, or peer reports). Triangulation of method involves using a different technique to describe, explore, or explain the relationships in the data, such as applying general analytic techniques like graphs along with descriptive statistics or participant narratives so as to show that the interpretation of the data is corroborated by technique. Yin (2009) suggests triangulation of theories, which involves collecting additional perspectives on the unit of analysis.

Other terms for validity and reliability used in social constructivist ideologies are isomorphic to some reality, trustworthy, related to the way others construct their social worlds, or fairly expressed (Guba & Lincoln, 2005).

In constructivist ideology, usually qualitative data are collected. Therefore, validity requires authenticity to show that the meanings and interpretations are trustworthy, rigorous, and free of researcher bias. Validity in advocacy and emancipatory methods means fairness for all stakeholders' views, perspectives, claims, concerns, and voices. In research methods, participants may have to be trained to understand the terminology or procedures so as to achieve validity (Guba & Lincoln, 2005).

Tracy (2010, p. 840) presents a best-practice model for achieving validity when collecting any type of data using interpretative research methods (regardless of the ideology), as briefly summarized below:

- worthy topic (significant, interesting, timely),
- rigor (theoretical constructs, data collection and analysis processes),
- sincerity (transparency of methods and researcher biases),
- credibility (positivist counterpart to validity and reliability: data and method triangulation, detailed descriptions, participant quotes, and reflections),
- resonance (natural aesthetic, authentic representation),
- literature contribution (identifies gap and conceptually or theoretically helps community of practice),
- ethical (treats participants with cultural dignity), and
- coherence (logical methods for purpose, links research questions and interprets findings to literature).

When constructivist research methods, such as phenomenology, are employed (generally to collect and interpret complex qualitative data type), validity is achieved by demonstrating authenticity. Researchers should quote key portions of participant responses (e.g., narratives), summarize analog data (e.g., images, geography, audio), and have participants verify the correctness of all interpreted data (Guba & Lincoln, 2005).

Descriptive statistics

Descriptive statistics are used to summarize the independent factors and dependent variables in the unit of analysis for any ideology. However, these techniques are utilized more in positivist and pragmatist designs since constructivist studies usually collect qualitative data that cannot be analyzed in these ways. The mean, median, and standard deviation were already mentioned as techniques to describe the characteristics of the sample. These are repeated here in the overall context of descriptive statistics.

These techniques summarize the central tendency and distribution shape of the collected data. Mode and categorical charts can be used if the data types are qualitative (nominal or ordinal). For example, gender (in surveys or experiments) or object type (in business studies) is often presented in descriptive statistics as percentages of each value count.

The other descriptive statistics are mean, median, variance, standard deviation, and confidence, which are depicted as a typology in figure 5.2. Parametric normality is the process of testing the values in quantitative data type samples (interval and ratio) to ensure that the shape approximates a normal distribution, using techniques such the skew, kurtosis, Kolmogorov-Smirnov, or Anderson-Darling Normality Test (Hair et al., 2006).

A result that is not considered normal could be due to outliers, such as bad data, or perhaps a survey participant who faked the questionnaire (or may be a bad fit for the study to generalize the findings). Outlying point values can be detected by using 3 standard deviations from the mean, or by calculating the

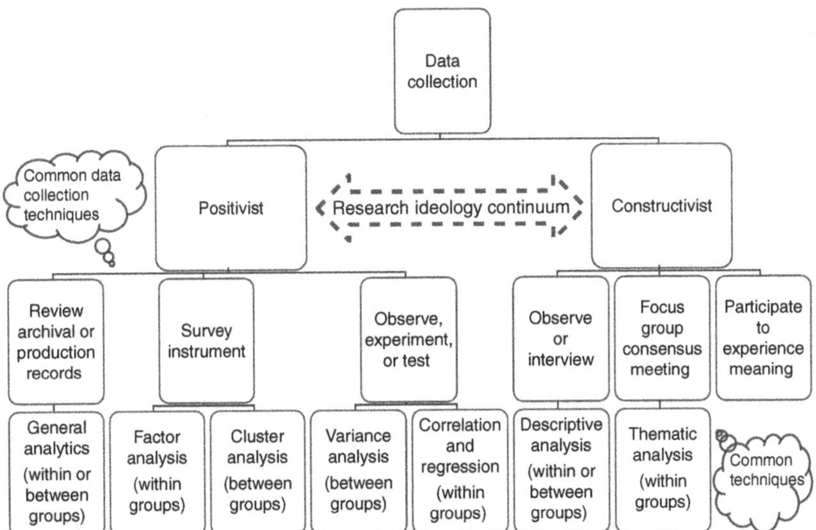

Figure 5.2 Descriptive statistical techniques.

interquartile in a box-whisker plot. Once outliers are detected, the researcher must consider ethics and the generalization goal of the research strategy to help make the decision about discarding or retaining the data.

Inferential statistics in positivistic and pragmatist ideologies

Experiments and general analytic methods require inferential statistical techniques to test hypotheses or to answer explanatory questions about the unit of analysis. These techniques are split into two categories; the first, which is called the parametric procedure, assumes that the sample is from a normal distribution, while the second, which is a nonparametric procedure, has few constraints, except that it requires specific data types as outlined in Strang (2009, p. 2).

Parametric inferential statistics correlation include ANOVA, ANCOVA, MANCOVA, multivariate regression, forecasting, structural equation model, cluster analysis, and various model validation procedures. Nonparametric inferential statistical techniques include Spearman Rho, signs test, and so on. A full explanation of these are beyond the scope of this handbook (Elliott & Woodward, 2007; Keppel & Wickens, 2004; Ullman & Bentler, 2003; Zechmeister, Zechmeister & Shaughnessy, 2001).

The most common inferential statistical techniques are illustrated in Figure 5.3 as a typology according to purpose. The typology uses three purpose categories, from left to right: theory/instrument creation, relationship detection, and predictive cause-effect. The purpose of techniques for instrument creation is to identify factors, from items, so as to reduce data into a parsimonious (simple) model (Keppel & Wickens, 2004). If an instrument or construct already exists a priori in the literature, then these techniques may be used to confirm that the model applies for new data samples (Hair et al., 2006); this is also called a replication or a confirmation study (Yin, 2009). Relationship detection techniques measure the direction (positive or negative) and strength of associations between the factors. Generally correlation is used for relationship detection as a prelude to using cause-effect techniques (Elliott & Woodward, 2007; Keppel & Wickens, 2004).

Predictive techniques test cause effect in the unit of analysis. Factors are the independent variables, while the dependent variable is the outcome of the factors. An experiment generally uses a predictive structure with the treatment being the independent factor and the behavior representing the outcome dependent variable. ANOVA, MANCOVA, ANCOVA, and regression techniques are commonly used to test cause-effect hypotheses or research questions (Hair et al., 2006).

The unit of analysis in casual-predictive often requires the researcher to manipulate the independent factors (or measure this intact from the existing process or group). Experimentation provides the most powerful support

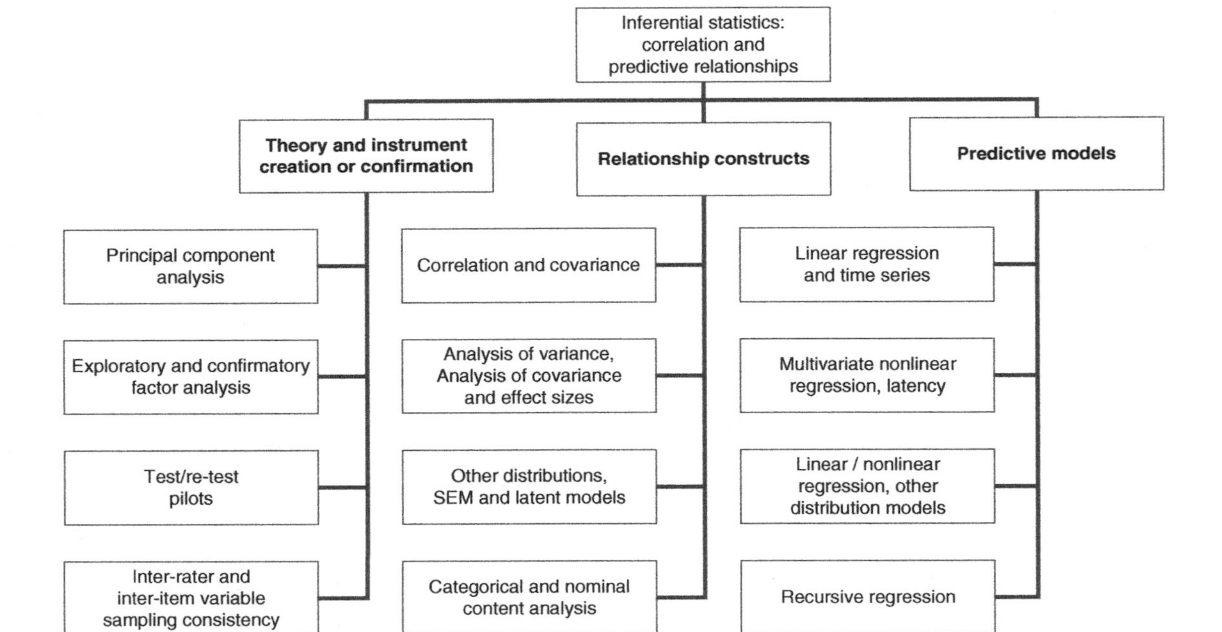

Figure 5.3 Inferential statistical techniques.

possible for a hypothesis of causation. With an ex post facto (intact process) design, investigators have no control over the variables in the sense of being able to manipulate them. They can only report what has happened or what is happening. It is important that the researchers using this design not influence the variables; to do so would introduce bias. The researcher is limited to holding factors constant by judicious selection of subjects according to strict sampling procedures and by statistical manipulation of findings (Zechmeister et al., 2001).

Certain types of independent factors may be important or the unit of analysis when applying cause-effect techniques. A mediating factor can be ratio data type and it covaries with the dependent variable; its existence affects the factor effect on the dependent variable. A moderating factor is usually a categorical or ordinal data type; the level affects the dependent variable. For example, in an experiment, if motivation is manipulated on a test group using rewards (treatment factor), and if gender affects their performance whereby females like the gifts better than males, then gender is a moderator.

The causal relationship that occurs between a factor and dependent variable may be symmetrical (independent or mutual covariate factors), reciprocal (opposite/negative effects), or asymmetrical. Of greatest interest to the research analyst are asymmetrical relationships, namely,

- stimulus-response (factor causes behavior);
- property-disposition (attribute impacts attitude);
- disposition-behavior (casual affective/attitude); and
- property-behavior (explanatory attribute or factor) (Hair et al., 2006).

Causal hypotheses are tested by measuring the covariation among variables, determining the time-order relationships among variables, and ensuring that other factors do not confound the explanatory relationships. The conditions for claiming cause-effect are (Keppel & Wickens, 2004; Zechmeister et al., 2001):

1. A relationship exists between the factor and the dependent.
2. The factor occurs before the dependent variable.
3. No other logical explanation exists (e.g., no confounding or interacting factors).

There are a large number of inferential statistical techniques, which are beyond the scope of this handbook, but the reader may consult the subject-matter experts (Cohen et al., 2003; DeVellis, 1991; Elliott & Woodward, 2007; Jöreskog & Moustaki, 2006; Keppel & Wickens, 2004; R. B. Kline, 2004; T. J. B. Kline, Sulsky & Rever-Moriyama, 2000; Strang, 2010; Ullman & Bentler, 2003). In addition to the techniques mentioned in figure 5.3, when ANOVA, MANCOVA, or ANCOVA produce a statistically significant result, there are

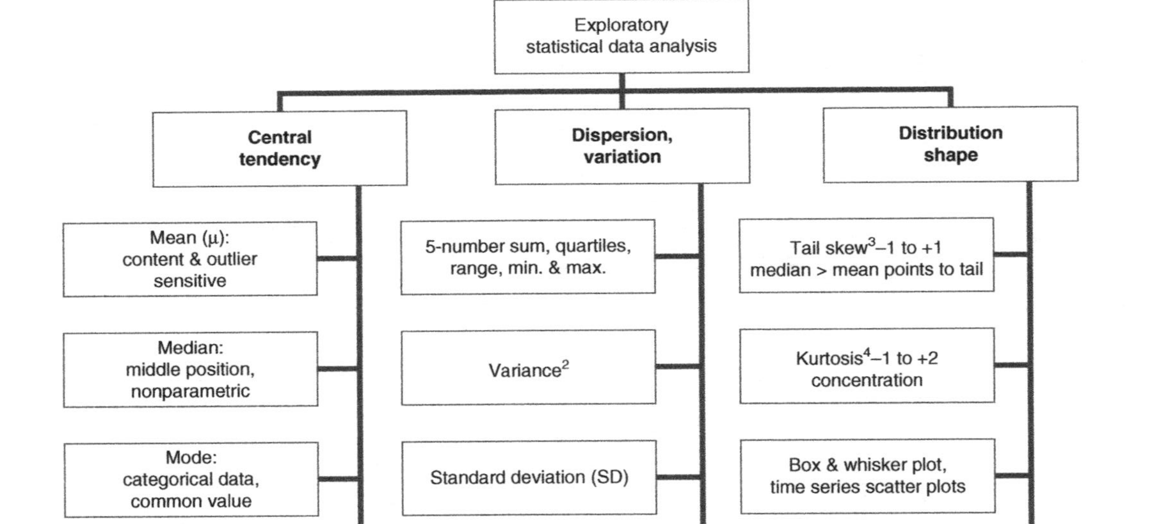

Covariance is variation to mean and is used in numerator of variation coefficient (compare variables with different units).
Scatter plots are used for comparing two variables, but may also illustrate the distribution shape in time series.
Empirical rule: ±3STD = 99.7%, ±2STD = 95%, ±1STD = 68%; chebychev: 1k = 0%, 2k = 75%, 3k = 89%

Figure 5.4 Exploratory statistical analysis techniques.

procedures to detect which factor and group was significantly higher or lower according to the hypothesis test (see figure 5.4).

The following techniques are commonly used to highlight which particular unit of analysis was higher or lower in terms of significant effect size: Fisher LSD, Bonferroni, Tukey HSD, Tukey-Kramer, Scheffé, Brown-Forsythe, Newman-Keuls, and Dunnett's C (Elliott & Woodward, 2007; Hair et al., 2006; Keppel & Wickens, 2004).

Conclusions

This chapter presented an overview of the generally accepted research techniques, most of which are specified within methods. The techniques were discussed separately because they may be used anytime as long as the assumptions required for their application are met (this is generally a concern for parametric statistics). Cross-method techniques were discussed, namely, sampling technique and data collection along with credibility, validity, and reliability checking.

The following chapters in this section of the handbook present special topics relevant for research design. Most of these chapters expand on the ethical standards of the *scientific method,* which is the underlying ideology of business and management research. For example, the next topic discusses multicultural issues in the design. Subsequent chapters in this section address other popular concerns that scholars have, such as how to substantiate the significance of a study. Yet others in this section explain how to organize a literature review and how to interpret and discuss findings in business and management.

The following sections of the handbook provide practitioner-scholar examples of applied research designs across the business and management disciplines. The sections are organized according to the ideology layer of the research design typology in figure 5.1, namely, positivistic, pragmatic, and constructivistic. The authors of these chapters delve into specific designs, methods, and techniques using applied visual examples whenever possible and practical.

References

APA. (2010). *Publication manual of the American Psychological Association* (6th ed.). Washington, DC: American Psychological Association (APA).

Babbie, E. (2007). *The practice of social research* (11th ed.). Belmont, CA: Wadsworth/Thompson.

Charmaz, K. (2006). *Constructing grounded theory: A practical guide* (2nd ed.). London: Sage.

Cohen, J. (1968). Weighted kappa: Nominal scale agreement with provision for scale disagreement or partial credit. *Psychological Bulletin, 70*(2), 213–220.

Cohen, J., Cohen, P., West, S. G., & Aiken, L. S. (2003). *Applied multiple regression/correlation analysis for the behavioral sciences* (3rd ed.). Mahwah, NJ: Lawrence Erlbaum Associates.

DeVellis, R. F. (1991). *Scale development: Theory and application*. Newbury Park, CA: Sage Publications.

Elliott, A. C., & Woodward, W. A. (2007). *Statistical analysis quick reference guidebook with spss examples*. London: Sage.

Gill, J., Johnson, P., & Clark, M. (2010). *Research methods for managers* (4th ed.). London: Sage.

Guba, E. G., & Lincoln, Y. S. (2005). Paradigmatic controversies, contradictions, and emerging confluences. In N. K. Denszin & Y. S. Lincoln (Eds.), *Handbook of qualitative research* (pp. 191–215). Thousand Oaks, CA: Sage.

Hair, J. F., Black, W. C., Babin, B. J., Anderson, R. E., & Tatham, R. L. (2006). *Multivariate data analysis* (6th ed.). Upper Saddle River, NJ: Prentice-Hall.

Hammersley, M., & Atkinson, P. (1983). *Ethnography principles in practice*. London: Routledge.

Jöreskog, K. G., & Moustaki, I. (2006). *Factor analysis of ordinal variables with full information maximum likelihood*. Hillsdale, NJ: Lawrence Erlbaum Associates.

Kemmis, S., & Wilkinson, M. (1998). Participatory action research and the study of practice. In B. Atweh & S. Kemmis (Eds.), *Action research in practice: Partnerships for social justice in education* (pp. 21–36). New York: Routledge.

Keppel, G., & Wickens, T. D. (2004). *Design and analysis: A researcher's handbook* (4th ed.). Upper Saddle River, NJ: Pearson Prentice-Hall.

Kline, R. B. (2004). *Beyond significance testing: Reforming data analysis methods in behavioral research*. Washington, DC: American Psychological Association.

Kline, T. J. B., Sulsky, L. M., & Rever-Moriyama, S. D. (2000). Common method variance and specification errors: A practical approach to detection. *Journal of Psychology, 134*(4), 401–421.

Neuman, W. L. (2000). *Social research methods: Qualitative and quantitative approaches*. Boston: Allyn & Bacon.

Strang, K. D. (2009). Using recursive regression to explore nonlinear relationships and interactions: A tutorial applied to a multicultural education study. *Practical Assessment, Research & Evaluation, 14*(3), 1–13. Retrieved from http://pareonline.net/getvn.asp?v=14&n=3.

Strang, K. D. (2010). Using recursive regression to explore nonlinear relationships and interactions: Applied multicultural education study [textbook supplement]. In W. Lee (Ed.), *Assessment and evaluation in higher education* (3rd ed., pp. 206–238). Upper Saddle River, NJ: Pearson and Association for Study of Higher Education. Retrieved from http://vig.pearsoned.com/store/product/1,1207,store-18100_isbn-055857579X,00.html.

Strang, K. D. (2012). Man versus math: Behaviorist exploration of post-crisis non-banking asset management. *Journal of Asset Management*, 13(5), 348–467. Retrieved from http://www.palgrave-journals.com/jam/journal/v13/n5/index.html.

Tracy, S. J. (2010). Qualitative quality: Eight big-tent criteria for excellent qualitative research. *Qualitative Inquiry, 16*(10), 837–851.

Ullman, J. B., & Bentler, P. M. (Eds.). (2003). *Structural equation modeling* (Vol. 2). New York: Wiley.

Whitley, B. E. Jr. (2002). *Principles of research in behavioral science* (2nd ed.). New York: McGraw-Hill.

Yin, R. K. (2009). *Case study research: Design and methods* (4th ed.). London: Sage.

Zechmeister, J. S., Zechmeister, E. B., & Shaughnessy, J. J. (2001). *Essentials of research methods in psychology*. New York: McGraw-Hill.

Zuber-Skerritt, O. (1993). Improving learning and teaching through action learning and action research. *Higher Education Research and Development, 12*(1), 45–58.

6

Design Issues in Cross-Cultural Research: Suggestions for Researchers

Linda Brennan, Lukas Parker, Dang Nguyen, and Torgeir Aleti

Chapter overview

This chapter builds on the first five chapters in this handbook that explained the research design typology. The focus here is on design issues in cross-cultural research. This chapter is intended to serve as a guide for practitioners to apply and integrate the research design typology layers into a scholarly manuscript. In contrast to the broad scope of the first five chapters, this chapter concentrates on how to integrate specific components of the typology, regardless of which ideology the researcher holds on the continuum (positivist, post-positivist, pragmatist, interpretivist, or constructivist).

Introduction

This chapter presents an overview of the issues that emerging cross-cultural researchers face in designing, developing, and conducting research in the field. It takes the perspective of providing formative advice for people new to the field of cross-cultural research. At the end of the chapter there is a summary of tips and techniques to guide researchers in making decisions about their research. The new researcher is advised to read widely in the field of research methods in addition to the field of culture in order to ensure that his or her research is conducted validly and rigorously.

The importance of cross-cultural research

Understanding a globalizing world requires understanding the various cultures that make up the globe. Cross-cultural research allows us to understand cultural diversity, global problems, comparative human behavior, and society. The development of understanding requires us to be able to access a variety of information sources from across the globe; of course, one of the most important information sources is empirical research gathered from the field. One of the traditional barriers to research is that of being able to access ethnographic and qualitative research in a format that can be used for your own research. Quantitative data is often available for data mining, and "big data sets" allow for cross-cultural analyses at a broader level than ever before. However, these "secondary" data sources, while useful, are not all there is to cross cultural research.

This chapter aims to contribute to an understanding of how data can be gathered from the field both validly and reliably. It incorporates the consideration of qualitative approaches as well as quantitative and mixed approaches. Phenomenography is one of the major theoretical fields underpinning this, and from this perspective it can be counting qualities (hence qualitative research), or it can be describing things so that others can be able to use your descriptions in the formation of their own ideas and the achievement of their own research goals. Cross-cultural research has a long history dating back to the nineteenth century and is probably founded in the anthropological sciences. However, it goes back even earlier than that when looking at explorers and their attempts to develop trade relationships and understandings of various cultures and reporting those understandings back to their home countries.

Cross-cultural research is particularly important to people wanting to understand other cultures or even their own in terms of the ways that cultures change, overlap, and affect each other. For a good example of how culture is impacted by research and issues in conducting cross-cultural research, we recommend the work of George Murdock (1949) who began the process of determining what cross-cultural research is and how it can be done appropriately within the anthropological tradition. Anthropology, as a tradition of research, often uses qualitative research. This is not to say that they do not count things within the societies that they are examining; it is more that the research is about the richness and the complexity of information available. Therefore, there is a greater capacity of developing an understanding of a particular society by looking at it from different perspectives. The depth of understanding that comes about as a result of looking at a culture from a variety of different aspects such as texts, language, para-language, semiotic signs, and symbols will be further discussed in this chapter. The knowledge developed from such forms of "data" enables a cross-cultural researcher to develop a strong, in-depth understanding of the variety of things that make up a culture. As a result, one can understand where cultural and cross-cultural research can make a contribution to practice. A particularly good journal to use here for reference is the *Journal of Cross-cultural Research*. It will enable an emerging researcher to develop a strong understanding of the recent issues that are being examined.

Human society and the globalized world in which we increasingly find ourselves are changing rapidly. However, there are also many things that remain the same. Finding what is the same and what is changing will enable researchers to provide strategies and theorize about human society and human behaviors. Cross-cultural research, therefore, particularly in marketing, enables the researcher to examine the individual within his or her social settings and understand the groups of individuals that make up the society. This knowledge will enable marketers and business researchers to develop strategies and practices that can be spread across national and cultural boundaries.

Cross-cultural research is multidimensional

The premise of this chapter is that cross-cultural research is designed to understand differences across (cross), between (inter), and within (intra) cultures. For the purposes of the chapter, we use the term "cross-cultural" to include all these various usages of conducting research in cultural settings. In order to develop an understanding of differences between cultures, one must first understand culture. In order to understand a culture, you need to understand the societal structures in which the culture occurs. These structures include norms, traditions, customs, and rituals, as well as institutions, organizations, and systems around which individuals in the society relate to each other and interact. These elements of culture all have some observable characteristics or artifacts that enable researchers to identify differences and similarities between cultures. Examples of cultural artifacts can be found at different levels: macro (societal), meso (organizational/institutional), and micro (individual). Table 6.1 illustrates the three levels of research into cultural issues.

In cross-cultural research, it is important to get the level of research correctly aligned with the inferences you wish to make. For example, if you want to predict how an individual from a particular culture background is likely to behave, you need to start with an individual measure. However, societal-level values are often inferred from observing the behaviors of individuals who are embedded within a specific culture. For new researchers to the field, there is a danger inherent in this inference. For example, an individual who is compliant with the laws of a society may appear to have adopted the values of the society. However, he or she may be doing so fearing his or her personal safety and out of a feeling that there is no choice. As such his or her attitude may not be in

Table 6.1 Example of levels of cross-cultural research

Macro	Meso	Micro
Societal	Organizational / Institutional	Individual
Values	Laws	Compliance
Morals	Codes of conduct	Behaviors
Ideals	Group beliefs about etiquette	Manners
Tenets	System of beliefs about <something>	Attitudes about <something>

line with the values of the society at all. Indeed, examining attitudes in cases where an individual's attitudes are in conflict with societal values may invoke social desirability bias and you may never know how an individual really feels. In certain Asian countries social desirability is also caught up with concepts of face, and this can also confound results.

The level of research conducted must be commensurate with the sampling frame in order to produce comparable results. Data gathered from individuals can only be used to infer something about the individuals. It cannot be used to infer something about the organizations or institutions or the society. An interesting theme of research where this has occurred is that of Hofstede, whose widely cited research is founded in work conducted while he was employed at IBM in the late 1960s to mid-1970s, and where he and his colleagues conducted a global study of IBM employees in each of the countries where IBM had a presence. He aggregated the results to produce insights about the organizational culture within the countries he studied. His website (http://geert-hofstede.com/) proclaims that it is about national and organizational culture. It is important to note that he does not infer that his findings are applicable to individuals. Despite this, Hofstede's work can be found being applied to individuals in many papers and theses aiming to understand the implications of culture. As with any generalized study, significant deviations from the normative categories exist and should be handled with caution, especially on an individual level.

Importantly, even with multiple country settings, international research is not always cross-cultural research. Examining how things work in international settings does not necessarily mean you are exploring culture. For example, examining how consumers buy cosmetics in India or Brazil does not require a deep knowledge of the culture to make certain inferences about how to market to them effectively. Understanding how to create marketing strategies does require straightforward market research of the type that is standard practice to those trained in market research. Research into culture is not as straightforward because many of the artifacts of a culture are often hidden from view, much like an iceberg (Hall, 1977). The advice provided in the following sections can also be applied to international market research. However, the aim of this chapter is to inform academic researchers aiming to design better cross-cultural research, not international market research practitioners.

Issues and suggestions for their remediation

There are many issues associated with cross-cultural research ranging from the most evident, that of there being different languages to work with, to the more hidden aspects, such as the underlying politics of using others to foster your own research agenda. The following sections give us a brief overview of such issues and discuss possible ways to tackle them. There is a summary of the suggestions in table 6.6 at the end of this chapter.

Language

The language of data collection is an important consideration in CCR. Researchers will be tasked with ensuring that their research is both valid and reliable within the context of the study. Formative validity must be established by ensuring that the concepts being researched are the same in each of the countries in the study (Brennan & Camm, 2007). Establishing semantic validity can be a concern when the languages are different. For an overview of the issues and procedures involved in translating cross-cultural research instruments, see the work of Harkness and colleagues (Harkness, 1999; Harkness, Pennell, & Schoua-Glusberg, 2004; Harkness & Schoua-Glusberg, 1998). An important component of semantic validity is that of the equivalence of key ideas and constructs. Equivalence, especially in the use of scale data, is important if accurate contrasts and comparisons are required. When there is no directly equivalent construct, long descriptions may be required to counter the lack of clarity. Harkness suggests annotated instruments when this is the case. This is where the investigator provides multiple alternative words for the translators. However, it is also important to note that sometimes there is no precise term to convey meaning, and sometimes compromises must be made as meaning is generated by the context and use of words and terms (see e.g., Tu et al., 2003). This is particularly prevalent in high context societies where many things are left unsaid.

There are some concepts that remain relatively stable across cultural boundaries. These are often referred to cross-cultural universals (Lloyd, 2010; Osgood, 1975). Brown (1991) provided a list of elements of culture that could be found in human societies around the world. While there is much argument about whether or not cross-cultural "universals" exist, there are similarities in addition to differences that can be traced in people's behaviors. In the mainstream, the best way to understand universals is that they overlap geographically and socially and are intervolved with each other. Customs shift incrementally as they become geographically distant from each other. Hence, contiguous countries may share more similarities than differences and countries farther apart may be very different from each other. For the new researcher, determining if one is trying to look at differences or similarities is a necessary first step in the research process.

Valuing research outcomes: philosophy and cultural traditions

Another issue confronting CCR is that of philosophical approaches to the conduct of research. Not the least of these is axiology—the valuing of the inputs, processes, and outcomes of the research. In some cultures, there is a high degree of reliance on "hard" quantitative research methods and a lesser valuing of "soft" qualitative research methods. Thus, a qualitative research study may not have the same level of acceptance in these societies. This issue is associated with the concept of paradigms, which are ways of viewing the world and therefore research practices (Brennan, Voros & Brady, 2011). There are many paradigms that research can be founded on, but the major ones can be categorized into three domains: positivistic (positivism and post-positivism); interpretivistic (criticalism and constructivism); and action/participatory. These are often characterized as being quantitative or qualitative in nature. Without engaging in an extensive debate about the rights and wrongs of various approaches and methods, we want to make the point that cultural traditions lead to such viewpoints and alternative perspectives may be needed when it comes to research. If truth exists and can be found (positivism), it may be that the researcher needs to consider the finding in the light of other lenses that may have been applied in the making of the truth (constructivism). "Your" truth and "my" truth is not "our" truth (interpretivism). In conducting cross-cultural research, it pays to check your assumptions at the outset.

Associated with axiological issues in conducting CCR are two other philosophical debates about knowledge generation: that of ontology and epistemology. Ontology is the study of the nature of being or existence. It influences CCR in that different cultures have different ways of being as well as different ways of knowing (epistemology) (Tudge & de Lucca Freitas, 2012). Cultural differences about the nature of the world can be found in many cultural artifacts well beyond the scope of any research project. An ontological approach deals with what makes a human a human, including institutional, social, and technical conventions.

Epistemology is the study of knowledge, and it is concerned with what is known and how it can be known. Each culture has its own research traditions and has developed ways that research is expected to be conducted over time. For example, in Hong Kong, the "traditional" conception of epistemological belief is associated with certainty as well as expert knowledge, and is overtly put in opposition to constructivism (Chan 2008). There are three main ways in which epistemology informs CCR. These are:

1. Beliefs about the nature of knowledge, the way that it can be structured and the forms that knowledge can take. For example, there is no point taking extensive "qualitative" field notes if no one takes them seriously as a form of knowledge.
2. Beliefs related to the nature of knowing, including how to evaluate and judge criteria for knowledge construction. For example, if only established experts or elders have the social authority to "own" knowledge and disseminate it, this will make the research task for the emerging researcher very difficult, because it is undesirable to challenge the authority. This is particularly relevant in societies with a Confucian heritage, such as China, Korea, or Japan.
3. Beliefs about knowledge within the cultural context and how it might be viewed (lens or paradigm) and conveyed to others (communication). For example, can a person deeply embedded in the culture actually understand it from an external point of view? Can a person who has never experienced the culture fully understand it? Can culture be conveyed to others at all?

In order to be aware of the epistemological stance of the source and target cultures, and therefore biases that will exist in the research, the researcher will need to be open to alternative points of view throughout the research process, from conceptualizing the research to analyzing the data and writing up the results. Bias is not a "bad" thing unless you do not know that it exists and can be accounted for in your research. Some form of bias will be evident in all forms of research, regardless of their nature. Recognizing bias as part of the researcher's identity, rather than as an undesirable by-product, is necessary for emerging researchers to conduct cross-cultural research with confidence.

Epistemology and ontology are inputs to axiological positions, that is, they are the philosophical foundations by which any research is valued. An emerging researcher should be aware of the potential for differences to be evidenced throughout the research process and to take into account different points of view. Table 6.2 summarizes the impacts of paradigm and philosophical approach on CCR.

Ethical dilemmas and cross-cultural research

Across the world academic research is usually conducted within an ethical decision-making framework using principles that can be traced back as far as ancient Mesopotamia, more than 5,000 years ago (Larue, 1993). Ethical decision making has distinct cultural traditions and there are differences in how ethical decisions are made depending on these traditions. Some of the main ethical, not necessarily religious, traditions are: Hinduism, Buddhist, Classical Chinese, Jewish, Christian, and Islamic (Singer, 1993). While there are religious underpinnings to some of these traditions, they can be found in secular

Table 6.2 Summary of the impact of paradigm and philosophical approach on CCR

Issue	Positivism	Interpretivism
Style of language	Third person Objective Complete answers—facts exist within the scope of this project Controls for bias and assumes that external influences on the research process are controllable People are subjects or respondents	First person Subjective Partial answers—nothing is a fact but may contribute to others understanding Recognizes external influences on the research process and accounts for them People are participants in the research process
Concepts of proof	Things can be proven Falsification (disproven)	Nothing is "real" except to the subject
Concepts of truth	Absolute—it exists and can be found somewhere in the researcher's universe	Relative—it all depends Triangulation can provide a relative point of reference
Methodological approaches	Survey Secondary data sets (e.g., econometric analyses)	Interview Group discussions Observations Semiotics
Perspective	Usually a third party—externalized research, attempts to create objectivity	Often self or participant
Types of knowledge	Concrete Knowable Transferable	Abstract Unknowable Subjective
Samples and sampling	Generalizable (to predict) Probability	Purposive (to explain or understand) Nonprobability

Source: Adapted from Brennan, Voros, and Brady (2011).

countries where such religions have had precedence at some point in the country's history. This chapter does not aim to contribute to the wide-ranging debate that surrounds theories of ethics and their application to research. However, there is a need to elucidate some of the ethical principles that are applied to academic research with humans. A set of principles that is widely used is that of the American Psychological Association (APA). Their principles are:

1. *Beneficence and nonmaleficence*. This means that researchers should make every effort to do no harm during the conduct of their research and ensure that their research benefits the participant.
2. *Fidelity and responsibility*. Researchers should ensure that they do not allow other researchers to behave in a way that can harm participants.

3. *Integrity.* Researchers should be accurate, honest, and truthful
4. *Justice.* Researchers should ensure that all persons benefit from the research where possible. Researchers should work within their competences and biases.
5. *Respect for persons and their dignity.* Researchers should respect the participants' right to privacy, confidentiality, and self-determination (autonomy and informed consent). Safeguards to protect the vulnerable will be established.

This is an edited version of the APA principles and the full version can be found at http://www.apa.org/ethics/code/index.aspx?item=3. These principles can be applied in CCR but there are some conditions where special caution needs to be taken. The first of these is that some Western notions of ethical research may seem to be cultural imperialism (Honan, Hamid, Alhamdan, Phommalangsy & Lingard, 2012). For example, the APA definition of respect for persons includes a right to privacy and confidentiality. Privacy is not a proclaimed human right throughout the world, and therefore in some countries this principle may seem to be imperialistic. An additional proviso in CCR is that of the participants' role in the process (Marshall & Batten, 2003). Applying the principles of autonomy and informed consent can be challenging in some countries where the cultural context does not allow for individual autonomy to a great extent (e.g., highly collectivist countries).

Power distance is a theoretical concept developed by Mulder (1959) and later popularized by Hofstede (see e.g., G. Hofstede, 1983; G. Hofstede, Bond & Luk, 1993; G. H. Hofstede, 2001). Power distance theory suggests that more powerful members of groups will attempt to maintain or extend psychological distance between themselves and less powerful group members. Conversely, less powerful group members will attempt to close this power gap as much as they can, unless the perceived power gap is so large that they cannot see any potential for becoming closer to the object of power. What this means for cross-cultural researchers is ethically complex. For example, people in low power positions (e.g., students, low-r level employees) may not be in a position to say "no" to participating in research. The ethical principle of "respect for persons" (Groves et al., 2013), a key platform in the ethical conduct of research, requires that participants are autonomous and not persuaded or coerced into participating. People in low power positions may feel obliged to participate in order to close the perceived power gap or because they feel they have no real choice given the powerful position of the person making the request to participate. This is particularly relevant in China, for example, where *guanxi* (an intricate system of overt and covert social networks governed by unwritten laws of reciprocity), acting as the glue that holds the society together, requires compromises from the part of the person seeking to establish *guanxi* with a person of higher social status (Liang & Lu, 2006). Power distance is likely to be an issue for those countries recording high power distance scores according to Hofstede's research on cultural dimensions. These are countries usually in Asia, Africa, the Middle East, and Latin countries such as Spain, Italy, and Latin America.

Concepts of privacy and seeking personal or sensitive information

Different countries also have different legal, regulatory, and cultural differences about what is and is not permissible to ask people. For example, in Vietnam where the age of the person is important in establishing social rank and knowing how to appropriately address someone (Sidnell & Shohet, 2013), asking a person's age is not a point of concern and people will willingly provide this information. Conversely, in Australia, age is considered to be a private matter and some justification is required before people will respond to this type of request for information. The types of information that are likely to be considered sensitive are listed in table 6.3.

Tied up with the issue of sensitive information is that of the trust reposed in the researcher by the participant. In some countries, especially where there may be power disparities as a result of class or caste systems, participants can be reluctant to provide information that can classify them as belonging to a particular group of people. They may feel this lack of trust because of societal mores about the use of information provided in surveys or as a result of information being misused from other research projects. Furthermore, information that can result in stigmatization of participants is unlikely to be accurately reported.

Table 6.3 Potentially sensitive information in CCR

Type of information	Examples
Personally identifying information	Location, address details, social security numbers, health cards, identity cards, biometric data, date of birth, phone numbers
Security information	Passwords, email addresses, usernames, IP addresses
Social status information	Income, occupation, education, titles, marital status
Financial security information	Credit card details, tax returns, financial or bank statements
Potentially negative information	Criminal records, visa denials, credit history, fines and misdemeanors
Potentially discriminatory information	Sexual preference, ethnicity, religion, citizenship status, disability

Source: Adapted from a variety of sources by the authors.

In addition, sometimes people are reluctant to provide information to strangers or outsiders (Martin, 2008). This can be as a result of family and filial ties and societal or group rights to knowledge. In some communities, there are rules about who can and cannot be told specific types of knowledge. For example, in Australian Indigenous communities specific knowledge is passed on by elders to initiates only; some other knowledge can be shared only with women or only with men; nonmembers of the community cannot be told at all. An outsider might easily ask an offensive question not knowing that he or she isnot entitled to the knowledge. An answer will be given, but it won't be the "truth." Furthermore, in such circumstances, the right to knowledge is not held by any individual and an individual is not entitled to share his or her community's knowledge with others without the entire community agreeing to it. This can make gaining informed consent problematic. Also, when some knowledge must be hidden from others, finding the "truth" can be challenging. There are likely to be many truths in such contexts: The truths that you, as an outsider, are entitled to know and the ones that the community is entitled to know. Linked to this is the potential for peoples to be exploited by emerging researchers seeking to build their careers. While we can assume that no one intends to exploit others, researchers need to work with the community to ensure that the target communities are appropriately represented in knowledge dissemination.

Signs, symbols, and finding meaning in CCR

Cultural artifacts come in many different forms. One form that is often overlooked by researchers is that of semiotics, including symbols and signs. Table 6.4 is a list of typical research techniques used in CCR. Signs, symbols, and cultural artifacts tend to be very important in "qualitative" techniques although they can be found in all types of research. Thus, if your research project involves any of the techniques listed in column 1 you may want to create a coding framework for how you will evaluate the semiotics throughout the research process.

Table 6.4 Typical CCR techniques

Qualitative	Quantitative	Secondary
Interviews	Surveys	Literature
Focus groups	Audits	Statistics
Projective techniques	Mechanical observations	Census data
Metaphor elicitation	Content analyses	Subscription data
Introspection	Experiment	Data mining
Semiotics		Business trends

The caution for emerging researchers into CCR issues is that signs and symbols tend to be readily visible only to those who are primed to see them (Parkany, 1998). Semiotics is the analysis of signs and symbols to explore and understand meaning. In order to understand meaning, the following is necessary:

1. The sender and the receiver are aligned in some way (usually through the communication context).
2. There are signs and symbols that each party is aware of and can describe (if not define).
3. There are ways of meaning that are understood between the sender and receiver. For example, metaphors and similes have shared understanding between cultures.
4. Conceptual structures are agreed upon and understood by each party, that is, what is true or false, what is subjective or objective, real or an illusion? For example, is the depiction of a naked woman in the Sistine Chapel different in meaning as compared with a picture of a naked woman in *Playboy* magazine?
5. The messages are framed in such a way that the receiver is aware of the sender's meaning. This framing may be influenced by semantic units, genre, style, stereotypes, ideologies, discourses, myths, or paradigms.

Another example of signs and symbols and shared meaning across cultures is the vexed issues of numbers and numerical symbols. In some cultures, especially those where numerology is a significant tradition (cf. South and Southeast Asia), constructing scales can be complex. In such cultural contexts a number is not simply a number; it may be a lucky number, a divine symbol, or an indicator of bad fortune (Cammann, 1961; Sivin, 1976). Thus, a survey designed in the Western method with intervals between the numbers, designed to produce linear results, may not yield the results you want at all because there are culturally embedded responses to numerical symbols and systems. The language of numbers is not universal.

East Asian survey participants have been found to be more likely to select middle responses in scales (Chen, Lee & Stevenson, 1995; Harzing, 2006) as compared to those from North American and Spanish-speaking countries who are more likely to have more extreme response styles. Furthermore, participants from individualistic, high uncertainty avoidance, or masculine cultures are less likely to be acquiescent in their responses (less likely to agree with statements) (Johnson, et al. 2005).

A mixture of positive and negative statements can mitigate against both acquiescence and disacquiescence (Smith, 2003); however, questionnaire items containing negations can be difficult to translate into some languages. To reduce the impact of extreme response styles evident in some cultures, Harzing

(2006) recommends the use of a larger number of categories, which can enable respondents with a relatively strong opinion to voice a more nuanced position. Also, scale anchors must be carefully selected to ensure that the correct meaning is conveyed, as small changes in wording can lead to considerable differences in responses.

Sources of information and the need for triangulation

CCR researchers must also be aware that in some countries exact and specific data may not be available. When the best you can do is an estimate, it changes the nature of the outcomes you can claim as a result of your research. For example, the World Bank has an excellent source of country statistics, CIA.gov is another very useful source of information, and many countries (but not all) have their own statistical collection agencies. However, as can be seen in table 6.5, each of these sources has slightly different numbers and if you look at the provenance of the figures (how rigorously they are derived), it may be that some are more reliable than others. Furthermore, some figures may be more up to date than others. As you can see, the cia.gov figures are quoted as of July 2013 and claim to be more up to date than the Vietnamese government source data. This would need to be verified before relying on the data. When creating statistical approximations about populations, triangulation is critical to assuring the veracity of the estimation.

The principle of triangulation is especially important in CCR because there are so many potential errors in the various sources of data. In many cases, it is

Table 6.5 Differences in sources of information: A Vietnam example

Demographic statistic	World Bank	CIA.gov	General Statistics Office of Vietnam
Population	88,775,500 (2012)	92,477,857 (July 2013)	88,526,883 (April 2012)
Average age of population	Not available	total: 28.7 years male: 27.6 years female: 29.7 years (2013 est.)	Not available (data on age group distribution available)
Average income per annum $US	$1,400 (2012)	Not available	$2,551 (2012) (calculation from monthly income in VND)
Average number of years in education or literacy rate	Not available	total population: 93.4% male: 95.4% female: 91.4% (2011 est.)	total population: 94%

not feasible to establish where the most accurate figure lies within the context. As a consequence, some caution needs to be exercised when using statistical data from secondary sources, even when the source is a government one.

Pragmatics and practicalities in CCR

Cross-cultural researchers should also be aware that trade-offs are always necessary in research. There are pragmatic reasons for undertaking research in different ways at different times. Perfect research is rarely feasible. The trade-offs most applicable to CCR are:

1. *Time*. This refere to the time you have to invest in the conduct of the study, collection of results, obtaining feedback, and acting on the conclusions. Also, the amount of time the researcher has to invest in the study. For example, in high context cultures where established relationships are essential to the quality of the outcome, it may take many years to develop a relationship to the point of being able to conduct in-depth qualitative research. As another example, in some countries, especially developing ones, online surveys may not be feasible (as there are too few personally owned and accessible computers) and postal systems may not be efficient enough to have timely returns. While faster, interpersonal data collection can be expensive and may result in interviewer bias.

   The concept of time is also perceived differently across cultures. This may have implications in both the logistics of conducting research and the accuracy of the research itself. For example, Levine, West, and Reis (1980) observed that Brazilians were less accurate than Americans in estimating the time of the day, have a more flexible perception of what constitutes being early and being late, and do not see lack of punctuality as a serious offense. What this may mean for researchers conducting research in Brazil is, for example, that they should design their research with flexibility, wherein research that requires time precision and pressure needs to be adaptable. Survey questions requiring participants to report personal activities at various times of the day, for example, can be subject to bias and inaccuracy without providing them with the equipment they need (e.g., watches, clocks).

   Pace of life also pays a role in the perception of time. Countries with high-paced lifestyles such as Japan, Switzerland, Ireland, and Germany tend to value time more than countries with a slower lifestyle, such as Mexico, Indonesia, or El Salvador (Levine & Norenzayan, 1999). And as pace of life correlates positively with economic achievement, the general pattern is that developing countries tend to resist the idea of time being seen as concrete and rigid.

2. *Availability of sample.* The number and type of people you need to know about is necessarily limited in some circumstances. Research is always constrained by researchers' ability to gain access to an acceptable number of appropriately sampled people. As mentioned previously, different methods of sampling are deployed for different reasons. If using a probability sampling methodology, defining the population will be critical to the ability to generalize to the broader population. However, if you are intending to predict how the general population of a country will respond to a particular issue, then using a convenience sample of highly educated university students is not a good start.
3. *The need for objectivity.* This is also important if you want to make a significant decision based on the research. However, objectivity sometimes requires expensive research methods in order to increase levels of precision and confidence in the research results. Of course, there are circumstances where you do not need or want to be objective in research methods. This decision will be related to the paradigm of research adopted for the research.
4. *The type of technology required.* This can also constrain or facilitate the research. Much research today is relatively sophisticated simply because the technology exists. For example, a structural equation model can be built using a non-normal, nongeneralizable data set; but as the fundamental principle behind modeling is that a linear relationship exists (both theoretically and practically), this is statistically inappropriate—unfortunately this is very commonly seen in CCR. Modeling of non-normal population data will not help you predict what will happen in the normal population. Further, while online surveys are increasingly useful sources of data, in many countries they are not representative samples and so any results derived from such sources must be treated with some caution.
5. *Response rates.* They vary according to the participant's level of interest in the issue as well as some more basic considerations of when, where, and how the contact is initiated. If a high response rate is required, it is often more expensive to conduct the research. In countries where there are issues with access to sample participants this can add much complexity to the research procedures. The greater the requirement for statistical generalizability, the greater the likelihood of an extensive and possibly expensive research project. Raising response rates can be problematic if there is a requirement for an incentive to be given the participant. For example, participants may need to be reimbursed for their time and effort in participating. However, in some countries this may be seen as an incentive to participate and therefore it crosses the ethical boundary of voluntary consent (autonomy). Determining the level and type of incentive can take some time and will

equire a strong knowledge of the cultural and ethical considerations that prevail in the target countries.

6. *Research ethics and integrity.* These are often traded off, particularly when research is conducted among vulnerable populations. Highly ethical research takes more time and is usually more expensive as a result. The principles of ethical conduct of research outlined earlier can assist with this set of trade-offs. In addition the Singapore Statement (http://www.singaporestatement.org/) provides some excellent guidelines for emerging researchers in CCR to understand the principles of research with integrity in the international setting.
7. *Human effort.* This is another important consideration. The more the human effort required—participants, researchers, and others, the more expensive and time consuming the research. In addition, the greater the human effort required the more the likelihood of error, as fatigue is an issue.
8. *The speed.* This will constrain the research. For example, a quick project will not be using a grounded theory or a deep ethnographic approach. Quantitative surveys are much faster to conduct than qualitative in-depth studies or meta-analyses. However, fast quantitative research may not solve an in-depth qualitative research problem. Fast statistical data collection may not be representative of the general population (response bias).
9. *The availability of expertise.* This is an important consideration. The best research is constrained by the researchers' ability to conduct it, analyze the outcomes, and act on the results. In CCR research, the expertise has to be available in all the cultures included in the study. Thus, the training of researchers can be an extensive (and expensive) constraint, especially if there is a requirement for specialist expertise.
10. *Navigating CCR research* Different countries' legal and regulatory frameworks can also be challenging. Some examples of this issue are:
    a. Funding bodies in different countries have different rules and regulations for whom they will and will not provide funding to, and what they will provide funding for.
    b. Cross-institutional agreements may need to be negotiated if there are different entities involved. Creating an agreement with different types of entities can also be challenging. For example, an EU-funded grant for research conducted in Southeast Asia on the outcome of a project on sustainability could involve several universities, the host government, the aid agency, local authorities for permissions to conduct research, and others. Each one of these has different needs from the agreement and one contract will not suffice. Also, the locus of the agreement has to be decided at the outset, as the laws of the country in which it is held will be the prevailing ones, should an issue arise.
    c. Authors will need to negotiate intellectual property agreements that are able to be applied in different countries.

d. Some countries do not permit research within their countries to be published without consent of the government.
e. Research partnerships and agreements may need to be formalized and documented in order to be accepted. For an emerging researcher this might be more than he or she is able to independently negotiate in the early stages of a CCR project.

Conclusion and suggestions for future reading

As you can see, CCR is very complex, as summarized in table 6.6. It requires a consideration of the level of research: societal (macro), institutional (meso), or individual (micro). Cultural differences and similarities can be found within and between each of these levels. Excellent marketing insights can be gained if you understand how to address each level according to the needs of the research project. The issues associated with language—whether to translate or not, how to translate, and what happens to your research when you do—have been the subject of entire books; so if you intend to undertake CCR in a language other than your own, you are advised to read further than this brief chapter (see references).

The philosophical foundations of research are not universal and different cultures have different traditions of conducting research. These traditions influence how people see and value research (axiology). There are many paradigms at play in the CCR field and the few described in this chapter are only the beginning of the research journey. Should you want to examine the underpinning philosophies that affect your research projects, you can find a rich source of information in the Philosophy of Science literature (Curd & Psillos, 2013). In the marketing discipline, authors such as Hunt (1993; 1992, 2003) have some interesting insights to add to how the discipline is constructed.

The ethics of CCR is an emergent field as globalization is increasingly dissolving social and geographic boundaries. Researchers need to be aware of the potential for cultural imperialism and to ensure that their research allows for autonomy and respect for persons. Researchers also need to be cognizant of the types of information that are considered sensitive in the target culture, as well as the possibility that the knowledge they are seeking may belong to a community that does not want to share it with outsiders.

Culture is often conceptualized as an iceberg and as a consequence many cultural artifacts are invisible to someone who is not primed to see them. Ensuring that meaning is found and conveyed to others will require a consideration of the signs and symbols (semiotics) that are embedded within the culture.

A shared frame of reference should be established at the outset of the research. The vast array of information that is available on the Internet can be confusing, and assessing the veracity of the data before relying on them is important

Table 6.6 Summary of issues and suggestions for remediation

	Issue	Remedy
1	Language	1. Forward and backward translation of research instruments 2. Construct development in source and target language 3. Translation committees including source and target language speakers
2	Concepts of truth and axiology of research traditions	1. Understand the dominant research paradigm in the target country 2. Ensure that the lens through which you view your own research is clearly understood and accounted for in designing your research 3. Ensure that you have an understanding of the epistemological and ontological stance(s) adopted for the research and evidenced in the target culture 4. Articulate your assumptions and check them for veracity prior to conducting research
3	Power distance and consent to participate	1. In countries where there is likely to be high power distance and resultant ethical considerations, ensure that participants are given the opportunity to "opt in" to research and not approached to participate by those in a position of power
4	Concepts of privacy and seeking personal or sensitive information	2. Ensure that you know what is permissible to ask before designing the instrument 3. Ensure that the rights of the participant are protected when collecting and analyzing potentially sensitive information 4. The ethical principles of justice, respect, and beneficence supersede those of the research 5. Ensure that you have the right to knowledge granted to you by the right people (e.g., community elders)
5	Signs symbols and finding meaning	1. Ensure that you understand the semiotic framework in the target culture 2. Ensure that you have sufficient facility with the target culture to be objective in your viewpoint and can understand the implications of descriptions as they are provided to you (e.g., metaphors and analogies) 3. Understand the conventions of communicating within the target and source cultures and ensure that there is a shared frame of reference
6	Sources of information	1. Ensure that you use multiple peer-reviewed sources of statistical information where feasible 2. Check that official figures are verifiable and collected in a rigorous manner 3. Ensure that at least three pieces of information (triangulation) are accessed before relying on the results 4. Develop a tolerance for ambiguity when it comes to data (it may never be correct)

Table 6.6 Continued

	Issue	Remedy
7	Pragmatics and practicalities	1. Ensure that you allow enough flexibility in your project to account for issues with sampling, data collection and response rates 2. Before you start the project decide on how much effort will be required in terms of a. Time b. Speed of research process c. Technology including software and data processing d. Researcher expertise (e.g., analysis, interviewing skills, translation capability) 3. Decide on your ethical stance and evaluate the costs and benefits of research using ethical principles applicable to your position

in CCR. All research has trade-offs to be made for pragmatic and practical reasons. Conducting good quality research takes an investment of time and effort, but it is worth it for the benefits it brings both to the community of scholars and the communities that the research aims to serve.

References

Brennan, L., & Camm, J. (2007). Pressure to innovate: Does validity suffer? *Australasian Journal of Market Research, 15*(1), 29–41.

Brennan, L., Voros, J., & Brady, E. (2011). Paradigms at play and implications for validity in social marketing research. *Journal of Social Marketing, 1*(3), 100–119.

Brown, D. E. (1991). *Human universals*. Philadephia, PA: Temple University Press.

Cammann, S. (1961). The magic square of three in old Chinese philosophy and religion. *History of religions, 1*(1), 37–80.

Chan, K.W. (2008). Epistemological beliefs, learning, and teaching: The Hong Kong cultural context. In M.S. Khine (Ed.), *Knowing, knowledge and beliefs: epistemological studies across diverse cultures* (pp. 257–272). New York: Springer.

Chen, C., Lee, S. -Y., & Stevenson, H. W. (1995). Response style and cross-cultural comparisons of rating scales among East Asian and North American students. *Psychological Science, 6*(3), 170–175.

Curd, M., & Psillos, S. (2013). *The Routledge Companion to Philosophy of Science*. New York: Routledge.

Groves, R. M., Fowler Jr., F. J., Couper, M. P., Lepkowski, J. M., Singer, E., & Tourangeau, R. (2013). *Survey methodology*. New York: Wiley.

Hall, E. T. (1977). *Beyond culture*. New York: Random House Digital, Inc.

Harkness, J. (1999). In pursuit of quality: Issues for cross-national survey research. *International Journal of Social Research Methodology, 2*(2), 125–140.

Harkness, J., Pennell, B.-E., & Schoua-Glusberg, A. (2004). Survey questionnaire translation and assessment. In Stanley Presser, Jennifer M. Rothgeb, Mick P. Couper, Judith T. Lessler, Elizabeth Martin, Jean Martin, & Eleanor Singer (Eds.), *Methods for testing and evaluating survey questionnaires*, Vol. 546, pp. 453–473, New York: Wiley.

Harkness, J. A., & Schoua-Glusberg, A. (1998). Questionnaires in translation. *ZUMA-Nachrichten Spezial, 3*(1), 87–127.

Harzing, A.-W. (2006). Response styles in cross-national survey research: A 26-country study. *International Journal of Cross Cultural Management, 6*(2), 243–266.

Hofstede, G. (1983). National cultures in four dimensions: A research-based theory of cultural differences among nations. *International Studies of Management & Organization, 13*(1–2), 46–74.

Hofstede, G. H. (2001). *Culture's consequences* (2nd ed.). Thousand Oaks, CA: Sage.

Hofstede, G., Bond, M., & Luk, C.-l. (1993). Individual perceptions of organizational cultures: A methodological treatise on levels of analysis. *Organization Studies, 14*(4), 483–503.

Honan, E., Hamid, M. O., Alhamdan, B., Phommalangsy, P., & Lingard, B. (2012). Ethical issues in cross-cultural research. *International Journal of Research & Method in Education,* 12(4), 1–14.

Hunt, S. (1993). On rethinking marketing: Our discipline, our practice, our methods. *European Journal of Marketing, (special edition on The New Marketing Myopia: Critical perspectives on theory and research in marketing, edited by D.T. Brownlie, M. Saren, R, Whittington and R. Wensley) 28*(3), 13–25.

Hunt, S. D. (1992). For reason and realism in marketing. *Journal of Marketing, 56*(April), 89–102.

Hunt, S. D. (2003). *Controversy in marketing theory: For reasons, realism truth and objectivity.* Armonk, NY: Me Sharpe.

Johnson, T., Kulesa, P., Cho, Y. I., & Shavitt, S. (2005). The relation between culture and response styles: Evidence from 19 countries. *Journal of Cross-Cultural Psychology, 36*(2), 264–277.

Larue, G. A. (1993). Ancient ethics. In P. Singer (Ed.), *A companion to ethics* (pp. 29–40). Oxford: Blackwell Publishers.

Levine, R. V., & Norenzayan, A. (1999). The pace of life in 31 countries. *Journal of Cross-Cultural Psychology, 30*(2), 178–205.

Levine, R. V., West, L. J., & Reis, H. T. (1980). Perceptions of time and punctuality in the United States and Brazil. *Journal of Personality and Social Psychology, 38*(4), 541.

Liang, B., & Lu, H. (2006). Conducting fieldwork in China: Observations on collecting primary data regarding crime, law, and the criminal justice system. *Journal of Contemporary Criminal Justice, 22*(2), 157–172.

Lloyd, G. (2010). History and human nature: Cross-cultural universals and cultural relativities. *Interdisciplinary Science Reviews, 35*(3–4), 201–214.

Marshall, A., & Batten, S. (2003). Ethical issues in cross-cultural research. *Connections, 3*(1), 139–151.

Martin, K. L. (2008). *Please knock before you enter: Aboriginal regulation of outsiders and the implications for researchers.* Teneriffe, QLD: Post Pressed.

Mulder, M. (1959). Power and satisfaction in task-oriented groups. *Acta Psychologica, 16*(1), 178–225.

Murdock, G. P. (1949). *Social structure,* New York: Macmillan.

Osgood, C. E. (1975). *Cross-cultural universals of affective meaning.* Urbana: University of Illinois Press.

Parkany, R. (1998). *An historic context concerning research in symbolic systems and semiotic meaning.* Sydney: Sage.

Sidnell, J., & Shohet, M. (2013). The problem of peers in Vietnamese interaction. *Journal of the Royal Anthropological Institute, 19*(3), 618–638.

Sin, L. Y. M., Cheung, G. W. H., & Lee, R. (1999). Methodology in cross-cultural consumer research: A review and critical assessment. *Journal of International Consumer Marketing, 11*(4), 75–96.

Singer, P. (Ed.). (1993). *A companion to ethics*. Oxford: Blackwell Publishers.

Sivin, N. (1976). Chinese alchemy and the manipulation of time. *Isis, 67*(4), 513–526.

Smith, T. W. (2003). Developing comparable questions in cross-national surveys, In J. A. Harkness, F. J. R. Van de Vijver, & P. P. Mohler (Eds.), *Cross-cultural survey mmethods* (pp. 69–92). New York: John Wiley & Sons.

Tu, S. P., Jackson, J. C., Teh, C., Lai, A., Do, H., Hsu, L., Chan, I., Tseng, B., Hislop, G., & Taylor, V. (2003). Translation challenges of cross-cultural research and program development. *Asian American and Pacific Islander Journal of Health, 10*(1), 58–66.

Tudge, J. R. H., & de Lucca Freitas, L. B. (2012). Internationalization, globalization and culture (Internacionalização, Globalização E Cultura). *Psicologia & Sociedade, 24*(3), 547–556.

7

Establishing Rationale and Significance of Research

Judith Hahn

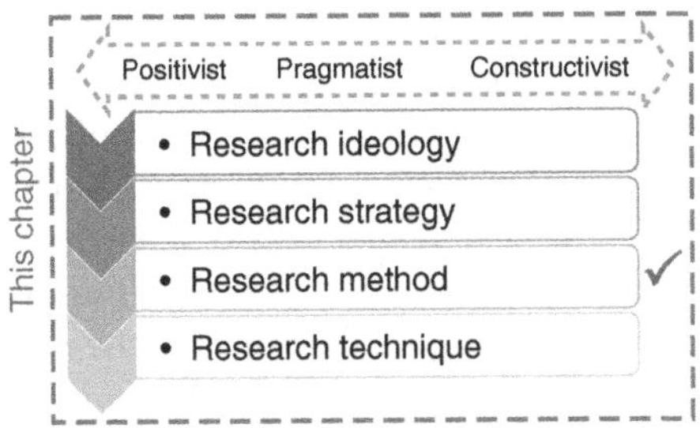

Chapter overview

This chapter builds on the first five chapters in this handbook that explained the research design typology. The focus here is on establishing rationale and significance of research. This chapter is intended to serve as a guide for practitioners to apply and integrate the research design typology layers into a scholarly manuscript. In contrast to the broad scope of the first five chapters, this chapter concentrates on how to integrate specific components of the typology, regardless of which ideology the researcher holds on the continuum (positivist, post-positivist, pragmatist, interpretivist, or constructivist).

Introduction

Research studies can influence and change the direction of the field of the research study; however not all research will change direction of research, some may have more influence than others. A research study should relate to the nature of the research question. Investigating the background of your topic and examining the chronological survey of the literature is a vital aspect of the review process of the research project. The methodology of your research should include a discussion of the literature about sampling errors, generalizability, and the empirical foundations that have been laid down during the study. Then develop your concepts and your knowledge base within the research topic area.

You may be influenced by some of the research literature you have read, and this may have an impact on your research ideology, as described earlier in this handbook. You may also reflect on your subjective position based on your practical experience. You may be swayed by authors of certain articles to take the position they have adopted on their study as they have some credibility. However, you may have to eliminate some of the ideas or conclusions drawn from these articles in your research study if you observe methodological failings in their research. You may need to include those articles that have a potential for future research based on them, or the ones whose ideas are potentially influential within a broader perspective.

Figure 7.1 is a conceptual diagram illustrating the key principles for establishing rationale and significance from a literature review for the introduction section of a paper. The basic idea is to, first, cite several good quality empirical studies (no older than five years) showing the state of the art in current factors or topics of interest in the study. Second, practitioners should be cited to establish the current practice gap (generally no older than three to five years). These practitioners may be government departments or associations that publish statistics or program evaluation data to outline the major problems. Third, thought leaders should be cited on how to study the problem, using relevant research designs, methods, and techniques. All these establish a reference for how the study has performed, and where the findings may be generalized.

Rationale

The rationale for doing research is to become familiar with what information was and is available pertaining to the subject that the researcher is interested in, for example, new treatments for cancer, diabetes, etc. Researchers developing a hypothesis can read up the latest and the oldest available material on how it relates to their way of thinking, patient experiences, and the connection between what the literature states and the focus of the research technology. This can be done based on their own findings and conclusions from the new information they have gathered during the research study versus being dependent on out-of-date material.

The initial step is to review first and secondary sources through peer-reviewed journals and educational materials. After the articles are found, a bibliography of each article is written in APA format; for formal papers, the decision to write notes about each article is strictly up to the researcher, but it does save time especially if there are dozens of articles that do not fit into the criteria of the research. When doing a literature review for a dissertation, the criteria becomes more extensive; the researcher will have to list the purpose, problem, need for the research hypothesis, type of research method used, strengths, and

Figure 7.1 Conceptual model of establishing significance and rationale.

weaknesses of the research project, and the results. The researcher will also have to look for trends, developments, contradictions, or similarities that other reviewers might have missed when doing the literature review, or he or she may disagree on an issue. Not all data have a clear conclusion.

Common pitfalls

Students list a series of writers in their literature reviews with short explanations as to the justification of their inclusion into the bibliography as their work within the topic, and a few sentences are devoted to them. The reviewer then has the chore of sorting out the rationale for inclusion. A literature review should be clear in structure, include an explanation for the structure, and it should be planned and presented for a clear rationale.

Emphasizing leading research studies

Research studies can influence and change the direction of the field of the research study for a variety of reasons: new concepts may be developed that may be widely applicable across all fields of research, may change the way researchers view the subject, and open different avenues for research and new methodologies.

Researchers also have options for the approaches they will use in their research; for example, some researchers may prefer *quantitative* approaches while others may favor *qualitative* ones using phenomenology or interactions. A research study should relate to the nature of the research question. Some research issues, for example, produce better results when a survey approach is used in order to gain an idea of broad trends. Qualitative approaches are better in investigating the human lived experiences. When researchers work within a particular methodological framework on a regular basis, they can become committed to that perspective.

When you start your literature review is started, it is better to first write the bibliography on each article that pertains to your topic of research, so that you have the main points and do not have to retrace your steps wasting valuable time trying to find the article amid the plethora of information and data that are available online, in journals, and in textbooks. The examples below are related to the medical field; however, bibliographies are all written in the the same format.

Example of establishing rationale and significance

In an article (Katz, 2010), the author states that the gross domestic product in 2009 was $2.5 trillion and the consumption projection was $2.5 trillion for out-of-pocket expenditures for health-care coverage for the average American care spending in the United States. The US 2019 future expenditure projection estimates will touch $4.5 trillion or 19.3% of the gross domestic product for health care, and "limiting health care expenditures can easily reach 100% of GDP in industrialized nations even without accounting for wasteful expenditures" (Katz, 2010, p. 70).

Medicaid is the only public health insurance program that taps state revenues for its financing; but it also serves an expansive population compared to other societal groups. Historically, administration of Medicaid, which is done by the federal government and the states, has been a controversial program because of the pressures of escalating program expenditures on the budgets of the federal and, particularly, state governments. Consequently, state health reformers resisted incorporating the expensive Medicaid population into reformed systems in order to reduce state financial liability (Kinney, 1995).

The Medicare program would have remained intact but with streamlined billing and claims administration procedures. If such procedures had been in place, Medicaid would have been incorporated into the private health insurance system over a period of time. Under the single-payer proposals, Medicare and Medicaid were incorporated into the single-payer system. According to this article, the cost of health care is high, and insurance providers are seeking ways to control the costs by capping the amount that providers can bill for services. This leads to denying patients services after reaching the allotment of funding available to them. This rationing of health care in theory is done so that more patients will receive health-care coverage. Health care is a business, and as with any business, the prices go up when the demand is high, and unfortunately, unlike most businesses, there are no sales in health care; what does happen is that the price increase limits the access to health care to individuals who can least afford to purchase it (Mclean, 2006).

Despite all these drawbacks, passing the Medicare and Medicaid program, represents a major expansion of the government's role in providing social supports—in this case, access to health care for vulnerable populations. The creation of these programs was clearly a major national milestone; supporters of these programs were essentially from several competing legislative proposals with very different ideological starting points (Mclean, 2006).

In the year 2002, the Hastings Center began a project to address health-care quality improvements in the areas of nursing, health policy and regulations, medicine, social science, health-care management, law, and health-services research. The goals of the project were to (1) ensure quality improvement in ethical issues, (2) make recommendations regarding quality improvements, and (3) promote communication on quality improvement regarding ethical issues in the community (The Ethics of Using QI Methods to Improve Health Quality and Safety, 2006).

Exploring key academic arguments

Investigating the background of your topic and examining the chronological survey of the literature is another important aspect of the review process of the research project. Researchers' opinions on the subject matter differ and provide an insight into the depth of the surveyed literature and the key ideas that form the basis for the study of that subject. Each distinctive area of a subject has its own range of concepts, which are used to express ideas in that subject. Some of these concepts may be shared with other academic areas, while some may be unique to the area in question.

In order to write about the topic and fully understand the subject, you first must comprehend what you are talking about. When reading the literature of your topic, it will be to your advantage to put it into your own words so that you can understand what you are reading and what you are going to discuss. Remember you are going to be the expert about this topic, so you will need to know and discuss this subject with authority.

You will also need to know how the subject of your research will affect society as it relates to your research. Your own value judgments are to be unbiased when interacting or dealing with the participants of your research. You must ensure that ethics and values are a component in the statement of consent to participate in the research project. When doing literature research in chronological or historical order, which is basic and popular method of gathering data there are certain disadvantages.

There may not be a link or connection between one section of your topic and the next; the sequence of dates is the only connection. The choice here is to narrow the time frame of the topic, then do the chronological sequence and themes that coordinate with the literature. Develop your concepts and knowledge base within the research topic area. Analyze all of your literature and determine the focus of your research. When all these concepts are on target, then you are ready to start sorting and gathering all of the information together in order to write your paper.

The ideas from your literature review reflect the analytical process undertaken by the researcher and the knowledge that will offer new concepts to define and add to the contribution to perform a new research project. You should use the literature as a basis and a link for drawing your conclusions.

References

Katz, M. (2010). Toward a new moral paradigm in health care delivery: Accounting for individuals. *American Journal Of Law and Medicine, 36*(1), 78–135.

Kinney, E. (1995). Protecting consumers and providers under health reform: An overview of the major administrative law issues. *Health Matrix (Cleveland, Ohio: 1991), 5*(1), 83–140.

Matteson, L. & Lacey, F. M. (2011*). Doing your literature review: Traditional and systematic techniques*. London: Sage

Mclean, T. R. (2006). The future of telemedicine and its Faustian reliance on regulatory trade barriers for protection. *Health Matrix: Journal of Law-Medicine, 16*(2), 443–509.

Saxton, J. & Johns, M. (2010). Barriers to change in engineering the system of health care delivery. *Studies in Health Technology and Informatics, 15*(3), 437–463.

The Ethics of Using QI Methods to Improve Health Quality and Safety. (2006). *Hastings Center Report*, Vol. 36, pp. S1–S40.

8

Organizing and Conducting Scholarly Literature Reviews

Linnaya Graf

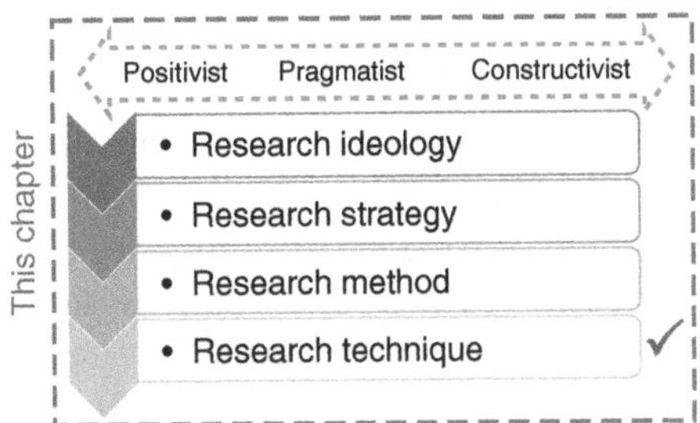

Chapter overview

This chapter builds on the first five chapters in this handbook that explained the research design typology. The focus here is on organizing and conducting scholarly literature reviews. This chapter is intended to serve as a guide for practitioners to apply and integrate the research design typology layers into a scholarly manuscript. In contrast to the broad scope of the first five chapters, this chapter concentrates on how to integrate specific components of the typology, regardless of which ideology the researcher holds on the continuum (positivist, post-positivist, pragmatist, interpretivist, or constructivist).

Overview

Understanding the literature review

The first key in understanding the expectation of completing a literature review is to consider what a literature review is not. Specifically, it does not include the act of sitting down to complete a review of a work of literature and provide your thoughts on whether it was "good" or "bad" (Fink, 2014). Reviewing literature is not the same as reviewing a movie. The assignment is not asking you to provide your opinion on the topic; rather you are expected to synthesize what is understood about the topic to date and provide reflection on what that accumulation of knowledge means (Boote & Beile, 2005). When an assignment or activity requires a literature review, the expectation is that the author will review a body of literature. This collection can be any type of material, such as military protocols, but is usually a collection of academic sources. Further, a literature review designed for industry purposes of making informed decisions must include a comprehensive, rather than selective review of all possible documents (Baker, 2000).

Garrard (2014) defines a literature review as "an analysis of scientific materials about a specific topic that requires the reviewer to carefully read each of the studies to evaluate the study's purpose, determine the appropriateness and quality of the scientific methods, examine the analysis of the questions and answers posed by the authors, summarize the findings across the studies, write an objective synthesis of the findings" (p. 5). This concept of an objective synthesis is important to understand, because in a literature review you are not being asked to provide a stance or an argument for your interpretation. Rather you are being asked to present what is currently known, identify what is not yet understood, and evaluate the literature using a systematic belief (Boote & Beile, 2005). A key benefit of any literature review is the further dissemination of gathered knowledge to a new audience (Hart, 2003).

Application and characterisitcs

Boote and Beile (2005) discussed the importance of students using the exercise of literature review as a necessary preparation for the dissertation process in being able to understand how to properly apply synthesis of the literature in an act of building methodological skill sets. One of the very best examples of how to systematically and methodologically create a literature review is provided by Garrard (2014) in the area of health sciences. While the matrix method by this author is designed for a specific industry, in reality this method can be adopted for any industry with minor adaptions and is a superior method of organizing and conducting a literature review in a way that can be validated and reproduced.

The significance of Garrad's (2014) theoretical framework for designing a literature review rests in owning the literature. Garrard provides a simple explanation of how to identify the best sources for literature, how to create a paper trail and document the review process, how to select the best documents for inclusion, abstracting, and summarizing research for tracking purposes, synthesizing the literature using the matrix method, and how to store data about the review for later reference. While Garrad's work is usually applied to the health sciences, it can certainly be adapted for business or other academic

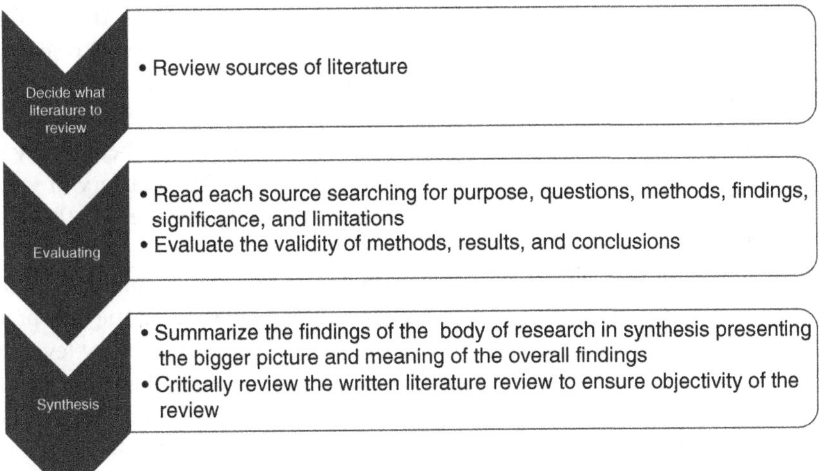

Figure 8.1 Visualization of the steps in creating a matrix method (Garrad, 2014) style literature review across any discipline.

disciplines as a practical and useful method for systematically conducting a review. Figure 8.1 depicts the matrix method various teps involved in the matrix method.

Characteristics of a good literature review

A sound literature review includes specific traits and characteristics. Specifically, it includes both depth and breadth of citation to demonstrate to the reader both the broad and specific applications of the research to the topic (Hart, 2003). A second trait includes relevant and recent literature that is appropriate for the time span being considered. For example, if looking at a historical view of theoretical application, then it is acceptable to have research that is 20 or more years old. However, if exploring an innovative topic it is more appropriate to keep research within the last few years. A third trait of good research is the integration of a variety of research across disciplines. For example, a review should include citations and examples of theoretical and conceptual frameworks, methodological applications, and practical skills and application (Baker, 2000; Hart, 2003). Other important traits of a good literature review include having a central theme, consistently tying back to that thesis, written with clarity and conciseness.

Individuals who have conducted a complete and proper literature review will feel a sense of ownership of the literature (Garrard, 2014). This means that the reviewer will be able to clearly and completely explain all of the main ideas captured in the literature, key findings and results, significance, and limitations of the given topic without referring to notes or the research itself. This ownership comes with the commitment of the reviewer to take the needed time and resources to not only read, but also master the area of research, including historical, current, and emerging studies on the topic. This is a common requirement of dissertation students who are required to demonstrate to a board their expertise in their research topic by demonstrating their ability to precisely identify gaps in the literature due to having a clear mastery of what the research has correctly and incorrectly identified and published on the subject, to date.

Case study example 1. Susie B is a masters thesis student who is conducting a literature review as part of her thesis. Her topic is a meta-analysis of the best practices in addressing bullying at the individual, school, and community level. In her work, Susie first identifies every academic and peer-reviewed journal that is relevant to her topic; she also finds dissertation and thesis sources for emerging work and explores government publications for reports on bullying. Next, she sets the inclusion criteria for her work. This includes sources available in the last eight years, peer-reviewed and academic sources making up 70% of her work and emerging scholarly works (dissertations and thesis) and government publications forming the remaining 30%. After setting parameters she tracks and documents each search she completes using the matrix method to include source, author, date, keywords, research questions, methods, results, significance, and limitations. Next, she writes summaries of each source she marks for inclusion while evaluating and dissecting each article to review for validity of what the authors did correct and where there was room for potential errors or limitations. Finally, she uses her matrix and summaries to write a comprehensive synthesis of the findings identifying clear gaps in the knowledge and limitations of the current research. She evaluates her work for objectivity and then uses her literature review as the basis for her meta-analysis.

In the above example Susie is able to provide documentation of her paper trail and tracking of her review to her committee and team; if requested, she can go back to any point in her review to retrieve additional information or reconsider a source, and an outside party can reproduce her work. This methodological documentation of the review process separates average literature reviews from quality literature reviews. Individuals who engage in this documentation process can more easily demonstrate ownership and mastery of the literature in their topic area.

Case study example 2. Archie Q. is a military installation expert who wishes to have a better understanding of why telecommunication reforms have been failing in several departments across military posts in the midwestern United States. In order to consider what the literature indicates about reform, Archie completes a comprehensive literature review of change management theories and case studies of technological implementation. Archie begins by determining what sources are most appropriate to the military field and industries with similar cultures. Next, he sets parameters to include both historical views of change management theory and more recent examples of technology adaption to include both successful and unsuccessful outcomes. Next Archie sets aside four days and documents searches of all possible materials, completing his developed review matrix as he finds each source. At the conclusion, Archie writes a synthesis of these findings in a report for his superiors outlining theoretical and practical traits of successful technological adaptations, as well as those which were not successful. So in this case, gaps in the literature related to the lack of knowledge specific to military installations, which were used to then justify a data-driven review to the board to more carefully study technological adaption and consider changes to improve telecommunication reform using the identified military installations as case studies.

Organizing a literature review

In searching for literature, a good review begins with mastering the tools, including abstracts, indexes, and search engines in order to properly find and cull all of the desired research in a given area (Hart, 2003). In order to locate these assets it is critical that a student or researcher in the twenty-first century have appreciable technological skill and mastery of the ability to use search indexes and conduct online searches. Building these skills should be a primary goal during earlier academic training, and a requirement at primary and secondary education.

As mentioned previously, documentation of this review is a critical step in a quality literature review. In this text, the matrix method (Garrard, 2014) is presented as one methods of documentation that could be applied to any industry and that is easy to understand. In the matrix method a documentation of process is used to track the review from definition to synthesis. During the review, there are four areas of work that should be organized and stored in a systematic way (Garrard, 2014):

- The first area of organization includes keeping a paper trail of dates for each search conducted, which includes a summary of keywords used, search engines explored, parameters of the search, number of findings, limitations, etc. This information should be accessible to an outside party to recreate the search that was conducted. This source might be a diary or a log kept in a word document.
- The second area of organization includes a copy of every document in the review. This might be a downloaded copy either scanned or saved in pdf or some other format.
- The third area of organization includes a review matrix. Creating this may best be accomplished using a spreadsheet. The review matrix is a document that provides specific details of every document, using a spreadsheet format,

that will allow a reviewer to see across studies. For example, using this type of tool will show the reader how many qualitative and quantitative studies have been used to explore the topic. This matrix is critical for capturing the big picture.

- The final area of organization is a folder that saves each draft of the synthesis written for the review as it evolves, for example as and when data are added or removed, when highlights are noted, or when major examples are spotted. This can be important for going back to a previous draft for information, as needed.

Creating a review matrix tool is highly customizable for each industry and purpose of literature review. The categories of that matrix can be determined by the reviewer, but should include basics such as purpose, research questions, methods, results, and significance. However, the columns can also include highly specified topics based on the purpose of the review, knowledge of the industry, and academic curiosity of the reviewer. Figure 8.2 is an example of a customized review matrix column subjects that our case study example, Susie B, might use to create her for literature on bullying.

Steps in conducting a review

The steps in conducting a literature review include establishing a rationale for the review, implementing a protocol and parameters to meet goals, developing a purpose or thesis statement, creating an outline, selecting key articles that

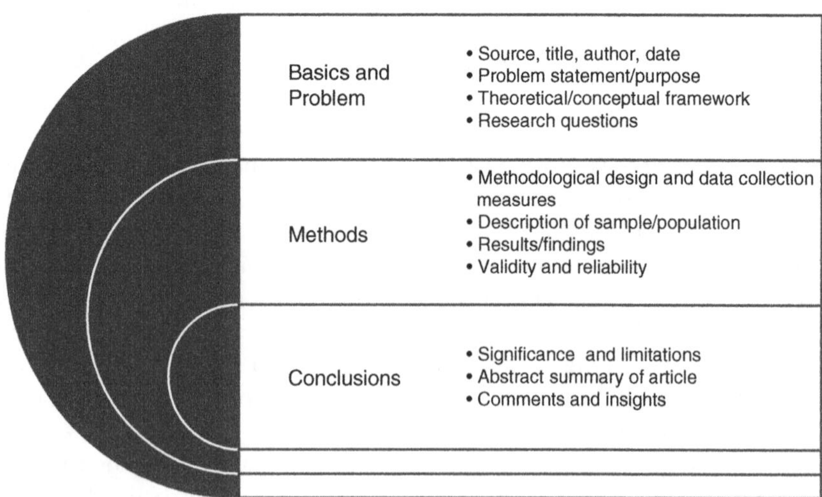

Figure 8.2 Review matrix topics: Examples.

meet the established parameters and support the thesis of the review, and making a clear synthesis of the literature that includes interpretation of the author's own voice (Boote & Beile, 2005; Fink, 2014; Garrard, 2014; Hart, 2003). Part of the determining parameters is to consider whether a deductive or inductive approach is being taken to the literature search. Specifically, an inductive review is one in which a conclusion is presented only after all of the information has been compiled and presented (Hart, 2003). Inductive approaches to literature reviews are typically used in qualitative and exploratory types of inquiries. In contrast, deductive reviews start with a statement or theory already believed to be true and the research is used to validate or question that hypothesis (Hart, 2003). Deductive approaches are more common in numerically based, quantitative studies that are use to test a hypothesis or are the basis of experimental testing.

Both these approaches, inductive and deductive, can have appropriate uses across industries. The important aspect is to choose one strategy that is most appropriate and apply that consistently throughout the work.

Figure 8.3 outlines the different steps involved in conducting a literature review.

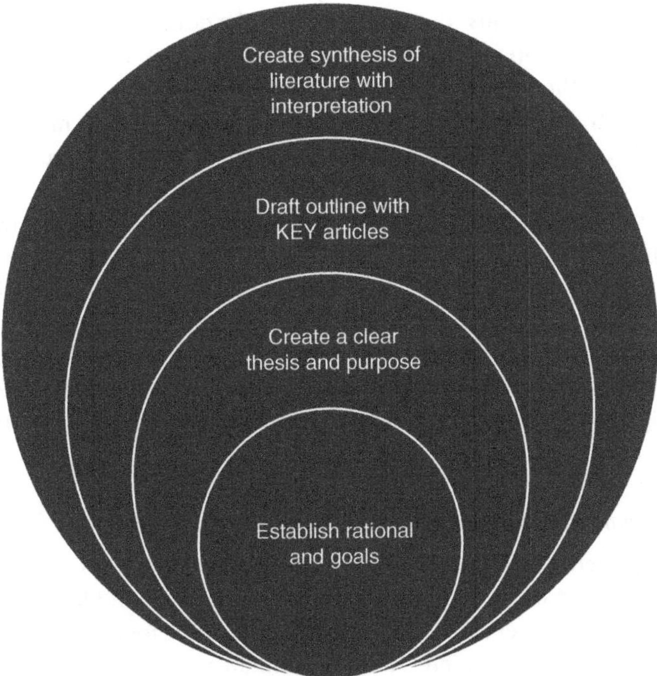

Figure 8.3 Steps in conducting a literature review.

Step 1: Establishing a rationale and purpose for the literature review

A proper literature review begins with a clear purpose, which goes beyond the accumulation and presentation of a variety of studies and knowledge about a subject. In reviewing the many sources for literature reviews, three purposes emerge for conducting the review. Specifically, quality literature reviews play an important part in synthesizing a large body of theory, models, data, and knowledge about a subject to accomplish one of three goals:

- provide a historical perspective for a given subject,
- explore and understand what is already known about a given subject, and
- identify where the gap in knowledge exists in a given area.

By providing a historical perspective, synthesizing what is known, and identifying where gaps are, a literature review can be used to drive future research and make empirical decisions using what is currently known. Keeping these purposes in mind, literature reviews are made using two specific rationales. The first rationale is to conduct direct research. Regardless of the purpose of the research, for example, academic merit, innovation, understanding, exploration, or validation, it should be directed by the identified gaps in knowledge. It is not acceptable for someone to simply conduct research based on a whim or to uncover a question "just because" one felt like doing so. A literature review provides a justification for what is being studied, why, in what order, and using what type of methodology.

Concurrently, industries across the globe must continue to make decisions without perfect knowledge. The second rationale for a literature review is that it is used to bring together and synthesize a large body of knowledge to allow more informed decisions and sound choices. This is useful in allocating funding, creating programs, designing policies, and determining future movements. This second purpose of conducting literature reviews is not to necessarily direct future research on the topic, but to use what is currently known to make the best decisions possible with what is already known. This speaks to the gaps as well, because it helps leaders to determine where not to create program or funding if too little is known about the effects of change for that given area.

Step 2: Implementing a protocol to meet literature review goals

The establishment of the goal for a given literature review helps to lay the foundation for how the literature review should be organized and laid out. It is not enough simply to gather all of the data on a given topic for a certain number of years and put it into paragraph. That is a summary of research, not a literature review (Boote & Beile, 2005). A literature review extends beyond a summary to provide interpretation, insight, and synthesis of multiple works (Fink, 2014). Developing a literature review is similar to painting a picture. Each citation used within a literature review is a single addition to the overall picture, similar to one dot in a big picture. Each contribution represents a unique color or texture. It is the blending of these colors and textures that creates something new to offer to the consumer of the review. The person creating the literature review is a crafter, who is crafting something of value from what came before.

To create this work of art, the literature review, the first step is to create a sound structure. Begin with clearly identifying the purpose of the review. This purpose becomes the thesis and central theme of the entire review (Boote & Beile, 2005).

Step 3: Developing a thesis statement and outline

After having a clear purpose, the next step is to develop a skeleton of support to build on the foundation. The first part of this skeleton is having a sound foundation, or thesis statement, for the literature review. The thesis statement should clearly capture and express the purpose of the literature review (Fink, 2014). It should also be the anchor to which all other aspects of the literature review tie back to throughout the final document. After establishing a thesis statement, the goals of the review can be used, along with identified key citations, to provide historical and philosophical importance or a framework that establishes the validity and importance of the thesis statement. Creating the skeleton of the literature can often best be accomplished by creating an outline (Cooper, 1998; Creswell, 2013). The outline then becomes the framework for synthesis and as the larger picture of research becomes visible, the next step will be to add empirical support to the framework.

Step 4: Examples of supporting outline

The third stage of development includes flushing out the meat of the literature review. A literature review is not every possible piece thrown into the mix. The key is selecting exactly the right textures, colors, and mediums to paint the picture you want to create. For the literature review, this means selecting the correct citations based on all of the available information. This is accomplished by providing a clear rationale for the inclusion and exclusion criteria that are used to select what makes its way into the literature review. Neither should one throw in everything nor should one cherry-pick only what looks good to include. On the contrary, deciding which citations will be marked for inclusion or exclusion for a literature review involves follwoing an established criterion process, which is described to the reader. This process is absolutely critical for providing a quality indicator for the reader about the integrity of the review. As was indicated prior, reviews are used to create policies, design programs, and direct future research. This means that the reader should have a crystal clear understanding of how the literature was designed and shaped in order to have confidence in the utility of the work.

Step 5: Selection of key articles

The next stage in the literature review is the selection of key articles that meet the established parameters and support the thesis of the review. This can use many of the different methods described in the literature such as the matrix method (Garrard, 2014) or coding (Cooper, 1998; Fink, 2014). The key is to document and set parameters for the study based clearly on the purpose, goals, and outline defined in the previous steps. These parameters will then dictate the beginning stages of the search, and as new keywords or information are uncovered the parameters of the search might change or evolve. This is one key reason for documentation. However, another is so that the reviewer can go back and confirm any possibility of error, ensure complete reviews, and provide keywords used to find articles in the event of more than one reviewer working together, or a committee being involved. When there is more than one researcher conducting the literature review, it becomes important to develop standardized tools that all reviewers agree to use, applying it systematically across the board. Again, as research might evolve each individual engaged in the process would have an important need to share findings, data, and desired changes with their team.

Step 6: Evaluation of literature

After clearly establishing and locating the desired articles, it is critical to evaluate the articles. In this case articles will be dissected piece by piece, focusing on each component (Fink, 2014). To define evaluation, this includes the act of objectively critiquing each component for meaning, validity, reliability, significance, and limitations. By noting and establishing issues like sample sizes, alignment of the design with the problem, theoretical framework, or conclusions coming naturally from the results, the reviewer is able to determine how valid the body of literature is in explaining the specific phenomenon or create a case for making a data-driven decision informed by clear evidence.

Step 7: Synthesis of the literature

The final stage of the literature review is a clear written report synthesizing all of the components of the body of literature that have been collected and evaluated in an integrated view, along with an objective evaluation and interpretation in the reviewers own voice addressing questions of validity, reliability, and significance. In the synthesis, the reviewer will not provide mini-summaries of each article. Rather, the reviewer will use the comparison across the body of literature to discuss implications of what the review tells us about the status, knowledge, gaps, and strengths of the literature to date.

Conclusions

One of the best way for any student or industry professional to master literature review skills is to review examples of good research or reviews in the literatures that are theoretical, skill-based, and applied from both a historical and modern perspective (Boote & Beile, 2005; Dessian, Krom, & Soini, 2013; Latif, Abbas, & Assar, 2014; Oxman, Sackett, & Gyuatt, 1993; Panne, Beers, & Kleinnecht, 2003; Simpson & Courtney, 2002; Slater, Mohr, & Sengupta, 2013; VanMeter & Garner, 2005), as well as to actively practice the development of tools and organizational techniques in creating literature review. Like any other skill, becoming a sound researcher and being able to synthesize the details of a large body of research into a comprehensive picture is one that comes with practice and hard work.

References

Baker, M.J. (2000). Writing a literature review. *The Marketing Review, 1*(2), 219–247. doi . org/10.1362/1469347002529189.

Boote, D.N. & Beile, P. (2005). Scholars before researchers: On the centrality of the dissertation literature review in research preparation. *Educational Researcher, 34*(6), 3–15. doi: 10.3102/0013189X034006003.

Cooper, H. M. (1998). *Synthesizing research: A guide for literature reviews*. Thousand Oaks, CA: Sage Publications.

Cresswell (2014). *Research design: Qualitative, quantitative, and mixed methods approach*. Washington, DC: Sage Publications.

Dessein, J., De Krom, M., & Soini, K. (2013). Rural sociological approaches to sustainable agriculture: A systematic literature review. XXV ESRS Congress (pp. 154–155). Presented at the 25th European Society of Rural Sociology (ESRS) Congress : Rural resilience and vulnerability : The rural as locus of solidarity and conflict in time of crisis, European Society of Rural Sociology (ESRS).

Fink, A. (2014). *Conducting research literature reviews*. Washington, DC: Sage Publications.

Garrad, J. (2014). *Health sciences literature review made easy: The matrix method*. Burlington, MA: Jones& Bartlett Learning.

Hart. C. (2003). *Doing a literature review: Releasing the social science research imagination*. Thousand Oaks, CA: Sage.

Latif, R., Abbas, H., Assar, S., & Ali, Q. (2014). Cloud computing risk assessment: A systematic literature review. *Future Information Technology, 27*(6), 285–295.

Oxman, A. D., Sackett, D. L., & Guyatt, G. H.(1993). Users guide to the medical literature: How to get started. *The Journal of American Medical Association, 270*(17), 2093–2095.

Panne, G., Beers, C., & Kliennecht, A. (2003). Success and failure of innovation: A literature review. *International Journal of Innovation Management, 7*(3), 309–314.

Simpson, E. & Courtney, M. (2002). Critical thinking in nursing: Literature review. *International Journal of Nursing Practice, 8*(2), 89–98. doi: 10.1046/j.1440–172x.2002.00340.x.

Slater, S. F., Mohr, J. J., & Sengupta, S. (2013). Radical product innovation capability: Literature review, synthesis, and illustrative research propositions. *Journal of Product Innovation, 31*(3), 553–566. doi: 10.1111/jpim.12113.

Van Meter, P. & Garner, J. (2005). The promise and practice of the learner-generated drawing: Literature review and synthesis. *Educational Psychological Review, 17*(4), 286–325.

9

Interpreting Findings and Discussing Implications for All Ideologies

Mary Ann Rafoth, George Semich, and Richard Fuller

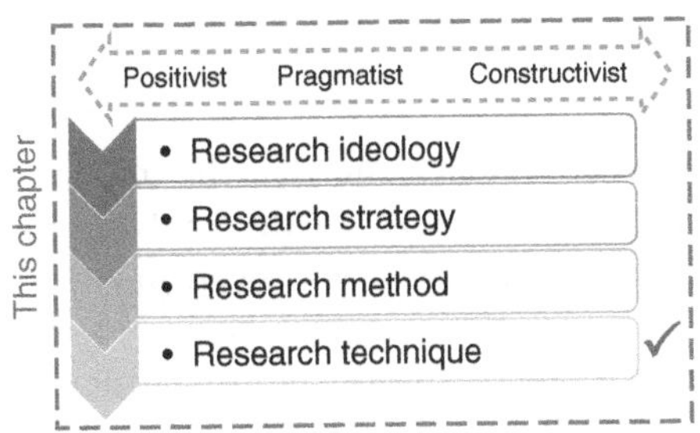

Chapter overview

In this chapter Rafoth, Semich, and Fuller build on the previous chapters in this handbook that explained how to design a scholarly study. In contrast to the broad scope of the first five chapters, this chapter is intended to serve as a guide for practitioner-scholars to interpret findings and discuss implications in the research technique layer, regardless of which ideology the researcher holds (positivist, post-positivist, pragmatist, interpretivist, or constructivist).

Introduction

This chapter discusses the end result of research—its interpretation and implications. This important phase in the research process is conceptually illustrated in figure 9.1. It is often tempting for researchers to leap to the crucial raison d'être of all research by anticipating results in such a way that interpretation is colored and implications are either understated or overstated. Interpretation of research findings begins with an accurate understanding of analysis and the rigor of the study. Clear descriptions of findings allow for better interpretation and increased replication. Thus, the probability that research results

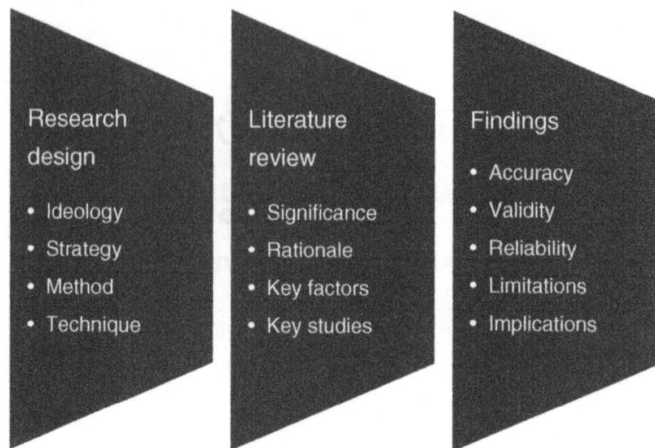

Figure 9.1 Conceptual processes in scholarly research.

can be interpreted with confidence and that the implications of research are valid is connected to both the power of the study and the amount of bias. Researchers must be objective and critical concerning their results before drawing conclusions.

To ascertain the significance of findings in quantitative research and provide an accurate interpretation of results, an appropriate analysis of effect size is required. Normative expectations, policy-relevant gaps, and effect size are three important benchmarks for judging significance of findings (Hill, Bloom, Black & Lipsey, 2008). In general, interpretations and implications for any piece of research can be judged to be more significant when there are a large number of studies in the field, when effect size is larger, when there are fewer tested relationships, and where there is less flexibility in design, definitions, outcomes, more analytical modes, and less financial and other interest or prejudice (Ioannidis, 2005). Interpretations of descriptive statistics, establishing statistical versus practical significance, assessing bias, identification of confounding explanations and factors, arguments for causal relationships, interpretation of risk factors, balancing test specificity and sensitivity in predictive studies, and interpretation of qualitative research are discussed in this chapter.

Avoiding bias in reporting

In reviewing and interpreting research it is important to analyze for any bias that might reduce the evaluation of the researcher's findings and implications as being accurate. Bias can be defined and seen in many ways but is generally viewed as any effect, circumstances, or condition that individually or in combination may skew the data or interpretation of the data. Bias implies a systematic effect on the data in one particular direction that predictably favors or opposes the study hypothesis (Riegelman, 2005).

Data and data-gathering techniques are, for the most part, rather sensitive and open to many subtle forms of bias despite the most diligent researcher's intentions. Bias can happen when the researcher expects or anticipates a certain outcome from the research. This expectation of results can inadvertently drive how a researcher acts or behaves while conducting the research. This researcher bias can not only affect how he/she acts in designing and implementing the study, but it can have an effect on the subjects causing a change in their behavior. Thus, bias can also have an influence on how the researcher interprets that behavior and hence reports findings in a published work.

Bias has many harmful effects and can actually distort the reported findings of a study despite the researcher's best efforts. Researchers, to the best of their abilities will develop research methods to remove the bias from their findings with the intention of improving the generalizability of results to the larger population. Those that cannot be removed need to be reported properly in such a way as to frame the results honestly.

The researcher's approach to minimizing bias begins with the choice of a theoretical orientation and the literature review. All research studies, including quantitative, qualitative, and mixed methods approaches, should begin with a theoretical perspective that guides or connects the study to previous research. Establishing a theoretical perspective and continuing to stay true to it as research findings are examined are essential to avoiding investigator bias. Creswell (2014) suggests that "some historical precedent exists for viewing a theory as a scientific prediction or explanation for what the researcher expects to find" (p. 53). For example, in an educational research study, a researcher may have looked at McClelland's acquired needs theory, which identified three key needs (achievement, power, and affiliation) and how these needs can be met by boys and girls in a middle-school classroom.

This same theory may then be applied as an experimental design to an elementary group of learners or a secondary group of learners with a researcher implementing this same design with the same set of conditions with the intent to see if similar scientific predictions or explanations may exist relative to different sex age learners. A researcher might also choose alternate theories that can likewise be explored through the literature to make predictions based on the research. This can be helpful in building new quantitative studies using new theoretical underpinnings supported by a new body of literature. Further options would include looking at a different approach relative to a quasi-experimental design for the same research study. The researcher might do a correlational study to examine a type of relationship between groups (boys and girls), or an independent samples *t*-test to show differences, or a chi-squared test of independence to examine possible associations between two variables as a way of looking for statistical significance in the association. Bias will be minimized if results are viewed through a theoretical perspective and the researcher critically evaluates how the current findings support or do not support the theory.

Quantitative methods often test a theory as it applies to a study. Thus, to a quantitative researcher, part of the literature may be to explore a theory, especially as it relates to the methodology section of the research study. Thus, a portion of the review of the related literature would primarily beabout how the theory supports the design and the conduct of the research study. To avoid bias, the researcher must make a clear connection between theory and application. Here is an opportunity for a researcher to break out of theoretical biases and look at the same study through a new theoretical lens.

Multiple theories may apply providing alternate approaches to understanding. To illustrate, in a research study regarding male and female teachers' willingness to integrate new handheld technologies in the classroom, a researcher might look at the study from both motivational theory and resistance theory. These very different theoretical underpinnings may explain why these teachers may or may not implement handheld devices. In other cases, researchers may have used different quantitative designs to study the same topic. To avoid bias in the literature review, researchers must examine and report how these other designs might have influenced results. In short, the literature review must present an unbiased account of the selection of methodological design in a quantitative study.

There are parallels with qualitative designs. Qualitative researchers must acknowledge personal biases that may influence their perception of issues as well as their reviewing the work of other researchers. Qualitative studies with methodological literature reviews are many times a springboard for discovery and further inquiry because in qualitative research a premium is placed on the objectivity of the researcher.

Objective reporting of results

It is not necessarily the bias that is seen that can be detrimental, but the bias that escapes the researcher's attention that is particularly harmful to the generalization of a study's reported results. The reader must be aware of not only the bias that is reported but that which may be subtly conveyed in the presentation. The existence of bias cannot be viewed as simply there or not there, but should be viewed by how the researcher presents the bias that may exist. Because some level of bias is nearly always present in a published study, readers must also consider how bias might influence the stated conclusions (Gerhard, 2008).

As noted earlier, bias can be found in both qualitative and quantitative research and understanding how bias can influence the results of a study becomes integral to the acceptance of research results as new knowledge and to the integration of the research into the current knowledge base. One of the areas that can be a source of bias is how randomization is applied to choosing a sample population. This is called sample bias, and consumers of research should cast a critical eye on research to appreciate how this may exist in the choosing of subjects. Obviously, no sample will be an exact match to the population all the time. The sample may be disproportionate in the number of males to females or have a higher mean age or income than the population as a whole, which may slant the findings. Using a larger sample or a stratified sample will however help to smooth out some of these unintended variables. To avoid bias in reporting, it is essential for the researcher to report a complete description of the sample, to assess its representation relative to the population, and to discuss the impact on interpretation of results.

Suppose a researcher wishes to survey a sample population of a university's students on a particular issue from a small school of around 5000 students. The researcher decides that a representative population may be 400 students. To randomly select participants the researcher may decide the best method is to stand in the middle of the quad during an afternoon and ask every fifth student who passes them to participate in the study. The researcher may assume that this is the best way to randomize choosing a sample population. At face value this may seem completely random but if we analyze further we begin to see that the bias may be in the details. This sampling method actually becomes limited to those who walk on the quad regularly during the day. Those adult students who work and only take evening classes may not be represented. Those students who don't have classes in any of the buildings on the quad but in other areas of campus, or possibly taking classes at an off-campus location, would not be represented. None of online students will be adequately represented if at all. The sample then consists of a greater number of potentially young students taking daylight classes by percentage than may actually exist in the overall population. This creates a sample bias and then begs the question as to whether or not the findings and results are truly indicative of all university students or only of a subset of the population. The question arises as to whether the sample is truly representative or to what degree it accurately characterizes the population being studied. The higher the degree of sample bias that exists, the less representative the data are to the actual population.

In a qualitative study, bias may also exist but in different ways. In qualitative research the researcher will use what is called a purposeful sample in choosing a group to interview, observe, or survey. Here the researcher wishes to observe or talk to subjects that have the body of knowledge that the researcher seeks to describe. If he/she seeks to know how CEOs of major companies who grew up in orphanages became successful, then talking to anyone other than those who fit the profile would not yield the depth of understanding, so randomizing would not work here. While this is not sample bias as discussed above it is not to say that bias cannot exist within a descriptive scenario. Judgment sampling involves selecting a sample that is believed to be representative of a given population (Gay, Mills & Airasian 2011). The issue with bias is that different researchers may use different criteria to choose a representative sample.

In observing a particular situation, the researcher's presence may change how people act during a study. This is sometimes called the Hawthorne Effect, which causes individuals to alter their actions or behavior due to the attention they may be getting from the researcher or simply from the researcher being there. For some, simply being observed causes them to change their behavior or to act in a way that they think is in line with the researcher's expectations. The subjects believe they are being evaluated on something and want to be viewed in the most favorable light to meet those expectations. As Babie (2012, p. 153) states, "when people are asked for information, they answer through a filter of what will make them look good." This is especially true in interview situations.

The types of bias present must be discussed in the interpretation and presentation of research data in qualitative studies. Bias can also be seen in an interview in the way in which an interviewer asks a question, the tone of voice, or the words chosen, which may affect the responses of an interviewee. If an interviewer changes his tone or asks questions based upon preconceived ideas, it may inadvertently alter the responses and the results. This is bias that will bring into question the integrity of the data collected and the descriptions or the accuracy of the researcher's analysis. Thus, a researcher must evaluate and report potential personal biases that could have affected the interpretation and presentation of results.

Accuracy of analysis

As has been discussed, most research being conducted within a quantitative or qualitative environment is rarely bias free. It is a part of every research study and generally is unavoidable. In order for the researcher to be true in his analysis of the research and ultimately for the reporting of the findings to serve as knowledge, he or she has to be open and honest about the likelihood and degree of bias that does exist within the data, how it was collected, and what the researcher in good conscience understands as the effect on the results. In analyzing a researcher's sample, it is important to see the larger picture and view all possible limitations to choosing a true sample. The researcher should review all possible considerations that are limiting.

When reporting the results of a survey research, the investigator should discuss and present not only those who did participate but also the percentage of subjects that declined to participate in the process or to complete a written survey. In many cases the written survey is conducted via regular postal mail services or through some online survey tool with the request to participate coming to potential subjects through email or other electronic forms of communication. Reporting the number of those who have not participated is as important as reporting the number that did, as not doing this can inject bias.

Generalizations from obtained data to a population are limited when nonrespondents differ systematically from respondents on survey-relevant variables. Remember though, nonresponse in and of itself does not necessarily indicate bias (Rogelberg & Luong 1998). This may simply result in having a small data set that provides little statistical significance. Either way this needs to be discussed within the published results. Rogelberg and Luong (1958) have further established some techniques and strategies that can provide insight into possible sources of nonresponse bias:

- Using a follow-up type approach, a small segment of the original nonrespondents can be randomly selected and contacted via phone, mail, or email for a smaller version of the original survey. This smaller data set can then be compared to the respondents and nonrespondents on the actual survey. If the data are similar to the original data collected the researchers may reasonably assume that their original survey data is representative of the larger population.
- Distinguish between those who respond early and those who respond late, possibly after a second or third request to participate. This may have an impact on how questions are answered. Differences between these two groups may indicate some type of bias in the data.
- The researcher should examine the survey topic and questions to determine whether certain characteristics such as respondents' educational level, career choice, or any other factors may be related to their willingness to participate.

Accurate description of results

Consider the source when describing and reporting results. External validity is an essential consideration as this again deals with the ability of the research to be transferred in the case of a descriptive study or to be generalized to other groups or populations in the case of a quantitative study. As described, the ability to transfer qualitative data is left to the reader. However the exact methods and conditions of how data were designed and collected and any potential sources of bias should be reported to allow the consumer to have an accurate understanding of how the findings can be extrapolated and applied appropriately in their own setting. The highest levels of rigor are usually seen in the quantitative experimental designs. Many times this is seen through some type of clinical trial or experimental design. These types of studies will use specific populations with minimal exclusionary criteria allowing them a high degree of similarity to the overall population being studied. This generally allows them a high degree of external validity or the ability to generalize findings.

As noted earlier, one of the areas of bias can come in the form of those included in the sample population. When analyzing the quantitative published literature, readers should assess whether bias is present due to how subjects are chosen. Criteria that are not specific and tight are a source of bias and limit internal validity (which refers to the reliability or accuracy of results). Readers should decide, based upon the author's considerations and descriptions, if this precludes generalization to the stated or to other populations. Again this is done by judging how well the sample accurately represents the population. Bias can occur in many phases of research, through design, data gathering, analysis of findings, and in drawing conclusions. It becomes the responsibility of the readers to view the published research with a discerning eye to draw their own conclusions as to what equates to new knowledge and what can or cannot be applied. A deeper understanding of where bias may exist within the different areas of a study will assist to this end.

Implications and importance of power of the study

Quantitative methods are in many cases supported by methodologies and findings from previous research and from meta-analyses. Rumrill and Fitzgerald (2001) argued that quantitative research must be concerned with critical areas such as sample size, effect size, and defining variables into measureable components. Reviewing various studies can provide a deeper or richer understanding of the nature of the research and is essential to establishing an effect size for the study and knowing the power of the findings. A researcher who examines and references multiple studies builds a case in which the findings and interpretations from other studies in the field are supported and therefore gains credibility. By examining multiple studies that use a similar research hypothesis, the researcher can data mine information for additional analysis and later for reporting findings.

Power defined

In quantitative research design, researchers typically are looking at some kind of comparison (usually between groups) and applying inferential statistics to determine if there is a meaningful difference (usually a statistically significant one). When a literature review does not provide enough evidence to determine the direction of a difference, researchers test a null hypothesis (one where no differences are predicted) or one that is nondirectional. Basically, research is generally an exercise to reject the null hypothesis. There is always a chance that errors will be made, of course. We sometimes are misled and cite a difference that does not really exist as demonstrated by other research (type I error) or find a difference that is not substantiated by other research (type 2 error).

The concept of power represents the likelihood that one of these errors will be made in the research. Research findings are judged to be valid when the power is at least .8, in other words, when there is at least an 80% chance of finding a true significant difference. Factors that affect power include sample size. A larger sample generally improves the likelihood that if there is a difference the researcher will find it. If a power value is below .8, then the sample size should be increased to decrease the chance of an error in the finding and interpretation. An important first step in determining power is to determine whether or not a study had a big enough sample to allow for adequate power. A power analysis provides the answer to how big your sample size should be. To determine power the researcher must know (1) which statistical test to use (*t*-test, ANOVA, multiple regression etc.), (2) how to choose a significance level (usually .01 or .05), (3) the sample size being targeted, and (4) determine something called an "effect size." Various software programs (e.g., G Power or Optimal Design software) permit easy power analysis once these variables are known (Buskirk 2008; Hedges & Rhoads, 2008).

Effect size

Effect size is an important construct that helps determine if statistically significant findings mean anything in practical terms (Shaughnessy, Zechmeister & Zechmeister 2012). Effect size lets the researcher and the consumer of the research know if the findings are valid and ready to be used in real-world decision making. Moreover, effect size is a standardized construct, so that the impact of different approaches on the same outcome can be compared. For example, a researcher evaluating the impact of a new instructional technique on learning math fractions finds that before the new technique students knew 80 out of 100 math facts and after the new instruction had learned 83 out of 100 facts. A large sample size might provide a statistically significant finding, but is it meaningful if it brought about only a slight increase in performance?

Calculation of effect size is essential for an accurate interpretation of data. One technique for calculating effect size is by taking the difference between the mean of the treatment or intervention group minus the mean of the control or comparison group divided by the standard deviation of the scores of the control or comparison group. Note that there are other techniques according to the method and context of the situation (e.g., ANOVA vs. MANOVA). An effect size should be at least .3 to be judged moderate and greater than .5 to be considered large. Effect sizes below .1 are considered to be inconsequential (Hill, Bloom, Black & Lipsey, 2008). To compute effect size prior to a study to establish adequate sample size, the researcher must identify studies on the same or similar topics in the literature and use their means and standard deviations to predict adequacy of the sample.

Statistical versus practical significance

In assessing the importance of a research finding, statistically significant results are considered critical. Statistical significance establishes the chances that the finding is due to chance. When establishing significance the researcher chooses a probability (alpha) level ahead of time (usually .05 meaning that there is a 5% chance that your findings are due to factors other than the program or intervention). To establish significance, the probability or *p*-value from the study is compared to the alpha level. If the *p* value is lower than the alpha level, the results are significant. This does not, however, mean that the results have practical significance or have implications for changes in practice. The smaller the sample size and the weaker the power of the study, the lesser the implications for a change in practice that can be suggested. In interpreting and presenting descriptive statistics the researcher should identify what kind of description is being provided. The statistic may describe a measure of location (showing the relative placement of data) through a measure like a percentile or quartile or a standard score (a *z* score, *T* score, or a stanine). Or, the statistic may describe a measure of central tendency (showing the normative tendency of the data) such as a mean (arithmetic average), the mode (a measure of frequency), or the median (the point at which half the data points are above, and half below). The descriptive statistic may also describe variability through the reporting range (the difference between the minimum and maximum, an interquartile range (the spread in the middle 50% of the data), or the standard deviation (the square root of variance that shows the index of variability in the score distribution) and coefficient of variation (that compares the relative variability within a sample). Researchers may also use descriptive statistics to report the shape of a sample distribution (its skewness—asymmetry of distribution or its kurtosis—flat distribution). Graphic options for displaying descriptive data include frequency polygons, pie charts, box plots, and stem and leaf charts (Trochim, 2006).

Using the literature review to interpret research results

The literature review is one of the most misunderstood, frequently maligned, and misrepresented part of research articles and dissertations. In both a research article and in a dissertation, the literature review not only stands alone to demonstrate the researcher's knowledge of the topic area and more specifically the issue to be examined, but also functions to explain the choice of methodology it serves to link the findings in the final chapter back to the literature. Clark (2012) in *Writing the successful thesis and dissertation* suggests that a literature review can best be understood when the author writes with some key terms as guides. These include: compare and contrast (present the author's views on an issue), criticize (present problems in methodology or perspectives from other works), highlight (note gaps in existing literature), show (explain how the researcher's study relates to past studies), identify (delineate gaps or problems in the literature), define (offer a unique perspective on the research area using a new lens), and question (evaluate the results of past studies) (p. 111). The literature review might also be understood as researcher reflection (deeper interpretation of the findings from the researcher's own thinking) and further investigation and reporting of the literature though projected review (examining the themes from qualitative approaches and alternate interpretations from quantitative method reporting). Creswell (2004) suggested that there are parts of the results of a study that are useful for future researchers and that the writer should point out potential avenues for further research. The literature review's most essential function is to provide a framework for the interpretation of the results of the researcher's study.

According to Machi and McEvoy (2012), "a literature review is a written argument that promotes a thesis position by building a case from credible evidence based on previous research" (p.3). The literature review should go beyond a mere support base as it relates to a particular issue. An argument has two sides, so in most cases the responsible researcher has to present both sides on the issue. Consideration of all sides of an issue is essential to appropriate interpretation of research results. To illustrate, perhaps a researcher posits that phonics is the best method to teach early readers how to spell words correctly. Certainly, there is a body of research that supports this statement. Conversely, there is a body of literature that supports the look/say method or the language experience approach, etc. To a researcher, this is the opportunity to bring current research on phonics to light while demonstrating an understanding of the other side of the research argument. This is the reason why a literature review can be freestanding or a part of a much larger research study (Imel, 2011), and it also the reason why a literature review is essential for interpretation and presentation of data. Narrowing a literature review to only support the research results as presented by the researcher limits the potential for expanding the research on a topic and establishes a single-side approach for the reader that might be a misrepresentation of research findings.

Unfortunately, speaking from our past experience advising doctoral students, we find that there is often a great temptation to include only supportive literature as they feel this builds a stronger case for their research hypothesis. There is a prevailing temptation to not include new literature that might help explain or interpret unexpected results in the discussion section that the triangulation process begins. In a perfect world, the literature review might always be congruent with research results. Research is done to explain our world in all its complexity, and the literature review should expose this complexity. Its role is not to help the researcher tie up his or her project with no loose ends. Arguments that depend on single sources and findings that are totally supported by the all the literature reported might lead one to question whether it was really necessary for the researcher to conduct the study at all. Finally, an inadequate presentation of existing research limits the reader's ability to extend the research beyond the parameters of the research manuscript and to judge the validity of the results. In addition, effective literature reviews go beyond simply listing sources or summarizing research studies from the literature. In fact, Rocco and Hatcher (2011) argue that many literature reviews cover the literature but fail to present insights into the literature. Generally, this type of literature review strings together quotes and ideas from many authorities in the field and, as mentioned above, uses these sources to support the argument in the conclusion. This is problematic in that it limits the reader from exploring new ideas or insights from the literature.

The literature review is more of annotated bibliography around an issue. When the researcher is seeking to discover rather than report the literature, there is a better chance that the reader will find greater opportunity to look at the topic through a new lens or new perspective. Onwuegbuzie et al. (2010) actually identified multiple benefits of a more quality literature review that include the following: identifying what is already done and what still needs to be done, locating variables that are germane to the topic, finding possible relationships between theory and concepts and practice, selecting exemplary research, preventing redundancy in the related literature, referencing other studies with similar designs and methodologies, and looking for any inconsistencies, possible strengths, and weaknesses in those research methods and designs (p. 1).

In some cases, the focus of a study can change in the process of unraveling the literature or when examining the findings. New ideas may emerge to the researcher that may lead to different analyses than originally proposed and would translate into the researcher subsequently defining a theory that would require new or additional support from the body of existing research. Again, this supports the notion that the literature can change under various circumstances with both quantitative and qualitative methodology. In fact, Glaser and Strauss (1998) note that constant comparison analysis of theory in a research study has several characteristics that include

- building theory, as opposed to testing it;
- providing researchers with analytic tools for analyzing data;
- assisting researchers in understanding multiple meanings from data;
- providing researchers with a systematic and creative process for analyzing data; and,
- assisting researchers in identifying, creating, and seeing the relationship among components in the data when constructing a theme.

This can viewed as opportunistic to the researcher in that understanding becomes primary rather than simple reporting and interpretation. Research is a continuous process and, in this case, the writer can actually expand the field of knowledge by introducing research to the reader and connecting it to data in new ways. This is where a literature review that follows a support approach with emphasis on evidence and relevance only satisfies a very narrow scope of the research process but does little if anything to go beyond to a more enlightening, interpretative, and expansive look at the literature.

Policy-relevant gaps

Narrative literature reviews also serve as a means of creating new theoretical relationships and even new theories as the researcher links relevant studies for the purpose of reinterpreting or interconnecting these studies to his/her personal research study and to either note or close a policy-relevant gap in the literature (Baumister & Leary 1997). This type of literature review enables the researcher to build new theories and to address gaps in the literature through his or her research as a part of the research methodology.

Selection of approach in a study may likewise be altered based on the researcher's perception of how the results might possibly be different by using different approaches and by knowing which approach may be more useful in addressing a gap in the literature. To illustrate, if a researcher is interested in doing a case study focused on his/her workplace over a period of time, the researcher will also need to examine the workplace issue through the eyes of participants who have been living the experience, to increase the likelihood that the study will fill a gap in policy-relevant practice. The researcher will need to combine case study with a phenomenological approach, such as the interpretative phenomenological approach (IPA), as a means to assess how individuals perceive the issue relative to their roles at the workplace. In short, the investigator delves deeper into the issue and provides possible new insights based on the experiences of the participants in this workplace setting in order to be able to draw policy-relevant conclusions. This gives the researcher opportunities to explore new ideas that directly relate to both the results and the interpretation of the findings from the study.

Researchers who use mixed-methods approaches may integrate the literature review in a convergent manner to address gaps in the literature and gaps relative to policy and practice in particular. Campbell and Fiske (1959) are considered to be the first to use mixed methods, and they argued that by collecting different forms of data both reliability and validity were increased via triangulation of findings.

A synthesis of literature across methodological approaches is more likely to reveal policy gaps. Baumeister and Leary (1997) noted that it is "not only permissible that a literature reviewer theorize after assembling evidence but positively desirable" (p. 314). Creswell (2014) suggests that the interpretation of this convergent approach using quantitative and qualitative methodologies would usually be located in the discussion section of the study or last chapter of the study. Additionally, the methodology section or chapter would discuss a rationale for two different methodologies and might seek new theories with a new lens at looking at a particular problem. When the quantitative results are not congruent with the data from the qualitative section, this provides obvious fodder for discussion. To illustrate, in the case of a mixed methods study that looked at undergraduate student participation with a student engagement initiative, while the quantitative analysis revealed levels and patterns of student engagement, only the qualitative piece ascertained the causes. This combination of information was relevant to both policy and practice changes and most clearly addressed the gaps in existing literature.

Arguments for causal relationships

Research studies generally fall into three main categories that include those that are descriptive in nature, those that are relational in nature or relationship studies, and causal studies. Trochim and Donnelly (2008) argue that in an era of evidence-based practice, causal-based studies have been elevated in status. Largely, this is due to the fact that causal studies have more of a direct impact on changing the lives of the participants of the study. By examining each variable, the researcher looks for what variable(s) might be causing a particular behavior to occur. Causal-based studies go beyond just stating that there is a relationship, and actually attempt to identify how the independent variable will affect another variable referred to as a dependent variable in the relationship. To illustrate, a researcher may look at how increased reading of scholarly writing will lead to improved writing among graduate students. The researcher takes a directional approach to analyze differences in student writing rather than simply predicting that there is a relationship between reading and writing as would be the case in more descriptive or exploratory studies.

To illustrate the above scenario, if a teacher is having difficulty with classroom management, the teacher may elect to follow Glaser's choice therapy as a means of changing personal teacher behavior and response to students in the classroom. This may have positive outcomes relative to student behavior, but it may or may not be due to theoretical implications of choice therapy. In fact, it may be more related to simple change in approach on the part of the teacher or may be related to a host of other school-related events such as a winning sports team, special school programs, or upcoming holidays, which can have an impact on student behavior. Furthermore, the observed behavior may be caused by external factors or an internal relationship between the variables. In this case, it might be that a third party, perhaps a principal who had an earlier intervention with the class, may have precipitated a relationship change between teacher and students and subsequently would have no connection to choice theory as an agent of change. Using this same illustration, the teacher might use a causal-comparative design to employ choice therapy to certain classes while using existing standard approaches with other classes. By using comparisons between groups and analyzing the cause and effect relationship, the teacher has a greater opportunity for predictability given that the relationship is expanded with more participants and a comparative design. It would be important to add that causal-comparative studies do pose serious threats to internal validity since the manipulation of the independent variable has already occurred (Fraenkel & Wallen 2003).

For causal studies, validity is based primarily on the inferences drawn by the researcher. There is also less reliance on the time factors with causal studies. However, with causal-comparative studies, relationships are often viewed over a time period. Also, causal-comparative designs, as noted by Schenker and Rumrill (2004), involve preexisting groups; thus differences among those groups are identified by the dependent variable in the cause and effect relationship. Because all participants would receive the treatment and then be compared to those who did not receive treatment, this is considered a fair context for research. Further within the context of fair treatment in the case of a researcher working with groups of students, all students would be given treatment, perhaps at different intervals, but treatment cannot be taken away from certain individuals or manipulated in any manner other than the procedures for fair and equal treatment established earlier on in the research study.

Mora (2012) addressed the question as to whether survey instruments can show causality in market research. Basically, the author findings indicated that surveys can show correlations with the data but cannot show causality even though both reside in experimental design. Relative to this case, there could be no manipulation of the independent or dependent variables since the survey instrument reports data subject to interpretation and speculation on the part of the researcher. The kindergarten to high school setting presents another set of problems since there may not be an opportunity to do experimental research among groups of students. Instead, Vogt (2007) suggests that specifying a model rather than conducting experimental research for determining program effectiveness may be best in a more regulated environment. This enables the researcher to create a model or diagram showing the relationship with the independent and dependent variable and from this diagram examine and speculate on the cause in the relationship. Review of the related literature as discussed in other sections of this chapter will also offer additional support to this process.

Causal-based studies and causal-comparative research might also be viewed to some degree as descriptive research since they describe conditions that presently exist. Relationships are examined in terms of cause and effect, thus these are conditions that already exist. Essentially, the researcher can also be trying to find a cause for preexisting differences among groups as in the case of causal-comparative research studies. Or, the researcher may be doing retrospective causal research that investigates various causes from a predefined effect. In short, causal research studies can evaluate a cause and effect relationship. Scriven (2008) actually sees causation as the middle of the road of investigative research methods in that it has a position between the theoretical and the highly localized or experimental approaches. Causal studies also have experimental roots since there is, as previously mentioned, a manipulation of variables between cause and effect. It may focus on the exploration of effects in study, or it may focus on the causes as a part of the research study. The causal approach usually serves to recognize differences among groups or individuals in a study. It also seeks causes and consequences in cause and effect relationships. The value of the causal studies design is perhaps the middle of the road position described above with the manipulation of the independent variable and an intervention with an outcome. In reporting and interpreting causal effects, it is essential the researcher delineate all of these factors.

In addition, confounding factors need to be considered in assessing results, especially in establishing causality. Confounding factors may be a problem when the researcher is comparing two groups and the groups differ in background factors (such as when there are more girls than boys in one classroom vs. another in a study), when those factors are not a focus of the study but turn out to influence results, or when the background factor (sex) turns out to influence the outcome. Confounding factors should be addressed in the study design when possible, or the researcher can adjust the analysis to control for the confounding factors. Failure to note confounding factors can lead the researcher to draw inaccurate conclusions about their results. Confounding factors can also harm accurate interpretation by an incorrect rejection of the null hypothesis and discussion of results by hiding real associations or creating false connections between independent and dependent variables (Wade, 2010). Another threat to an accurate interpretation of causality is the presence of risk factors that are correlational rather than causal. Also, the researcher may find strong associations between variables that may simply establish risk factors rather than causal relationships. Many risk factors present as confounding factors (age, sex, ethnicity, SES, occupation). Risk factors are especially significant in health studies and the social sciences as well as some areas of finance.

Predictive validity is often used in association with risk factors to predict future outcomes and thus generate recommendations for current behavior and decision making and as inferences of causality. In any predictive study, there are always four possible outcomes: correct identifications, correct rejections are made, incorrect identifications are made, and incorrect rejections are made. Incorrect identifications are false positives, while incorrect rejections are false negatives. The number correctly identified and correctly rejected equals the total number correctly identified. The number incorrectly identified and incorrectly rejected equals the total number incorrectly identified. Computing the first case provides an indication of the overall effectiveness of the predictive measure. The index of sensitivity is the number correctly identified or predicted to be in the group that was to be identified (e.g., future poor readers). The index of specificity on the other hand is the number correctly identified as not to being in that group (e.g., future good readers). Thus, in interpreting the validity of screening data and assessing predictive validity the following indices should be computed (Gredler 1992):

- overall effectiveness (number valid positives + number false negatives/total number in sample).
- sensitivity index (number valid positives/number valid positives + false negatives)
- specificity index (number of valid negatives/number of false positives + valid negatives)
- percentage of true predicted at risk (number of valid positives/number of valid positives + false positives)
- percentage of true not at risk (number of valid negatives/ number false negatives + valid negatives).

Each of these indices provides an important method to assess the validity and utility of predictive measures, but all must be computed and discussed to provide an accurate interpretation of results.

Conclusion

In conclusion, there are different factors affecting judgment of the significance and accuracy of research findings. Research findings that are supported by a number of studies with similar results are most likely to be valid. Studies with an adequate effect size demonstrate that the study has sufficient power for the results to be meaningful. Studies that examine fewer tested relationships are more likely to produce more valid and reliable results related to the relationships. Studies that follow similar design plans and use definitions and outcome measures that are somewhat standard and that are used in other studies are more likely to produce meaningful results. A proper analysis is essential for the discussion of results. Discussion of significance must include not only statistical significance but also the practical implications. Finally, evidence that both the study design and interpretation of results are free of bias should be presented to allow the reader to judge significance.

References

Baumeister, R. F. & Leary, M. R. (1997). Writing narrative literature reviews. *Review of General Psychology, 1*(3), 311–320.

Buskirk, T. D. (2008). *Statistical power from* Encyclopedia of survey research methods *by Paul Lavrakas.* Thousand Oaks, CA: Sage, pp. 845–847.
Clark, I. (2012). *Writing the successful thesis and dissertation: Entering the conversation.* Upper Saddle, NJ: Prentice-Hall Publishers, p. 111.
Creswell, J. (2014). *Research design: Qualitative, quantitative, & mixed methods approaches,* 4th edn. Thousand Oaks, CA: Sage Publishers, pp. 28, 53.
Fraenkel, J. R. and Wallen, N. E. (2003). *How to design and evaluate research in education,* 5th edn. New York; McGraw-Hill Publishers, p. 374.
Gredler, G. (1996). *School readiness: Assessment and educational issues.* Brandon, VT: CPPC.
Imel, S. (2011). Writing a literature review. Chapter 11 from *The Handbook of Scholarly Writing and Publishing* by Tonnette S. Rocco & Tim Hatcher & Associates. San Francisco, CA: Josey-Bass Publishers, p. 145.
Gay, L. R., Mills, G. &. Airasian, P. W. (2011). *Educational research: Competencies for analysis and applications* 10th edn., Upper Saddle, NJ: Prentice Hall.
Gerhard, T. (2008). Considerations for research practice. *American Journal of Health. Systems Pharmacology, 65*(1), 2159–2168.
Glaser, B. G. & Strauss, A. L. (1967). *The discovery of grounded theory: Strategies for qualitative research.* Chicago, IL: Aldine.
Hedges, L. & Rhoads, C. (2010). *Statistical power analysis in research.* Washington, DC: US Department of Education.
Hill, C. J., Bloom, H. S., Black, A. R., Lipsey, M. W. (2008). Empirical benchmarks for interpreting effect sizes in research. *Child Development Perspectives, 2*(1), 172–177.
Ioannidis, J. P. A. (2005). Why most published research findings are false, *PLoS, 2*(8). doi:10.1371/journal.pmed.0020124.
Machi, L. & McEvoy, B. (2012). *The literature review: Six steps to success.* Oakmont, CA: Corwin Press—A Sage Company, p. 3.
Mora, Michaela (2012). Can surveys uncover cause and effect? January 18, 2012. Retrieved April 1, 2014 from http://www.relevantinsights.com/tag/causality-research
Onwuegbuzie, A. J., Leech, N. L., & Collins, K. M. T. (2012). Qualitative analysis techniques for the review of the literature. *The Qualitative Report, 17*(56), 1–28.
Riegelman, R. K. (2005). *Studying a study and testing a test: How to read the medical evidence* 5th edn. Lippincott Williams and Wilkins, Philadelphia.
Rogelberg, S. G. & Luong, A. (1998). Nonresponse to mailed surveys: A review and guide. *Current Directs in Psychological Science, 7*(1), 60–65.
Rumrill Jr., P. D. & Fitzgerald, S. M. (2001). Using narrative literature reviews to build a scientific knowledge base. *Work, 16*(2), 165–170.
Schaughnessy, J. J., Zechmeister, E. & Zechmeister, J. (2012). Data analysis and interpretation: Part II. Tests of significance and the analysis story. *Research methods in psychology* 6th ed. New York: McGraw Hill Higher Education, pp. 347–377.
Scriven, M. (March 2008). A summative evaluation of rct methodology: & An alternative approach to causal research. *Journal of multidisciplinary evaluation, 5*(9), 11–24.
Schenker, J. D. & Rumrill, P. D. (2004). Casual-comparative research design. *Journal of Vocational Rehabilitation, 21*(1), 117–121.
Strauss, A. & Corbin, J. (1998). *Basics of qualitative research: Grounded theory procedures and techniques,* 2nd edn., London: Sage. pp. 273–284.
Trochim, M. K. (2006). Statistical Power, November 24, 2008. Retrieved March 15, 2014 from http://www.socialresearchmethods.net/kb/power.php.
Trochim, M. K. & Donnelly, J. P. (2008). *The research methods of knowledge base.* 3rd edn. Cincinnati, OH: Cengage Learning Publishers, p. 5.
Vogt, P. W. (2007). *Quantitative research methods for professionals.* Boston, MA: Pearson Publishers, pp. 42–47.

Part II

Positivist Applications

10
Implications of Experimental versus Quasi-Experimental Designs

Jeremy W. Grabbe

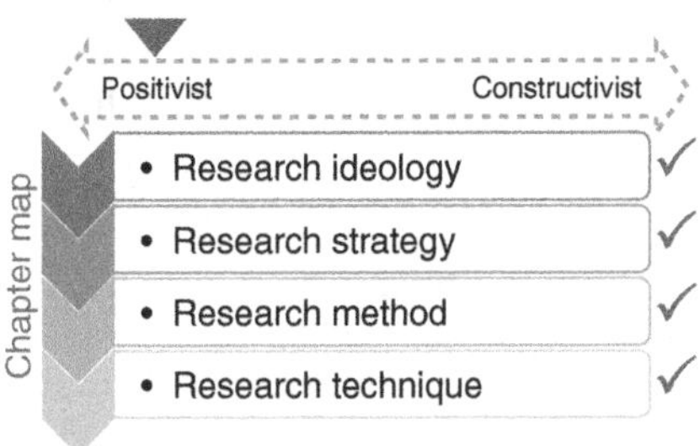

Chapter overview

In this chapter Grabbe contrasts the rationale for using the true experiment or a quasi-experiment method in a research design based on several of his studies. He clearly holds a positivist ideology. The unit of analysis in his research strategy was the treatment or preexisting condition for the nonequivalent groups. The level of analysis was group in these designs and the focus was between-groups rather than within-group. The heavy use of a priori factors from his literature review would suggest a deductive purpose with a generalization target to similar groups in business and management.

Introduction

Comparisons of experimental and quasi-experimental designs are of paramount importance to understanding implications of research in the field of business and management. Confusion in choosing between these two methods in research designs has tremendous ramifications, which often result in exceeding the limits of what may be extracted from the findings of a study. The first part of this chapter will elaborate on the definition and the differences between designing research with these two methods. These two methods are often used synonymously (Pedhazur & Schmelkin, 1991). Therefore confusion between the two methods is common for both researchers and laymen. Key to this understanding will be a detailed explanation of what defines the treatment within a study. This chapter will discuss the advantages and disadvantages of different types of experimental and quasi-experimental designs. Quasi-experimental designs have been described as being overused by some (Campbell & Boruch, 1975). This chapter will explore how that debate affects research in business and management. Issues of implementation, such as availability of subjects and selection, will be addressed along with an elaboration of how to choose a research design around those implementation issues. A discussion of how the implementation of an experimental or quasi-experimental design will relate to issues of external validity. An overview of the general analytic methods for both designs will be given. Finally, both experimental and quasi-experimental designs will be reviewed in terms of various threats to internal validity.

Experimental research design basics

Among those attempting to develop a broader background in research designs, one source of confusion is the implications of experimental and quasi-experimental designs. It is important to understand the differences between designs, which can have profound implications for the inferences one can draw from research studies. The use of experimental and quasi-experimental methods is often discussed in the context of quantitative versus qualitative research. However, as Bryman (2006) has noted, the distinction between quantitative and qualitative research has become less distinct. This is due to a remarkable number of studies utilizing both quantitative and qualitative methods. This combination can also lead to greater confusion about the differences between experimental and quasi-experimental methods.

An ongoing debate in business research has been how the selection of the right method and design will assist in enhancing scientific rigor and applicability of results. Hevner and March (2004) have advocated more field research among other methods. It is important to consider the goal of the study as well as the feasibility of the execution of the study when considering the method chosen.

Treatment

The selection of a research design requires the understanding of many factors (Venable & Baskerville, 2012). A source of confusion, but a concept that is integral to understanding experimental and quasi-experimental designs, is treatment. Treatment refers to the manipulation of the independent variable and is often referred to in other fields as manipulation. One of the first issues that arise when contemplating treatment is scale of measurement. "How does one measure the different levels of an independent variable?" This is a critical question to answer when deciding to use an experimental or quasi-experimental design. A ratio scale such as the one used in a pharmaceutical experiment in which subjects can receive 0 mg, 15 mg, or 30 mg of a drug is a manipulation that can indicate the use of an experimental design easily.

Other scales such as the nominal scale can be confusing. A nominal scale is used for qualitative, categorical differences. A study in which gender is the independent variable will invariably be a quasi-experimental design. There is no quantitative difference in levels of this variable such as coding 1 for male and 2 for female does not imply that females have twice as much "gender" as males. However, a true experimental design can have a categorical independent variable treatment. One could manipulate refreshments given to subjects in a study that examines if beverages served affect productivity. In this case productivity (dependent variable) is influenced by our manipulation of beverages served (independent variable). We could randomly assign subjects to receive hot cocoa, coffee, green tea, water, or a sports drink. This could be coded so that receive hot cocoa = 1, coffee = 2, green tea = 3, water =4, and sports drink = 5. This is a categorical manipulation like gender in the previous example. In this example water is not twice the amount of "beverage" as coffee. However, because of the random assignment to different levels of the independent variable, even though they are categorical levels, this would be indicative of a true experimental design.

This brings up the debate about the strength of treatment. In an experimental design the sterile nature can artificially increase the strength of a treatment. However, beyond the concept of experimental versus quasi-experimental design, the scope of the study itself and implementation of treatment may affect the strength of the treatment. This can depend upon the intervention/manipulation such as Yeaton and Schrest (1981) discuss when comparing strength of psychotherapy in terms of strength compared to varied strengths of chemotherapy as a contrast of two distinct research aims:

> The problem of specificity of strength. Treatments are not universally strong. Treatments are strong for some problems but not for others. Morphine is a strong treatment for pain. Aspirin is a weak treatment for pain. Larger dosages might, however, enhance the strength of aspirin therapy for pain, at least up to a point. If a treatment is inappropriate for the presented problem, strength is simply an irrelevant dimension of treatment. Aspirin in any dose is not an effective treatment for a staphylococcus infection. Without knowledge of the kinds of problems likely to be modified by a given treatment, clinicians are doomed to failure.

Causality

A second important distinction between experimental and quasi-experimental design is causality. Because of the high internal validity and control found in experimental designs the direction of causality can be determined. Quasi-experimental designs in contrast are able to suggest relationships exist but the direction of the causality of that relationship is beyond the purview of quasi-experimental designs. Imai, Tingley, and Yamamoto (2013) have warned of the desire for causality over understanding causal mechanisms:

> The identification of causal mechanisms is at the heart of scientific research. Applied researchers in a variety of scientific disciplines seek to explain causal processes as well as estimating causal effects. As a consequence, experimental research has often been criticized as a black box approach that ignores causal mechanisms. Despite this situation, both methodologists and experimentalists have paid relatively little attention to an important question of how to design an experiment to test the existence of hypothesized causal mechanisms empirically.

Experimental design

Listed below are some of the advantages of quasi-experimental designs:

1. greater external validity,
2. feasibility of studying things that are not given to random assignment (e.g., gender, ethnicity),
3. greater accessibility to participants by use of field research, and
4. use of different variable approaches (Marais, 2012).

These are some of the disadvantages of quasi-experimental designs:

1. low control over conditions,
2. sampling bias issues,
3. low internal validity, and
4. error from covariates and confounds.

Types of experimental designs

Treatment-control post-manipulation only:

- treatment group: $IV_1 \rightarrow DV_1$
- control group: DV_2

This design uses a treatment group and a control group. The manipulation of the independent variable requires the administration of the treatment to the experimental (treatment) group, and the measurement of the dependent variable is taken for both groups (see Grabbe et al., 2010 for an example of Treatment-Control Post-manipulation only study). For example, if our independent variable is listening to a motivational speech before being interviewed for a job, only subjects in the treatment condition will listen to the motivational speech. Subjects in the control condition will not listen to anything, nor would they receive any interaction as part of the study prior to being measured on the dependent variable (performance on the job interview).

Single categorical or continuous variable post-manipulation only:

- Level 1: $IV_1 \rightarrow DV_1$
- Level 2: $IV_2 \rightarrow DV_2$
- Level 3: $IV_3 \rightarrow DV_3$

In this design one independent variable is used and given at the different levels of the independent variable to different groups. This design does not use a control group, but instead compares different levels of the independent variable to each other (i.e., a between-subjects design). An example of a single continuous variable post-manipulation only design would be a study of safety training (independent variable) and safety outcomes (dependent variable). The independent variable can be divided into three levels of 2 hours of safety training, 4 hours of safety training, and 6 hours of safety training. This example uses three levels of the independent variable, but the number of levels depends entirely of the experimenter's manipulation, so one could theoretically have as few as two levels or up to an infinite number of levels.

Treatment-control. Measures at pre-manipulation and post-manipulation:

- *Pre Post*
- Treatment group: $DV_1 \rightarrow IV_1 \rightarrow DV_1$
- Control group: $DV_2 \rightarrow DV_2$

This time-series design compares a treatment group to a control group as well as provides a manipulation check. The control group is measured at two different times with no experimental manipulation in the intervention time between the measurements. In contrast the treatment group is measured at two different times like the control group. During the intervening interval between the manipulations the treatment group is subjected to the manipulation of the independent variable by the experiment. The benefit of this experiment is that, first, there is a baseline for comparison, and, second, that the control group serves as a check for practice effects for measurement.

A study of ergonomic design intervention and productivity can serve as an example of a design using pre-and post-manipulation of treatment and control groups. Two departments within a company are randomly selected. Both are measured at pre-manipulation for their productivity. Then, one of the groups is randomly assigned to the treatment condition and receives an ergonomic design intervention. The other group is designated as a control condition. It receives no treatment intervention. After the treatment design is implemented, both groups are assessed for their respective productivity. This has the advantage of measuring for any variability that may occur during normal operations to be measured in the control group. Furthermore the pre-post-manipulation measurement provides a time-series change to examine the extent of the manipulation.

Factorial design

A factorial design utilizes different factors involved in treatment conditions. For example a study may look at different types of leadership and interactions (independent variables) and how they affect satisfaction with managerial feedback (dependent variable). Let us assume that leadership had three levels: affiliative, democratic, and pacesetting. Our factor of interaction has two levels: face-to-face and online. This would results in an experiment where subjects could be randomly assigned to one of six different treatment conditions (see table 10.1). Within the cells of the six treatment conditions we will find the means of our dependent variable of managerial feedback satisfaction for each of the six possible combinations of treatments. Each cell in the table represents the mean satisfaction of managerial feedback for each of the six conditions.

A major issue with a factorial design is the logistics of implementation of all the cells. This requires a large population with large-scale implementation, which may not result in informative data. Instead von Eye (2008) argues that a fractional factorial design is a feasible alternative to a full factorial analysis:

> Full factorial designs are often not only cost-intensive and wasteful when many factors are taken into account. They also yield little information above and beyond designs that allow one to only consider main effects and lower order interactions. Consider, for example, the cross-classification of six dichotomous factors. The analysis of this design comes with 1 df for

Table 10.1 Experimental treatment conditions

Treatment conditions	Affiliative	Democratic	Pacesetting
Face-to-face	Affiliative—Face-to-face	Democratic—Face-to-face	Pacesetting—Face-to-face
Online	Affiliative- Online	Democratic—Online	Pacesetting—Online

the intercept, 6 df for the main effects, 15 df for the two-way interactions, 20 df for the three-way interactions, 15 df for the four-way interactions, 6 df for the five-way interactions, and 1 df for the six-way interaction. Now, suppose that only the intercept, the main effects, and the first order interactions are of interest. In this case, two thirds of the degrees of freedom in this design are used to estimate parameters that are not of interest and will not be interpreted.

Fractional factorial designs use only a subset of the treatment combinations, or cells, of a completely crossed design. This subset can be chosen based on the sacristy of effects principle. Specifically, fractional designs allow the data analyst to estimate the effects of interest. Based on the scarcity of effects principle, these effects are assumed to be of low order. In fractional factorial designs, higher-order effects are either not estimable or they are confounding. More details are listed next.

Quasi-experimental design

Some have argued that quasi-experimental designs lack rigor (Stanley, 1966). The works of Campbell and Stanley (1963) served to raise the merits of quasi-experimental design. Quasi-experimental designs had been previously derided because of the lack of causality seen in true experimental designs. The rise of quasi-experimental designs has roots in two changes in research focus: (1) the desire to leave the laboratory and to seek ecological validity and (2) to ask questions that cannot be addressed (at least feasibly) by true experimental designs. These two factors have led some to call quasi-experimental designs as controlled investigations (Kish, 1975) or observational studies (Cohran, 1983).

These are some of the advantages of experimental designs:

1. greater internal validity,
2. greater control of extraneous variables,
3. ability to define causality, and
4. easier replicability (Campbell & Stanley, 1963).

Some of the disadvantages of experimental designs include:

1. a lack of realism,
2. low external validity,
3. sampling bias (some participants who may not participate in a laboratory study would have participated in a field study),
4. may demonstrate causality, but not explain causal effects (Imai et al., 2013).

Some of the types of quasi-experimental designs include:

Nonequivalent groups designs. This is a design in which the assignment to experimental and control groups is not random. In this case one group serves as a control group and another group(s) serves as the treatment groups. Much like the treatment-control design with measures at pre-manipulation and post-manipulation mentioned earlier, subjects in each group are measured upon the dependent variable initially. The control group receives no treatment and is measured again at a later time on the dependent variable. The treatment group is measure on the dependent variable and then receives the experimental treatment. After manipulation the treatment group is measured again on the dependent variable. An advantage of this design is that it utilizes the pre-manipulation measurement as a means of trying to control for group differences that may affect the results of the treatment manipulation.

Pretest-posttest design. A pretest-posttest design uses one group that is selected based upon a preexisting condition for selection. In this case one may select a specific group based upon a desire to examine whether the treatment affects the dependent variable in a select condition. An example of a pretest-posttest design would be to study the effects of acupuncture as a means of stress reduction in air traffic controllers. Here acupuncture is our treatment independent variable and stress levels are our dependent variable. Why this is considered a quasi-experimental design is because the population in question is air traffic controllers and only air traffic controllers are selected to receive the treatment, therefore selection is not truly random.

Interrupted time-series design. Sometimes a researcher will desire to take several measurements both prior to and after a manipulation. This has the advantage of measuring variance over time as well as understanding possible trends. The interrupted time-series design allows for multiple observations. In the example given below, let O stand for observation and T represent the treatment manipulation. Then,

O1 O2 O3 T O4 O5 O6

From the review of the various quasi-experimental designs it can be seen that multiple measurements have an advantage of sampling variability. It must be noted that in quasi-experimental designs there is a greater likelihood the subjects may ascertain the goal or the experiment or at least assume a possible goal. It is very important to check whether the manipulation had its intended effect. This is especially true in sociobehavioral research where very frequently the manipulation is meant to affect some construct (e.g., anxiety, motivation, aspirations). An aspect of checking whether the manipulation had its intended effect is the determination of whether it did so with the intended strength. Manipulation checks are also aimed at uncovering whether a manipulation had unintended effects, that is, whether it affected other variables in addition to, or in lieu of, the intended one. Further, it is also possible for the manipulation check itself to have unintended effects.

In true experimental designs it is more likely that subjects may be blind to the goals of the experiment. However, due to the selection of participants based on preexisting conditions found in quasi-experimental designs, it is possible that subjects' responses may be affected by the measurement of the dependent variable. This is known as reactivity. Sometimes the measurement of the dependent variable may lead to outcomes and behaviors that are triggered (reactive) by the nature of the measurement. For example a researcher may be studying diversity. While measuring diversity a subject may begin to ascertain the factor of diversity. This could lead to the subject responding "no" in their true impressions of diversity, but may be utilizing social desirability or reacting to priming and/or stereotype threat. This has led some to argue that researchers should utilize manipulation checks. The use of manipulation checks works to assess the reactivity of a dependent variable measure. This has the advantage of reducing the threat of reactivity to validity.

Contrast of error between experiment designs

Figure 10.1 shows a comparison of experimental and quasi-experimental designs and their relationships. The research model portrayed in study 1 is an experimental design. In this we see that the independent variable's effect upon the dependent variable is assumed to be free of random error. This assumption of freedom is theorized to result from a lack of bias in the sample due to random sampling. The influence of random error is placed directly onto the dependent variable as a moderator effect. This is an influence that is outside the effect of the independent variable. In contrast study 2 is a quasi-experimental design. In this model, random error influences or is influenced by the independent variable. The effect of random error can come about through a bias in the sample due to a lack of random sampling. This could lead to the error appearing to be

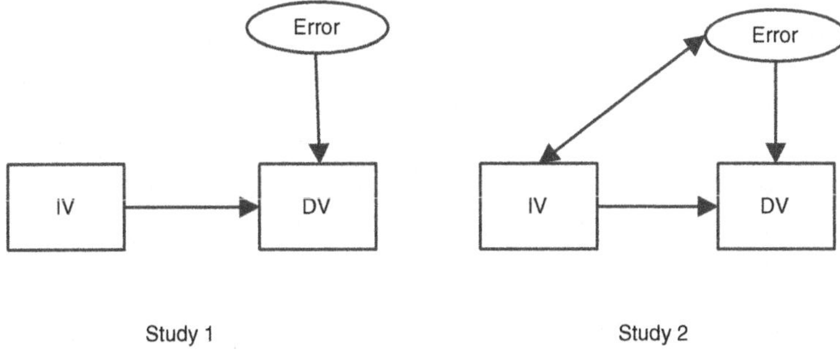

Figure 10.1 Comparison of experimental study designs.

more systematic and can mimic the systematic influence one would expect of an independent variable.

Consider two fictional experiments that highlight the differences between the two designs in terms of the error and influence mentioned above. The first study is an experimental design. Different music (upbeat or down tempo) is played for different groups in a waiting room of the laboratory before the subjects are shown different products and rate the desirability of those products. The independent variable is the background music in the waiting room. It has two levels: upbeat and down tempo. The dependent variable is the subjects' rating of product desirability.

In the second study, a quasi-experimental design, the age of the subject is the independent variable (two levels: younger and older adults) and its effect on product desirability (dependent variable) is studied (it is important to note that background music was not used in this study and is not a factor). Because age is a preexisting condition that cannot be manipulated, there is no random assignment to either age group. Subjects are assigned an arbitrary age point of demarcation (Grabbe & Allen, 2012; Grabbe & Allen, 2013). Factors affecting the selection of subjects can contribute to the error affecting the dependent variable. For example, women statistically live longer than men. Therefore it is possible (and rather common) to find a gender bias in older adult groups. This could results in a measured effect of age (the manipulation/treatment of study 2) along with an unmeasured effect of gender (error associated with nonrandom sampling.

Contrast of validity between experiment designs

As mentioned earlier in the chapter, one desire of the researchers was to leave the laboratory to conduct field research. This shift helps to highlight the differences in validity between the two designs. True experimental designs have demonstrated high levels of internal validity (Mohr, 1982). Quasi-experimental designs have shown just the opposite by showing high external validity. The concerns over validity are related to the purpose of the study at hand. Researchers focusing on the everyday value of a study, particularly in the world of finance and economics, may favor quasi-experimental designs because of the applicability of results due to higher external validity.

An important way in which both internal and external validity could be improved is in the use of controlled, naturalistic settings (Meyer, 1994). Researchers in the realm of business have advocated for the use of more naturalistic settings in which to base an experiment (Sun and Kantor, 2006). This use of naturalistic settings need not be "in the field" or even devoid of the random selection of subjects in true experimental designs. Bugelski (1981) has stated, "the laboratory is not a building or a room with fixed walls and do-not-disturb signs" (p.63). Venable and Baskerville (2012) have differentiated between artificial and naturalistic evaluation. Sun and Kantor (2006) have gone on to further define the use of naturalistic settings implying that a real task can be used in a laboratory setting. This would serve to maximize both internal and external validity.

Conclusion

This chapter has covered the differences and similarities between true experimental and quasi-experimental designs. Several factors for implementation have been discussed along with issues of causality and validity. This would lead one to believe (perhaps naïvely) that researchers' selection of method to use would reflect consideration of the requirements of the study as well as the feasibility and goals of the study (Jones, 2003). Blumberg, Cooper, and Schindler (2008) have noted that selection of method may depend upon factors other than those discussed above, "Many scholars show a strong preference for either type of study. However, these preferences more likely reflect their own capabilities and experiences than a general idea about which type of research is more useful" (192).

References

Blumberg, B., Cooper, D. R., & Schindler, P.S. (2008). *Business research methods*, Berkshire: McGraw-Hill.

Bryman, A. (2006). Integrating quantitative and qualitative research: How is it done? *Qualitative Research*, *6*(1), 97–114.

Bugelski, B. R. (1981). Life and the laboratory. In I. Silverman (Ed.), *Generalizing from laboratory to life* (pp. 51–65). San Franciso, CA: Jossey-Bass.

Campbell, D. T., & Boruch, R. F. (1975). Making the case for randomized assignment to treatments by considering the alternatives: Six ways in which quasi-experimental evaluations in compensatory education tend to underestimate effects. In C. A. Bennett & A. A. Lumsdaine (Eds.), *Evaluations and experiment: Some critical issues in assessing social programs* (pp. 195–296). New York: Academic Press.

Campbell, D. T., & Stanley, J. C. (1963). Experimental and quasi-experimental designs for research on teaching. In N. L. Gage (Ed.), *Handbook of research on teaching* (pp. 171–246). Chicago, IL: Rand McNally.

Cochran, W. G. (1983). *Planning and analysis of observational studies*. New York: Wiley.

Grabbe, J. W., & Allen, P.A. (2012). Cross-task compatibility and age-related dual-task performance. *Experimental Aging Research*, *38*(1), 469–487.

Grabbe, J. W., & Allen, P.A. (2013). Age-related sparing of parafoveal lexical processing. *Experimental Aging Research*, *39*(1), 419–444.

Grabbe, J., McCarthy, A., Brown, C., & Sabo, A. (2010). Olfaction and emotion content effects for memory of vignettes. *Current Research in Psychology*, *6*(1), 53–60.

Hevner, A. R., S. T. March, et al. (2004). Design science in information systems research. *MIS Quarterly*, *28*(1), 75–105.

Imai, K., Tingley, D., & Yamamoto, T. (2013). Experimental designs for identifying causal mechanisms. *Journal of the Royal Statistical Society*, *176*(1), 5–51.

Jones, B. (2004). Perspectives on management research design and orientation: Quandaries and choices. *The Electronic Journal of Business Research Methods, 2*(1), 111–118.

Kish, L. (1975). Representation, randomization, and control. In H. M. Blalock, A. Aganbegian, F. M. Borodkin, R. Boudon, & V. Capecchi (Eds.), *Quantitative sociology: International perspectives on mathematical and statistical modeling* (pp. 261–284). New York: Academic Press.

Marais, H. (2012). A multi-methodological framework for the design and evaluation of complex research projects and reports in business and management studies. *Electronic Journal of Business Research Methods, 10*(2), 64–76.

Meyer, B. D. (1995). Natural and quasi-experiments in economics. *Journal of Business & Economic Statistics, 13*(2), 151–161.

Mohr, L. B. (1982). On rescuing the nonequivalent-control-group design. *Sociological Methods & Research, 11*(2), 53–80.

Pedhazur, E. J., & Schmelkin, L. P. (1991). *Measurement, design and analysis: An integrated approach*. Hillsdale, NJ: Lawrence Erlbaum Associates, Publishers.

Sun, Y. & P. B. Kantor. (2006). Cross-evaluation: A new model for information system evaluation. *Journal of the American Society for Information Science and Technology, 57*(5), 614–628.

Venable, J. & Baskerville, R. (2012). Eating our own cooking: Toward a more rigorous design science of research methods. *Electronic Journal of Business Research Methods, 10*(2), 141–153.

Von Eye, A. (2008). *Fractional factorial designs in the analysis of categorical data*. Retrieved from http://interstat.statjournals.net/YEAR/2008/articles/0804003.pdf.

Yeaton, W. H., & Sechest, L. (1981). Critical dimensions in the choice and maintenance of successful treatments: Strength, integrity, and effectiveness. *Journal of Consulting and Clinical Psychology, 49*(2), 156–167.

11

Structural Equation Modeling: Principles, Processes, and Practices

Sewon Kim, Edward Sturman, and Eun Sook Kim

Chapter overview

Kim, Sturman, and Kim clearly hold a positivist ideology. They explain how to design a study for a within-group factor comparison unit of analysis research strategy. This is an excellent discussion of the best practices for applying structural equation modeling (SEM). SEM is usually inductive in principle, although confirmatory factor analysis (the first phase of SEM) is deductive since it measures the reliability of an a priori construct using the sample data. They use applied examples drawn from their own studies.

Introduction

Structural Equation Modeling (SEM) is a powerful analytic method that is entering into its middle age. Researchers have often utilized SEM to examine if hypothesized conceptual models and structural relationships at the conceptualization stage are supported by the empirical data provided by their study sample (Bollen, 1989; Kline, 2010). Although SEM has been around for decades, its use has continued to increase as researchers have come to recognize it as a powerful tool in testing their model and relations. However, SEM still remains a complicated and esoteric statistical technique for some.

The purpose of this chapter is to provide a practical guide to SEM regarding principles, processes, and applications. A three-step approach is taken to explore the key question, "How can we apply SEM principles for our research practices?" The approach to answering this question includes: (1) introducing fundamental concepts associated with SEM; (2) demonstrating basic applications of SEM using SEM programs (e.g., AMOS); and (3) discussing other important topics related to SEM analysis (e.g., bootstrapping procedures).

The chapter is divided into five major parts. The first part introduces the basics of SEM. The next part presents an introduction to path analysis. The third section is devoted to confirmatory factor analysis (CFA) for testing measurement models. The fourth part illustrates the two-step approach of SEM for testing models with structural and measurement components. The last part discusses other relevant issues that are frequently considered in SEM.

Using nonmathematical terminology, the chapter is written to serve people who do not have extensive quantitative backgrounds—junior researchers, graduate students, and practitioners. With continued growth of SEM anticipated, readers will benefit from a better understanding regarding the value of SEM. By addressing the aforementioned question, we hope to provide readers with a good working knowledge of the principles, processes, and applications of SEM to expand their research practices.

Basics in structural equation modeling (SEM)

Sample size

As with most statistical analyses, SEM analytic findings derived from using a larger size of sample tend to produce more reliable statistical results (as compared to findings from utilizing a smaller sample). Hence, when designing a research project or study involving SEM, researchers will first need to answer the following question: "How large a sample does the current study require?"

Although more complex models need larger samples, general guidelines about absolute sample size are as follows: (1) large, $n > 200$ cases; (2) medium, $n =$ approximately 150 cases; and (3) small, $n < 100$ cases. To attain statistically stable estimates and less sampling errors, it is often recommended that researchers have 200 cases or more for their respective study sample (Tabachnick & Fidell, 2001). Alternatively, taking the complexity of study models into account, the ratio of the number of survey items (or free parameters) to the number of respondents (or cases) can be considered. Although there are no absolute standards regarding the item-respondent ratio—different researchers suggest different ratios (e.g., 1:5, 1:10, or 1:20)—it is believed that SEM analyses using a ratio of less than 1:5 may not be able to produce accurate results (Bentler & Chou, 1987).

Assumptions and limitations

Multivariate normality

There are several important conditions that SEM assumes for its statistical estimation process. Most of the SEM estimation methods (e.g., maximum likelihood) assume multivariate normality of the sample data. Although it is not always practical to examine all aspects of multivariate normality (e.g., normal distribution of all the univariate variables; normal distribution of all jointed pairs of variables; and linearity of all bivariate scatterplots), much of multivariate nonnormality can be detected by examining univariate distributions.

Univariate normality

Skew and kurtosis are two possible ways that univariate distributions can be nonnormal. *Skew* indicates that the form of a unimodal distribution (that has one peak) is unbalanced about its mean: negative skew implies that the left tail of the distribution is longer; and positive skew implies that the right tail of the distribution is longer. Since it is unlikely that the data are perfectly balanced (skewness = 0), researchers can consider the distribution is approximately symmetric when the sknewness is between – 0.5 and 0.5 (Bulmer, 1979).

For a unimodal, balanced distribution, nonnormality may still occur through *kurtosis*: positive kurtosis implies a higher central peak and heavier tails (when the value of the standardized kurtosis is greater than 3; or > 3); and negative kurtosis implies a lower central peak and lighter tails (when the value of the standardized kurtosis is less than 3; or < 3) (Kline, 2010). To achieve normality of the data, researchers can choose either to delete those extreme cases that are outliers (e.g., skew or kurtosis) or perform data transformations. Bootstrapping is another option for dealing with the nonnormal distribution of the sample data, and will be discussed in more detail in a later part of the chapter.

Linearity

SEM estimation methods also assume all relationships among the study variables to be linear and homogeneous. In fact, SEM techniques take into account only linear associations among the variables and, thus, nonlinear effects not represented in the estimation process could result in underestimating the extant strength of the association. Although it is difficult to assess linearity and homoscedasticity of all relationships among the variables, it is desirable that researchers examine bivariate scatterplots to check if the linearity assumption has been met in the data.

Multicollinearity

In SEM, statistic matrices are required to be inverted in the calculation process. However, if the variables are too highly correlated, the required matrices for the given analysis cannot be inverted appropriately. Multicollinearity may occur when two or more variables, which look distinctive or separate from one another, in fact measure the same thing. Multicollinearity can be detected by calculating the squared multiple correlation (*SMC* > 0.90, Kline, 2010), variance inflation factor (*VIF* > 5, Tabachnick & Fidell, 2001), or bivariate correlation (*r* = 0.9, Hair, Black, Babin, Anderson & Tatham, 2006). Once multicollinearity has been detected, researchers can choose to drop redundant variables or create a composite score of those relevant variables.

Path analysis

Path analysis can be thought of as the graphical representation of a series of regression analyses, though all estimations in path modeling are simultaneously calculated in one analysis (Hair et al., 2006). The path coefficients are regression coefficients, and they are either standardized or unstandardized. As in regression analyses, we are often interested in the magnitude of the relationship between one or more predictors and an outcome and whether it is statistically significant (a *p*-value of less than .05 is typically used as the standard for demonstrating statistical significance). When conducting path analysis with programs such as AMOS or LISREL we can also test how well a hypothesized model fits the actual data.

Although the directional arrows in path analytic models would seem to imply cause and effect, path analyses cannot automatically demonstrate cause-and-effect relationships. As in multiple regression, this causal modeling ability ultimately depends on the theoretical rationale and study design underlying the data. It is for this reason that researchers must be careful to ensre that their hypothesized model and structural relations are theoretically sound and plausible. If the data were generated from a tightly controlled experiment then we could more confidently make causal statements when interpreting the results.

Theoretical applications

Consider the following example of a path analysis demonstrating the relationship between measures used to select new employees at a company (interview and personality test), organizational fit, and performance after year 1 (also see figure 11.1). The interview and personality variables are termed *exogenous* as they are not predicted by any other variables in the model. The covariance or correlation between these two variables is represented with a bidirectional arrow and remains unanalyzed. Any variable with a unidirectional arrow pointing toward it, such as organizational fit and year 1 performance, is termed *endogenous*. The effects of extraneous factors on the endogenous variables, including measurement error, are included in the error terms (e1 and e2).

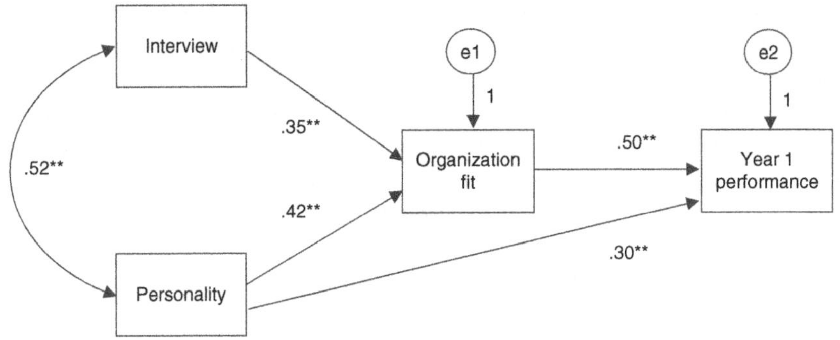

Figure 11.1 Path analysis. Model fit indices are as follows: χ^2/df = 1.74; NFI = .97; CFI = .96; SRMR = .03; and RMSEA = .02.
*p < .05. **p < .01. ***p < .001.

In this example we can see that all hypothesized relations turn out to be statistically significant (p < .01). First, organizational fit has *direct effects* from both interview and personality. Likewise, year 1 performance has direct effects due to organizational fit and personality. However, personality and interview also have an *indirect effect* on year 1 performance through their relationship to organizational fit. We may say that organizational fit *mediates* the relationship between personality and year 1 performance. The concept of mediation and various statistical techniques that have been developed to test for mediation (or indirect) effects are discussed later in the chapter. The combined direct and indirect effects on year 1 performance are called the *total effects*.

Model identification and fit

Asides from the obvious advantage of determining the magnitude and significance of the relationships between variables in our studies (including indirect effects) path analysis can also tell us how well our hypothetical models fit our actual data. Evaluating the fit of a model involves comparing the variance/covariance matrix from a sample to the estimated model-implied variance/covariance matrix. There are a number of indices that we can use to evaluate the fit of a model, all of which can be found in the output of SEM software packages such as AMOS, LISREL, or Mplus. We are chiefly concerned with providing readers a relatively straightforward explanation of the various indices and the most widely used standards for evaluating a "good fitting" model. Before turning to model fit, we briefly cover model identification.

Model identification

A model is "identified" when there is a unique solution for each parameter in the model (Tabachnick & Fidell, 2001). We determine this, in practical terms, by comparing the number of estimated parameters to the number of data points. When analyzing the covariance structure, a parameter is any of the following: (a) any directional effect, such as the direct effect of personality on organizational fit in figure 11.1; (b) variances of exogenous (or independent) variables and residual (or error) variances of endogenous variables; and (c) all covariances (e.g., the bidirectional arrow between personality and interview in figure 11.1). Hence, our example in figure 11.1 can be said to have 9 parameters.

We determine the number of data points by combining the variances and covariances, which can easily be calculated using the following formula:

$$[k(k + 1)] / 2$$

where k is the number of observed variables in the model. In our example there are 4 observed variables, which can be plugged into the above formula to yield 10 data points. Therefore, in our example we have 9 parameters to be estimated and 10 data points.

The degrees of freedom (df) is the number of parameters subtracted from the number of data points. In our example, $df = +1$. When the degrees of freedom are positive a model is said to be overidentified and our analysis of fit can proceed. When the degrees of freedom are equal to 0 (e.g., the number of parameters equals the number of data points) our model is said to be "just identified." This is not very helpful for researchers as all fit indices are bound to be perfect and will not provide any information of value. When the degrees of freedom are negative, the model is said to be "underidentified" and analysis of fit cannot proceed unless some parameters are either removed or constrained. It should be noted that this rule (called the counting rule or the *t*-rule) is a necessary but not a sufficient condition for the identification of a path model.

Model fit

Once model identification is complete, we can proceed to testing how well our hypothesized model fits the actual data. One way of doing this is to compare the model covariance matrix to the estimated population covariance matrix (Hair et al., 2006). The χ^2 of the model should not be significant as this indicates that the hypothetical model deviates from the actual data. Due to problems with this statistic relating to sample size, χ^2/df has been used as an alternative metric with acceptable values ranging from 2 to 5 (Bollen, 1989; Kline, 2010). It should be noted that for smaller sample sizes (e.g., less than 150 participants) the optimal values for these fit indices are lower than that for large samples (Sivo, Fan, Witta & Willse, 2006).

Other indices, known as incremental fit indices, compare the χ^2 of the model to some baseline (or null) model in which all measured variables are unrelated to one another (see Hooper, Coughlan & Mullen, 2008 and Tabachnik & Fidell, 2001 for straightforward explanations of these indices). One of the more commonly used indices is the Normed Fit Index (NFI; Bentler & Bonnet, 1980), which compares the χ^2 of the model and χ^2 of a baseline model. It should be noted that the NFI may be problematic for smaller sample sizes. The Cumulative Fit Index (CFI; Bentler, 1990) also uses a baseline model for comparison, but it is not adversely affected by smaller sample sizes. Both the NFI and CFI can range from 0 to 1 with values above .90 indicating a good fitting model, although values above .95 are preferred (Bentler, 1992; Hu & Bentler, 1999; Kline, 2010).

Absolute fit indices directly compare a hypothesized model to the sample data. The Goodness-of-Fit Index (GFI) was the very first standardized fit index, and it compares the proportion of variance in the observed sample covariance that can be accounted for by the estimated model-implied covariance. GFI shows a slight bias such that higher values may be obtained with a higher number of parameters. The Adjusted Goodness of Fit Index (AGFI) attempts to adjust for the bias by including the degrees of freedom in its calculation and favoring more parsimonious models; however, the AGFI did not perform well in some statistical simulation studies. The standard for a good fitting model using GFI is a value of .90 and above, although more conservative approaches advocate using .95 and above (Hooper et al., 2008; Miles & Shevlin, 1998).

Other types of indices, which penalize for a lack of parsimony, have attracted much interest lately, as more complex models generally produce a better fit than less complex models. These indices favor the simplest model when two or more models have similar descriptive power for the same data. The Root Mean Square Error of Approximation (RMSEA) tells us the degree of fit between our model, with optimally chosen parameters, and the data. The RMSEA is in fact a badness-of-fit index in that a higher value represents a worse fit of the model to the data while a lower value indicates a better fit (e.g., a zero value indicates the best fit). The most commonly used standards for this index have varied over time but currently a value of .08 or lower has received some support (Browne & Cudeck, 1993).

Residual-based fit indices are based on the square root of the differences between the sample variance and covariance and the hypothesized variance and covariance (with smaller values being indicative of a better fit). The Root Mean Squared Residual (RMR) is one such method, but it will produce different values based on the number of response options associated with the items in a measure. The Standardized Root Mean Squared Residual (SRMR) corrects for this drawback, with values of .10 or lower indicating a good fit (Kline, 2010). The popular overall model fit indices and commonly recommended cut-off values are provided in table 11.1.

Table 11.1 Popular fit indices and commonly accepted standards

Fit index	Standard
χ^2	Nonsignificant value ($p > .05$)
χ^2/df	< 5, 3, or 2
NFI	> .90
CFI	> .90
GFI	> .90
RMSEA	≤ .08
SRMR	< .10

Application examples

Although some of the preceding discussion may verge on the esoteric, the actual use of path analysis may be relatively straightforward using the appropriate statistical software, such as AMOS, LISREL, or Mplus. For instance, AMOS allows the user to interface with SPSS datasets and simply click and drag variables to create a path diagram such as that in figure 11.1. These user-friendly software programs will allow researchers to test their own models, keeping in mind that they should focus on the following information:

1. The magnitude and significance of relationships in a complex model of observed variables. Path analysis incorporates only observed variables and not latent variables (or underlying constructs). Thus, researchers ought to use a composite score of measurement items for each study variable (e.g., one merged score for the organizational fit variable in figure 11.1).
2. Possible meditational effects, which will be discussed later in this chapter.
3. The fit of the model, for example, using either all or some of the indices in table 11.1 for making a holistic evaluation.

Confirmatory factor analysis

Perhaps the easiest way to explain confirmatory factor analysis (CFA) is to distinguish it from exploratory factor analysis (EFA). The latter technique is often used to reduce a large number of observed variables into a more manageable, or theoretically meaningful, set of underlying factors. There are numerous approaches to EFA, which we will not delve into here, but it is important to stress that the technique is positivistic, in that statistical software reduces the number of observed variables into underlying components based on the correlation matrix. It is also interpretivistic because the researcher must interpret what these underlying factors represent. In EFA we are primarily concerned with finding out things like how many factors underlie a (typically large) set of variables or how strongly each observed variable loads onto a factor (for more of EFA see Costello and Osborne's article, 2005).

In CFA we specify the relationships a priori between a set of observed (or indicator) variables and one or more latent variables (or underlying constructs). For this reason we say that it is a *confirmatory* factor analytic technique. What are we trying to confirm? Primarily two things:

1. the observed variables load on the latent variables in the manner predicted by theory or previous observations; and
2. our hypothesized model, which includes all of the relationships among our observed variables and latent variables, fits the actual data.

Therefore, the major difference between exploratory and confirmatory factor analyses is that the former is primarily data driven and empirical, whereas the latter is primarily theory driven (Thompson, 2004). Also, note that CFA models represent only the *measurement model*. In contrast, path analyses represent only *structural models*—we will discuss these in more detail later in the chapter.

CFA applications

First order CFA

We will attempt to demonstrate how researchers can use CFA with the following example. Suppose we have data from a large set of measures that are used in selecting sales associates at a large firm. The company requires all applicants to

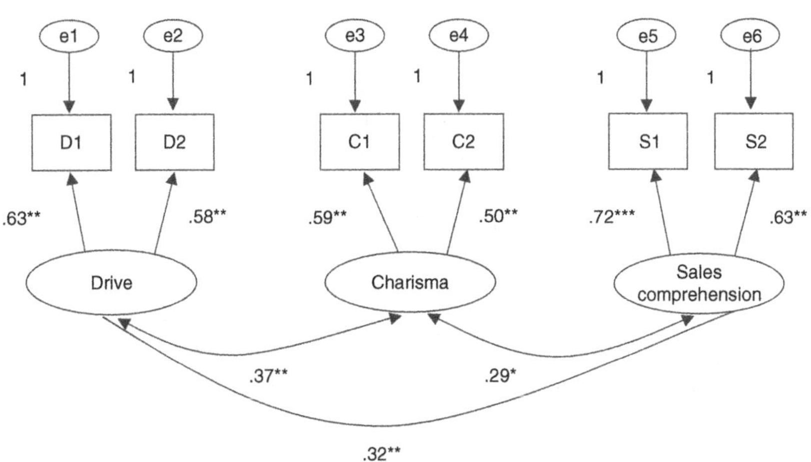

Figure 11.2 First order CFA model of sales characteristics. Model fit indices are as follows: χ^2 p = .04; χ^2/df = 1.89; NFI = .96; CFI = .95; SRMR = .04; and RMSEA = .03.

*p < .05. **p < .01. ***p < .001.

complete measures of money motivation, ambition, likeability, persuasiveness, sales knowledge, and sales experience. We may theorize that motivation (D1) and ambition (D2) will load on a common latent variable, which we will call Drive, likeability (C1) and persuasiveness (C2) will load on a latent variable, which we can call Charisma, and sales knowledge (S1) and sales experience (S2) will load on a latent variable, which we will call Sales Comprehension. In our model, as in standard CFA models, the latent variables will display unanalyzed correlations with one another. Suppose we obtained the results found in figure 11.2.

In this example, researchers would immediately key in on several important pieces of information. First, the observed variables loaded strongly and significantly (indicated by the asterisk mark) on their respective latent variables ($p < .01$). What constitutes a strong loading is somewhat arbitrary, but a general rule of thumb may be that the standardized path coefficients should be at least .30 ($\beta \geq .30$; which we might consider somewhat weak) and preferably .50 or higher ($p \geq .50$, Hair et al., 2006). Second, the model fits the data well. The χ^2 value is significant ($p < .05$), which indicates a poor fit, but as mentioned this is a sensitive measure to the study sample size, and it is not uncommon to obtain significant results in an otherwise good-fitting model. The other measures of fit are all in the acceptable range ($\chi^2/df < 3$; NFI > .90; CFI > .90; SRMR < .10; and RMSEA ≤ .08; Bollen, 1989; Browne & Cudeck, 1993; Hu & Bentler, 1998; Kline, 2010).

Second order CFA

It is possible to introduce a higher-order factor into confirmatory factor analysis. In this case we are simply regressing the other latent variables on a higher-order latent variable. Again, we will primarily be interested in the strength of the path coefficients from the second-order latent variable to the first-order latent variables, as well as the overall fit of the model. Because the first-order latent variables now become endogenous, it will be necessary to add error terms, which we call disturbances (d1 and d2).

In our example, we may have theorized that both Drive (P1-Drive) and Charisma (P2-Charisma) are just different aspects of an underlying variable, which could be called Personality. As can be seen in figure 11.3, both Drive and Charisma loaded fairly strongly on Personality ($p < .01$; $\beta \geq .50$, Hair et al., 2006), lending some support to this idea. Further, the overall fit of the model improved, with all indices now suggesting a good fitting model ($\chi^2/df < 3$; NFI > .90; CFI > .90; SRMR < .10; and RMSEA ≤ .08; Bollen, 1989; Browne & Cudeck, 1993; Hu & Bentler, 1998; Kline, 2010).

To summarize, CFA is a useful technique for researchers who have an apriori measurement model that could be checked against data. In some cases, it may be inspired by an EFA, but this is not necessary. Perhaps the most important

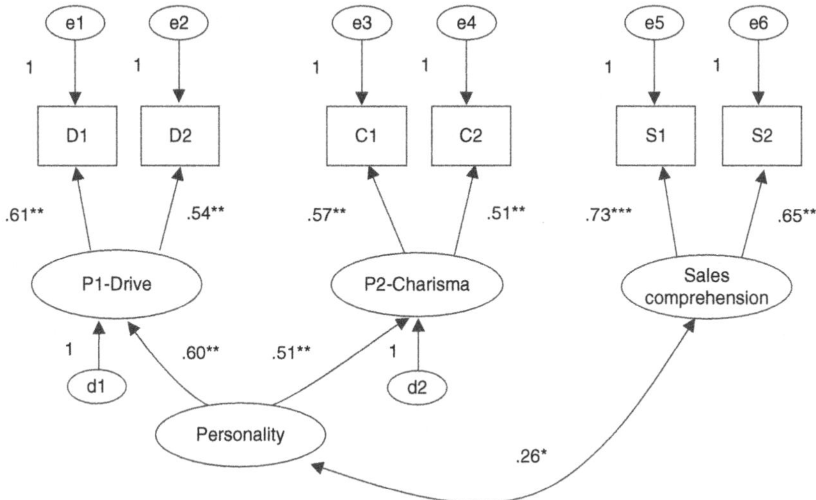

Figure 11.3 Second order CFA model of sales characteristics. Model fit indices are as follows: $\chi^2/df = 1.61$; NFI = .97; CFI = .96; SRMR = .02; and RMSEA = .02.
$^{*}p < .05$. $^{**}p < .01$. $^{***}p < .001$.

consideration in developing a CFA model is to have a logical and well formulated theoretical basis for the model. Conducting the CFA itself may be a relatively straightforward process with programs such as AMOS, which interface with other statistical packages (e.g., SPSS) allowing researchers to use a graphical user interface to draw the hypothesized relationships between the variables instead of entering commands.

Two-step approach of sem: testing models with structural and measurement components

Concepts

Researchers often use the SEM analysis to test the hypothesized structural regression model. As shown in figure 11.4, the structural regression model can be viewed as a combination of *measurement model* and *path model*. As in the measurement model, the structural regression model has a measurement component that represents the hypothesized associations between latent variables and observed variables. Like the path analytic model, it also has a structural component that embodies the hypothesized relations between the latent variables. Thus, it is a distinctive strength of SEM to test two sets of hypotheses about measurement and structural associations with a single model.

It is recommendable that researchers take *a two-step modeling approach* in SEM (Anderson & Gerbing, 1998): (1) first, we validate the hypothesized

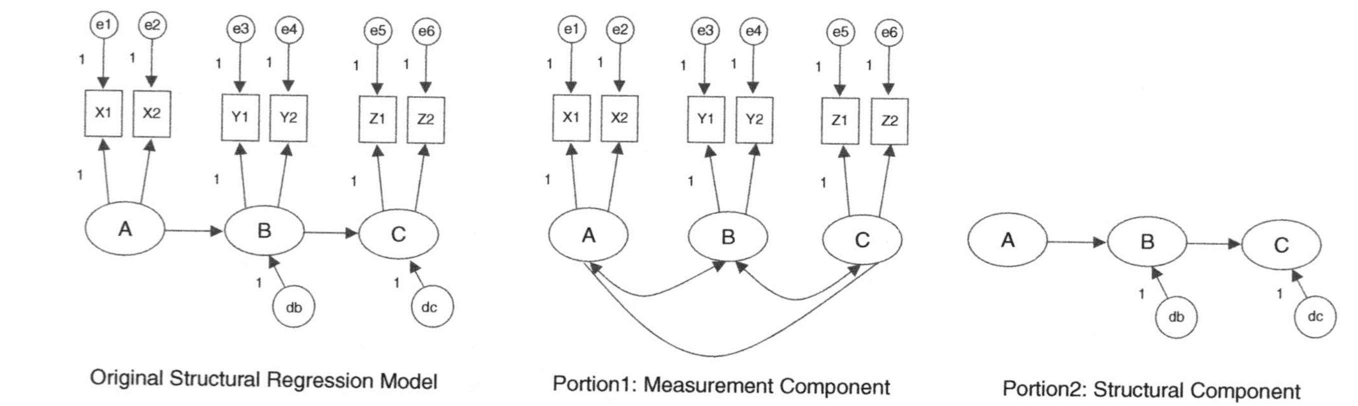

Figure 11.4 Illustration of the composition of a structural regression model. One hypothesized original structural regression model is composed of two portions of the hypothesized measurement component (portion 1) and the hypothesized structural component (portion 2).

measurement model using CFA; and (2) then establish the goodness-of-fit of the hypothesized structural regression model. Using *two-step modeling* we can accurately locate the root of inadequate model fit, when the overall fit of the hypothesized structural regression model is poor. The hypothesized structural regression model can be mis-specified in the measurement component (portion 1), the structural component (portion 2), or both (portions 1 and 2). Figure 11.4 provides pictorial depictions of an original structural regression model decomposed into two subcomponents.

Further, each of the hypothesized relations between the latent variables in the structural regression model can be examined via regression estimates—these estimations are part of one SEM analysis of the overall model; thus their calculated values might be different from the results of a series of simple regression analyses that examines each path in the model separately (e.g., multiple regression analyses). As in the earlier path analysis and CFA, *p-values* of less than .05 ($p < .05$) can be used as the criterion to determine the statistical significance for those hypothesized relations.

Two-step applications

We will attempt to demonstrate how researchers can use two-step modeling with the following comprehensive example. Suppose we conduct an empirical study to test the hypothesized conceptual model and the structural relationships between effective managerial behavior and employee attitude and performance-related responses through the use of SEM. We acknowledge that the hypothesized model and statistical results used here were derived from Kim, Egan, Kim, and Kim (2013a). Their data and models were adapted for our illustration in this chapter. Let's say we choose the total 22 survey items to assess the four latent variables in this study: 8 items for Transformational Leadership; 6 items for Self-Efficacy; 3 items for Work Engagement; and 5 items for In-Role Behavior. Using these survey items, 534 cases of the sample data are collected; thus, the item-respondent ratio used in our study is 1:24 (22:534), and this well exceeds the recommended ratio (1:5, Bentler & Chou, 1987). Figure 11.5 provides the hypothesized conceptual model with structural and measurement components.

First, we conduct measurement modeling using CFA to confirm the specified relationships between a set of latent variables (or underlying constructs) and observed variables (or measurement items). The fit indices for CFA are presented in table 11.2 (also see figures 11.2 and 11.4 for a reminder of CFA pictorial depictions). The holistic fit examination indicates that the measurement model has a good fit to the data ($\chi^2/df < 3$; NFI > .90; CFI > .90; SRMR < .10; and RMSEA ≤ .08; Bollen, 1989; Browne & Cudeck, 1993; Hu & Bentler, 1998; Kline, 2010). All of the items are statistically significantly associated to their respective factor ($p < .01$) and standardized item loadings range from .51 to .92 (≥ .50,

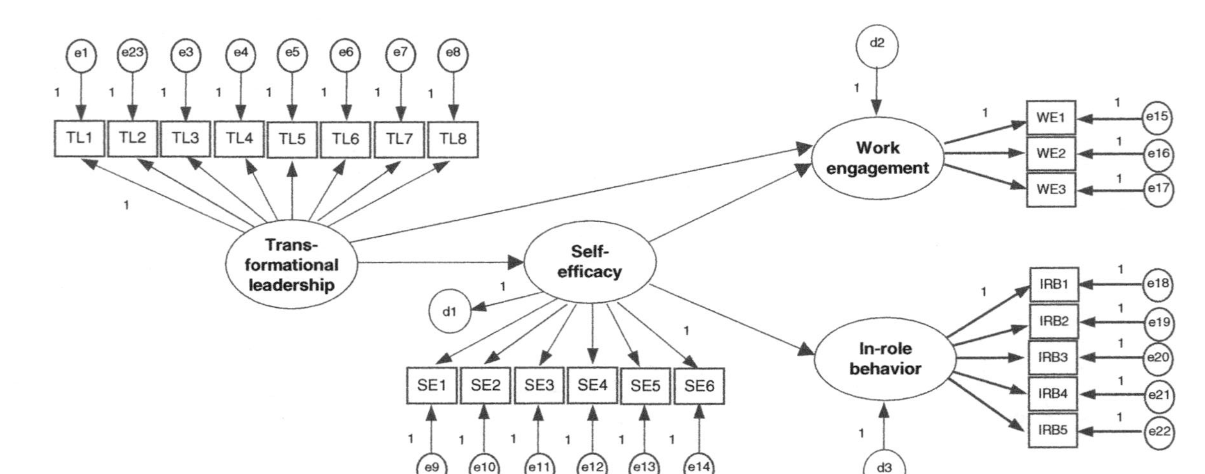

Figure 11.5 Hypothesized model and structural relations with structural and measurement components .This is a pictorial representation of actual inputs for SEM programs (e.g., AMOS; LISREL; Mplus).

Table 11.2 Fit indices for the measurement model: Confirmatory factor analysis

	χ^2	*df*	NFI	CFI	SRMR	RMSEA
Model	612.66	203	.96	.97	.04	.04

Table 11.3 Fit indices for the structural regression model: Structural equation modeling analysis

	χ^2	*df*	NFI	CFI	SRMR	RMSEA	Δdf	$\Delta\chi^2$
1. Model 1[a]	857.20	358	.96	.96	.05	.04		
2. Model 2[b]	855.55	356	.87	.85	.10	.11		
3. Model 3[c]	1,185.93	359	.83	.82	.14	.15	1	328.73***

Note: Δdf reflects the difference between the *df* of the alternative nested structural equation models and the *df* of the hypothesized structural equation model (Model 1). $\Delta\chi^2$ reflects the difference between the χ^2 of the alternative nested structural equation models and the χ^2 of the hypothesized structural equation model (Model 1).

$^*p < .05$. $^{**}p < .01$. $^{***}p < .001$.

[a]Model 1 is the hypothesized model as depicted in figure 11.5.

[b]Model 2 is a partial mediation model with direct paths added between work engagement and in-role behavior as well as between transformational leadership and in-role performance.

[c]Model 3 omits the path between transformational leadership and self-efficacy.

Hair et al., 2006). Hence, we can conclude that the hypothesized measurement model is adequately supported and confirmed by the study sample.

Once the measurement model is identified, we conduct estimations of the hypothesized structural regression model. The overall model fit indices for the hypothesized model, as well as alternative models, are provided in table 11.3. We can see that the fit indices from the analysis exceed the recommended cut-off values; χ^2/df is 2.39 (< 3); NFI is .96 (> .90); CFI is .96 (> .90); SRMR is .05 (< .10); and RMSEA is .04 (≤ .08) (Bollen, 1989; Browne & Cudeck, 1993; Hu & Bentler, 1998; Kline, 2010). These results indicate that the hypothesized model has an adequate goodness-of-fit to the study sample; in addition, the hypothesized model is also significantly better than two alternative models (for more details on the alternative models and overall study design, see the original article Kim, Egan, Kim and Kim, 2013a).

Now, we proceed with a further examination of regression estimations. The direct and indirect effects of regression estimates in the overall structural regression model are presented in table 11.4; the total effects can also be calculated by combining direct and indirect effects. The results show that all of the hypothesized relationships between the study variables are statistically significant in the reported sample ($p < .01$). Thus, we conclude that the hypothesized structural relations receive full support in the present study.

Table 11.4 Direct and indirect effects

	Outcome					
	Self-efficacy		Work engagement		In-role behavior	
Predictor	**Direct**	**Indirect**	**Direct**	**Indirect**	**Direct**	**Indirect**
Transformational leadership	.73** (.15, 31)		.30** (.42, .61)	.33** (.23, 40)		.13** (.21, 35)
Self-efficacy			.46** (.10, 32)		.10** (.14, 28)	

Note: Standardized regression coefficients are shown. The lower and upper bounds of the 95 % confidence intervals (shown in parentheses) are based on the findings from a bootstrapping analysis using the bias-corrected method. * $p < .05$. ** $p < .01$. *** $p < .001$.

Additional examples of two-step modeling can be found in similar SEM studies conducted by Kim, Egan, and Moon (2013b), Egan and Kim (2013), and Lang et al. (2011).

Other important SEM topics

Missing data

In almost any research, the sample data may have missing or incomplete observations. A small amount of missing observations may not be a major concern in a large sample data set (< 10%, Cohen & Cohen 1983). However, it is desirable for researchers to carefully examine a pattern of missingness in their study sample. There are three primary patterns that can address most of the missingness. *Missing completely at random* (MCAR) is the most restrictive assumption and asserts that the pattern of missingness is unrelated to both the presence and absence of any variables in the data set. Next, *missing at random* (MAR), which is somewhat less restrictive than MCAR, claims that the pattern of missingness is unrelated to the absence of (or unobserved) variables and is related to the presence of (or observed) variables in the data. These two patterns of MCAR and MAR assume that the missingness of the data is ignorable. The last pattern, which is the least restrictive assumption, is *nonignorable* and it refers to the missingness that is nonrandom. Nonignorable indicates that there is an underlying or systematic mechanism behind the incompleteness of the data.

In order to handle missing data, researchers can consider using one of the following methods. First, *listwise deletion* removes cases with missing observations on any variable and allows researchers to analyze the data available in a complete form. Next, in *pairwise deletion*, cases with missing observations are removed only when a particular analysis or computation is involved with those missing observations; thus, different analyses may result in different numbers of cases used for the calculations. The *single imputation* method replaces an unobserved value with an estimated value; the most basic technique for this approach is mean imputation that replaces a missing value with the overall sample mean.

The *multiple imputation* method averages the outcomes across multiple imputed data sets (e.g., the average outcome value from 5 imputed data sets) to deal with the problem of amplified noise from imputation activities. Lastly, *maximum likelihood* (also known as *full information maximum likelihood*) is an estimation method that uses available data without either excluding or replacing the missing values from analysis. Among these, the maximum likelihood estimation and multiple imputation outperform other missing values treatments (Rubin, 1996; Schafer & Graham, 2002) and are strongly recommended in SEM (Allison, 2003). Of note is that full information maximum likelihood is available by default for missing data in many SEM software packages (e.g., AMOS, LISREL, Mplus, EQS).

Bootstrapping

Another important topic for SEM applications is bootstrapping. Bootstrapping is a resampling procedure that considers the original sample to represent the population. Its basic concept is that the original sample gives rise to one or more additional sample data sets. One of the main reasons for the use of bootstrapping is to deal with the presence of multivariate nonnormality of the data (Byrne, 2001). Researchers can also use bootstrapping when the sample size is insufficient, where parametric inference necessitates complex formulas (e.g., when computing standard errors), or when power analysis needs to be performed. In the following section, we provide more detailed applications of bootstrapping for mediation testing.

Mediation model

Analysis of mediation (or indirect) effects is an important subject for management studies. In the past, the Sobel test was the most commonly used estimator for indirect effects. However, bootstrapping confidence intervals are preferred over the Sobel test recently, as the Sobel test makes the assumption of normality of the data (e.g., the z distribution) and this normal sampling distribution assumption is often violated during the mediation testing procedures (MacKinnon, Lockwood & Williams, 2004). Thus, in mediation testing with SEM, it is suggested that researchers utilize the bootstrapping method, particularly *bias-corrected* (BC) estimation with 1,000 (or more) resampling and 95% confidence intervals. Recent simulation studies report that the BC bootstrap confidence intervals perform better than other methods, such as the bootstrap-t method or percentile method (Cheung & Lau, 2008).

As presented in table 11.4, the significance of indirect effect can be determined by examining the lower and upper bounds of the 95% confidence intervals (shown in parentheses in the table). If the confidence interval does not include zero, we can conclude that the corresponding indirect relation is statistically significant. On the other hand, if it overlaps zero, the indirect relation is considered to be statistically nonsignificant. For more guidelines and examples for the mediation model testing, we recommend recent organizational research articles by Cheung and Lau (2008).

Effect size

In addition to conventional significance test results, we also recommend that effect size indicators be interpreted and reported in SEM studies. By doing so, practical significance can be derived for practitioners and researchers (Kim & Egan, 2013; Preacher & Kelley, 2011). By reporting effect sizes, readers are also able to gauge the stability of study results across samples and contexts. Although it is difficult to provide interpretative guidelines that can be used across study genres or areas, regression coefficients with values greater than .50 (> .50) could indicate a large effect; values around .30 (around .30) may imply a medium effect; and less than .10 (< .10) could suggest a small effect (Kline, 2010). Preacher and Kelley's article (2011) provides a more in-depth discussion on this topic area.

Conclusion

In this chapter we have attempted to show the reader the potential use of path analysis, CFA, and SEM along with some practical issues related to these powerful techniques. Each of these techniques allows researchers to explore relationships between the study variables in ways that other statistical methods could only partially provide. This is the real advantage of SEM: in one technique we have a combination of multiple regression and factor analyses, which can tell us whether we have viable models. In the business world, the uses and potential benefits of such a technique are vast.

Although SEM is accompanied by a good deal of technical jargon and may appear daunting to those who are contemplating its use for the first time, in actuality it can be quite straightforward in its application if we just remember the kinds of questions we are seeking to answer. First, we are interested in the nature of the relationships in our models: Are they weak, moderate, or strong? Are they statistically significant? What are the indirect effects of one variable on another or the meditational role of another variable? Second, how well does our model, whether it be path analysis, CFA, or SEM, fit the actual data? To answer this question we need only to run the appropriate statistical analysis (a relatively easy task using any SEM software) and determine whether some or all of the indices obtained for our models approximate the standards in table 11.1.

It is also important to keep in mind that path analysis, CFA, and SEM are interrelated techniques that can each be used to tackle some of the questions above. Path analyses embody the structural model, and we are primarily concerned with the relationships between the observed variables and the fit of our model. CFA is only concerned with the measurement model, and here the strength of the association of the observed variables to the latent variable and the fit of the model are the primary concerns. SEM is a natural extension of both of these techniques that incorporates both the structural model and measurement model. So, for example, if we added fourth-quarter Sales Performance as an outcome in figure 11.3, with Personality and Sales Comprehension as predictors, we move from CFA to SEM. As described in another example of two-step modeling (also see figure 11.5), SEM can also demonstrate how managerial behavior influences ėmployee attitude and performance-related responses. The examples we provided in the chapter clearly illustrate the potential use of this technique for business. Having modeling techniques that allow management researchers to predict variables such as performance, work engagement, retention, etc., could have innumerable benefits to organizations.

References

Allison, P. D. (2003). Missing data techniques for structural equation modeling. *Journal of Abnormal Psychology, 112*(4), 545–557.

Anderson, J., & Gerbing, D. (1988). Structural equation modeling in practice: A review and recommended two-step approach. *Psychological Bulletin, 103*(3), 411–423.

Bentler, P. M. (1992). On the fit of models to covariances and methodology to the Bulletin. *Psychological bulletin, 112*(3), 400–404.

Bentler, P.M. (1990). Comparative fit indexes in structural models. *Psychological Bulletin, 107,* 238–246.

Bentler, P.M., & Bonett, D.G. (1980). Significance tests and goodness of fit in the analysis of covariance structures. *Psychological Bulletin, 88,* 588–606.

Bentler, P. M., & Chou, C. (1987). Practical issues in structural modeling. *Sociological Methods & Research, 16*(1), 78–117.

Bollen, K. A. (1989). *Structural equations with latent variables.* New York: John Wiley & Sons.

Browne, M. W., & Cudeck, R. (1993). Alternative ways of assessing model fit. In K. A. Bollen & J. S. Long (Eds.), *Testing structural equation models* (pp. 136–162). Beverly Hills, CA: Sage.

Bulmer, M. G. (1979). *Principles of statistics.* Mineola, NY: Courier Dover.

Byrne, B. M. (2001). *Structural equation modeling with AMOS: Basic concepts, applications, and programming.* Mahwah, NJ: Lawrence Erlbaum Associates.

Cheung, G. W., & Lau, R. S. (2008). Testing mediation and suppression effects of latent variables: Bootstrapping with structural equation models. *Organizational Research Methods, 11*(2), 296–325.

Cohen, J., & Cohen, P. (1983). *Applied multiple regression/correlation analysis for the behavioral sciences.* Hillsdale, NJ: Erlbaum.

Costello, A. B., & Osborne, J. W. (2005). Best practices in exploratory factor analysis: Four recommendations for getting the most from your analysis. *Practical Assessment, Research & Evaluation, 10,* 1–10.

Egan, T. M., & Kim, S. (2013). The impact of managerial coaching on employee voice, motivation to learn, and psychological safety. Paper presented at *the 2013 Academy of Management Annual Meeting—Lake Buena Vista, Florida*.

Hair, J. F., Black, W. C., Babin, B. J., Anderson, R. E., & Tatham, R. L. (2006). *Multivariate data analysis*. Upper Saddle River, NJ: Prentice Hall.

Hooper, D., Coughlan, J. and Mullen, M. R. (2008). Structural equation modeling: Guidelines for determining model fit. *Electronic Journal of Business Research Methods, 6*, 53–60.

Hu, L., & Bentler, P. (1998). Fit indices in covariance structure modeling: Sensitivity to under parameterized model misspecification. *Psychological Methods, 3*(4), 424–453.

Kim, S., & Egan, T. M. (2013). Invited reaction—The contrasting effects of coaching style on task performance: The mediating roles of subjective task complexity and self-set goal. *Human Resource Development Quarterly, 24*(4), 459–468.

Kim, S., Egan, T. M., Kim, W., & Kim, J. (2013a). The impact of managerial coaching behavior on employee work-related reactions. *Journal of Business and Psychology, 28*(3), 315–330.

Kim, S., Egan, T. M., & Moon, M. (2013b). Managerial coaching efficacy, work-related attitudes, and performance in public organizations: A comparative international study. Review of Public Personnel Administration. Advance online publication. doi:10.1177/0734371X13491120.

Kline, R. B. (2010). *Principles and practice of structural equation modeling*. New York: Guilford Press.

Lang, J., Bliese, P. D., Lang, J. W., & Adler, A. B. (2011). Work gets unfair for the depressed: Cross-lagged relations between organizational justice perceptions and depressive symptoms. *Journal of Applied Psychology, 96*(3), 602–618.

MacKinnon, D. P., Lockwood, C. M., & Williams, J. (2004). Confidence limits for the indirect effect: Distribution of the product and resampling methods. *Multivariate Behavioral Research, 39*(1), 99–128.

Miles, J., & Shevlin, M. (1998). Effects of sample size, model specification and factor loadings on the GFI in confirmatory factor analysis. *Personality and Individual Differences, 25*, 85–90.

Preacher, K. J., & Kelley, K. (2011). Effect size measures for mediation models: Quantitative strategies for communicating indirect effects. *Psychological Methods, 16*(2), 93–115.

Rubin, D. B. (1996). Multiple imputation after 18+ years. *Journal of the American Statistical Association, 91*, 473–489.

Tabachnick, B., & Fidell, L. (2001). *Using multivariate statistics*. New York: HarperCollins.

Thompson, B. (2004). *Exploratory and confirmatory factor analysis: Underlying concepts and applications*. Washington, DC: American Psychological Association.

Shevlin, M., & Miles, J. N. (1998). Effects of sample size, model specification and factor loadings on the GFI in confirmatory factor analysis. *Personality and Individual Differences, 25*(1), 85–90.

Sivo, S. A., Fan, X., Witta, E. L., & Willse, J. T. (2006). The search for "optimal" cutoff properties: Fit index criteria in structural equation modeling. *Journal of Experimental Education, 74*(3), 267–288.

Schafer, J. L., & Graham, J. W. (2002). Missing data: Our view of the state of the art. *Psychological Methods, 7*(2), 147–177.

12

Correlation to Logistic Regression Illustrated with a Victimization–Sexual Orientation Study

Creaig A. Dunton and Mark Beaulieu

Chapter overview

Dunton and Beaulieu hold a positivist ideology. In their chapter, they explain a common positivist technique: correlation. They go on to discuss regression and a specialty technique: logistic regression. Correlation and regression are generally deductive within-group unit of analysis strategies, since factors of interest are measured as predictors of the dependent variable. The factors and dependent variable of interest in the unit of analysis are established through a scholarly literature review. As with all true positivistic ideologies, hypotheses are developed to test the unit of analysis. A unique aspect of their example was the ex post facto use of logistic regression on existing data. Using correlation and regression is not considered mixed methods or multi-methods because researchers with a positivist ideology generally use correlation first to show evidence of the hypothesized relations between factors or between factors and the dependent variable, otherwise it may not be feasible to continue the analysis. Logistic regression has specific assumptions that must be met in order to be applied, and they discuss this.

Introduction

In the social sciences, there are few methods of analysis that are more ubiquitous than regression. With its basic, familiar equation structure and ease in interpretation, paired with its flexibility and application to a multitude of data, it forms the basis of most research in the discipline. It allows researchers to determine the effects on a single dependent variable using multiple independent variables, with the strength of each measured as the others are held constant. By controlling for a wide variety of potential causes, the actual effects of independent variables can be quantified. In its most basic form, regression is closely related to correlation in that it quantifies the relationship between two variables. However, a significant difference is that correlation is a standardized measure and also makes no insinuation of cause versus effect, while regression examines the role of multiple predictor variables. The logic behind both is quite similar, and both will be examined in this chapter.

We will focus largely on the conceptual nature and interpretation of both correlation and regression analysis. While equations will be presented, we will not take a heavily mathematical approach in our examination. Our examples will be presented and interpreted without specific use of equations or calculations, as most analyses in the social sciences are performed by statistical software. The mathematical theory required to calculate regression analyses can be easily found in any statistics textbook. For the sake of convenience, terms such as independent variable, predictor, and cause will be used interchangeably, as will dependent variable, outcome, and effect.

Throughout this we will utilize examples from a study examining the role that sexual orientation had on victimization on a college campus in upstate New York, specifically sexual assault and sexual harassment. This is excerpted from a paper examining if GLBT (gay, lesbian, bisexual, and transgender) students were more likely to be victims of sexual harassment and assault. Beyond their orientation, we also include variables known to affect victimization, including age, race, fraternity/sorority membership, being a member of a school sports team, if they are an international student, and if they live alone (Brown, Clarke, Gortmaker, & Robinson-Keilig, 2004; Coston, 2004; Duncan, 1990; Fasting, Brackenridge, & Sungot-Borgen, 2003; Lehrer, Lehrer, Lehrer, & Oyarzun, 2007; Makepeace, 1987; Monks, Tomaka, Palacios, & Thompson, 2010; Tomsich, Gover, & Jennings, 2011).

Correlation and regression basic principles

While we will speak of regression later as its own distinct concept and method, its most basic form is the basis of correlation. At its core, regression is mathematically quite simple. In algebra and geometry, the equation of a line is presented as: $y = mx + b$,

where x and y represent the two axes of a Cartesian plane. Within this equation, m is defined as a slope, or the change in y associated with an increase in x, and b is the intercept, or the value of y if x is zero. Associating this equation with the relationship between two variables rather than a plotted line, it is clear that the slope represents the change in a dependent variable associated with an increase or decrease in the independent variable, and thus measures the direction and strength of the relationship.

This is known as the regression line, and when plotted onto a two-dimensional Cartesian plane, it visually presents the relationship between the two variables. Considering y as an outcome variable and x as a predictor variable, the effect of a change in the cause (x) on the dependent variable (y) can be predicted by a regression equation. A scatter plot can be produced by using the regression equation to illustrate the direction and strength of the relationship between the data points based on the slope.

In our example of sexual orientation and victimization, this point can be best illustrated by examining the relationship between student age, their score

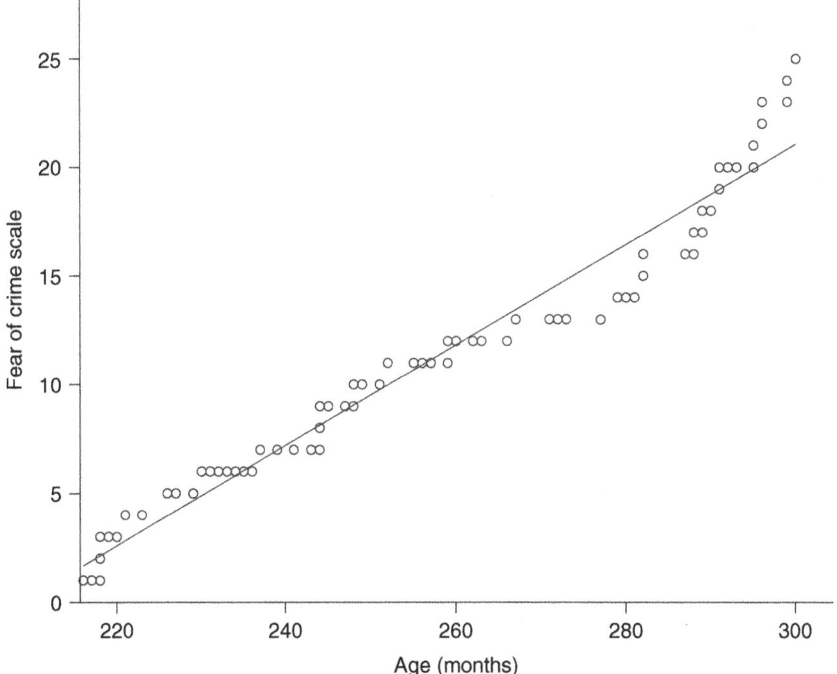

Figure 12.1 Scatter plot with regression line (positive relationship).

on a fear of crime questionnaire, and their score on a risk-taking behavior scale. (Please note that these variables were created in order to illustrate this point, they do not reflect the actual data we will examine later.)

As can be seen in figure 12.1, there was a close relationship between a student's age (measured in months) and their perceived fear of victimization. As students grew older, they were more fearful of potential victimization.

Figure 12.2 illustrates the relationship between the students' age in months and their risk-taking behavior. As can be seen, these two have a close, but negative relationship. As students become older, their risk-taking behaviors decreased.

Correlation

While a slope represents the relationship between the two variables, the direction and strength of the relationship is not immediately interpreted, as it is a continuous variable that can have nearly any value and thus interpretation is heavily dependent upon the data being analyzed. For this reason, a standardized statistic is created to be easily interpretable, which is Pearson's *r*.

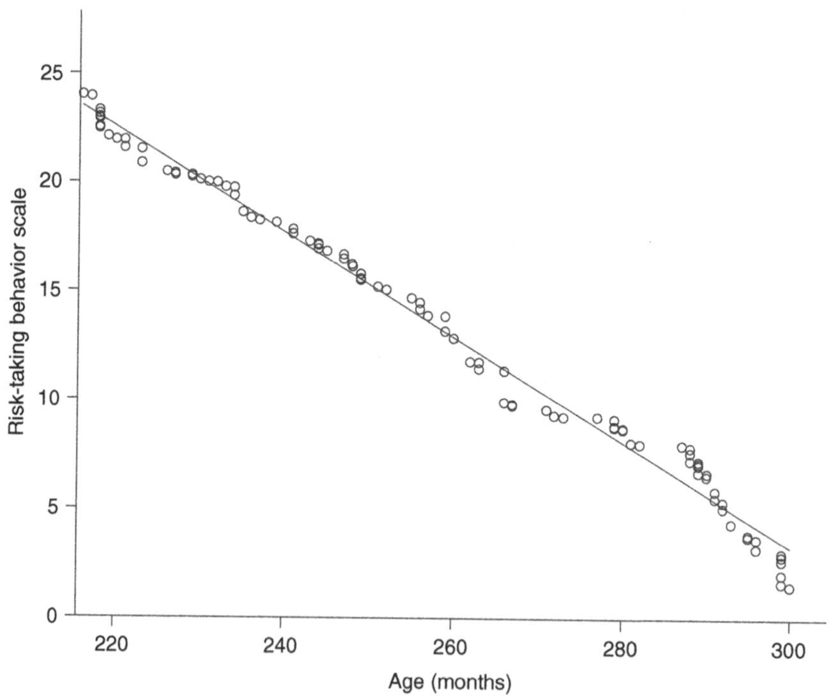

Figure 12.2 Scatter plot with regression line (negative relationship).

To calculate Pearson's *r* based upon a regression line, one would use the following equation:

$$r = \frac{\sum (X - \bar{X})(Y - \bar{Y})}{\sqrt{\left[\sum (X - \bar{X})^2\right]\left[\sum (Y - \bar{Y})^2\right]}}$$

Pearson's *r* is generally referred to as a correlation coefficient, and it is an easily interpreted measure of the direction and strength of the relationship between two variables. Pearson's *r* is a standardized coefficient ranging between –1 and 1 that indicates how closely two variables are related to one another. A correlation of 1 demonstrates that each increase in the independent variable raises the dependent variable by the exact same amount. Conversely, a correlation of –1 means that for each increase in the independent variable, the dependent variable is reduced by the exact same amount. A Pearson's *r* of zero indicates no relationship between the two variables (Lewis-Beck, 1995).

Realistically, perfect correlations almost never occur in nature, and while the standard benchmark to establish a relationship can vary, an *r* value of 0.50 indicates a moderately strong relationship between the two variables examined (Gill, Johnson, & Clark, 2010; Healey, 2015) Correlation is often presented as a descriptive statistic to not only show how closely related two variables are without making any claims of causation, but also provide an essential first step before proceeding with a causal analysis. If two variables have little relationship with each other, it may not be worth further analysis without having an extremely compelling theoretical reason to do so.

Rarely in empirical research is a single correlation presented, instead the correlations between multiple variables are usually used. For this reason, we will examine correlations using a correlation matrix, which presents the individual correlations between multiple variables.

The frequently used caveat that "correlation does not equal causation" is extremely relevant in this context (Gill, Johnson, & Clark, 2010, p. 43). Pearson's *r* simply measures the association between two different variables, and can make no distinction as far as spuriousness or time-order, the two other major components needed for causation.

Correlation makes no assumption that one variable causes the other, and thus there is no independent or dependent variable in a correlation analysis (Kutner, Nachtsheim, & Neter 2004).

Correlation example

While correlations do not necessarily imply causation, they are a useful first step in determining the likelihood of a relationship. For example, in table 12.1 one can see that the four measures of victimization (psychological abuse,

Table 12.1 Correlations for all cases

Variable	Psychological abuse	Physical abuse	Sexual harassment	Sexual assault	Sexual orientation (Hetero-sexual = 0; LGBT = 1)
Psychological abuse	1	.300**	.304**	.073*	.185**
Physical abuse	.300**	1	.106**	.115**	.161**
Sexual harassment	.304**	.106**	1	.218**	.144**
Sexual assault	.073*	.115**	.218**	1	.215**
Sexual orientation (Heterosexual = 0; LGBT = 1)	.185**	.161**	.144**	.215**	1
Gender (Male = 0; Female = 1)	.121**	0.021	.392**	.124**	.110**
Belongs to a fraternity/ sorority (No = 0; Yes = 1)	.095**	0.067	.100**	0.042	0.06
On a sports team (intercollegiate or campus) (No = 0; Yes = 1)	−0.06	0.025	−.083*	0.004	0.006
International student (No = 0; Yes = 1)	0.059	.073*	0.066	0.039	.144**
Lives on campus (No = 0; Yes = 1)	−.071*	−0.046	0.007	.085*	−.071*
Lives alone (No = 0; Yes = 1)	0.045	0.067	−0.005	.079*	0.064
Race (Non-white = 0; White = 1)	−.087*	−0.06	−.135**	−.100**	−.112**

$^{*}p < .05$, $^{**}p < .01$

Gender (Male = 0; Female = 1)	Belongs to a fraternity/ sorority (No = 0; Yes = 1)	On a sports team (inter-collegiate or campus) (No = 0; Yes = 1)	International student (No = 0; Yes = 1)	Lives on campus (No = 0; Yes = 1)	Lives alone (No = 0; Yes = 1)	Race (Non-white = 0; White = 1)
.121**	.095**	–0.06	0.059	–.071*	0.045	–.087*
0.021	0.067	0.025	.073*	–0.046	0.067	–0.06
.392**	.100**	–.083*	0.066	0.007	–0.005	–.135**
.124**	0.042	0.004	0.039	.085*	.079*	–.100**
.110**	0.06	0.006	.144**	–.071*	0.064	–.112**
1	0.008	–.090**	0.06	–.069*	–0.029	–.146**
0.008	1	.086*	0	.091**	0.048	–.076*
–.090**	.086*	1	–0.031	.156**	0.013	0.051
0.06	0	–0.031	1	-0.04	-0.03	–.366**
–.069*	.091**	.156**	–0.04	1	.092**	0.01
–0.029	0.048	0.013	–0.03	.092**	1	–0.014
–.146**	–.076*	0.051	–.366**	0.01	–0.014	1

physical abuse, sexual assault, and sexual harassment) are all related to each other. For psychological abuse, there are statistically significant relationships with the other three measures of victimization (physical abuse (0.300), sexual harassment (0.304), and sexual assault (0.073)).

Based on these results, one could say that individuals who experienced psychological abuse were more likely to report physical abuse, sexual harassment, and sexual assault. The further from zero, the stronger the relationship. While this example only has positive relationships, the rule can still be applied. In this case, 0.304 is further from zero than 0.073 so physical abuse has a stronger relationship with sexual harassment than sexual assault. Turning to physical abuse, the relationships are similar, but the strength of relationships differs. Physical abuse is most strongly related to psychological abuse (0.300) and exhibits weaker relationships with sexual harassment (0.106) and sexual assault (0.115). Once again, this is because 0.300 is further from zero than either 0.115 or 0.106.

In the logistic regression section, the examples will be limited to the dependent variables sexual assault and sexual harassment, so the discussion that follows here is between the independent variables and these two dependent variables. Thus, the first set of coefficients of interest will come from the column for sexual harassment. A quick perusal of the column shows that sexual orientation (0.144), gender (0.392), belonging to a fraternity/sorority (0.100), being on a sports team (–0.083), and race (–0.135) are related.

Unlike the relationships between the measures of victimization, there are both positive and negative relationships between sexual harassment and the independent variables. Thus, these results indicate that GLBT students, females, and members of a fraternity or sorority are all more likely to report sexual harassment. In these variables, the dummy variables are coded 1 for GLBT, female, and belonging to a fraternity/sorority. Thus, a higher value on these variables is related to higher levels of reported sexual harassment. The negative coefficients are coded as 1 = participation on a sports team and 1 = White. Thus, being on a sports team lowered reported victimization, as did being white.

Once again the strength of relationships can be determined, and this time there are both positive and negative relationships. Here, 0.392 is the furthest from zero, so gender has the strongest bivariate relationship with sexual harassment. The weakest relationship is between being on a sports team and sexual harassment (–0.083). However, race (–0.135) has a stronger relationship with sexual harassment than belonging to a fraternity/sorority (0.100). This is because –0.135 is further from 0 than 0.100. In other words, the absolute value of –0.135, which is 0.135, is larger than the absolute value of 0.100.

Let us move to sexual assault since that will be also be used as a dependent variable in the logistic regression example that will be discussed later.

Move to the column for sexual assault and then go across to sexual orientation to examine the first relationship between an independent variable and sexual assault. Sexual orientation (0.215), gender (0.124), lives on campus (0.085), and lives alone (0.079) all exhibit positive relationships with sexual assault. Race (–0.100) has a negative relationship with sexual assault. In this example, GLBT students, females, living on campus, and living alone are all related to higher levels of sexual assault. Whites, again race is coded 1 = White and 0 = non-White, were less likely to report sexual assault. Sexual orientation has the strongest relationship with sexual assault since 0.215 is further from zero than any of the other bivariate correlations. The weakest relationship is with living alone since 0.79 is closest to zero. The negative relationship between race and sexual assault is stronger than either lives on campus or living alone, since –0.100 is further from zero than either 0.085 or 0.079 respectively.

Single regression

If time-order and nonspuriousness can be ascertained, the logic behind correlation can be utilized to examine causal relationships via regression. Single regression examines the casual relationship between a single predictor variable and an outcome dependent variable at a later point in time by estimating the amount of variance explained in the dependent variable by each change of value in the independent predictor (Gill, Johnson, & Clark, 2010). Thus, regression is logically similar to a correlation coefficient that presents the actual impact of the independent variable on the dependent variable, albeit in a non-standardized metric. Realistically, regression is employed mostly to examine the relationship between multiple predictor variables and an outcome variable, which is known as multiple regression and will be discussed in detail (Gill, Johnson, & Clark, 2010).

While structurally similar to the equation of a line, in a case of single regression the model (as it is known) would be presented as:

$$Y = a + bX + e$$

where Y is the dependent variable, X is the independent variable, a is the intercept (the value of the dependent variable when the independent variable is zero), and e represents the error term, or the difference between the predicted and actual value. In regression terminology, b is analogous to the slope in a linear equation, but is referred to as a regression coefficient. Special caution should be made about interpreting the intercept, as it is may have little theoretical relevance. It is largely included for mathematical purposes and is usually reported, but may not be interpretable, such as having a negative value or a zero value when it is impossibility (Lewis-Beck, 1995).

The equation is devised by finding the most effective predictive line that best fits the data, while minimizing errors in measurement. This is known as Ordinary Least Squares (OLS) regression. Modern computer software calculates the most efficient slope and intercept far easier than by hand, and also more accurately. The formula used to calculate the slope is:

$$b = \frac{\sum(X-\bar{X})(Y-\bar{Y})}{\sum(X-\bar{X})^2}$$

And the intercept is

$$a = Y - bX$$

Errors are calculated by using the sum of squared errors (SSE) between the actual value in the data and the value predicted by the regression line. It is calculated using the following formula:

$$SSE = \sum(Y-\hat{Y})^2$$

Ordinary Least Squares is not the only method utilized to calculate a regression model. Another, which we will come back to later, is Maximum Likelihood Estimation (MLE). MLE calculates the regression model by estimating values of the population that are consistent with sample data (Kutner, et al., 2004).

Multiple regression

Multiple regression is among the most essential tools of analysis within the social sciences (Haase, 2011). Multiple regression utilizes a similar logic, but includes multiple predictor and control variables to develop a model that avoids spuriousness while still using the OLS method of estimation. Spuriousness is addressed by including multiple independent variables that are defined theoretically as being potential causes of the dependent variable being examined.

These additional independent variables may be theoretically relevant variables that are precipitators of the dependent variable, or they may be control variables. Control variables are those that are known, or at least expected to contribute, to the dependent variable. By measuring them, their effects on the dependent variable are controlled for, and spuriousness is removed. It is presented as:

$$Y = a + b_1X_1 + b_2X_2 ... b_nX_n + e$$

Multiple regression at this stage can still be thought of in the same context as the aforementioned equation of a line example, although with the equivalency of slopes to coefficients means that a multiple regression model will include dimensions that cannot be visualized. Regardless of the number of independent variables utilized in a model, there is still only a single intercept value and a single error term.

The interpretation does not differ significantly from that of simple regression, it just should be noted that the effect of change in a single independent variable is found while all other independent variables are held constant, and the intercept represents the dependent variable's value with all independent variables at zero. That is why it is important in a multiple regression model to include all of the predictor variables that could potentially have an impact on the outcome variable (Lewis-Beck, 1995). A key factor of multiple regression is that it can be used to predict what value of the dependent variable an individual would have based upon the relationships found within the data being analyzed.

Significance tests are also applicable for the coefficients in a multiple regression equation. In this case, they can be quite simply interpreted as indicating which of the independent variables may truly have an effect on the dependent variable. This test is performed using a standard t distribution, with a null hypothesis of the coefficient having a value of zero, and the alternate hypothesis of it not equaling zero.

Regression is based upon a series of assumptions that should be acknowledged. First, the model is correctly specified, meaning that Y is the dependent variable, the X variable(s) are independent and have an effect on the dependent, and the relationship is linear. Second, the variables are measured correctly and are quantitative in nature. Third, there cannot be any perfect collinearity (two or more independent variables having a Pearson's r of 1.0), and fourth, the error term is homoskedastic (error variance is constant across values of the independent variable) and not correlated with any of the independent variables (Lewis-Beck, 1995).

One of the most widely used tests for how effective a regression model is at prediction is R^2, also known as the coefficient of determination, or explained variance (Lewis-Beck, 1995). The coefficient of determination is a standardized measurement that calculates the amount of variability in the dependent variable predicted by the regression equation. It has a minimum value of zero (indicating that the regression model explains none of the variation in the dependent variable), and a maximum of one (the regression model explains all of the variation in the dependent variable). Like most measurements, in the real world it lies between these two extremes, and a hypothetical R^2 value of 0.59 would be interpreted as meaning that 59 percent of the variation in the dependent variable can be attributed to the regression equation.

Multiple regression example

We will next examine the relationship in our data between the independent variables and our dependent variable of victimization using multiple regression. For the OLS regression, there are three important areas that this section must cover: unstandardized coefficients, standardized coefficients, and explained variance. In table 12.2, the unstandardized coefficients are the numbers that are not in parentheses (e.g., the unstandardized coefficient for sexual orientation is 2.251). The standardized coefficients are the values in the parentheses. The explained variance of $R^2 = 0.152$ is listed at the bottom of the table.

The unstandardized coefficients are the slopes for the OLS regression equation. In other words, the unstandardized coefficients provide the change in total victimizations by a one unit change in the independent variable. The example here uses mostly dummy variables, so for most of the variables the slope provides the difference between the predicted victimizations for the two categories, controlling for all other variables in the analysis. The one exception

Table 12.2 OLS regression

Independent variable	**B (Beta)**
Sexual orientation	2.251**
	(0.229)
Gender	1.040**
	(0.221)
Belongs to fraternity/sorority	0.510*
	(0.072)
On a sports team (intercollegiate or campus)	–0.152
	(–0.024)
International student	0.625*
	(0.065)
Lives on campus	–0.070
	(–0.015)
Age	–0.105*
	(–0.079)
Lives alone	0.201
	(0.025)
Race	–0.394*
	(v0.077)
Constant	2.235
R^2	0.152

+$p < .10$, *$p < .05$, **$p < .01$

is age, where a one year increase in age is associated with a decrease in reported victimization.

In the example, there are six statistically significant relationships between reported victimization and the independent variables. Sexual orientation (2.251), gender (1.040), belongs to a fraternity/sorority (0.510), and international student (0.625) all exhibited positive relationships with reported victimization. In other words, GLBT students, females, fraternity/sorority members, and international students all reported more victimization than heterosexual students, males, nonfraternity/sorority members, and noninternational students. The other two relationships are negative. Both age (–0.105) and race (–0.394) were found to be negatively related to reported victimization. Simply put, the older a student was, or if the student was white, the less the victimization he or she reported.

Predictions

One nice thing about unstandardized coefficients is that it allows one to make predictions about total reported victimization. Let us do this for two different hypothetical students. First, the beta coefficients from table 12.2 must be put into an equation to calculate the predicted value. All one has to do to create this equation is know the unstandardized coefficients and the constant. It can be interpreted that the constant is the predicted value of total abuse if all variables were equal to zero. In other words it is the intercept. Based on the data presented in table 12.2, the equation would be:

$$\begin{aligned}&\text{Total Victimization}\\&\quad = 2.235 + 2.251x(\text{sexual orientation}) + 1.040x(\text{gender})\\&\qquad + 0.510x(\text{fraternity or sorority}) - 0.152x(\text{sports team})\\&\qquad + 0.625x(\text{international student}) - 0.070x(\text{lives on campus})\\&\qquad - 0.105x(\text{age}) + 0.201x(\text{live alone}) - 0.394x(\text{race})\end{aligned}$$

Before moving on, let us take one quick look at two things in the above equation that may cause confusion. The first issue is the inclusion of the constant. It should be noted that the first number in the equation is 2.235 and that there is no multiplication after that value. This is because if all of the values of the variables are 0, then the predicted value will be 2.235 + 0 (all of the multiplications would be 0 since each unstandardized coefficient is being multiplied by 0). Thus, putting the constant first in the equation lets the reader know what the predicted value of the dependent variable is if all independent variables are equal to 0. The second point that should be made is that there are negative values in the previously presented equation. Let us start with the sports team coefficient. There could be a plus sign before the sports team coefficient, but then it must have the following notation: + (–0.152) × (sports team). That is less efficient than simply realizing that the slope has a negative value, so the minus sign saves time and has the same impact.

Hypothetical student 1: Let us say that a student had the following characteristics for our independent variables: gay, male, belongs to a fraternity, on a sports team, noninternational student, lives on campus, 18 years old, does not live alone, and is White. The values for those variables would be as follows:

- Sexual orientation = 1
- Gender = 0
- Fraternity/sorority = 1
- Sports team = 1
- International student = 0
- Lives on campus = 1
- Age = 18
- Lives alone = 0
- Race = 1

Let us put those values into the equation and the result will be the predicted total reported victimization.

$$\begin{aligned}\text{Total Victimization}\\ &= 2.235 + 2.251x(1) + 1.040x(0) + 0.510x(1) - 0.152x(1) + 0.625x(0)\\ &\quad - 0.070x(1) - 0.105x(18) + 0.201x(0) - 0.394x(1)\end{aligned}$$

If we do the multiplication first, the equation becomes

$$\begin{aligned}\text{Total Victimization}\\ &= 2.235 + 2.251 + 0 + 0.510 - 0.152 + 0 - 0.070 - 1.89 + 0 - 0.394\\ &= 2.49\end{aligned}$$

For this student, we would predict 2.49 instances of reported victimization.

Hypothetical student 2: Now, except for age, let us make our next hypothetical student the opposite of our first student and make the student old enough to be a senior in college. Thus, hypothetical student 2 is heterosexual, female, not in a fraternity/sorority, not on a sports team, an international student, does not live on campus, 22 years old, lives alone, and is non-White. The values for those variables would be as follows:

- Sexual orientation = 0
- Gender = 1
- Fraternity/sorority = 0
- Sports team = 0
- International student = 1

- Lives on campus = 0
- Age = 22
- Lives alone = 1
- Race = 0

Once again, let us put those values into the equation and the result will be the predicted total reported victimization.

$$\begin{aligned}&\text{Total Victimization}\\&\quad = 2.235 + 2.251x(0) + 1.040x(1) + 0.510x(0) - 0.152x(0) + 0.625x(1)\\&\qquad - 0.070x(0) - 0.105x(22) + 0.201x(1) - 0.394x(0)\end{aligned}$$

If we do the multiplication first, the equation becomes

$$\begin{aligned}&\text{Total Victimization}\\&\quad = 2.235 + 0 + 1.040 + 0 - 0 + 0.625 - 0 - 2.31 + 0.201 - 0 = 1.791\end{aligned}$$

For this student we would predict 1.791 reported victimizations. As you can see the power of unstandardized coefficients is the ability to predict the dependent variable. Obviously the real responses will differ from the predicted values, but the OLS regression is simply a means to give us estimates of our dependent variable. From the above two hypothetical students, it is rather obvious someone could not have 2.49 or 1.791 victimizations. However, our OLS regression predictions will be better the higher our explained variance. We will discuss explained variance later, after the discussion of standardized coefficients.

The purpose of standardized coefficients is to allow one to examine the relative strength of relationships between the independent variables and the dependent variable. When determining the strength of relationships, we can think of standardized coefficients in the same way we did bivariate correlations. Obviously, standardized coefficients are controlling for the other variables in the equation, but in terms of interpretation there is really no reason to worry about that right now. The further the standardized coefficient is from zero, the stronger the relationship. Let us point out the standardized coefficients in table 12.2. The standardized coefficients are the values in parentheses. For example, the standardized coefficient for sexual orientation is 0.229.

Next, let us discuss only the statistically significant relationships, since those would be the ones of concern in any research done later on with OLS regression. As stated above, six of the relationships are statistically significant: sexual orientation (0.229), gender (0.221), belongs to a fraternity/sorority (0.072), international student (0.065), age (–0.079), and race (–0.077). Now that we have seen the standardized coefficients, let us rank them in the order of strongest to weakest relationship: sexual orientation, gender, age, race, fraternity/sorority membership, and international student.

Once again, all we have to do is see which values are furthest from zero. In this case, sexual orientation's standardized coefficient of 0.229 is the furthest from zero. One area that confuses some people is when a value is negative. As discussed with correlation, being positive or negative indicates not the strength, but the direction of the relationship. Focus on the absolute value of the number. In this case both age (–0.79) and race (–0.77) are negative relationships, but they have a bigger impact on victimization than either belonging to a fraternity/sorority (0.072) or being an international student (0.065).

Finally, a discussion of explained variance is important. After the OLS regression has been run, it is important to note how well the equation explains the phenomena examined. To do this, we use R^2. Since R^2 is always positive, the larger the number the better job the equation does in explaining the variance of the dependent variable (Gill, Johnson, & Clark, 2010). In other words, higher the R^2, stronger the model. In our example, R^2 is 0.152. R^2 is actually just a proportion, so we can multiply the given value by 100 to get a percent of variance explained by the model. For the model presented here, we would say that our independent variables explained 15.2 percent of the variance in total reported victimizations.

Speciality regression

The aforementioned form of regression is intended only for continuous numeric dependent variables, which may not be appropriate for the data set that needs to be examined. A multitude of specific variants of regression exists that are more suited for specific types of data. It is the popularity and ease in interpretation of regression models that have led to the development of specialized forms that are a better fit to data that are not exclusively linear or interval in nature (Long, 1997).

The previously discussed regression models for single or multiple independent variables are based on what is known as classic regression analysis that assumes linear models with continuously distributed numeric dependent variables (Haase, 2011). For our example, we will focus on logistic regression. Logistic regression is utilized when a dependent variable has a dichotomous outcome (yes or no), or a categorical one in which the values cannot be put into any specific quantitative order. Other specific forms of regression are focused on dependent variables that are counts (numerical data that is discrete in nature) and that include negative binomial and Poisson distributions and special considerations for time-series data.

Logistic regression (also called logit) is one of multiple strategies utilized to examine what affects the presence or absence of a dependent variable based upon the impact of one or more independent variables. Closely related to probit models, logit and probit models assume the presence of a latent variable that, upon reaching a specific threshold, changes the outcome from a zero to a one, or a "no" to a "yes." Together, these are referred to as the binary response model (Long, 1997).

It is not uncommon that a dependent variable being studied would be measured by its presence or absence, such as the decision to contact police or whether or not an individual was a victim of a crime. In other cases it may make more sense to recode an existing interval or ratio variable into a dichotomous one to simplify interpretation or analysis. In these situations a variable is "dummy coded" in which a zero indicates the absence and a value of one indicates the presence of the variable in question. Both logit and probit also have variations that allow for the analysis of dependent variables that are not binary, but ordinal in nature, but those are beyond the scope of this chapter. Logit and probit models differ slightly in their calculations, and neither one is better than the other. Logit is often chosen initially due to its popularity, but maximum likelihood estimates are a better indicator of which method fits the data best (Long, 1997).

As mentioned previously, these specialized forms of regression are based upon Maximum Likelihood Estimation (MLE) rather than Ordinary Least Squares. MLE is used because the logistic model is based on a nonlinear (dichotomous) dependent variable, and thus has a non-normal distribution of error terms, which is a requirement of OLS (O'Connell, 2006)

One thing that differs significantly with logistic regression and its ilk is in how the results are interpreted. Since there is a binary outcome rather than a continuous one, a coefficient cannot be interpreted the same way if the dependent variable is just a zero or a one with no numeric value attached. In logistic regression, coefficients are presented as odds ratios, which are usually then converted to simple odds for ease in interpretation. For example, a coefficient of –1.19 when converted to simple odds would become 0.30, and interpreted as an odds ratio for a "yes" outcome is 30%.

$$\text{EXP}\ (-1.19) = 0.30$$

Editor's note: Dunton and Beaulier frequently use the term Exp(B) which refers to an accepted mathematical *Expression* for estimating the odds ratio of a *beta coefficient* from logistic regression, calculated by raising the natural logarithm of constant e (approximately 2.71828) to the power of the *beta*; for example in SPSS or spreadsheet software entering the function = EXP(1.171) would produce 3.226 (Strang, 2012).

As a diagnostic measure, the aforementioned R^2 has questionable use because in the logistic regression model it is only partial information and cannot be relied upon, so it is necessary to utilize a different strategy in order to determine the effectiveness of a logistic regression equation (Long, 2007). While the debate is beyond the scope of this chapter, it remains a point of argument for researchers (O'Connell, 2006). A simple, but effective means of assessing the overall effectiveness of a logistic regression model is chi-square, which is reported in most statistical packages such as SPSS.

Logistic regression example

The following tables refer to an example based on college students' self-reported victimization for sexual assault and sexual harassment. Columns present the results for three samples: all cases (both genders in one sample), males, and females. This allows an examination of the possible different results in victimization by gender and how those may differ from the combined gender sample (all cases).

Let us begin with the results for sexual assault (table 12.3). Since these are the results of logistic regression, there are two different coefficients of importance for interpreting the findings. The first is the coefficient *B*, which is the slope. If *B* is equal to zero there is no relationship. If the value for *B* is positive, that would indicate a positive relationship. In other words, a higher value on the independent variable is associated with a higher value on the dependent variable. If *B* is negative, then we would have a negative relationship. In other words as the independent variable goes up in value, the dependent variable decreases in value.

Table 12.3 Victimization outcomes for sexual assault

Independent Variable	All cases		Male		Female	
	B	Exp(B)	B	Exp(B)	B	Exp(B)
Sexual orientation (1=Gay/Lesbian/Other)	1.782	5.941**	2.758	15.770**	1.261	3.529**
Gender (1=female)	0.728	2.071**				
Fraternity/Sorority	0.094	1.098	−0.697	0.498	0.573	1.774
On a sports team (intercollegiate or campus)	−0.104	0.901	−0.096	0.908	−0.054	0.948
International student	−0.183	0.833	−0.412	0.662	0.002	1.002
Lives on campus	0.863	2.371**	1.113	3.042*	0.654	1.924
Age	−0.027	0.973	0.038	1.038	−0.131	0.878
Lives alone	0.630	1.877+	0.774	2.168	0.816	2.261
Race (1=White)	−0.519	0.595+	−0.050	0.952	−0.749	0.473*
Chi-Square	50.385		23.057		23.527	
DF	9		8		8	
N	816		482		334	

$+p < .10$, $*p < .05$, $**p < .01$

When examining reported victimization for sexual assault for all cases (table 12.3, column 1), five of the independent variables (sexual orientation, gender, fraternity/sorority membership, living on campus, and living alone) all exhibit a positive relationship with reported sexual assault victimization. Without considering the statistical significance of the relationships, a quick look would indicate that GLBT students ($B = 1.782$), females ($B = 0.728$), those in a fraternity or sorority ($B = 0.094$), those that live on campus ($B = 0.863$), and those that live alone ($B = 0.630$) all face increased risks of sexual assault victimization.

Four of the independent variables have negative relationships with reported victimization for sexual assault: on a sports team, international student, age, and race. Once again, let us ignore the statistical significance for these results and just focus on the coefficients. Based on these findings, being on a sports team (intercollegiate or campus), being an international student, being older, and Whites all had lower risks of sexual assault victimization.

The second important coefficient for discussion is Exp(B) or the odds ratio. The odds ratio can often be easier to interpret than the slope (B) depending on the units of the independent variables. While the example above uses mostly dichotomous variables (age being an exception), this is not always the case. The odds ratio provides the increased likelihood that the outcome of interest will occur when you move up a value in the independent variable. Let us go back to table 12.3, column 1 (sexual assault, all cases) and interpret the coefficients. The first thing that should be noticed is that there are no negative numbers among the odds ratios. This is because in an odds ratio, a value of 1 indicates no relationship between the independent variable and the dependent variable. Thus, a positive relationship between an independent variable and the dependent variable would be greater than 1 and a negative relationship will be between 0 and 1.

If we turn back to our positive relationships from the previous paragraph (sexual orientation, gender, fraternity/sorority membership, living on campus, and living alone) we can see that the positive relationships range from 1.098 (membership in a fraternity/sorority) to 5.941 (sexual orientation). In this example, we can simply say that GLBT students are 5.941 times more likely to be victims of sexual assault than heterosexual students. We can do this because we have assigned the value of 1 to GLBT students and 0 to heterosexual students. Thus as we move from the category assigned 0 (in this case heterosexual students) to the category assigned a value of 1 (in this case GLBT students) the odds of being a victim of sexual assault increase by 5.941 times.

In even simpler terms we could say that GLBT students are almost six times more likely to report being a victim of sexual assault. Turning to membership in a fraternity/sorority, we can see that while the relationship is positive, it is weak (again, let us ignore the statistical significance for the time being).

An odds ratio of 1.098 means that members of fraternities and sororities were more likely to report sexual assault victimizations, but not by much; they were 1.098 times more likely to report victimization than people who do not belong to fraternities or sororities. Being female (gender [Exp(*B*) = 2.071]) and living on campus (Exp(*B*) = 2.371) both increased the likelihood of reported sexual victimization by over two times. Living alone also showed an increased likelihood of reported sexual assault victimization (Exp(*B*) = 1.877). Thus living alone made a student 1.877 times more likely to report sexual assault victimization. In other words, living alone increased the odds of sexual assault victimization by 87.7%.

The negative relationships between the independent variables and sexual assault could be found simply by looking for odds ratios (Exp(*B*)) that are below 1. In this case there are the four relationships already discussed above in the paragraph on the *B* coefficient. However, one could find that information without examining the *B* coefficient. In this case, the negative relationships range from race (Exp(*B*) = 0.595) to age (Exp(*B*) = 0.973). The stronger relationships are those furthest away from 1 (or if preferred, the smaller the number the stronger the relationship). In this case, race has the strongest impact on reported victimization. Whites are 0.595 times as likely to report victimization as non-Whites.

Alternately, we could say that whites are victimized 59.5 percent of the time as often as non-Whites. For age, which has the highest odds ratio, for those with a negative relationship, we can see that it is almost the same as 1. A student that is 19 will be about 3% less likely to be victimized as someone that is 18. In other words, a 19-year–old's victimization risk is 97.3 percent that of an 18-year-old. For the other two negative relationships, being on a sports team decreases the likelihood of victimization by about 10% (Exp(*B*) = 0.901) and international students (Exp(*B*) = 0.833) were 16.7 percent less likely to be victimized than other students.

These results are similar to a linear regression model, except we are not discussing slopes. Since the dependent variable is dichotomous, we can simply see how much more or less likely an outcome is when controlling for the other independent variables. In this case, are there relationships between the independent variables and the dependent variable? While we can see both positive and negative relationships between the independent and dependent variables, not all of them are meaningful and the nonstatistically significant relationships do not allow one to make claims that the relationships truly exist. For example, age does not decrease the likelihood of victimization by a large amount (Exp(*B*) = 0.973) and not surprisingly it is not statistically significant.

When discussing results, normally one would ignore the coefficients that are not statistically significant. That was not done here to provide extra examples, but let us do that now. The independent variables that are related to reported victimization in a statistically significant way would be sexual orientation, gender, living on campus, living alone, and race. Normally, these would be the coefficients discussed when focusing on the results. There is no legitimate reason to discuss that age lowers risk of victimization, when the results of the regression do not indicate that the relationship is statistically significant. Thus, we should treat those coefficients as 0 since we cannot say with confidence that the coefficients are not actually 0.

For future examples, let us start with determining statistical significance and then only discuss the results for statistically significant relationships. For males (see table 12.3, column 2), only sexual orientation and living on campus are statistically significant predictors of reported sexual assault victimizations. In fact GBT males (Exp(*B*) = 15.770) are 15.770 times more likely to report sexual assault victimizations. If one were to put this into percentages, it would mean GBT males are 1,477% more likely to be victims of sexual assault. Males that live alone are 3.042 times more likely to report sexual assault victimizations. None of the other independent variables have an impact on male reported sexual assaults.

For females, the results are different (see table 12.3, column 3). Similar to males, sexual orientation (Exp(*B*) = 3.529) has a strong impact on reported victimization. However, the relationship, while still very strong, is much smaller than it was for males. LBT females are 3.529 times, or 252.9% more likely to report sexual assault victimization. While a far cry from 15.770 times more likely, this is still a very large increase in victimization risk. White females (Exp(*B*) = 0.473) are significantly safer, in terms of sexual assault victimization, than non-White females. Being White made females significantly safer (they were almost 53% less likely to report sexual assault, controlling for other factors). Note that living alone was significant in the combined sample (all cases); it was not significant in either of the gender specific subsamples.

Let us move to table 12.4, which examines reported sexual harassment victimization. Unlike the sexual assault example above, we will discuss only those coefficients that are statistically significant. Looking at the sample with both genders (table 12.4, column 1), sexual orientation, gender, membership in a fraternity/sorority, being on a sports team (intercollegiate or campus), and race all impacted reported sexual harassment victimization. Three of those relationships are positive: sexual orientation (*B* = 1.206), gender (*B* = 1.660), and membership in a fraternity/sorority (*B* = 0.680). While these are all positive, the odds ratio can tell us how much increased risk there is for students that are GLBT, females, and members of fraternities or sororities. For sexual harassment, gender (Exp(*B*) = 5.258), has the strongest impact on victimization. Females are 5.258 times more likely to report sexual harassment than males.

Turning to sexual orientation, GLBT (Exp(*B*) = 3.341) students are 3.341 times more likely to report sexual harassment victimization. Finally, members of a fraternity/sorority (Exp(*B*) = 1.973) are almost twice as likely to report victimization. Moving to the negative relationships, being on a sports team (Exp(*B*) = 0.690) significantly lowered victimization. Participating on a sports team made one 0.690 times as likely to be a victim of sexual harassment. This means that controlling for all other factors, participation on a sports team meant the reported victimization was 31% less than those who were not participants on a team. For race, Whites (Exp(*B*) = 0.729) reported significantly less victimization than non-Whites. One could say that Whites were 27.1% less likely to report sexual harassment.

Sexual harassment for males (table 12.4, column 3) shows similar results to the combined sample (obviously the gender independent variable has been removed). Sexual orientation (Exp(*B*) = 4.994) and membership in a fraternity/sorority (Exp(*B*) = 1.753) increased the likelihood of sexual harassment. GBT males are almost five times (4.994) more likely to report sexual harassment victimization than heterosexual males. Membership in a fraternity increased victimization by 1.753 times or 75.3%. The negative relationships are the same as for the combined sample: being on a sports team (Exp(*B*) = 0.630) and race (Exp(*B*) = 0.569). Being on a sports team reduced male sexual harassment victimization by 37%. Turning to race, Whites were once again significantly less likely to be victimized. White males are 43.1% less likely to be sexually harassed than non-White males.

Finally, for females (table 12.4, column 3), the results are not similar to those for the full sample or for males. First of all, for females, sexual orientation has no relationship with sexual harassment. For males, sexual orientation is the strongest predictor of sexual harassment. For females, only membership in a sorority (Exp(*B*) = 3.139) and living on campus (Exp(*B*) = 2.538) have statistically significant relationships with reported sexual harassment victimization. Both of these variables are positively related to sexual harassment victimization. We can tell this by looking at the slope (*B*). For both, *B* is above 0 (sorority (*B* = 1.114) and living on campus (*B* = 0.931)). We can also recognize that the relationships are positive by noting that both of the odds ratios are above 1. Females in a sorority are over three times (3.139) times more likely to be sexually harassed, and females living on campus are 2.538 times more likely to be victimized.

Conclusion

As it stands, the various forms of regression are among the most frequently used statistical techniques in the social sciences due to their power and ease of interpretation. Conceptually simple but extremely powerful for prediction, they have remained one of the most popular methods in research. The refinement to the methods has led to the aforementioned logistic, probit (similar

Table 12.4 Victimization outcomes for sexual harassment

Independent variable	All cases		Male		Female	
	B	Exp(B)	B	Exp(B)	B	Exp(B)
Sexual orientation (1=Gay/Lesbian/Other)	1.206	3.341**	1.608	4.994**	0.939	2.557
Gender (1=female)	1.660	5.258**				
Fraternity/sorority	0.680	1.973**	0.561	1.753+	1.144	3.139*
On a sports team (intercollegiate or campus)	-0.372	0.690+	-0.462	0.630+	-0.304	0.738
International student	0.118	1.126	-0.089	0.915	0.244	1.276
Lives on campus	0.188	1.207	-0.269	0.764	0.931	2.538**
Age	-0.025	0.975	-0.099	0.906	0.137	1.147
Lives alone	-0.053	0.948	0.113	1.120	-0.262	0.769
Race (1=White)	-0.316	0.729+	-0.564	0.569*	-0.015	0.985
Chi-Square	158.138		25.689		18.979	
DF	9		8		8	
N	816		482		334	

+$p < .10$, *$p < .05$, **$p < .01$

to logit but having different data assumptions), and many other variants that apply a form of regression to nearly any data or research question possible. We presented only a brief overview of the various refinements of regression, and while we might have limited our examples to an example in the discipline of criminal justice, it is not hard to see the multitude of other scenarios that regression is applicable to.

References

Brown, R. D., Clarke, B., Gortmaker, V., & Robinson-Keilig, R. (2004). Assessing the campus climate for gay, lesbian, bisexual and transgender (GLBT) students using a multiple perspectives approach. *Journal of College Student Development, 45*(1), 8–26.

Coston, C. T. M. (2004). Worries about crime among foreign students studying in the United States: A comparative study. In C. T. M. Coston (Ed.), *Victimizing vunerable groups* (pp. 173–193). Westport, CT: Praeger.

Duncan, D. F. (1990). Prevalence of sexual assault victimization among heterosexual and gay/lesbian university students. *Psychological Reports, 66*(1), 65–66.

Fasting, K., Brackenridge, C. H., & Sungot-Borgen, J. (2003). Experiences of sexual harassment and abuse amongst Norwegian elite female atheletes and non-athletes. *Research Quarterly for Exercise and Sport, 74*(1), 84–97.

Gill, J., Johnson, P., & Clark, M. (2010). *Research methods for managers* (4th ed.). London: Sage.

Haase, R. F. (2011). *Multivariate general linear models*. Thousand Oaks, CA: Sage.

Healey, J. F. (2015). *Statistics: A tool for social research* (10th ed.). Stamford, CT: Cengage Learning.

Kutner, M. H., Nachtsheim, C. J., & Neter, J. (2004). *Applied linear regression models* (4th ed.). New York: McGraw-Hill Irwin.

Lehrer, J. A., Lehrer, V. L., Lehrer, E. L., & Oyarzun, P. B. (2007). Prevalence of and risk factors for sexual victimization in college women in Chile. *International Family Planning, 33*, 168–175.

Lewis-Beck, M. S. (1995). *Data analysis: An introduction*. Thousand Oaks, CA: Sage.

Long, J. S. (1997). *Regression models for categorical and limited dependent variables*. Thousand Oaks, CA: Sage.

Makepeace, J. M. (1987). Social factors and victim offender differences in courtship violence. *Family Relations, 36*(1), 87–91.

Monks, S. M., Tomaka, J., Palacios, R., & Thompson, S. E. (2010). Sexual victimization in female and male college students: Examining the roles of alcohol use, alcohol expectancies, and sexual sensation seeking. *Substance Use & Misuse, 45*(13), 2258–2280.

O'Connell, A. A. (2006). *Logistic regression models for ordinal response variables*. Thousand Oaks, CA: Sage.

Strang, K. D. (2012). Logistic planning with nonlinear goal programming models in spreadsheets. *International Journal of Applied Logistics, 2*(4), 1–14.

Tomsich, E. A., Gover, A. R., & Jennings, W. G. (2011). Examining the role of gender in the prevalence of campus victimization, perceptions of fear and crime, and the use of constrained behaviors among college students attending a large urban university. *Journal of Criminal Justice Education, 22*(2), 181–202.

Appendix

Description of variables for logistic regression example

- Sexual orientation
  1 = GLBT
  0 = heterosexual
- Gender
  1 = female
  0 = male
- Belongs to a fraternity/sorority
  1 = yes
  0 = no
- On a sports team (intercollegiate or campus)
  1 = yes
  0 = no
- International student
  1 = yes
  0 = no
- Lives on campus
  1 = yes
  0 = no
- Age
  Measured in years
- Lives alone
  1 = yes
  0 = no
- Race
  1 = White
  0 = non-White
  Categories of victimization experienced (0–4, sum of dichotomous variables for presence of psychological abuse, physical abuse, sexual assault, or sexual harassment)
- Psychological abuse
  1 = yes
  0 = no
- Physical abuse
  1 = yes
  0 = no
- Sexual harassment
  1 = yes

0 = no

- Sexual assault

1 = yes

0 = no

END OF DATA

13
Survey Method versus Longitudinal Surveys and Observation for Data Collection

John F. Gaski

Chapter overview

In this chapter Gaski applies the positivist ideology using the critical analysis research method. This method applies the literature review and general analytic techniques (including pairwise *t*-tests and other parametric statistics). The unit of analysis in the research strategy was the "inconsistent use of semantics across the years and journals for the survey, observation and experiment methods versus the incorrect use of these terms for data collection techniques," a deductive between-groups focus. The level of analysis was the social science literature. The generalization target was all practitioner-scholars intending to use these methods in their research design. Since the unit of analysis was qualitative and complex, very few positivistic techniques were applicable. However, the ideology remains positivist rather than Pragmatist due to evidence cited and the lack of interpretation on the data content done by the researcher.

Introduction

Although humanity's scientific progress and the advancement of knowledge over the millennia may seem relentless, world history also offers examples of knowledge lost. The consequences of the Roman Empire's fall and the subsequent Dark Ages would be the most familiar archetype. Think of Hellenic culture, Roman engineering, or almost any technical knowledge (in the Western world) that existed before the Middle Ages. Consider concrete, which became a nearly dormant substance for over 1000 years after having been perfected by ancient Rome. Or retrieve any archived episode of the History Channel's "Ancient Discoveries."

Knowledge loss can come about through less drastic means than slaughter of knowledge-bearing populations or the sacking and arson of the library at Alexandria in 642 A.D. (or 391 A.D. or 48 B.C., depending on the source. Precise knowledge about the date seems to have been lost!) Neglect, irresponsibility, and normal forgetting—albeit concurrently by a large group—can be sufficient modes of destruction.

A close-to-home example of a less substantive type helps to illustrate the tendency. Have you noticed that more and more social science scholars are mispronouncing the proper name, "Likert," as in Likert scale? Younger readers especially may not even be aware that Rensis Likert pronounced his last name with a short i, not a long i. Everyone else in the field seemed to do likewise only 20 or 30 years ago. Now, however, with the passage of more time separating us from Professor Likert, his work, and his contemporaries, knowledge of the original pronunciation is being lost among succeeding generations, and more frequently we hear the bastardized long i applied to the psychometrician's name.

The field of behavioral science indeed appears no more immune to "knowledge lost" syndrome than the rest of Western civilization is, at least in one epidemic instance. Namely, it has become clear that a large segment of the field's professoriate no longer knows what the term "survey" or "survey research" means. Then, in turn, the meaning of longitudinal research has also come to be corrupted. Fortunately, knowledge loss can sometimes be reversed.

The underlying issue

The essential definition of survey research, from a recognized authoritative source (at least according to votes in the textbook market), is this: "Survey is a large-sample, cross-sectional study.... The survey attempts to be representative of some known universe, both in terms of the number of cases included and in the manner of their selection" (Churchill 1976, pp. 75, 78; 1987, p. 91, 97). "Surveys... rely on a sample of elements from a population of interest that are measured at a single point in time" (Churchill & Iacobucci 2002, p. 122). The official American Psychological Association dictionary, conferring perhaps the ultimate imprimatur, corroborates with this definition of survey research: "a research method in which the investigator attempts to determine the current state of a population with regard to one or more attributes; a study in which a group of participants is selected from a population and some selected data... are collected, measured, and analyzed" (VandenBos 2007, p. 912).

More remote provenance from traditional behavioral science comes from Walter (1949, p. 315): "The survey uses a number of specific devices to bring together many kinds of data regarding its particular subject of interest. It attempts a comprehensive understanding of interlocking forces and facts." Kerlinger, in his familiar masterwork (1964, p. 393), distills the essence and provides a baseline: "Survey research is that branch of social scientific investigation that studies large and small populations (or universes) by selecting and studying samples chosen from the populations." Katz (1967, p. 148) adds: "Survey methodology includes any set of quantitative measurements taken of people in their natural habitat." (As a psychologist, that author artificially, but naturally, delimits the method to human study—while it is recognized that some include lower animals within the subject matter scope of psychology.)

The relevant feature to note about these varied but reconcilable definitions is this: they do not specify how data are to be collected. Survey does not require nor imply whether measurement or data collection will be done by communication (i.e., questionnaire) or observation, the two basic approaches to primary data acquisition. That is because survey is a research design, not a data collection/measurement method. A definite implication of this true realization of the survey definition, therefore, is that either questionnaire or observation can be used within the confines of a survey design.

For readers beginning to experience dissonance, denial, resistance, or even epiphany, total and sudden immersion may be best: contrary to prevailing misunderstanding, survey is not synonymous with questionnaire, or even roughly equivalent. The survey can be executed via either observation or questionnaire. See Schreier (1963, p. 34): "Surveys may be conducted by questioning or observing individuals"; and Wentz (1972, p. 75): "Survey data can be gathered by observation or inquiry." Vadum and Rankin (1998, p. 41) also recognize both data approaches as survey tools: "Surveys are passive-observational studies.... The subjects [*sic*] in a survey can be interviewed."

For an authority from classic behavioral science widely perceived as approaching the gold standard, consult Simon (1969, p. 229): "The survey can observe behavior.... The survey can also collect data on what people say.... The important distinction between the survey and the experiment is that the survey takes the world as it comes." This last nuance is an indication of the extent to which information on the subject seems to have been dissipated over the years. For emphasis, it is a large part of the essence of what "survey" really means: measuring the world as it is, irrespective of data-gathering approach, as opposed to the artificial intervention of the experiment.

Clearly, when Glock (1967, p. xix) says of the survey, "no restrictions on how the data are collected . . . no requirement that questionnaires be used at all," he is specifically allowing for the observation method. Katz (1967, p. 148) concurs: "The survey method may utilize behavioral observation, or verbal or written questioning." Kaplan (1964, p. 165) explicitly reminds that cross-sectional work may proceed by "observation of behavior in the circumstances in which it occurs." Kerlinger (1964, p. 395) also attests that observation is one way of obtaining survey data. Gee (1950, p. 307) seems to go even further in circumscribing the survey technique: "The procedures by which . . . gathering of data is accomplished may be classified as non-controlled and controlled observation"; but he does also acknowledge the questionnaire method. Early on, Lundberg (1929, p. 162) suggested, "Since the form of inquiry known as the social survey is nothing but . . . investigations or researches into related problems, all methods . . . of observing and recording data . . . may properly be applied."

As Boyd and Westfall (1964, p. 60) try to clarify and distinguish, yet obliquely preview the problem, "'survey' is also used . . . to denote any study in which data are gathered by interviewing. This is a more limited connotation than covered by the present use." Survey, in fact, is rightfully treated as virtually synonymous with cross-sectional research (e.g., Morgan and King 1971, p. 308). For intersubjective convergent verification, just refer again to the traditional definitions. Explicitly, "the cross-sectional study . . . is often called a sample survey" (Churchill & Iacobucci 2002, p. 117). Stevens et al. (1997, p. 65) reinforce: "Cross-sectional analysis . . . is sometimes referred to as a sample survey."

The critical error

Of course there are many sources that define survey contrarily, and that is the problem. Prominent examples abound, such as the following: (These are delivered anonymously. Enough erroneous definitions of survey can be found that it would be unfair, and would give undue focus, to single any out.)

- From a general behavioral science research text, "survey: all methods of securing information wherein it is obtained by asking others for it."
- From a psychology text: "Surveys are questionnaires and interviews that gather information by asking."
- From a handbook on survey research, "Survey: research technique where information requirements are specified, a population is identified, a sample selected and systematically questioned, and the results analyzed, generalized to the population, and reported."
- From a research dictionary: "surveys, also called questionnaires."

[These definitions would include experimental research if the dependent variable is measured by questionnaire. For that matter, they could also allow exploratory design within the definitional domain if focus group is the approach used.]

- From another psychology textbook: "To design a questionnaire and give it to a large sample of people...is the survey method."
- From a survey research text: "survey research—gathering information about a large number of people by interviewing a few of them."
  [These definitional entries also encompass experimental design if and when a dependent variable is measured by any type of interview-administered questionnaire (e.g., personal, web-interactive, or telephone).]
- From applied research texts: "Surveys require asking people, who are called respondents, for information using either verbal or written questioning." "Survey research is the systematic gathering of information from respondents...with some version of a questionnaire."
  [At least these two erroneous definitions (incorrect, that is, per preceding and subsequent material) technically rule out experiment by virtue of specification of "respondents"—as opposed to subjects.]

And then countless published articles use "survey" as mis-defined. In 2008 alone, for example, 66 *Journal of Applied Psychology* articles purported, described, or discussed survey-related method(s) and 50 (76%) incorrectly used the term as a synonym for a questionnaire at least once. In the *Psychological Bulletin*, in contrast, only one of seven such articles (14%) in the 2008 volume misused "survey" in that way. But other leading journals in allied behavioral science fields were also inspected, and implicated. Of 51 *Public Opinion Quarterly* articles purporting, describing, or discussing survey-related methods during the 2008 publication year, 24 (47%) incorrectly used "survey" as a synonym for questionnaire at least once. For another APA-sponsored journal, the *Journal of Consumer Research*, the erroneous proportion that same year within the targeted "survey"-use category was a remarkable 83%, or 24 of 29. (A few of these referenced items also wrongly used "survey" in the context of longitudinal research, to be detailed later.) Authors of the other 54 (of the 153 total) seem to know what the word "survey" means—that is, used it in accord with the original definition. The PB performance can be recognized as substantially superior or more accurate than that of the other journals, at the $p = 0.01$ level of significance or better, from table 13.1 results. It is not surprising that these errors would be viral, but the proportion of published misunderstanding may be troubling. Somehow, in short, many social science scholars have lost sight of the meaning of the word "survey."

By comparison, four decades earlier, in the year 1968, of 11 *Psychological Bulletin* articles that claimed or discussed survey method, only one misused the word as synonym for questionnaire. With *JAP* that year, it was only one of 12. For *POQ* in 1968, none of 21 made that particular mistake. *JCR*, in print

Table 13.1 Proportion of articles incorrectly using the word "survey" for "questionnaire"

2008	*PB**	*JAP*	*POQ*	*JCR*
1/7	50/66	24/51	24/29	
(14%)	(76%)	(47%)	(83%)	
1978				*JCR*
2/11				
(18%)				
1968	*PB*	*JAP*	*POQ*	
1/11	1/12	0/21		
(9%)	(8%)	(0%)		

**Psychological Bulletin, Journal of Applied Psychology, Public Opinion Quarterly,* and *Journal of Consumer Research,* respectively.

since 1974, allows but a three-decade retrospective scanning the 1978 volumes: Only two of the 11 pertinent articles that year exhibited the described mistake, that is, displayed ignorance of the correct meaning of "survey". Evidently, behavioral scholars of the '60s and '70s generally knew what the word "survey" means.

Paired comparisons: significance levels of differences among the listed journal/year proportions

$p < 0.001$: '08 *PB* vs. '08 *JAP*; '08 *PB* vs. '08 *JCR*; '08 *JAP* vs. '08 *POQ*; '08 *JAP* vs. '78 *JCR*; '08 *JAP* vs. '68 *PB*; '08 *POQ* vs. '68 *POQ*; '08 *JCR* vs. '78 *JCR*; '08 *JCR* vs. '68 *PB*; '08 *JCR* vs. '68 *JAP*; '08 *JCR* vs. '68 *POQ*.

$p < 0.01$: '08 *PB* vs. '08 *POQ*; '08 *POQ* vs. '78 *JCR*.

$p < 0.1$: '78 *JCR* vs. '68 *POQ*.

(All other comparisons were nonsignificant: '08 *PB* vs. '78 *JCR*; '08 *PB* vs. '68 *PB*; '08 *PB* vs. '68 *JAP*; '08 *PB* vs. '68 *POQ*; '08 *JAP* vs. '08 *JCR*; '78 *JCR* vs. '68 *PB*; '78 *JCR* vs. '68 *JAP*; '68 *PB* vs. '68 *JAP*; '68 *PB* vs. '68 *POQ*; '68 *JAP* vs. '68 *POQ*.)

Elaborative argument

Could this counterposed numerical record not be fairly seen as a waxing popular certification of the putative neo-definition of survey, or is it more a testament to the extreme extent of a counterfeit usage and the ensuing lost-knowledge scourge in a major field, on this matter? The latter will continue to be argued presently. Beyond the documentation listed above, much more of which could have been offered argumentatively for overkill, the author posits that any reader's professional experience should confirm that the "survey"-as-questionnaire misunderstanding is now very widespread in some fields. It demonstrably is true of leaders in social science research, as verified by evidence from the preceding targeted literature review and examples to come. As the review also reveals, it was not always this way.

But, again, with so many seemingly corroborative definitions equating survey with measurement by questionnaire, why would this not therefore constitute an established, though nouveau, consensus? Meaning follows usage, after all. Why prefer a possibly archaic definition over a modern one? The rebuttal to this rationalization and contrived casuistry is straightforward. (Analogously, when a pandemic surpasses majority incidence, does it thus automatically transmute into something legitimized as desirable?)

First, basic principles of evaluating secondary information sources—which is the task at hand—provide guidance. The relevant rule is that original or primary sources of secondary data are given precedential credibility over derived or secondary sources of secondary data (Churchill 1976, p. 129; 1987, p. 183; Churchill and Brown 2007, p. 151; Simon 1969, pp. 343–345). Accordingly, "survey" means cross-sectional design (along with the representativeness condition, that is), not data collection by questionnaire. (Cross-sectional design that also fulfills the representative sample requirement qualifies as survey, in other words.) Because the original definition was, in fact, the original, due credit must be bestowed.

Moreover, these come-lately revisionist definitions and uses, and presumptive definers, simply forfeit the debate by default. Despite extensive search, none have been found that attempt to refute or even address the original definition, to even present an argument for the superior viability of the newer proto-definition over the classic one. They just blithely or fatuously offer a clumsy and, to be shown, incoherent neologism in evident disregard of the lexicographic conflict. On this basis alone, the case should be closed by walkover in favor of the position argued here and the first-mover, vanguard, primal definition of survey, which does happen to have indelible "squatter's rights."

No matter how much we may wish to paper over the problem by imposing a deconstructive rendering to the effect that the survey definition has evolved naturally and legitimately, substantive support for such a claim is absent. As shown throughout, there is much basis for the contrary conclusion. The field of linguistics, unfortunately, has no definite rule for when a neologismic rival meaning for a word is allowed to supplant an established one. It is more of a mass tug-of-war or aggregate mud-wrestling match (Mair 2006, pp. 3, 19, 39–40, 73, 87–88, 93, 153, 205; blame this author, not the cited one, for the imagery). This paper is an attempt to supply rightful force on the established, original, traditional side. Just because nonstandard use of an expression has become widespread does not mean that scholars must surrender to it. Science must never ratify the unsupported, let alone the incorrect.

To elaborate further, if even necessary at this point, if survey now means questionnaire measurement, then those terms are redundant. There would then be two terms for questionnaire and none for (non-field study) cross-sectional research. That combination produces inefficient and incongruous nomenclature, and is thereby objectively disallowed. Acquiescence to the evolved use pattern in this case simply produces incoherent terminology, in other words.

One other squelch, perhaps: What does a geological surveyor do? Does that surveyor employ observation or questionnaire? *Q.E.D.* Or is that case too far afield to serve as exemplar? Instead, significantly, one must acknowledge that the word "survey" long predates social science research (ca. 1386; *Online Etymology Dictionary*, 2012) and its etymology should therefore be respected, or at least not ignored. Ultimate derivation traces to the French supervidre and in turn the Latin supervidre, meaning literally over-looker or overseer (Schuman 1997), and obviously connotes measurement by observation!

Touché? If not, more: What is the generic meaning of the term "survey course"? Ponder "surveillance." What of the astronomical survey, for that matter? Or, ironically, see the book titled, *Survey of Social Science* (Smith 1945). Wheeler, Goodale, and Deese (1975, pp. 13–14) provide yet another clincher to the case, without even trying, with two less than exotic examples of the survey method: "studying the contents of animals' stomachs to determine their feeding habits [and] random inspection of assembly-line products to maintain quality control." No questionnaire communication involved at all, is there? (In fact, these illustrations signify why readers from the physical sciences may wonder what the commotion is all about.)

All eight definitions of "survey," as verb and noun, in a leading dictionary (ten including "surveying," 12 including "surveyor") involve measurement by observation only (*Britannica World Language Dictionary*, 1959, p. 1263). *Webster's* (1965, p. 748), matches this eight-for-eight, ten-for-ten, and 12-for-12 performance. *Merriam-Webster* (1974, p. 689) also goes eight-for-eight in favor of observation. The unabridged *Webster's Third New International* (1993) lists 19 observation-based "survey" definitions (27 and 30, respectively, also including the two derivatives), and none manifestly involving communication. The most up-to-date English language resource, Dictionary.com (2012) incorporating the latest editions of preeminent print dictionaries, lists 39 survey definitions, as noun or verb, and all either explicitly state the observational method or are compatible with it. None mentions the communication approach. Then, the primary definition of "survey" as transitive verb, from an even more primary source (*Webster's*, 1941), is (was) "to examine...with a scrutinizing eye, inspect"—which even more concretely designates observation as an allowed method within the rubric.

Roget's Thesaurus (1977, p. 1247) also weighs in with support. The cross-listed entries for "survey" include collection, examination, measurement, scrutiny, and view (as noun); examine, measure, and scrutinize (as verb). Linked words for "surveying" and "surveyor" are assessment, location, mensuration; measurer, and supervisor, respectively. The only indexed items in the whole set suggestive of communication more than observation are "canvass" and "discuss," so the overall profile is one of strong vindication of this paper's position.

Now, what if we were to find a dictionary that does include survey-as-questionnaire among the definitions? We can, in fact, such as *Webster's Online Dictionary* (2012), which lists the questionnaire method as twentieth out of 20 entries, including specialty field definitions. Does this discovery invalidate the position advanced in this paper? No; first, the fact that survey defined as questionnaire appears well down the list in a legitimate source does not contest the primacy of the other, originalist definition presented here. In fact, it confirms it. Second, where do you suppose modern-day lexicographers found that contrary definition, other than newer sources in the research field who report the heretical definition out of ignorance? Third, if we are counting definitions, "survey equals questionnaire" is outvoted or out-pointed by a huge margin. Finally, even if one were to accept survey-as-questionnaire as an authentic secondary (actually, well below tertiary), subordinate, down-the-list, colloquial, idiosyncratic definition, it would not challenge in any way the primary point argued here that survey research may involve measurement by observation.

Merely excavating a lower-level dictionary definition that endorses survey as questionnaire is not exculpatory. To the contrary, you can usually find someone, somewhere, who will say anything! A single maverick or renegade deviancy of this type signifies a scandal more than authentication, but that, sadly, is the thin reed of defense those who misuse "survey" in the way described must rely upon, especially if resorting to the now-rebutted posture that the word has genuinely evolved. From the wide-angle perspective, that is also the indefensible checkmated situation the behavioral science field finds itself in concerning this scientific fundamental. Of course, it is no real surprise that a newer definition would be contaminated by the destructive linguistic tendency spotlighted in this review, dramatizing the lost knowledge effect.

Yes, meaning often follows usage in ordinary language, sometimes reasonably and productively, sometimes senselessly and evasively, but such casual and even sloppy lexicography as exposed here cannot be abided with scientific argot. For that technical purpose, more of a formal language system is desirable (Nagel, 1961, p. 93; Popper, 1959, p. 71; Rudner, 1966, pp. 15–16). The pioneering Lundberg (1929, p. 54) foresaw "the futility of much argument...resulting from a poor definition of the terms employed." Echoing and applicable is Hunt's critique of a different but analogous scientific malapropism: "Such abuse may result in little harm in ordinary conversation, but may have serious, unintended consequences in research and scientific writing" (1976, p. 134).

In the formative period of behavioral research, Eubank (1927, pp. 386–400) proposed "criteria by which a term is to be accepted or rejected...[or] tests of a true scientific concept: (1) Is the term reasonably precise? Does it convey an exact and clear-cut meaning? (2) Does the term convey only one final idea? (3) Is the term perfectly general...always employed in the same sense wherever it is used?" Applied to the issue of "survey" misuse in behavioral science, these questions could be regarded as a bill of indictment. No, "survey" has not come to mean questionnaire, and continued dereliction will not make it so. The word has come to be misunderstood, misused, and therefore misunderstood further.

To be sure, it is understandable that the psychological research field in particular would naturally come to equate survey with questionnaire, if for no other reason than verbal convenience. Students of the individual's mental processes, engaged in "study of the soul" (per literal meaning of the word "psychology"), after all, must often measure unobservable characteristics, and that almost inevitably requires communication instead of observation. It would be no surprise, therefore, if nearly 100% of all research in psychology—survey, experimental, or otherwise—employed questionnaire measurement for at least some variables. Hence, the survey-questionnaire distinction becomes muddled. But even if survey research in a field would somehow correspond universally to one data collection method, that does not equalize the two or excuse outright misapplication of language.

Actually, the way the research profession has treated, or mistreated, the word "survey" is not even adequate for the semantics of a common or natural language system. Lifting Hunt's poignant expression of frustration with a similar case of dysfunctional ambiguity: "This usage is by no means a consensus position because there is no consensus concerning the term" (1976, p. 134). Distinctively, in the present "survey" dilemma, there may in fact be a modern, trendy consensus. It just happens that the consensus would be wrong.

Semantics are not trivial—another truth that seems to have been misplaced or repressed. A classic reference nominates primary and basic aims of semantics: "(1) To help the individual think straighter. (2) To improve communication between individuals and between groups" (Chase, 1948, p. 249). It is at this rudimentary level that a branch of social science research and scholarship has failed in this instance.

The scientific importance

So, where are we? Is our definitional situation a pure standoff? We find some sources for and some against each interpretation of survey.

On the contrary (a) survey as cross-sectional design is favored and (b) survey as questionnaire is rejected on the basis of (1) primacy of definition a and (2) no extant rationale for the alternative usage b; (3) the stated logical basis for disallowing usage b; (4) the deep historical etymology supporting definition a; and (5) contemporary lexicography in the form of overwhelming mainstream dictionary guidance.

But what difference does any of this really make? So what, if the definition or interpretation of survey has "evolved," shall we say, over time? No self-respecting veteran of philosophy of science training would be so dismissive, but the questions will be answered nevertheless.

The conceptual level

One major concern arising from the linguistic imprecision at issue would be conceptual confusion. Clear and definite classification is the starting point for theory, explanation, and understanding (Bunge, 1967, p. 75; Harvey, 1969, p. 326). If definition is ambiguous, clean classification is likewise undermined, maybe even impossible. "Definition and classification of terms... [are]... an essential step in any area of inquiry that purports to use the scientific method.... [T]here must be an agreed-upon point of departure" (Engel, Kollat, & Blackwell, 1973, pp. 659–660). Corroboration can be found even in sundry sources in the physical sciences:

> Classification is one of the fundamental concerns of science. Facts and objects must be arranged in an orderly fashion before their unifying principles can be discovered and used as a basis for prediction.... [U]nless some system is created among them, they would be unlikely to provide any useful information. (Sokal, 1966)

Teas and Palan (1997) diligently discuss the damage done to theory by a poor language system, definitional ambiguity in particular. Lewis and Erickson (1969) also capture the importance of the scientific basics:

> Unless there is agreement as to the "meaning" of a term, the result will be confusion rather than clarity and order. To encourage an arbitrary definition... is to retreat from the first requirement of making a discipline scientific—that is, to provide a taxonomy within which one can classify. (pp. 11–12)

Alternative, incompatible impressions of what the word "survey" means disturb and even vitiate the metatheoretical utility of any other construct that intersects with, or approaches, the conceptual space of survey. This literally creates conceptual and theoretical incoherence, resulting in a scrambling of conceptual sets. (Later, that will be explicitly demonstrated with the term "longitudinal" and the concepts of observation and data collection generally.) In effect, if the box connected to the arrow is squishy, of what value is the arrow or possibly even the box at the other end? Such amorphousness then warps the surrounding space of nearby constructs in a perverse way. This condition is an untenable, intolerable foundation for thinking, let alone scientific thinking.

The epistemological aspect

Not to be overlooked either is miscomprehension of the literature accruing from misunderstanding of a fundamental and universal technical term. To be sure, one who believes in "survey = questionnaire" would have an understanding consistent with much of the social science research literature, though consistently erroneous. This compounding and snowballing misperception would tend to abet the knowledge-loss phenomenon unremittingly into the future, and apparently this mechanism is what has been functioning historically. Toward an accurate potential understanding of the full behavioral science literature, and beyond, the recognition transmitted in this paper is encouraged.

The implications

A more pragmatic consequence, especially growing from the conceptual issue, for researchers, research educators, and research students would be confusion among research designs and data collection methods. Figure 13.1 reproduces a research methods schematic from a leading introductory behavioral science textbook (again, anonymously similar figures are fairly common.) The authors fall victim to the confusion described herein, and this error induces cascading misclassification. Because the authors appear to erroneously equate survey with measurement by questionnaire (based on their surrounding text, as well), they are at sea and stultified in trying to locate observation.

As can be seen in the upper bracket, observation is positioned mistakenly as co-equal with a research design when it is merely a form of data collection or measurement method. (Or is experiment falsely reduced to the data collection method level?) But if one believes that survey means questionnaire, not realizing that it is a research design, this quandary is inescapable. As Glock (1967, p. xi) laments, "there are widespread misconceptions among social scientists who consider themselves informed, as to what it means to use survey methods in scientific research. Sometimes, survey research is conceived of too narrowly as being solely a data collection device."

Or perhaps the figure 13.1 authors correctly understand survey to be a design but misunderstand it as one that necessarily implies and requires questionnaire measurement. This is simply a different abortive route to the same misclassification of observation and the resulting incoherence. Regardless, the focal column in the figure 13.1 conflates a measurement approach with two research designs, and this problem is ultimately attributable to mixing "survey" and "questionnaire."

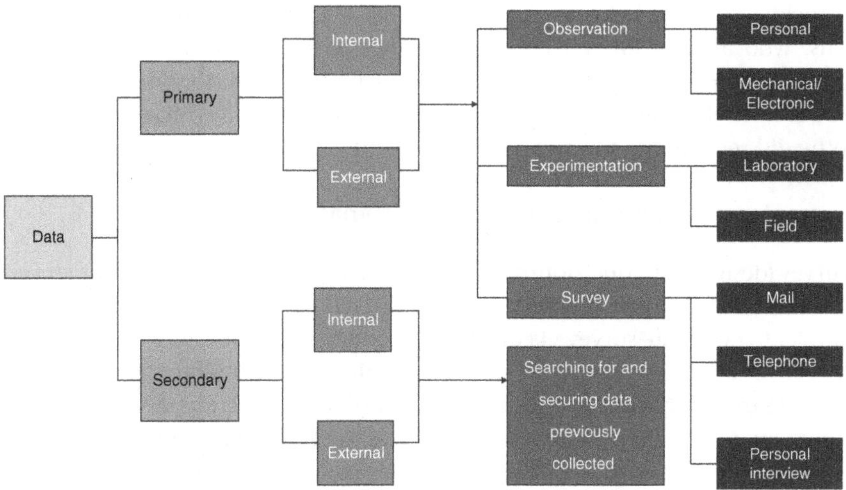

Figure 13.1 Commonly perceived organization of research design and measurement.

Table 13.2 Corrected research design and measurement method relations

Method in research design	Measurement technique	Administration process
Survey	Communication (questionnaire); Observation	Written (mail, email, fax), website, telephone, personal interview
Observation	Humans Nonhumans (objects, animals)	Personal or automated; Personal or automated (mechanical)
Longitudinal survey	Communication (questionnaire); Observation	Written (mail, email, fax), website, telephone, personal interview
Experiment	Laboratory observation, sample, or questionnaire Field observation, sample, or questionnaire	Written, personal interview, automated (computer or mechanical), intrusive sample (e.g., blood draw).

Table 13.2 provides a corrected framework. Aside from adding longitudinal as a design, for more exhaustiveness, it accurately collects research designs at one methodological level, then portrays data collection (i.e., measurement) approaches at the next in a way that clarifies how either questionnaire or observation can be employed with either survey or experiment—in fact, any of the three designs—addressing another source of confusion for some neophyte social science students.

Incidentally, for behavioral science–based readers who already knew all of this, who already knew that survey allows observational measurement, (1) please bear with the presentation; and (2) why have you not done something about it, that is, about the near-ubiquitous and oppressive misapprehension? Why did remedy have to await this treatment?

Examples of design-measurement combinations

Survey (design) with questionnaire (measurement): about 99+ % of all survey (per the correct definition) research published in the social science literature. (It is correct to designate survey via questionnaire measurement as "survey" research, by definition. It would also be accurate to call it "questionnaire research." One refers to the design, one to the measurement or data collection method. What is not accurate is to delimit survey to that measurement approach.)

Survey (design) with observation (measurement): (1) an arena owner's study of whether seat location relates to beer consumption by monitoring a random sample of seats via human (or remote camera) observers during an event; (2) a study of whether residential house size relates to number and style of automobiles driven, with all variables measured by observation (though likely laboriously). (In each case, measurement could have been done by questionnaire. With either observation or questionnaire measurement, a cross-sectional, one-time data set obtains; hence, a survey.)

Longitudinal (design) with questionnaire (measurement): (1) Michigan Survey Research Center Index of Consumer Sentiment involving five questions administered to repeated national samples; (2) daily pre-election political tracking polls. Longitudinal (design) with observation (measurement): same-store sales performance analysis.

Laboratory experimental (design) with questionnaire (measurement): controlled testing of effect of alternative prototype TV ads on brand preference, with dependent variable measured by written questionnaire item(s). Laboratory experimental (design) with observation (measurement): controlled testing of effect of alternative prototype TV ads on quasi-purchase behavior, with dependent variable measured by simulated shopping, behavioral sample product choice.

Field experimental (design) with questionnaire (measurement): test marketing of advertising effect on attitude, with mail or email questionnaire measurement of dependent variable. Field experimental (design) with observation (measurement): conventional new product test marketing, with sales response the dependent variable.

Summary reflection

The foregoing conceptual and taxonomic morass is a direct derivative of misunderstanding of the word "survey." The following assertion should be seen as less than radical: language is important. Semantics, particularly definition, amounts to a component assembly part of the launch pad for science. Obviously, if that foundation or scaffolding is deficient, defective, or weak, the scientific enterprise can be subverted.

How so, in this case? A tendency to associate the communication/questionnaire approach to data collection with cross-sectional research can cause a myopic tendency to underutilize observation as a measurement method. Again, as the great Simon says, "I want to decrease the likelihood that students will rush blindly to use the questionnaire survey.... [T]oo often people do questionnaire research just because they do not realize that there may indeed be much better methods for getting the knowledge they want" (1969, p. 246). Concordantly, the author has witnessed a naïve student (and even faculty) presumption that experimental research dictates measurement only by observation (for the dependent variable)—because students and faculty tend to think that measurement by communication is a survey! This is the kind of harm foretold by Simon and Hunt, as cited above.

A needlessly bemusing riddle for those who equate the survey and questionnaire methods is apt: When you do measure an experimental dependent variable by questionnaire, do you also refer to that instrument as a "survey"? (Some in the accompanying bibliography do exactly that.) If not, why not? Oh, "survey" only refers to nonexperimental, for example, cross-sectional, research with communication-based measurement? Communication as opposed to what? So you do implicitly acknowledge that the cross-sectional design also allows the other measurement approach, that is, observation.

This hypothetical exchange sequence brings the targeted misunderstanding, and above false paradox, into bolder relief and very close to enlightenment. That is, if questionnaire is ever used in an experiment, then it cannot be equivalent to survey, which is a different design. Or is this all an exercise in academic navel gazing, à la how many definitions can fit on the head of a pin? As referenced, Chase, Churchill, Eubank, Glock, Hunt, Lundberg, Schuman, and Simon would disagree. Or review the "Importance" section. Actually, the argument presented here has the forensic playing field to itself, so far, even though the contrary linguistic behavior saturates journal pages. That contrary position, it should be noted, does not bother with any shred of basis or justification.

Derived, focal issue: Longitudinal loose ends and closure

The established APA-certified, Churchillian, and Simonesque definition of survey relied upon here, itself the offspring of others even more foundational and original, does yield the conclusion that survey is tantamount to cross-sectional design, as defended in the foregoing argument and despite its prevalent misunderstanding. More precisely, as mentioned, survey and cross-sectional are nearly synonymous, save for the one particular exceptional case noted earlier. (The design called the field study, per its own strict original meaning, qualifies as cross-sectional but not survey, technically, for reasons given.)

As inferable from previous exposition, there can be no such thing as a longitudinal survey, by definition, because longitudinal and survey research are different, mutually exclusive designs (Churchill & Iacobucci, 2002, pp. 110, 117; Simon, 1969, pp. 284–286). Survey involves one-time measurement and longitudinal means repeated measures over time (Hollingworth, 1927, pp. 34–35; Menard, 1991, p. 4). There may be differing interpretations of "survey" regnant, with one unfounded and obtuse, but any conflation of survey and longitudinal research, as done in recent as well as prominent articles over the decades, seems to be less pandemic but far more than a novelty. Yet this treatment was probably inevitable given the widespread misappropriation of "survey" as questionnaire. Some exemplars of the self-contradictory "longitudinal survey" locution are Toch (1953), Holland (1968, pp. 1–10), Judge and Livingston (2008, p. 999), Rindfleisch et al. (2008), and Rasinski, Lee, and Krishnamurty (2012, p. 229), along with the familiar National Longitudinal Survey of Youth misnomer (e.g., as cited in Goldberg et al., 2008; Hom, Roberson & Ellis 2008; and Judge & Hurst 2008). (Next, will survey and experiment be parties to an illicit merger, terminologically, per the nonreason of the preceding riddle feature? Remarkably, this tendency already can be found in the supplementary bibliography (Erez et al., 2008; Fan & Wanous, 2008; Levi & Fried, 2008)—quite apart from the legitimate use to identify experiment overlaid upon a survey.) Clear enough, but some subtlety intrudes upon contemplation of variations.

What if a survey is repeated at a subsequent time, but with different sample elements? The term "longitudinal survey" would actually make some intuitive sense in that case, but still cannot be allowed as semantically authentic, as of now, per the basic survey definition requiring one point in time, or cross-sectional, measurement. The proper term for such temporally repeated data collection is simply "longitudinal research" or even "multiple cross-sectional," although a new term may be needed to distinguish it from intertemporal study of a single entity or a panel, respectively. "Cross-wave" has also been seen as label for this design (Fienberg & Tanur, 1986, pp. 77–78) as has "trend analysis" (Bock, 1979, pp. 211–214) and "successive independent sample design" (Shaughnessy & Zechmeister, 1977, pp. 147–150). "Cross-sectional time-series," more recently displayed by Luo and Homburg (2008, p. 33), has inherent meaning but would not appear to adequately differentiate between panel and independent intertemporal samples. "Repeated measures" has been used for the panel designation purpose in the past (Maxham & Netemeyer, 2002) to distinguish from (a) the preceding or even (b) single-entity longitudinal (such as national economy time series). The panel per se is also what is sometimes meant by "longitudinal survey" (e.g., Johns Hopkins University, 2008), we must acknowledge. Clear as mud, is it not?

The expression "longitudinal survey" does have some reputable afield precedent (Bureau of Labor Statistics, 2008; Fienberg & Tanur, 1986), though used even there in a way that duplicates the error of equating survey with questionnaire. It is ultimately problematic, however, whether the term is a considered, innovative linguistic hybrid or just an imprecise mongrel or mutation. Perhaps the usage will take hold even more widely and be justified, for once, but it would need some official or formal ratification, perhaps at the professional association level—again, if we aspire toward a formal language system.

However, this prospective usage of "longitudinal survey" would still appear to be terminally redundant. Accepting Simon's (1969) transcendental interpretation of survey as "taking the world as it comes," that methodological approach also is inherent in any longitudinal research. In other words, "longitudinal survey" as opposed to what, longitudinal experiment? (This does not contest the familiar before-and-after time dimension that may exist technically within experimental design; Campbell & Stanley, 1963, p. 58.) So the "longitudinal" descriptor would therefore presuppose the "world as it comes" tack versus experimental intervention, and the survey-longitudinal dichotomy remains one of single vis-à-vis multiple measurement occasions. Again, the only possible underlying basis for a "longitudinal survey" terminology is seen as the fundamental misconstrual of survey as questionnaire, which renders the term "longitudinal" alone sufficient for the intertemporal measurement design. (And for the microtemporal aspect within experimental design, the preferred language "pre-post" or "before-after" is the norm, which avoids confusion with true longitudinal research; Campbell & Stanley, 1963, p. 13.)

Why not the facile resolution of using "survey" for one-time (nonexperimental) data gathering and "longitudinal survey" for repeated measurement of the same type? A rhetorical question may dispatch. Those unconvinced by the preceding volume of material should be compelled to answer the question: What meaning is transmitted by the term "longitudinal survey" beyond that contained in "longitudinal"? Measurement approach, for example, questionnaire, is already dismissed analytically and voluminously. Or could the referent be independent sequential samples instead of fixed panel—or vice versa? No substantive defense (rather than crude custom) of conferring "survey" designation on one but not the other is found in the major literature. Hence, the redundancy conclusion.

Taxonomic detail: Longitudinal versus panel

Does not longitudinal research also require a fixed sample or panel, by definition? Some scholars do bracket the two (e.g., Shaughnessy & Zechmeister, 1997, pp. 150–152) but, although panels are commonly used in longitudinal designs, their fixed sample characteristic traditionally is not mandated by the definition of longitudinal (Simon, 1969, p. 284). Whether studying change with a continuing panel or different sequential samples, it is still a matter of investigating intertemporal phenomena and data for a population proxy, therefore longitudinal. (This idiographic design is occasionally and simply called time-series analysis in some fields; Frederiksen & Rotondo 1979, pp. 133–134—although others reserve the term for particular factor-decompositional analytics, e.g., ARIMA.) Raskind et al. (1998, p. 268) and Menard (1991, p. 4) recognize that longitudinal design allows inclusion of "the same or at least comparable [units] from one period to the next" (emphasis supplied), and therefore is not categorically identical to panel research. White and Arzi (2005, p. 138), however, are among those who believe that only "the same individuals or entities" qualify under the "longitudinal" rubric. Another surprising source that equates longitudinal research with panel design is the official American Psychological Association glossary (2013).

One reason for adducing this ad hoc maxim concerning the longitudinal-panel relation, or just noting the reality, is that there is no bright-line distinction between longitudinal research with and without panel, yet the two variants clearly exist. What of panel "mortality" (attrition, alternatively), for example? How much panelist drop-out with replacement is allowed before one period's sample is substantially distinct from a prior period's—5%, 10%, 20%, more? At what point is this phenomenon materially no different from independent samples with some inadvertent common elements? The prototype cases are defined but the categorical demarcation could be fuzzy. Consider, for instance, the "revolving panel" (McKinney, 1994).

To illustrate an extreme, the author has worked for decades with a so-called panel of one of the ten largest commercial polling and market research firms in the world, utilizing independent annual samples of 2000 out of a panel pool of 200,000 US households. Yet this method is loosely but universally referred to as a "panel." (Note, to augment an earlier point: This author does not reveal here whether measurement has been accomplished by questionnaire or observation!)

Again, though, this is not the sole issue regarding what is ordinarily if paradoxically termed longitudinal "survey." Many authors cited throughout were also equating survey with the questionnaire measurement instrument itself, contrary to the original meaning. For example: "Participants were sent four…mail surveys" (Fan & Wanous, 2008, p. 1394); "fill out a survey" (Oyserman & Lee, 2008, p. 313); "surveys completed by a…respondent," "surveys that employ a single-scale format" (Rindfleisch et al., 2008, pp. 262–263). Also, we encounter "surveys consisting of the 30…items" (Neubert et al., 2008, p. 1223); "filled in one general survey," "surveys were returned" (Sonnentag,

Binnewies, & Mojza 2008, p. 676); "mailed envelopes containing the...survey" (Tepper et al., 2008, p. 723). Ferris et al. (2008); Keutzer, Lichtenstein, and Mees (1968, p. 527); Maslach and Leiter (2008, p. 503); Montes and Irving (2008, pp. 1371–1372); and Orvis, Dudley, and Cortina (2008, p. 1186) illustrate further.

To sum up, we seem to have superfluous terminology for some methods and not enough or absent descriptors for others. Richer, more precise, and generally accepted nomenclature may be needed to distinguish time-series study of a single entity, a fixed panel, and multiple sequential samples. Surveying (!) the broad panorama of mainstream behavioral science, Menard (1991, p. 5) decries "the lack of consensus regarding what constitutes longitudinal research." Then, "there is no single concrete definition of the longitudinal method" (Baltes & Nesselroade, 1979, p. 1). (Perhaps there was at one time.) And to be clear, the vexatious, sometimes subtle details of this section compound and aggravate the earlier issue of a field's wholesale violation of definitional—therefore philosophy of science—norms concerning "survey." This is the crux or key insight for emphasis: because of misunderstanding and misuse of the word "survey," the term "longitudinal" has also been hashed in the scientific literature. As a result, a plenary semantic initiative and resolution is advocated here.

The lesson, in brief: "survey" is not interchangeable with "questionnaire." It is a research design, not a data collection method. Therefore, survey is incompatible with longitudinal research, which is a different design—so the term "longitudinal survey" is an oxymoron, misused by those who conceptually confound "survey" with a particular data collection approach. Likewise, with "survey panel" (e.g., Rossi & Crain, 1968, p. 267; Wang et al., 2008). Fortunately, the word "panel" or sometimes even "longitudinal" alone suffices, so correction is straightforward. (If data collection via communication is also meant, try "longitudinal-questionnaire" or "questionnaire panel," as appropriate.) Perhaps this paper will provide momentum for the more parsimonious, and correct usage to regain the acceptance it formerly enjoyed for decades. If it fails, it may signify future linguists' demarcation of a new formal definition—and even more abiding confusion.

Final reflection

To any reader annoyed by the elementary level of much of the preceding discussion, it is necessitated, unfortunately, by the long-term record of error and even negligence of a preponderant segment of empirical literature, as reported. This is in marked contrast to the otherwise impressive record and proud tradition of social science and its subfields examined here. (See the high-impact factors for *JAP* and *PB*.) It is understandable why the layman would mistakenly tend to equate survey with questionnaire or questionnaire-based research. After all, the overwhelming majority of surveys, such as opinion polls, that laymen—and even university students and researchers—are exposed to would employ data collection by communication, not observation (Grosof & Sardy, 1985, p. 109). For the layman it is probably close to 100%, thus when seeing or hearing "survey" he or she naturally thinks questionnaire. But scholars, especially those supposed to be expert in research methods, should have been able to meet a higher standard of discernment. The "clumsy neologism" description applied earlier may be mild for such an enduring, fundamental lapse by nearly an entire field that infects not only research, but generations of those scholars' students (as confirmed by corresponding generations of leading textbooks and journals). If not true, then why do we find the basic errors so readily identifiable here?

The ultimate ontological question left by this exercise may be: Is it important, or not, for a behavioral science research field to use scientific language accurately, in particular to know what the word "survey" means? Is it important, or not, for research scholars to know what they are talking about—at the most fundamental level? The issue is no less than that. In this review and argument the various forms of damage caused by the central misunderstanding are elaborately itemized, so no reader can credibly retort that the consequences do not matter. The corollary concern of possible harm to a field's image before those with a more grounded understanding of research lexicon can be considered a second-order effect that all should want to resolve immediately.

Might it be quixotic for this piece to attempt to dismantle and amend even a small fragment of the nomenclature of an entire field, and then presume for the product to be accepted by that audience? Perhaps, no such presumption is involved. If demonstrably incorrect and incoherent usage can be carelessly adopted by nearly an entire scientific population, spanning several fields actually, why not eventual acceptance of alternative usage that does have rational support? The only presumption is confidence in audience judgment, once the issue is finally mapped out accurately, as this paper has sought to do. "A journey of a thousand miles begins with a single step." The author also hopes the benefits of the atavistic but classical terminology as outlined can provide incentive for rhetorical conversion.

To punctuate the gravity of the prevailing juncture, the following needs to be recognized objectively. The amount of error-laden literature such as cited here across different fields, in view of its content, inescapably suggests that many scholars must have suffered confused internalization of some very basic research nomenclature. That condition is not suitable for a serious behavioral science or a mature discipline—thus, the motivation for this effort to reclaim lost knowledge.

References

American Psychological Association. (2013). *Glossary of psychological terms.* http://www.apa.org/research/action/glossary.aspx (accessed June 25, 2013).

Baltes, P. B., & Nesselroade, J. R. (1979). History and rationale of longitudinal research. In J. R. Nesselroade & P. B. Baltes (Eds), *Longitudinal research in the study of behavior and development* (pp. 1–39). New York: Academic Press.

Bock, R. D. (1979). Univariate and multivariate analysis of variance of time-structured data. In J. R. Nesselroade & P. B. Baltes (Eds), *Longitudinal research in the study of behavior and development* (pp. 199–231). New York: Academic Press.

Boyd, H. W. Jr. & Westfall, R. (1964). *Marketing research,* Homewood, IL: Richard D. Irwin, Inc.

Britannica World Language Dictionary. (1959). Vol. 2 Chicago: Encyclopedia Britannica, Inc.

Bunge, M. (1967). *Scientific research I: The search for system.* New York: Springer-Verlag.

Bureau of Labor Statistics, U. S. Department of Labor (2008). *National longitudinal surveys.* http://www.bls.gov/nls/ (accessed November 9, 2008).

Campbell, D. T., &. Stanley J. C. (1963). *Experimental and quasi-experimental designs for research.* Chicago, IL: Rand McNally.

Chase, S. (1948). *The proper study of mankind.* New York: Harper & Brothers.

Churchill, G. A. Jr. (1976). *Marketing research: Methodological foundations.* Hinsdale, IL: The Dryden Press.

Churchill, G. A. Jr. (1987). *Marketing research: Methodological foundations* (4th ed.). Hinsdale, IL: The Dryden Press.

Churchill, G. A. Jr., & T. J. B. (2007). *Basic marketing research* (6th ed.). Mason, OH: South-Western.

Churchill, G. A. Jr., & Iacobucci, D. (2002). *Marketing research: Methodological foundations* (8th ed.). Mason, OH: South-Western.

Dictionary.com (2012). http://dictionary.reference.com/browse/survey (accessed December 16, 2012).

Engel, J. F., Kollat, D. T., & Blackwell, R. D. (1973). *Consumer behavior* (2nd ed.). New York: Holt, Rinehart, & Winston.

Eubank, E. E. (1927). The concepts of sociology. *Social Forces, 5*(3), 386–400.

Fienberg, S. E., & Tanur, J. M. (1986). The design and analysis of longitudinal surveys: Controversies and ssues of cost and continuity. In R. W. Pearson & R. F. Boruch (Eds), *Lecture notes in statistics,* Vol. 38 (pp. 60–93). Berlin: Springer-Verlag.

Frederiksen, C. H., & Rotondo, J. A. (1979). Time-series models and the study of longitudinal change. In J. R. Nesselroade & P. B. Baltes (Eds), *Longitudinal research in the study of behavior and development* (pp. 111–153). New York: Academic Press.

Glock, C.Y. ed. (1967). *Survey research in the social sciences.* New York: Russell Sage Foundation.

Goldberg, W. A., Prause, A., Lucas-Thompson, R., & Himsel, A. (2008). Maternal employment and children's achievement in context: A meta-analysis of four decades of research. *Psychological Bulletin, 134*(1), 77–108.

Grosof, M. S., & Hyman, S. (1985). *A research primer for the social and behavioral sciences.* Orlando, FL: Academic Press.

Harvey, D. (1969). *Explanation in geography,* New York: St. Martin's Press.

Holland, J. L. (1968). Explorations of a theory of vocational choice. *Journal of Applied Psychology, 52*(1, Part 2), 1–37.

Hollingworth, H. L. (1927). *Mental growth and decline: A survey of developmental psychology.* New York: Appleton.

Hom, P. W., Roberson, L., & Ellis, A. D. (2008). Challenging conventional wisdom about who quits: Revelations from corporate America. *Journal of Applied Psychology, 93*(1), 1–34.

Hunt, S. D. (1976). *Marketing theory: Conceptual foundations of research in marketing.* Columbus, OH: Grid, Inc.
Jinyan, F., & Wanous, J. P. (2008). Organizational and cultural ntry: A new type of orientation program for multiple boundary crossings. *Journal of Applied Psychology, 93*(6), 1390–1400.
Johns Hopkins University. (2008). *Welfare, children, & families.* http://web.jhu.edu/three citystudy/ (accessed November 9, 2008).
Judge, T. A., & Hurst, C. (2008). How the rich (and happy) get richer (and happier): Relationship of core self-evaluations to trajectories in attaining work success. *Journal of Applied Psychology, 93*(4), 849–863.
Judge, T. A. & Livingston, B. A. (2008). Is the gap more than gender? A longitudinal analysis of gender, gender role orientation, and earnings. *Journal of Applied Psychology, 93*(5), 994–1012.
Kaplan, A. (1964). *The conduct of inquiry,* San Francisco, CA: Chandler Publishing Co.
Katz, D. (1953). Field studies, in research methods in the behavioral sciences. In L. Festinger & D. Katz (Eds) *Research methods in the behavioral sciences,* (pp. 56–97). New York: Holt, Rinehart and Winston.
Katz, D. (1967). The practice and potential of survey methods in psychological research. In Charles Y. Glock (Ed.), *Survey research in the social sciences* (pp. 145–215).New York: Russell Sage Foundation.
Kerlinger, F. N. (1964). *Foundations of behavioral research.* New York: Holt, Rinehart, and Winston, Inc.
Keutzer, C. S., Lichtenstein, E., & Mees, H. L. (1968). Modification of smoking behavior: A review. *Psychological Bulletin, 70*(6), 520–533.
Lance, F. D., Brown, D. J., Berry, J. W., & Lian, H. (2008). The development and validation of the workplace ostracism scale. *Journal of Applied Psychology, 93*(6), 1348–1366.
Levi, A. S., & Fried, Y. (2008). Differences between African Americans and Whites in reactions to affirmative action programs in hiring, promotion, training, and layoffs. *Journal of Applied Psychology, 93*(5), 1118–1129.
Lewis, R. J., & Erickson, L. G. (1969). Marketing functions and marketing systems: A synthesis, *Journal of Marketing, 33*(7), 10–14.
Lundberg, G. A. (1929). *Social research,* New York: Longmans, Green and Co.
Luo, X., & Homburg, C. (2008). Satisfaction, complaint, and the stock value gap. *Journal of Marketing, 72*(7), 29–43.
Mair, C. (2006). *Twentieth-century English: History, variation, and standardization.* Cambridge: Cambridge University Press.
Maslach, C., & Leiter, M. P. (2008). Early predictors of job burnout and engagement. *Journal of Applied Psychology, 93*(3), 498–512.
Maxham, J. G. III, & Netemeyer, R. G. (2002). A longitudinal study of complaining customers' evaluations of multiple service failures and recovery efforts. *Journal of Marketing, 66*(10), 57–71.
McKinney, J. D. (1994). Methodological issues in longitudinal research in learning disabilities. In S. Vaughn & C. S. Bos (Eds), *Research issues in learning disabilities: Theory, methodology, assessment, and ethics* (pp. 202–230). New York: Springer-Verlag.
Menard, S. (1991). *Longitudinal research.* Newbury Park, CA: Sage Publications.
Misangyi, E. A. V. F., Johnson, D. E., LePine, M. A., & Halverson, K. V. (2008). Stirring the hearts of followers: Charismatic leadership as the transferal of affect. *Journal of Applied Psychology, 93*(3), 602–615.
The Merriam-Webster Dictionary. (1974). New York: Simon & Schuster, Inc.
Montes, S. D., & Irving (2008). Disentangling the effects of promised and delivered inducements: Relational and transactional contract elements and the mediating role of trust. *Journal of Applied Psychology, 93*(6), 1367–1381.

Morgan, C. T., & King, R. A. (1971). *Introduction to psychology* (4th ed.) New York: McGraw-Hill.

Nagel, E. (1961). *The structure of science*, New York: Harcourt, Brace and World.

Neubert, M. J., K., Kacmar, M. Carlson, D. S.,Chonko, L. B., & Roberts, J. A. (2008). Regulatory focus as a mediator of the influence of initiating structure and servant leadership on employee behavior. *Journal of Applied Psychology, 93*(6), 1220–1233.

Online Etymology Dictionary. (2012). http://www.etymonline.com/index.php (accessed October 27, 2012).

Orvis, K. A., Dudley, N. C., & Cortina, J. M. (2008). Conscientiousness and reactions to psychological contract breach: A longitudinal field study. *Journal of Applied Psychology, 93*(5), 1183–1193.

Oyserman, D., & Lee, W. S. (2008). Does iculture influence what and how we think? Effects of priming individualism and collectivism. *Psychological Bulletin, 134*(2), 311–342.

Popper, K. R. (1959). *The logic of scientific discovery*. New York: Harper and Row.

Rasinski, K. A., Lee, L., & Krishnamurty, P. (2012). Chapter 13: Question order effects. In C. Harris (Ed.), *APA Handbook of Research Methods in Psychology*, Vol. 1 (pp. 229–248). Washington, DC: American Psychological Association.

Raskind, M. H., Gerber, P. J., Goldberg, R. J., Higgins, E. L., & Herman, K. L. (1998). Longitudinal research in learning disabilities: Report on an international symposium. *Journal of Learning Disabilities, 31*(5–6), 266–277.

Rindfleisch, A., Malter, A. J., Ganesan, S., & Moorman, C. (2008). Cross-sectional versus longitudinal survey research: Concepts, findings, and guidelines, *Journal of Marketing Research, 45*(6), 261–279.

Roget's International Thesaurus. (1977). (4th ed.). Revised by R. L. Chapman. New York: Harper & Row.

Rossi, P. H., & Crain, R. (1968). The NORC permanent community sample. *Public Opinion Quarterly, 32*(2), 261–272.

Rudner, R. (1966). *Philosophy of social science*. Englewood Cliffs, NJ: Prentice-Hall.

Schreier, F. T. (1963). *Modern marketing research*. Belmont, CA: Wadsworth Publishing.

Schuman, H. (1997). Polls, surveys, and the English language. Working paper, *Institute for Social Research*, University of Michigan.

Shaughnessy, J., & Zechmeister, E. (1977). *Research methods in psychology*. (4th ed.). New York: McGraw-Hill.

Sheatsley, P. B. (1974). Survey design. Chapter 1, Part B. In R. Ferber (Ed.), *Handbook of Marketing Research*. Vol. 2 (pp. 66–81). New York: McGraw-Hill.

Simon, J. L. (1969). *Basic research methods in social science*, New York: Random House.

Smith, M. B. (1945). *Survey of social science*, Boston, MA: Houghton Mifflin Co.

Sokal, R. R. (1966). Numerical taxonomy. *Scientific American, 215*(12), 106–116.

Sonnentag, S., Binnewies, C., & Mojza, E. J. (2008). "Did you have a nice evening?" A day-level study on recovery experiences, sleep, and affect. *Journal of Applied Psychology, 93*(3), 674–684.

Stevens, R. E., Wrenn, B., Ruddick, M. E., & Sherwood, P. K. (1997). *The marketing research guide*. New York: The Haworth Press.

Teas, R. K. & Palan, K. M. (1997). The realms of scientific meaning framework for constructing theoretically meaningful nominal definitions of marketing concepts. *Journal of Marketing, 61*(4), 52–67.

Tepper, B. J., Henle, C. A., Schurer Lambert, L., Giacalone, R. A., & Duffy, M. K. (2008). Abusive supervision and subordinates' organization deviance. *Journal of Applied Psychology, 93*(4), 721–732.

Toch, H. (1953). Attitudes of the "fifty plus" age group: Preliminary considerations toward a longitudinal survey. *Public Opinion Quarterly, 17*(3), 391–394.

Vadum, A. C., & Rankin, N. O. (1998). *Psychological research.* Boston: McGraw-Hill.
VandenBos, G. R., ed. (2007). *APA Dictionary of Psychology.* Washington, DC: American Psychological Association.
Walter, P. A. F. Jr. (1949). *The social sciences.* New York: D. Van Nostrand Co.
Wang, M., Zhan, Y., Liu, S., & Shultz, K. S. (2008). Antecedents of bridge employment: A longitudinal investigation. *Journal of Applied Psychology, 93*(4), 818–830.
Webster's Collegiate Dictionary. (1941). (5th ed.) Springfield, MA: G. & C. Merriam Co.
Webster's New World Dictionary. (1965). Nashville, TN: The World Publishing Company /The Southwestern Company.
Webster's Online Dictionary. (2012). http://www.websters-online-dictionary.org/definition /survey (accessed December 16, 2012).
Webster's Third New International Dictionary. (1993). Springfield, MA: Merriam-Webster, Inc.
Wentz, W. B. (1972). *Marketing research: Management and methods.* New York: Harper & Row.
Wheeler, L., Goodale, R., & Deese, J. (1975). *General psychology.* Boston, MA: Allyn and Bacon.
White, R. T., & Arzi, H. (2005). Longitudinal studies: Designs, validity, practicality, and value. *Research in science education, 35*(3), 137–149.
Wikipedia. (2012). Likert, R., http://en.wikipedia.org/wiki/Rensis_Likert (accessed December 13, 2012).
Wilson, G. (1950). *Social science research methods.* New York: Appleton-Century-Crofts, Inc.

14

Cross-Sectional Survey and Multiple Correspondence Analysis of Financial Manager Behavior

Kenneth D. Strang

Chapter overview

This chapter is an applied example that explains how an empirical study was designed. The author's ideology was stated in the study as positivistic. The cross-sectional survey is a technique that employs a questionnaire to collect data from human participants. Correspondence analysis is considered a de facto method although it is often described in the literature as a statistical technique in the general analytics method. An outline of the topics from the manuscript is given to illustrate the customary structure of a peer-reviewed article in the business and management discipline. Subsequent sections explain how each part of the paper relates to the research design typology. The applied example was based on an article published in the *Journal of Asset Management*. This was a relevant article to illustrate how various qualitative and quantitative techniques were integrated in the general analytics method, and especially how to collect qualitative data representing self-reports of professional behavior (financial portfolio asset managers were sampled from New York Stock Exchange listed companies).

Journal manuscript analysis

I use the first person in this chapter, which is a modern post-positivist writing style endorsed by the American Psychological Association (APA) and cited in their Edition 6 Manual (APA, 2010). This contrasts with the earlier positivistic impersonal style of saying "the researcher" or "this author." The reader should also note that the reference format in this chapter is not APA because the handbook style is Harvard (which is very similar to APA). The communities of practice in the business and management discipline do not all use the same style guide for publishing (these vary by the journal and publisher). Likewise, organizations and associations (such as APA, Marketing Academy of Management, etc.) also specify their own scholarly writing styles. Furthermore, these practices sometimes differ across countries.

The manuscript was published in 2012, as "Man versus math: Behaviorist exploration of post-crisis non-banking asset management," in the *Journal of Asset Management* on pages 348–467 (http://www.palgrave-journals.com/jam/journal/v13/n5/index.html). This is a popular business and management peer-reviewed journal indexed by several associations and listed with Cabell's (a benchmark often used by accredited university business schools to classify as scholarly work towards performance evaluations and promotions).

Manuscript structure

The topic structure is outlined below with a brief explanation of the purpose of each section. While this structure is typical it is not universal because most journals have customized requirements. I have many publications, so I have to carefully manage my style guides for the journals that I am submitting my work to. For example, most journals strictly follow APA, which does not use the "introduction" heading (albeit the section is still included). Additionally, the caption "methods" is used instead of "methodology." Some journals prefer to see limitations at the end of the discussion, contrary to this example. A few journals that I have published to do not accept a methods section while others do not accept a literature review section. This is the general layout:

1. Abstract—an executive summary of the paper including key findings.
2. Introduction—establishes the rationale, the problem, and gap in literature.
3. Literature Review—deductive critical analysis of relevant articles (from last 5–7 years).
   3.1. Behaviorist Financial Theories—articles identifying qualitative, behaviorist factors.
   3.2. Quantitative Techniques—articles and explanations of quantitative technique factors.

   3.3. Applied Correspondence Analysis—how MCA can/has been used by thought leaders.
4. Methodology—research design, including strategy, formal methods, and techniques.
   4.1. Participants and Instrumentation—sample context, how they were selected, instruments.
   4.2. Validity and Reliability Procedures—discussed since a new questionnaire was created.
5. Results and Discussion—everything from here on is after the study was completed.
   5.1. Exploratory Dimensional Analysis—basic analysis of data, descriptive statistics, etc.
   5.2. Interpretation of Asymmetric Estimates—core of analysis to answer research questions.
   5.3. Naming Asymmetric Dimensions—inductive analysis where a new model was built.
6. Conclusions—summary of the study and implications of findings to generalized target(s).
   6.1. Limitations and Recommendations—pitfalls to disclose and suggestions for next study.
7. References—the details from only the citations (not a bibliography), in Harvard style.

Executive summary of manuscript

The title and abstract of indexed articles are considered public domain for obvious reasons, so they may be reproduced without the permission of the publisher as long as they are correctly cited. The abstract is an executive summary, so it is the best way to introduce the case, as quoted below:

> Rationalists may argue the best way to manage an investment portfolio is to use risk balancing strategies such as asset class diversification. Positivists would likely insist on probabilistic concepts—perhaps a mean-variance statistical technique. A third less-studied approach in the financial literature is to apply a behaviorist philosophy such as heuristics or rating the quality of the management team. An interesting variation is to study the behavior of effective asset managers, particularly their methodologies, and then imitate those best-practices. This is a fundamental principle underlying case studies, ethnography, grounded theory, and other interpretative research philosophies, so it was useful to apply it to study the investment discipline. Furthermore, extant financial studies pre-dated, or tested data prior to, the global financial crisis, which may invalidate older models. Therefore the researcher interviewed 39 non-banking asset managers from

> high-performing NYSE-listed companies to explore their perception that current portfolio management techniques would be effective in volatile financial markets. A statistically significant asymmetric plot was produced, which revealed gender and market outlook were key factors. (Strang, 2012a, p. 348).

Research design of journal manuscript

Now that you have a general idea what the manuscript was about, I will switch to using the research design typology as a framework for analyzing this example. The research design process is the same for developing a thesis or dissertation, except that the style guides are usually different and much more detail is required (with mandatory topics—e.g., see Vajjhala's and also Hahn's chapter in the constructivist section of this handbook).

Manuscripts are not always top-down as per the research design typology. In fact, most scholarly studies commence with either a preliminary literature review or as a follow-up to your one of your published papers (which has a literature review). The literature review is done with an ideology preset to identify the strategy (unit of analysis and level of analysis). However, sometimes researchers change their ideology on the continuum. As mentioned earlier, ideology is not innate but rather it is socialized. I often vary between post-positivism and pragmatism. This is why the researcher needs to state to avoid communication barriers with reviewers. Figure 14.1 is a conceptual drawing of the research design workflow for this manuscript.

Research ideology

As noted above, I stated in the manuscript, under the methodology topic, that I held a positivistic ideology: "The research was designed as an exploratory survey of purposively-sampled asset managers, using qualitative data gathering techniques. The researcher employed a theory-dependent positivist philosophy consisting of a deductive literature review (above) to assist in coding the interview responses" (Strang, 2012a, p. 356).

I should disclose that my preferred ideology was and is post-positivist (at times I am considered pragmatic). I reverted to the positivist philosophy style for writing the paper, and I used the customary language, such as "the researcher," because I had revised other papers in the journal, which convinced me that the editorial review board were traditional and would expect conformance in order to accept manuscripts for publication. This was a reputable journal that was being read by the practitioners and scholars around the world that I wanted to generalize to.

As a quick review of the first handbook section, ideologies represent the sociocultural philosophical attitude of the researcher that may be categorized

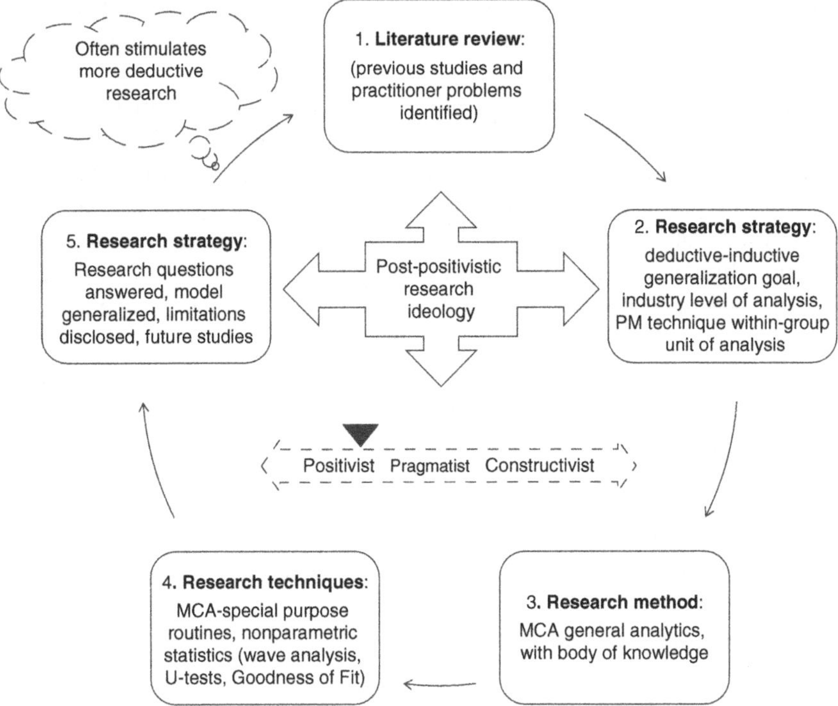

Figure 14.1 Conceptual drawing of research design workflow for manuscript.

as axiology, epistemology, and ontology. Researchers generally just state their ideology or philosophy (Creswell, 2009, 2012; Creswell & Tashakkori, 2007). However, I will explain it here in a bit more detail, but I would not go to this length in the positivistic paradigm, although I would indeed do that if I held a constructivist ideology.

Axiology in general refers to the theory of beliefs, such as religion and soci-cultural values. In business and management, axiology means the priority of values conditioned by organizational and global culture socialization. Although I lived in Australia for almost ten years, I grew up and have been grounded in the culture of the United States, where I live. I have published many empirical papers analyzing global culture and learning styles (e.g., Strang, 2009a, 2010, 2012b), but for this chapter I will simply indicate that my cultural dimension indexes are closer to the younger generation as compared with the average values calculated by Hofstede on his survey of IBM employees (Hofstede, 1991; Strang, 2012c). For example, my cultural profile, as compared to the US mean is: PDi is low (consultative rather than authority preference), MFi is same as US MFi (higher toward results oriented instead of nurturing), ICi is slightly lower (more collective than individualistic), UAi is about the same as US average (higher uncertainty avoidance than acceptance of risk), and my LTi is much higher than the US norm (long-term, future focused, rather than short-term profit-driven).

Axiology impacted the study design but not the actual data since all participants were US-based asset managers. Additionally, since I used a questionnaire as a survey instrument to collect data, I knew I had to be careful of assuming that the participants would understand the priority—such as would they feel comfortable revealing their average salary, age, gender, and education. Additionally, some words may be interpreted differently between cultures, and I had no way of confirming the sociocultural profile of the respondents before I issued the survey. So as a research design, axiology triggered specific techniques to be implemented: "An interview questionnaire was pilot-tested with a sample of asset managers at a local management meeting (*N*=4), to improve the wording" (Strang, 2012a, p. 356).

Epistemology in business and management refers to the disciplinary terminology for communicating knowledge. This was indeed an issue for this study—in fact the focus of the study was to discover what portfolio management techniques asset managers were using. I used some quantitative ordinal scales for the descriptive aspects of the survey instrument but the main question was open-ended. Here is what I stated in the paper (Strang, 2012a, p. 356):

> During the interview, each participant was asked to describe their asset management techniques in a brief paragraph in the Skype message window (which was captured by the researcher). The researcher verified the contents of the demographics and the technique paragraph. Writing was used with verbal confirmation to avoid misunderstandings.

Thus, in this case, I was concerned about epistemology, my own ideology, so I added this process as a way to improve the accuracy in the data (not to improve the meaning as in constructivism). I did this by asking the participants to verbally confirm their written answer on the phone to make sure that "they" were using the correct terminology from the literature review keywords and not that I was understanding them correctly. This is a positivistic ideology at heart. Although it is premature to discuss research technique, this was method triangulation.

I had noted in earlier chapters that epistemology and ideological differences impact the choice of statistical technique, such as in engineering or math vector analysis may be used to analyze participant response data agreement while in economics or psychology correlation or exploratory factor analysis would be de facto. Epistemological differences can also impact the researcher's ideology when trying to establish validity and reliability processes along with the requisite benchmarks. It was clear from my quote above that I created a questionnaire and improved its wording. Therefore I did not have an a priori instrument, so I knew I would have to validate it in order to communicate this as "credibility" to other positivistic researchers.

Epistemology also impacts the choice of deductive theory-driven versus the inductive theory-creating approach, which becomes the purpose of the research strategy. A positivist will generally require an a priori theory to test against to approve or falsify (e.g., in hypothesis testing). However, some positivists try to generate theory, such as through factor analysis. A pragmatist could use either approach, depending on the nature of the study, and the availability of a priori theories or instruments from the literature review. A post-positivist or pragmatist is not likely going to cancel his or her study just because no relevant theory exists in the literature. Thus, the deductive versus inductive debate has a small impact on the epistemology of the ideology, but it will greatly impact how the strategy is designed (discussed later).

Ontology in business and management means how a researcher understands things exist as tangible versus intangible and tacit versus explicit. In this study I anticipated that participants may not immediately recognize the name of the portfolio technique they were using, not that they did not know, but rather it was the espoused-theory versus theory-in-use phenomenon (Argyris & Schön, 1996). I did not have ex post facto data that I could use to verify what participants did to manage their portfolios. Table 14.1 is a list of the common portfolio management techniques (adapted from Strang, 2012a, p. 358). I did not share this list with the participants. Instead my goal during the interview was to simply make sure there were no incorrectly spelled keywords in the participant response, and if they mentioned a new technique not on my list, then I verified the correct spelling of it with the participant and recorded it.

The demographic questionnaire used built-in scales and the items were calling for basic characteristics so there were no axiology, ontology, or epistemology issues (unless an asset portfolio manager was to lie about his or her salary if belonging to the high-MFi culture dimension). Any outlier salaries would show up in the data, so I had planned to look for reasonable values and I felt that the personal interview (albeit online via Skype) would improve the participant's honesty as compared with completing an online survey instrument or a mail in questionnaire.

I did some basic transformation of the response data when it came to the question about optimistic and pessimistic about using the existing portfolio techniques in the next 2–5 years.

The degree of confidence for future volatile market conditions was transformed into a three-level ordinal: low, medium, high. Then these codes were grouped into the taxonomy developed from the literature (Strang, 2012a, p. 358).

Table 14.1 Common portfolio management techniques

Code	Common portfolio management technique a participant would provide
Technique	
Brainstorm	Brain storming, nominal group, executive discussion, consensus building, meeting, emails, blogs, stakeholder participation, criteria, focus group, Delphi, group creativity
CAPM	Capital Asset Pricing Models, cost-benefit analysis, yields, profitability indexes
GAAP	Accounting, earned value, tax treatment, tax credits, tax incentives, Economic Order/Production Quantity, cost-benefit analysis, financial ratios (ROE, EPS, etc.)
Heuristics	Guess, reflection, experience, instinct, judgments, client interview, research, risk-avoidance, individual creativity, leader/manager profiling
Linear	Payback period (PP), breakeven point analysis, moving average/linear forecasts, linear equations, polynomial equations, linear/integer programming
Liquidity	No analysis, hold guaranteed investment certificates, treasury bills, cash, bank accounts, gold, silver
Marketing	Attribute design templates, QFD, lead user, House of Quality, surveys, factor analysis
Mixed method	Quantitative-qualitative data analysis, transformations, AHP, MDCM, priority matrix, normalized ratings, fuzzy set, Prospect Theory, clustering
Monetary	Capital budgeting, Discounted Cash flow (DCF), Net Present Value (NPV), Internal Rate of Return (IRR), average rate of return (ARR), Weighted Average Cost of Capital (WACC), expected monetary value (EMV), return on investment (ROI)
Nonlinear	Sensitivity analysis, scenario analysis, goal programming, network flow, nearest neighbor search, and neural network analysis, metaheuristic conditional search routines, Markov analysis, quadratic
Probability	Probability distributions, statistics, risk analysis, Bayesian Probability Theory (BPT), Monte Carlo simulation, minimax, maximax, regret, Hurcwitz, mean-variance, beta risk, diversification
Strategy	SWOT, TOWS, VRIO, Cash-Cows, sacred cow, stage gate, GE matrix, BCG
Visual	Diagrams, charts, plots, trees, tables
Perception	
Optimistic	Highly confident existing techniques will be effective in next 2–5 years in any type of conditions
Pessimistic	Not confident existing techniques will be effective in next 2–5 years, need to research new methods

Source: Adapted from Strang, 2012d, p. 357.

Research strategy

The research strategy defines the goals, research questions (or hypotheses), based on the unit, level of analysis, and generalization goal (deductive or inductive or both, and who or where the results will be generalized). A positivist will define these elements based on a priori research but any order is possible during the development of the research strategy if following a pragmatic ideology.

The original study was stimulated by my wondering if portfolio managers were behaving differently with respect to risk management,after the 2008 global fiscal crisis had passed and the world was in economic recovery mode. I had read an Internet article by Dr. Angelo Calvello about the "The Death of the Portfolio Manager" (http://ai-cio.com/channel/TECHNOLOGY_PRODUCTS/Column__The_Death_of_the_%C2%ADPortfolio_Manager.html). I began to wonder what techniques portfolio managers were applying in this new post global economic-crisis paradigm. I stated in my paper that "the global financial crisis has changed the risk tolerance and behavior of investment managers because there seems to be no pattern to the continuing volatility since the 2008–2011 US sub-prime failure" (Strang, 2012a, p. 348). I had also noted that "another rationale for conducting this study was that published theory generally lags behind practical innovations, which impedes the advancement of a body of knowledge" (Strang, 2012a, p. 348). An insight I came up with was (p. 348):

> A limitation with any mathematical technique applied to analyze quantitative data is that at best it is limited by the currency of the data and likelihood that past performance will project or generalize future performance (Strang, 2009b). Therefore, based on the above literature, more studies were needed of modern portfolio management techniques.

The generalization goal starts with a deductive versus inductive approach, the former to base the research questions and hypothesis on testing the data "against" a priori theories, and the latter to build theoretical meaning "from" the data. It also should include where or who the results, if significant or credible, would apply to (generalization). My generalization goal was deductive-inductive in nature because I wanted to first find out what were the generally accepted portfolio management techniques (I did not know all of them) and then to find out what practitioners were doing. The last quotation above shows that using only deductive a priori theories could limit what can be found in the data. I wanted to be able to generalize my findings to portfolio managers as well as to other researchers for replication of the study with different larger samples. Here is another quote identifying this:

> In this study the objective was to describe asset manager behavior across different industry portfolios and then summarize their best-practices. Asset

> managers in this study refer to the non-banking discipline, where professionals manage an income stream, such as rental property, transportation/logistics systems, franchises, as well as the traditional financial instruments (bonds, stocks, mutual funds, certificates, etc.). Furthermore, an important goal of this study was to demonstrate the descriptive-interpretative research philosophy (Creswell, 2009) which is uncommonly utilized in the finance discipline. Descriptive in this context meant asking practitioners to discuss their theories-in-use (Gill, Johnson & Clark, 2010), rather than force a list of espoused-theories for portfolio management upon participants through a survey instrument. (Strang, 2012a, p. 348)

As I explained earlier, the levels of analysis are attributes referring to where the scholarly focus of the study is, such as the individual, group, or a larger partition. Level of analysis conceptually relates to the goal for the sampling method. This is because the level of analysis defines where the researcher intends to generalize the findings to, assuming they are reliable and significant (positivism). The level of analysis can be determined by looking at the method and technique, along with the generalization goal. Since I wanted to generalize to portfolio managers and other researchers, I was referring to the common asset manager techniques or the pattern of their use after the global crisis. This would be the industry or society level of analysis. This does not refer to how the data is collected, since it will be taken from individuals, but rather, how the findings and results will be summarized. "MCA is from a family of multivariate exploratory techniques capable of producing statistical estimates and graphical diagrams of nonnumeric variable relationships" (Strang, 2012a, p. 355).

The unit of analysis identifies the factor, variable, process, relationship, or tacit phenomena at the heart of a study. It results in research questions and hypothesis when taking the positivist ideology. Note I did not form hypotheses here due to the nature of the MCA method. Simple correspondence analysis (CA) should not be confused with MCA, although both are nonparametric with no statistical distribution expectations and practically no constraints except requiring slightly different arrangements of input data. From a research strategy standpoint, the difference is somewhat analogous to a parametric ANOVA versus MANOVA. MCA uses one independent factor with multiple levels such the multiple dependent variables in MANOVA, whereas CA expects more than two independent factors but a single inductive dependent variable (like ANOVA), and CA converts nominal data to binary number patterns (Strang, 2012d). I published a study using CA to identify risk-management preferences in a sample of program managers, as summarized by this quote to illustrate the difference:

> Therefore, to implement the above approach, the researchers interviewed a theoretically-selected sample of program managers (n=211) using

> demographic and open-ended questions to capture the portfolio risk management techniques used in their organization after the global crises cited earlier. The sample frame was drawn from "solvent" companies registered in the stock markets of 20 countries. Descriptive statistics were used to summarize demographic characteristics of the participants. A literature review was used to identify the core categories of portfolio risk management techniques and the common industry functional disciplines (factors of interest). The unit of analysis was the nature and quality of the relationship between risk management technique and functional discipline. CA was used to identify relationship quality and plot the results. The rationale and method for applying CA was cited to the literature to facilitate replication of this study. Validity and reliability estimates were also reported. (Strang, 2012d, p. 2)

My research questions quoted earlier, "describe asset manager behavior across different industry portfolios and then summarize their best-practices" (p. 348). Units of analysis may be variables of any data type, nominal, ordinal, integer, continuous, or a relationship. However, here my variable was "portfolio management (PM) technique/behavior" a nominal data type, which would provide an indication of asset manager process behavior. Since my unit of analysis was the "PM technique," my level of analysis was industry, and my generalization goal was also industry (community of practice); this was a within-group analysis focus. It would not make sense to compare one PM against another, or a PM technique against another, or to do this by groups. I was interested in the entire community of asset managers using PM techniques.

Research method

All de facto scholarly research methods start with or at least include a relevant and current literature review. Some methods require citing the method from thought leaders (as was the case in my study due to its novelty), while others require citing similar types of studies or at least defining the key factors. Factors in this sense would mean the findings of other articles surrounding the topic, namely, portfolio management techniques is that I was focused on.

As I explained in the first section of this handbook, methods and techniques tend to fall in line with ideology and strategy. In particular, formal methods commonly associated to the unit of analysis in the research strategy. The Multiple Correspondence Analysis (MCA) is a method along with a family of techniques, also commonly titled general analytics, which may be supplemented by descriptive statistics. MCA was also a "PM technique," but as I discovered through my literature review, it was not well known either in the financial industry or as a research method. Here is what I found in paraphrased format (Strang, 2012a, pp. 355–356):

> MCA is a multivariate graphical technique designed to explore the relationships among categorical variables [but it] appears to be an underused technique (Sourial et al., 2010, p. 639). A search of a well-known multidisciplinary literature index (www.sciencedirect.com) returned 7,245 peer reviewed journal articles applying "correspondence analysis" as a statistical method; 3,084 of those were published within the last five years (from 2007 to June 1, 2012). Ironically though, only five business-oriented journal manuscripts were identified in these results. Thus, while MCA is a proven statistical technique applied in the social sciences, it is rarely mentioned in research from other fields. By comparison, when the search term was changed to "factor analysis" (FA) as a statistical method—the parametric counterpart to MCA—83,537 manuscripts were found; 32,158 of those were published within the last five years and numerous business-oriented manuscripts were present in the results. The interpretation of this is that MCA is well-known in the social science literature yet other more traditional techniques such as FA are eleven times more popular, while MCA is rarely utilized in business research. The implications of this (even before this study initiated) were that there would not likely be any comparative studies of applying MCA in the business literature to analyze portfolio management. This was true in that there were no MCA studies of asset management techniques located. MCA is from a family of multivariate exploratory techniques capable of producing statistical estimates and graphical diagrams of nonnumeric variable relationships. Common variations include "dimensional analysis," "multidimensional scaling," simple or multiple "correspondence analysis," "conjoint analysis," "choice models,", "discriminant analysis," "Euclidian distance analysis," "spatial segmentation" as well as "vector analysis" of contingency tables. (Greenacre & Blasius, 2006; Hair, Black, Babin, Anderson & Tatham, 2006; Williams, Abdi, French & Orange, 2010)

I also had justification for selecting this method, beyond that it was suited for an exploratory factor analysis of nominal data. Nonparametric procedures such as chi square test of independence or goodness of fit can be used on the nominal two-factor data; chi square methods do not explain the "nature" of the relationship within the content of the factors, only that a relationship may exist in the overall model (Hair et al., 2006). In my own testing I had found that MCA was useful for transforming complex qualitative data that lacked any a priori structure into relationship-interdependence diagrams (at least in SPSS and Minitab software). In this way MCA seemed as powerful as factor analysis but it worked with nominal qualitative data types. It was the perfect method for my study.

I also selected some aspects of the survey method insofar as I developed a questionnaire and pilot tested it to improve its validity. As noted above, both MCA and the survey method, or any scientific method for that matter, requires a thorough literature review. My literature review was approximately 3000 words, and it included approximately 50 relevant, recent citations.

Research technique

Here I will explain why and how the techniques were applied to the study, rather than define them. As I discussed in the first few chapters, there are common cross-method technique categories such as sampling, data collection, data analysis, validity-reliability analysis, and ethics. First my sample frame was non-banking asset managers in the United States. I used a random sampling technique but it was not true random since I applied purposive selection as discussed below. I was interested in effective asset managers of successful companies who were available:

> The sample consisted of non-banking industry asset managers selected by randomly contacting companies listed on the New York Stock Exchange (NYSE). This was done by first selecting companies with the highest earnings-per-share ratio (over the last fiscal year ending in 2011). Since the search was done for all companies on the same day, November 1, 2011, the profitability and context relating to the global financial or natural disaster crises were roughly equal. Note that earnings-per-share is not the only indicator of a solvent company since it measures profitability (there are others in various categories such as liquidity, leverage, and activity), but this was selected for the purposes of this study. Next the researcher purposively selected only those companies who were willing to provide an asset manager to be briefly interviewed for this study. Only one participant was selected from each company. The rationale for the purposive sampling method was to select at least one profitable company that showed positive annual earnings per share (above zero) for their fiscal year ending in 2011, and were generally considered solvent. (Strang, 2012a, p. 358)

There were sufficient guidelines in the literature about how to apply MCA as a methodology (Greenacre & Blasius, 2006). The first goal was to show that the sample participants (N=39) were similar in high ability. I listed the descriptive statistics on the asset managers to show they were senior (mean age 45, SD=5.0) and their mean years of experience was 23 (SD=2.1). Since I used the survey method, via a questionnaire, it is necessary to perform to check bias against respondent dropout and for late responses. I used wave analysis to test response bias. The theory behind wave analysis is: "those who return surveys in the final weeks of the response period are nearly all nonrespondents, [so] if the responses begin to change a potential exists for response bias" (Creswell, 2009, p. 152). As I explained in the paper:

> [Response bias] is a serious threat to the inferential goal of survey research because if late responders (including those that did not respond at all) had different perceptions this implies that the sample is not representative of the intended global population. Since the duration of the interviews spanned several weeks, this was a logical validity test to conduct. (Strang, 2012a, p. 358)

To do this, I used a nonparametric technique, the Mann-Whitney U-test, to compare medians of the first 3/4 to last 1/4 of responses received, for all key variables (age, experience, and disciplines), and this "confirmed there was no response bias (n1=29, n2=10; Wa=1626.0, P=0.61, We=19722.1, P=0.51, Wd=9882.0, P=0.48" (Strang, 2012a, p. 358). I then made the assertion that these tests satisfied internal and external validity, when considering that the questions were based on a pilot-tested questionnaire, and I did not plan for parametric tests.

Since MCA is a nonparametric statistical procedure, it has very few assumptions concerning the normality of the data; so I did not have to meet any distribution assumptions that are common with other methods such as *t*-tests, ANOVA, and regression.

The main problem though, in terms of validity, was to make sure I had coded the "PM technique" keywords in table 14.1 correctly based on the participant responses. With respect to coding reliability and validity, the nature of the qualitative data made it impossible to apply quantitative reliability checking techniques such as the inter-rater agreement. Instead I followed the advice in the literature. Creswell recommended that data validity checking could be performed through "peer debriefing" (Creswell, 2009, p. 192). I did this by getting my research assistants to help. I asked "two management science doctoral students to thoroughly review the data versus the coded transformations for the portfolio selection technique responses" (Strang, 2012a, p. 358). They did not find any errors or questionable coding. There was 100% agreement, so naturally I accepted the result as being unbiased at least in the research context.

The process of interpreting the MCA output was complex, and it took several pages in the original manuscript. The end result was an informative visual "asymmetric plot of asset manager techniques and perceptions (N=39, λ=0.79, T= 35%)" (Strang, 2012a, p. 362). Once I had built a model using MCA, I had to use additional techniques to ensure the model itself was valid. I used the *Goodness of Fit* test on the two-axis dimensional model and I found both axes were statistically significant with an X^2=(38)=69.22, p=.0015 (Strang, 2012a).

As I noted in the manuscript, the "statistical estimates from axis 1 were: λ^1=0.40, T^1=0.18; and for axis 2: λ^2=0.39, τ^2=0.17; with a total variance of 35%

captured by the two factor model. Therefore the dimensional model adequately represented the qualitative interview data" (Strang, 2012a, p. 363). If interested you should consult the original manuscript as it serves as a tutorial for how to decode the MCA data and inductively build the model to explain the patterns of responses in the data.

Conclusions

Rather than summarize this chapter, I will continue to apply the research design typology to the manuscript. The last part of the research design is actually the first part—again. This means that the researcher must go back and examine the research strategy, confirm what was found, and explain how that can be generalized as implications.

To accomplish that, I summarized what the study set out to do, again following the impersonal positivistic writing style. "In this study, the researcher interviewed 39 experienced asset managers each from different profitable companies listed in the NYSE. The goal was to explore the relationship between asset management technique and their perceptions of effectiveness for continuing market conditions" (Strang, 2012a, p. 363). I also reminded the readers that I had tested this method as the "first known application of MCA in the study of asset management practices, the manuscript included justification of the method, and the procedure was explained in detail" (Strang, 2012a, p. 363).

I can say I found some interesting patterns in this model that were explained by the data. The asset managers were polarized in their use of two very different PM techniques: deterministic versus probabilistic. Gender was an unexpected but significant factor. Risk adverse asset managers used behaviorist strategies such as liquidity, brainstorming, and heuristics. At the other extreme, efficient frontier analysts relied on statistically driven techniques (e.g., linear regression). Male asset managers were pessimistic concerning future stock market performance so they preferred nonlinear mixed-methods and diversification. In contrast female asset managers were optimistic about the market outlook; they favored GAAP and visual techniques such as decision trees. CAPM was equally accepted by everyone, and it was the most popular technique with an 11.4% "moment of mass."

From a research design perspective, I also needed to address the limitations. I noted that it was a small sample of 39 US-based asset managers and I called for a larger study and replication in the future. I noted that there was potential for error in my surveying technique (transcribing the technique codes) as well as in the coding process although my two research assistants had been in 100% agreement. I also pointed out several other limitations. I then closed with recommendations for future studies.

References

APA. (2010). *Publication manual of the American Psychological Aassociation* (6th ed.). Washington, DC: American Psychological Association (APA).

Argyris, C., & Schön, D. (1996). *Organizational learning II: Theory, method, and practice.* Reading, MA: Addison-Wesley.

Creswell, J. W. (2009). *Research design: Qualitative, quantitative, and mixed methods approaches* (3rd ed.). New York: Sage.

Creswell, J. W. (2012). *Designing qualitative studies.* New York: Sage.

Creswell, J. W., & Tashakkori, A. (2007). Differing perspectives on mixed methods research. *Journal of Mixed Methods Research, 1*(4), 303–308.

Gill, J., Johnson, P., & Clark, M. (2010). *Research methods for managers* (4th ed.). London: Sage.

Greenacre, M., & Blasius, J. (2006). Multiple correspondence analysis and related methods. Boca Raton, FL: Taylog & Francis, pp. 40. Retrieved from http://books.google.com/books?id=ZvYV1lfU5zIC&printsec=frontcover&source=gbs_ge_summary_r&cad=0#v=onepage&q&f=false.

Hair, J. F., Black, W. C., Babin, B. J., Anderson, R. E., & Tatham, R. L. (2006). *Multivariate data analysis* (6th ed.). Upper Saddle River, NJ: Prentice-Hall.

Hofstede, G. (1991). *Culture and organizations: Software of the mind.* New York: McGraw-Hill.

Strang, K. D. (2009a). How multicultural learning approach impacts grade for international university students in a business course. *Asian English Foreign Language Journal Quarterly, 11*(4), 271–292. Retrieved from http://www.asian-efl-journal.com/December_2009_ks.php.

Strang, K. D. (2009b). Using recursive regression to explore nonlinear relationships and interactions: A tutorial applied to a multicultural education study. *Practical Assessment, Research & Evaluation, 14*(3), 1–13. Retrieved from http://pareonline.net/getvn.asp?v=14&n=3.

Strang, K. D. (2010). Global culture, learning style and outcome: An interdisciplinary empirical study of international students. *Journal of Intercultural Education, 21*(6), 519–533. Retrieved from http://www.tandfonline.com/doi/abs/10.1080/14675986.2010.533034#preview.

Strang, K. D. (2012a). Man versus math: Behaviorist exploration of post-crisis non-banking asset management. *Journal of Asset Management, 13*(5), 348–467. Retrieved from http://www.palgrave-journals.com/jam/journal/v13/n5/index.html

Strang, K. D. (2012b). Student diaspora and learning style impact on group performance. *International Journal of Online Pedagogy and Course Design, 2*(3), 1–19. Retrieved from http://www.igi-global.com/article/student-diaspora-learning-style-impact/68410.

Strang, K. D. (2012c). Multicultural face of organizations. In M. A. Sarlak (Ed.), *The new faces of organizations in the 21st century.* Vol. 5 (pp. 1–21). ON: North American Institute of Science and Information Technology (NAISIT). Retrieved from http://naisit.org/book/detail/id/6.

Strang, K. D. (2012d). Nonparametric correspondence Analysis of global risk management techniques. *International Journal of Risk and Contingency Management, 1*(3), 1–24. Retrieved from http://www.igi-global.com/journal-contents/international-journal-risk-contingency-management/53135.

Williams, L. J., Abdi, H., French, R., & Orange, J. B. (2010). A tutorial on multi-block discriminant correspondence analysis (MUDICA): A new method for analyzing discourse data from clinical populations. *Journal of Speech Language and Hearing Research, 53*(1), 1–21.

15
Control Variables: Problematic Issues and Best Practices

Leon Schjoedt and Krittaya Sangboon

Chapter overview

Schjoedt and Sangboon hold a positivist ideology. In this chapter they discuss an important aspect of the unit of analysis strategy in research designs: How does one account for or control factors that the researcher is aware of in the model but are beyond the focus of a within-groups or between-groups comparison? In other words, control factors are confounding, moderating, or mediating variables. The reason it is important to identify and control (or account for) these factors is so that the researcher can generalize to other populations, that is, by identifying the confounding factors that are present but are beyond the unit of analysis interest. When participants are samples for a between-group unit of analysis comparison, individual attributes in each participant often differ. Designing control variables is one approach among others to address this.

Introduction

Graduate school offers a plethora of valuable lessons for emergent researchers, but many times these lessons are cut short due to the limited time available. We learn about how to conduct empirical research and about the principles of conducting statistical analysis, for example, regression analysis. We learn that we can limit the impact of alternative explanations of the relationship under empirical investigation by including control variables when conducting a multiple regression analysis by entering control variables (CVs) as step one and the independent variables (IVs) as step two (Becker, 2005). This way we can determine the unique variance accounted for in the dependent variable (DV) by the IVs while controlling for the effects of other variables, the CVs (Hair, Black, Babin, Anderson & Tatham, 2006). Alternatively, we can estimate the strength of the relationship between the IVs and DV while controlling for noise from the measurement of other variables affecting the relationship.

As researchers, we are frequently interested in understanding causal relationships. Conducting an experiment provides better insights into the causal relationships by providing an opportunity to eliminate alternative explanations among the predictor—the independent variables—and the criterion—the dependent variable—by randomly assigning individuals to experimental conditions and manipulating the variables (Schwab, 2005). Despite this, we tend to conduct nonexperimental research. This is done many times because, for a variety of reasons, we cannot conduct an experiment (Austin, Scherbaum & Mahlman, 2002; Stone-Romero, 2007). Yet, nonexperimental research has a major drawback; nonexperimental research does not benefit from the opportunity to control the effects of variables to the same extent as experimental research. When we attempt to control for alternative explanations, we statistically control the influence of variables outside the relationship that is our principal interest; we seek to control the effects of extraneous nuisance variables. When we statistically control these extraneous nuisance variables, we refer to them as control variables.

The use of control variables in nonexperimental research is widespread in business research as evidenced by several authors (e.g., Atinc, Simmering, & Kroll, 2012; Becker, 2005; Breaugh, 2006, 2008; Carlson & Wu, 2012; Schjoedt & Bird, 2014; Spector & Brannick, 2011). In preparing this chapter we reviewed the 63 articles published in 2013 in two leading academic research oriented journals—*Journal of Accounting and Economics* and *Journal of Business Venturing.* Our review showed that all but one of the 45 empirical studies published included control variables. This shows that an important aspect in academic empirical business research is control variables.

Due to the widespread use of control variables in the academic business literature, we would expect that in graduate school a substantial amount of time is allocated toward the issue of control variables, at least to the same degree as attention that is allocated to the independent variables. Despite the fact that control variables are extraneous variables that account for unique variance in the dependent variables just like the independent variables, attention given to them is limited in graduate school and in published research. This observation is based on our personal experiences, conversations with doctoral students and faculty, and readers of published and unpublished manuscripts in the capacity of editors, reviewers, and consumers of academic research, and our survey of the published research in 2013 in two leading international academic journals—*Journal of Accounting and Economics* and *Journal of Business Venturing*. The limited attention to control variables in graduate school resulting in limited attention to control variables by emergent researchers and, in turn, in published research is a problematic issue in establishing valid replicable research findings and in advancing the literature. This is unfortunate as these problematic issues can readily be remedied. Thus, there seems to be a need for guidelines in using control variables in nonexperiential research.

Purpose

The purpose of this chapter is to draw attention to the issue of control variables in nonexperimental research, assess the present use of control variables, and provide nine recommendations for use of control variables in future research. Most importantly, the purpose of drawing attention to the use of control variables is to lay the groundwork for enhancing future research by appropriate use of control variables. By drawing attention to the problematic use of control variables and by providing a set of nine recommendations for use of control variables, we seek to assist emergent researchers in reducing, or even eliminating, the problematic issues surrounding the current practice of using control variables to improve the validity and replicability of future research. Such improvements will benefit academic business research by providing greater confidence in research findings gained from research employing more appropriate use of control variables for the purpose of advancing the literature and our understanding of business (Hunter & Schmidt, 2004; Meehl, 1970, 1971; Schjoedt & Bird, 2014).

Approach

Our approach to this chapter is to first provide an introduction to control variables in terms of their purpose and relevance in nonexperimental research with an emphasis on their use in regression analysis—perhaps the most widespread technique for statistical data analysis in business research. As our intent is to illustrate the use and purpose of control variables, we will also address what constitutes statistical control in a nontechnical manner. For readers who are interested in the technical (mathematical) aspects in controlling the influence of variables, we refer you to other works (e.g., Cohen, Cohen, Aiken & West, 2003). Three approaches to the use of control variables and their inherent issues are presented next. With an appreciation of control variables established, we consider two distinct points of view regarding the use of control variables.

We continue by outlining the best practices of using control variables before we provide an assessment of the use of control variables in research published in 2013 by surveying the two leading business journals—*Journal of Accounting and Economics* and *Journal of Business Venturing*. The choice of journals was based on the leading journals in each of our areas of research interests. Based on this assessment, we identify problematic issues in the current use of control variables in published research and we discuss how our findings compare with other researchers' findings. Lastly, in discussing our assessment findings, we echo other scholars in providing a set of nine recommendations for use of control variables in nonexperiential research to enhance the validity of future research and to advance the literature and our collective understanding of business.

Significance

Business researchers have improved their attention to methodological issues (Ketchen, Boyd, & Bergh, 2008). Yet, there is substantial room for improvement in areas of research methods and in research publications in academic business journals. One area that needs improvement is how CVs are used. To advance the business literature, substantive developments are necessary. Substantive developments refer to studies addressing the nature of the relationships among constructs—independent and dependent variables (Schwab, 1980). In empirical research, conclusions drawn are only as robust as the methods employed in conducting the research (e.g. design, sampling, measurement, analysis, and interpretation of results). Even though progress has been made in business research, improvements in employing research methods have room for improvement. This constitutes a problem because appropriate use of research methods is essential for replicable substantive developments and, in effect, advancement of the business literature and our understanding of business. To enhance future business research we offer an empirical assessment of the use of CVs in published research to illustrate the problematic issues and, in concert with other methodologists (Atinc et al., 2012; Becker, 2005; Carlson & Wu, 2012; Schjoedt & Bird, 2014; Spector & Brannick, 2011), a set of nine recommendations for use of control variables in future research to enhance the validity of research findings as well as advance the literature.

Control variables

In most studies, we are interested in examining a relationship among constructs, the principal relationship of interest, especially, if one or a set of constructs causes change in another construct. When these constructs are empirically examined we refer to them as variables. This means that we are interested in assessing the strength of the relationship among variables or estimating the amount of variation in one variable that is contributed by another variable or set of variables. The two types of variables we use to this end are typically referred to as the independent variable (IV) and dependent variable (DV). The IVs and DV are measureable representations of the constructs of interest in an empirical study. Even though nonexperimental research does not permit claims of causality, the labels of IVs and DV are commonly used. In our hypotheses regarding the relationship between the constructs, we typically state or hold that the IVs are related to the DV, which means that changes in the DV are dependent on changes in the IVs.

Control variables (CVs) constitute a third type of variable. Factors extraneous may influence the principal relationship. These extraneous factors may cause changes in the DV when the IVs change, which is referred to as nuisance variance (Breaugh & Arnold, 2007; Meehl, 1970, 1971). Therefore, we seek to control for the effects of these extraneous factors when examining the principal relationship in nonexperimental research. We mostly refer to the variables representing these extraneous (or nuisance) factors as CVs.

To control for the extraneous factors, CVs may be employed in two ways: elimination or inclusion (Pedhazur & Schmelkin, 1991). Elimination refers to holding some of the variables constant, thus, controlling for their potential effects. For example, examining male entrepreneurs provides insights only into the relationship of work-and-family conflict and life satisfaction of male entrepreneurs as was done by Schjoedt (2013). Alternatively inclusion refers to the CV that is assessed and included in the data analysis providing opportunity to account for the variance caused by the CV. (Another form of inclusion is matched-group design. In this approach, entities of extraneous factors (e.g., people, organizations) that vary in terms of the IVs and DV are matched (Breaugh & Arnold, 2007). In this chapter, we only address CVs in terms of statistical inclusion rather than matched-groups design or elimination.) Continuing the example, if both females and male entrepreneurs were included in the sample, data on the respondents' sex were collected, and sex was included as a CV, the potential effect of sex on the DV—life satisfaction—could have been examined.

Unlike in experiments, in nonexperimental research we cannot control for extraneous factors through manipulation of the experimental conditions. Therefore, in our efforts to control for the extraneous factors, we use statistical control. This involves identifying extraneous factors that may influence the IV-DV relationship and the CVs that represent these extraneous factors. Then, when we conduct our data analysis, we control for these extraneous factors (using the CVs) mathematically by partialling out the variance associated with the CVs when estimating the relationships among the IVs and DV. For a more detailed nonmathematical explanation of statistical control, please see the work by Schjoedt and Bird (2014).

Control variables and their roles in nonexperimental research

Control variables and their role in statistical control depend on our intentions for the study. Statistical control has been used in three ways. First, prediction of unique variance in the DV that stems from the IVs (i.e., ΔR^2, R^2; D'Andrade & Dart, 1990; Hair et al., 2006). With the CVs entered as the first set of variables, providing a baseline and one or more IVs as a second or later set of variables in a regression analysis, the primary interest is whether the addition of IVs provides a meaningful increase in the variance explained by the regression model. This approach brings forth two challenges. The first challenge is to identify all meaningful variables predicting the DV. If a meaningful CV is left out, it will affect the estimate of the variance explained by the IVs and, thus, limit the explanatory value of the unique variance accounted for by the IVs. On the other hand, adding a large number of CVs limits the amount of unique variance explained by the IVs (Becker, 2005). The second challenge is that CVs are not all equal. Many CVs are included based on theoretical considerations of their association with the DV, while other CVs are artifacts of research design and sample characteristics (e.g., measurements, organizational characteristics) that covary with the DV but do not explain the relationship of interest between the IVs and the DV. When testing for incremental variance contributed by IVs, failing to include meaningful CVs could results in an overestimation of the IVs' unique contribution and inclusion of artifact CVs could result in an underestimation of the unique variance accounted for by the IVs when the artifact CVs are entered prior to the IVs. Even when meaningful CVs are correlated with IVs, the regression coefficients may not provide evidence of unique contributions.

Second, many times a measurement problem is (implicitly) assumed by researchers. The variable assessed does not represent the construct of interest, one or more of the IVs or the DV; and by removing the contaminant by partialling, the true relationship among variables of interest can be observed. This is referred to as purification (Spector & Brannick, 2011). To control this contaminant requires a CV that covaries perfectly with the contaminant but is unrelated with the variable of interest. Depending on the contaminant affects the IV-DV relationship or only an IV or the DV, partialling or semi-partialling the correlations is the appropriate statistical control (Carlson & Wu, 2012; Cohen et al., 2003). The challenge in purification is to identify the appropriate CV or CVs as many times, as a CV captures only a part of the contaminant. Another challenge is that CVs share variance with the variable of interest and when partialling results in removal of variance associated with the variable of interest (Spector, Zapf, Chen & Frese, 2000). Thus, identifying appropriate CVs is complicated by, many times, an IV and CV sharing both meaningful and contaminant variance, which is similar to the problem that occurs in examining common method variance (Doty & Glick, 1998; Podsakoff, MacKenzie, Lee &

Podsakoff, 2003; Spector, 2006). Considering that the regression coefficients are closely related to the semipartial correlation between the IV and DV means that when a CV is entered first in a regression analysis it controls the IV (not the DV) for the effect of the CV (Breaugh, 2005, 2008; Spector & Brannick, 2011). Consequently, when nuisance variance exists only in the DV or in both the IV and DV, the regression coefficient does not capture the intended relationship.

Third, we may want to assess the unique contribution of the IV in the presence of other variables or rule out alternative explanations (Becker, 2005; Breaugh, 2008; Cohen et al., 2003; Meehl, 1970, 1971; Spector et al., 2000). When we seek to control for the effects of a variable (the CV) on the IV to identify the unique contribution of the IV or rule out alternative explanations, it is unclear if the effect on the DV from residual IV (after partialling out the CV effect) is similar to the manipulation of the IV in experimental research. Controlling for (partialling out) the effects of a CV in an IV, especially when they are correlated, is profoundly problematic because effects are removed from variables that cannot be removed in real life (Breaugh, 2008; Meehl, 1970, 1971; Newcombe, 2003). This means when using control variables, a sample becomes a sample of "fictional people assigned fictional scores" (Meehl, 1970, p. 401) and results based on these "fictional people" do not generalize and are, consequently, of little interest in contributing to advancement of the field (Cohen et al., 2003; Hunter & Schmidt, 2004; Meehl, 1970). This issue becomes even more problematic as the magnitude of the correlations between the IVs and CVs increase (Breaugh, 2008; Schjoedt & Bird, 2014). In contrast to purification and the assumption that the use of CVs is an issue of measurement, this third approach is based on the assumption that variables are valid representations of the constructs. As this shows, employing CVs that are correlated with the IVs can result in regression coefficients that not equivalent to the original unpartialled variable; phrased differently, partialling changes the meaning of the regression coefficients.

Two points of view

Based on the preceding section, it appears that the use of CVs is problematic. This has led to two distinct points of view regarding their use. Select methodologists have adopted a conservative stance regarding CVs and promote the rule of thumb: "When in doubt, leave them out" (Carlson & Wu, 2012, p. 413). Essentially what these scholars note is that without clear evidence that the inclusion of CVs produce control, the CVs should not be used for statistical control. Another point of view is apparent if we judge the practice of using CVs in nonexperimental research. It is more liberal and widespread, and it encourages the use of CVs. Further considering the preceding section, it is worth looking at best practices before we examine the use of CVs in published research in the business literature.

Best practices

Whether one holds the conservative or liberal point of view regarding CVs or whether the purpose of the CVs is one of the three listed in the preceding pages, the best practices when employing CVs in nonexperimental research may be grouped into two: justification and reporting of CVs. Several methodologists (Becker, 2005; Breaugh, 2008; MacKinnon, Krull & Lockwood, 2000; Meehl, 1971; Spector & Brannick, 2011; Schwab, 2005) recommend that researchers provide theoretical evidence for the need and relevance of CVs. They also note that CVs should not be included without thought or explanation because without the theoretical justification, the empirical evidence of the relationship with the DV cannot be adequately appreciated (Breaugh, 2008; Swab, 2005). This means that consideration of CVs should not be confined to the methods section alone; they should be integrated in hypothesis development, hypotheses, results section, and discussion because CVs fundamentally alter the relationships between the IVs and the DV (Breaugh, 2006, 2008; Carlson & Wu, 2012; Meehl, 1970, 1971; Newcombe, 2003). This altered relationship between the IVs and the DV when partialling out the effects of the CVs is rarely, if ever, addressed as part of the considerations of the limitations to a study. We will provide nine recommendations for use of CVs after we have assessed the use of CVs in recent research publications.

A survey of the use of control vaiables in published research

Leading academic journals in business are revered and stand as hallmarks of excellent research. Thus, it is expected that articles published in these journals follow the best practices of employing CVs as part of the studies and of advancing the literature. This is furthered with several authors having noted that the use of CVs is widespread (e.g., Atinc, Simmering, & Kroll, 2012; Becker, 2005; Breaugh, 2006, 2008; Carlson & Wu, 2012; Spector & Brannick, 2011). These scholars have also noted that there are problematic issues surrounding the use of CVs in research published in leading academic journals. In our study, presented in this section, we assess the use of CVs in recent articles published in leading academic journals. After our assessment and identification of problematic issues in the current use of CVs in published research, we compare our results with other assessments of the use of CVs.

Method

For our assessment of the use of CVs, we coded all 63 articles published in 2013 in two leading business journals as mentioned earlier—*Journal of Accounting and Economics* (*JAE*) and *Journal of Business Venturing* (*JBV*). We chose the year 2013 because it is the most recent full year prior to writing this chapter and we chose these two journals because they are the leading journals in each of our areas of research interests, accounting and entrepreneurship. Since we are only interested in published empirical research that includes CVs, we did not consider conceptual research, editorials, no-empirical reviews, meta-analyses or the like. *JAE* published 32 and *JBV* published 13 articles with empirical research. To maintain consistency among the studies, we focused on studies employing regression analysis. Among the empirical research articles we found only two. One article did not include CVs resulting in data from 12 studies from *JBV*. This means that 98% of all the empirical research articles published in *JAE* and *JBV* in 2013 included CVs. To maintain consistency among the studies, we focused on studies employing regression analysis as the principal method of data analysis. One study published in *JBV* employed structural equation modeling. This study was also excluded from our assessment. Exclusion of these two studies resulted in our assessment based on 32 *JAE* and 11 *JBV*—a total of 43—articles published in 2013.

To assess inter-rater reliability, we independently coded three articles from the *Strategic Entrepreneurship Journal* from the year 2009. This resulted in an inter-rater reliability of 88%. We clarified the differences before coding the articles published in *JAE* and *JBV*. For our assessment, we identified items used in other assessments of use of CVs (Atinc et al., 2012; Becker, 2005; Carlson & Wu, 2012). This resulted 65 coded items per article and in consistency with previous assessments. We coded a variety of information on the type of study (micro/macro) and correlational; the type of analysis (e.g., regression); the discussion section, and on IVs, DV, and CVs (e.g., number of variables). Considering that our focus in this chapter is on CVs, we only included measures that pertain to CVs in the following.

Measures

Separate section. We coded 1 for an article that included a separate section on CVs and 0 when a separate section on CVs was not provided in the article (Atinc et al., 2012).

Described. We coded 1 for articles that included a description of, at least, one of the CVs and 0 for those that did not include any description.

Relevance described. When the relevance of at least one CV was described, we coded 1, otherwise 0 (Atinc et al., 2012; Becker, 2005; Carlson & Wu, 2012).

Measurement. If description of the measurement of the CVs was included, it was coded as 1, if not, then it was coded as 0 (Atinc et al., 2012; Becker, 2005).

Psychometric properties. We coded 1 if an article included any psychometric properties for the CVs, for example, Cronbach's alpha. On the other hand, if no psychometric properties were provided, we coded it as 0 (Atinc et al., 2012; Breaugh, 2006).

Citation support. If the authors provided citations to other studies as support for the CVs, we coded 1, otherwise 0 (Atinc et al., 2012; Becker, 2005).

Data source. If the data used for the control variables were primary data, we coded 1, if not, then 0 (Atinc et al., 2012; Carlson & Wu, 2012).

Basis for inclusion. As noted by other scholars, the basis for inclusion of CVs should be mentioned in a research publication. We coded 0 for articles that did not include any basis for the inclusion; 1 when authors mentioned that the CV, or CVs, might be related to the IVs or DV; 2 when a conceptual argument for the inclusion was provided; and 3 when the authors provided empirical evidence for the inclusion of the CVs (Atinc et al., 2012; Becker, 2005; Carlson & Wu, 2012).

Relationship direction stated. When the direction of the relationship among the CV and DV was predicted, we coded 1, if not prediction of the relationship was provided, it was coded 0 (Atinc et al., 2012).

Perceptual variable. If one or more of the CVs were perceptual variables—a perceptual variable is based on respondents provide a judgment or rating—it was coded as 1. If all the CVs were nonperceptual variables, the article was coded as 0 (Atinc et al., 2012; Breaugh, 2006).

Proxy variable. Often nonperceptual variables are employed as proxies for another variable that the researchers want to control for in the study. If at least one CV was a proxy for another variable, it was coded as 1, otherwise it was coded as 0 (Atinc et al., 2012; Pedhazur & Schmelkin, 1991; Spector & Brannick, 2011).

IV-CV relationship. If the relationship between an IV and CV was described in the article as part of the hypothesis development or literature review, it was coded as 1, if not, then 0 (Atinc et al., 2012).

DV-CV relationship. If the relationship between the DV and a CV was described in the article as part of the hypothesis development or literature review, it was coded as 1, if not, then 0 (Atinc et al., 2012).

CVs in hypotheses. When the CVs were included in a stated hypothesis, it was coded as 1, if not, then 0 (Atinc et al., 2012; Becker, 2005).

All CVs in descriptive stats. If the authors reported the descriptive statistics and correlations for all the CVs, we coded it as 1, if not, we coded it as 0 (Atinc et al., 2012; Becker, 2005).

CVs correlations in text. If correlations discussed in the text included one or more CVs, then it was coded as 1, if not, then it was coded as 0 (Atinc et al., 2012; Becker, 2005).

One CV-relationship in text. If a relationship with a CV and another variable was addressed in the text, then we coded it as 1. If no relationships were commented on in the text, then we coded it as 0 (Atinc el al., 2012; Becker, 2015).

Relationships among all CVs in text. If all the relationships—correlations or regression coefficients—were addressed in the text, then it was coded as 1, if not, then it was coded as 0 (Atinc et al., 2012; Becker, 2005).

R^2 for CVs reported. If the authors reported the R^2 for a block of CVs, we coded 1, if not, we coded 0 (Atinc et al., 2012; Becker, 2005).

ΔR^2 for CVs reported. If incremental R^2 for the CVs was reported by the authors, then we coded it as 1, on the other hand, we coded it as 0 (Atinc et al., 2012; Becker, 2005).

Addressed in results. When results pertaining to CVs were addressed in the results section, it was coded as 1. When the CV results were not part of the text in the results section, it was coded as 0 (Atinc et al., 2012; Becker, 2005).

Addressed in discussion. This was coded as 1 when results pertaining to CVs were included in the discussion section and 0 when not included (Atinc et al., 2012; Becker, 2005).

CV-DV relationship addressed in discussion. If any of the relationships among any of the CVs and the DV was included as part of the discussion section, we coded it as 1; if not, then we coded it as 0 (Atinc et al., 2012; Becker, 2005).

IV-CV relationship addressed in discussion. When a relationship between an IV and a CV was addressed in the discussion section, we coded 1, if not, we coded 0 (Atinc et al., 2012; Becker, 2005).

Results

In table 15.1 we present the total numbers of IVs and CVs and the average number of IVs and CVs per article, as well as the standard deviation. We do so for *JAE*, *JBV*, and for all 43 articles used in our assessment. It is noteworthy that the average number of IVs per research publication is approximately the same for both journals—*JAE* employed an average of 4.1 IVs and *JBV* an average of 4.3 Ivs, whereas the number of CVs per article is substantially higher for the articles published in *JAE*. Empirical research published in *JAE* had on average 9.3 CVs; whereas the average number of CVs in *JBV* was 6.1. One reason for this may be in the type of study. In their assessment of the use of CVs in management research, Atinc et al. (2012) distinguished between macro- and microstudies. Macrostudies refers to studies with organizational or industry-level outcomes); and, microstudies refers to research with individual or group-level outcomes. Visually examining whether a study was macro or micro, we observed that all 32 research publications in *JAE* were macrostudies. For *JBV*,

Table 15.1 Total number, means, and standard deviations

	IVs			CVs		
	Number	Mean	s.d.	Number	Mean	s.d.
JAE	131	4.1	2.8	299	9.3	5.8
JBV	67	4.3	2.5	47	6.1	3.0
All	198	4.1	2.7	346	8.5	5.4

seven articles described macrostudies and four microstudies. We also observed that the microstudies had fewer CVs than macrostudies. Because of the difference between the macro- (39) and micro (4) studies and the very small number of microstudies, we did not compare the mean number of CVs statistically.

In table 15.2 we present the frequencies and percentages on the variables we measured to assess the use of CVs in published research for the 43 empirical research articles published in *JAE* and *JBV* in 2013. We present these frequencies and percentages for *JAE, JBV,* and all the articles. Collectively, there does not seem to be a pattern in how CVs are used, addressed, or reported across the journals. However, there are some consistencies. No one reports psychometric properties of CVs. No hypothesis includes CVs. Also, no one addresses all the relationships among the CVs in the text, and no one considers the relationships among the CVs and the DV as part of the discussion.

In *JAE* less than half of the articles included a separate section on CVs; whereas in *JVB* more than 90% included such a section. Only about 60% of the research published in *JAE* included a description of the CVs; while all the articles in published in *JBV* included CV-descriptions. Less than one-in-five of the publications included a description of how or why the CVs were relevant to the study. Less than 10% of the research published in both journals included a description of how the CVs were measured; for the most part, the CVs were just mentioned. Research published in *JAE* included citations as support for the CVs in more than 95% of the articles. This was only the case in about 82% of the articles published in *JBV.* Secondary data were used in the vast majority of publications in *JAE*; yet, the majority of studies used primary data for the CVs in *JBV.* About a third of the published articles included an argument for inclusion of the CVs with only 31% in *JAE* and 46% in *JBV.* In only 3 articles were the direction of the relationship with CVs stated; all these were in *JAE.* In a total of 11 publications, CVs were employed as proxy variables [10 (31%) in *JAE* and 1 in *JBV* (9%)]. Four articles—two in each journal—included a description of the IV-CV relationships, which is less than 10% of the publications. The DV-CV relationships were described in a quarter of the articles published in 2013—22% in *JAE* and 27% in JBV. In about 80% of the publications—81% in *JAE* and 73% in *JBV*—the correlations among all the CVs were reported as part of the descriptive statistics. However, only one study in each of the journals included considerations of the correlations among CVs in the text. While the majority of the published articles included R^2 for the CVs, only three (27%) articles in *JBV* (and none in *JAE*) included R^2-change. More than 80% of the research published in 2013 included mentioning of the CVs in the text in the section describing the results—88% in *JAE* and 73% in *JBV.* On the other hand, the CVs were only considered in the section discussing the study findings in one-in-five articles [8 articles (25%) in *JAE* and 1 article (9%) in *JBV*]. Lastly, only two research publications included considerations of the IV-CV

Table 15.2 Frequencies and percentages of use of CVs

Coded variable	Value	*JAE* n = 32		*JBV* n = 11		All articles n = 43	
		Count	%	Count	%	Count	%
Separate CV section	Yes (1)	13	40.6	11	90.9	23	53.5
	No (0)	19	59.4	1	9.1	20	46.5
CVs described	Yes (1)	20	62.5	11	100.0	31	72.1
	No (0)	12	37.5	0	0.0	12	27.9
CV relevance described	Yes (1)	4	12.5	2	18.2	6	14.0
	No (0)	28	87.5	9	81.8	37	86.0
CV measurement	No info (0)	0	0.0	2	18.2	2	4.7
	Mentioned (1)	29	90.6	8	72.7	37	86.0
	Described (2)	3	9.4	1	9.1	4	9.3
Psychometric properties of CVs	Provided (1)	0	0.0	0	0.0	0	0.0
	Not provided (0)	32	100.0	11	100.0	43	100.0
Citation support for CVs	Yes (1)	31	96.9	9	81.8	40	93.0
	No (0)	1	3.1	2	18.2	3	7.0
Data source for CVs	Primary (1)	2	6.3.	7	63.6	9	20.9
	Secondary (0)	30	93.8	4	36.4	34	79.1
Basis for inclusion of CVs	Provided (1)	10	31.3	5	45.5	15	34.9
	Not provided	22	68.8	6	54.5	28	65.1
CV relationship direction stated	Yes (1)	3	9.4	0	0.0	3	7.0
	No (0)	29	90.6	11	100.0	40	93.0
CV as a perceptual variable	Yes (1)	0	0.0	0	0.0	0	0.0
	No (0)	32	100.0	10	100.0	43	100.0
CV as a proxy variable	Yes (1)	10	31.3	1	9.1	11	25.6
	No (0)	22	68.8	10	90.9	32	74.4
IV-CV relationship	Described (1)	2	6.3	2	18.2	4	9.3
	Not described (0)	30	93.8	9	81.8	39	90.7

continued

Table 15.2 Continued

Coded variable	Value	*JAE* $n = 32$		*JBV* $n = 11$		All articles $n = 43$	
		Count	%	Count	%	Count	%
DV-CV relationship	Described (1)	7	21.9	3	27.3	10	23.3
	Not described (0)	25	78.1	8	72.7	33	76.7
CVs in hypotheses	Yes (1)	0	0.0	0	0.0	0	0.0
	No (0)	32	100.0	11	100.0	43	100.0
All CVs in descriptive stats	Yes (1)	26	81.3	8	72.7	34	79.1
	No (0)	6	18.8	3	27.3	9	20.9
CV correlations in text	Yes (1)	1	3.1	1	9.1	2	4.7
	No (0)	31	96.9	10	90.9	41	95.3
One CV-relationship in text	Yes	3	9.4	0	0.0	3	7.0
	No	29	90.6	11	100.0	40	93.0
Relationships among all CVs in text	Yes (1)	0	0.0	0	0.0	0	0.0
	No (0)	32	100.0	11	100.0	43	100.0
R^2 for CVs reported	Yes (1)	30	6.3	7	63.6	37	86.0
	No (0)	2	93.8	4	36.4	6	14.0
ΔR^2 for CVs reported	Yes (1)	0	0.0	3	27.3	3	7.0
	No (0)	32	100.0	8	72.7	40	93.0
CVs addressed in Results	Yes (1)	28	87.5	8	72.7	36	83.7
	No (0)	4	12.5	3	27.3	7	16.3
CVs addressed in Discussion	Yes (1)	8	25.0	1	9.1	9	20.9
	No (0)	24	75.0	10	90.9	34	79.1
CV-DV relationship addressed in Discussion	Yes (1)	0	0.0	0	0.0	0	0.0
	No (0)	32	100.0	11	100.0	43	100.0
IV-CV relationship addressed in Discussion	Yes (1)	2	6.3	0	0.0	2	4.7
	No (0)	30	93.8	11	100.0	41	95.7

relationships as part of the section in which the study findings were discussed. Both these were in *JAE*.

Discussion and recommendations for future research

The purpose of this chapter is to draw attention to the use of CVs and to provide a set of nine recommendations for use of CVs in future research. This is for the purpose of improving the use of CVs to enhance the quality and contributions of future nonexperimental research. We have pointed out three roles of CVs in nonexperimental research. We also introduced best practices for employing CVs. Despite these best practices being widely known, our assessment of the use of CVs in published research revealed some troublesome characteristics.

Our assessment revealed that 98% of the published empirical research published included CVs. It also showed that 96% of the empirical research employed regression analysis as the principal means of data analysis and all studies employing regression analysis included CVs. These numbers illustrate the importance of CVs in research and understanding of how CVs influence research findings. Collectively, our assessment illustrates that while there some characteristics of the use of CVs in research that are good, there is substantial room for improvement of the use of CVs if we want to enhance the validity of our research findings and, in turn, advance the literature and our understanding of business.

Control variable selection

The first recommendation for use of CVs is to justify their inclusion. This is perhaps the most important recommendation we can offer. Provide theoretical evidence for the need and relevance of the CVs, or, at least, explain briefly why the CVs were selected. The best scenario is when the CVs are included in the development of the hypotheses and also included in the hypotheses (Atinc et al., 2012; Becker, 2005; Breaugh, 2006, 2008; Carlson & Wu, 2012; Gordon, 1968; Meehl, 1970, 1971; Schjoedt & Bird, 2014; Spector & Brannick, 2011; Spector, et al., 2000).

Our assessment revealed that about 35% of the research publications included a justification for inclusion of the CVs. This is less than the rate found by other scholars (Atinc et al., 2012; Becker, 2005; Carlson & Wu, 2012). Closer examination of the frequencies reveals that there is a substantial difference between the journals. The basis for inclusion of CVs is more widespread in entrepreneurship (*JBV*) than in accounting (*JAE*), and the frequency seen in entrepreneurship is in line with the management literature (Atinc et al., 2012; Becker, 2005; Carlson & Wu, 2012). If citations supporting the use of CVs are considered, then again the entrepreneurship publications are in line with the management literature, while more of the accounting research publications included citations than other assessments of the use of CVs (Atinc et al., 2012; Becker, 2005). This indicates there is some room for improvement in our use of CVs.

The second recommendation for use of CVs is to avoid artifact CVs. Inclusion of artifact CVs—CVs that are conceptually unrelated with the DV—limits the potential for the IVs to account for variance in the DV (a type II error; concluding there is no effect when there is, in fact, an effect). Avoid inclusion of multiple control variables to cover all eventualities. Only include a CV when there is a logical reason and/or empirical or conceptual evidence supporting the inclusion, as inclusion of more CVs comes at a price, reduction of statistical power and potential for reduced generalizability of the findings (Bandura, 1997; Becker, 2005; Carlson & Wu, 2011; Cohen et al., 2003; Pedhazur & Schmelkin, 1991; Schjoedt & Bird, 2014).

While we did not assess whether a CV was an artifact CV, we did observe there was, on average, more CVs than IVs in the publications, and there were more CVs in the accounting publications than in the entrepreneurship studies. When placing these results in the context of the results provided by Carlson and Wu (2012), we note that artifact CVs is an issue in published research, which also indicates we may improve our use of CVs by limiting the number of artifact CVs employed in our future research.

Measurement of control variables

The third recommendation is to provide a clear and concise description of the CVs: how each control variable was measured and how they were used, for example, to explain differences between analyses with one set versus another set of control variables (Becker, 2005; Schjoedt & Bird, 2014).

Our assessment revealed that in more than 60% of the articles, the CVs were described; however, their measurement was only described in about 9% of the published articles. This is substantially less than the 90% found by Atinc et al., (2012). One aspect that may account for why our assessment revealed that CV measurements were only mentioned, not described, maybe due to the vast majority of the studies that examined firm level variables. However, the assessment by Atinc et al. (2012) showed that over 95% of the research examining firm level variables included descriptions of how CVs were measured. Becker's (2005) research also illustrates that omission of descriptions of CV measurement is widespread, yet, more prevalent than in our assessment. While mentioning the CVs, which is done widespread, there is room for improvement in how we describe the employed CVs in our research and this could be done by including a clear description of how all the CVs were measured.

The fourth recommendation is not to use proxies in place of the real CVs (nuisance variables). The problem inherent in using proxy variables for CVs is that it is not clear to what extent the proxy variable truly controls the real nuisance variance; if at all possible, researchers should measure the actual nuisance variable that is to be controlled for in a study instead of using proxies (Breaugh, 2006, 2008; Carlson & Wu, 2011; Meehl, 1970, 1971; Pedhazur & Schmelkin, 1991; Spector & Brannick, 2011; Schjoedt & Bird, 2014).

In the research publication in our assessment about a quarter of the research publications included proxy variables. While no other assessment of CVs provides frequencies for the use of proxies as part of the CVs, we observe that about a third of the accounting publications and less than 10% of the entrepreneurship articles included proxy variables as CVs instead of the actual nuisance variables. Because a proxy variable may not adequately capture the true nature of the variable it is intended to represent, especially in regard to the proxy variable's relationship with the IVs and DV, the use of proxy variables is problematic for the validity of the research findings as their inclusion in a study may lead to misinterpretation of the study results (Atinc et al., 2012; Breaugh, 2006, 2008; Pedhazur & Schmelkin, 1991; Spector & Brannick, 2011). Again, there is room for improvement in our use of CVs.

Data analysis

The fifth recommendation is to run the data analyses with and without CVs. Prior to analyzing the data using regression analysis; carefully examine the zero-order correlations. Further, to determine if the impact of the control variables is meaningful in the regression analysis, run a regression analysis with the IVs and DV without CVs; and, then, introduce CVs as a second step into the regression analysis. If the regression results do not differ, the CVs do not account for the findings. If they do differ, it indicates the manuscript describing the study should include examination of how the CVs influence the variables of interest (Becker, 2005; Carlson & Wu, 2012; Meehl, 1971; Schjoedt & Bird, 2014).

In our assessment, we went beyond only considering whether correlations were considered as part of the descriptive statistics. We found very few research publications included considerations of the zero-order correlations with CVs in the text (less than 5%). This is furthered by only three research publications that included assessment of the impact of the CVs (ΔR^2 for CVs). Based on this observation, it seems there is limited consideration of whether CVs are meaningful in the research. Placing this finding in the context of whether CVs are meaningful in a study (Becker, 2005), there is room for improvement by considering the simple relationships CVs have with and the impact CVs have on other variables (IVs and DV) in a study.

Reporting

The sixth recommendation is to provide descriptive statistics (i.e., means and standard deviations) for all continuous control variables. Provide summary descriptive statistics for categorical control variables (e.g., percentage of observations for each category). This offers an opportunity for readers to make their own assessment of the CVs impact and relationships (Atinc et al., 2012; Becker, 2005; Breaugh 2006, 2008; Gordon, 1968; Schjoedt & Bird, 2014).

It is good to see that about 80% of the research publications in our assessment included CVs in the descriptive statistics, which was typically in a table with means, standard deviations, and zero-order corrections. This is consistent with the results provided by other researchers (Atinc et al., 2012; Becker, 2005, Carlson & Wu, 2012). Despite this, there is still room for improvement by including all CVs in a table with correlations to provide an overview and a basis for assessment whether the CVs are meaningful in the study. Further, when correlations among all variables—IVs, DV, and CVs—are presented in a correlations table, it helps readers identify discrepancies between the regression results and correlations. Such discrepancies may indicate variable suppression and issues in interpretation of the regression results (Atinc et al., 2012; Becker, 2005; Breaugh, 2008; Carlson & Wu, 2011; Schjoedt & Bird, 2014; Spector & Brannick, 2011).

The seventh recommendation is to provide evidence of the psychometric properties of all variable measures including the CVs. If the validity of the CVs measures is questionable, the results generated using the CVs are also questionable (Becker, 2005; Breaugh 2006, 2008; Pedhazur & Schmelkin, 1991; Schjoedt & Bird, 2014; Stone-Romero, 2007).

In our assessment, no research publication included any psychometric properties for the CVs. Considering that psychometric properties are important in establishing measurement validity, the observation that no study included consideration of psychometric properties may be due to no study employed perceptual variables as CVs. Even though the vast majority of articles considered in our assessment described studies focused on firm level CVs and, in many articles, they were, what is referred to as, objective variables, there may still be a need to consider whether they are valid measures, especially if they are proxy variables. Using multiple measures to assess objective variables, a form of triangulation of the variable measurement, is desirable. While our assessment does not provide an opportunity to consider CVs based on multi-item measures (because there were none), we still echo other scholars when pointing out there is also room for improvement in reporting psychometric properties or other information that illustrates the CVs are assessed using valid measures.

The eighth recommendation is to give CVs the same attention as IVs when reporting the results. Both the IVs and CVs have independent effects on the DV. In the results section, it is beneficial to the readers to include the same results (e.g., beta, significance level, variance explained) for the continuous and dichotomous control variables that are typically provided for in the IVs.

This provides readers an opportunity to make their own assessment (Atinc et al., 2012; Becker, 2005; Meehl, 1970, 1971; Breaugh, 2008; Carlson & Wu, 2011; Schjoedt & Bird, 2014; Spector et al., 2000).

While our assessment showed that CVs do get attention when the results are reported, in correlation tables and to a very limited degree in the text, it is far from the attention given to the IVs despite both CVs and IVs having independent effects on the DV. Further, rarely were results reported showing CVs' independent effect by reporting the unique incremental variance (ΔR^2) accounted for by the CVs after the IVs had been entered. Also, rarely was at least one relationship with a CV considered in the text presenting the results. This pattern is similar to those found in other assessments (Atinc et al., 2012; Becker, 2005; Carlson & Wu, 2012).

Interpretation of results

The ninth recommendation is to interpret the results that pertain to the hypotheses. Most researchers do not include CVs in the hypotheses. This means when the regression results are interpreted to determine the study findings, only results without CVs should be used to determine whether a hypothesis is supported. In effect, when hypotheses do not include CVs and data analyses include CVs, the results that are based upon inclusion of the CVs cannot support the hypothesized relationship researchers as the inclusion of the CVs profoundly alters the relationship among the IVs and DV (Atinc et al., 2012; Becker, 2005; Carlson & Wu, 2012; Schjoedt & Bird, 2014; Spector & Brannick, 2011).

In our assessment of the use of CVs in published research, we found no hypothesis that included CVs. Yet, we found that all the findings were based on data analysis that included CVs. This means that while relationship A is hypothesized, relationship B is empirically tested to draw conclusions whether there is support for the hypothesis pertaining to relationship A. Another assessment of the use of CVs also shows that 96% of the articles considered did not include CVs in the hypotheses, while the article authors stated that the hypotheses were supported or not using results based on findings from data analysis that included CVs (Atinc et al., 2012).

General discussion, limitations, and suggestions for future research

It appears that from our assessment that CVs receive limited consideration from researchers, and this limited consideration has the potential to limit the validity of research findings, at times led to misinterpretation of the results, and limit the potential to advance the literature. The limited attention CVs receive may result in invalid research results and findings, which, in turn limit advancement of the literature, if not reverse progress by providing findings that contradict the literature. This and the appearance of a set way of considering CV in published research (Atinc et al., 2012; Carlson & Wu, 2011) are the reasons why we chose to draw attention to the current use of CVs with this chapter and our assessment and to provide nine recommendations for improving the use of CVs in empirical research. With this in mind, a tenth recommendation is to include CVs in the considerations of the limitations to a study. Such considerations could include thoughts about the effects of CVs as proxies for other variables, relationships, if any, among CVs and IVs, measurement of CVs, etc.

Since we point out how limitations pertaining to CVs need to be considered in future research publications, let us also point out limitations in our assessment. In our assessment, we focused on research articles published in 2013 in two journals. This presents a bias as it does provide a broad assessment across multiple years for each journal. It only provides an indication of the problematic issues pertaining to the use of CVs in published research. Yet, that is enough to illustrate there are problematic issues in the use of CVs in published research as we chose to use elite journals in two separate areas of business—accounting and entrepreneurship. Our assessment was also biased by our focus on regression analysis in the selection of which research publications to include in our assessment. We could have included studies in which structural equation modeling (SEM) was the principal method of data analysis. This would have resulted in one additional publication to be included in our assessment. We determined the cost-benefit of the added value of adding one more article to our assessment. At the expense of consistency the method of data analysis was limited to such a degree that we chose to focus on regression analysis-based research only. Also, one publication does not suffice to make a comparative study among the use of CVs in regression analysis and SEM. We note that other scholars also observed a very limited number of publications based on SEM (Atinc et al., 2012). While we focused on research based on regression analysis only, we observed that our findings are similar to those that include SEM-based research (e.g., Atinc et al., 2012). An assessment of CVs in SEM-based research may be a topic for another chapter in another volume since SEM-based research is increasing in research publications. Unbeknownst to us at the outset, the vast majority of research was macrostudies in which the variables of interest are at the firm level, not the individual or group levels. This also presents a limitation to our assessment. As part of our presentation of the recommendation and discussion of our results we included considerations of research results on the use of CVs. Because we found similar patterns in the results we are confident that our findings are consistent and not biased in revealing the problematic issues in the current use of CVs or in supporting the need for improving the use of CVs by following the nine recommendations we echo in this chapter (Atinc et al., 2012; Becker, 2005; Breaugh,

2006, 2008; Carlson & Wu, 2012; Meehl, 1970, 1971; Schjoedt & Bird, 2014; Spector & Brannick, 2011). Thus, we suggest that scholars will employ the recommendations in future research to enhance the validity of their research findings and the literature.

Concluding comments

The purpose of this chapter was to draw attention to the issue of control variables in nonexperimental research, assess the present use of control variables, and provide nine recommendations for use of control variables in future research. We considered CVs in a nonmathematical manner, two points of view regarding the use of CVs, and best practices of using CVs prior to providing an assessment of the current use of CVs in research publications in business. From our assessment we observed that CVs receive limited consideration from researchers, and this limited consideration is based on the appearance of a set way in considering CVs published research. This is evident in the relationships between CVs and other variables (IVs and DV) and is rarely considered beyond presenting the correlations as part of a table in which the descriptive statistics are presented. Very rarely are CVs considered as part of the hypothesis development or discussion. For example, no published study in our assessment included CVs as part of the hypotheses. This is despite CVs being, in fact, independent variables. We ended our assessment by presenting nine recommendations by echoing other methodologists (Atinc, et al., 2012, Becker, 2005; Breaugh 2, 2006, 2008; Carlson & Wu, 2012; Meehl, 1970, 1971; Pedhazur & Schmelkin, 1991; Schjoedt & Bird, 2014; Spector & Brannick, 2011). As this chapter comes to an end, we want to emphasize that the major issue in the current use of control variables is not the inclusion of control variables, but that the use of CVs is often inappropriate leading to problematic research findings. In concert with many authors (e.g., Atinc et al., 2012; Becker, 2005; Breaugh, 2006, 2008; Carlson & Wu, 2011; Meehl, 1970, 1971; Schjoedt & Bird, 2014; Spector & Brannick, 2011), our assessment illustrates that there is room for improvement in using CVs in research studies and the nine recommendations echoed in this chapter hold potential to improve the use of CVs in research publications to enhance validity of research findings and to advance the business literature.

References

Atinc, G., Simmering, M. J., & Kroll, M. J. (2012). Control variable use and reporting in macro and micromanagement research. *Organizational Research Methods, 15*(1), 57–74.

Austin, J. T., Scherbaum, C. A., & Mahlman, R. A. (2002). History of research methods in industrial and organizational psychology. In S. G. Rogelberg (Ed.), *Handbook of research methods in industrial and organizational psychology* (pp. 3–33). Malden, MA: Blackwell Publishers.

Becker, T. E. (2005). Potential problems in the statistical control of variables in organizational research: A qualitative analysis with recommendations. *Organizational Research Methods, 8*(1), 274–289.

Breaugh, J. A. (2006). Rethinking the control of nuisance variables in theory testing. *Journal of Business and Psychology, 20*(1), 429–443.

Breaugh, J. A. (2008). Important considerations in using statistical procedures to control for nuisance variables in non-experimental studies. *Human Resource Management Review, 18*(3), 282–293.

Carlson, K. D. & Wu, J. (2012). The illusion of statistical control: Control variable practice in management research. *Organizational Research Methods, 15*(2), 413–435.

Cohen, J., Cohen, P., West, S. G., & Aiken, L. S. (2003). *Applied multiple regression/correlation analysis for the behavior sciences.* Mahwah, NJ: Lawrence Erlbaum.

D'Andrade, R., & Dart, J. (1990). The interpretation of *R* versus *R*2 or why percent of variance accounted for is a poor measure of effect size. *Journal of Quantitative Anthropology, 2*(1), 47–59.

Doty, D. H., & Glick, W. H. (1998). Common methods bias: Does common methods variance really bias results; An investigation of prevalence and effect. *Organizational Research Methods, 1*(2), 374–406.

Hair, J. F., Black, W. C., Babin, B. J., Anderson, R. E., & Tatham, R. L. (2006). *Multivariate data analysis* (6th ed.). Upper Saddle River, NJ: Pearson/Prentice Hall.

Hunter, J. E., & Schmidt, F. L. (2004). *Methods of meta-analysis.* Thousand Oaks, CA: Sage.

Ketchen, D., Boyd, B., & Bergh, D. (2008). Research methodology in strategic management: Past accomplishments and future challenges. *Organizational Research Methods, 11*(3), 643–658.

MacKinnon, D. P., Krull, J. L., & Lockwood, C. M. (2000). Equivalence of the mediation, confounding and suppression effect. *Prevention Science, 1*(2), 173–181.

Meehl, P. E. (1970). Nuisance variables and the ex post facto design. In M. Radner & S. Winokur (Eds.), *Analyses of theories and methods of physics and psychology* (pp. 373–402). Minneapolis: University of Minnesota Press.

Meehl, P. E. (1971). High school yearbooks: A reply to Schwarz. *Journal of Abnormal Psychology, 77*(4), 143–148.

Newcombe, N. S. (2003). Some controls control too much. *Child Development, 74*(1), 1050–1052.

Pedhazur, E. J., & Schmelkin, L. P. (1991). *Measurement, design, and analysis: An integrated approach.* Hillsdale, NJ: Lawrence Erlbaum.

Podsakoff, P. M., MacKenzie, S. G., Lee, J. Y., & Podsakoff, N. P. (2003). Common method biases in behavioral research: A critical review of the literature and recommended remedies. *Journal of Applied Psychology, 88*(3), 879–903.

Schjoedt, L. (2013). The influence of work-and-family conflict on male entrepreneurs' life satisfaction: A comparison of entrepreneurs and non-entrepreneurs. *Journal of Small Business & Entrepreneurship, 26*(1), 45–64.

Schjoedt, L. & Bird, B. (2014). Control variables: Use, misuse, and recommended use. In A. Carsrud & M. E. Brännback (Eds.), *Handbook of research methods and applications in entrepreneurship and small business* (pp. 136–155). Northampton, MA: Edward Elgar.

Schwab, D. B. (2005). *Research methods for organizational studies.* Mahwah, NJ: Lawrence Erlbaum Associates.

Schwab, D. P. (1980). Construct validity in organizational behavior. *Research in Organizational Behavior, 2*(1), 3–43.

Spector, P. E. (2006). Method variance in organization research: Truth or urban legend? *Organizational Research Methods, 9*(1), 221–232.

Spector, P. A., & Brannick, M. T. (2011). Methodological urban legends: The misuse of statistical control variables. *Organizational Research Methods, 14*(2), 287–305.

Spector, P. E., Zapf, D., Chen, P. Y., & Frese, M. (2000). Why negative affectivity should not be controlled in job stress research: Don't throw the baby out with the bath water. *Journal of Organizational Behavior, 21*(3), 79–95.

Stone-Romero, E. F. (2007). Non-experimental designs. In S. Rogelberg (Ed.), *The encyclopedia of industrial and organizational psychology* (pp. 519–522). Beverly Hills, CA: Sage Publishing.

16
Monte Carlo Simulation Using Excel: Case Study in Financial Forecasting

Seifedine Kadry

The nature of simulation

Modeling is the process of producing a model; a model is a representation of the construction and working of some system of interest. A model is similar to but simpler than the system it represents. One purpose of a model is to enable the analyst to predict the effect of changes to the system. On the one hand, a model should be a close approximation to the real system and incorporate most of its salient features. On the other hand, it should not be so complex that it is impossible to understand and experiment with it. A good model is a judicious tradeoff between realism and simplicity. Simulation practitioners recommend increasing the complexity of a model iteratively. An important issue in modeling is model validity. Model validation techniques include simulating the model under known input conditions and comparing model output with system output. Generally, a model intended for a simulation study is a mathematical model developed with the help of simulation software. Mathematical model classifications include deterministic (input and output variables are fixed values) or stochastic (at least one of the input or output variables is probabilistic) and static (time is not taken into account) or dynamic (time-varying interactions among variables are taken into account). Typically, simulation models are stochastic and dynamic.

A simulation of a system is the operation of a model of the system. The model can be reconfigured and experimented with; usually, this is impossible, too expensive, or impractical to do in the system it represents. The operation of the model can be studied, and hence, properties concerning the behavior of the actual system or its subsystem can be inferred. In its broadest sense, simulation is a tool to evaluate the performance of a system, existing or proposed, under different configurations of interest and over long periods of real time. As an example of the use of simulation, consider a manufacturing company that is contemplating building a large extension onto one of its plants but is not sure if the potential gain in productivity would justify the construction cost. It certainly would not be cost-effective to build the extension and then remove it later if it does not work out. However, a careful simulation study could shed some light on the question by simulating the operation of the plant as it currently exists and as it would be if the plant were expanded (Banks, 1998).

Steps in simulation study

Before simulation is applied to the problem, a simulation analysis needs to be conducted to ensure that the changes will be beneficial. This section will show how to perform a proper simulation analysis through different steps (Banks, Carson, Nelson, & Nicol, 2005; Cellier, & Kofman, 2006):

Step 1: Formulate the problem

This step is vital. For simulation to be effective, it needs to solve the right problem. In this step, we take a look at the problem to understand it and then to formulate the problem statement. For example, find the average profit of a product subject to random parameters.

Step 2: Select the input variables

Use the problem statement to create variables for the simulation. There are two types of variables. Decision variables are variables that can be controlled by the programmer, for example fixed cost. Uncontrollable variables are variables that are random and can be approximated, but not controlled by the programmer, for instance sales quantity, variable cost.

Step 3: Make constraints on decision variables

Assign values and constraints to the variables that can be controlled.

Step 4: Identify the output variables

Establish what variables you want the simulation to output. During this step, consider your problem statement. What are you trying to solve? Try to program output variables that are broad enough to help see the problem. For example, profit.

Step 5: Collect real data

Gather information from the system to input into the simulation. This can be done using a survey, historical sales, etc.

Step 6: Model development

In this step, we re-write the problem statement using mathematical equation. For example:

Profit = revenue – (Variable cost – fixed cost)

Step 7: Model implementation

Choose simulation software, like Excel, to run the model. We may need to assign different capabilities, such as a random number generation, which would help model the randomness of reality in the simulation.

Step 8: Model verification

Setup Excel to run an initial simulation and compare the results to the actual system. Confirm if the data found are comparable to real data; otherwise rework your simulation until it resembles the real-world data.

Step 9: Model experimentation and output analysis

Test the simulation to find the best possible solution to the problem. Try altering some of the variables. Graph all findings to see all possible solutions, as there may be more than one solution to the problem. The programmer and the problem responsible, that is, the head of finance, decides the best possible option.

Monte Carlo and spreadsheet simulation

Monte Carlo simulation is a general term that has many meanings. The word "simulation" signifies that we build an artificial model of a real system to study and understand the system. The "Monte Carlo" part of the name alludes to the randomness inherent in the analysis: The name "Monte Carlo" was coined by the physicist Nicholas Metropolis (inspired by [Stanislaw] Ulam's interest in poker (Ulam, 1991)) during the Manhattan Project of World War II, because of the similarity of statistical simulation to games of chance, and because the capital of Monaco was a center for gambling and similar pursuits. Monte Carlo is now used routinely in many diverse fields, from the simulation of complex physical phenomena such as radiation transport in the Earth's atmosphere and the simulation of the esoteric subnuclear processes in high-energy physics experiments, to the mundane, such as the simulation of a Bingo game or the outcome of Monty Hall's vexing offer to the contestant in "Let's Make a Deal" (Drakos, 1995).

Monte Carlo simulation is a statistical method for analyzing random phenomena such as market returns. The computer will randomly select annual returns based upon the given statistical parameters of return, volatility, and correlation. This process is then repeated thousands of times, allowing one to see the range of possible outcomes. While not a perfect tool, we believe this is the best way to evaluate issues such as acceptable spending rates in retirement, wealth values at retirement, and appropriate asset allocations.

Traditionally, practitioners have used what are known as straight-line estimates (Bianchi, Boyle, & Hollingsworth, 1999) of returns to calculate future wealth. This method has three key flaws. It ignores the importance of the returns sequence. Below-average returns in the early retirement years combined with portfolio withdrawals can have a devastating effect on portfolio survival. Actual annualized returns may be less than the estimated return. Straight-line estimates, by definition, assume no volatility. But in reality, returns vary from year to year. Monte Carlo simulation assumes that returns are volatile. This causes the annualized return—or the portfolio growth rate—to be lower than the expected annual returned.

Furthermore, Monte Carlo simulations allow investors to see the tradeoffs that occur when creating specific goals for their retirement plans. Many people have more than one retirement goal. For example, an investor could plan to spend a certain amount of money during retirement and also leave an inheritance to his or her children. Monte Carlo simulations can help estimate the odds of success for achieving both of those goals. In addition, these simulations can also estimate how increasing the odds of success for one goal may decrease the odds of success for the second goal.

Monte Carlo simulation also accounts for the sequence of returns. Some Monte Carlo simulations will include scenarios where returns are below average or even negative in the early years of retirement, which has a significant impact on the success of a portfolio. It will also have runs where the annualized returns during the entire time period are less than expected.

Monte Carlo simulation is a method of analysis based on artificially recreating a chance process (usually with a computer), running it many times, and directly observing the results (Law & Kelton, 2000).

Monte Carlo simulation can be done in spreadsheets programs such as Excel if the problem of interest is not too complex. In this regard, Excel provides a random-number generator, the ability to generate random values from some basic probability distributions like normal, uniform, exponential, binomial, and Poisson, and summary statistics like mean and variance and graphical plots such as a histogram. Spreadsheet simulations are widely used to performing risk analyses in application areas such as finance, manufacturing, project management, etc.

Table 16.1 Formulas of uniform random number generation in Excel

Example of Random Number Generation in Excel	
Random Numbers between 0 and 1	**Random Numbers between 4 and 9**
=RAND()	=RAND()*(9–4)+4
=RAND()	=RAND()*(9–4)+4
=RAND()	=RAND()*(9–4)+4
=RAND()	=RAND()*(9–4)+4
=RAND()	=RAND()*(9–4)+4
=RAND()	=RAND()*(9–4)+4
=RAND()	=RAND()*(9–4)+4
=RAND()	=RAND()*(9–4)+4
=RAND()	=RAND()*(9–4)+4
=RAND()	=RAND()*(9–4)+4

Table 16.2 Uniform random number generation in Excel

Example of Random Number Generation in Excel	
Random Numbers between 0 and 1	**Random Numbers between 4 and 9**
0.131512552	4.173016427
0.270186835	7.931975861
0.484249045	6.587979509
0.983187095	7.856934051
0.100073065	7.921725595
0.947085204	5.88804872
0.349751998	8.787073944
0.990223804	4.901153565
0.920426562	6.607277672
0.875165723	6.617723156

Random number generation in Excel

Because Monte Carlo simulation is based on repeatedly sampling from a chance process, it stands to reason that random numbers are a crucial part of the procedure. This section will briefly explain various aspects of generating uniform (tables 16.1 and 16.2) and nonuniform random numbers in Excel worksheets.

The standard Excel RAND function can be used to generate random numbers from the uniform distribution. The RAND function returns numbers from the interval [0, 1), and if you need to generate numbers from another interval, you should use the following formula: =RAND() * $(b–a) + a$. This will return

Table 16.3 Excel functions to generate random numbers

Distribution	Excel function
Normal	=NORMINV(RAND(); mean; standard_deviation)
Lognormal	#NAME?
Exponential	=-LN(1-RAND()) / lambda
Weibull	#NAME?

random numbers from the interval [*a*, *b*)—greater than or equal to *a*, and less than *b*.

Even though the RAND function can be useful for generating uniform random numbers, most of the time you will need to model various nonuniform distributions, such as the normal, lognormal, exponential, gamma, and others. In fact, the uniform distribution arises in a very limited number of applications, so the chances are your worksheet models will rarely deal with this distribution. Excel doesn't provide any functions for directly generating random numbers from the popular continuous and discrete distributions; however, you can use the standard capabilities of Excel and the inverse transform method to create such a function yourself. Table 16.3 shows different Excel functions to generate nonuniform distributions:

Application one: Monte Carlo and integration

Monte Carlo methods can be directly applied to finance problems involving evaluation of multidimensional integrals. For instance, Paskov uses Monte Carlo simulation to find the present value of securities, which involves up to 360 dimensional integrals (Paskov, 1994). In this section, we will study how to apply Monte Carlo simulation to estimate single (tables 16.4 and 16.5) and double integral (tables 16.6 and 16.7) alongside their implementation in Excel.

Monte Carlo and single integral

The Monte Carlo method can be used to estimate numerically the value of a single integral, that is, $\int_a^b f(x)dx$. For a function of one variable the steps are:

1. Choose x_n points randomly distributed, $x_1, \ldots, x_n$, in the interval [*a*, *b*]
2. Determine the average value of the function: $\hat{f} = \frac{1}{n}\sum_{i=1}^{n} f(x_i)$
3. Calculate the estimation of the integral: $\int_a^b f(x)dx \approx (b-a)\times\hat{f}$

Larger value of n will produce more accurate approximations. Example: find $\int_0^1 \sqrt{x+\sqrt{x}dx}$ using the previous steps. We will solve it first in Excel then symbolically using Mathematica:

Mathematica result:

$$\int_0^1 \sqrt{x+\sqrt{x}dx} = 1.045301308$$

Table 16.4 Formulas for evaluation of single integral using M-C in Excel

xi	*f(xi)*
=RAND()	=SQRT(A2+SQRT(A2))
=RAND()	=SQRT(A3+SQRT(A3))
=RAND()	=SQRT(A4+SQRT(A4))
=RAND()	=SQRT(A5+SQRT(A5))
=RAND()	=SQRT(A6+SQRT(A6))
=RAND()	=SQRT(A7+SQRT(A7))
=RAND()	=SQRT(A8+SQRT(A8))
=RAND()	=SQRT(A9+SQRT(A9))
=RAND()	=SQRT(A10+SQRT(A10))
=RAND()	=SQRT(A11+SQRT(A11))
=RAND()	=SQRT(A12+SQRT(A12))
=RAND()	=SQRT(A13+SQRT(A13))
=RAND()	=SQRT(A14+SQRT(A14))
=RAND()	=SQRT(A15+SQRT(A15))
=RAND()	=SQRT(A16+SQRT(A16))
=RAND()	=SQRT(A17+SQRT(A17))
=RAND()	=SQRT(A18+SQRT(A18))
=RAND()	=SQRT(A19+SQRT(A19))
=RAND()	=SQRT(A20+SQRT(A20))
=RAND()	=SQRT(A21+SQRT(A21))
=RAND()	=SQRT(A22+SQRT(A22))
=RAND()	=SQRT(A23+SQRT(A23))
=RAND()	=SQRT(A24+SQRT(A24))
=RAND()	=SQRT(A25+SQRT(A25))
=RAND()	=SQRT(A26+SQRT(A26))
=RAND()	=SQRT(A27+SQRT(A27))
=RAND()	=SQRT(A28+SQRT(A28))
=RAND()	=SQRT(A29+SQRT(A29))
=RAND()	=SQRT(A30+SQRT(A30))
Value of the integral	**=(1/29)*SUM(B2:B30)**

Table 16.5 Evaluation of single integral using M-C in Excel

xi	*f(xi)*
0.232939200228894	0.845917816825487
0.17916347883758	0.776170438654687
0.877501035228949	1.34694145661676
0.93786028071032	1.38068539050352
0.448642000201082	1.05756769776935
0.593790018557203	1.168061529184
0.791135221569091	1.29637689198466
0.0531004523780982	0.532480803775058
0.635772758901347	1.19713255575967
0.480354925498706	1.08325036192413
0.152888514173888	0.737494490131171
0.142473704123024	0.721062129458825
0.0312535849576134	0.456114480974696
0.865277538177908	1.33995540729805
0.267662003283073	0.886015020020861
0.774099382228269	1.28605153866262
0.155796007206651	0.741960939994192
0.585693864180154	1.16232536322765
0.642293349150374	1.20155125176554
0.00448813947580984	0.267360650331544
0.625708183372595	1.1902627298633
0.503681932252332	1.10153867715948
0.578346511674149	1.15708144881448
0.0675083196527986	0.572129313594467
0.596351148880892	1.16986704500815
0.982798343692982	1.40504811548761
0.676647180489378	1.22443164286866
0.666222631088019	1.2175579048137
0.0196941543670608	0.40003751960672
Value of the integral	**0.997325193519967**

Monte Carlo and double integral

The Monte Carlo method can be used to estimate numerically (tables 16.6 and 16.7) the value of a double integral, that is, $\int_a^b \int_c^d f(x,y)dydx$ For a function of one variable the steps are:

4. Choose n points randomly distributed, $(x_1, y_1)\ldots\ldots(x_n, y_n)$, in the rectangle $[a, b] \times [c, d]$
5. Determine the average value of the function: $\hat{f} = \frac{1}{n}\sum_{i=1}^{n} f(x_i, y_i)$
6. Calculate the estimation of the integral: $\int_a^b \int_c^d f(x,y)\,dydx \approx (b-a)(d-c)\times\hat{f}$

Larger value of n will produce more accurate approximations. Example: find $\int_0^{1.25}\int_0^{1.25} \sqrt{-x^2 - y^2 + 4}\,dydx$ using the previous steps. We will solve it first in Excel then symbolically using Mathematica (see tables 16.6 and 16.7):

Table 16.6 Formulas for evaluation of double integral using M-C in Excel

xi	*yi*	*f(xi,yi)*
=(5/4)*RAND()	=(5/4)*RAND()	=SQRT(-A2^2-B2^2+4)
=(5/4)*RAND()	=(5/4)*RAND()	=SQRT(-A3^2-B3^2+4)
=(5/4)*RAND()	=(5/4)*RAND()	=SQRT(-A4^2-B4^2+4)
=(5/4)*RAND()	=(5/4)*RAND()	=SQRT(-A5^2-B5^2+4)
=(5/4)*RAND()	=(5/4)*RAND()	=SQRT(-A6^2-B6^2+4)
=(5/4)*RAND()	=(5/4)*RAND()	=SQRT(-A7^2-B7^2+4)
=(5/4)*RAND()	=(5/4)*RAND()	=SQRT(-A8^2-B8^2+4)
=(5/4)*RAND()	=(5/4)*RAND()	=SQRT(-A9^2-B9^2+4)
=(5/4)*RAND()	=(5/4)*RAND()	=SQRT(-A10^2-B10^2+4)
=(5/4)*RAND()	=(5/4)*RAND()	=SQRT(-A11^2-B11^2+4)
=(5/4)*RAND()	=(5/4)*RAND()	=SQRT(-A12^2-B12^2+4)
=(5/4)*RAND()	=(5/4)*RAND()	=SQRT(-A13^2-B13^2+4)
=(5/4)*RAND()	=(5/4)*RAND()	=SQRT(-A14^2-B14^2+4)
=(5/4)*RAND()	=(5/4)*RAND()	=SQRT(-A15^2-B15^2+4)
=(5/4)*RAND()	=(5/4)*RAND()	=SQRT(-A16^2-B16^2+4)
=(5/4)*RAND()	=(5/4)*RAND()	=SQRT(-A17^2-B17^2+4)
=(5/4)*RAND()	=(5/4)*RAND()	=SQRT(-A18^2-B18^2+4)
=(5/4)*RAND()	=(5/4)*RAND()	=SQRT(-A19^2-B19^2+4)
=(5/4)*RAND()	=(5/4)*RAND()	=SQRT(-A20^2-B20^2+4)
=(5/4)*RAND()	=(5/4)*RAND()	=SQRT(-A21^2-B21^2+4)
=(5/4)*RAND()	=(5/4)*RAND()	=SQRT(-A22^2-B22^2+4)
=(5/4)*RAND()	=(5/4)*RAND()	=SQRT(-A23^2-B23^2+4)
=(5/4)*RAND()	=(5/4)*RAND()	=SQRT(-A24^2-B24^2+4)

continued

Table 16.6 Continued

xi	*yi*	*f(xi,yi)*
=(5/4)*RAND()	=(5/4)*RAND()	=SQRT(-A25^2-B25^2+4)
=(5/4)*RAND()	=(5/4)*RAND()	=SQRT(-A26^2-B26^2+4)
=(5/4)*RAND()	=(5/4)*RAND()	=SQRT(-A27^2-B27^2+4)
=(5/4)*RAND()	=(5/4)*RAND()	=SQRT(-A28^2-B28^2+4)
=(5/4)*RAND()	=(5/4)*RAND()	=SQRT(-A29^2-B29^2+4)
=(5/4)*RAND()	=(5/4)*RAND()	=SQRT(-A30^2-B30^2+4)
Value of the integral		**=(5/4)*(5/4)*(1/29)*SUM(C2:C30)**

Table 16.7 Evaluation of double integral using M-C in Excel

xi	*yi*	*f(xi,yi)*
1.195642506	0.366281218	2.301173412
1.172636015	0.702446616	2.209444269
0.649473868	0.972371788	1.864486366
0.783050039	0.307473092	2.125706391
1.148268599	0.953086181	2.10003512
0.960089986	0.981521665	1.989569804
0.959921235	0.961709693	1.999140626
1.085932172	0.929085641	2.077510182
0.541172071	0.402367844	2.032478125
0.770353345	0.978054487	1.907053669
0.265050025	0.456457117	1.965171345
0.791045566	0.770683787	2.007934159
0.993880777	0.524978015	2.170759564
0.427015278	0.012621177	2.04503857
0.823610763	0.122668764	2.159464531
1.0491668	0.38668825	2.225134417
0.567302772	0.632622442	1.98030838
0.816104611	0.533303016	2.093230668
0.388848117	0.977102659	1.787868354
0.538446779	0.367031555	2.038433902
0.263627193	0.479900354	1.95938637
0.86623045	0.073400483	2.178294645
0.104077916	0.182542033	1.99436973
1.03738339	1.055447169	1.990526456
0.709284146	1.0514025	1.843267963
0.682407971	1.102719857	1.802689534
1.140414945	0.839260088	2.143872373
0.980498615	0.435238478	2.184478199
0.944834694	1.020409849	1.962517857
Value of the integral		**3.186387122**

Mathematica result:

$$\int_0^{\frac{5}{4}}\int_0^{\frac{5}{4}} \sqrt{4-x^2-y^2}\,dydx = 2.66905414$$

Monte Carlo and portfolio evaluation (finance)

In this section, we will illustrate Monte Carlo simulation through portfolio evaluation problem. Consider three stocks, A, B, and C. Let $S_a(t)$, $S_b(t)$, and $S_c(t)$ be the prices of A, B, and C at time t, respectively. Initially, that is at time $t = 0$, we buy n_a units of A, n_b units of B, n_c units of C so our initial wealth is $W(0) = n_aS_a(0) + n_bS_b(0) + n_cS_c(0)$. After T years (investment horizon), our terminal wealth, $W(T) = n_aS_a(T) + n_bS_b(T) + n_cS_c(T)$. Assume that S_a, S_b, and S_c follow Geometric Brownian Motion (GBM), GBM is used in mathematical finance to model stock prices in the Black-Scholes model:

$$S_{a\_}\text{GBM}(\mu_a,\sigma_a),\ \text{i.e. } S_a(T) = S(0)e^{\left(\left(\mu_a-\sigma_a^2\right)T+\sigma_a W_a(T)\right)}$$

$$S_{b\_}\text{GBM}(\mu_b,\sigma_b),\ \text{i.e. } S_b(T) = S(0)e^{\left(\left(\mu_b-\sigma_b^2\right)T+\sigma_b W_b(T)\right)}$$

$$S_{c\_}\text{GBM}(\mu_c,\sigma_c),\ \text{i.e. } S_c(T) = S(0)e^{\left(\left(\mu_c-\sigma_c^2\right)T+\sigma_c W_c(T)\right)}$$

where $W(T)$ is a standard Wiener process, $W(T) \sim \sqrt{T}\ N(0, 1)$, where $N(0, 1)$ is a normal distribution with zero mean and unit variance. μ the percentage drift and σ the percentage volatility are constants. Let us assume the following parameter values (see table 16.8).

This implies $W(0) = 3000\$$. We would like to estimate (tables 16.9–16.16), using Monte Carlo simulation, the probability that the value of the given portfolio rises by more than 10%, that is, $P\left(\frac{W(T)}{W(0)} \geq 1.1\right)$

Case study in financial forecasting

The Monte Carlo method is one of many methods for analyzing uncertainty propagation, where the goal is to determine how random variation, lack of knowledge, or error affects the sensitivity, performance or reliability of the system that is being modeled. Monte Carlo simulation is categorized as a sampling method because the inputs are randomly generated from probability distributions to simulate the process of sampling from an actual population. So, we try to choose a distribution for the inputs that most closely matches data we already have, or best represents our current state of knowledge. Now, we will

Table 16.8 Portfolio parameters

Parameter	Value
T	2 (years)
μ_a	0.24
μ_b	0.18
μ_c	0.14
σ_a	0.3
σ_b	0.2
σ_c	0.5
$S_a(0)$	150$
$S_b(0)$	100$
$S_c(0)$	50$
n_a	100 units
n_b	100 units
n_c	100 units

Table 16.9 Portfolio evaluation input parameters in Excel

W(0)$=	=B9*B12+B10*B13+B11*B14
Number of Simulation	
1000	
P(W(T)/W(0)>=1.1)/1000	
=COUNTIF(L2:L1001,">=1.1")/1000	

Table 16.10 $S_a(T)$ generation formulas (partial information shown due to volume)

$S_a(T)$
=B$9*EXP((B$3-(B$6^2)/2)*B$2+B$6*SQRT(B$2)*NORMINV(RAND(),0,1))
=B$9*EXP((B$3-(B$6^2)/2)*B$2+B$6*SQRT(B$2)*NORMINV(RAND(),0,1))
=B$9*EXP((B$3-(B$6^2)/2)*B$2+B$6*SQRT(B$2)*NORMINV(RAND(),0,1))
=B$9*EXP((B$3-(B$6^2)/2)*B$2+B$6*SQRT(B$2)*NORMINV(RAND(),0,1))
=B$9*EXP((B$3-(B$6^2)/2)*B$2+B$6*SQRT(B$2)*NORMINV(RAND(),0,1))
=B$9*EXP((B$3-(B$6^2)/2)*B$2+B$6*SQRT(B$2)*NORMINV(RAND(),0,1))
=B$9*EXP((B$3-(B$6^2)/2)*B$2+B$6*SQRT(B$2)*NORMINV(RAND(),0,1))
=B$9*EXP((B$3-(B$6^2)/2)*B$2+B$6*SQRT(B$2)*NORMINV(RAND(),0,1))
=B$9*EXP((B$3-(B$6^2)/2)*B$2+B$6*SQRT(B$2)*NORMINV(RAND(),0,1))
=B$9*EXP((B$3-(B$6^2)/2)*B$2+B$6*SQRT(B$2)*NORMINV(RAND(),0,1))
=B$9*EXP((B$3-(B$6^2)/2)*B$2+B$6*SQRT(B$2)*NORMINV(RAND(),0,1))
=B$9*EXP((B$3-(B$6^2)/2)*B$2+B$6*SQRT(B$2)*NORMINV(RAND(),0,1))
=B$9*EXP((B$3-(B$6^2)/2)*B$2+B$6*SQRT(B$2)*NORMINV(RAND(),0,1))

continued

Table 16.10 Continued

$S_a(T)$
=B$9*EXP((B$3-(B$6^2)/2)*B$2+B$6*SQRT(B$2)*NORMINV(RAND(),0,1))
=B$9*EXP((B$3-(B$6^2)/2)*B$2+B$6*SQRT(B$2)*NORMINV(RAND(),0,1))
=B$9*EXP((B$3-(B$6^2)/2)*B$2+B$6*SQRT(B$2)*NORMINV(RAND(),0,1))
=B$9*EXP((B$3-(B$6^2)/2)*B$2+B$6*SQRT(B$2)*NORMINV(RAND(),0,1))
=B$9*EXP((B$3-(B$6^2)/2)*B$2+B$6*SQRT(B$2)*NORMINV(RAND(),0,1))
=B$9*EXP((B$3-(B$6^2)/2)*B$2+B$6*SQRT(B$2)*NORMINV(RAND(),0,1))

Table 16.11 $S_b(T)$ generation formulas (partial information shown due to volume)

$S_b(T)$
=B$10*EXP((B$4-(B$7^2)/2)*B$2+B$7*SQRT(B$2)*NORMINV(RAND(),0,1))
=B$10*EXP((B$4-(B$7^2)/2)*B$2+B$7*SQRT(B$2)*NORMINV(RAND(),0,1))
=B$10*EXP((B$4-(B$7^2)/2)*B$2+B$7*SQRT(B$2)*NORMINV(RAND(),0,1))
=B$10*EXP((B$4-(B$7^2)/2)*B$2+B$7*SQRT(B$2)*NORMINV(RAND(),0,1))
=B$10*EXP((B$4-(B$7^2)/2)*B$2+B$7*SQRT(B$2)*NORMINV(RAND(),0,1))
=B$10*EXP((B$4-(B$7^2)/2)*B$2+B$7*SQRT(B$2)*NORMINV(RAND(),0,1))
=B$10*EXP((B$4-(B$7^2)/2)*B$2+B$7*SQRT(B$2)*NORMINV(RAND(),0,1))
=B$10*EXP((B$4-(B$7^2)/2)*B$2+B$7*SQRT(B$2)*NORMINV(RAND(),0,1))
=B$10*EXP((B$4-(B$7^2)/2)*B$2+B$7*SQRT(B$2)*NORMINV(RAND(),0,1))
=B$10*EXP((B$4-(B$7^2)/2)*B$2+B$7*SQRT(B$2)*NORMINV(RAND(),0,1))
=B$10*EXP((B$4-(B$7^2)/2)*B$2+B$7*SQRT(B$2)*NORMINV(RAND(),0,1))
=B$10*EXP((B$4-(B$7^2)/2)*B$2+B$7*SQRT(B$2)*NORMINV(RAND(),0,1))
=B$10*EXP((B$4-(B$7^2)/2)*B$2+B$7*SQRT(B$2)*NORMINV(RAND(),0,1))
=B$10*EXP((B$4-(B$7^2)/2)*B$2+B$7*SQRT(B$2)*NORMINV(RAND(),0,1))
=B$10*EXP((B$4-(B$7^2)/2)*B$2+B$7*SQRT(B$2)*NORMINV(RAND(),0,1))
=B$10*EXP((B$4-(B$7^2)/2)*B$2+B$7*SQRT(B$2)*NORMINV(RAND(),0,1))
=B$10*EXP((B$4-(B$7^2)/2)*B$2+B$7*SQRT(B$2)*NORMINV(RAND(),0,1))
=B$10*EXP((B$4-(B$7^2)/2)*B$2+B$7*SQRT(B$2)*NORMINV(RAND(),0,1))
=B$10*EXP((B$4-(B$7^2)/2)*B$2+B$7*SQRT(B$2)*NORMINV(RAND(),0,1))

Table 16.12 $S_c(T)$ generation formulas (partial information shown due to volume)

$S_c(T)$
=B$11*EXP((B$5-(B$8^2)/2)*B$2+B$8*SQRT(B$2)*NORMINV(RAND(),0,1))
=B$11*EXP((B$5-(B$8^2)/2)*B$2+B$8*SQRT(B$2)*NORMINV(RAND(),0,1))
=B$11*EXP((B$5-(B$8^2)/2)*B$2+B$8*SQRT(B$2)*NORMINV(RAND(),0,1))
=B$11*EXP((B$5-(B$8^2)/2)*B$2+B$8*SQRT(B$2)*NORMINV(RAND(),0,1))

continued

Table 16.12 Continued

$S_c(T)$
=B$11*EXP((B$5-(B$8^2)/2)*B$2+B$8*SQRT(B$2)*NORMINV(RAND(),0,1))
=B$11*EXP((B$5-(B$8^2)/2)*B$2+B$8*SQRT(B$2)*NORMINV(RAND(),0,1))
=B$11*EXP((B$5-(B$8^2)/2)*B$2+B$8*SQRT(B$2)*NORMINV(RAND(),0,1))
=B$11*EXP((B$5-(B$8^2)/2)*B$2+B$8*SQRT(B$2)*NORMINV(RAND(),0,1))
=B$11*EXP((B$5-(B$8^2)/2)*B$2+B$8*SQRT(B$2)*NORMINV(RAND(),0,1))
=B$11*EXP((B$5-(B$8^2)/2)*B$2+B$8*SQRT(B$2)*NORMINV(RAND(),0,1))
=B$11*EXP((B$5-(B$8^2)/2)*B$2+B$8*SQRT(B$2)*NORMINV(RAND(),0,1))
=B$11*EXP((B$5-(B$8^2)/2)*B$2+B$8*SQRT(B$2)*NORMINV(RAND(),0,1))
=B$11*EXP((B$5-(B$8^2)/2)*B$2+B$8*SQRT(B$2)*NORMINV(RAND(),0,1))
=B$11*EXP((B$5-(B$8^2)/2)*B$2+B$8*SQRT(B$2)*NORMINV(RAND(),0,1))
=B$11*EXP((B$5-(B$8^2)/2)*B$2+B$8*SQRT(B$2)*NORMINV(RAND(),0,1))
=B$11*EXP((B$5-(B$8^2)/2)*B$2+B$8*SQRT(B$2)*NORMINV(RAND(),0,1))
=B$11*EXP((B$5-(B$8^2)/2)*B$2+B$8*SQRT(B$2)*NORMINV(RAND(),0,1))
=B$11*EXP((B$5-(B$8^2)/2)*B$2+B$8*SQRT(B$2)*NORMINV(RAND(),0,1))
=B$11*EXP((B$5-(B$8^2)/2)*B$2+B$8*SQRT(B$2)*NORMINV(RAND(),0,1))

Table 16.13 *W(T)* generation formulas (partial information shown due to volume)

W(T)	***W(T)/W(0)***
=B$12*H2+B$13*I2+B$14*J2	=K2/E$2
=B$12*H3+B$13*I3+B$14*J3	=K3/E$2
=B$12*H4+B$13*I4+B$14*J4	=K4/E$2
=B$12*H5+B$13*I5+B$14*J5	=K5/E$2
=B$12*H6+B$13*I6+B$14*J6	=K6/E$2
=B$12*H7+B$13*I7+B$14*J7	=K7/E$2
=B$12*H8+B$13*I8+B$14*J8	=K8/E$2
=B$12*H9+B$13*I9+B$14*J9	=K9/E$2
=B$12*H10+B$13*I10+B$14*J10	=K10/E$2
=B$12*H11+B$13*I11+B$14*J11	=K11/E$2
=B$12*H12+B$13*I12+B$14*J12	=K12/E$2
=B$12*H13+B$13*I13+B$14*J13	=K13/E$2
=B$12*H14+B$13*I14+B$14*J14	=K14/E$2
=B$12*H15+B$13*I15+B$14*J15	=K15/E$2
=B$12*H16+B$13*I16+B$14*J16	=K16/E$2
=B$12*H17+B$13*I17+B$14*J17	=K17/E$2
=B$12*H18+B$13*I18+B$14*J18	=K18/E$2
=B$12*H19+B$13*I19+B$14*J19	=K19/E$2
=B$12*H20+B$13*I20+B$14*J20	=K20/E$2

Table 16.14 Result of first replication

$S_a(T)$	$S_b(T)$	$S_c(T)$	$W(T)$	$W(T)/W(0)$
116.0842	138.6495471	19.74371041	27447.74117	0.91492471
137.2631	127.9634045	30.27641612	29550.29007	0.98500967
156.5835	113.4472853	55.72428889	32575.50595	1.0858502
171.3581	104.8640184	91.4316055	36765.37327	1.22551244
178.7382	111.7994655	85.81762969	37635.52805	1.2545176
349.6326	175.0107136	27.5665886	55220.99032	1.84069968
99.91662	150.9055699	104.1275571	35494.97428	1.18316581
215.4292	170.6453982	56.76047092	44283.50944	1.47611698
525.127	94.26486172	30.79324015	65018.51073	2.16728369
152.4688	177.2018957	105.2821253	43495.27833	1.44984261
295.1447	125.5673344	83.47028753	50418.23237	1.68060775
87.91017	163.5324092	32.17714775	28361.97248	0.94539908
224.4255	169.7437502	53.48809693	44765.73792	1.49219126
102.0705	130.283927	56.60759963	28896.19809	0.9632066
346.4788	146.2515758	76.70295448	56943.32982	1.89811099
353.2605	180.9794981	36.10829706	57034.82604	1.90116087
290.8719	138.9028047	12.75365049	44252.83444	1.47509448
248.5232	174.9930795	81.83655994	50535.28015	1.68450934
119.5891	177.0686605	110.6794455	40733.71956	1.35779065
160.2389	156.0308998	47.80278991	36407.26284	1.21357543
229.3136	144.4026876	109.8721494	48358.8456	1.61196152

Parameter	Value
T	2
μ_a	0.24
μ_b	0.18
μ_c	0.14
σ_a	0.3
σ_b	0.2
σ_c	0.5
$S_a(0)$	150
$S_b(0)$	100
$S_c(0)$	50
n_a	100
n_b	100
n_c	100

W(0)$=	**30000**
Number of Simulation	
1000	
P(W(T)/W(0)>=1.1)/1000	
0.846	

Table 16.15 Result of second replication after clicking F9 (partial data shown due to volume)

$S_a(T)$	$S_b(T)$	$S_c(T)$	$W(T)$	$W(T)/W(0)$
294.5824	105.8110976	57.57801981	45797.15114	1.5265717
182.5329	103.9754798	38.7183776	32522.67588	1.0840892
278.4623	85.74075359	32.62497922	39682.8004	1.32276001
308.2367	113.557523	257.7648814	67955.91243	2.26519708
185.0825	139.9127748	60.02634074	38502.15973	1.28340532
258.478	130.643203	36.28640921	42540.75965	1.41802532
234.4929	284.1912976	11.29337962	52997.76088	1.76659203
153.1906	110.8291399	26.68010955	29069.98488	0.9689995
340.8527	158.3569095	106.0986946	60530.83137	2.01769438
308.2086	257.9521773	55.00764209	62116.8375	2.07056125
268.9843	122.8945798	39.77032849	43164.91776	1.43883059
419.8857	247.6603095	320.557862	98810.38932	3.29367964
230.3563	129.8636139	78.295093	43851.49683	1.46171656
268.4693	122.0522161	33.64258674	42416.40705	1.41388024
152.1882	178.411674	20.5672694	35116.71207	1.17055707
322.6315	98.36084616	25.5362831	44652.86243	1.48842875
183.9737	127.4499145	110.9769802	42240.05462	1.40800182
292.3022	127.6740217	189.5630824	60953.93497	2.03179783
236.3793	141.3830501	110.0499807	48781.23716	1.62604124
204.7038	143.7115071	10.6549816	35907.02804	1.19690093
343.3839	147.0483523	22.97502116	51340.72826	1.71135761

Parameter	Value
T	2
μ_a	0.24
μ_b	0.18
μ_c	0.14
σ_a	0.3
σ_b	0.2
σ_c	0.5
$S_a(0)$	150
$S_b(0)$	100
$S_c(0)$	50
n_a	100
n_b	100
n_c	100

***W(0)*$=**	**30000**
Number of Simulation	
1000	
P(W(T)/W(0)>=1.1)/1000	
0.832	

Table 16.16 Result of third replication after clicking F9 (partial data shown due to volume)

$S_a(T)$	$S_b(T)$	$S(T)$	$W(T)$	$W(T)/W(0)$
180.7438	142.9802181	72.87419381	39659.81748	1.32199392
224.3536	172.9441552	34.95035997	43224.81125	1.44082704
181.4517	171.3077681	38.3479162	39110.73775	1.30369126
346.5778	148.6285008	36.67492756	53188.12757	1.77293759
359.6572	84.14916054	167.8487638	61165.51111	2.03885037
305.5232	206.8110736	29.04734793	54138.16317	1.80460544
404.5978	123.515923	50.38315925	57849.68359	1.92832279
578.0705	171.6037212	134.9646927	88463.89491	2.9487965
304.7525	144.1223743	38.45911489	48733.401	1.6244467
107.8753	113.2406218	74.30798122	29542.39496	0.9847465
151.4575	78.54738923	38.13240075	26813.72741	0.89379091
253.5258	116.4672363	29.5842987	39957.73303	1.33192443
201.7433	132.1521781	34.96330895	36885.87447	1.22952915
184.4463	231.853593	30.05727493	44635.71448	1.48785715
286.5837	136.9781109	41.53390198	46509.57092	1.55031903
210.1896	157.6280889	19.622883	38744.06097	1.2914687
207.3423	90.4721846	108.9255659	40674.00312	1.3558001
283.8027	219.0284584	138.6968594	64152.80147	2.13842672
116.7787	216.077654	24.24543035	35710.17453	1.19033915
651.1841	126.6921812	471.0159577	124889.219	4.16297397
213.1551	127.498984	71.52551407	41217.95561	1.37393185
289.6618	158.2314212	69.58506123	51747.82975	1.72492766

Parameter	Value
T	2
μ_a	0.24
μ_b	0.18
μ_c	0.14
σ_a	0.3
σ_b	0.2
σ_c	0.5
$S_a(0)$	150
$S_b(0)$	100
$S_c(0)$	50
n_a	100
n_b	100
n_c	100

***W(0)*$=**	**30000**

Number of Simulation

1000

P(W(T)/W(0)>=1.1)/1000

0.863

apply Monte Carlo to a financial forecasting problem. Let us say that a factory manager of a firm *X* is planning to introduce a new product. He wants to forecast the first year profit from this product, which will depend on:

- sales in units
- price per unit
- unit cost
- fixed costs.

The net profit formula is Profit = Sales * (Price – Unit cost) – Fixed costs. The fixed costs (salaries, rental, advertising, etc.) are given as $100,000. However other factors like sales, selling price, and cost involve some uncertainty. For example, sales in units can cover quite a range, and the selling price per unit will depend on competitor actions. Unit costs will also vary depending on vendor prices and production experience. We will use a Monte Carlo simulation (tables 16.17–16.20) to forecast the profit and evaluate the risk caused by the uncertain variables. Our next step is to identify uncertain functions—also called functions of a random variable. Net profit is calculated as Profit = Sales * (Price – Unit cost) – Fixed costs. Sales volume, selling price, and unit cost are all uncertain variables, so net profit is an uncertain function. For

Table 16.17 Financial forecasting initial values

Financial Forecasting of Sales			
	Value	**Uniform Between**	
Fixed Cost	100000	–	–
Sales Volume	125891	70000	100000
Selling Price	10.502	10	15
Unit Cost	9.8359	7	10

Table 16.18 Formulas of financial forecasting

Financial Forecasting of Sales			
	Value	**Uniform Between**	
Fixed Cost	100000	–	–
Sales Volume	=INT((E4-D4)*RAND()+E4)	70000	100000
Selling Price	=(E5-D5)*RAND()+D5	10	15
Unit Cost	=(E6-D6)*RAND()+D6	7	10

Table 16.19 Financial forecasting setup (partial data shown due to volume)

Monte Carlo Simulation			
Sales Volume	**Selling Price**	**Unit Cost**	**Profit**
112623	11.1222038	7.702329	285157
119315	14.2464967	7.091067	753750
116713	10.8769502	8.501031	177301
129921	10.3440736	7.127791	317863
121121	13.8872206	8.592415	541312
102552	12.7043222	8.225031	359360
105470	11.0169627	9.105198	101634
110847	11.6373747	7.687213	337864
102035	11.6905918	7.93663	283036
115706	11.4465755	7.589212	346320
122166	13.7472874	7.567072	655012
110300	14.8323165	7.56984	701051

Profit Times	Percentage
4874	97.48

Profit Times	Percentage
=COUNTIF(E10:E5009,“>0”)	=(G10/5000)*100

Table 16.20 Financial forecasting setup (formulas – partial information shown due to volume)

Monte Carlo Simulation			
Sales Volume	**Selling Price**	**Unit Cost**	**Profit**
=INT((E$4-D$4)*RAND()+E$4)	=(E$5-D$5)*RAND()+D$5	=(E$6-D$6)*RAND()+D$6	=B10*(C10-D10)-C3
=INT((E$4-D$4)*RAND()+E$4)	=(E$5-D$5)*RAND()+D$5	=(E$6-D$6)*RAND()+D$6	=B11*(C11-D11)-C3
=INT((E$4-D$4)*RAND()+E$4)	=(E$5-D$5)*RAND()+D$5	=(E$6-D$6)*RAND()+D$6	=B12*(C12-D12)-C3
=INT((E$4-D$4)*RAND()+E$4)	=(E$5-D$5)*RAND()+D$5	=(E$6-D$6)*RAND()+D$6	=B13*(C13-D13)-C3
=INT((E$4-D$4)*RAND()+E$4)	=(E$5-D$5)*RAND()+D$5	=(E$6-D$6)*RAND()+D$6	=B14*(C14-D14)-C3
=INT((E$4-D$4)*RAND()+E$4)	=(E$5-D$5)*RAND()+D$5	=(E$6-D$6)*RAND()+D$6	=B15*(C15-D15)-C3
=INT((E$4-D$4)*RAND()+E$4)	=(E$5-D$5)*RAND()+D$5	=(E$6-D$6)*RAND()+D$6	=B16*(C16-D16)-C3
=INT((E$4-D$4)*RAND()+E$4)	=(E$5-D$5)*RAND()+D$5	=(E$6-D$6)*RAND()+D$6	=B17*(C17-D17)-C3
=INT((E$4-D$4)*RAND()+E$4)	=(E$5-D$5)*RAND()+D$5	=(E$6-D$6)*RAND()+D$6	=B18*(C18-D18)-C3

instance sales volume is a uniform random variable between 70,000 and 100,000 items; Selling price is a uniform random variable between 10$ and 15$; unit cost is a uniform random variable between 7$ and 10$. The distribution of these parameters can be determined by experience and using historical data.

The better way to present and analyze the result of this simulation is to draw a dynamic histogram in Excel.

Create a Dynamic Histogram in Excel

In this section, we will study how to draw a dynamic histogram in Excel in order to observe actively the behavior of the data. Excel comes bundled with an add-in called the Analysis Toolpak (or ATP), accessible through the Data Analysis command on the Tools menu. The Analysis Toolpak provides many statistical functions not available directly through Excel. Depending on our installation, the Analysis Toolpak may or may not be installed. There are times when you may want to bypass the ATP and build your own tables and histograms. The ATP calculates its values and pastes them into the output range as values (static), not as formulas (dynamic). If the underlying data change, the ATP output ranges do not change. This may be desired behavior in some cases, but other times it can be inconvenient. This technique places formulas into the output range, so the values adjust to changing data.

Step 1: specify the minimum and maximum (table 16.21). In our example, max = 700000$ and min = –80000$.

Step 2: build up the bins (tables 16.22–16.23). In our example, we will use 50 bins. The first bin is the minimum value, then for each bin (50 bins) we add the width of the bin to the previous bin value. The width of each bin is given by (max–min)/50.

Step 3: to fill up the frequency column (table 16.24), we select the whole column, then use the frequency function by writing it in the function bar and then click shift+Ctrl+enter simultaneously.

Step 4: create the column chart (figure 16.1). Select the whole frequency column, then insert column chart from the insert menu and then change the data source for *x*-axis to be the bins column. To create more replication, we just click on F9 to regenerate new values.

After creating the histogram, the next step is to analyze the results visually. We can glean a lot of information from this histogram:

- It looks like profit will be positive, most of the time.
- The uncertainty is quite large, varying between –48000 and 381000.
- The distribution does not look like a perfect Normal distribution.
- There do not appear to be outliers, truncation, multiple modes, etc.

Table 16.21 Minimum and maximum values for profit (partial data shown due to volume)

Monte Carlo Simulation			
Sales Volume	**Selling Price**	**Unit Cost**	**Profit**
112718	12.60507789	7.293205333	498743.7
101967	10.83146991	8.327987328	155272.6
127094	11.81807691	8.694758837	296955
122795	11.54914646	7.583331063	386982.3
112705	11.32389662	9.208461529	138420.1
120910	10.26792293	7.043703027	289840.4
102731	13.9220564	9.720978137	331581

Profit Times	Percentage
4882	97.64

min	**–80000**
max	700000

Table 16.22 Create the bins values (partial data shown due to volume)

Monte Carlo Simulation			
Sales Volume	**Selling Price**	**Unit Cost**	**Profit**
112718	12.60507789	7.293205333	498743.7
101967	10.83146991	8.327987328	155272.6
127094	11.81807691	8.694758837	296955
122795	11.54914646	7.583331063	386982.3
112705	11.32389662	9.208461529	138420.1
120910	10.26792293	7.043703027	289840.4
102731	13.9220564	9.720978137	331581
121250	13.6603893	8.760605372	494098.8
107541	12.59609009	9.937500791	185907.4
101262	13.49271658	9.612850152	292883
123160	13.05823365	8.293691926	486801
114481	11.77906659	9.53097104	157364.2
125379	14.23414819	7.559911817	736809.1

Profit Times	Percentage
4882	97.64

min	**–80000**
max	700000

Bins	Frequency
–80000	
–64400	
–48800	
–33200	
–17600	
–2000	
13600	

Table 16.23 Create the bins values (formulas—partial information shown due to volume)

Monte Carlo Simulation			
Sales Volume	Selling Price	Unit Cost	Profit
112718	12.6050778853399	7.29320533291252	498743.650364511
101967	10.8314699071365	8.32798732798306	155272.608148542
127094	11.8180769082209	8.6947588366114	296954.986993141
122795	11.549146455781	7.58333106310347	386982.301143835
112705	11.3238966193107	9.20846152895843	138420.111858158
120910	10.2679229279655	7.04370302666991	289840.428265647
102731	13.9220563993786	9.72097813683046	331580.970989831
121250	13.6603893004813	8.7606053717131	494098.801363144
107541	12.5960900945125	9.93750079111575	185907.352276595
101262	13.4927165751828	9.6128501523512	292883.033708773
123160	13.0582336531133	8.29369192607004	486800.959102647
114481	11.7790665902246	9.53097104034093	157364.226646228
125379	14.2341481907294	7.55991181733146	736809.082260258

Profit Times	Percentage
4882	97.64

min	-80000
max	700000

Bins	Frequency
=J12	
=(J13-J12)/50+I16	
=(J13-J12)/50+I17	
=(J13-J12)/50+I18	
=(J13-J12)/50+I19	
=(J13-J12)/50+I20	
=(J13-J12)/50+I21	

Table 16.24 Find the frequency values

Monte Carlo Simulation			
Sales Volume	**Selling Price**	**Unit Cost**	**Profit**
112718	12.60507789	7.293205333	498743.7
101967	10.83146991	8.327987328	155272.6
127094	11.81807691	8.694758837	296955
122795	11.54914646	7.583331063	386982.3
112705	11.32389662	9.208461529	138420.1
120910	10.26792293	7.043703027	289840.4
102731	13.9220564	9.720978137	331581
121250	13.6603893	8.760605372	494098.8
107541	12.59609009	9.937500791	185907.4
101262	13.49271658	9.612850152	292883
123160	13.05823365	8.293691926	486801
114481	11.77906659	9.53097104	157364.2
125379	14.23414819	7.559911817	736809.1
119795	14.73084668	9.961103009	471391.4
114885	14.36959566	8.054426952	625518.2
115525	14.81735526	9.719969236	488875.5
122220	10.79588341	7.659086208	283379.4
108658	11.05300152	9.775734717	38785.26
114709	12.34877129	8.131848169	383719

Profit Times	Percentage
4882	97.6

min	–80000
max	700000

Bins	Frequency
–80000	6
–64400	10
–48800	16
–33200	20
–17600	32
–2000	31
13600	44
29200	42
44800	70
60400	70
76000	68
91600	68
107200	89

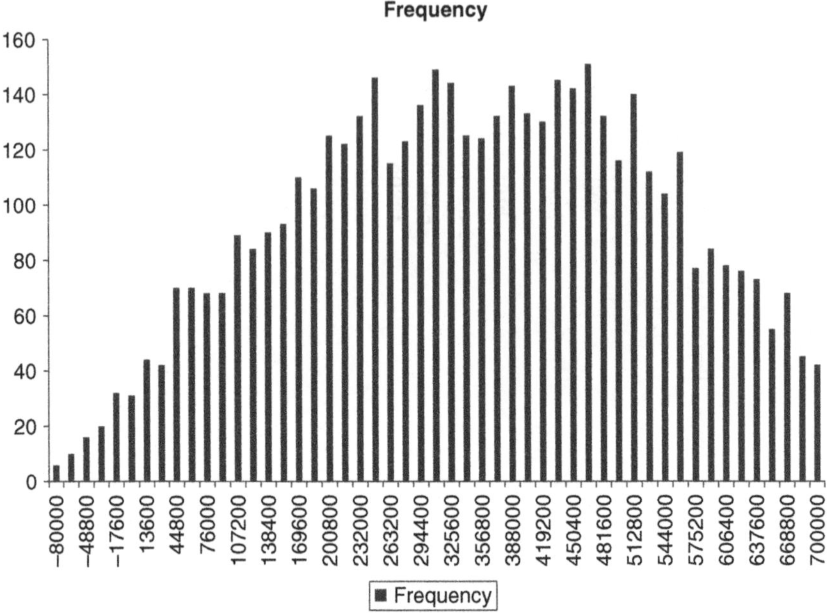

Figure 16.1 The column chart of the frequency.

The histogram tells a good story, but in many cases, we want to estimate the probability of being below or above some value, or between a set of specification limits.

In our Monte Carlo simulation example, we plotted the results as a histogram in order to visualize the uncertainty in profit. In order to provide a concise summary of the results, it is customary to report the mean, median, standard deviation, standard error, and a few other summary statistics to describe the resulting distribution.

Conclusions

This chapter presented an overview of the Monte Carlo simulation in Microsoft Excel. Some applications are given, such as random number generation, integration calculation, and portfolio evaluation, and implemented using Monte Carlo. A detailed application about sales financial forecasting is studied and analyzed. This application is not comprehensive, and there are many other factors affecting sales that have not been covered. However, we hope this model has given the reader a good introduction to the basics.

References

Banks, J., Ed. (1998). *Handbook of simulation: Principles, methodology, advances, applications, and practice.* New York: John Wiley & Sons.

Banks, J., Carson, J.S., Nelson, B.L. & Nicol, D.M. (2005). Discrete-event system simulation. (4th.ed.). Upper Saddle River, NJ: Prentice-Hall.

Bianchi, M., Boyle, M., & Hollingsworth, D. (1999). A comparison of methods for trend estimation. *Applied Economics Letters, 6*, 103–109.

Cellier, F.E. & Kofman, E. (2006). *Continuous system simulation*. New York: Springer-Verlag.

Drakos, Nikos (1995). *Computer based learning unit*. University of Leeds. Introduction to Monte Carlo Methods. csep1.phy.ornl.gov/mc/node1.html.

Landau, D. P. & Binder, K. (2005). A guide to Monte Carlo simulations in statistical physics. (2nd ed.). Cambridge: Cambridge University Press.

Law, A. M. & Kelton, W.D. (2000). Simulation modeling and analysis. (3rd ed.). New York: McGraw-Hill.

Paskov, S. (1994). *Computing high dimensional integrals with applications to finance*. (Preprint Columbia University).

Stanislaw, Ulam. (1991). *Adventures of a mathematician*. Originally published in 1976, University of California Press, p. 199.

Part III

Pragmatistic Applications

17
Critical Analysis Using Four Case Studies across Industries

Linnaya Graf

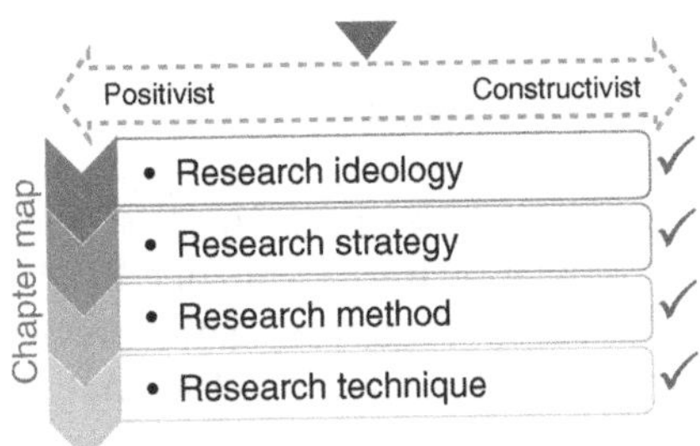

Chapter overview

In this chapter Graf discusses how she applied the pragmativist ideology using an integrated critical analysis with multiple case studies. This method applies the critical analysis literature review and interpretive critical thinking techniques (from the perspective of the researcher), as a multiple case study ($N = 4$). The cases were drawn from business, engineering, health care industries and from higher education. The unit of analysis in the research strategy was the "creative use of critical thinking skills in critical analysis across four case studies," an inductive within-group focus (since there was an overall analysis and not a comparison between cases). The level of analysis was the organization. The generalization target was to all practitioner-scholars in academia and in organizations intending to use these methods.

Background

The best research tool in the world is a sharp mind that applies critical thinking to information in order to evaluate and interpret findings. We call this process critical analysis. Critical analysis is used across every discipline. It is applied to populations and individuals in personal and professional spheres (Khine, 2014; Paterson, Barrts, Lanunso & Verheof, 2009).

Critical analysis is used across different industries for various reasons. In business, critical analysis might commonly be applied to proposals and project summaries (Arnott & Pervan, 2005). Engineers conduct critical analysis of performance measures and solutions (Coleman & Steele, 2009). Health-care systems conduct critical analysis to determine effectiveness of staff and programs (Kohn, 1997; Melander, 2004). Researchers, doctoral students, graduate faculty, and those in the human service and behavioral services fields often conduct written critical analysis to evaluate works or literature (Sapsford & Jupp, 2006). Regardless of the purpose, critical analysis is a scientific process that includes specific steps in order to achieve the most valid interpretation. In this chapter, the application of critical analysis to evaluating and interpreting evidence is explored using both theoretical consideration and real-world application. The use of case studies provides examples of real-world application using critical analysis across business, engineering, health care, and academics. We also review the specific steps to writing a critical analysis, or interpretative analysis, of literature. The key consideration in any form of critical work is to understand the key concept that critical thinking, imagination, review, and evaluation all work together to create a critical analysis. Critical analysis goes beyond a synthesis of the literature to include an argument, interpretation, and "criticism" of the subject being reviewed (Fairclough, 2013). In the following sections, consider how critical analysis is applied in real-life situations across business, engineering, health care, and academics as a way of illustrating its use across a spectrum of industries in real-world application.

Critical analysis in business

Overview

The value of critical thinking in business cannot be overstated. Business professionals, whether small and single-owner entrepreneurs or large company CEOs work in an environment where they must continually make decisions, often that have significant consequences. Alasdi and Abdelrahim (2007) provided a significant look into the variables that predicted success in business and found that critical analysis and a planning model is the cornerstone of business success across the globe. Critical analysis in business runs across extensive and multilevel platforms, often simultaneously. For example, business analysis requires assessing assumptions, sales, volumes, and pricing; projecting growth and patterns; evaluating programs and financial structures; and assessing vulnerabilities. Businesses must consistently analyze past circumstances, present occurrences, and future projections. While the art and science of critical thinking in the area of everyday is an important part of critical analysis in business, there are also evaluation and analysis tools used in business that help with project implementation, management, and evaluation.

Application

There are many types of tools used in critical analysis for business. However, some of the most common are used for project management applications. One example of a critical analysis tool in business is called the critical path method, or critical path analysis. Critical path analysis is a complex process of mapping the alternative pathways to a specific end (Thornley, 2007). It is often used as an algorithm for a conducting an effective project management. This tool is used to help determine if a projected timeline is correct for a project and whether the project can be completed in a timely manner. This tool includes (Thornley, 2007):

- a complete list of all activities required to complete the project,
- an explanation of relationship and dependencies between all activities, and
- an estimated time for completion of each activity.

A tool very similar to critical path analysis is the program evaluation and review technique or PERT. To illustrate the use of PERT, consider an initial draft of a project table from a case study in the archives of PrePEAR, LLC (Graf, 2013, see table 17.1). As part of a large-scale program evaluation, a 360-degree evaluation of a nonprofit business plan was designed that included several outcome and processes evaluation measures.

When looking at the chart it becomes easier to plan and consider a few practical realities. First, the earliest possible time for the completion of this project is 13 weeks. In reality, the project requires 16 weeks for completion due to a longer data collection and longer debriefing times than required. After the initial chart was approved by the client's board, the project required a more specific timeline for staff interviews and client, training, documentation review, and analysis of data. The above draft, applying the PERT method, was used to create a complex timeline for the project, which ultimately was completed under time and budget. Part of critical analysis in business is proper planning. By carefully consider all possible resources, activities, deliverables, and goals prior to implementing any of the above actions the board and project manager were able to consider potential impediments. For example, a symposium was scheduled during the timing slotted for staff training, and accommodations had to be made for the staff who would be absent during the training sessions due to the symposium. Critical analysis applied to project proposals, management, and evaluation in the area of business plays a crucial role not only in making sound business decisions, but also in successfully accomplishing goals, meeting budget requirements, and planning for potential challenges. Whether

Table 17.1 Sample PERT pathway model

	Define all components	Task dependence	Type	Earliest time to start	Estimated time to complete
A	Evaluate current resources		Parallel	Week 1	1 week
B	Review of current materials		Parallel	Week 1	1 week
C	Development of measures	A,B	Sequential	Week 2	1 week
D	Training of interviewers		Sequential	Week 3	2 weeks
E	Data collection: Interview of staff	D	Parallel	Week 5	4 weeks
F	Data collection: Interview of clients	D	Parallel	Week 5	4 weeks
G	Data collection: Measurement of outcome changes, archival	D	Parallel	Week 5	4 weeks
H	Analysis of data	E, F, G	Sequential	Week 9	2 weeks
I	Debrief of staff/clients	H	Sequential	Week 11	3 days
J	Reporting development	H	Sequential	Week 12	1 week

implemented across daily tasks or complex project management, critical analysis in business includes purposeful and systematic evaluation of past, present, and future realities and then making decisions based on the provided information in a way that allows for maximizing success and minimizing losses. Critical analysis may not prevent all emergencies or challenges, but it can minimize both the occurrence and the effects of negative outcomes.

Case studies

One of the best methods for understanding critical analysis applied to real-life settings is to consider case studies. The following three case studies are taken from the professional career of the author as the owner of a small research company operating since 2009. Names and some details have been changed to protect clients' personal information. Case study 1 explores a small nonprofit, nongovernmental organization that desired to evaluate its agency's process and outcomes for the purpose of creating deliverables for grant applications and private funders. Case study 2 presents a review of the critical analysis case study method, often used in making business decisions that affect expansion, alignment, or organizational change. Case study 3 considers the steps involved in critical analysis and the application of research to marketing practices. For each of the following case studies consider how critical analysis was an important part of ensuring successful planning, implementation, and evaluation.

Case Study 1. Client NP-NGO had a small nonprofit that had been able to secure two years of seed money in order to start a small community service agency. At the end of their first 18 months, the board of the NP-NGO convened faced with the realization that the grant funding provided to start the nonprofit service center was only six months from being depleted, but the agency had not yet secured another source of sustainable funding for future work. Originally, the NGO contracted PrePEAR, LLC with the desire to complete a process and outcome evaluation of their program service. NP-NGO had an overall goal of producing deliverables to be used in applying to multiple grant agencies to secure future funding. An example of the work completed in the initial drafting of the project is listed in the explanation of the PERT tool above. However, planning the project was only one small part of applying critical analysis in this case. After completing the data collection and analysis the board was required to take the information gathered from the study and create some fairly radical changes to meet the requirements of current grantors the agency was hoping to secure funding from in a very short time. Two specific sources of grant funding were tentatively available to the agency based on an existing relationship with a state coalition that had two open grant options. However, the grant application was a combined application, since all funding was coming from the state coalition. In other words, the NP-NGO could only apply to one grant source funding and had to choose an option. In a careful review of the grant details the major differences included amount and length. Specifically, Grant A offered a larger amount of grant money, but was a single-year grant without possibility of a renewal. In contrast, Grant B was designed specifically as a sustainability grant. Grant B provided only half of the amount available for Grant A, but was and had an ongoing disbursement over five years, assuming requirements of the grant committee were met each year. Both grant options would allow for the agency to pursue further outside funding, but excluded each other as possible options. In this case the board has a very difficult decision to make: acquire another year of full funding, or five years of conditional partial funding. If you were advising this board, what information would you need to decide which option was more appropriate for the NP-NGO? (Ultimately, the agency elected the second sustainability grant with the intention of securing additional funding through individual funders and fundraising).

Case Study 2. Company X requested that PrePEAR, LLC conduct a case analysis of their agency protocol and business strategy during a five-year review of the company's strategy. The company was a small business (< 20 employees) and was considering the possibility of expanding a second operation in a nearby town. The owner of the company had a standing professional relationship with the research company. Company X had conducted its own internal analysis and audit previous to the contracted request. However, the owner of company X decided an outside review would help bring together the deciding factors. In completing a critical case analysis there are specific steps to be followed that allow for a systematic review of the agency. The following steps were taken:

- Documentation review of the company's historical foundation and the political, financial, community, philosophical, and personal influences that affected the growth of the company.
- A SWOT analysis of the company's strengths, weaknesses, opportunities, and threats.
- An analysis of all external factors including an economic review of the industry, competition, projected growth for the industry, a geographic review, and overall employment opportunities for the potential staffing pool.
- A breakdown and clarification that reviewed alignment between the company's mission, goals, corporate-level strategy, business practices, and daily activities.
- A brainstorming session with the top staff and owner of all possibility scenarios, and a review of the SWOT analysis and potential pro/con outcome list for each scenario.
- A written case study with charts, visuals, and a pathway chart for potential outcomes was presented to the top staff and owner.

This analysis required a critical review, especially of the strengths and weaknesses that removed all personal opinion and was analytical in nature. Due to the standing professional relationship between the owners of these two companies, it was important to express and consider any potential bias in the analysis. Providing an honest and critical review allowed this company to make a sound business decision. In the end, the business decided to expend available resources in making a singular expansion of one division within their existing business model, rather than starting a secondary site. This type of systematic business modeling and evaluation often can make the difference between sound business decisions based on empirical data and sustainable economies and decisions made on desire.

Case Study 3. Case study 3 is a review of a single owner of a small, for-profit, community service agency that provided educational and financial services to a three-county area on the East Coast. We will call the owner Agent Z. To understand the background, Agent Z had operated a very successful 300-client educational and financial service for approximately 15 years before relocating to a new geographic area within the three county radiuses being served. Services offered by the agency included trainings, workshops, and lunch and learn sessions, individual and corporate business analysis, as well as sales of insurance and financial products. In this case, the research company was contracted originally to provide training for the agent in a specific statistical analysis tool. During the training sessions, Agent Z disclosed that client retention had been a challenge over the last few months because of the geographical location of the agent's office. After discussion of a few possible challenges, the research company agreed to review the agent's marketing plan and evaluate business practices for the purpose of offering possible recommendations in changes to improve continued client retention and marketing of services from the new location. In conducting the evaluation, a documentation review was conducted of two main sources, these included distribution and communication strategies and archival documentation of client communication. Following the document review, a client survey was conducted based on a random selection of 45 of the agent's existing clients. This evaluation uncovered that roughly 30% of clients remained unaware of the geographical move of the agent's office, clients were not receiving periodic communication from the agent, and materials were being used that still had the old contact information from the agent's previous location. Using this information a recommendation pathway model was put together that included:

1. Discarding all old materials with the previous contact information. While it can be tempting not to waste materials already printed, this was creating confusion for clients and came across as if the agent was not professionally organized or competent.
2. Along with obtaining all new materials with contact information, the agent was encouraged to take the time and have each client touched twice with the new geographical location. One with a personal call and the other by mail or email. Temporary help or an automated system could be used to call each client with the "We've Moved" message, along with an invite to come to a grand re-opening.
3. A grand reopening was encouraged to invite existing and potential clients to a meet and greet with a local political figure, athlete, or community service (such as finger-printing for children). This type of activity would allow

new clients to see the new office setting in a low-pressure situation and create exposure among community members in the new area.

4. To sustain communication and exposure to clients, a "touch" system was designed to allow for clients to be touched by mail, email, or phone at least once per quarter. This included an automated annual newsletter, a handwritten birthday card organized by the agent's secretary but signed by the agent, and letter reminding the client about next quarter's upcoming policy review, and an annual phone call asking the client to meet for a review of current policies. The automated systems were a small fee option for the agent, but were provided by a third party system that allowed the agent to maximize time and resources. Alternatives to an automated system would be hiring a part-time assistant to help with more consistent and systemized contact of clients.

In each of these case studies, the consistent theme is systematic, planned, decision making using careful data collection, analysis, comparison, interpretation, and planning based on the data in order to make sound business decisions. While these examples provide more concrete methods of evaluating funding, change, marketing, and complex business practices, these skills are also used on a daily basis in business. For example, deciding where to place time and resources for each list of daily activities requires a careful reflection on current and potential outcomes (Arnott & Pervan, 2005). It could be sometimes something as simple as whether to change the timing of creating a report, which activities to prioritize, and even who to have lunch with, all choices that should be made carefully rather than casually. Those business professionals who apply purposeful and reflective thinking, reading, review, and evaluation of their actions each day will find success more easily and critical thinking becomes more natural the more often it is used. Consider something simple, like determining how to handle a coming snow storm if your business does not have a formal snow policy. What are the decisions that have to be made? The first step is critical questioning, or asking purposeful targeted questions that allow for gathering data needed to make a systematic, data-driven decision. Following is an example of a pathway model that a business owner who is applying critical thinking to the effects of a snow storm on operational efficiency might consider (see figure 17.1):

Conclusion

The provision of an overview, examples of applied tools, and case study reviews opens a clear window into how critical analysis is used in both daily business operations and strategic planning. The purpose of this section is not so much to provide an education on business skills and management, as much as it is to illustrate the need and reality of how critical analysis affects the business

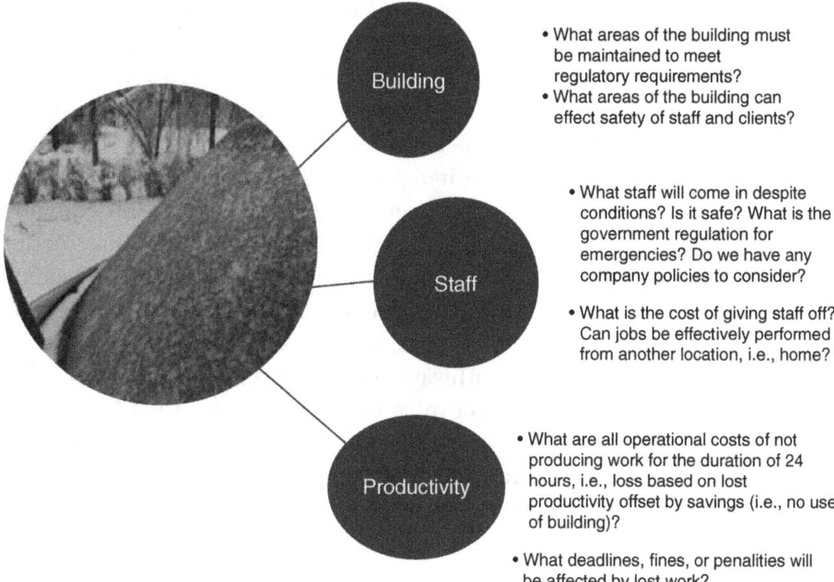

Figure 17.1 Sample of critical thinking questions related to operational efficiency.

world on a micro- and macrolevel. Understanding and applying these skills is important, as well as practicing them consistently. Individuals who are interested in critical analysis for business are strongly encouraged to review further texts that focus specifically on critical analysis in this subject (Dyer, 2011; Paul & Elder, 2002; Williams, 2001).

Critical analysis in engineering

Overview

One specific industry that uses critical thinking by the very nature of its work is engineering. In reality, the majority of people who decide to pursue the engineering field are by nature analytical and systematic in their thoughts and behavior (Paul, Niewoehner & Elder, 2007). For example, much of the daily work in engineering relies on experimental testing of uncertainties, validation of methods, exploration of errors, and testing the predictions of future outcomes (Coleman & Steele, 2009). Other industries could learn a great deal from how most engineers approach a project, and that is one reason why this industry is included in this applied look at using critical analysis in our work. In their daily operations engineers work in a position where they are attempting to meet a specific need through the development of a precisely crafted design. This design must yield a product that will meet that need with the best possible precision for outcomes (including safety, utility, process, and production), while keeping cost for the engineering company and client as low as possible without sacrificing the needed output. That is a very tall order. Most engineers approach new projects with some form of critical assessment. Specifically, their first tasks are to determine what the precise needs, budgets, resources, and parameters of the desired product include. Next, is to assess priorities of the client, including budget over output or vice-versa. Subsequently, the engineer uses this information and begins to employ critical imagination in order to begin drafting or conceptualizing a possible design to meet the need of the client. This process is the same no matter what the product. For example, this product might be roadways, a pipeline, a dam structure, a bottle or a container, electrical wiring pathways, a new testing method, or any other. The key in this step is the engineer must begin to use his or her knowledge, experience, past projects, and collected data to apply methods of thinking beyond what has already been previously conceptualized to create the best possible design for the product (Shaughnessy, Zechmeister & Zechmeister, 2003).

Application

Design work is only one part of engineering, but it is a unique skill demonstrating the importance of using a scientific process to make a creative product, which is a practical application of the concepts in critical analysis. In real-world application of these concepts, engineers use critical processes in areas of asking questions for clarity, determining accuracy and precision, determining relevance, including breadth and depth in their scope, providing logical validity for their work, and creating fairness across all vested interest (Paul et al., 2007). In most types of engineering, the engineer works from the creation of a model or a simulation, which is used to test the output of a specific design or assumption. One of the most common applications of this is the use of simulation tools. There are numerous examples of simulation tools. However, to provide one example, consider the application of simulation to determine the life of a product. This is called fatigue analysis. Fatigue analysis is used to test the point at which a product will stop working, or from where its load can no longer be borne (Gerber, 2012). Elements of fatigue analysis testing include determining the load-life, stress-life, strain capability, and crack points (Gerber, 2012). One example of a tool that can successfully predict fatigue is the ANSYS nCode DesignLife tool (Ansys, 2014). This tool was developed to predict the finite elements of fatigue. Tests are performed using structural stimulation that calculates each material model, repetitive loading, stresses, and breaking points using software technology that removes the painstaking labor of calculating individual scenarios (Ansys, 2014).

Case studies

Case studies are a typical method of teaching engineering in the classroom, because they help students take on a perspective role and most importantly help them see how critical thought and creativity are used together to acquire desired outcomes. Case studies are used to demonstrate analysis, decision-making processes, and judgment in developing design work. The following cases were provided by a manager at an engineering firm working in fluid dynamics. Names and details have been removed to protect the identity of the client and company.

Case Study 1. One area where an engineer must use critical analysis is in determining how to balance accuracy and productivity in testing designs. Specifically, more accurate testing takes time and resources, often at the sacrifice of releasing the design in a timely manner and/or limiting the investigated design space. A good engineer has to find the delicate balance between testing for accuracy, without testing to the point of losing production time. In fluid engineering, one design tool that is used for design testing is Computational Fluid Dynamics (CFD). Specifically, in our case, CFD is used to predict the flow field created by hydraulic machinery. The flow field within hydraulic machinery is a complex problem, especially if the goal is to predict the performance of an entire system. One challenge is that calculations for this simulation require data points, called grid nodes or mesh. The larger the volume or system, the more grid nodes are required if attempting to capture an accurate prediction. When in the iterative, or design portion of the project, the engineer desires quick calculations that allow for small, but frequent adjustments of the design until the design criteria are achieved. Due to limitations in computing power, simulation of the entire machine is somewhat restricted due to the time and resources required. One alternative is to test individual components that are being iteratively designed. However, a CFD simulation of individual components alone will not take into consideration all of the interactions that occur between adjacent components. Applying critical analysis, the solution for this problem is to use a technique that assumes periodicity in a multi-passage component. This allows the single passage of a multi-passage component to be analyzed with CFD rather quickly with minimal reduction in accuracy. As more components are added to build the entire hydraulic machine in CFD, the use of periodicity allows one to reduce a large, resource intensive problem to one that is easily managed to meet the engineer's desired turnaround time. This works because the accuracy of a flow-field simulation mainly depends on two subjects:

- exact simulation of the internal flow for the examined components and
- correct choice of boundary conditions, which is especially difficult at inlets and outlets.

These design assumptions are further reinforced and shown to be appropriate by comparing CFD results with those obtained during physical, scale model testing. By using a simplified assumption when modeling these boundary conditions the engineer is able to make accurate predictions faster, allowing for the required balance between production and accuracy.

Case Study 2. A primary purpose in hydraulic and mechanical engineering (multidisciplinary engineering) is to continually improve the efficiency of designs and processes. This requires critical evaluation of the original design, critical imagination to consider a new design, and testing to ensure that the new design will produce results. For example, a recent design was considered for a power plant that sought to improve efficiency using a newly designed guide vane. To predict the performance of a design change, first the existing guide vane geometry was numerically tested using Computational Fluid Dynamics (CFD) for the hydraulic performance and Finite Element Analysis for the structural performance. The same process was then performed for design iterations on a new guide vane. After investing the design space for the new guide vane, the achieved results did not show a high potential for a significant reduction in hydraulic efficiency losses when using a new guide vane design. This is because in some applications the guide vane design is driven by the structural requirements and one must balance the structural and hydraulic performance of a component to meet all design specifications. Subsequently, when the financial analysis was performed for a smaller improvement in power generation it showed that the payback period exceeded the customer's requirement to install a new guide vane. In engineering, the goal is not always to create something new, but critical analysis is used to develop purposeful, systematic, data-driven decision making that helps determine where efforts and resources should be placed to improve efficiencies. In this case the recommendation was not to implement a new design.

Conclusion

Critical analysis reasoning in engineering applies across all engineering disciplies, be it applying systematic decision making to electrical, civil, materials science, mechanical, or forensic engineering. The key to engineering reasoning is applying a scientific evaluation and decision-making process. However, creation is only one part of the process in engineering. A good engineer must not only create a sound process for decision making, but also be able to develop a result and report that makes a clear argument for his or her recommendations (Barnet & Bedau, 2011). Individuals interested in having a better understanding of engineer reasoning are encouraged to read textbooks dedicated to this subject (Paul et al., 2007) and explore websites related to critical thinking and engineering students.

Critical analysis in health care

Overview

A current area of active research and application for critical analysis is the health-care industry. Critical analysis has been applied across both individual care and organizational management (Carroll, 2009; Preusser, 2008; Sollecito & Johnson, 2013; Wilkinson, 2011). For example, critical care in nursing has been a hot topic in the field of health care over the last decade, with an emphasis on creating a new workforce of nurses who have strong critical thinking skills (Preusser, 2008). Critical analysis in nursing is related mostly to the act of clearly understanding and defining problems, determining what data are needed to solve problems, recognizing and evaluating assumptions, formulating sound hypothesis, drawing valid conclusions, and evaluating the soundness of decision making (Preusser, 2008). Clinical medical practice frequently requires split-second decision making, often with limited or incomplete knowledge. Training individuals to engage in a daily practice of analytical thinking will improve clinical practice and problem solving when confronted with the complex and challenging situations of medical practice.

However, critical analysis is a skill taught in health care not only to individuals who are practicing medicine or medical skills. Critical analysis occurs across health care as an industry at the organizational level (Sollecito & Johnson, 2013). Evaluation of an agency's risk and quality management systems, often called performance management, is a practice required by most accrediting boards in the health-care field. The global evolution of the health-care industry has challenged directors and leaders like never before to meet or exceed expectations while reducing possible risks (Sollecito & Johnson, 2013). Quality and risk management programming requires careful and deliberate planning, evaluation, and improvement, all of which require a cycle of applied critical analysis. To demonstrate both the narrow and broad field of critical analysis in health care, the application of performance management tools is presented, followed by case studies from the nursing field.

Application

To demonstrate application in the health-care industry, consider the example of a performance management tool used by a health organization in the northeastern United States. Names and details have been altered slightly to protect the identity of the company and clients. Performance management is systematic, strategic, and continuous (Carroll, 2009; Sollecito & Johnson, 2013). In this application of a performance management system, the health organization includes a board, made up of five members, who are accountable for designing, implementing, and for the continuous evaluation of the system.

Traits of their quality and risk management plan include a cyclical process that accounts for all of the following traits:

- transparent evaluation of current systems,
- surveys and focus groups to gather experiences,
- systematic tracking of all resources and expenditures, real and assumed,
- review of regulation and accreditation standards,
- short- and long-term goal setting,
- training and education for all leaders and staff,
- strategic and purposeful activities, tracked for compliance,
- consistent and standardized communication,
- technology, software, platform, and system review/training on a quarterly basis,
- data collection and assessment of processes on an annual basis,
- data collection and assessment of outcomes on an annual basis,
- analysis of data and report development on a monthly basis,
- a plan that is aligned with the mission, values, and goals of the organization,
- a cultural norm within the organization that risk and quality control crosses every staff member, across every level of the organization,
- expectations are designed from the bottom up (customer defined),
- implementation is designed from the top down (leader implemented),
- implementation is system wide and standardized (every department has the same requirements and expectations), and
- improvements are process-focused rather than individual-focused (in other words an effort is made to create better processes rather than singling out individual successes or failures).

For a successful risk and quality control system, the system must allow for input from all internal and external stakeholders, alignment, legal regulations, and a process focus (Carroll, 2009; Sollecito & Johnson, 2013). One of the best ways to understand how critical analysis is applied is to explore multiple case studies and view real-world examples of how critical analysis is applied in an organizational method. One of the best available resources for health care evaluation research, resources, and case studies is Press Ganey (http://www.pressganey.com/). Specifically, you will find case studies of enterprise-wide operations approaches, payment-system reforms, therapeutic improvements, cultural-change programs, communication strategies, readmission challenges, patient-flow challenges, collaboration experiences, empowering employees, patient satisfaction, administrator restructuring, revolutionizing the concept of excellence, modernizing processes, upgrading systems, and much more. These extensive real-world case studies are a superior resource for how hospitals have created dramatic changes applying a critically thought-driven process

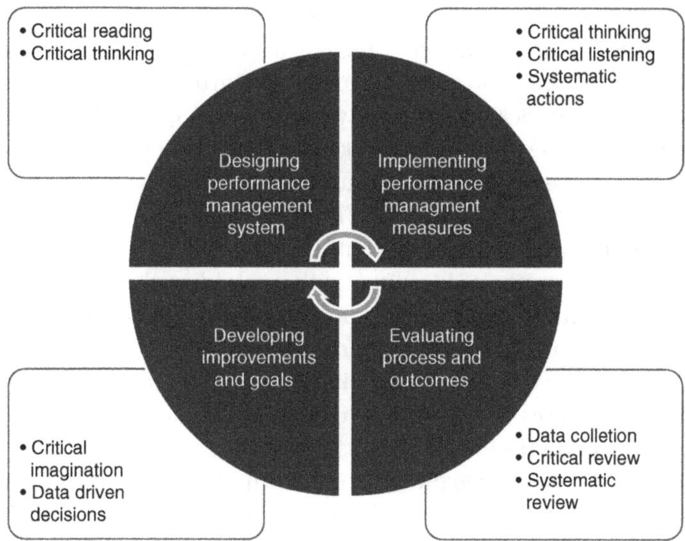

Figure 17.2 Relationship between performance management and critical analysis concepts.

of change. Find below an example of how each area of risk and quality management relates to critical analysis (see figure 17.2).

Case studies

Like most fields, the use of case studies provides superior methods of understanding and teaching critical thinking skills across the health-care sector (Popil, 2011). According to Popil (2011), the use of case studies provides more active learning than theoretical application. The practice also increase clinical problem solving, encourages the practice of critical thinking, and employs real-world consequences that health-care professionals can identify with. In considering how critical analysis is applied in a more individualized manner, consider the following cases provided by a nurse working in the pediatric care floor of a hospital in the northeast United States. Case studies are taken from her personal working experience with names, dates, and details altered sufficiently to protect the identities of the clinical nurse and patients.

Case Study 1. Patient L is a young mother with 3 children and who is currently 12 weeks pregnant. She presents at an urgent care center with pain in her abdomen and persistent migraines. She reports she has been seen for a threatened miscarriage twice in the last month and is currently taking a migraine medication as needed, along with an iron supplement and prenatal vitamin. Client has no history of a prior completed miscarriage and her current etiology is negative for any form of placenta disruption via ultrasound and there is an absence of bleeding. The patient discloses that prior pregnancies included cervical disruptions and pregnancies in the 32–34 week range, but with viable pregnancies and all children living. During examination the client becomes mildly hysterical and starts crying, expressing remarks that she "feels she is going to lose the baby" and "she knows something is wrong." As the lead clinical nurse there is no immediate cause for the woman's concern that can be detected via the exam or ultrasound. The emergency physician on board confirms the findings and also reports that there appears to be no detected cause for pain and no presence of bleeding, with a fetal heartbeat detected. At the absence of any clinical symptoms to support diagnoses, the patient is referred to seek follow-up with a regular obstetrician as soon as possible and report to the hospital delivery ward if any bleeding occurs in the next 48 hours. (What are possibly the causes of this pain with lack of diagnosis? What other pathways could the staff take to care for this patient?)

Case Study 2. Family Z brought their 17-month-old female child with pain in the arm and bruises to the face. The family reports that the child "fell down the stairs," the pattern of bruising and description of pain appears consistent with the story provided by the family. Upon examination, including a CAT scan and x-rays, the diagnosis for arm pain is a torn elbow tendon with treatment to include a brace and pediatric anti-inflammatory medication. While the facial bruising appears significant, x-rays and CT scan do not reveal any abnormal swelling or bruising of the brain, or presence of facial fractures. Upon an exam there is a negative presence of any ripped tissue, blood, or foreign bodies. The facial symmetry appears abnormal with swelling under the left side of the face and cheekbone. The tongue, nasal bridge, ear, and eye exam all appear superficially intact, but because of the age of the child it is difficult to determine what level of pain and feeling might be impacted. The adult male member of the family presents a caring, appropriate affective state with the child. The child does not exhibit signs of fear or anxious reactions when held by the adult male member. However, during a discussion of discharge directives, the adult male member of the family leaves to go to a restroom, and the female member of the family who reports she is the sister of the 17-month-old child reports she thinks the male hit the child in anger causing the child to fall down the stairs. (Based on this disclosure what are the actions you must follow through on as a mandated child-abuse reporter?)

Case Study 3. Nurse P has reported to work with bloodshot eyes and erratic behavior three times in the last week. Nurse P reports she has a sick child at home and "has not been sleeping well". During a clinical assessment Nurse P mixes up two charts and hands out the wrong lab orders and medical information to two different patients. The mistake is caught by one of the patients who notes that the name is wrong on the order. The mistake is corrected before the patients leave the building and Nurse P begs the patient not to say anything to the lead nurse supervisor as she has already been written up twice this week and is fearful of losing her job. (What is your legal or ethical obligation to disclose your knowledge of this incident? Is reporting errors that have been mitigated important? Why or Why not?).

Conclusion

In industry-level performance management critical analysis is applied in a standardized and systematic method. But, that standardization must always allow for the individuality of each organization's mission, values, and goals along with the constant changes that occur in the health-care field (Carroll, 2009; Sollecito & Johnson, 2013). Further, as noted from each of these case studies for critical care there is often no clear-cut or standardized answer for individual medical care decisions. However, actions must continue to be based on best practices, quality and risk management policies, regulations, and personal values that result in data-driven decisions. Health-care professionals and the industry as a whole operate under a framework of critical analysis at all times. Their work requires gathering all possible knowledge, developing sound hypotheses, considering multiple pathways and potential solutions.

Critical analysis as an academic exercise

Overview

Critical thinking as a practice is both a science and an art. As an academic exercise critical analysis includes critical thinking, critical reading, critical imagination, critical writing, and critical revision The purpose of academic critical thinking is to be able to use deductive and inductive reasoning, identify fallacies and contradictions, and construct a valid and logical argument based on sound inference and interpretation (Barnet & Bedau, 2011; Lavery, Hurge & Doran, 2009; Lewis, 2007). When crafting and developing an argument, a scientific process that includes very specific and systematic steps should be used for gathering all possible knowledge, evaluating current information, applying inductive and deductive pathways to possible interpretations, and coming to conclusions that are based on sound evidence. There are multiple methods written and available in the literature regarding this process, which can be used and adapted by someone trying to create their own system. (Barnet & Bedau, 2011). However, for illustrative purposes this chapter provided a personal system based on years of experience of the author working in research methodology and teaching college courses.

Practical steps for writing an interpretative (critical) analysis

Each step in the critical analysis process has a unique and important place in the process. The following compilation is the current author's system for developing a critical analysis step by step (see figure 17.3). This practice guide is

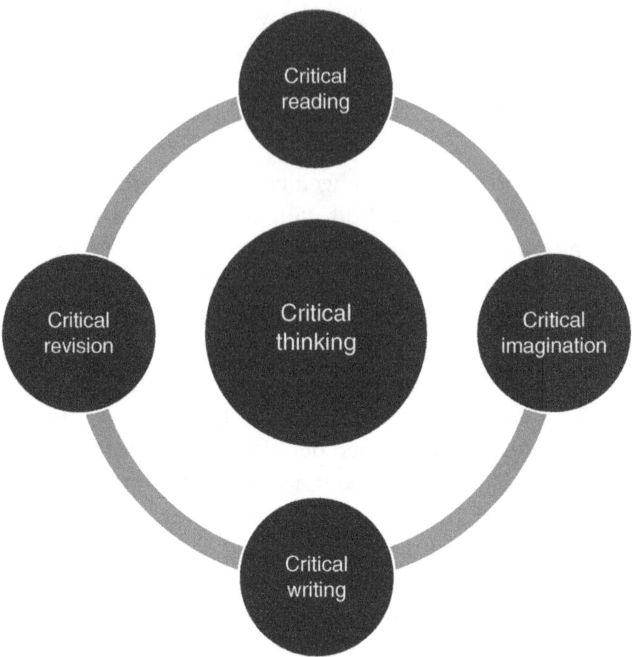

Figure 17.3 Diagram of the tools required for conducting critical analysis. Critical thinking as applied using critical reading, critical imagination, critical writing, and critical revision.

provided to assist any individual in visualizing the breakdown of this process and in learning how to implement the various aspects of the writing process as an academic exercise. The following visualization is a conceptual view of the process as a cyclical undertaking that includes at its center the practice of critical thinking at every stage. Further in this section, the process of critical analysis is deconstructed step by step to assist in ensuring the application of rigor and proper purpose in writing.

The term critical in this case denotes a purposeful and mindful activity, in which the mental processes are self-corrective and involve a set of rigor and standards in their application. Following is a breakdown of the critical analysis as an academic process.

Step 1. Critical Thinking. Critical thinking is a "process of actively and skillfully conceptualizing, applying, analyzing, synthesizing, reasoning, or communicating, as a guide to belief and action (Barnet & Bedau, 2011; Criticalthinking.org, 2013). This process is cyclical and ongoing. Critical thinking occurs throughout the entire process of a critical analysis. It occurs as part of setting the parameters for how a problem will be studied, setting the parameters for the research that will be collected to begin critical reading on the subject, to supplement critical imagination and hypothesis development, and as part of the writing and revision process. However, critical thinking is not all thinking. Critical thinking is a specific, self-disciplined process of actively engaging, mentally exploring a topic, using very conscious and mindful effort for evaluating and defining the topic.

Step 2. Critical Reading. Critical reading includes both reading and thinking. Critical reading could be defined as the act of evaluating literature as it is being verbally or visually absorbed. In other words, the reader is not simply taking in the words or plot through the senses. In contrast, the reader is actively evaluating the words and meanings for context and validity, comparing the information to all previously known data, and developing a hypothesis about relevance, accuracy, and meaning.

There is a multitude of challenges in critical reading that begins with evaluating the author or publisher of a given work. Have you heard the phrase, "consider the source"? Considering the source is an important part of critical reading for two reasons. First, some sources include a test of validity before publication. For example, a peer-reviewed journal article must be accepted by experts in the field that it is a valid and valuable contribution to the field. A newspaper article goes through an editorial process to meet the criteria of the publisher. However, open source Internet sites, personal business sites, and blogs simply are self-published works that are edited only by the author. Knowing the criteria for evaluating the validity of the work is critical. Realistically even journals and newspapers have very different reviewing processes. Determining the source includes knowing this process. The second consideration is related to translation. Specifically, in a peer-reviewed article the author has typically engineered, designed, implemented, and evaluated any data being presented. This is important because data provided secondhand can become confused, misinterpreted, misconstrued, purposefully twisted, or lost in translation. We know that bias and personal agenda can be introduced at every stage of information dissemination (Barnet & Bedau, 2011). Thus, it stands the reasons that the only way to ensure you are evaluating the most accurate version is to review and interpret the original data yourself, as much as possible. Peer-reviewed articles almost always include a clear window into the data collection, analysis, and interpretation process. This transparency is critical to the field for the very reason of ensuring validity.

After "considering the source" of the article and any data being evaluated, the next critical thought pertains to how the current information fits into the larger picture of data presented in the field. For example, if ten reports are run that examine the effectiveness of an ad campaign and nine reports come back showing a positive effect while one report shows a negative effect, logic dictates it is more likely that nine reports are correct than the single report. That doesn't mean that the further research should be halted. Indeed, discrepancies should always be carefully evaluated. A statistical assumption would indicate that the most likely answer is that the single report included an outlier or a mistake. However, a critical reader will ask "what is the report showing that is different from the other string of reports." Is it possible that the last report is more accurate than the previous nine due to random change, a change in criteria, how questions were asked, how information was evaluated, or the method of analysis? Thus, critical reading requires both a thorough and specific look at a single publication, as well as an evaluation of the publication against the larger field of available information.

A list of questions to ask when critical reading:

- Who is the author?
- Who is the publisher?
- What is the purpose of the work?
- How old is the information?
- Where the data did come that are being presented?
- Who funded the data collection and analysis?
- Who benefited from the data outcome and interpretation, were they associated with the collection or publication?
- How does the article fit into the broader field of literature?
- Are the methods used to collect or analyze any data transparent and able to be reproduced?

Step 3. Critical Imagination. Similar to critical thought, critical imagination is the "ability to think beyond the boundaries of conventional thinking and consider creative alternatives" (Shaughnessy et al., 2003, p. 37). However, critical thinking occurs as a continuous process before, during, and after critical reading; in contrast, critical imagination should stem from critical reading and contribute to the development of hypothesis, theories, and lines of thought that create new and further inquiry. Critical imagination includes thought that contributes to considering previously unidentified meanings and outcomes, identification of potential flaws or errors, alternative hypotheses or potential solutions, or creative application of outcomes. Thinking about a problem in a new way can lead to a new insight, a novel problem-solving technique, or open up a new line of inquiry.

Step 4. Critical Writing. Critical writing is very different from creative writing. Creative writing is designed be expressive, imaginative, inspired, and often artistic. Critical writing does not include any of these qualities. Keep in mind that critical writing can and should still include aspects of writing style that engage and interest the reader. However, critical writing should be analytical, investigative, methodical, and clear. Critical evidence should be built carefully from a foundation of valid evidence and presented in such a way that the future reader can conduct hie or her own critical review of your work.

The step of critical writing applies the knowledge learned in critical reading and the hypothesis, interpretations, and mental explorations of critical imagination into a deliverable to be given to someone else, and which explains and outlines your conclusions.

Step 5. Critical Revision. The technique of critical revision is the application of proper structure, content, organization, accuracy (Jacobsen, 2012). This step of critical revision is not the place to produce an interpretative stance. In contrast, this step requires a clear adherence to the rubric and guidelines of the publication and audience for which the critical analysis is being designed. Jacobsen (2012, pp. 245–248) provides one example of a checklist that can be used to edit and review a manuscript before submission. However, there is no sample checklist that will suffice for all aspects of publication. Each industry, university, and publication requires their own formatting and style. However, an example does provide an excellent starting point for designing a more personalized checklist and can be used as a model.

Checklist items should include all aspects of structure and content, style, and clarity. The checklist for submission should be designed based on the compilation of formatting and style instructions from the submission requirements of the work being done and the writing manual for the discipline (APA, AMA, MLA, etc.). Table 17.2 provides another example of how to design a checklist

Table 17.2 Sample table for critical revision

Formatting	**Style**	**Clarity**
Are paginations and indentions formatting using the appropriate style manual?	Is the proper font size and type applied using the appropriate style manual?	Is there an introduction that explains the purpose and importance of the work?
Are tables, figures, and graphs laid out using the appropriate style manual and publication requirements?	Is the tone of writing appropriate to the topic and audience?	Do titles appropriately represent each topic?
Are levels of headings applied using the appropriate style manual?	Is grammar and spelling carefully reviewed and all correct?	Has unnecessary jargon, technical language been removed and all uncommon terms defined?
Is white space applied using the appropriate style manual?	Is past/present tenses used appropriately and consistently throughout the manuscript?	Is there a clear thesis sentence for each paragraph?
Does the word count meet the manuscript requirements?	Has all potential bias (gender, disability, racial) been removed from the wording?	Are statistics included in both visual and narrative form, as appropriate?

using a simple table insert in a word document or by modifying it for an Excel spreadsheet. Please note that the sample provides an example of the categories and is not meant to be an exhaustive list. Understand that many websites and textbooks can provide you great formatting and writing advice. However, the final authority on these topics are the manuscript guidelines and the style manual for your school of thought provided for you by the organization where you intend to submit it.

Application

Critiquing the literature. In applying critical analysis, often students are required to complete critical reviews of a specific article or body of literature. In conducting this exercise the student should begin by creating or applying a given checklist for analysis. This will often be provided for the student in the form of a rubric or academic tool in the academic institution's writing center. I always encourage students to ensure they seek the individual institutions' or professors' checklist or rubric before designing their own. While the steps for critical analysis are universal, each institution or faculty member may weigh various items differently. The formatting and expectations from each assignment will vary by industry and degree type. Following is an example of the matrix you can use when conducting a critical review (see table 17.3):

Crafting an argument. A second common critical analysis assignment in academics is to review a given topic, interpret the findings, and write a persuasive argument for why your findings are correct. Again, always base work from the rubric or checklist attached to the assignment. However, if there are no specific expectations provided before writing, create a peer-review checklist. After crafting your argument, compare your paper to your checklist and then ask a peer to review your work against the checklist. An example of questions for your checklist would include:

- Is there a clear thesis statement to describe the purpose of the argument?
- Does the review provide poor, sufficient, or extensive evidence to back the claims in the argument?

Table 17.3 Sample table for critical review of the literature

Author	Source/ peer-reviewed?	Issue being addressed	Main thesis	Intended audience	Findings and significance	Source and validity of evidence	Defined limits

- Is there a wide variety of persuasive tools used (rhetorical questions, clear descriptors, specific verbiage)?
- Is there any ambiguousness in the word choices?
- Is the vocabulary interesting and does it engage the reader?
- Does the work provide a "Why should you care" statement and attempt to convince the reader that the argument is relevant for the reader?
- Is the mechanics and spelling of the context correct?
- Is there an introduction, a transition between topics, and a conclusion that are clear and easy to identify?
- Is the work organized in such a way that the reader is pulled through the text easily and follows the argument logically?
- Does the work use scientific evidence rather than inflammatory language to make a case for the findings?
- Does the argument clearly include interpretation (the voice of the author) as well as cited evidence to support statements (i.e., not cited every sentence)?
- Describe the main purpose and findings of the argument.

The ability for your peer-reviewer to clearly explain the topic argument is a litmus test for clarity. If you must tell the reader what you meant to write, then your writing lacks clarity.

Case study

To illustrate a clear example, consider the case study of Student B. Student B was required to complete a capstone requirement that included a comprehensive critique of a topic of choice related to his degree of field. The student was provided a rubric, a quality control checklist, and a formatting template to complete the assignment. The student had a mentor assigned to assist him with accountability in completing the capstone in the required 12-week timeframe. The student followed a systematic process in approaching and completing the assignment, which served the student well, submitting a well-crafted, sound argument and findings from the literature review. First, the student identified a topic that held a personal interest and that he found enjoyable. Second, the student developed a matrix to review the literature and gather as much information as possible related to the topic to uncover a central question to be explored in the research. Third, using the matrix to get a big picture of findings across multiple studies, the student designed a clear thesis statement that used the research findings for support.

Fourth, a second review of the literature was conducted with expanded search terms and then analyzed to ensure that a full picture of all possible knowledge was gathered. Fifth, the student culled the literature for the most recent, well-crafted arguments, and studies based on the strongest science. These studies were marked for inclusion in the body of the paper. In the next step, the student crafted a clear introduction that presented the central question and the purpose of the paper. Next, he presented the research in his own words, synthesizing his thoughts with the research findings to provide a clear argument that was supported by the research. (Note, the student did not write a list simply summarizing the different research). In the eighth step, the student described how the research supported the argument. Finally, the student wrote a powerful summary that brought together the research, significance of the findings, and acknowledged the limitations. If there were appendices they would also be added, but in this case the student did not use any figures or appendix attachments. Appropriate attachments for this work might have included the review matrix used to critique the literature and the parameters used for the literature search.

Conclusions

The above examples outlined the clear and specific steps used in academic work to write a formal critical analysis and to include a critical review of the literature as the data. While there are other problems in the business and management discipline that include critical analysis, these are the most common types found. The skills described for use in both of these examples generalize to all forms of academic and organizational work. Specifically, the use of critical thinking as applied in critical reading, critical imagination, critical writing, and critical revision is the cornerstone of success in any academic assignment.

Summary

This chapter provided the reader with a theoretical definition and applied examples of the critical analysis method. The examples were drawn from across a spectrum of industries for the purpose of providing the reader with a real-world understanding of this research skill set. The use of critical analysis was explored in business, engineering, health care, and as an academic exercise for those individuals working as researchers, doctoral students, graduate faculty, or in thehuman service and behavioral services fields. The purpose of this chapter was to illuminate easy examples of how critical analysis is used to evaluate scholarly work or literature, review a project, or engage in data-based decision making (Sapsford & Jupp, 2006). Case studies were provided to spark an interest and explain the utility of critical thinking in real-world settings. The takeaway from this chapter is that critical thinking, imagination, review, and evaluation form a cyclic, systematic process required in purposeful and mindful thinking that leads to intentioned outcomes. The art and science of critical analysis exceeds the steps of a critical review to provide an argument, interpretation, or "criticism" of the given topic (Fairclough, 2013). The reader is encouraged to take the information learned in the previous pages and apply it to further learning specific to the reader's industry and field.

References

Alasdi, R. & Abdelrahim, A. A. (2007). Critical analysis and modeling of small business performance (Case study: Syria). *Journal of Asia Entrepreneurship and Sustainability, 3*(2), 1–76.

Ansys, Inc. (2014). ANSYS nCode DesignLife. Products. Ansys, Inc. Retrieved from http://www.ansys.com/.

Arnott, D. & Pervan, G. (2005) A critical analysis of decision support systems research. *Journal of Information Technology, 20*, 67–87, doi:10.1057/palgrave.jit.2000035.

Barnet, S., & Bedau, H. (2011). *Critical thinking, reading, and writing: A brief guide to argument* (7th ed.). Boston, MA: Bedford.

Carroll, R. (Ed). (2009). *Risk management handbook for health care organizations*. San Fransisco, CA: Jossey-Bass.

Coleman, H. W., & Stelle, W. G. (2009). Experimentation, validation, and uncertainty analysis for engineers (3rd ed.). Hoboken, NJ: Wiley & Sons, Inc.

Dyer, L. (2011). *Critical thinking for business students* (2nd ed.). Thornhill, ON: Captus Press, Inc.

Gerber, B. (2012) To live forever: Fatigue stimulation can increase product life, reduce costs, and decrease risk. *Ansys Advantage*, 51–52.

Jacobsen, K. H. (2012). *Introduction to health research methods*. Sudbury, MA: Jones & Bartlett Learning.

Khine, M. S. (Ed.) (2014). *Critical analysis of science textbooks: Evaluating instructional effectiveness*. Cambridge, MA: Springer.

Kohn, L. T. (1997). *Methods in case study analysis*. The Center for Studying Health System Change [Technical report No. 2]. Retrieved http://www.hschange.com/CONTENT/158/158.pdf.

Lavery, J., Hughes, W., & Doran, K. (2009). *Critical thinking: An introduction to basic skills* (6th ed.). Peterborough, ON: Broadview Publisher.

Melander, S. D. (2004). *Case studies in critical care nursing: A guide for application and review* (3rd ed.). San Francisco, CA: Elsevier Health Sciences.

Paul, R. W., & Elder, L. (2002). *Critical thinking: Tools for taking charge of your professional and personal life*. Uppersaddle River, NJ: Prentice Hall.

Paul, R. W., Niewoehner, R. J., & Elder, L. (2007). *The thinkers guide to engineering reasoning*. Sonoma, CA: Foundation for Critical Thinking.

Paterson, C., Baarts, C., Launso, L., & Verheof, M. J. (2009). Evaluating complex health interventions: A critical analysis of the "outcomes" concept. *BMC Complementary and Alternative Medicine, 9*, 18. doi:10.1186/1472–6882–9–18.

Popil, I. (2011). Promotion of critical thinking by using case studies as teaching methods. *Nurse Education Today, 31*(2), 204–207.

Preusser, B. A. (2008). *Winningham and Preusser's critical thinking cases in nursing* (4th ed.). St. Louis, MO: Mosby Elesevier.

Sapsford, R., & Jupp, V. (Eds) (2006). *Data collection and analysis*. London: Sage Publications.

Shaughnessy, J. J., Zechmeister, E. B., & Zechmeister, J. S. (2011). *Research methods in psychology* (9th ed). London: McGraw Hill.

Sollectio, W. A. & Johnson, J. K. (2013). *McLaughlin and Kalunzy's continuous quality improvement in health care* (4th ed.). Burlington, MA: Jones & Bartlett Learning.

Thornley, G. (2007). *Critical path analysis in practice* [Digitial]. Routledge: Tavistock Publications.
Wilkinson, J. M. (2011). *Nursing process and critical thinking* (5th ed.). Upper Saddle River, NJ: Pearson Education, Inc.
Williams, S. J. (2001). *Making better business decisions: Understanding and improving critical thinking and problem solving skills*. Boston, MA: Sage Publications.
Vaugh, L. (2007). *The power of critical thinking*. NewYork: Oxford Press.

18
Integrating Multiple Case Studies with a Merger and Acquisition Example

Lars Schweizer

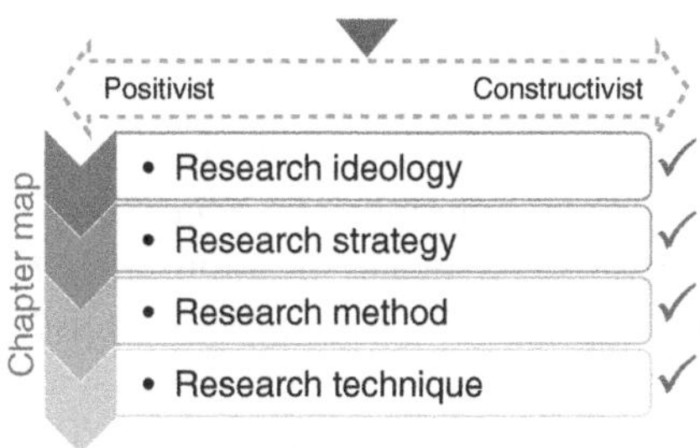

Chapter overview

Schweizer appears to hold a post-positivist philosophy, which he nicely integrates into the pragmativist research design ideology. He does a thorough job at explaining the single and multiple case study methods, using several merger and acquisition examples to illustrate each, respectively. Researchers have a different epistemology in their ideology when using the case study method; the within-case focus is used instead of within-group, and cross-case analysis refers to a between-groups comparison. When researchers follow the post-positivist ideology, a single case study may be conducted like an experiment, observation, or field study method, using deductive theory-driven research questions (or hypotheses). In contrast, when researchers adpot a pragmatic ideology, they are more likely to use multiple case studies, with either a deductive or inductive unit of analysis, with a goal to generalize the findings to other populations.

Introduction

"For the most part, the cases of interest in education and social service are people and programs. Each one is similar to other persons and programs in many ways and unique in many ways. We are interested in them for both their uniqueness and commonality. We seek to understand them. We would like to hear their stories" (Stake, 1995, p. 1).

Miles & Huberman (1994) suggest that researchers should use a qualitative research design when there is a clear need for an in-depth understanding, for local contextualization, for the potential for casual inferences, as well as for the points of view of the people under study. Yin (2009) argues that case study research can be used to analyze why and how contemporary, real-life phenomena occur in cases where researchers have minimal control. Lee (1999, p. 54) points out that case study research addresses many of the issues usually taken up by laboratory or field experiments and that "the case study's in-depth nature and emphasis on situational embedded process justify some level of casual inference." Larsson (1990) states that case studies are particularly appropriate for the study of the merger and acquisition (M&A) integration processes, given the need for detailed, contextual descriptions of, as is frequently the case in M&As, very sensitive data The use of case studies in the context of M&As is also in line with the recommendations of Bower (2004), Hunt (1990), Javidan et al. (2004), and Napier (1989). Hence, the appropriate research methodology for a study that attempts to extend existing post-acquisition integration literature is the comparative case study research methodology (Eisenhardt, 1989; Glaser & Strauss, 1967; Lee, 1999; Stake, 1995; Yin, 2009). Thus, this chapter will provide a detailed description of an application of the case study method by illustrating the integration of multiple case studies as an example of post-acquisitions integration. In line with Lee (1999, p. 55), it is crucial to point out that no "hard-and-fast rules governing case study research" exist. Instead, it is only possible to offer general guidelines on how to conduct case study research. In this context, Eisenhardt and Graebner (2007, p. 27) emphasize that "the purpose of the [case study] research is to develop theory, not to test it."

Theoretical background of qualitative case study research

Miles and Huberman (1994) point out a couple of important and recurring features of qualitative research: (1) Qualitative research is done through an intense contact with the research field or real-life situation. (2) The researcher's role is to gain a systematic overview of the context under study. (3) This is done by attempting to capture data on the perceptions of local actors from within. (4) By reading and analyzing the data with the help of certain instruments, the researcher is able to isolate and identify specific patterns that emerge from the data.

Silverman (2010) raises a few critical points concerning quantitative research: (1) It can lead to a "quick fix," involving little or no contact with people in the "field." (2) Statistical correlations may be based upon variables that, in the context of the naturally occurring interaction, are arbitrarily defined. (3) After-the-fact speculation about the meaning of correlations can involve the very common-sense processes of reasoning that science tries to avoid. (4) The pursuit of measurable phenomena can mean that unperceived values creep into research by simply taking on board highly problematic and unreliable concepts. (5) While it is important to test hypotheses, a purely statistical logic can make the development of hypotheses a trivial matter and fail to help in generating hypotheses from data.

Given these identified shortcomings of quantitative research, Silverman (2010) states that a preference for qualitative research has some implications: (1) a preference for qualitative data is simply understood as the analysis of words and images rather than numbers; (2) a preference for naturally occurring data, that is, observation rather than experiment, unstructured rather than structured interviews; (3) a preference for meanings rather than behavior—attempting "to document the world from the point of view of the people studied" (Hammersley, 1992, p. 165); (4) a rejection of natural science as a model; and (5) a preference for inductive, hypothesis-generating research rather than hypotheses testing.

Moreover, qualitative and quantitative research differs in more than their research methodology and data analysis. On the one hand, qualitative research is often characterized as interpretative, whereas quantitative research is considered as being positivist. Thus, regarding qualitative research as interpretative might even imply that quantitative research is not interpretative. Although the selection of specific variables as likely causes of some designated effects, the formulation of hypotheses, and the use of statistics might create this impression, the design of the research strategy as well as the subsequent interpretation of the collected data have interpretative aspects (Eisenhardt & Bourgeois III, 1988).

Yin (2009) mentions three major concerns a case study strategy has to deal with. First, there is the complaint about the lack of rigor in case study research. Thus, every investigator must work hard in order to ensure methodological rigor, which for example can be realized through the help of well-identified research questions and well-developed interview schedules as well as questionnaires (Eisenhardt, 1991). Taking this into account, the problems in case study research are not different from experiments, surveys, or historical research. In this context, Yin (2009, p. 105) points out that "much depends on an investigator's own style of rigorous thinking, along with the sufficient presentation of evidence and careful consideration of alternative interpretation." Second, there is the frequently asked question of how to generalize from just one case. According to Yin (2009, p. 21) the answer is explained below:

> Case studies, like experiments, are generalizable to theoretical propositions and not to populations or universes. In this sense, the case study, like the

experiment, does not represent a "sample," and the investigator's goal is to expand and generalize theories (analytic generalization) and not to enumerate frequencies (statistical generalization).

The third concern about case studies is that they take too long and result in massive, unreadable documents. This represents another challenge for the investigator who has to look for alternative ways of getting information. He could for example make more use of the telephone or the data available in libraries instead of being a participant-observer. Moreover, he should keep in mind who the audience of the case study is going to be.

Eisenhardt (1989, p. 536) emphasizes that "theory-building research is begun as close as possible to the ideal of no theory under consideration and no hypotheses to test." Because of this, case study research very often leads directly to the cases and the contextual descriptions of the industries of which the considered companies are part. After a rich and theoretically unbiased understanding of the case activities has been gained, there will be the confrontation of theories and case results. This procedure of "postponed" literature review will lead to the extension of theory and thus to a theoretical contribution of its own. Of course, even Eisenhardt (1989, p. 536) must admit that "it is impossible to achieve this ideal of a clean theoretical slate." Thus, her advice is that the case study researcher "should avoid thinking about specific relationships between variables and theories as much as possible" (Eisenhardt, 1989, p. 536).

For reasons of convenience—and perhaps for an aura of rigor—there is an undeniable temptation to conduct cross-sectional research that "proceeds from a distance, with a remote researcher gathering abstract data from organizations he knows almost nothing about" (Miller & Friesen, 1990, p. 1014). With the help of within-case and cross-case analyses, the goal is pursued to find diverging as well as similar patterns on the basis of which tentative hypotheses can be formulated. The end result—a set of testable propositions—represents the actual goal of the case study's work describing and comparing several organizational post-acquisition integration processes.

According to Eisenhardt (1989, 1991) as well as Eisenhardt and Graebner (2007) case studies can be regarded as a powerful mean in order to create theory, because they permit replication and extension among individual cases. The rich background context of cases is provided by stories (storytelling), but the deeper theoretical insights of case studies are gained from methodological rigor and multiple-case comparative logic.

Stake (1995) describes three major differences between qualitative and quantitative research. First, there is a distinction between explanation and understanding as purpose of inquiry. Second, one can notice a distinction between a personal and an impersonal role for the researcher. Third, there is a distinction between knowledge discovered and knowledge constructed. Following Denzin and Lincoln (1994) qualitative research—just like quantitative research—should provide (1) internal validity (degree to which findings correctly map the phenomenon in question), (2) external validity (degree to which findings can be generalized to other settings similar to the one in which the study occurred), (3) reliability (extent to which findings can be replicated, or reproduced, by another inquirer), and (4) objectivity (extent to which findings are free from bias).

As far as validity is concerned Yin (2009) points out four standard tests of validity: (1) construct validity by developing a correct set of operational measures, (2) internal validity by establishing a casual relationship, which Jick (1979) refers to as "within-method triangulation," (3) external validity by establishing the domain to which a study's findings can be generalized, which Jick (1979) calls "between-method triangulation," and (4) reliability by demonstrating that the operation of a study can be repeated. The concern of validity can be addressed in several ways. That is, triangulation is used to increase construct validity. In this sense, triangulation is used not only to examine the same phenomenon from multiple perspectives, but also to enrich the understanding by allowing for new and deeper insights to emerge. The issue of internal validity is handled by conducting multiple iterations and follow-ups during the analyses. The problem of reliability and repeatability is addressed (1) by drawing up a detailed case study protocol and (2) by strictly following the required documentation and transcription standards. External validity is increased by studying multiple companies and analyzing comparative findings. This search for meaning within a case can be considered as a search for patterns or for consistency. If similar results are to be obtained from multiple cases, replication is said to have taken place. The multiple case study contains multiple narratives, which are presented as separate sections about each case.

In a further step, a cross-case analysis is required. Strauss (1987) describes this in three steps. First, the researcher will tend to construct for each case an overall descriptive picture, including both the inner and outer context. Second, each case is to be analyzed separately. Within-case analysis typically involves detailed case study write-ups for each site. The central focus is to become intimately familiar with each case as a stand-alone entity, which allows the unique patterns of organizational integration and collaboration in each case to emerge before the investigator generalizes patterns across cases. To avoid being overwhelmed by the large amounts of information and data, the within-case analyses are focused around the identified subresearch questions that serve as essential elements of the phenomenon under study. Third, the case study researcher will draw general conclusions about all these cases. With the help of this cross-case analysis, the crucial part of multiple firm case studies, the investigator will capture the novel findings that may exist in the cases by looking at the data in many divergent ways.

From the within-case analysis in connection with the cross-case analysis, tentative hypotheses begin to emerge. Overall, the triangulating investigator is left to search for logical patterns in mixed-methods results. According to Eisenhardt (1989, p. 543) it must be considered that "shaping hypotheses in theory building research involves measuring constructs and verifying relationships." After that, the comparison of the emergent hypotheses with the extant literature is an essential feature of theory building in case study research. By this, the internal validity, generalizability, and theoretical level of theory building from case study research will be enhanced. The theoretical saturation is reached when the incremental improvement through a new iteration process to theory is minimal. The issue of external validity, that is, establishing the domain for generalizability, is a frequently overextended topic in the criticism of case studies. Case study research does not always claim to produce generalized theory; rather its aim is to produce hypotheses and theory extension for subsequent testing to then develop a general theory. However, this does not imply that external validity is not an issue to be addressed in case study research. In order to increase external validity, case study research is supposed to use multiple companies and comparative findings to the extent available.

Multiple case study research in practice

Finding and developing the research question

The research of this study starts from a perceived inappropriateness of existing studies in the field. In the context of post-acquisition integration activities, where testable theoretical propositions have not been sufficiently developed, the paradigm of critical rationalism, as proposed for example by Popper (1976), seems inappropriate. This paradigm considers the purpose of scientific research as explaining reality by formulating theories and then attempting to falsify them (Kretschmann, 1990). However, falsification is hardly possible when relatively few hypotheses on a phenomenon have been stated. Thus, for the post-acquisition integration study, which is taken as the example in this chapter, theory building using mainly qualitative research is more appropriate than theory-testing (Eisenhardt, 1989; Snow & Thomas, 1994). Gioia and Pitre (1990) argue for a multiparadigm approach to theory building as a means of establishing correspondence between paradigms and theory-construction efforts. From their point of view, qualitative research corresponds to "theory-building in the interpretative paradigm," whereas quantitative research is viewed as "theory-building in the functionalist paradigm." Qualitative research has become increasingly accepted in disciplines such as psychology, sociology, and business administration (Miles & Huberman, 1994).

According to Yin (2009, p. 19) "defining the research question is probably the most important step to be taken in a research study." Stake (1995) refers to the "research question" as "issue question" or "issue statement." The central research question of this study focuses on how the post-acquisition integration between biotechnology companies and big pharmaceutical companies takes place. In this context, it is necessary to consider what consequences this implies for the knowledge transfer and the organizational changes that might affect the innovative and organizational competencies and flexibility of the acquired company. In analyzing and trying to answer this question, the following research fields, which can also be considered as a kind of subresearch questions, and which Stake (1995) refers to as "topical questions," are of interest:

1. the impact of motives, sequence, and timing of the M&A process on the integration process,
2. the analysis of the integration process itself with respect to the dimensions of:
   - strategic integration,
   - organizational/structural integration,
   - knowledge/competence transfer,
   - cultural integration,
   - personal/HR integration, as well as
3. the organization of the integration process itself.

The set of research questions guides the entire research process from field work to case description over analysis to theory extension. Moreover, it helps the investigator to specify the kind of organization to be approached and the kind of data to be gathered. The formulation of the research question is crucial, because, on the one hand, the researcher may risk to become overwhelmed by the complexity of the data with questions that are too broad and general in nature, and, on the other hand, with questions that are too focused, too specific, the issue of bias reappears. In such a dilemma,a carefully compromising solution appears appropriate and, in fact, is proposed by Eisenhardt (1989). The research questions need to serve as "guiding lights" without overly restricting the necessary degrees of freedom of the research process. In Mintzberg's (1979, p. 585) words:

> No matter how small our sample or what our interest, we have always tried to go into organizations with a well-defined focus—to collect specific kinds of data systematically.

A contextually rich description of the biotechnology as well as the pharmaceutical industry as the outer context of this study, of the firms operating in them, and of their M&A activity is needed if a deeper understanding is to be gained. Thus, detailed descriptions or "stories" are indispensable for eventually creating rich theoretical insights, even if this means that researchers have to collect seemingly circumstantial technical information on the industries or companies they are observing in a time-consuming effort. Piore (1979) points out that each piece of information collected in the case study process can be considered as a certain piece in the pattern of these cases.

Due to the fact that this study does ask not only "what'"questions, but also "why" and "how" questions, it can be considered analytic in nature. The appropriate research methodology for a study that attempts to extend theory by description and analysis, that describes in detail "what" an M&A activity of the pharmaceutical companies in the biotechnology sector looks like, that analyzes "why" the observed integration patterns occur, and that analyzes "how" the described behavior unfolds regarding both the forms and the sequences it takes on, is the comparative multiple case study research methodology (Eisenhardt, 1989; Eisenhardt & Graebner, 2007).

The choice for this research strategy is also supported by the work of Yin (2009), who distinguishes five research strategies: experiments, surveys, archival analyses, history, and case studies. From his point of view there are three basic conditions that determine the selection of an appropriate strategy for a study: (1) the types of research questions, (2) the extent of control an investigator has over actual behavioral events, and (3) the degree of focus on contemporary as opposed to historical events. This study asks "how" and "why" questions, which are more explanatory in nature, and thus—according to Yin (2009)—favor the use of case studies as the appropriate research strategy. Moreover, he points out that the case study's unique strength is its ability to deal with a full variety of evidence—documents, artifacts, interviews, and observations.

As in all exploratory studies of this kind, the case chapter is not only the longest chapter—it must also be considered as being the "heart and soul" of the research. The goal is to develop a rich, complicated understanding of the integration of the biotechnology firms in the structure of the industry incumbents through the description and analyses of the different integration histories. Why the case study approach is chosen can best be expressed in the words of Stake (1995, p. xi):

> We study a case study when it itself is of very special interest. We look for the detail of interaction with its contexts. Case study is the study of the particularity and complexity of a single case, coming to understand its activity within important circumstances.

The study is directed at the post-acquisition integration process of small biotechnology companies in the structure of industry incumbents and the subsequent collaboration between them. The aim is to generate testable propositions and to extend theory in this field. Thus, the selection of an appropriate research methodology—such as the multiple case study approach—is necessary. It is widely accepted that qualitative data are most appropriate for generating an initial understanding of the rationale or theory of a process. After that, the results can be tested by quantitative support (Eisenhardt, 1989). But, with a research focus that seeks to grasp the "how" and "why" of processes, a story that narrates the sequence of events is needed (Van de Ven & Huber, 1990).

Select cases

Another crucial issue is to choose the right number of cases—the different case study approaches are summarized in figure 18.1. According to Eisenhardt (1991, p. 622) it is important to notice that "the appropriate number of cases depends upon how much is known and how much new information is likely to be learned from incremental cases." Comparing this with her former statement (Eisenhardt, 1989, p. 545), this must somehow be seen in relative terms:

> A number of 4 to 10 usually works well. With fewer than 4 cases, it is often difficult to generate theory with much complexity, and its empirical grounding is likely to be unconvincing.

Considering both statements, one may even draw the conclusion that any number of case studies is right as long as new insights are gained. This study investigates the M&A and organizational integration activities of four pharmaceutical firms as well as their subsequent collaboration with the acquired company. The study is intentionally focused on this small number of firms in order to allow a detailed analysis and contextually rich description of the complex processes. Moreover, this study is limited to five cases (one pharmaceutical company has acquired and integrated two different biotechnology firms) because of the given time and particularly the funding restraints. Having to choose between more cases and richer context this study tries to put its emphasis on a more contextualist research, which, according to Pettigrew (1990), is more capable of capturing the embeddedness and temporal interconnections of corporate change processes. In this study, context refers to outer context, on the one hand, especially the development of the pharmaceutical and biotechnology industry, and to inner context, on the other hand, for example, the organizational structure of a company.

Due to the limited number (five) of cases that are included in this study, the selection of the firms is one of the most critical elements of the case study research process. As far as large-sample quantitative research is concerned random sampling is used to overcome the problem of bias. Following the advice of Pettigrew (1990) and Eisenhardt (1989), the investigator should choose cases such as extreme situations or polar types in which the process of interest is

	Single case (Harvard Business School tradition)	**Eisenhardt's open multi-case study approach**	**Yin's theory based multi-case study approach**
Aim	Detecting contingency	Theory building	Theory enhancing
Number of variables	Many	Several	Limited set
Level of detail	Deep open analysis, mainly qualitative data	Detailed open analysis, qualitative and quantitative data	Specific, focused analysis, qualitative and quantitative data
Number of cases	1	Approximately 4–10	Not specified
Theoretical foundation	Ex ante not existing	Ex ante mostly not existing	Ex ante already analyzed
Generalization	Not feasible	Feasible	Feasible
Researchers	e.g., Dyer&Wilkens(1991), Harvard Business School case tradition	e.g., Eisenhardt (1989, 1991), Pettigrew (1990)	e.g. , Lee (1999), Yin (2009)

Figure 18.1 Different case study approaches.

observable because the goal of a case study research is to replicate or extend the existing theory.

This study selects two widely known industries: the pharmaceutical industry, a well-developed industry, on the one hand, and the biotechnology industry, an emergent industry with lots of interconnections with the first one, on the other hand. Thus, we have large diversified firms as well as small start-up companies, which clearly represent the polar types recommended by Eisenhardt (1989). As a starting point this study has a look at the M&A activities within and between these industries. This procedure results in a 2 × 2 matrix (see figure 18.2) determined by biotechnology/pharmaceutical companies as potential buyers on one axis and by biotechnology/pharmaceutical companies as potential targets on the other axis.

Now, the question arises, which quadrant is of analytical interest. In order to determine this, the buyer-axis as well as the target-axis is each added by a second dimension. The buyers are differentiated according to their financial strength expressing their capacity of being able to finance an acquisition. It is not very surprising that pharmaceutical companies are ranked among those with great financial strength, whereas the biotechnology companies are rather "poor" financial performers. On the target side, the additional dimension is the innovative capability concerning both research as well as organizational capabilities. Here, the pharmaceutical companies are considered as having rather low innovative capability, whereas the biotechnology companies are

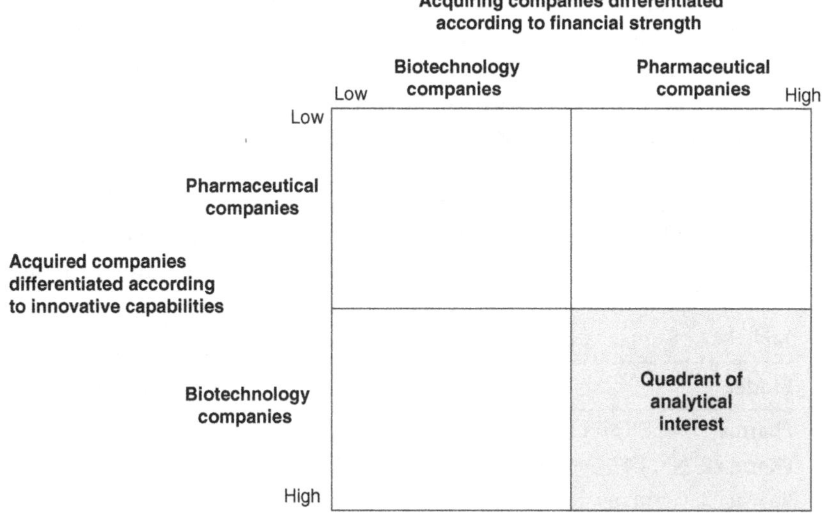

Figure 18.2 Classification matrix for M&A activities in the pharmaceutical and biotechnology industry.

some kind of "stars" in the field of innovation. Thus, the quadrant of analytical interest is the one where pharmaceutical companies being rich in cash acquire biotechnology companies having lots of innovative capabilities that pharmaceutical companies do not have, but would like to possess. This again reveals the polar types recommended by Eisenhardt (1989) and Pettigrew (1990). To generate a pool of potential sites for filling this quadrant a process of scanning documents had to be employed. Once a sufficiently large number of firms had been identified within this quadrant, a more detailed analysis of the kind of M&A and integration activities is undertaken. Companies promising new, interesting insights are approached with a request for cooperation for the research study.

The sampling of the case studies is crucial for later analysis, as the choice of the sample tends to influence the results of the study (Miles & Huberman, 1994). When analyzing a rather small sample of cases—as already depicted in the section before—"extreme" research sites, also called "polar types," are to be chosen (Pettigrew, 1990, 1992).

In order to select the cases, all M&A activities between pharmaceutical and biotech companies during the 1990s were identified. Following Powell, Koput, and Smith-Doerr (1996), the analytical focus was put on firms engaged in human therapeutics and diagnostics. As European pharmaceutical companies have been especially active in acquiring biotech firms and in view of the practical fact that there was access to informants in European pharmaceutical companies, these companies have mainly been chosen as acquirers.

Based on these reflections, the table 18.1 provides an overview of major M&A deals between big pharmaceutical/health-care focused companies, mainly with European origin, and US-based biotechnology companies, which are to be analyzed in the context of this study. The focus on US biotechnology companies as targets can be explained by the fact that the US biotechnology industry is more advanced compared to the European biotechnology industry. This reveals quite well why European pharmaceutical companies have made their acquisitions in the United States and not within Europe. Among a lot of other companies that had been contacted, these four companies agreed to participate in the study. Apart from that, the facts that target and bidder are of the same

Table 18.1 Sample of major M&A deals

Bidder	Target	Value US $ billion)
Pharma 1, NJ, US and UK	Biotech 1CA, US	0.650
Pharma 2, NY, US/ Germany	Biotech 2MA, US	1.100
Pharma 3, Germany	Biotech 3MA, US	Undisclosed
Pharma 4, Switzerland	Biotech 4CA, US	0.625
Pharma 4, Switzerland	Biotech 5MD, US	0.283

origin and have the same differences in size enhance the comparability of the cases. Furthermore, this sample includes successful as well as failed deals. This corresponds to the "polar types" recommended by Pettigrew (1990, 1992). Moreover, these "polar types" are represented by the fact that the acquired biotechnology companies are of US origin, whereas the acquiring pharmaceutical companies come from Europe. Because of this, the analytical focus of this study is not put on potential problems that might arise due to the fact that the acquiring companies are of European origin, whereas the acquired biotechnology companies are of US origin. These potential cultural problems and differences are quite similar for all acquiring companies.

Case analysis

Given the qualitative nature of most of the data sought, triangulation was one of the most important means of increasing construct validity and substantiating findings and subsequent hypotheses (Denzin, 1978). The archival documents used are presented at the beginning of each case write-up and are included in the case-study databank. The most common documents used were: SEC filings (forms 10-K and 10-Q), annual reports according to German law, "red herring" prospectuses pursuant to Part Ia of the 1933 act registration statements, articles from the business and trade press, internal documents such as presentation slides, catalogs, executive speeches, and company press releases available through the websites of the case study companies, their subsidiaries, partners, and competitors. Moreover, analysts' reports of different investment banks were used. The advantages of the documented sources include their tendency to be more comprehensive and less subjective to memory-based bias. The amount of relevant documents differed by firm. All collected documents are included in the case database.

While the preliminary interviews and conversations were unstructured, the interviews with the company representatives employed a semi-structured design in order to allow for an appropriate degree of comparability and, at the same time, to allow for ample opportunity for an unobstructed flow of narrations. Such a questionnaire is included in the case study database.

Interviews were conducted "face-to-face" (with one exception via telephone) in German or English and usually lasted 1.5 to 2.5 hours, the longest exceeding 3 hours. The interviews were taped and fully transcribed. Citations in German were translated into English. This procedure of full transcription is imperative for reasons of internal validity and reliability. Bortz and Döring (1995, p. 230) state: "If an interview also contains open questions and narrative parts, an audio recording is unavoidable." In addition to the added rigor and internal validity, one of the main benefits of taping and transcribing interviews is that the interviewer can concentrate on what is being said, rather than being continuously distracted by note-taking. All transcripts are included as part of the case study database. Similar to the well-established Harvard Business School case research approach, all interviewees were granted anonymity, in that nothing they said was attributed to them personally until and unless they approved of the transcript (Leonard-Barton, 1990). Interviewees received copies of the case description with requests for approval. If they objected to certain parts of the case descriptions they were asked to mark the parts which were then omitted from the final version. In addition, interviewees were asked to make additions or clarifications, which were then integrated into the final case descriptions. In order to increase the overall quality of the study, the draft case reports were reviewed by the participants and informants in the case. Furthermore, from a methodological viewpoint, these corrections enhance the accuracy of the study, hence increasing the construct validity of the study (Yin, 2009).

Often, case studies confront the investigator with a choice regarding the anonymity of the case. Should the case study and its informants be accurately identified, or should the names and the entire case be disguised? The most desirable option is to disclose the identities of both the case and the individuals. By this, the reader is able to recall any other previous information he or she may have already learned about the same case in reading and interpreting the case report. Nevertheless, there are some occasions when anonymity is necessary. The most common rationale is that, when the case study has been on a controversial topic or involves big failures linked with the loss of money, anonymity serves as a measure to protect the real case and its participants. On such occasions when anonymity may appear justifiable—as it is in the cases studied—a compromise should be first sought (Yin, 2009). In such a situation, the investigator should determine whether the anonymity of the individuals alone might be sufficient, thereby leaving the case itself to be identified accurately.

While the objective of the data collection phase is to create an accurate portrayal of the "what" question concerning the post-acquisition integration processes of the different deals, the objective of the data analysis is to enable the generation of hypotheses concerning the "how" and "why" questions. However, as recommended by Pettigrew (1990), the data collection and data analysis phases were overlapped chronologically in order to allow for follow-up data collection. The entire process of data collection and analysis lasted for 1.5 years.

Within-case analysis

The analysis phase consists of two parts: within-case analysis and cross-case analysis. The first part of the data analysis is the transcribing of the fully taped interviews. To increase quality, interview transcripts are reviewed by the interviewees and amended, if necessary. Based on cyclic reading and rereading, each interview is structured and coded in order to facilitate within-case as well as subsequent cross-case analysis (Strauss & Corbin, 1990). Building on the detailed case descriptions, the within-case analyses aim at identifying patterns in the integration process of each firm. In order to avoid being overwhelmed by the large amounts of information, the within-case analyses are focused around the same specified categories that serve as essential elements of organizational integration activities. The goal is to develop a rich understanding of the organizational integration process of these enterprises through the descriptions and analyses of five firm-level integration histories. This is done by gaining insights into the motives, forms, and processes of organizational integration activities of four big pharmaceutical firms that are active in the biotechnology industry by selecting a firm-level perspective. In a first step, the development of the pharmaceutical and biotechnology industry is presented in order to provide the appropriate setting for the different case studies. The analysis and description of the industry development and the M&A activities in these industries not only serve as a useful background for the rich understanding of the cases, but also make clear why the cases are worthwhile analyzing. In line with grounded theory research (Glaser & Strauß, 1967; Miles & Huberman, 1994) the analysis resulted in the identification of acquisition motives, organizational integration, biotech know-how and knowledge transfer, and cultural integration as main categories that formed the basis for the within- and cross-case analysis.

Each case starts with a short corporate profile of the companies involved and is subsequently divided into two major parts. The first major part is the case description, which contains a detailed depiction or story about the integration process and collaboration between the considered firms. The second major part is the subsequent within-case analysis section, which—in contrast to the almost pure descriptive section of the first part—is much more analytical in nature and tries to analyze the given data, which can be considered as being one of the most crucial steps in building theory from case studies. The necessary prerequisite for the within-case analysis is the detailed case study description as is done at the beginning of each case study section. This is crucial for the generation of insights, because it allows the researcher to cope early in the analysis process with the enormous volume of data. The overall idea is to become familiar with each case as a separate, stand-alone entity (Eisenhardt, 1989) and to allow unique patterns of each case to emerge and to be explained before the cross-case analysis is performed. A separation of case description and within-case analysis is necessary, because of the huge amount of data and information involved. Besides this overwhelming amount of data a combined descriptive and analytical section would reduce the border between the pure description of the facts and the respective analysis. Thus, the reader would no longer be able to distinguish between what has been described based on the interviews as well as documents, on the one hand, and what has been the analytical contribution and conclusions of the author, on the other hand.

The framework selected for the within-case analysis is based on the semi-structured questionnaire used for the interviews. The within case-analysis utilized a matrix technique for comparative analysis across interviews within one case (Miles & Huberman, 1994). The resulting matrices allow visual identification of patterns in the post-acquisition integration process of each firm. The topics chosen for the questionnaire have been developed by making a first review of the post-merger/post-acquisition and M&A literature and studies as well as preliminary discussions with industry experts and has also been continuously updated based on useful remarks that came up during the different interviews. To start with, there is the question about the motives and, by this, the strategic rationale behind the acquisition and the subsequent integration and collaboration. After that, there is the analysis of the integration process, which can be subdivided in two major perspectives. On the one hand, it is necessary to analyze the integration topics of organizational/structural integration, knowledge/competence integration and transfer, cultural integration, as well as people integration. The key subject in this context is the aspect of organizational integration, because all the other issues are in some way centered on this. On the other hand, there is a clear need to analyze the organization of the integration process itself, which only allows, supports, and enables the different integration issues to be realized.

Cross-case analysis and shaping of tentative hypotheses

The crucial part of multiple firm case studies is the cross-case analysis. Eisenhardt (1989, p. 541) points out that: "Across-case searching tactics enhance the probability that the investigators will capture the novel findings which may exist in the data." Furthermore, the cross-case analysis builds on the results of the within-case analyses by focusing on the same categories. After having analyzed each respective case on its own using case description and within-case analysis, this section of the case study research turns to the comparative analysis of the five case studies of organizational integration and collaboration after the M&A deal. The analytical focus will be on the detection of commonalities or differences concerning (1) acquisition motives, (2) realization of the organizational integration according to the different integration topics of organizational/structural integration, knowledge/competence integration and transfer, cultural integration as well as personnel integration, and (3) the organization of the post-acquisition integration process itself.

The organizational integration patterns that gradually emerged from within and cross-cases analyses are iteratively (re-)confronted with the cases in order to assess their fit with the observations. If necessary, some of the emerging patterns are either dropped or refined and adjusted until their fit with the data appeared close enough to base some tentative hypotheses on them. This process of field work and data analysis reaches closure when additional iterations do not result in a better accord between the tentative hypotheses and the cases, that is, when theoretical saturation is achieved and marginal improvements become minimal. Indeed, the entire case study research part is devoted to shaping a set of tentative hypotheses. These tentative hypotheses constitute the basis for an extensive unfolding of the literature as the next step, leading to a creation of a new post-acquisition integration framework—the ultimate aim of the described M&A study.

However, before starting to shape these tentative hypotheses (leading to testable propositions) one may ask the question whether the case studies discussed can serve as the basis for generalizing the findings. Certainly not, since the problem remains that the sample consisted of only five cases. However, the point is that generalization should not be the goal for a case-based study, because sample size is almost too small for claiming that the findings can be generalized. It is an advantage of case-based studies that they are able to generate rich narrations (stories) and analyses in order to develop grounded hypotheses (testable propositions) and theory extension. Still, the issue of external validity is not irrelevant for case study research. Thus, an increase in sample size and a replication of findings across a higher number of units of analyses makes such findings more robust. Because resource restraints prohibit the execution of large sample case studies, Leonard-Barton (1990) recommends the use of "replicated multiple sites" in order to overcome the problem of external validity. By this, the findings of a case study approach based on one or more in-depth cases can be corroborated by the use of supporting evidence from additional "mini-cases."

Enfolding literature

The final step in the research process for this post-acquisition integration study begins concurrently with the cross-case analyses and can be best described as "enfolding the literature'. An essential feature of hypothesis formation and theory extension from testable propositions lies in the comparison of the emerging hypotheses with both conflicting and similar findings in the extant literature (Eisenhardt, 1989).

After having described and analyzed the different cases it is now time to refine the findings of the case study chapter. As already pointed out in the discussion of the methodological foundations of this chapter, case descriptions and analyses should ideally be "theory-free," allowing the researcher to capture the richness of the cases without any kind of bias. Only after tentative hypotheses have been drawn from the cases should theory or, in other words, the existing literature, be enfolded (Eisenhardt, 1989). It is an essential component of case-based hypothesis formation and theory extension that the tentative hypotheses are juxtaposed with conflicting and similar theoretical findings. Hence, it is the overall goal of this part that the tentative hypotheses can be challenged, corroborated, and, eventually, refined in such a way that together they serve as an extension to theory as testable propositions or even result in the formulation of a new theory.

The literature to be enfolded by confrontation with the case study results consists of a broad body of theoretical writings in the fields of M&A, and post-merger/post-acquisition integration. All these streams of scholarly work are well-established fields. The first step is to confront the extant studies of M&A motives and reasons with the case findings. The next part turns to a discussion of how post-merger and post-acquisition integration literature might contribute to the understanding of the observations during the case analysis process. The discussion of these fields will have to be restricted to the most prominent theoretical approaches due to the large size of these different disciplines. Having shown that the extant theory is unable to explain large parts of the observations made, the final step is devoted to the construction of a new approach with the help of other concepts such as the value chain concept or the concept of core competencies.

This procedure of "postponed" literature review leads to the formulation of testable propositions, to the extension of theory and thus to a theoretical contribution of its own. In the terminology used by case study methodologists, the last step has been engaged in the enfolding of conflicting and supportive literature up to the point where further discussions of extant literature do not produce additional support for the explanation of the case-based tentative hypotheses. Thus, theoretical saturation in the sense of Eisenhardt (1989) and Yin (2009) has been reached. What remains to be done is to utilize what has been learned for constructing a new integration approach, capable of explaining the post-acquisition integration of small biotechnology or, more generally speaking, high-technology firms into the structure of pharmaceutical firms or, in other words, large corporations. In order to do that the theoretical arguments need to be taken back to the level of the case findings, that is, to the set of the tentative hypotheses, in an iterative loop. This step serves to ascertain the validity of this study and to detect any potential remaining weakness of the new approach. This part tries to answer that question and, by this, is concerned with increasing internal validity. This is done by using iterative loops, in which the results of a study's analytical generalizations are repeatedly checked against the observed phenomena. For this study this means that the "framework for post-acquisition integration of small high-technology companies" into the structure of large corporations is checked against the set of tentative hypotheses. This confrontation allows identifying and, thus, supporting what the novel approach does explain and, equally important, where the model remains unclear or where it does not hold the explanatory power. The

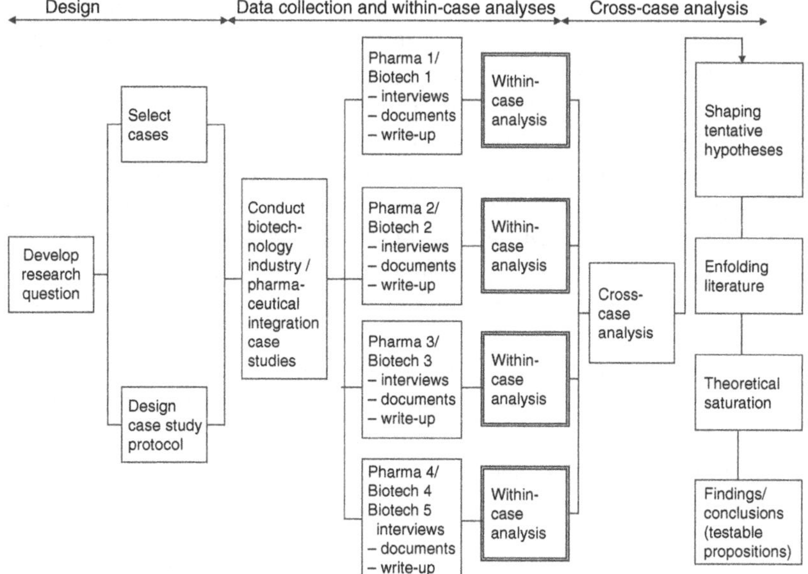

Figure 18.3 Research outline of the study about post-acquisition integration activities.

overall aim of this section is to check the new "framework for post-acquisition integration of small high-technology companies" into the structure of large corporations against the case-based tentative hypotheses in order to increase the model's internal validity. The confrontation performed in this final iterative loop led to a substantial corroboration of the new framework as it offers profound explanations of almost all tentative hypotheses that are formulated as testable propositions.

These different research steps are again summarized in figure 18.3.

Conclusions

As mentioned above, figure 18.3 describes in detail the different steps that need to be followed when carrying out a multiple-case study research project. Following Mason (1996), we can summarize that qualitative research

- should be systematically and rigorously conducted,
- should be strategically conducted, yet flexible and contextual,
- should involve self-scrutiny by the researcher, or active reflexity,
- should produce social explanations to intellectual puzzles,
- should produce social explanations that are generalizable in some way, or that have a wider resonance, and
- should be conducted as an ethical practice.

Eisenhardt and Graebner (2007, p. 30) conclude that "theory building from case studies is an increasingly popular and relevant research strategy that forms the basis of disproportionately large numbers of influential studies."

Of course, the generalizability of the developed testable propositions is limited by relatively small size and scope of the sample. As a consequence, the results of case-based research can very often serve as a guideline for larger-scale empirical efforts. These might be necessary to statistically assess the presented relationships and to help define the contexts in which these relationships vary. Moreover, given the complexity of M&As, the results of such a study may vary across different industries with different attributes and characteristics and across different types of M&As. Thus, future research may focus on how the developed post-acquisition integration approach is put in place in different industries and different types of acquisition pursuing different motives. In order to do that, such a study may combine qualitative and quantitative methods drawing on qualitative field work, survey data, and secondary data in order to gain a richer understanding of complex phenomena.

References

Bortz, J., & Döring, N. (1995). *Forschungsmethoden und Evaluation* [Research methods and evaluation] (2nd ed.). Berlin: Springer.

Bower, J. L. (2004). When we study M&A, what are we learning? In A. Pablo & M. Javidan (Eds.), *Mergers and acquisitions. Creating integrative knowledge* (pp. 235–244). Oxford: Blackwell Publishing.

Denzin, N. K. (1978). *The research act.* New York: McGraw-Hill.

Denzin, N. K. & Lincoln, Y. S. (eds.) (1994). *Handbook of qualitative research,* Thousands Oaks, CA: Sage.

Dyer, G. W. & Wilkens, A. L. (1991): Better stories, not better constructs, to generate better theories: A rejoinder to Eisenhardt. *Academy of Management Review, 16*(4), 613–619.

Eisenhardt, K. (1991). Better stories and better constructs: The case for rigor and comparative logic. *Academy of Management Review, 16*(3), 620–627.

Eisenhardt, K. M. (1989). Building theory from case study research. *Academy of Management Review, 14*(4), 488–511.

Eisenhardt, K., & Bourgeois III, L. J. (1988). Politics of strategic decision making in high velocity environments. Toward a midrange theory. *Academy of Management Journal, 31*(4), 737–770.

Eisenhardt, K., & Graebner, M. E. (2007). Theory building from cases: Opportunities and challenges. *Academy of Management Journal, 50*(1), 25–32.

Gioia, D. A. & Pitre, E. (1990). Multiparadigm perspectives on theory building. *Academy of Management Review, 15*(4), 584–602.

Glaser, B. G., & Holton, J. (2005). Basic social processes. *The Grounded Theory Review. International Journal of Grounded Theory Review, 4*(3), 1–27.

Glaser, B., & Strauss, A. (1967). *The discovery of grounded theory: Strategies of qualitative research.* London: Wiedenfeld and Nicholson.

Hammersley, M. (1992). Some reflections on ethnography and validity. *Qualitative Studies in Education, 5*(3), 198–204.

Hunt, J. W. (1990). Changing pattern of acquisition behaviour in takeovers and the consequences for acquisition processes. *Strategic Management Journal, 11*(2), 69–77.

Javidan, M., Pablo, A., Singh, H., Hitt, M., & Jemison, D. (2004). Where we've been and where we're going. In A. Pablo & M. Javidan (Eds.), *Mergers and acquisitions: Creating integrative knowledge* (pp. 245–261). Oxford: Blackwell Publishing.

Jick, T. D. (1979). Mixing qualitative and quantitative methods: Triangulation in Action. In J. Van Maanen (Ed.), *Qualitative methodology* (pp. 135–148). Beverly Hills, CA: Sage.

Kretschmann, J. (1990). *Die Diffusion des kritischen Rationalismus in der Betriebswirtschaftslehre* [The diffusion of critical rationalism in business administration]. Stuttgart: Schäffer-Poeschel.

Larsson, R. (1990). *Coordination of action in mergers and acquisitions: Interpretive and systems approaches towards synergy.* Doctoral dissertation, University of Lund, Sweden.

Lee, T. W. (1999). *Using qualitative methods in organizational research.* Thousand Oaks, CA: Sage Publications.

Leonard-Barton, D. (1990). A dual methodology for case studies: Synergistic use of a longitudinal single site with replicated multiple sites. *Organization Science, 1*(3), 248–266.

Mason, J. (1996). *Qualitative researching.* Thousand Oaks, CA: Sage.

Miles, M. B., & Huberman A. M. (1994). *Qualitative data analysis. An expanded sourcebook.* (2nd ed.). Beverly Hills, CA: Sage.

Miller, D., & Friesen, P. (1983). The longitudinal analysis of organizations. A methodological perspective. *Management Science, 28*(9), 1013–1034.

Mintzberg, H. (1979). An emerging strategy of "direct" research. In J. Van Maanen (Ed.), *Qualitative methodology* (pp. 105–116). Beverly Hills, CA: Sage.

Napier, N. K. (1989). Mergers and acquisitions: Human resource issues and outcomes; A review and suggested typology. *Journal of Management Studies, 26*(1), 271–289.

Pettigrew, A. (1990). Longitudinal field research on change: Theory and practice. *Organization Science, 1*(3), 267–292.

Pettigrew, A. (1992). The character and significance of strategy process research. *Strategic Management Journal, 13*(1), 5–16.

Piore, M. J. (1979). Qualitative research techniques in Economics. In J. Van Maanen (Ed.), *Qualitative methodology* (pp. 71–85). Beverly Hills, CA: Sage.

Powell, W., Koput, K., & Smith-Doerr, L. (1996). Interorganizational collaboration and the locus of innovation: Networks of learning in biotechnology. *Administrative Science Quarterly, 41*(1), 116–145.

Popper, K. R. (1976). *Die Logik der Forschung* [The logic of scientific discovery]. Tübingen: Mohr.

Silverman, D. (2010). *Doing qualitative research* (3rd ed.). London: Sage.

Snow, C. C., & Thomas, J. B. (1994). Field research methods in strategic management: Contributions to theory building and testing. *Journal of Management Studies, 31*(4), 457–480.

Stake, R. E. (1995). *The art of case study research.* Thousand Oaks, CA: Sage Publications.

Strauss, A. L. (1987). *Qualitative analysis for social scientists.* Cambridge: Cambridge University Press.

Strauss, A., & Corbin, J. (1990). *Basics of qualitative research: Grounded theory procedures and techniques.* Newbury Park, CA: Sage Publications.

Van de Ven, A., & Huber, G. (1990). Longitudinal field research methods for studying processes of organizational change. *Organization Science, 1*(3), 213–219.

Yin, R. K. (2009). *Case study research: Design and methods* (4th ed.). London: Sage.

19

Iterative-Pragmatic Case Study Method and Comparisons with Other Case Study Method Ideologies

Harm-Jan Steenhuis

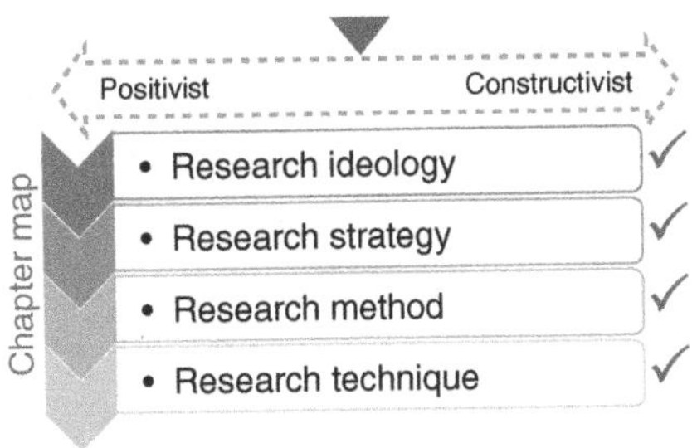

Chapter overview

In this chapter Steenhuis succinctly explains the differences in research ideology and strategy (deductive vs. inductive-driven) case study research methods. The post-positivist ideology form of case study method uses a deductive a priori theory-driven and strategy for the unit of analysis that has been popularized by thought leader Robert Yin (1994). The pragmatic ideology form of case study method (further right on the continuum, close to constructivist) uses an inductive-oriented, theory-grounded unit of analysis research strategy. This latter interpretivist form of case study follows the work of thought leaders Glaser and Strauss (2007) as well as Locke (1996). Steenhuis clearly has a pragmativist ideology, which he labels as leaning toward the Straussian and Glaserian school of grounded theory. After reviewing and contrasting the post-positivist versus interpretative-pragmatic forms of case study approaches in the literature, he introduces a new research methodology (with relevant techniques) to implement his approach: interactive-pragmatic case study method.

Introduction

The case study method is a formal research method that has been applied in many different fields, including in business and management studies. Despite the frequent use of case studies, there is limited agreement on what a case study actually is or how it should be conducted and there is a wide variety in how case study research results are presented in scientific journals. For example Darke, Shanks, and Broadbent (1998), Fox-Wolfgramm (1997), Leonard-Barton (1990), McClintock, Brannon, and Maynard-Moody (1979), McCutcheon and Meredith (1993), and Meredith (1998) discuss different types of case studies with different characteristics, different techniques, and different levels of deepness or richness. Part of the reason for this lack of general agreement is that case studies have been used across all research ideologies as was noted in chapter 1 of this handbook.

The purpose of this chapter is to increase the awareness for different case study research methods and to describe a specific case study method, that is, the progressive-iterative case study. To place the progressive-iterative case study in perspective, several other case study methods are also described. In order to explain the different case study methods, I will start with a background section that contains a more general discussion on research approaches.

Theoretical background

In order to understand the differences that occur in case study research, it is necessary to first gain a broader understanding of the underlying research ideology. Understanding research ideology is important for academics because it affects what is scientifically accepted and, for example, where and what can be published. For instance, Soteriou, Hadjinicola, and Patsia (1999, p. 235) raise the issue that the publication rate of European researchers in highly ranked US journals are low. It has also been noted that in the field of business studies there are considerable differences between acceptable research ideology in the United States and Europe. Bengtsson, Elg, and Lind (1997, p. 473) note that "while European studies run the risk of being regarded as weird and 'unscientific' by North Americans, many Europeans may feel that North American research leans too much towards rigorous but rather uninteresting statistical exercises." Bengtsson, Elg, and Lind (1997) note that the transatlantic gap is not only geographical but also a gap between methodological approaches.

In the next two subsections I will discuss the differences between natural and social sciences and following this, from a different perspective, the objectives of research. Some studies make a distinction between different types of case studies based on the purpose or objective of the study (Cunningham, 1997) but in my view, the research objective is related to research ideology. The discussion on ideology is connected to the discussion of the research design framework that was presented in chapter 1 of this handbook (Strang, 2014). In addition to the identification of social science, another distinction that is made is that for design sciences (van Aken, 2004; Holmström, Ketokivi, and Hameri, 2009). I will cover this perspective when discussing research objectives.

Natural sciences versus social sciences

The aim of scientific research is to search for truth. This leads to two questions. First, what is truth? Second, what search method must we use so that we can be sure to find it? It is necessary to discuss these questions because of the different opinions that exist on the acceptability of scientific studies in social science areas such as management. What is argued by one author to be a scientific study with valid results is disregarded as such by another and vice versa. In the natural sciences such as physics there is agreement on what constitutes a scientific study. The approach followed is essentially termed "the scientific method" and follows the positivist/post-positivist hypothetico-deductive approach, that is, a priori hypotheses are formed that are subsequently tested.

According to Meredith, Raturi, Amoako-Gyampah, and Kaplan (1989, p. 304) the testing oriented research is often claimed to be true research. For example in the field of operations management, despite calls for more interdisciplinary, applied case studies, interviewing methodologies, and a greater emphasis on benefit to the production and operations management practitioner, the dominant research strategies in mainstream production and operations management academic journals continue to include quantitative models and laboratory simulations (Ansari, Lockwood, and Modaress, 1992, p. 57). In the quantitative testing approach the researcher is considered objective and simply observes or measures the outcomes of experiments. The assumption is that the researcher does not influence the experiment in any way other than through controlled manipulation.

In contrast with the natural sciences, there is hardly any agreement on what can be termed scientific work in social science topics such as business management. A problem with social science is that it involves humans, and due to this the relationship between observer and observed is different from that in the natural sciences. In particular, the researcher can affect the outcomes, even if there is no direct interaction and it only involves observing. A well-known example of this is the Hawthorne effect. This complication of human interaction has led to a broader spectrum of approaches in social sciences, compared to the natural sciences, and disagreements on what is acceptable.

As an aside, I want to point out that in the natural sciences, the observer can also influence the experiment. Take for example a very simple electric system with a battery and a light. The experimenter can measure the voltage in this system but by placing a measurement instrument in the system, the experimenter has changed the system. For this particular example, there are theories available that allow for adjustments to correct for this observer influence. These methods for adjustment are general and agreed upon in physics. This means that there is consensus on how to measure in these instances. However, with the development of quantum mechanics, it has become clear that even in physics there are more serious situations where the observer, through measuring, influences the end state of a quantum system. An example of this is the issue of wave function collapse. There is currently no consensus on how to deal with this measurement problem.

The naturalist viewpoint on social science is that the same rules apply as in the natural sciences, that is, the (post)-positivist principles should be applied. The assumption is that there is a reality (ontological stance) that the observer and observed are separate (epistemological stance) and that hypothesis can be verified with experiments (methodological stance) (Guba & Lincoln, 1994, p. 109). Following Popper, some modifications were made. The result can be characterized as post-positivism: there is a reality but it cannot be understood perfectly (ontology), the observer and observed are separate (epistemology), and the hypothesis can be falsified (methodology) (Guba & Lincoln, 1994, p. 109), see also chapter 1 of this handbook.

The anti-naturalist viewpoint on social sciences is that the naturalist approach is not appropriate because the object of research is different. Whereas the natural sciences (*Naturwissenschaft*) deal with observable issues, the social sciences deal also with inner meanings (*Geisteswissenschaft*). To get access to the inner meaning, a researcher has to use the *Verstehende* method (Hamilton, 1994). In line with chapter 1 of this handbook, the reasoning of anti-naturalists can be seen as pragmatism or constructivism, which is more inductively oriented. Figure 19.1 provides a schematic overview that extends the ideology layer of the research design typology developed earlier by Strang in figure 2.1 of chapter 2 and in figure 3.1 of chapter 3.

In different academic disciplines, similar ideas may occur although different terms might be used. For example, Meredith, Raturi, Amoako-Gyampah, and Kaplan (1989), with an orientation on operations management, provide a similar type of distinction as the naturalist versus socialist science. They provide a framework for research ideologies based on two dimensions: the rational/existential dimension (relating to the epistemological structure) and the natural/artificial dimension (relating to the source and kind of information used). Rational research conforms to the traditional deductive approach whereas existential research conforms to an inductive approach (Meredith, Raturi,

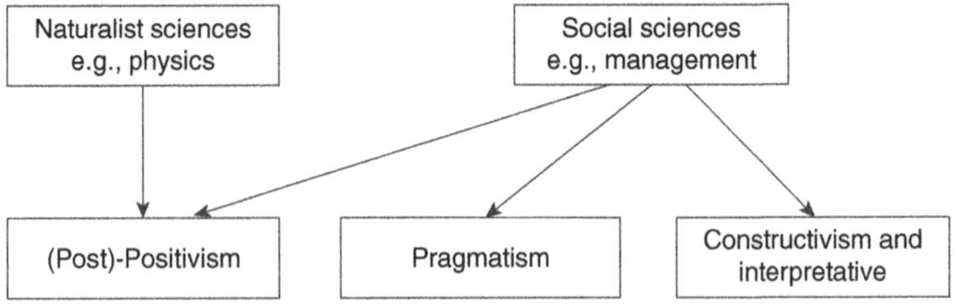

Figure 19.1 Research ideology for natural and social sciences, based on Strang (2014).

Amoako-Gyampah & Kaplan, 1989, p. 305). Natural research is empiricism, that is, deriving explanation from concrete, objective data, whereas artificial research is subjectivism, that is, deriving explanation from interpretation and artificial reconstruction of reality. According to Meredith, Raturi, Amoako-Gyampah, and Kaplan (1989), compared to survey research, case study research is more existentially oriented because it includes the context of the phenomenon as part of the object of study. It doesn't assume that the phenomenon under study can be isolated from the context or that the facts or observations are independent of the laws and theories used to explain them as is the case for survey research. Case study research is more naturally oriented compared to survey research because it deals more with direct observations of object reality compared to people's perceptions of object reality.

Research objective

After a broad discussion of research ideologies in the previous section, as well as a more elaborate discussion in chapter 1 of this handbook, I am going to provide another way of looking at research. Discussion in the earlier section was based on the ideology or beliefs of the researcher and this determines their stance in what is, or should be, acceptable research. In a way, this can be viewed as a top-down approach, that is, the researcher first establishes what he or she believes in and then conducts the research accordingly. In this section, discussion follows another orientation, primarily that of what the objective of the research is. In a way, this can be viewed as more of a bottom-up approach, that is, the researcher first determines what the objective of the research is and then determines what research approach fits with that objective.

In a broad sense, objectives of research can be theory oriented or practice oriented (Gummesson, 2000). Verschuren and Doorewaard (2005) provide a schematic overview of the different research objectives (see figure 19.2).

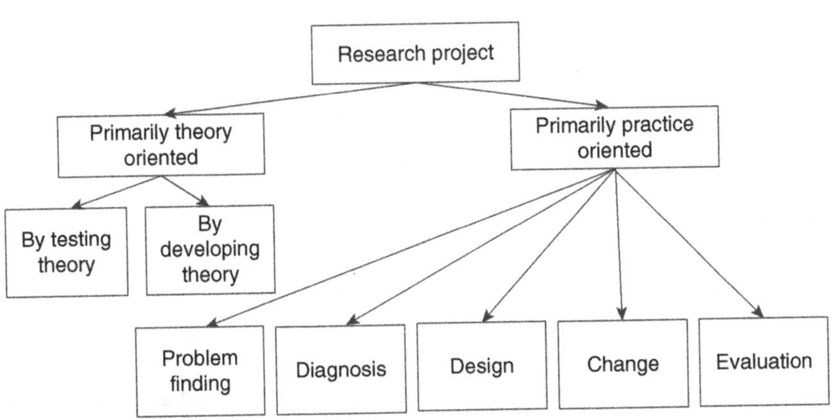

Figure 19.2 Objectives for doing research, based on Verschuren and Doorewaard (2005).

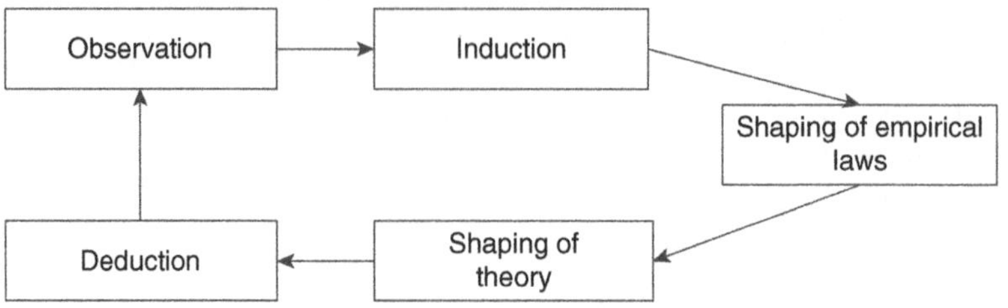

Figure 19.3 The empirical cycle, based on de Groot (1969).

Research that is primarily oriented toward making a contribution to theory can be developing oriented or it can be testing oriented. The difference relates to the starting point on the empirical cycle (see figure 19.3).

Developing a theory

The inductive approach to developing new theory is followed in new areas of research where limited preliminary theory is available. In this approach, initial observations are used to induce empirical laws. In a next step these can be tested.

One of the problems with case study research, and a developing research design, is the limited ability to generalize the results. Especially since theory is developed from the in-depth analyses of practical situations, it means that only a limited number of practical situations (or cases) can be analyzed. The more situations one analyzes, the more "solid" the theory will probably be. However, the limited number of situations that can be analyzed is a problem with this type of research. Since in-depth analyses are required, analyzing only one situation can be very time consuming depending upon the complexity and scope of the situation. The study of multiple situations might therefore not always be possible due to time constraints on the research.

Testing a theory

The deductive, (post)-positivist approach to testing a theory starts with the development of theory in the form of hypotheses, which are then tested based on observations. The theory can come from two different sources. First, the theory that results from the developing research can be tested in other situations so that it leads to more general conclusions. Second, based on literature a "new" theory can be constructed for testing. This requires a large amount of available theory or a high theoretical sensitivity of the researcher.

The testing can be done in different ways. It is, for example, possible to test a theory that depends on multiple context factors. A case study can, in that instance, be used for testing purposes (Yin, 1994). One could also for example test the relationship between two units by means of a survey.

Dubin makes a distinction between attribute units and variable units in a theory (Dubin, 1978). An attribute is a property of a thing distinguished by the quality of being present, for example, the presence of electricity, or not. A variable is a property of a thing that may be present in some degree (Dubin, 1978), for example, the temperature in a factory. Dubin (1978) explains that the kind of units employed in a theory make a difference to the extensiveness of the tests that can be made. Consider a theory that employs only two attribute units. This leads to the matrix in table 19.1.

In a classical experiment, having two groups (one experimental group and one control group) where one group receives a treatment and the other group does not, the comparison is between cell 1 and cell 4. Attribute A can be computers and attribute B can be operators in Company X (a specific company). A comparison could now be made between the productivity of the operators in Company X who have a computer (cell 1) and operators in Company Y (another company) who do not have a computer (cell 4).

If a theory is only focused on variable units, it is focused on ONE of these cells. In this case the situation is as given in figure 19.4, whereby in each cell the internal distribution of the population is shown. Variable A is for example the age of the operator and variable B the number of hours that he or she uses a computer. It must be noted in this case that if for example in cell 1, the variable A and/or B has the value zero, it is not an instance of cell 2, cell 3, or cell 4. Because of the different consequences of the tests, it is important to determine exactly what is being tested. Note that Dubin (1978) distinguished, besides the difference of attribute and variable, five types of units and three general types of relationships.

Research design often involves statistical tests. The relevance of these tests usually increases when the tests involve a large sample size. In the particular

Table 19.1 A two-by-two matrix for attribute units

	Attribute A	**All not-As**
Attribute B	CELL 1	CELL 2
All not-Bs	CELL 3	CELL 4

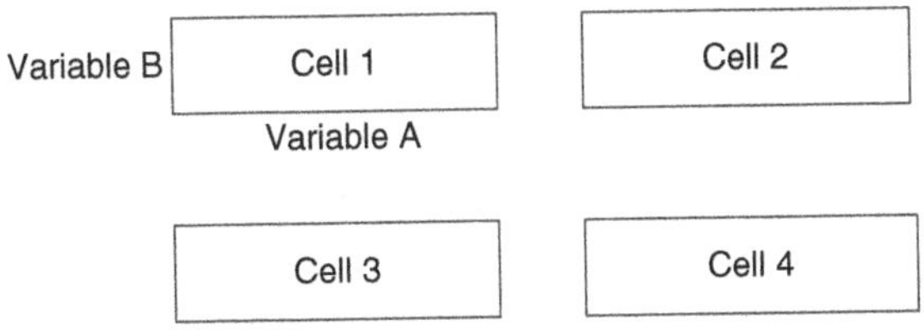

Variable B	Cell 1 Variable A	Cell 2
	Cell 3	Cell 4

Figure 19.4 Variable and attribute units.

example of a falsification of a theory, a test could involve a sample size of one but generally the sample size needs to be quite large to show a statistically significant result. These tests are most often aimed at a limited number of relationships. The knowledge generated is thus, although very rigid, narrower than that which is developed under the developing theory approach.

Applying a design

A third option is knowledge that is created through the application of a design. This is in particular relevant for academic disciplines such as management because businesses are often interested in solutions for their problems. Thus, the application of a design (thought-out solution path) has practical value. In many instances this type of research involves action research, that is, the researcher is involved in the design and implementation of the solution, which can also be case studies, for example (Huxham & Vangen, 2003). The steps for this type of research start with the initial identification of a problem. After this, diagnoses are made. Then a design is created and subsequently implemented. After this there is an evaluation step. A well-constructed design is based on the available theory, and the application of this design teaches us lessons about that design. It is however also possible to use a less-developed design (meaning that there is limited theoretical support for that design). In this case lessons can also be learned from the implementation of the design. This is based on a trial-and-error sequence and adaptations can be developed from the lessons learned. A design can thus gain increasing value through the use of iterative steps. The regulative cycle illustrates this approach (see figure 19.5).

Van Aken (1994) goes a step further and states that knowledge in a "design science" is created by the interaction between professionals (in the practical field) and scientists (van Aken, 1994). The professional solves practical problems and the scientist analyzes how the professional solves the problem. The professional aims to solve one particular problem and the scientist aims to develop scientific knowledge that can be used to solve a class of similar problems (van Aken, 1994). Therefore, there is a difference in solving one problem for a particular practical situation versus the more scientific approach of

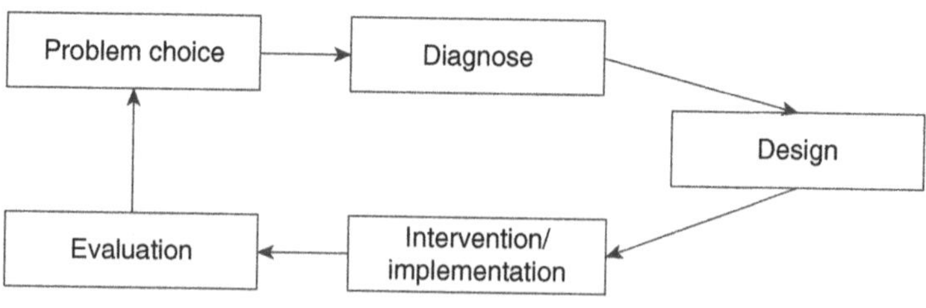

Figure 19.5 Regulative cycle, based on Van Strien (1986).

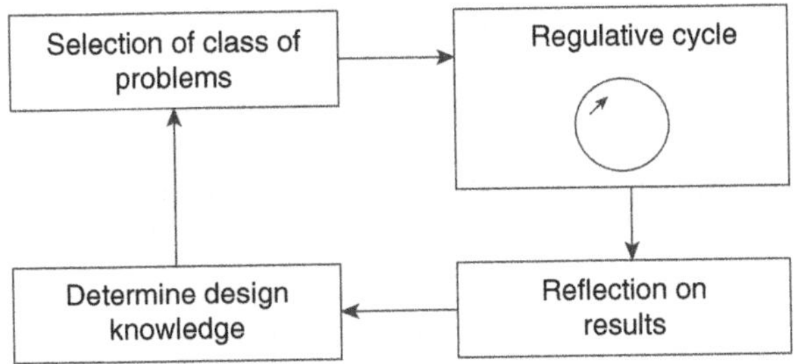

Figure 19.6 Reflective cycle, based on Van Aken (1994).

gaining knowledge about a class of problems. Van Aken's reflective cycle illustrates this (see figure 19.6).

The reflective cycle uses a series of cases to develop design knowledge. The reflection on the results is important. This is not just a conclusion on whether the goal (the change in the practical situation) is achieved. It is the linking of the results (the success of the implementation) back to the design. This generates knowledge about the particular design that was used. This makes it useful, for example, for its application in other situations.

Practical implications

When looking at conducting research, two approaches can be found in the literature. In one approach, which can be characterized as top-down, the researcher identifies the ideology and conducts research in accordance with the ideology. The discussion of ideologies showed that in contrast with the natural sciences, there are several different ideologies for social sciences, that is, (post)-positivism, pragmatism and constructivism/interpretative. What is considered acceptable research in one ideology is often not acceptable for another ideology. It is therefore important for the researcher to state which ideology is being followed.

A second approach, which can be considered bottom-up, is to identify the purpose of the research and based on this apply an ideology that aligns with that purpose. Three main approaches can be identified here: to develop new theory, to test a proposed theory, and to apply a design. These three approaches are related to research ideology because they relate to what is considered acceptable. For example, in the (post)-positivist research ideology, a qualitative approach may be considered exploratory or preliminary research rather than "true research". Similarly, the application of a design through action research for one specific problem in a company may not be considered "true research" from the (post)-positivist research ideology because the generalizability would be questioned as well as the objectivity of the researcher.

Case study research approaches

In this section, I will compare three case study methods. Although there are other case study methods too, I focus on these three because they are frequently used and cited in management research. The first approach that I will describe is Yin's (1994) case study method. Yin (1994) is probably the most cited source for the case study method in management studies. Based on its characteristics and to distinguish it from the other two methods, I will call his method the (post)-positivist case study method. The second and third case study methods that I will discuss are based on different ideologies that is, pragmatic and interpretative. One main difference between these two methods is how they use the literature at the start of the research and the degree to which the data analysis and subsequent data collection is planned. The second method that I will describe is the original grounded theory method, which was developed by Glaser and Strauss (1967) and further developed by Glaser (1992). This approach is different from the grounded theory approach supported by Strauss and Corbin (1990). Based on its characteristics and to distinguish this case study method from the other two, I will call it the emergent interpretative case study method. The third method that I will describe is the method proposed by Eisenhardt (1989). Based on its characteristics and to distinguish this method from the grounded theory method I will call this method the planned pragmatic case study method (see figure 19.7).

My discussion of these three case study methods will follow figures 1.1 and 1.2 from this handbook (Strang, 2014), that is, the research ideology, and

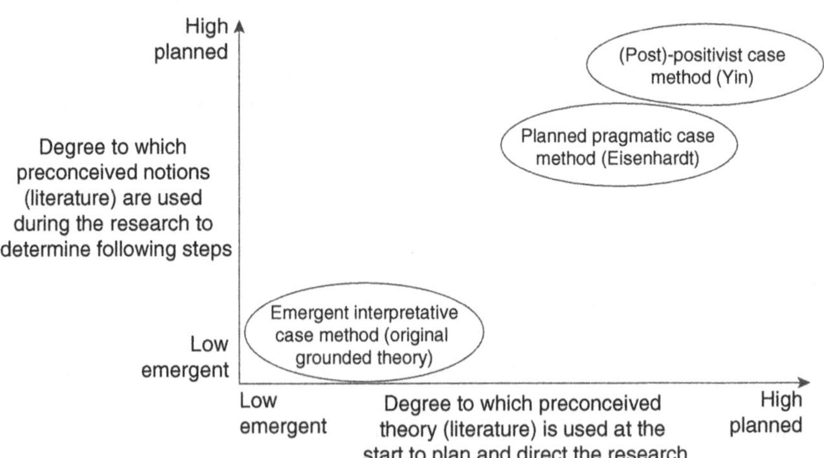

Figure 19.7 Comparative position of three case study methods.

techniques such as the criteria applied, the role of literature and how cases are selected, and how data are analyzed will be discussed for each method.

(Post)-positivist case study method (yin)

Yin (1994) states that case studies can be used for exploratory, descriptive, or explanatory purposes (p. 4). Nevertheless, researchers should realize the specific ideology and approach that Yin mainly supports.

Research ideology

A clear indication of the research ideology supported by Yin (1994) is his following statement: "Case studies can be viewed as 'quasi-experimental,'" that is, situations in which the experimenter cannot manipulate behavior but in which the logic of experimental design may still be applied (p. 9). This indicates that Yin views case studies similar to experiments, that is, he follows the approach of the natural sciences. This relates to a deductive or testing oriented method. In other words, Yin's case study method is based on the positivist/post-positivist research ideology.

Another sign that demonstrates Yin's (1994) positivist/post-positivist ideology comes from his concern with objectivity. Yin's discussion is permeated by this concern, which is characteristic of the positivist and post-positivist ideology. In the positivist/post-positivist ideology the researcher is considered independent of the research object and this independence is very important for objectivity. Yin's discussion on research design shows a similar stance on independence. Yin (p. 20) proposes several measures to "demonstrate" the researcher's "independence" from the research data and how his more rigorous and methodologically sound case studies lead to "objective" conclusions. In contrast Yin does not highlight "interpretative" issues that are considered by others such as Guba and Lincoln (1994) as a characteristic of an interpretative case study.

Lastly, Yin's case study method is oriented on investigating each case in a similar way. This is shown through the necessity for a detailed case-study protocol.

Research techniques: Criteria of validity and reliability

Yin (1994) discussed four criteria to judge the quality of the case study research. These criteria are: construct validity, internal validity, external validity, and reliability. These criteria are commonly used in the positivist and post-positivist research ideology. From the positivist/post-positivist research ideology, there are at least two challenges with these criteria. First there is the issue of external validity, that is, the degree to which results can be generalized. Yin has an extensive discussion on this challenge and discusses the replication logic as a tactic to improve this validity. The other challenge is reliability, which, in the positivist/post-positivist ideology, is more an issue of the potential for other researchers to replicate the study. Replication is pointless for case studies (Janesick, 1994) and so Yin (1994, p. 36) argues that the results should be reliable, that is, with minimal errors and bias. This would mean following established procedures and documenting the data in such as way that an auditor could repeat the procedures and arrive at the same conclusions.

Research techniques: Role of literature and selection of cases

In accordance with the (post)-positivist ideology, Yin's (1994) case study method contains a detailed plan on how to conduct the case study. This is similar to the detailed preparations for setting up and, in particular, controlling an experiment. Yin's method includes a heavy emphasis on the existing substantive literature in the preparation phase and he states, "This role of theory development, prior to the conduct of any data collection, is one point of difference between case studies and related methods such as ethnography...and 'grounded theory'...For case studies, theory development as part of the design phase is essential...the complete research design embodies a 'theory' of what is being studied" (p. 27). In other words, the substantive literature in Yin's case study method is extremely important and is equivalent to a set of hypotheses that are subsequently tested in quasi-experiments, that is, cases. To make sure that these experiments are comparable, Yin's approach contains an extensive amount of planning. For example, he provides guidelines for a case study research design (an action plan for getting from the initial set of questions to be answered to some set of conclusions [answers] about these questions) (p. 20). The design has five components: the study's questions, its propositions (if any), its unit(s) of analysis, the logic linking the data to the propositions, and the criteria for interpreting the findings.

The selection of multiple cases is mainly driven by the available substantive theory and the resulting theoretical framework and follows the experimentation logic, that is, replication logic. Each case must be carefully selected so that it either (a) predicts similar results (a literal replication) or (b) produces contrasting results but for predictable reasons (a theoretical replication) (p. 46). This means that cases can be selected at the beginning of the research study, that is, in the design phase, based upon the developed theoretical framework and the expected results. Yin explains that replication logic is different from the sampling logic used in surveys. In sampling logic, a number of respondents are assumed to "represent" a larger pool of respondents. This allows statistical generalization. Case studies, using replication logic, allow analytic generalization, in which a previously developed theory is used as a template to compare the empirical results of the case study. "If two or more cases are shown to support the same theory, replication may be claimed. The empirical results may be considered yet more potent if two or more cases support the same theory but do not support an equally plausible rival theory (p. 31). The number of cases (replications) depends on the certainty that a researcher wants to have about the multiple case results. Yin states, "For example, you may want to settle for two or three literal replications when the rival theories are grossly different and the issue at hand does not demand an excessive degree of certainty. However, if your rivals have subtle differences, or if you want a high degree of certainty, you may press for five, six, or more replications" (p. 50). Note that the replication logic implies validation and that each case study should cover the same exact research questions and approach, which is in accordance with the (post)-positivist ideology.

Research techniques: Analysis of data

The goal of Yin's (1994) case study method is that, similar to experiments, developed theory must be tested through replications (p. 36) in the empirical case situations. Yin's case research design is based on making sure that replications are achieved, that is, the same methods are applied in each case so that findings can be compared. Yin states, "An important step in all of these replication procedures is the development of a rich, theoretical framework. The framework needs to state the conditions under which a particular phenomenon is likely to be found (a literal replication) as well as the conditions when it is not likely to be found (a theoretical replication). The theoretical framework later becomes the vehicle for generalizing to new cases, again similar to the role played in cross-experiment designs" (p. 46).

Practice implication

Yin's (1994) case study method follows the (post)-positivist ideology. In line with this research ideology he conducts a literature review of the substantive theories at the beginning of the research project. This leads to a theoretical framework, which is essentially a set of hypotheses. The theoretical framework is tested and validated based on a set of cases that serve as quasi-experiments. These experiments are selected based on replication logic, that is, similar results through literal replication or different (but expected) results through theoretical replication. The research design follows a detailed plan, provided in the case study protocol, so that each study is approached in the same way and with the same questions. To help the development of the case study protocol, one or more pilot case can be used. The pilot case is not part of the actual cases (p. 76). The criteria to judge the quality of the case study follows the (post)-positivist ideology, that is, validity and reliability, with an emphasis on minimizing bias so that, for example, somebody else should be able to read the data and come to the same conclusion.

The emergent interpretive case study method (grounded theory)

Compared to the method by Yin(1994), at the other end of the spectrum is the emergent interpretative case study, that is, the original grounded theory approach developed by Glaser and Strauss (1967) and further explained by Glaser (1978, 1992, 2001, 1998, 2003, 2005). Since the original work, the two authors have followed different approaches leading to a Straussian and Glaserian school of grounded theory (Locke, 1996). In my discussion below I follow the Glaserian grounded theory school.

Research ideology

In contrast with the deductive/testing approach proposed by Yin (1994), Glaser and Strauss emphasize an inductive, theory developing approach (Glaser and Strauss, 1967, p. 5) that fits the interpretative research ideology. This means that the reality is interpreted by the researcher. This is accomplished through reporting the participants' behaviors or responses and perhaps using coding (Strang, 2014). This ideology is evident in the grounded theory approach through the use of memos. As Glaser (1978, p. 84) states: "In the grounded theory approach, since the major objective is to generate substantive theory, we use the descriptive information gained through careful, systematic data collection as the grounding for the theoretical analysis and some illustration. Thus the successive raising of the description through conceptual abstraction to categories and then theory is explicitly developed in memos."

Research techniques: criteria of credibility, plausibility, and trustworthiness

Glaser and Strauss (2007, 224) state that there is often criticism of qualitative research such as grounded theory. Furthermore, this criticism stems from the guidelines based on the (post)-positivist ideology quantitative approach dealing with issues such as hypothesis construction, sampling, reliability, validity, and verification but that these criteria are not applicable. Instead, they argue that the main issue for grounded theory is credibility (2007, p. 223). Conveying credibility to the reader of a grounded theory research study is not an easy task and the main difficulty is in making readers understand the transition from data to theory. Researcher can use techniques such as quoting telling phrases dropped by informants and giving background descriptions of places. As a side note, Glaser (1992, p. 116) explains why the approach by Strauss and Corbin (1990) is not grounded theory because criteria for their approach are similar to the (post)-positivist research criteria related to verification.

Research techniques: role of literature and selection of cases

In contrast to the (post)-positivist ideology and many other types of research, in the original grounded theory approach the argument is made that a literature review at the start of a research project should *not* be in the substantive area (Glaser, 1998, p. 67). In grounded theory, reading the theoretical literature should be avoided until after the discovered framework is stabilized (Glaser,

1978, p. 51) so that the researcher can enter the research setting with as few predetermined ideas as possible (p. 3). The (initial) role of literature in grounded theory is to create theoretical sensitivity. Theoretical sensitivity is "an ability to generate concepts from data and to relate them according to the normal modes of theory" (Glaser, 1992, p. 27). Three types of literature are distinguished: (1) nonprofessional and popular, (2) professional literature related to the substantive area under research, and (3) professional literature that is unrelated to the substantive area (Glaser, 1992, p. 31). At the beginning of a grounded theory study, it is vital to be reading, but in unrelated fields (Glaser, 1992, p. 35). In grounded theory there is no initial preconceived framework of concepts and hypotheses (Glaser, 1978, p. 44). Only after the concepts have emerged from the empirical data should the researcher read the literature in the substantive area under research (Glaser, 1992, p. 33). Essentially what this means is that in this case study method, the researcher limits the preliminary notions by not reading the substantive literature. This enables keeping a more open mind to different interpretations that arise from the field study, that is, the theory emerges instead of becoming forced out due to preconceived notions. This is another area where Glaser (1992, p. 4) argues that the approach as proposed by Strauss and Corbin (1990) deviates from the original idea because it includes preconceived substantive questions that lead to a forced conceptual description.

Data collection and subsequent case selection in the grounded theory approach is based on theoretical sampling. This is the process of data collection for generating theory whereby the analyst jointly collects, codes, and analyzes his data and decides what data to collect next and where to find them, in order to develop his theory as it emerges (Glaser and Strauss, 1967, p. 45). This is another area where Glaser (1992) argues that the approach by Strauss and Corbin (1990) is not grounded theory because their categorization process, imposed on a labeling process by asking preconceived questions, produces a fully preconceived conceptual description rather than grounded theory (Glaser, 1992, p. 43). The grounded theory method is also in sharp contrast with the replication logic used by Yin, which requires comparable cases. In the grounded theory approach cases are not used to compare across the same domain, but rather, they are used to create additional insight, that is, to enrich theoretical concepts. In other words, information collected in different cases is not similar but rather involves new areas for exploration. According to Glaser and Strauss (1967, p. 48), "By contrast, data collected according to a preplanned routine are more likely to force the analyst into irrelevant directions and harmful pitfalls. He may discover unanticipated contingencies in his respondents, in the library and in the field, but is unable to adjust his collection procedures or even redesign his whole project. In accordance with conventional practice the researcher is admonished to stick to his prescribed research design, no matter how poor the data. If he varies his task to meet these unanticipated contingencies, readers may judge that his facts have been contaminated by his personal violation of the preconceived impersonal rules" (p. 49). The latter is indeed reflected in Yin's (1994) work where he states, "A final reminder is that a case study design is not something completed only at the outset of the study. The design can be altered and revised after the initial stages of a study, but only under stringent circumstances...In the event of a multiple case design, the selection of cases may have to be modified because of new information about the cases. In other words, after some early data collection and analysis, an investigator has every right to conclude that the initial design was faulty and to modify the design...At the same time, an investigator must be careful, not to shift, unknowingly the theoretical concerns or objectives. If these rather than the cases themselves, are changed, the investigator can correctly be accused of exercising a bias in conducting the research and interpreting the findings. The point is that the flexibility of case study designs is in selecting cases differently from those initially identified (with appropriate documentation of this shift) but not in changing the purpose or objectives of the study to suit the case(s) that were found" (Yin, 1994, p. 52). In other words, although Yin allows for some changes, this is only under stringent circumstances and the cases still need to be comparable.

The number of cases in a grounded theory study cannot be stated at the outset of the research. The criterion for judging when to stop sampling pertinent to a category is the category's theoretical saturation. Saturation means that no additional data are being found whereby the researcher can develop properties of the category. As he sees similar instances over and over again, the researcher becomes empirically confident that a category is saturated (Glaser and Strauss, 1967, p. 61).

Research techniques: Analysis of data

As explained above, the analysis of data occurs simultaneously with the collection of data, that is, the direction that the research takes emerges as the research progresses. The method for generating a theory that is proposed by Glaser and Strauss (1967, p. 21) is comparative analysis. They contrast this method with analytic induction, which is similar to the notion of analytic generalization as mentioned by Yin (1994).

Glaser and Strauss (1967, p. 104) explain analytic induction as: "concerned with generating and proving an integrated limited, precise, universally applicable theory of causes accounting for a specific behavior. It tests a limited number of hypotheses with all available data, consisting of numbers of clearly defined and carefully selected cases of the phenomena. The theory is generated by the reformulation of hypotheses and redefinition of the phenomena forced by constantly confronting the theory with negative cases, cases which do not confirm the current formulation."

In contrast to analytic induction, Glaser and Strauss propose the use of the constant comparative method. They state: "The constant comparative method is concerned with generating and plausibly suggesting (but not provisionally testing) many categories, properties, and hypotheses about general problems. Some of these properties may be causes, as in analytic induction, but unlike analytic induction others are conditions, consequences, dimensions, types, processes etc.... Further, no attempt is made by the constant comparative method to ascertain either the universality or the proof of suggested causes or other properties" (1967, p. 104).

Practice implication

Overall, the original grounded theory approach (Glaser, 1978, 1992; Glaser and Strauss, 1967) provides a very different method of doing case study research than the method provided by Yin (1994). The main differences are that grounded theory method is inductive and not deductive; grounded theory is not based on validation (through the replication logic) of an existing theoretical framework but on generating a theoretical framework by constantly comparing and interpreting empirical data and by simultaneously developing theoretical concepts/constructs that emerge from these data. This means that most hypotheses and concepts not only come from the data, but are systematically worked out in relation to the data during the course of the research (Glaser and Strauss, 1967, p. 6). In other words, this kind of case study is such that each case is not investigated in a similar way but rather, the learning from one case is used for the investigation of the next case. In the original grounded theory approach the researcher has to refrain from the substantive theory until the end; this is so that preconceived notions do not enter the process. The grounded theory approach proposed by Strauss and Corbin (1990) tends toward increased prescription instead of emergence (Locke, 2001, p. 64). The end result of grounded theory is an ever-developing, unproven theory that can be formulated as a set of propositions or hypotheses where the importance of the theory is the generated insights through new concepts. It is not a theory that has been validated through empirical testing in a quasi-experimental format that leads to a degree of certainty about the validity of this particular theory or theoretical framework.

In short, the grounded theory approach is based upon a continuous cycling between empirical data collection and data analysis to develop concepts through a coding process that allows the generation of theory. Multiple cases allow a deeper understanding of some concepts but can also lead to new insights or refinement of earlier insights. This is quite different from the replication/ validation technique followed by Yin (1994) where theory is "developed" at the beginning of the research and subsequently tested in case settings. This validation process can lead to new insights as well, but it is primarily driven by preexisting theoretical notions, concepts, or codes, which is something that the grounded theory method is trying to avoid.

The planned pragmatic case study method (Eisenhardt)

Eisenhardt (1989) provides a case study method that lies somewhere between Yin's (1994) method and the original grounded theory method (Glaser & Strauss, 1967). Some of her thinking aligns with the grounded theory method, that is, it is inductive. But there are several elements where she follows a more planned approach. For example, she proposes selecting cases early in the research design, that is, before entering the field. This is not in accordance with the grounded theory approach where case selection is based upon earlier findings, that is, after entering the field. An overview of the Eisenhardt (1989) approach is provided in table 19.2.

Research ideology

Eisenhardt (1989) has an inductive approach similar to the grounded theory approach (Glaser & Strauss, 1967). That means, her method is inductively oriented where theory emerges at the end, not at the beginning of the study (Eisenhardt, 1989). She states: "The case study is a research strategy which focuses on understanding the dynamics present within single settings" (p. 534) and thus appears to fit the interpretative research ideology. However, Eisenhardt's (1989) method also has many commonalities with Yin's (1994) approach. For example, table 19.2 demonstrates that she is concerned with issues such as validity and generalizability. Furthermore, Eisenhardt (p. 546) states "the process described here adopts a positivist view of research. That is, the process is directed toward the development of testable hypothesis and theory which are generalizable across setting." In other words, it appears that Eisenhardt (1989) positions herself within the positivist research ideology and she views the case study method as more or less an exploratory part of the positivist hypothesis testing approach, that is, to develop the hypothesis that needs to be tested. Thus, it seems that the case study itself is not viewed by Eisenhardt as the scientific ultimate or even acceptable goal of research, but in order to improve the contribution that this exploratory research can make, she provides certain guidelines. All in all this can be interpreted as falling into the pragmatic research ideology as described in chapter 1 of this handbook (Strang, 2014).

Research techniques: Criteria of validity and generalizability

As can be seen from table 19.2, Eisenhardt (1989), similar to Yin (1994), is concerned with the criteria that are used in the (post)-positivist research ideology such as validity and generalizability. What is also apparent from the table is that she is not concerned with the issue of subjectivity or interpretation.

Table 19.2 Process of building theory from case study research

Step	Activity	Reason
Getting started	Definition of research questions	Focuses efforts
	Possibly a priori constructs	Provides better grounding of construct measures
	Neither theory nor hypotheses	Retains theoretical flexibility
Selecting cases	Specified population	Constrains extraneous variation and sharpens external validity
	Theoretical, not random, sampling	Focuses efforts on theoretically useful cases, i.e., those that replicate or extend theory by filling conceptual categories
Crafting instruments and protocols	Multiple data collection methods	Strengthens grounding of theory by triangulation of evidence
	Qualitative and quantitative data combined	Synergistic view of evidence
	Multiple investigators	Fosters divergent perspectives and strengthens grounding
Entering the field	Overlap data collection and analysis, including field notes	Speeds analyses and reveals helpful adjustments to data collection
	Flexible and opportunistic data collection methods	Allows investigators to take advantage of emergent themes and unique case features
Analyzing data	Within-case analysis	Gains familiarity with data and preliminary theory generation
	Cross-case pattern search using divergent techniques	Forces investigators to look beyond initial impressions and see evidence through multiple lenses
Shaping hypotheses	Iterative tabulation of evidence for each construct	Sharpens construct definition, validity, and measurability
	Replication, not sampling logic, across cases	Confirms, extends, and sharpens theory
	Search evidence for the "why" behind relationships	Builds internal validity
Enfolding literature	Comparison with conflicting literature	Builds internal validity, raises theoretical level, and sharpens construct definitions
	Comparison with similar literature	Sharpens generalizability, improves construct definition, and raises theoretical level
Reaching closure	Theoretical saturation when possible	Ends process when marginal improvement becomes small

Source: Based on Eisenhardt (1989).

Although the researcher has to understand the case (Eisenhardt, 1989, p. 534) this can be accomplished objectively. Another technique that Eisenhardt proposes in this regard is the use of multiple investigators, and "the convergence of observations from multiple investigators enhances confidence in the findings" (Eisenhardt, 1989, p. 538).

Research techniques: role of literature and selection of cases

Eisenhardt's (1989) method is less driven by a fully developed theoretical framework at the beginning of the research than what Yin (1994) proposes. However, she uses the literature to define the research question and area. She states, "The rationale for defining the research question is the same as it is in hypothesis-testing research. Without a research focus, it is easy to become overwhelmed by the volume of data" (Eisenhardt, 1989, p. 536). This illustrates that although a priori constructs are not required, Eisenhardt (1989) supports the use of substantive literature at the beginning of the research. As her second step indicates, theory is also used for selection of cases and this happens, similar to Yin (1989), early in the process, that is, before entering the field, which she identifies as step four.

Similar to Yin (1994) Eisenhardt's method is planned with specific research questions, well-designed instruments such as interview schedules and questionnaires, considering theoretical sampling and controls etc. (Eisenhardt, 1991, p. 620). Case selection is also very much conducted following Yin's (1994) guidelines of replication logic and theoretical sampling (Eisenhardt, 1989, 536). Replication logic is central in her view on building theories (Eisenhardt & Graebner, 2007, p. 25).

Research techniques: analysis of data

In Eisenhard's (1989) approach, data analyses frequently overlap with data collection. She states: "Analyzing data is the heart of building theory from case studies, but it is both the most difficult and the least codified part of the process" (p. 539). For single cases Eisenhardt (p. 540) states: "Within-case analysis typically involves the detailed case study write-ups for each site. These write-ups are often simply pure descriptions. In other words, in line with the positivist research ideology, the task of the researcher seems to be to simply describe what is observed. Eisenhardt (1989) further finds that the overall idea is to become intimately familiar with each case as a stand-alone entity whereas for cross-case analysis the key is to look for patterns. This then leads to the shaping of the hypothesis.

Practice implication

The case study method by Eisenhardt (1989) has some similarities with the grounded theory approach, that is, its inductive approach, but it has much more in common with the (post)-positivist ideology oriented case study method of Yin (1994). Both Yin (1994) and Eisenhardt (1989) have an approach where the literature in the substantive area is reviewed at the start of the study and this literature is used to plan the case study. Follow-up cases are selected by the replication logic, which is similar as that for experiments. This means that cases are selected based on their theoretical contribution. Cases are mainly comparable and similar information should be collected in all cases. Compared to Yin's (1994) more deductive and verification oriented method, Eisenhardt (1989) allows more induction.

Practitioner recommendation

The comparison of the three case study methods has shown that different authors have different approaches toward case studies. The three methods that are supported by each of the authors have differences, which in some instances not only relate to the research ideology but also relate to specific techniques such as the role of literature and how subsequent cases are selected. When a researcher is considering applying a case study method, the differences between these methods should be carefully considered and a clear stance on which specific case study method is followed should be taken as well as explained.

The iterative pragmatic case study method

The previous section has highlighted some of the main differences between the two extremes, that is, Yin's (1994) deductively oriented approach that follows the positivist/post-positivist research ideology and the inductively oriented grounded theory approach that follows the interpretative research ideology. In this section I propose another method that combines some of the strengths of both of these approaches.

One of the strengths of Yin's (1994) approach is that his replication logic provides a "degree of certainty" about the theoretical framework. The disadvantage is that the preconceived theoretical framework may be theoretically limiting compared to the openness to new insights in the grounded theory approach. I therefore propose a mix of the two methods.

Research ideology

My proposed method follows the pragmatic research ideology. The ontological viewpoint taken here is that there is a reality. This reality can only be understood imperfectly. Although a researcher is constructing theories this does not mean that research is not dealing with a "real" reality.

The epistemological viewpoint is that the researcher cannot be completely detached from the observed world. In social sciences such as management, information has to be interpreted. Thus, I support the notion that objectivity is essentially an elusive concept in social sciences such as management studies. Instead, the goal is to make meaning of the case(s), that is, to interpret it as good as possible. The proposed case study method is iterative, which means that theory is inductively developed and lessons from the data collection and analysis are used to determine what to collect next and which direction to take next, that is, it shares emergent characteristics with the grounded theory approach. The outcome of the case study is a theory that should not be considered validated, but rather it contains concepts and possible relationships that create new insight (grounded in empirical data) and that can be tested in subsequent research.

Research technique: criteria of credibility

In accordance with Janesick (1994) I consider credibility of the study the most important criterion because this is an indication of the quality of the interpretation. Note that the credibility of findings can probably not be communicated by providing the data from the study and letting the reader judge for him- or herself as is common in positivist/post-positivist studies. Instead, the credibility of the findings has to be established by the credibility of the research process, that is, the researcher has to demonstrate how findings were interpreted, and how there is a high degree of freedom, for example, by explaining how triangulation was used. In the section on data analysis below, the degree of freedom is explained a little more. In particular for studies that involve interpretation, credibility can be achieved by following research techniques such as the member check, that is, informants are consulted whether the interpretations of the researcher make sense, and triangulation, that is, the use of multiple types of measurements such as observations, interviews, and document analyses to improve accuracy of interpretation. Therefore, presenting a case study that is based on just one or a couple of interviews within an organization is inherently weak. Similarly, if only one type of data source, for example public records, is used, then the credibility of the findings is low.

Research techniques: role of literature and selection of cases

For Yin (1994) it is necessary to conduct an extensive substantive literature review at the start of the research because this literature review allows the development of a theoretical framework, which is then validated and adjusted through empirical case study data. In the grounded theory approach, a substantive literature study is discouraged because it has limited ability to generate new insights and creates preconceived notions that may inhibit the emergence of new theoretical insights. Yet, despite the openness of the grounded theory approach and consequently the potential for new insights, it is possible that the results of this type of research are a duplication of what is already known because the substantive literature is only reviewed at the end of the study. Ultimately, scientific contributions are evaluated based upon the contributions made to the existing body of knowledge, that is, the substantive literature. I therefore propose an intermediate approach. Rather than using the literature to develop a theoretical framework for testing purposes (i.e., literature is carefully analyzed and used for design purposes) and rather than not using any substantive theory at all (with the purpose of staying completely open to any issues that may arise in the field), I propose that some substantive theory is read at the beginning of the research. The purpose of this is to create some awareness of what is known. Therefore, the literature is not analyzed and used to generate a theoretical framework, but it is read so that the author is sensitive to important areas in the substantive field. Thus, if several important areas of similar importance emerge from and during the field study, then this sensitivity can be used to direct the case study data collection in those areas that might lead to the largest impact in terms of theoretical contribution.

The preparation for the case study is therefore much less directed than that proposed by Eisenhardt (1989) and Yin (1994). It does not involve a detailed case study protocol but rather it serves primarily to create awareness of the broad issues in the substantive area and may formulate "sensitizing concepts." Whereas definitive concepts provide prescriptions of what to see, sensitizing concepts are concepts that need to be developed further during the case (Bowen, 2006, see figure 19.8).

In addition, the researcher will, if not yet aware of it, have to become familiar with data analysis techniques, and the researcher will have to formulate a broad research objective and find an appropriate first case.

Although there are some special circumstances where a single case can be used, see Yin (1994) and Stake (1995), one advantage of the proposed method is the iterative aspect which requires multiple cases. The selection of subsequent cases is similar to that in the grounded theory approach. Essentially the selection of a case is similar to the selection of the next data to be collected inside a case, that is, it depends on what is already known, which concepts provide promising new insights, which concepts need further development, how much theoretical saturation has already occurred, and what kind of practical data are

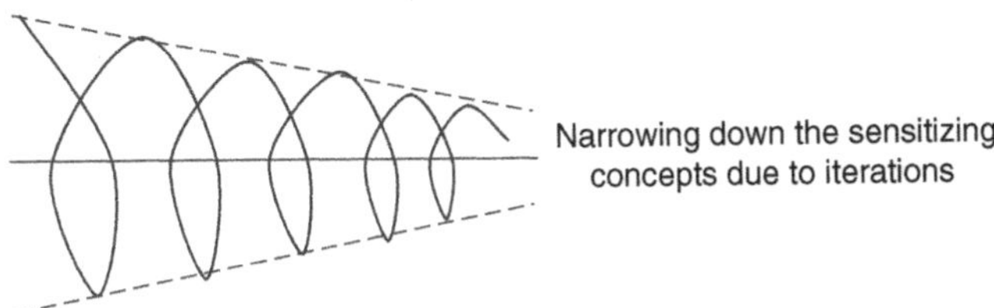

Figure 19.8 Iterative process with regard to sensitizing concepts.

available. This is also known as snowball sampling (Miles & Huberman, 1994). Selection of cases occurs not at the beginning of the research project, but, rather, happens throughout the project whenever there is a need for another case. I also suggest that for the multiple case study, an aspect of replication is used. In other words, subsequent cases serve two purposes: (1) they allow further development of concepts and new insights, and (2) they allow the replication of earlier findings.

Figure 19.9 illustrates how a certain set of variables is included in the first case. The further development of concepts and new insights is one of the strengths of the grounded theory approach and is used here in a similar fashion. Hence, additional cases may lead to previously unidentified concepts and/or further development of previously identified concepts. Note that the credibility of these insights has to be built in every case in a similar way, that is, through triangulation. The emergent nature of new aspects is shown in the second case at the top of the bar for the second case. There might, however, also be some variables that do not occur in the second case. This is shown as the white spot at the bottom of the bar for the second case. This same pattern repeats itself as more cases are added, hence the iterative nature of this case study method.

At the same time, the application of replication logic provides a mechanism to build credibility as well but in a different way, that is, through validating earlier findings in a new setting. This validation is not the primary purpose and does not need to be accomplished by an "exact copy" of the case approach in each case, that is, following a strict protocol. This would mean that each

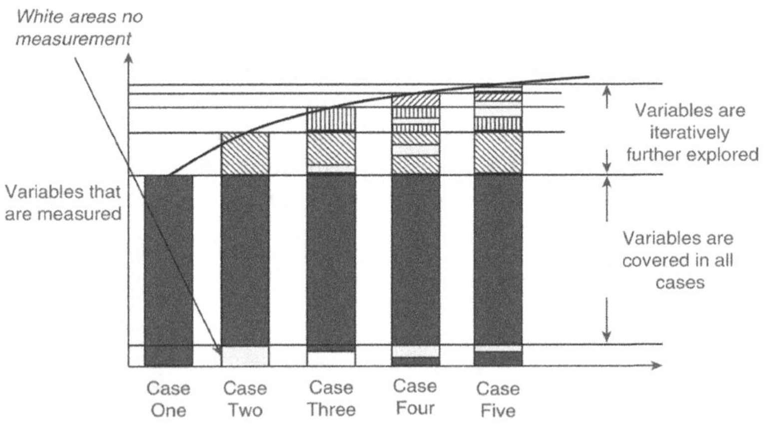

Figure 19.9 Illustration of iterative and replication aspects.

bar in figure 19.9 would be the same. Instead, it can be handled more quickly in subsequent cases by providing limited "tests" to determine whether similar concepts played a role. If there are indications that different factors play a role, then this should lead to the development of new insights, that is, concepts. Therefore, at the case level, constant comparisons of cases are also conducted. The proposed iterative pragmatic case study method thus combines on the one hand the emergent aspect of the grounded theory approach by iteratively adding new variables, while on the other hand it strengthens the validity of the findings that are common across all the cases. Using multiple cases in this manner provides strengthening of previously established concepts in subsequent cases while simultaneously allowing the development of new insights. This is why I term this approach "iterative."

It might even be possible at the end of the multiple case study to go back to earlier cases to specifically check for the missing variables in order to strengthen the overall findings. This is illustrated in figure 19.10.

Figure 19.10 illustrates how compared to figure 19.9 more data were collected at the end of the study to increase the overall credibility by increasing the variables that are measured across all cases. The figure illustrates for each new layer of variables (as they occurred as new cases were initiated) how data for those variables might also be available in the earlier studies, but, as shown through several white blocks in figure 19.10, some data might not be available. The reason why some data might be available but was not collected previously is because in the earlier cases these variables did not occur, or were not prominent. At later stages when more emergent notions have developed the researcher might become sensitive to these issues and then find that they were also present in earlier cases.

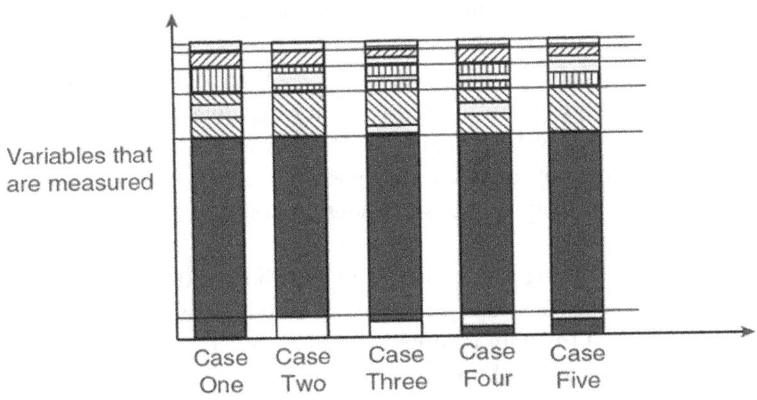

Figure 19.10 Situation at the end of the study where additional information from previous cases is collected.

Research techniques: analysis of data

The grounded theory approach offers an excellent mechanism for generating theory by using the constant comparative method. I propose the use of a similar technique in the iterative pragmatic case study method. An important characteristic is that this method involves a continuous cycle between data collection and data analysis. In every single case, the data that are collected next are determined by the analysis of the previous data, that is, on a day-to-day basis. Note that this is quite different from the traditional positivist/post-positivist ideology as for example is evident in surveys. In surveys all data are collected first, and then analyzed. A similar method is proposed by Yin (1994). I follow the grounded theory approach because it allows the emergence and development of new insights. It is also an important mechanism to "build" credibility in the findings. As mentioned earlier, triangulation techniques, for example, the use of multiple data sources or methods, should be used as well.

In practice, what this means is that the researcher starts with a rough idea about what he/she wants to learn from the empirical world. This learning will come through interpretation of data, which leads to codes. Let's say the researcher goes into the field and has an open interview with an informer. This interview leads to a certain insight, that is, a concept, about a situation that is deemed important by the researcher based on his/her research goal. Glaser and Strauss (1967) stress the importance of field memos in this regard. The researcher then decides to gain more knowledge about this concept, that is, to develop this concept further. This is established through triangulation. For example, the researcher interviews several other people to gain insight into their ideas about this concept. Note that this doesn't mean that direct questions have to be used. Furthermore, the researcher may decide to look at available documentation, which potentially provides additional insight into this concept. The researcher may also apply additional techniques or other sources. Each of these new "bits of information" are analyzed and compared with earlier findings about the concept. This leads to a further development of the concept. Analysis techniques such as for example developing a causal network can be used as well for creating further insight. Miles and Huberman (1994) provide a range of helpful techniques. Combining the insights of the different data sources and methods provides credibility in the interpretation of the researcher.

Another way of viewing this comes from Swanborn (2010). He describes a fundamental problem with case studies in an insightful way. He states: "The number of degrees of freedom is, simply defined, the number of independent equations concerning the unknowns. To summarize, in a case study we seem to have many theories to explain only one research result. In other words, we have more equations than unknowns, or, as it is commonly expressed, 'the number of units is smaller than the number of variables.' As a consequence, the researcher can fit almost any model or theory to the data of the studied case" (p. 98). Swanborn (2010) therefore suggests using techniques that increase the degrees of freedom. For example, he suggests using multiple researchers, using different data sources, etc. From my perspective this means that the interpretation of the data is more credible because techniques such as triangulation, etc. are used because these increase the degrees of freedom.

Whether the researcher continues to focus on a particular concept or not depends upon the interest of the researcher. (Is the concept an important new idea?) It also depends upon whether new things keep coming up in the data or not (theoretical saturation). At the end of the first case, the researcher has a number of concepts that are more or less developed based upon the available data in that case. Each of these concepts has to be relevant to the overall research objective.

Practice implications

In this section I have presented a fourth case study method. This method combines several elements of the previously discussed case study methods. Similar to the grounded theory approach it is inductive and emergent in nature. However, to reduce the risk of reinventing the wheel, I proposed that some substantive literature is reviewed at the start of the research project to create some theoretical sensitivity in the area. I also propose that the replication logic can be partially applied. This means that there will be a set of variables that will be measured across all cases thus enhancing the validity of the findings for those cases. Figure 19.11 shows the position of the iterative pragmatic case

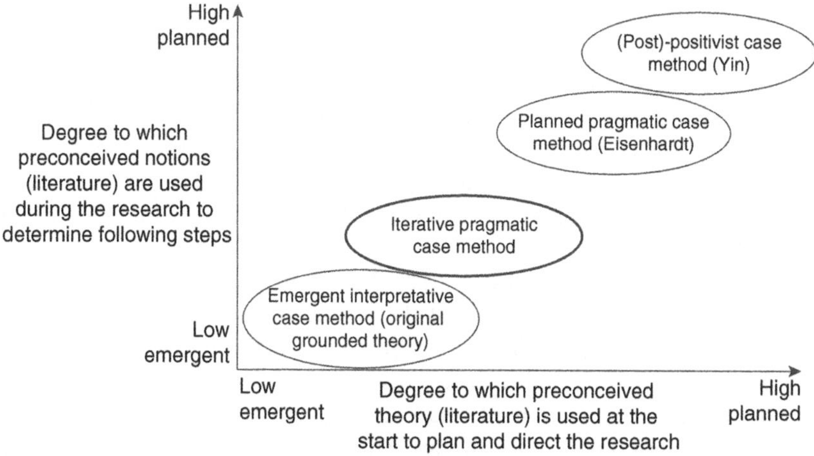

Figure 19.11 Comparative position of the iterative-pragmatic case study method.

study method compared to the already discussed other types of case study methods.

Example of the iterative pragmatic case study approach

To provide a sense of the amount of time it takes, the amount of data collected, the triangulation issue, and how the iterative process works, I will provide a brief description of one of my research projects that followed the iterative pragmatic case study method. The project was a multiple case study that consisted of four cases. This multiple case study was focused on the process of technology transfer, that is, the relocation of production activities from one country to another country. This happens in for example subcontracting or licensing. During each of these case studies I was positioned inside the case company.

The first case study took three months and involved the transfer of an entire aircraft manufacturing line, that is, this was a large and complex case. During these three months, two different data collection methods were used. People were interviewed and company archives were analyzed. The case was historical and although the manufacturing line still existed, no manufacturing was taking place any more. Therefore observations were limited. The interviews were initially open but were often followed by more closed-oriented interviews to confirm or reject concepts. Overall, approximately 34 interviews were held with 10 people. These people held different positions at the time of the transfer. Most were involved in technical aspects but some people concerned with quality aspects were also interviewed. It must be noted that the word "interview" is loosely used here. In some instances these interviews were somewhat structured to explore concepts and lasted more than an hour. In other instances they included short conversations with people to gain additional insight or to get feedback on an idea. Roughly 4500 pages of documentation were compiled on this technology transfer project. These included the initial contract, information on the technology, planning and progress documents, communication documents, and field memos that contained information based on interviews and conversations with respondents. It did not involve technical documents such as drawings and other design information, and it also did not include additional industry information (this was collected but not included in the case data-base).

After the first case study was conducted, several concepts were known that needed further development. One of these concepts was that the technology transfer of an entire aircraft manufacturing line was so complex that it appeared very difficult to manage and control this type of project. For example, it was very hard to keep track of small delays and how they could eventually influence the completion date of an aircraft. Therefore the "size" of the technology was chosen as a primary mechanism for the selection of the second case, that is, a "small" technology was selected. The second case involved the transfer of aircraft cockpit manufacturing. This transfer was based in the same company but provided a different context that allowed further insight into this particular aspect of "size". Because I was already familiar with the company, I was able to complete this case in approximately 1.5 months. Time savings occurred due to familiarity with people and easier identification and access to those people for interviewing purposes as well as easier identification and access to documents sources. Overall, approximately 78 interviews were held with 18 people in a variety of roles. Roughly 1750 pages of field data were compiled, which included the contract, technology information, planning and progress information, written communication, and field memos. Additionally, observation techniques were used because the project was ongoing. This is summarized in table 19.3.

After the second case study sufficient insight was gained on the issue of "size" but another issue came up. This issue was the "quality of the information" that was transferred. This issue was also encountered after the first case, but at that time deemed less important for further development than the issue of "size." Now, since "size" was better understood, a selection was made for a third case to look at the "quality of information" issue. The issue was that in both the first and second case, informants indicated that much of the information that was transferred (both included old technologies) was outdated and this created problems in production. A third case was therefore selected with a relatively new technology to be able to explore this issue further. The third case was again based in the same company but it involved a newly developed small technology, that is, the transfer of aircraft tail production (of a newly designed aircraft). Beingfamiliar with the people and the different aspects of the case, I was able to complete this case in approximately 1.5 months. Overall, approximately 181 interviews were held with 34 people. These included interviews outside the company because toward the end of this case, awareness was raised about the issue with the overall environment (i.e., national issues such as culture and working conditions) and several people from other organizations were interviewed to gain additional insight. Approximately 1500 pages of documentation were compiled similar to the earlier cases. In this instance, observation techniques were also used.

After the third case study, it was felt that the concepts of "size" and "quality of information" were sufficiently developed, but another concept, "environment conditions," was raised. Therefore a fourth case was selected that allowed further development of the environmental conditions. The first three cases involved technology transfer from a developed country to a developing country. Since the application of technology in the developing country was less smooth than in the developed country, the fourth case was chosen involving technology transfer from a developed country to a developed country. The

Table 19.3 Example of sensitizing concepts and case selection

	"Size of technology"	**"Accuracy of information" which is linked to "age of technology"**	**"Environment conditions"**
Case 2	Small	Established technology	Developing country
Case 1	Large	Established technology	Developing country
Case 3	Small	New technology	Developing country
Case 4	Small	Established technology	Developed country

case involved the production of a skin panel, that is, a small technology that was well-established. For the four cases, this means that although each of them added insight into particular aspects, they also had much in common. If the second case is taken as a "base for comparison" it follows that each case is comparable with the second case but adds insight into one additional concept. An analysis of these cases is summarized in table 19.3.

This fourth case took three months, that is, similar to the first case. Overall, approximately 69 interviews were held with 31 people in various positions. Observation techniques were also applied and approximately 3250 pages of documentation were compiled similar to the earlier cases.

During and after each case study, a case study report was written containing the methodology, the findings of the study, the lessons learned, and, for example, the case selection criteria. This process of writing the case study reports took approximately as much time as the time spent in the field. A confidential part of the case study report included keys to connect the findings as reported in the case study report with the actual data collection. For example, in a case study report, it would mention "interview 18." A key was provided giving information on when this interview was held, with whom, the topic (linking it with the research questions), and where the actual interview information was stored, that is, where in the collection of field data. In other words, the findings of each case study included essentially the interpretation of the data and the development of new concepts, but the case reports provided "evidence" for the interpretations by referencing the specific data that led to those conclusions. For example, a conclusion may have been reached based on several interviews in combination with some documents; therefore these interviews and documents were referenced in the case report, and through the "confidential key," the actual interview data and documents could be traced. Each of these case reports was approximately 100 pages in A4 (legal paper size).

This example shows the richness of data that can be achieved with the in-depth iterative pragmatic case method. This is because of the extended exposure to empirical data. For example, if a survey is conducted and replies are received from 600 respondents and each respondent took approximately 10 minutes to fill in the survey, then we could say that the exposure to data was approximately 6000 minutes or approximately 2.5 weeks. This is much less than the exposure of 9 months in the multiple case study described above.

Despite this richness there are some disadvantages of doing this type of inductive research. One of the biggest obstacles is that, as noted by Meredith, Raturi, Amoako-Gyampah, and Kaplan (1989, p. 304), the testing approach (deductive) is generally considered "true research." Publishing inductive research is therefore faced with challenges with regard to the acceptability of the inductive research design. This is related to the reviewers' and editors' understanding of inductive research. Another challenge with this type of research is that enormous amount of data can make it very difficult to publish the findings in a journal article that is by necessity limited in length. On the other hand, the amount of data that is collected with this iterative and emergent approach may include many new scientific insights and has the potential of a number of smaller and more topic specific articles. For example, the research study described above resulted, besides the case study reports and conference publications, directly in ten articles in peer-reviewed scientific journals.

Practitioner recommendations

When conducting social science oriented research study it is important to identify the research ideology that is being followed. This is important because in contrast to the natural sciences there are multiple research ideologies in the social sciences. However, what is accepted in one ideology is often not accepted by another ideology. This chapter looked at one particular research method, that is, the case study method. It showed that there are different types of research methods and that these types are related to the underlying research ideology. On the one hand is the more deductively (validation) oriented approach from Yin (1994) and on the other hand is the more inductively oriented (developing) approach from Glaser and Strauss (1967). An approach by Eisenhardt (1989) lies in between these two approaches. Based on the discussion of the characteristics of these methods, another method was proposed: the iterative-pragmatic case study method. This method is mostly aligned with the inductive approach. It uses grounded theory principles to develop new theory and uses snowball sampling for case selection. However, it also uses validation techniques by checking similar information in subsequent cases (i.e., replication logic). Case study research leads to potentially much more, and richer, empirical data than, for example, surveys, but there can be drawbacks. In particular more inductive and interpretative oriented case methods are typically considered of lesser quality than testing oriented designs. Furthermore, the particular techniques, as for example highlighted by the grounded theory approach, are less well known, which makes publishing results in journals more challenging, and it is challenging to condense the amount of data into an article format.

References

Aken, J. E. van (2004). Management research based on the paradigm of the design sciences: The quest for field-tested and grounded technological rules. *Journal of Management Studies, 41*(2), 219–246.

Ansari, A., Lockwood, D., & Modarress, B. (1992). Characteristics of periodicals for potential authors and readers in production and operations management. *International Journal of Production and Operations Management, 12*(6), 56–65.

Bengtsson, L., Elg, U., & Lind, J. E. (1997). Bridging the transatlantic publishing gap: How North American reviewers evaluate European idiographic research. *Scandinavian Journal of Management, 13*(4), 473–492.

Cunningham, J. B. (1997). Case study principles for different types of cases. *Quality & Quantity, 31*(1), 401–423.

Darke, P., Shanks, G., & Broadbent, M. (1998). Successfully completing case study research: Combining rigour, relevance and pragmatism. *Information Systems Journal, 8*(1), 273–289.

Dubin, R. (1978). *Theory building.* New York: The Free Press.

Eisenhardt, K. M. (1989). Building theories from case study research. *Academy of Management Review, 14*(4), 532–550.

Eisenhardt, K. M. (1991). Better stories and better constructs: The case for rigor and comparative logic. *Academy of Management Review, 16*(3), 620–627.

Eisenhardt, K. M. & Graebner, M. E. (2007). Theory building from cases: Opportunities and challenges. *Academy of Management Journal, 50*(1), 25–32.

Fox-Wolfgramm, S. J. (1997). Towards developing a methodology for doing qualitative research: The dynamic-comparative case study method. *Scandinavian Journal of Management, 13*(4), 439–455.

Glaser, B. G. (1978). *Theoretical sensitivity: Advances in the methodology of grounded theory.* Mill Valley, CA: The Sociology Press.

Glaser, B. G. (1992). *Basics of grounded theory analysis: Emergence vs forcing.* Mill Valley, CA: Sociology Press.

Glaser, B. G. (1998). *Doing grounded theory: Issues and discussions.* Mill Valley, CA: Sociology Press.

Glaser, B. G. (2001). *The grounded theory perspective: Conceptualization contrasted with description.* Mill Valley, CA: Sociology Press.

Glaser, B. G. (2003). *The grounded theory perspective II: Description's remodeling of grounded theory methodology.* Mill Valley, CA: Sociology Press.

Glaser, B. G. (2005). *The grounded theory perspective III: Theoretical coding.* Mill Valley, CA: Sociology Press.

Glaser, B. G., & Strauss, A. L. (1967). *The discovery of grounded theory: Strategies for qualitative research.* Chicago, IL: Aldine Publishing Company.

Glaser, B. G., & Strauss, A. L. (2007). *The discovery of grounded theory: Strategies for qualitative research.* New Brunswick, NJ: Aldine Transaction.

Groot, A. de (1969). *Methodology: Foundations of inference and research in the behavioral sciences.* Belgium: Mouton & Co.

Guba, E. G. & Lincoln, Y. S. (1994). Competing paradigms in qualitative research. In N. K. Denzin & Y. S. Lincoln (Eds.), *Handbook of qualitative research* (pp. 105–117). Thousand Oaks, CA: Sage Publications.

Gummesson, E. (2000). *Qualitative methods in management research* (2nd ed.). Thousand Oaks, CA: Sage Publications.

Hamilton, D. (1994). Traditions, preferences, and postures in applied qualitative research. In N. K. Denzin & Y. S. Lincoln (Eds.), *Handbook of qualitative research* (pp. 60–69). Thousand Oaks, CA: Sage Publications.

Holmström, J., Ketokivi, M., & Hameri, A. P. (2009). Bridging practice and theory: A design science approach. *Decision Sciences, 40*(1), 65–87.
Huxam, C., & Vangen, S. (2003). Researching organizational practice through action research: Case studies and design choice. *Organizational Research Methods, 6*(3), 383–403.
Janesick, V. J. (1994). The dance of qualitative research design: Metaphor, methodolatry, and meaning. In N. K. Denzin & Y. S. Lincoln (Eds.), *Handbook of qualitative research* (pp. 209–219). Thousand Oaks, CA: Sage Publications.
Leonard-Barton, D. (1990). A dual methodology for case studies: Synergistic use of longitudinal single site with replicated multiple sites. *Organization Science, 1*(3), 248–266.
Locke, K. (1996). Rewriting the discovery of grounded theory after 25 years? *Journal of Management Inquiry, 5*(3), 239–245.
Locke, K. (2001). *Grounded theory in management research.* London: Sage Publications.
McClintock, C., Brannon, D., & Maynard-Moody, S. (1979). Applying the logic of sample surveys to qualitative case studies: The case cluster method. *Administrative Science Quarterly. 24*(1), 612–629.
McCutcheon, D. M., & Meredith, J. R. (1993). Conducting case study research in operations management. *Journal of Operations Management, 11*(1), 239–256.
Meredith, J. (1998). Building operations management theory through case and field research. *Journal of Operations Management, 16*(1), 441–454.
Meredith, J. R., Raturi, A., Amoako-Gyampah, K., & Kaplan, B. (1989). Alternative research paradigms in operations. *Journal of Operations Management, 8*(4), 297–326.
Miles, M. B., & Huberman, A. M. (1994). *Qualitative data analysis: An expanded sourcebook* (2nd ed.). Thousand Oaks, CA: Sage Publications.
Soteriou, A. C., Hadjinicola, G. C., & Patsia, K. (1999). Assessing production and operations in management related journals: The European perspective. *Journal of Operations Management, 17*(1), 225–238.
Stake, R. E. (1995). *The art of case study research.* Thousand Oaks, CA: Sage Publications.
Strang, K. D. (2014). Why practitioner-scholars need a research design typology. In K. D. Strang (Ed.), *Palgrave Handbook of Research Design in Business and Management* (pp. 1–15). New York: Palgrave.
Strauss, A. and Corbin, J. (1990). *Basics of qualitative research: Grounded theory procedures and techniques.* Newbury Park, CA: Sage Publications.
Strien, P. J. van (1986). *Praktijk als wetenschap: Methodologie van het sociaal-wetenschappelijk handelen.* Assen, Netherlands: Van Gorcum.
Swanborn, P. G. (2010). *Case study research: What, why and how?* Los Angeles, CA: Sage.
Verschuren, P., & Doorewaard, H. (2005). *Designing a research project.* Utrecht, Netherlands: Lemma.
Yin, R. K. (1994). *Case study research: Design and methods* (2nd ed.). Thousand Oaks, CA: Sage Publications.

20

Action Research Applied with Two Single Case Studies

Angeline Lim and Dae Seok Chai

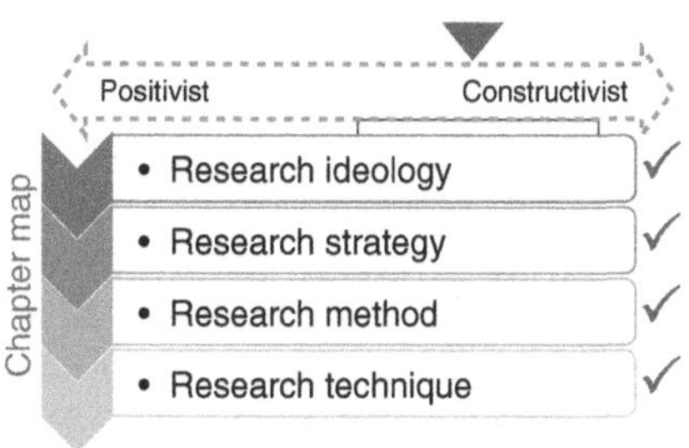

Chapter overview

Lim and Seok Chai clearly follow the pragmatist research ideology. They expose many of the controversies in classifying the action research method, and then they apply it in two case studies (in Singapore and South Korea). As they cite from the literature, some writers position action research method under the pragmativist ideology, but as advocated in chapter 1, a pragmatic method can come under either the pragmativistic or constructivistic ideologies, according to how it is applied, because it requires the researcher to involve the participants in the process of the problem that they are trying to solve. There is agreement in the literature that action research uses an organizational problem as the unit of analysis to develop a solution for a deductive-inductive theory-building purpose. It starts as deductive so as to review any a priori best practices that may exist, but usually existing procedures require modification (inductively developing a new process model). Otherwise why would an action research project be needed? The generalization is often organization specific although the implications apply to the industry or more broadly. As the authors of this chapter clarify, action research requires the researcher to participate with and within the target community. This is similar to the continuous improvement paradigm of total quality management in the post-positivist ideology where operations research methods are applied.

Introduction

"No action without research; no research without action" (Lewin as quoted in Marrow, 1969, p. 193). Action research is, as Kurt Lewin says, an intermingling of action and research. Action research is not action research without action, and certainly not without research. Often hailed as the founder of action research, Lewin is generally acknowledged to have introduced the term "action research" in his 1946 article "Action research and minority problems" published in the *Journal of Social Issues* (Greenwood & Levin, 1998; Susman & Evered, 1978; Yorks, 2005). It is important, however, to note that action research has diverse theoretical foundations and implementations (Dickens & Watkins, 1999; Reason & Bradbury, 2001; Yorks, 2005), and it is with this awareness and understanding that we attempt to define and elucidate action research.

In this chapter, we seek to provide readers with an understanding of action research by answering the following questions: What is action research? How did action research come about? What are the different forms of action research? Who engages in action research? How is action research conducted? The first part of the chapter focuses on clarifying the theoretical underpinnings of action research and its broad characteristics; the second part attempts to bring action research to life by taking readers through the process by which action research is conducted and illustrates the process through two case studies. Readers should also note that even though action research is used in many domains—for example, social, political, business—this chapter focuses on action research in the context of business organizations.

Overview of action research

What is action research?

Action research is a form of pragmatic research typically undertaken to improve communities of practice such as business organizations, educational institutions, and social institutions. Action research actively engages participants of the target community in this endeavor by seeking their input at various stages of the research process, and in the creation and refinement of an action plan that is derived from research findings. While the results of an action research project may contribute to the body of scientific knowledge available, they tend to be specific to, and are used for the betterment of, the target community.

From a conceptual standpoint, both theory and practice are involved in a reciprocal relationship in action research, interacting with each other to create knowledge that not only achieves the practical aims of the target community, but also contributes to the research goals of the researcher (Yorks, 2005). It is this understanding of action research that differentiates action research from applied research. While action research combines both thought (theory) and action (practice) in an interactive and reciprocal manner, applied research often separates thought and action into two different processes (Greenwood & Levin, 1998). It is critical to distinguish between action and applied research because while the goals of action research and applied research may be similar (to improve the target community), action research involves enquiry with the target community, and applied research often tends to involve the application of science on the target community (Eden & Huxham, 2002; Roll-Hansen, 2009). Applied research also often implies a one-way relationship from science to practice, while action research is commonly epitomized by the idea of "theory to practice and practice to theory."

Over the years, action research has been criticized as lacking academic rigor due to its lack of generalizability beyond the target community and lack of research objectivity (as researchers and members of the target community are involved in the research; Nykiel, 2007). Nevertheless, the purpose of action research differs from basic research, and standards by which basic research is evaluated (e.g., reliability, generalizability, and hypotheses testing) should not be applied to action research. Perhaps, as Eden and Huxham (2002) commented, action research should be understood as a research approach rather than as a research method.

In looking at examples of action research, it is fairly common for readers to assume that action research is a purely qualitative methodology. Many of the examples tend to describe action research as using qualitative methods such as interviews, focus groups, and participant observations. However, that is far from the truth. Action researchers are open to employing the full spectrum of research techniques including both qualitative and quantitative methods and are often encouraged to adopt a mixed-method approach to better triangulate the data (Nykiel, 2007; Yorks, 2005). As such, while action research can be seen as falling within either the pragmatistic or constructivist ideologies (see chapter 1), all the research methods in this book can be seen as potentially useful for action research from either ideological standpoint.

Theoretical foundations of action research

A research paradigm refers to "the set of common beliefs and agreements shared between scientists about how problems should be understood and addressed" (Kuhn, 1962). Research paradigms guide researchers to contribute to the development of their own field in different ways, and all the elements of research such as research topics, research questions, methods, analyses, and interpretation will depend on the paradigm that the researchers possess. In this vein, an understanding of action research is not complete without an understanding of its origins and theoretical perspectives.

Origins

As mentioned earlier, Kurt Lewin is generally credited as the first scholar who created and used the term in the 1940s. However, the history of action research is not as linear as one would like to think. As Yorks (2005: 193) aptly noted, "the family tree of action research has many roots and branches." Action research has its origins not only in social psychology but also in anthropology and social anthropology where researchers have played an active role in the target community that they are researching by providing them with new knowledge to solve various problems (Eden & Huxham, 2002). As a specific research approach, however, several researchers can be said to have contributed to its development. Cornerstone studies or handbooks on action research commonly cite Karl Marx, John Dewey, Charles Sanders Peirce, William James, Elton Mayo, William Foot Whyte, and Kurt Lewin for influencing action research. Their philosophies and research have been said to influence action research significantly and have become the theoretical foundations for action research (Eden & Huxham, 2002; Greenwood & Levin, 2007). Credit is also given to the Tavistock Institute in Great Britain (Trist & Murray, 1993), the industrial democracy research tradition in Sweden and Norway (Greenwood & Levin, 1998; 2001), the American Indians, and the Southern participatory action research in the southern hemisphere, including Africa, Latin America, and Southeast Asia for influencing action research (Greenwood & Levin, 2007).

Since its inception, action research has been used by researchers in the fields of education (e.g., pedagogical research), social science (e.g., feminist research, minority research, social work research), medicine (e.g., nursing studies), and more recently, in business management (Eden & Huxham, 2002; Holter, & Schwartz-Barcott, 1993; Reinharz, 1992; Yorks, 2005). Lewin's premise for action research is that real-life problems should drive research instead of a gap in the literature, as is often the case in basic research (Eden & Huxham, 2002; Roll-Hansen, 2009). However, in reality, action research can take many different forms and is often a balance between the desires of the target community and the researcher. Depending on who initiates the action research, the research may be driven more by a problem within the target community or a theoretical research question that bears testing in a realistic scenario. In spite of this, action research will usually serve its twofold purpose of: (1) contributing to a scientific body of research and (2) solving a problem or improving a situation within the target community.

Theoretical perspectives

According to figure 1.1 in chapter 1, action research is a research method that falls within the right side of pragmatism or the left interpretative side of constructivism ideologies. It may fall into the same category as methods such as critical analysis, grounded theory, phenomenology, ethnography, and case studies according to the manner in which it is applied. Depending on the focus of the action research project, scholars have suggested that there are two possible theoretical perspectives that may be adopted—a pragmatist perspective and a critical perspective.

First, since action research emphasizes practice and action, action research may be viewed from the perspective of pragmatism (Blumer, 1969; Crotty, 1998). According to Rescher (1995, p. 710), pragmatists assume that "efficacy in practical application—the issue of which works out most effectively—somehow provides a standard for the determination of truth in the case of statements, rightness in the case of actions, and value in the case of appraisals." Pragmatism as the foundation of action research has been articulated by Dewey (1976), Peirce (1950), James (1948), and Lewin (1948). In particular, Dewey's approach of a pragmatic philosophy to science as a form of human inquiry had a significant impact on action research. This philosophy remains foundational for action research with its linkage of knowledge and action.

Second, action research is linked with critical inquiry or critical paradigm (Crotty, 1998). The purpose of the critical paradigm is to uncover hidden interests, expose contractions, enable more informed consciousness, change injustice of the existing social structure, and challenge hegemony, such as the assumptions and values behind policies or systems (Fine, 2006; Giroux, 1982). Therefore, action researchers who adopt a critical perspective in their work tend to implement various types of methods to seek true knowledge or consciousness leading the oppressed to recognize the hegemony and injustice, and finally to make actions for social change (Kilgore, 2001; Swanson & Holton, 2005). In the context of organizational research, action researchers often engage members of the target community in reflective practice, where they observe and reflect on their own actions in order to improve the way things are being done.

Characteristics of action research

Given the diverse ways in which action research has developed and been implemented, it is not surprising that there is a lack of agreement on the definition of action research. Nevertheless, most writers of action research have agreed that there are fundamental elements of action research that distinguish it from other types of research methods and approaches (Eden & Huxham, 2002; 2008). In this section, we attempt to highlight these key characteristics of action research. From our review of the action research literature, there are four fundamental elements of action research that are present in all the different types of action research: (1) action, (2) research, (3) community participation, and (4) localization of context.

Action

As conceptualized for the first time by Lewin (1946), the term "action research" begins with the word "action" because it is a critical characteristic of action research. The "action" in "action research" can be described in several ways. First, action literally means that action research requires action. Action researchers believe that thought and action must not be separated, which is not required by other types of research in social science. Therefore, solving a practical issue is a key driver of action research, and new knowledge can only be generated and examined through action (Greenwood & Levin, 2007). This approach to research is clearly different from basic research approaches.

Second, action research requires change. As Lewin (quoted in Yorks, 2005, p. 376) was often quoted saying, "the best way to understand something is to try to change it." The purpose of action research is to improve the current status or initial situation of the target group, department, organization, community, society, or nation whereas the purpose of basic research tends to explain phenomenon or discover causation among constructs (Schmuck, 2009). To change and improve, we need action as well as thought or theory supporting the action. Therefore, action research seeks to provide solutions and interventions for planned change or improvement whereas basic research's aim is to contribute to the literature of specific fields.

Research

As the second word in "action research," research is another key characteristic of action research. Like other research methodologies, action research must proceed with appropriate purpose, research questions, theoretical framework, data collection methods, and analysis to contribute to the literature or academic fields through generating new knowledge. As French and Bell (1995) clearly indicated in their definition of action research, action research must build a body of scientific knowledge while pursuing effective action simultaneously.

For good action research to occur, researchers need to gather validated and reliable data from multiple sources using various research methods. Unlike basic research, which employs either a quantitative or a qualitative research method, action researchers often utilize a combination of methods—both qualitative and quantitative. In fact, the research technique used in an action research project is chosen based on the specific purpose of the project and the accessibility of the data. More importantly, the research method must be selected to avoid oppressing participants, usually minority or suppressed members of an organization (Greenwood & Levin, 2007). Therefore, most of the research methods described in this book could be implemented in action research.

Like Lewin's idea of "nothing is as practical as a good theory," researchers must balance between action and research in any action research project.

While balancing action and research or practice and theory, AR has been controversial. One of the common arguments is that AR lost its ability to become good research when research is involved in practical action because it is not fully following the widely accepted social science research criteria for credible empirical research (Gustavsen, 2003; Yorks, 2005). For example, action research generally has two goals: improving current status with action and accumulating knowledge with research. While these goals could be often incompatible, researchers for action research generally sacrifice the quality of research in terms of a design or method to achieve high-impact action and its objectives (Deutsch, 1968; Greenwood & Levin, 2007; Seashore, 1976). Like the ongoing and never-ending debate of legitimacy and credibility between qualitative and quantitative methodologies, the controversial debates between action and research are not likely to end. The important thing to keep in mind though is that action research must fulfill both the requirements of contributing to science and practice.

Participation

Another key characteristic of action research is the participation of members of the target community. Since one of the main aims of action research is continuous improvement or planned change, members of the target community have to be involved right from the beginning (Burnes, 2004; Kanter, Stein, & Jick, 1992; Kotter, 1996; Schein, 1996). This entails a collaboration between the action researcher and the various stakeholders in all the steps in the action research process such as assessing needs for improvement, collecting and analyzing data, sharing feedback, and creating, implementing, and evaluating the action plan. Doing so will enhance the effectiveness of any organizational development or change project.

Localization of context

One other characteristic of action research that sets it apart from other forms of research is the localization of context. Action research is generally conducted to improve or change the current status of groups or organizations whereas basic research tends to focus on the generalization of findings for the creation of universally accepted theory (Schmuck, 2009).

The key characteristics of action research should be viewed as a whole and not as stand-alone parts. One without the other would not constitute action research. For example, action as a characteristic may also apply to applied research; localization of context may apply to case studies, and so on. What makes action research unique is that all these elements come together to create a way of conducting research—an approach that straddles both science and practice, and attempts to fulfill the core aims of scientific research as well as contribute to the effective betterment of a community.

Conducting action research

There are many ways by which action research can be conducted. These differ across disciplines and context and are often labeled in various ways. Examples of various types of action research include participatory research (or participatory action research), critical action research (or critical participatory action research), classroom action research, action learning, action science, soft systems approach, industrial action research, societal action science, management action science, real-time action science, and retrospective action science (Eden & Huxham, 2002). While the types of action research may vary, there are similarities in the way they are being conducted.

Many of the models for conducting action research are derived from the Systems Model of Action-Research Process that Lewin developed in his publications (Eden & Huxham, 2002). This model comprises the following stages: planning, action, evaluation (e.g., observing, reflecting), and further planning (see figure 20.1).

The first stage is the planning stage. At this stage, the researcher and the key members of the target community jointly engage in a series of planning actions aimed at diagnosing the problem and identifying suitable actions for positive change. Activities at this stage include conducting a preliminary diagnosis of the organization, gathering data, analyzing data, providing feedback on results, and joint action planning.

The second stage is the action stage. In this stage, the researcher and the community members engage in activities related to the planning and execution of behavioral changes in the client organization and to learning processes that will help improve the plan of action. Activities at this stage include learning activities that their enable alignment with change objectives, action planning, and execution of the plan.

The third stage is the evaluation stage. In this stage, actual behavioral changes resulting from actions taken in the second stage should have taken place. Data are gathered to monitor progress and to determine if adjustments in the learning activities should be made.

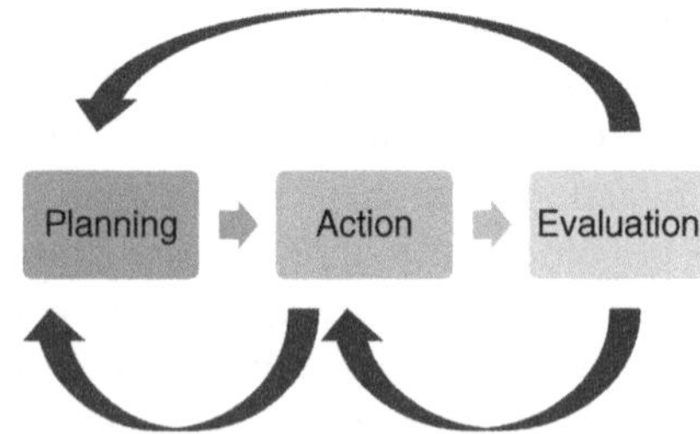

Figure 20.1 Lewin's systems model of action-research process (simplified).

As can be seen from figure 20.1, this research process is iterative in nature. Data are constantly gathered to refine the actions needed for change, and modifications are made to these actions to ensure that the actions taken are aligned with the intended change. This whole process is often done in collaboration with the target community.

Action research process

Drawing on Lewin's model and building on the ideas put forth by Eden and Huxham (2002), Elden (1981), and Yorks (2005), we outline the following action research process (see figure 20.2). The action research process is broken down into four main phases: (1) initiate and organize the project, (2) define and conduct the research, (3) create and implement an action plan, and (4) reflect and evaluate actions. Each of the phases are further broken down into specific steps. These are described below.

Initiate and organize the project

In an action research project, the action researcher is typically one of three groups of people: in-house HR/OD practitioner, external consultant, or external researcher. The action researcher usually has the relevant research training and often enters the project with a pre-understanding of relevant research theories and the organization. However, in recent years, more action research projects are undertaken by internal members of the organization (e.g., those who are enrolled in academic education programs, MBAs; e.g., Bartunek, et al., 2000).

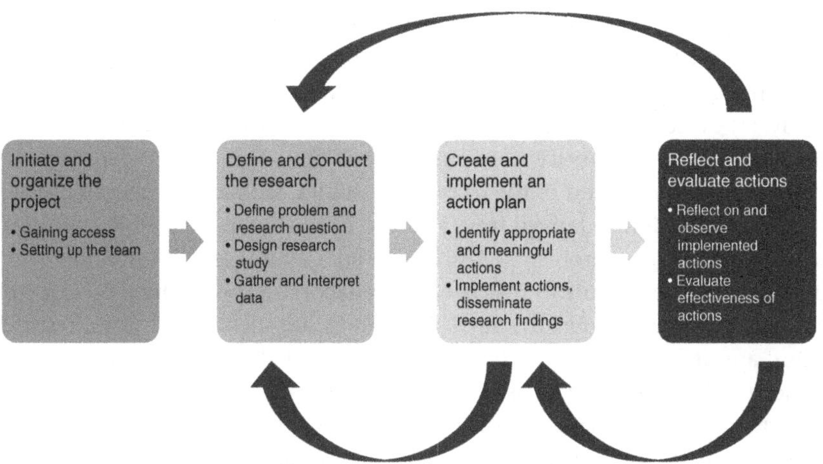

Figure 20.2 Action research process.

Depending on whether the action research project is initiated by the organization or the researcher, access to the organization may well be the first step in an action research process. This is typically the case for external researchers who are interested in studying an organization for the purpose of advancing scientific research, but who, at the same time, will contribute to the improvement of the organization based on the findings. In the context of organization-initiated action research, the action researcher may still need to seek access to the specific departments or teams that have been singled out by the organization for study. While formal access may have been given, action researchers may find themselves faced with resistance from the target department or team. They will then have find ways to obtain the buy-in and cooperation of the target members.

Once access to the organization is granted, the next step would be to set up the action research team. This entails defining the roles and relationships of the various action research team members (Yorks, 2005). Team members often include the researcher, members of the management team commissioning the research, and members of the target department or team. Sometimes, organizations would form a steering group to work alongside the researcher, to provide him/her with inside knowledge of the organization, and to help in the process (Eden & Huxham, 2002). It is critical to clarify the roles, responsibilities, and relationships of each of the team members because of the inherent tension in action research—the researcher's main aim may be to contribute to the field of science, while the organization's aim is to identify actions that can improve the organization. Having the roles and responsibilities laid out from the beginning will make it easier for the team to function going forward.

Define and conduct the research

The next phase in the action research process is to define and conduct the research. The three steps in this phase are similar to the process for conducting basic research: (1) define problem and research question, (2) design research study, (3) gather and interpret data. To kick off this process, the action research team will need to identify the issue (or problem). This is a crucial step as it sets the stage for the rest of the research activities. Unlike basic research where problem definition is derived from a review of the literature and identification of a theoretical gap, problem definition in an action research often involves a diagnosis of the organizational issue in collaboration with the target organizational members. Typically, key stakeholders are identified by the research team, and interviews or focus groups are conducted with the stakeholders to understand the problem areas within the organization. Sometimes, even when the organization initiates action research, the research team may perform a diagnosis as the organization may have a more biased view of the situation. Problem definition may also be a delicate discussion between external action researchers, who want to advance their research goals, and organizational members, who seek to focus on addressing their issues. The balance between action and research thus becomes critical.

Once the problem and research questions have been defined and agreed upon, the next step is to design the research study. In this step, the action research team will have to decide how the problem will be studied and choose research methods that will allow them to obtain the necessary data to answer the research questions (Yorks, 2005). Here, the action researcher typically will be able to leverage on their research training to suggest and advice the team on methods that will help them to collect the relevant data; organizational members will then assess the appropriateness of using those methods to collect data within the organization. As mentioned earlier, action research does not subscribe to a specific type of research technique (e.g., qualitative or quantitative); action researchers can select any research method from the whole spectrum of methods that suits their needs and is appropriate to the organizational context.

Data gathering and interpretation are the next steps in the action research process. Unlike basic research, data gathering and interpretation are often conducted in conjunction with the target members of the organization, and not independent of them. A key action that is added into this process is the feedback of data to the organizational members and enlisting their help in making sense of the data. This is crucial to the success of an action research project as the organizational members would have inside knowledge to provide deeper insights into the data. The researcher's role in this case would also involve good facilitation skills to be able to draw out the insights from the organizational members. Data gathering and interpretation not only occur at this stage of the research process, but also earlier on in the project during the problem definition phase (e.g., reviewing of archival information, diagnostic interviews, surveys), and later on in the evaluation phase (e.g. post-action evaluation survey, interviews).

Create and implement an action plan

The third phase in the action research process is the creation and implementation of an action research plan. Since the main purpose of action research is to contribute to the effectiveness of the organization, meaningful actions need to be identified from the research findings and implemented in a way that can effect change within the organization (Yorks, 2005). The development and implementation of the action plan should strongly involve key organizational stakeholders. This is to ensure that the actions in the plan are appropriate to the organization and that the organization follows through on the plan (Eden & Huxham, 2002). It is important to note that unlike basic research where practical implications signal the end of the researcher's involvement in practice, the action researcher is highly involved in the creation and implementation of the plan. The action research is also iterative, and the action research team may need to gather more data to refine the action plan.

Another step in this phase is for the research team to agree on how and when they want to disseminate the research findings. They may choose to share it with a select group of senior managers, or they may choose to share it publicly with the entire organization. Often, this decision will be made after consulting with the senior management. Researchers who are interested in publishing the finding may also seek permission from the organization in the process.

Reflect and evaluate actions

A hallmark of action research is the reflective process that takes place at multiple levels within the organization—at the personal level (where employees reflect on their own actions and see improvement), at the group level (where departments, teams, groups reflect on the actions of their own group), and at the organizational level (where the organization reflects on the culture, processes, and practices of the organization as a whole). It is through the reflections that the organization learns, grows, and improves. Reflections on the implemented actions may help the organization to refine the action plan.

The final step in the action research process is evaluation. A key step mentioned in Lewin's model, evaluation will allow the action research team to assess the effectiveness of the action plan and to make changes to the action plan where necessary. This step is critical because it ensures that the ultimate aim of the action research project—that is, to improve the organization—is met.

As can be seen, the action research process may follow a sequence of steps but is also highly iterative. Researchers and key organizational members would have to work closely throughout the process for the action research project to be a success. The next section describes two case studies that illustrate this process.

Applied action research case studies

The case of a Singapore-based multinational company

The following case describes a Singapore-based multinational company in the health-care industry. This company has offices in two locations in the city-state of Singapore—one in an expensive office building within the central business district, and a newer office in a relatively lower-cost industrial estate near one of the residential estates in the suburbs of Singapore. The company had undergone restructuring such that the individual accounting and IT departments attached to each business unit were now clustered into a larger group called Internal Shared Services (ISS), and their colleagues were now considered their clients. Employees in the ISS group were also moved to the new office in the suburbs of Singapore. Following these changes, more than 50% of the ISS staff resigned or asked for a transfer to another department. The head of ISS was perturbed and while she surmised that the reason for the high turnover had to do with the changes, she was not certain and wanted a more evidence-based view on what was happening.

Through the regional head of HR, she became acquainted with a couple of researchers from a local university. These researchers, while novices at action research, were experts in organizational behavior research and were excited at the prospect of being involved in research that had real-life practical implications. A small action research team was then formed comprising two researchers, the local head of HR, the head of IT, and the head of the ISS group. The researchers were asked to sign a confidentiality agreement, but were allowed to use the findings for academic purposes so long as the organization remained anonymous. The roles of the researchers and the action research team were broadly clarified at the beginning—researchers would diagnose, conduct the research, conduct a sharing session with employees to feed back the findings; the organizational members of the team would provide input on the research questions, research methods, and help in the research implementation process by informing ISS employees of the research and organizing the sharing sessions. It was also agreed that the researchers will be the only ones who have access to the raw data to encourage employees to share openly.

Diagnostic interviews were conducted with members of the action research team and the CEO, who oversaw the ISS group. Findings from the diagnostic interviews led the researchers to propose an employee pulse survey, which would get at various attitudes, intentions, and outcomes. Items for the survey were drawn from validated scales, and irrelevant items were removed to make the survey an appropriate length for the ISS employees. A draft of the survey items were shown to the organizational members of the action research team and their input was obtained on whether the items made sense, were relevant to the organizational context, and whether there were items missing.

Once the survey was finalized, the organizational team members arranged town hall meetings for the researchers to come in and brief the employees on the survey, and answered any questions that they might have. The researchers then administered the survey online and collected the data. After the data were analyzed, the researchers then shared the results of the survey with the rest of the action research team and obtained their input on how the data were interpreted. Results confirmed some of the ISS head's guesses about causes of turnover, but there were also surprising findings. Commuting time tended to be a key driver of turnover, and within the ISS group, there was a small team that had very high dissatisfaction levels due to one or two people who were disrupting the work of others. A few more town hall meetings were arranged for the researchers to share the results of the survey with the employees. During these sessions, the researchers answered questions from employees and assured them that the action research team will be working on a plan to address the issues that were raised.

Indeed, an action plan was subsequently created to address the issues. The development of the action plan was led by the organizational members of the research team, in consultation with the researchers. Examples of actions taken include allowing employees to work from home once a week (to compensate them for the additional commute), having a family day every Friday to allow employees to leave work early to have dinner with their family members, and having the manager of the dissatisfied team hold a private meeting with the team to understand the differences within the team.

As with any action research project, evaluation is a critical step. The researchers followed up with the ISS group a year later to administer another employee survey. This time, overall dissatisfaction levels decreased, engagement levels increased, and the ISS head reported that turnover had reduced to less than 10%—a 40% drop from the previous year! It turned out that many of the employees who were upset by the changes that had taken place had by then left the organization. Results of the evaluation were then shared with the ISS head and HR head (by then the IT head had also left), and with employees of the ISS group.

The HEFE adaptation project

The following case is a well-described example of action research conducted by an internal consultant of a Korean global organization located in Seoul. The internal consultant, Ms. Jung, was a Human Resource Development (HRD) assistant manager in the global HRD team at the HRD center of the company. The HEFE adaptation project is a project supporting the highly educated and newly recruited foreign employees by helping them adapt to new national and organizational cultures. Before describing this case further, it is important to understand the context of Korea and the company briefly.

Korea was a labor-exporting country, with the intent of contributing to the national economy, until the 1970s. Since the late 1980s, however, unskilled foreign employees have been imported mostly from the third world because of increased salaries for Korean line workers caused by a huge labor movement in the country. Furthermore, the trend of globalization in the 1990s touched off a transformation of large corporations in Korea from domestic or international to multinational or global. Within this trend, most large-scale Korean companies began to recruit foreign employees who were skilled and highly educated. However, several issues emerged because Korea has been homogeneous in terms of ethnicity, and most Koreans did not have any experience working with foreigners.

Since the company is one of Korea's top conglomerates, it attempted to transform itself into a global company and began recruiting foreign employees. These foreign employees are highly educated, having completed their bachelors or masters degrees in their native countries or in Korea. As such, most of them had a certain amount of experience living in Korea. Before recruiting these foreign employees, the company developed a long-term plan for them with several objectives. The primary objective was to recruit and develop them as highly educated local managers who understand both the Korean culture and their own culture well so that they can send these highly educated foreign employees back to their home country as local managers. This is mainly because the Korean expatriate managers do not fully understand the local cultures and local employees and managers do not understand the Korean culture and the company's organizational culture. It is with this purpose that the HRM practitioners of the company developed the foreign employees' career plans. According to this plan, the foreign employees will work with Korean employees at the company headquarters in Korea for two years. After learning the foundational skills, Korean culture, and the organizational culture, they would be sent to the local subsidiary in their country of origin as an assistant manager.

Another objective in hiring foreign employees was to create a diverse working environment. As mentioned previously, Korean society has been ethnically homogeneous in and the Korean employees of the company have not been exposed to a more international environment, which was becoming a critical issue as the company faced global competition. This was therefore a good opportunity for employees to internationalize and acquire the relevant cultural skills, and a way for the company to become the global corporation that it envisioned.

One year after the recruitment of these foreign employees, Ms. Jung was called to her manager to report on the current status of the foreign employees and the establishment of their development plan. In order to approach this project holistically and systematically, she met with the director of the HRD center, explained her intention and tentative plan, and secured the support of the director. From a strategic point of view, this assignment could potentially increase the influence of the HRD Center, so the director encouraged her to provide solutions based on thorough research.

Ms. Jung collected the data in three ways. First, she interviewed three groups of employees—the highly educated foreign employees, the Korean mentors of the foreign employees, and the HR managers who designed the recruitment and development program for foreign employees. Through these interviews, Ms. Jung sought to explore and understand the needs of each of the groups. Second, Ms. Jung requested access to the internal documentation of the program design and the progress report of the foreign employees. Through these documents, she was able to observe their work and their working environment. Third, she designed a survey questionnaire to identify the needs and wants from the foreign employees and Korean employees who work with the foreign employees. Even though a formal action research team was not formed within the company, Ms. Jung obtained input from other key organizational stakeholders such as her direct manager and the director in all parts of the research process.

Based on her findings, Ms. Jung identified that the foreign employees did not really mingle well with other Korean employees and discovered several related issues and problems. Below is a list of the problems:

1. The foreign employees did not know Korean culture well enough.
2. The foreign employees want to stay in Korea rather move back to their own country.
3. The foreign employees do not clearly understand HR policies or the plans for them.
4. Some of the foreign employees do not speak Korean fluently enough to communicate with their Korean colleagues or mentors.
5. Korean employees incorrectly assumed that the foreign employees needed to behave like Koreans and think like Koreans if they want to be a part of a Korean company.
6. The Korean mentors for the foreign employees have not been trained on how to deal with foreign employees who are new to the job.

Ms. Jung reported these problems based on the data collected and analyzed and created an action plan. Issues that were not her responsibility were shared with the HRM department; issues that were within the domain of HRD (e.g., training and development issues) were looked into further and a more detailed action plan was developed. Some parts of the action plan included:

1. providing the mandatory quarterly workshop for the foreign employees to learn Korean culture and cross-cultural competencies,
2. providing cross-cultural awareness training for the whole organization,
3. providing an opportunity for foreign employees to take an external Korean language class, and
4. checking up on foreign employees' status periodically.

After Ms. Jung reported these issues and suggestions to the director, the director met with the director of the HRM department and discussed the issues since it was crucial to work collaboratively with the HRM department. In this vein, Ms. Jung met with several HRM managers and discussed further steps of what the HRM department could do, the HRD department could do, and how those two programs could be strategically aligned.

With the full support of the manager and the director, Ms. Jung designed and implemented several programs to assist foreign employees to adapt to Korean culture as well as the organizational culture. For the newly launched quarterly workshop, the HRD department could provide cross-cultural training. The HRM department also participated in the workshop and explained the HR policies and plans for the foreign employees. These workshops were also the places for mutual communication between the foreign employees and the organization because both HRD and HRM departments could receive feedback from the foreign employees and get an opportunity to update any news to the foreign employees. More importantly, a new cross-cultural awareness training program was designed for the whole organization. This action research enabled the organization to improve its cultural competency and continue its pursuit to become more globalized.

Conclusion

Action research, messy as it is, is by far one of the more exciting research approaches. As Lewin says, "the best way to understand something is to try to change it," so the best way to understand organizational behavior is to try to change it. Action research presents itself as a research approach that allows us to not only bridge the gap between science and practice through the application of theory to practice, but to learn from practice to build better theories.

References

Blumer, H. (1969). *Symbolic interactionism: Perspective and method.* Englewood Cliffs, NJ: Prentice-Hall.

Burnes, B. (2004). Kurt Lewin and complexity theories: Back to the future? *Journal of Change Management, 4*(4), 309–325.

Crotty, M. (1998). *The foundations of social research: Meaning and perspective in the research process.* Thousand Oaks, CA: Sage Publication.

Deutsch, M. (1968). Field theory in social psychology. In G Lindzey & E Aronson (Eds), *The handbook of social psychology,* Vol. 1 (2nd ed.). (pp. 412–487). Reading, MA: Addison-Wesley.

Eden, C., & Huxham, C. (2002). Action research. In D Partington (Ed.). *Essential skills for management research* (pp. 193–209). Thousand Oaks, CA: Sage.

Fine, M. (2006). Bearing witness: Methods for researching oppression and resistance; A textbook for critical research. *Social Justice Research, 19*(1), 83–108.

French, W. L., & Bell Jr. C. H. (1995). *Organizational development: Behavioral science interventions for organizational improvement* (5th ed.). Englewood Cliffs, NJ: Prentice Hall.

Giroux, H. A. (1982). *Theory and resistance in education.* Boston: Bergin & Garvey.

Greenwood, D. J. & Levin, M. (2007). *Introduction to action research: Social research for social change* (2nd ed.). Thousand Oaks, CA: Sage.

Gustavsen, B. (2003). New forms of knowledge production and the role of action research. *Action Research, 1*(2), 153–164.

Kanter, R. M., Stein, B. A., & Jick, T. D. (1992). *The challenge of organizational change.* New York: Free Press.

Kilgore, D. W. (2001). Critical and postmodern perspectives on adult learning. In S Merriam (Ed.), *The new update of adult learning theory: New directions in adult and continuing education* (pp. 53–61). San Francisco, CA: Jossey-Bass.

Kotter, J. P. (1996). *Leading change.* Boston, MA: Harvard Business School.

Kuhn, T. S. (1996). *The structure of scientific revolutions* (3rd ed.). Chicago: University of Chicago Press.

Lewin, K. (1946). Action research and minority problems. *Journal of Social Issues, 2*(4), 34–46.

Lincoln, Y. S., & Denzin, N. K. (2005). Introduction: The discipline and practice of qualitative research. In N. K. Denzin & Y. S. Lincoln (eds.), *Handbook of qualitative research* (3rd ed.). (pp. 1–32). Thousand Oaks, CA: Sage.

Marrow, A. J. (1969). *The practical theorist: The life and work of Kurt Lewin.* New York: Basic Books.

Rescher, N. (1995). Pragmatism. In T. Honderich (Ed.). *The Oxford Companion to Philosophy* (pp. 710–713). Oxford: Oxford University Press,.

Roll-Hansen, N. (2009). *Why the distinction between basic (theoretical) and applied (practical) research is important in the politics of science,* Centre for the Philosophy of Natural and Social Science Contingency and Dissent in Science Technical Report 04/09. Available from: http://www.lse.ac.uk/CPNSS/research/concludedResearchProjects/ContingencyDissentInScience/DP/DPRoll-HansenOnline0409.pdf. (accessed March 30, 2014).

Schein, E. H. (1996). Kurt Lewin's change theory in the field and in the classroom: Notes towards a model of management learning. *Systems Practice, 9*(1), 27–47.

Schmuck, R. A. (ed.) (2009). *Practical action research: A collection of articles* (2nd ed.). Thousand Oaks, CA: Sage.

Seashore, S. E. (1976). The design of action research. In A. W. Clark (Ed.). *Experimenting with organizational life* (pp. 103–117).New York: Plenum.

Smith, J. K., & Heshusius, L. (1986). Closing down the conversation: The end of the quantitative-qualitative debate among educational inquirers. *Educational Researcher, 15*(1), 4–12.

Swanson, R. A., & Holton, E. F. (2005). *Research in organizations: Foundations and methods of inquiry.* San Francisco, CA: Berrett-Koehler Publishers.

Yorks, L. (2005). Action research methods. In R. A. Swanson & E. F. Holton III (Eds). *Research in organizations: Foundations and methods of inquiry.* (pp. 375–398). San Francisco, CA: Berrett-Koehler.

21
Transportation Queue Action Research at an Australian Titanium Dioxide Mining Refinery

Kenneth D. Strang

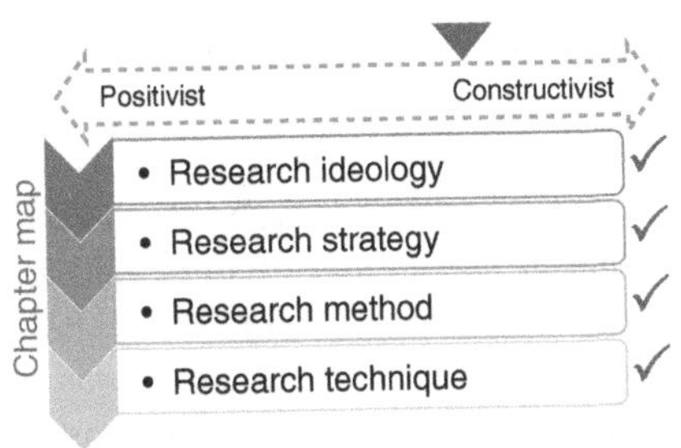

Chapter overview

This chapter discusses an applied example of an empirical study featuring a combination of operations research (general analytics) with the action research method. The author holds an interpretative pragmatist ideology. An outline of the manuscript is provided to demonstrate the normative structure of a peer-reviewed article in business and management. Subsequent sections explain how each topic relates to the research design typology layers. Two example studies are used, but the majority of the chapter discusses the operations research article. The main article was taken from the *European Journal of Operational Research*, where queue theory was utilized to develop a model for a sand refinery plant in Western Australia. A contrast article was added from the *International Journal of Internet and Enterprise Management* to demonstrate the rationale of using grounded theory instead of action research or ethnography. The second study was designed using a far-right pragmatic ideology (close to constructivist), with a unit of analysis focused on discovering how a new product development team at a multinational company in Australia used creativity to develop cellular phone products.

Journal manuscript analysis

As with my other chapters in this handbook, I use the first person in this chapter (a modern post-positivist writing style), and the recommended method endorsed by the American Psychological Association (APA) as cited in their APA Manual Edition 6 (APA, 2010). There is some controversy in the literature about whether to use "I" or "the author" in a scholarly manuscript.

The answer is that it depends on the sociocultural research ideology of the generalization audience—the reader. Often this is articulated as a style guide for a community of practice (e.g., APA) for a journal; or a corporation will have its unique organizational culture (e.g., standard operating procedures) to govern this. My experience is that traditional journals and companies in business, natural sciences, and psychology are positivistic, so they prefer to hear the nomenclature "the researcher" or "this author," while nonprofit companies and journals in the liberal arts disciplines prefer a personal tense. Nonetheless, APA has recently switched to using "I" or "we." The reader should also note that the reference format at the end of this chapter is not APA because the handbook style is Harvard (which is very similar to APA).

The core manuscript discussed in this chapter was published in 2012, as "Importance of verifying queue model assumptions before planning with simulation software," in the *European Journal of Operational Research* (on pages 493–504), which is a decision-sciences journal for operations research (http://www.sciencedirect.com/science/article/pii/S0377221711010319). The journal is well-respected in mathematics and operations research. It is a peer-reviewed journal indexed by several associations and listed with Cabell's (a benchmark used by accredited university business schools to signal scholarly work in performance evaluations and promotions).

Manuscript structure

The topic structure is outlined below explaining briefly the purpose of each section. This structure is typical. It is not a universal model because most journals have customized requirements. I have many publications employing various methods such as *t*-tests, ANOVA, CANOVA, MANOVA, along with the less common nonparametric and qualitative approaches, so I have to carefully manage my style guides to match the journals in each community of practice. Most journals strictly follow APA, which does not allow the "introduction" heading (albeit the section content is still included). Additionally, the "methods" section title is used instead of "methods and materials" in this applied example. Note in this example all section titles are numbered (except abstract and references), which was mandatory for the *European Journal of Operational Research*:

- Abstract—an executive summary of the paper including key findings.
- 1. Introduction—establishes the rationale, the problem, and gap in literature.
- 2. Literature review—deductive critical analysis of relevant articles (from last 5–7 years).
  - 2.1 Queue theory—queues, waiting-line theories, *Little's Law* (Little, 2004).
  - 2.2 Simulation software—operations planning software e.g., Caterpillar, Bethlehem Steel.
  - 2.3 Arrival and service distributions—how software uses simulations and distributions.
  - 2.4 Contemporary queue research—how scholarly researchers were studying the above.
  - 2.5 Research questions—synthesis of above formed questions and a hypothesis.
- 3. Materials and methods—design: strategy, sample, action research method, and techniques.
  - 3.1 Participants—sample context, how they were selected, and descriptive statistics.
  - 3.2 Theory and calculations—how queues and distributions were configured for testing.
- 4. Results—everything from here on is after study was completed: the analysis outcomes.
  - 4.1 Arrival rate analysis—tests first part of queue model, arriving trucks to refinery.
  - 4.2 Service rate analysis—tests second part of queue model, loading ramps at refinery.
- 5. Discussion—interpretation of queue model test results to answer questions and hypothesis.
- 6. Conclusions—summary of study, implications generalized to refineries, limitations.
  - References—details from only citations made in journal-specific style (not a bibliography).

Executive summary of manuscript

The title and abstract of indexed articles are considered public domain for obvious reasons, so they may be reproduced without permission of the publisher as long as they are correctly cited. Since an abstract is an executive summary, quoting it is the best way to introduce this case:

> This case study uses empirical data gathered at an Australian refinery to verify the assumptions for queue distributions before using special-purpose software to plan the off-road-truck hauling of titanium dioxide to a refinery ($n = 773$). Easy-to-use spreadsheet software is utilized to verify assumptions for queue models. Managers are able to make decisions based on economic implications of queue models to avoid making costly planning mistakes. Analysts can use nonparametric hypothesis-testing techniques to verify distribution assumptions for optimization without having to write hard-to-maintain and complex algebraic linear equations or nonlinear search routines. (Strang, 2012a, p. 493)

Research design of journal manuscript

Now that you, the reader, will have a general idea about what the study was focused on, I will analyze the manuscript using the research design typology as a framework. Figure 21.1 is a conceptual drawing of the research design workflow for this manuscript. Manuscripts are not always top-down as per the research design typology. In fact, most scholarly studies commence with either a preliminary literature review or a follow-up to one of the published papers (which has a literature review). The literature review is done to identify the strategy (unit of analysis and level of analysis). However, sometimes researchers change their ideology on the continuum.

As mentioned earlier, ideology is not innate but rather it is socialized through scholarly reading and practice. I often vary between post-positivism and the interpretative (almost constructivist) zone of pragmatism. I have also applied many of the generally accepted methods, across disciplines, so I am familiar not only with designing research, but also with being rejected by journal reviewers who do not have the same ideology as me. Thus, based on my experience, I advise researchers to declare their ideology to avoid misunderstandings.

The manuscript is technical but well worth a read keeping this chapter in hand. I should warn the reader that operations research papers are often very mathematically oriented, and they involve statistical techniques applied differently as compared with the experiment or observation method. More so, this is not a typical action research method application either, as compared to the handbook chapter by Lim and Seok Chai (where they used a traditional approach illustrated by two different articles as examples). Furthermore, the reader may enjoy the philosophical contrasts to action research that Sandiford presents in his chapter, where he discusses observations or participation as data

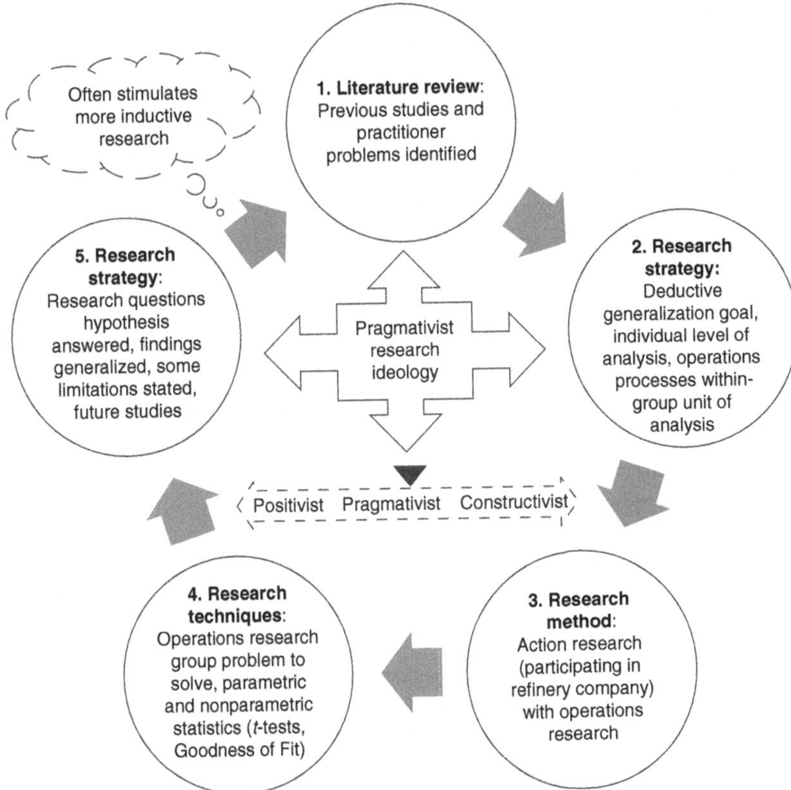

Figure 21.1 Conceptual drawing of research design workflow for manuscript.

collection methods in ethnography. You may now understand the rationale of why I position action research as predominately a pragmatistic ideology.

Research ideology

Although I did not directly state my philosophy in the manuscript, I hold a pragmativist research ideology. I open with this line of reasoning to show readers the scholarly rationale for the study, which was cited as being a gap in literature (Strang, 2012a, p. 493):

> This study addresses this "validation gap" in operations logistics and complexity theory literature—and departs from mathematical programming. A shortcoming in the literature is that operations research focuses heavily on technical or hypothetical/abstract models instead of practical advice. (Mercer, 1977; Sharp & Dando, 1979)

There is another place in the manuscript where I articulated my ideology, and it was driven by as well as substantiated by the literature review. The excerpt clearly frames my ideology as pragmatic since I wanted to develop a practical solution:

> The first conclusion drawn from the above review is that queue models in the extant literature are often conceptual (not empirical), and they are not pragmatic for use by "non-scientific" managers in the mining industry (especially mining businesses with limited resources). (Strang, 2012a, p. 497)

The research was designed as a deductive action research case study at a sand refinery. The reason it was deductive is because I was basing my analysis on queue theory and several well-known probability distributions, namely Poisson, Weibull, Bernoulli, normal, exponential, Erlang, and others from the operations research community of practice.

As a quick review of the first handbook section, ideologies represent the sociocultural philosophical attitude of the researcher that may be categorized as axiological, epistemological, or ontological. Researchers generally just state their ideology or philosophy (Creswell, 2009, 2012; Creswell & Tashakkori, 2007). I will explain this in detail as I did in the paper.

Axiology in general refers to the theory of beliefs, such as religion and sociocultural values. In business and management, axiology means the priority of values conditioned by organizational and global culture socialization. Although I lived in Australia for many years, I understand the culture of the United States, where I live. I have published many empirical papers analyzing global culture and learning styles (e.g., Strang, 2009a, 2010, 2012b), but for this chapter I will simply indicate that my cultural dimension indexes are closer to the younger generation as compared with the average values calculated by Hofstede on his survey of IBM employees (Hofstede, 1991; Strang, 2012c). For example, my cultural profile, as compared to the US mean is: PDi is low (consultative rather than authority preference), MFi is same as US MFi (higher toward results oriented instead of nurturing), ICi is slightly lower (more collective than individualistic), UAi is about the same as US average (higher uncertainty avoidance than acceptance of risk), and my LTi is much higher than the US norm (long-term, future focused, rather than short-term profit-driven). As will be discussed below, the sample participants had mixed cultures, and I did not assess those due to the nature of the study.

Axiology impacted the study design and the data collection, since this was an action research method; I was a participant, and the study took place in Australia. Many of the employees in the case study company were ex patriates (from other countries, working in Australia). The following excerpt from the methods section of the paper describes the case study. Although I lived in

Sydney NSW (eastern Australia) most of the time, I had relocated to Gellorup, Western Australia, a few kilometers south of Perth. This is where the case study company was based. As you will see from the excerpt, like many companies in Australia, they were foreign-owned. One thing I left out of the paper was the descriptive statistics of the sample—the engineering team. These were 20% Australian, 80% foreigners (half British and Middle Eastern), and all male:

> Cristal Global is a large surface mining multinational company with over 4000 employees. They are Arabian-owned, based in Saudi Arabia. They have large mining plants located in most continents including these countries: Australia, USA, South Korea, PRC (China), Singapore, Belgium, France, United Kingdom (England), and Brazil. Cristal Global primarily mines titanium dioxide which is used to provide super-white color to appliances or any plastic material. They also produce coatings such as paints and tints. Their main resource is sand crystals which they mine to extract the color pigments.
>
> This case study is based on the Cristal Global mining plant located in west Australia outside Bunbury WA Australia (on the coast just south of Perth). The plant is located near the Bunbury River delta beside the Indian Ocean. Cristal Global extract sand crystal from a surface pit in Bunbury (sometimes they purchase it), transport it through a multi-stage refining process, and refine the concentrate into purity grades grouped by density and color (customized for particular manufacturing uses). (Strang, 2012a, pp. 497–498)

Epistemology in business and management refers to the disciplinary terminology for communicating knowledge. This was indeed an issue for this study—in fact the focus of the study was to work with and observe engineers at the refinery, to improve their planning processes using spreadsheet-based software models. In this case I was not overly concerned about differences in epistemology because in keeping with the action research method, I was immersed in the team process, so it was very easy to remain on the "same page" with respect to sharing a common understanding of the queue models as they were mathematical, without much room for interpretation.

I had asserted in earlier chapters that epistemological and ideological differences impact the choice of statistical technique, such as in engineering or math vector analysis may be used to analyze participant response data agreement while in economics or psychology correlation or exploratory factor analysis would be de facto. Another way in which epistemological differences impact the researcher's ideology is in establishing validity and reliability processes along with the requisite benchmarks. I did not use an a priori instrument such as a questionnaire. Instead we—the team—used queue models that I had built by modifying their processes. I also collected data by observing my team, as we worked toward a better solution. On the other hand, I intended to test the validity of the model using statistics. Here is a quote (Strang, 2012a, p. 497):

> Thus, while it is acknowledged that linear/integer programming is more commonly used to optimize known constraints (Patriksson, 2008), here observational data are collected and factored as stochastic distributions (probabilistic not deterministic or heuristic) to verify commercial underlying constraint and distribution assumptions.

Epistemology also impacts the choice of deductive theory-driven versus the inductive theory-creating approach, which becomes the purpose of the research strategy. A positivist will generally require an a priori theory to test against to approve or falsify (e.g., in hypothesis testing). However, some positivists try to generate theory, such as through factor analysis. A pragmatist could use either approach, depending on the nature of the study, and the availability of a priori theories or instruments from the literature review. In this case, I was using existing queue theories and probability distributions that I had developed into spreadsheet software program models. This is deductive. I wanted to test the accuracy of these, as I stated in the paper:

> It is further accepted that mathematical programming can be used to search for feasible solutions of complex operational problems yet this study instead leverages the semi-structured easy-to-use context of spreadsheet software to verify queue model assumptions using hypothesis testing techniques based on probability density distribution shape. This is done by observing empirical data, leveraging probability, modeling a refinery with queue theory, and then using spreadsheet software to test the requisite hypotheses—before employing any further logistical operations planning. (Strang, 2012a, p. 494)

Ontology in business and management refers to how a researcher understands things that exist as tangible versus intangible and tacit versus explicit. In this study I was using the action research method and working with experienced engineers, using mathematical and statistical models that I had created in a spreadsheet. The likelihood of running into espoused-theory versus theory-in-use phenomenon was very little (Argyris & Schön, 1996). This is because computer software processes were the focus instead of human behavior or human perceptions.

The study was stimulated by my frustration when consulting with mining companies. They used very expensive software but it did not suit their needs for planning. Here is some background about the planning software from the paper:

> Contemporary mining industry operations are composed of physical processes that can be conceptually modeled using software. This allows the

> variables to be captured and manipulated in order to locate weak points and try new approaches, without affecting actual production (wasting time or money). Managers often recognize this as "what-if analysis," artificial intelligence, or goal-seeking models. A good example is the well known Flight Design Simulator software that allows engineers to experiment with designs without crashing real planes. (Strang, 2012a, p. 495).

As seen above, there were several justifications for doing this study, beyond making the process easier (such as simulation software often uses distributions that may not properly model a surface mine transportation queue). It may help to explain the main theories of a queue and how it is mathematically modeled in spreadsheet software. This approach is similar to the simulation discussed by Kadry in his chapter (using a post-positivistic ideology).

First we will look at the visual model, and then we will examine the main components of queue theory applied in the study.

In simplistic terminology, I wanted to participate in a project with the team at this surface mine refinery to test one of my visual operations research queue models (driven by statistical distribution) to improve their off-road truck sand transportation process. The visual aspect is that I wanted the model to generate a graph so they could easily see if their planning assumption was accurate by comparing how similar the two line series were. In addition, there would be statistical estimates to mathematically indicate the statistical similarity between the two series of lines (planned vs. actual for the loading queue system).

Research strategy

The research strategy defines the goals, research questions (or hypotheses), based on the unit, level of analysis, and generalization goal (deductive or inductive or both, and who or where the results will be generalized). A positivist will define these elements based on a priori research but any order is possible during the development of the research strategy if following a pragmatic ideology (as I was here) or a constructivist philosophy.

My research strategy was to develop a practical solution to be generalized specifically within the mining refinery plant. The industry I meant was surface sand mine refinery, not oil and gas refinery industry (a very different field). The quote below illustrates this generalization goal:

> It is argued that practitioners need pragmatic models that can be applied in-situ (on-site) by plant managers and engineers. Most importantly, underlying queue distribution assumptions (used in any model or software program) must be verified with real data. Planning mistakes can be costly. (Strang, 2012a, p. 497)

Thus, as I explained in the paper, the purpose was to develop a model that operational analysts could use to verify the underlying distribution model assumptions. By this I mean that the analysts could statistically verify the distributions they actually used and then select the best arrival and service queue configuration to use in their expensive planning software.

Levels of analysis are attributes referring to where the scholarly focus of the study is, such as the individual, group, or a larger partition. Level of analysis conceptually relates to the goal for the sampling method. This is because the level of analysis defines where the researcher intends to generalize the findings to, assuming they are reliable and significant (positivism). The level of analysis can be determined by looking at the method and technique, along with the generalization goal. Since I wanted to generalize to "operations analysts" (and other researchers), I was referring to the group level of analysis. I sampled the team as a whole, a within-group focus, and my unit of analysis was the accuracy (and usability) of the queue planning model.

The unit of analysis identifies the factor, variable, process, relationship, or tacit phenomena at the heart of a study. My hypotheses were associated with verifying the accuracy of the distributions for the arrival and service queues. The unit of analysis as identified above was to test the queue model assumptions as the hypotheses. These are excerpts from my paper that discuss this:

> From the above, the research question which emerges is: can simple statistical tests in spreadsheet software be used to validate the assumptions of a queue model in the mining industry (in order to identify opportunities for improvement in operations productivity)? Can a nonparametric hypothesis testing methodology be utilized as a technique to verify the queue model assumptions? (Strang, 2012a, p. 497)

Research method

All de facto scholarly research methods start with or at least include a relevant and current literature review. Some methods require citing the method from thought leaders (as was the case in my study due to its novelty), while others require citing similar types of studies or at least defining the key factors. Factors in this sense would mean the findings of other articles surrounding the topic, namely portfolio management techniques, which I was focused on.

As I explained in the first section of this handbook, methods and techniques tend to fall in line with ideology and strategy. In particular, formal methods were commonly associated with the unit of analysis in the research strategy. Operations research use mathematical and statistical tests, along with the *scientific method*, to ensure accuracy. They are mathematical, positivistic, but necessary to address the research strategy of showing if and how queue models could be used by the refinery team to verify their planning assumptions prior to engaging more complex software.

Action research, on the other hand, is pragmatic. There is (as Sandiford will tell you in the next chapter) a somewhat obscure line between the formal methods when it comes to collecting qualitative data through participation. In this study I was a researcher, a participant as a project manager, and I was also a qualified analyst (albeit not an operations research engineer). Thus, to distinguish between McDonald's (2005) variations of participation as ethnography (observing) versus participation as job-shadowing versus taking a hands-on full-participation approach as in action research, I was hands-on full participation.

As Lim and Seok Chai point out in their chapter, action research is a form of pragmatic research typically undertaken to improve communities of practice in organizations by actively engaging the participants during the research process to develop action plans or solutions to the problem. The problem statement is key to identifying action research. Generally, in action research, the unit of analysis is a process that is not functioning well at the group or organizational level of analysis. This is why most researchers cite Eden and Huxham (2002) for action research since this follows the systems thinking approach, to understand group and nonhuman processes, earlier popularized by Checkland (1999).

Since this study required some a priori theory (queues, waiting line) along with a community of practice special-purpose procedures (operations research in mine refinery planning), I needed to include a context that encompassed the problem (not having a feasible planning model). Although I approached this study with a deductive approach, since I had queue theory models in mind, I could have instead asked the engineers for theirs. Nevertheless, I needed to test this model with engineers, and I needed their motivational support in testing it, and not just a perfunctory hit-the-button kind of participation. The engineers participated with me in building the queue models, so as to ensure they were functional and suitable for Cristal Global analysts, before we started the data collection and testing activities.

Thus, action research was better than ethnography or grounded theory because I needed to integrate leadership and team motivation, while being part of the community to adjust the queue models if and where needed. So, in this sense, action research is the best method to describe how I conducted the study, since I used leadership but I was also a team member, and we collaborated on refining and determining the best solution to the problem. This was also due to my operations research knowledge (not an expert as the engineers were but sufficient to know what was going on since I had consulted as a project manager with other mining and supply chain companies). In contrast, if I were approaching a study to improve the process of something that I was not familiar with, then action research would not be the best method. Instead I might conduct a pilot study using ethnography or grounded theory to understand and articulate how the planning process systems worked, and after that, initiate a follow-up project using action research.

Speaking of grounded theory, I want to briefly mention another article here to help other researchers (instead of writing another chapter). I applied grounded theory using a far-right pragmatic ideology (close to constructivist) in two different studies. One was focused on discovering how a new product development team at a multinational company in Australia created cellular phone products (Strang, 2011). The abstract from the study is below. The study titled "A grounded theory study of cellular phone new product development" was published in the *International Journal of Internet and Enterprise Management* on pages 366–387 in 2011:

> The grounded-theory case study methodology was applied to examine a profitable company in cellular phone new product development (NPD). The goal was to participate in focus groups of NPD teams to document how they reverse-engineered competitive designs. The focus group theme analysis was linked to taxonomies applied by similar empirical case studies in the literature. A brain storming technique was used with the case study focus group to capture and contrast the ideation processes with knowledge creation and educational psychology theories. Several models were created to externalize the NPD team design processes. (Strang, 2011, p. 366)

The reason I selected the grounded theory method for that study was because I had conducted a pilot study that indicated the NPD teams relied on creativity, knowledge-sharing principles, and a cognitive learning processes (to stay ahead of competitors). My idea was to use educational psychology as a backdrop to have a better understanding and to describe the what and how of their processes. I selected the *Taxonomy for Learning*, popularized by Anderson and Krathwohl (2001).

Since the topic for the NPD study was very tacit—creativity—I needed to observe as best as I could to discover exactly what the NPD teams did, but I also needed to have the participants tell me what was in their cognitive schema (what they were thinking and why). I did not have the subject matter expert knowledge in the NPD study as compared to my greater operations research experience that I held for the mining study. Thus, I needed to have the *Taxonomy of Learning* to use as scaffolding to have a better understanding of what the NPD teams were doing, and in turn to use that as the epistemological baseline for all of us to articulate the NPD mental model in use (theories-in-use). This was theory grounded but very inductive, thus, it was grounded theory. Now I will not discuss that grounded theory manuscript any longer, as I switch back to the operations research mine refinery study.

Research technique

I will explain why and how I applied the operations research techniques to the study. As I discussed in the first few chapters, there are common cross-method technique categories such as sampling, data collection, data analysis, validity-reliability analysis, and ethics.

My sample frame was the mining industry. However, my sample was a case study, one organization, in the surface mining industry, specifically Cristal Global in West Australia. I picked this out of convenience since I was located there. It was not random. This was a case study but not the case study technique. I did not try to understand the organization in terms of their total processes, nor did I compare Cristal Global to any other organization. It was a within-group case, carried out using participatory action research, because I wanted to work with the team to improve work processes. However, I relied entirely on operations research method for the selection of techniques, which were statistical in nature.

There were sufficient guidelines in the literature about how to design a queue model. I will paraphrase a short section from the article to illustrate the key factors:

> Queue models are constructed by several key parameters: an input arrival rate λ, an average, constant or arbitrary service rate μ (occasionally a standard deviation σ), along with one or more servers (sometimes called channels). Queue models cannot represent every situation as most implementations are designed on a first-come-first-serve (FIFO/FCFS) philosophy, in a steady-state system without balking (no customers jumping into other queues). Here we will assume a FIFO based model. (Strang, 2012a, p. 494)

The above section explained the operations research theory that should be used to develop a queue model. Now I needed to consider how to develop a queue model for Cristal Global. This required me to spend time with the team to understand their processes at the Bunbury plant. In surface mining operations, the key productivity measures for planning are: truck payload (load size), cycle time (driving time), and operator efficiency. The cycle time includes waiting time at the shovel, truck, loader, and dumping tip—I was most interested in modeling this with a queue. By the way, the Caterpillar 793C trucks they use (with a payload of 215 tons) are taller than a single-story house (I even included a picture of one beside my vehicle—a pragmatic ideology).

The most critical bottleneck seemed to be at the sand refiner ramps where the off-road trucks arrive (at an average arrival rate) and the truck is positioned around the conveyor system for dumping the load (at an average service rate). I selected the Poisson distribution to model the arrival rates because it was identical to Erlang (the default in the operations research literature) but it was easier to model in the spreadsheet (this a pragmativist ideology).

Since the 793C truck payload maximum is 215.46 tons, and the haul roads have a maximum 4% rolling resistance, but the loading ramps at the sand refiner have a 6% grade resistance, there was a delay for weighing, which requires the truck remain still before dumping onto the sand-refiner conveyor. Since there was only one ramp currently activated in this particular first-stage aggregate sand refiner, this was the service component and the bottleneck. There were typically 34 trucks and 11 loaders in a fleet to service operations. The round-trip between the pit and sand refiner is on average 1000 meters (1KM) at a 4% grade which would take roughly 3 minutes using an effective speed of 12 M/H, which is equal to 20 KM/H (D=T*R; T = D/R; T=1/20*60 minutes = 3 minutes). The actual duration from pit to sand refiner is typically triple that due to maneuvering and having the shovel load the truck (which takes only a few minutes when the truck is properly positioned).

That was sample data I had obtained from the project files. However, there are many legitimate reasons why variability occurs in these processes. I will quote what I found from participating in this project:

> Truck arrival rates and sand refiner service ramp loading rates vary due to shift start up, lunch breaks, shut-downs, refueling, weather, operator mood, and special events (e.g., unknowns). Required random equipment inspections (trucks, ramps and sand refiner) also impact this. Large equipment periodically has to be relocated (e.g., shovel, high voltage electrical cables, blasting buffers) which can impact any nearby operations. Other obvious delays include equipment breakdown-repair, maintenance (greasing is very commonly done daily in the field to both trucks and sand refiner hydraulic joints). Finally lighting impacts service rates. (Strang, 2012a, p. 498)

I made the pragmatic decision to develop two queue models because these represented vastly different queue and distribution configurations to facilitate hypothesis testing:

- M/M/1 (a simple single channel/single server assuming Poisson arrivals and Exponential service); and
- M/G/1 (a single channel server with general distribution assumptions that can accept variation).

I followed the guidelines of Taylor (2010) to develop the probability distributions and I followed the recommendations of Strang (2009b) to apply nonparametric *Goodness of Fit* tests in a spreadsheet. In keeping with the pragmatic ideology, and following operations research techniques, I sampled truck arriving and servicing processes for several intervals:

> First, the expected time for the arrival to the queue is 7.92 minutes, from the Fleet Costing and Planning User Guide. A fleet of Caterpillar 793C Off-Highway Trucks and several 992G Wheel Loaders with High Lifts are being used in a simple route where mining takes place at a maximum depth of 10 meters, which involves an average rolling resistance of 4%, with a specified maximum grade of 8% (data indicates grade was 6% maximum) over an average one-way distance of 500 meters. (Strang, 2012a, p. 498)

The rest of the data analysis becomes complicated. Basically there were 773 observations in the sample. I used this data to generate the actual arrival and service times, first for a Poisson distribution and next for a bell-shaped normal distribution. I then compared the actual to the expected distributions using nonparametric statistical techniques because the data were observation counts (frequencies, integers but not ratio). This was called a fit-analysis in the operations research industry. I compared the distributions by applying the Goodness of Fit test. I created two charts for both of these comparisons. The *Goodness of Fit* produces statistical estimates of similarity, using a form of *t*-test. I used the 95% level of confidence for all statistical tests (which converts to a 5% level of significance: 1–95% = 5%). I did not analyze power since I did not have any a priori basis and since I was able to obtain a large sample over 100 (recall that $n = 773$). The null hypothesis (H0) was both distributions were similar, while the alternate hypothesis (H1) was that they were significantly different. This is a two-tailed test with less risk of rejecting a false claim that was true or vice-versa.

The charts produced in the study each had two lines series, the first was the "expected" based on queue theory, and the second was the "actual" from my sample. There were two different colored lines. If the lines were similar, and if the *Goodness of Fit Chi Square* X^2 statistic were low, this would mean the actual truck performance was a good fit with the predicted model (no significant difference in the distributions). Thus, the operations analysts would then know how to plan their workload, assuming that the actual processes did not vary. If the processes did vary then another operations research technique would be needed to check that, called statistical process control (Strang, 2009b), which was beyond the scope of my original study. The processes at the case study company were very stable because the quality measurements were within the upper and lower control limits.

The spreadsheet models that I had setup for my project team were automated but flexible enough to change. All they had to do was to import observations from actual production and the recalculate the models with the press of one key. The charts would automatically display along with the X^2 *Goodness of Fit* estimate for statistical significance confirmation. There were several interesting findings from the study, and I will let you read the original manuscript if you are interested, since they are not specifically related to research design. I can say that, not surprisingly, the model was accepted and put in use by the company, which was a fantastic outcome for an action research study.

Conclusions

Rather than summarize this chapter, I will continue to apply the research design typology to the manuscript. The last part of the research design is actually the first part. This means that the researcher must go back and examine the research strategy, confirm what was found, and explain how that can be generalized as implications. Generally, recommendations are given for future research, and in many instances (speaking for myself) this has inspired new studies.

To accomplish that, I summarized what the study set out to do, again following the impersonal positivistic writing style. Here is a quote from the conclusion section of the paper:

> This paper attempted to build a practical queue model to plan cost-benefits and verify simulation software assumptions in a refinery. This was in answer to the case study stakeholders and in the literature. In the literature Worthington (2009) noted the need for practical models especially for businesses that lack know-how or funds to hire scientists to concentrate on developing, testing, rationalizing and implementing mathematical models for an optimal solution. The managers and operations analysts in the case study expressed the same desire. This is in line with other literature that encouraged a practical understanding and application of operations research theories (Mercer, 1977; Sharp & Dando, 1979). Most importantly, the case confirmed that the underlying queue distribution assumptions (used in any model or software program) must be verified with data to avoid costly planning errors. Validation testing was developed here for the front end of operations research, such that small-to-large businesses could continue to use commercial or programmed software when assumptions are verified. More specifically the surface mine truck arrival rates and refinery service times were observed ($n = 773$) and their distributions compared to the expectations of the underlying planning software (namely, Poisson for arrivals, and exponential for service times). This was done using non-parametric *Goodness of Fit* hypothesis-testing statistical technique. (Strang, 2012a, pp. 502–503)

From a research design perspective, I also needed to address the limitations. I disclosed that this was a case study at a specific mining company, in Australia, thus the models I had created would not necessarily generalize to any other company, although the concept of using queue models in spreadsheet software certainly would. I also offered some mining industry advice with regard to using automated (simulated) models for operations research planning:

> The other limitation is that taking a non-mathematical programming approach to operational problem solving could decrease innovation (if propagated widely in the mining industry). It is logical to point out the alternative research of polynomial linear and non-linear algebraic search techniques that could provide innovative solutions to complex operations research problems (such as: Kleijnen, Beers & Nieuwenhuyse, 2010; Kleijnen, Pierreval & Zhang, 2011; Souza, Coelho, Ribas, Santos & Merschmann, 2010), beyond just hypothesis-testing.

References

Anderson, L., & Krathwohl, D. (2001). *A taxonomy for learning, teaching and assessing: A revision of Bloom's taxonomy of educational objectives*. New York: Longman.

APA. (2010). *Publication manual of the American Psychological Association* (6th ed.). Washington, DC: American Psychological Association (APA).

Argyris, C., & Schön, D. (1996). *Organizational learning ii: Theory, method, and practice*. Reading, MA: Addison-Wesley.

Checkland, P. (1999). *Systems thinking, systems practice*. Chichester: John Wiley & Sons Ltd.

Creswell, J. W. (2009). *Research design: Qualitative, quantitative, and mixed methods approaches* (3rd ed.). New York: Sage.

Creswell, J. W. (2012). *Designing qualitative studies*. New York: Sage.

Creswell, J. W., & Tashakkori, A. (2007). Differing perspectives on mixed methods research. *Journal of Mixed Methods Research, 1*(4), 303–308.

Eden, C., & Huxham, C. (Eds.). (2002). *Action research*. Thousand Oaks, CA: Sage.

Hofstede, G. (1991). *Culture and organizations: Software of the mind*. New York: McGraw-Hill.

Kleijnen, J. P. C., Beers, W. V., & Nieuwenhuyse, I. V. (2010). Constrained optimization in expensive simulation: Novel approach. *European Journal of Operational Research, 202*(1), 164–174.

Kleijnen, J. P. C., Pierreval, H., & Zhang, J. (2011). Methodology for determining the acceptability of system designs in uncertain environments. *European Journal of Operational Research, 209*(2), 176–183.

Little, J. D. C. (1961). A proof of the queuing formula: L = W. *Operations Research, 9*(3), 383–387.

Little, J. D. C. (2004). Models and managers: The concept of a decision calculus. *Management Science Journal, 50*(12), 1841–1853.

McDonald, S. (2005). Studying actions in context: A qualitative shadowing method for organizational research. *Journal of Qualitative Research, 5*(4), 455–473.

Mercer, A. (1977). An education in operational research: A personal viewpoint. *European Journal of Operational Research, 1*(6), 352–360.

Patriksson, M. (2008). A survey on the continuous nonlinear resource allocation problem. *European Journal of Operational Research, 185*(1), 1–46.

Sharp, R. G., & Dando, M. R. (1979). Decision resource management and practical intervention in conflicts—a model and its implications. *European Journal of Operational Research, 3*(4), 283–295.

Souza, M. J. F., Coelho, I. M., Ribas, S., Santos, H. G., & Merschmann, L. H. C. (2010). A hybrid heuristic algorithm for the open-pit-mining operational planning problem. *European Journal of Operational Research, 207*(2), 1041–1051.

Strang, K. D. (2009a). How multicultural learning approach impacts grade for international university students in a business course. *Asian English Foreign Language Journal Quarterly, 11*(4), 271–292. Retrieved from http://www.asian-efl-journal.com /December_2009_ks.php.

Strang, K. D. (2009b). Using recursive regression to explore nonlinear relationships and interactions: A tutorial applied to a multicultural education study. *Practical Assessment, Research & Evaluation, 14*(3), 1–13. Retrieved from http://pareonline.net /getvn.asp?v=14&n=3.

Strang, K. D. (2010). Global culture, learning style and outcome: An interdisciplinary empirical study of international students. *Journal of Intercultural Education, 21*(6), 519–533. Retrieved from http://www.tandfonline.com/doi/abs/10.1080/14675986.2010.53 3034#preview.

Strang, K. D. (2011). A grounded theory study of cellular phone new product development. *International Journal of Internet and Enterprise Management, 7*(4), 366–387. Retrieved from http://www.inderscience.com/browse/index.php?journalID=39&year =2011&vol=7&issue=4.

Strang, K. D. (2012a). Importance of verifying queue model assumptions before planning with simulation software. *European Journal of Operational Research, 218*(2), 493–504. Retrieved from http://www.sciencedirect.com/science/article/pii/S0377221711010319.

Strang, K. D. (2012b). Student diaspora and learning style impact on group performance. *International Journal of Online Pedagogy and Course Design, 2*(3), 1–19. Retrieved from http://www.igi-global.com/article/student-diaspora-learning-style-impact/68410.

Strang, K. D. (2012c). Multicultural face of organizations. In M. A. Sarlak (Ed.), *The new faces of organizations in the 21st century* (Vol. 5, pp. 1–21). Toronto, ON: North American Institute of Science and Information Technology (NAISIT). Retrieved from http:// naisit.org/book/detail/id/6.

Sturgul, J. R. (1999). Discrete mine system simulation in the United States. *International Journal of Surface Mining, Reclamation and Environment, 13*(1), 37–41.

Taylor, B. W. (2010). *Introduction to management science* (10th ed.). New York: Prentice-Hall.

Vidal, R. V. V. (1992). History of mathematical programming: A collection of personal reminiscences. *European Journal of Operational Research, 62*(1), 124–125.

Worthington, D. (2009). Reflections on queue modelling from the last 50 years. *Journal of the Operational Research Society, 60*(1), S83-S92.

22

Participant Observation as Ethnography or Ethnography as Participant Observation in Organizational Research

Peter John Sandiford

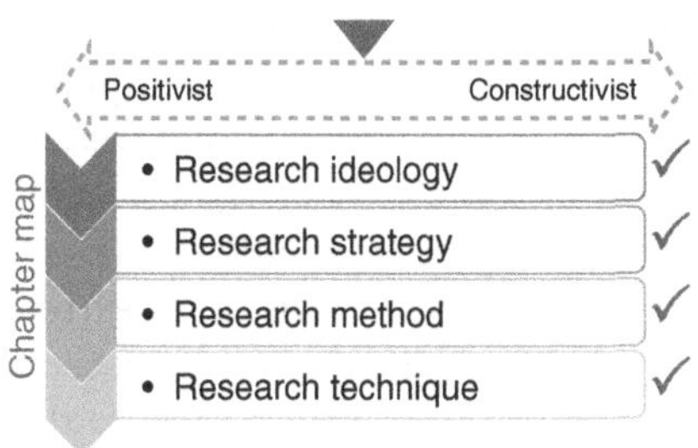

Chapter overview

Sandiford's contribution is a good example of the interpretative variation of the pragmatist research ideology, which is obviously his philosophy underlying this, and that which underlies the ethnography-observation-participation dilemma he critically analyzes in this chapter. His within-group qualitative unit of analysis focuses on "the implications of participating or only observing when conducting ethnography during organizational field studies" (editor's interpretation). It is customary for a researcher at the far right of the pragmatist ideology—but not quite constructivist—to take an interpretative approach while encouraging participants to assist in the reflection and clarification in the meaning of the data and phenomena collected. His approach seems close to action research insofar as he advocates the researcher to participate in ethnography so as to promote a better expression of the phenomena from the sociocultural perspectives of the participants as a whole. Speaking from my own experience, I advise researchers to clarify their research design ideology, otherwise they are likely to have their manuscripts returned from fundamentalists at the end of a double-blind peer-review process due to incorrectly applying a formal methodology.

Introduction

> The whole development of physical science has been a process of combining theory and observation; and in general every item of physical knowledge—or at least every item to which attention is ordinarily directed—has a partly observational and partly theoretical basis...Thus our axiom that all physical knowledge is of an observational nature is not to be understood as excluding theoretical knowledge. I know [emphasis original] the position of Jupiter last night. That is knowledge of an observational nature; it is possible to detail the observational procedure that yields the quantities (right ascension and declination) which express my knowledge of the planet's position.
>
> As a matter of fact I did not follow this procedure...I looked it up in the Nautical Almanac. That gave me the result of a computation according to planetary theory: It is the essence of acceptance of a theory that we agree to obliterate the distinction between knowledge derived from it and knowledge derived from actual observation. It may seem one-sided that the obliteration of the distinction should render all physical knowledge observational in nature. But not even the most extreme worshipper of theory has proposed the reverse—that in accepting the results of an observational research as trustworthy we elevate them to the status of theoretical conclusions. The one-sidedness is due to *our acceptance of observation, not theory, as the Supreme Court of Appeal* [emphasis added]. (Eddington, 1958, pp. 10–11)

Why observe?

Direct observation is an integral part of many types of research, indeed as shown in the opening quotation, it is often seen as the most convincing form of evidence (I believe what I can see), although it is often sidelined in the business and management field. It is not always clear why this is the case, although the preponderance of a questionnaire survey and interview studies in the literature could suggest that it is often considered more appropriate (perhaps, if more cynically, researchers may consider it easier) to ask research subjects questions about their experiences, attitudes, motivations etc. However, it would probably be foolish to ignore the methodological advantages of observation for many investigations into human areas of activity. Certainly researchers in other fields cannot really avoid observation of one form or another; researchers could hardly ask atoms and molecules (physics, chemistry), weather systems (meteorology), animals, plants (biology), or long dead people (history) why they behave the way they do/did; of course, positivist researchers in the natural sciences have long recognized the significance of observation within experimental design, with observation formally preceding and following, and, more informally during experimental interventions. However, despite the obvious advantages of being able to ask questions of our research subjects, we do need to be aware of the limitations of resultant data—it is clear that all questionnaire/interview data are perceptual to some extent, something that often seems to be ignored when reporting research involving hypothesis testing. Asking a customer about a purchasing behavior will inevitably result in partial data affected by such factors as imperfect memory, influences of mood, post-purchase experiences, interviewer impact, questionnaire design and question/item wording, possible intentional distortion of events (lying), etc. It would be unreasonable to expect subjects to recall and explain all such influences in a retrospective interview or questionnaire survey. Behaviorist researchers focus their attention on avoiding such issues by experimental design involving careful control of variables, rather than asking questions of their interview subjects while phenomenologists embrace them as enriching a co-constructed understanding of the world, while participant observers seek to be actively present and "by observing and reflecting on what he/she is observing, the researcher may capture service innovation activities [or other organizational phenomena] and issues that are taken for granted by the team members, and thus would never surface in a retrospective interview" (von Koskull & Strandvik, 2014, p. 144).

There is a long and rich tradition of observation in the social science literature, much of it involving some level of fieldworker participation in the research context. Certainly, much of the observation research conducted in business and management has a tendency toward some level of participation. The positivist ideal of objectivity and researcher separation from the observed is often difficult if not impossible in this sort of context, unless using non-intrusive tools such as hidden camera equipment. The stereotypical image of a time-and-motion researcher observing workers with a stopwatch and clipboard is a clear example of a low-level type of participation (certainly it could not be seen as unobtrusive) albeit less obviously than ethnographic fieldworkers. This chapter explores the value and practice of observation, and participant observation in particular, as a data collection technique for organizational based research. It draws on my own personal experiences conducting and supervising students utilizing participant observation in organization settings. To differentiate these from other examples given in the literature, short excerpts will be included from my own research publications. The next section seeks to define and conceptualize participant observation, especially focusing on different types and levels of participation and their relative advantages and limitations. This then develops into a discussion of the practicalities and challenges of conducting observational research and analyzing the resultant data. I should note here that a single chapter cannot hope to provide a full and balanced account of why and how researchers can engage in participant observation; rather it provides a personalized perspective, albeit based on relevant literature and personal experience. I will focus on what I have found to be important and challenging methodological issues, often framed around apparent paradoxes, rather than striving to give "the whole story" of this method.

Conceptualizing participant observation

Participant observation as ethnography: Ethnography as participant observation?

As with other areas of research, the terminology and jargon of participant observation can be confusing. For example, some researchers seem to use participant observation as a synonym for ethnography (it is also used more or less interchangeably with "fieldwork" in social research as well). Without getting too involved in a methodological discussion of ethnography here, it is probably sufficient to see ethnography as an approach to or strategy for research (or a methodology), while participant observation is a specific technique used to collect data. However, researchers planning to conduct participant observation would be well advised to explore the ethnographic literature, if only because this is the primary data collection technique of the ethnographer. For example, Spradley's (1980) readable text titled "Participant Observation" also reads as an introduction to ethnographic fieldwork more generally. His introduction sees this as "participating in activities, asking questions, eating strange foods, learning a new language, observing play, interviewing informants and hundreds of other things" (p. 3), with most of these activities representing participatory elements of the research, while the observation element is about trying to watch, record, and make sense of these experiences. The idea that participation involves activities beyond observation is further complicated by the apparent inclusion of interviewing. Certainly, it would be almost unthinkable for an observer to participate in a social situation without engaging in conversation with other participants, and such conservations are very likely (almost inevitably) to involve some sort of informal interviewing from time to time, with the fieldworker asking about an observed and/or shared phenomenon. Thus, participant observation could also be seen as "observation +," with participation effectively seen as a means of attempting to make sense of and contextualize observed data.

Taking part in the observed social group (whether a village, neighborhood, or work organization) has two key elements in itself, and these are not always easy to separate analytically. First, participant observers tend to be physically and socially close to their research subjects/participants, something that enables probing questioning when seeking explanations of phenomena observed. Thus, interviews (both formal and informal) can more readily be about shared phenomena and experiences rather than "stand-alone" interviews. Second, observers actually experience many (and the level and depth of these is closely linked to the time spent in the field and approach to participation) of the sociocultural experiences that they are researching firsthand. As Spradley (1980, p. 51) points out, "participation allows you to experience activities directly, to get a feel of what events are like, and to record your own perceptions," essentially personalizing the research for the researcher (something that positivists who seek objectivity and separation of researcher from researched would be very uncomfortable with). However, this approach to research is very similar to the way humans learn in social situations; it could be argued that we are all conducting participant observation of a kind when we learn to live in society—we are likely to consider that living and working in a new culture is a very effective way of learning about it. Thus, fieldworkers seeking to understand customer experience or the demands of working in a particular job can, to some extent, actually experience these themselves; a researcher investigating an organization's formal induction program for new staff and/or informal socialization processes can go through these in person. A useful way of thinking about this is to see the fieldworker not just as collecting data, but recognizing that "it is the researcher who is the main instrument of social investigation" (Burgess 1984, p. 79). So, rather than questionnaires or interviews as instruments, by participating, the observer actually takes on this role in person. Such a view suggests that participant observation is necessarily a duality, as Taylor (2006, p. 85) suggests "a pair of essentially inseparable things—'two sides of the same coin' perhaps," or even multiple possible dualities, such as observer-member (participant), colleague-researcher, customer-researcher, investigator-as-instrument, etc.

Observers who participate; Participants who observe

As suggested above, the level, type, and approach to participation plays a significant role in the research project. Different researchers have suggested models of differing types and levels of participation during fieldwork. Junker's (1960) typology, developed and popularized by Gold (1958), is often cited in the literature, based on a continuum from a complete observer (who "attempts to observe people in ways which make it unnecessary for them to take him into account," 1958, p. 221) through to a complete participant (who fully joins the group/culture being studied). Along this continuum he suggests two conceptual increments of observer as participant and participant as observer, each suggesting an emphasis on either participation or observation. It is significant that Gold (1958, p. 219) stresses that "the true identity and purpose of the complete participant in field research are not known to those whom he [*sic*] observes" and that participant as observer is "similar" in role, but without any pretense. Thus, the type/level of participation is similar for both, only differentiated by whether the fieldwork is overt or covert. In addition to this, the observer as participant is also narrowly defined, though not in terms of any pretense or not; rather, it is specified as "one-visit" data collection, involving more "formal" observation and interviews (1958, p. 221). Based on these definitions, the majority of research involving participant observation seems likely to fall into the participant as observer category, partly due to the likelihood of much covert research being discouraged by increasing expectations/requirements regarding informed consent by universities and publishers, and partly due to a recognition that very short-term fieldwork is likely to be rather superficial, lacking the richness depth of longer-term studies.

Popular as this model is, Spradley's (1980, pp. 58–62) participation types seem to be a little more nuanced and analytically sensitive, not least because it is not limited to the overt-covert issue outlined above. His approach is also based on a scale including:

- nonparticipation, normally requiring some sort of separation from the observed individuals, perhaps watching video recordings or televised activities;
- passive participation where the observer is present in the field, but avoids interaction as far as possible, perhaps acting as a shadower;
- moderate participation involves rather more interaction with other actors/participants in the field, perhaps involving a slight change over time, with passivity being overcome by taking part in some of the activities observed;
- active participation occurs when the fieldworker actively seeks to do and experience what the observed people are doing, perhaps seeking to learn a skill associated with that group in order to seek greater understanding (first hand); and
- complete participation tends to occur when ethnographers research a context that they already participate in, turning their own "ordinary situations in which they are members into research settings" (p. 61).

Here, the types of participation are somewhat more subtle, for example, nonparticipation and passive participation both seem to be included in the complete observer role as Gold's (1958) definition implies that presence in the field is possible without participation if observation is covert and with a conscious effort to avoid any interaction (hence including passive participation). The key apparent difference in the complete participant here seems to be intent; he specifically links these to two particular dangers of fieldwork, namely "going native" if the fieldworker "incorporate[s] the [participant] role into his self-conceptions and achieve[s] self-expression in the role, but find[s] he has so violated his observer role that it is almost impossible to report his findings (Gold

1958, p. 220); he defines the second danger as "ethnocentrism," or the opposite of going native, "whenever a field worker cannot or will not interact meaningfully with an informant" (p. 222) and is in danger of ignoring the informant/research participant's perspective.

Another advantage of the latter model is an apparent acknowledgment that participant-observers can move along the scale (in either or both directions) as their fieldwork emerges and develops. It presents a more flexible and sensitive typology that allows for fluid and changing roles without the apparently rather narrow, covert-overt focus on Gold's (1958) definitions. For instance, Spradley's variation of complete participation may or may not be covert. Indeed, any of Spradley's roles could be either overt or covert while presenting a rather more conceptually sensitive model for researchers to use, especially when reflecting on their own fieldwork planning and experiences and seems to be more helpful in identifying any shifts in their roles during fieldwork.

Figure 22.1 provides a comparison of the two models that demonstrates differences in emphasis and apparent conceptual overlapping of Gold's (1958) categories, highlighting the apparent issues of field relations from an ethnocentric/going native perspective and indicating the covert/overt divide; this issue will be explored more later in the chapter.

The above discussion may at first seem rather fussy and lacking in significance. However, it has considerable implications for any fieldworker. As with many aspects of research, there is a certain tension between the methodological pulls of research demands/requirements. Peberdy (1993, p. 55) points out that "the participant observer is attempting to combine both involvement and detachment" and this separation of roles is very challenging, if indeed it is

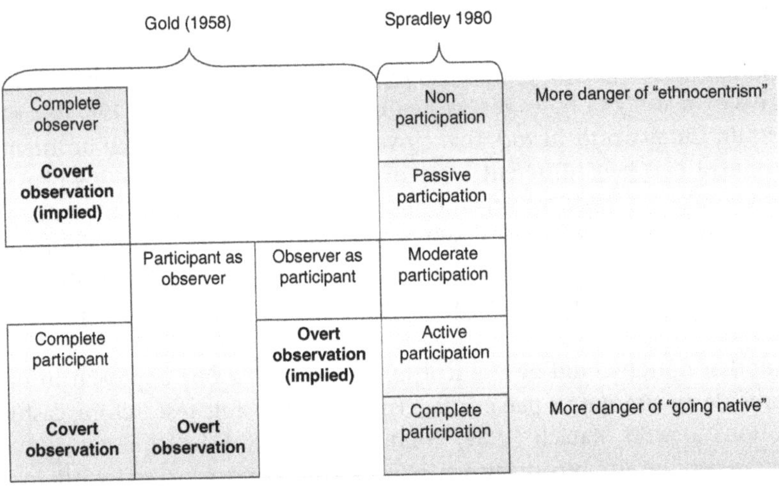

Figure 22.1 Fieldworker roles.

possible at all. This is often seen as a key limitation, or at least a challenging dilemma, of the technique. Bourdieu (2003, pp. 281–282) agrees with this:

> Inherent difficulty of such a posture has often been noted, which presupposes a kind of doubling of consciousness that is arduous to sustain. How can one be both subject and object, the one who acts and the one who, as it were, watches himself acting? What is certain is that one is right to cast doubt on the possibility of truly participating in foreign practices, embedded as they are in the tradition of another society and, as such, presupposing a learning process different from the one of which the observer and her dispositions are the product; and therefore a quite different manner of being and living through the experiences in which she purports to participate.

Although the decision about participation must fit the researcher's philosophical orientation and specific research questions, it will also inevitably be influenced by practicality. Such practicality will relate closely to the setting being researched—for example, a researcher setting out to investigate the work of a lawyer overtly by observing lawyers at work in their natural setting would find it difficult to do so as a full participant observer unless qualified and working as a lawyer already. Thus access to the field would be dependent partly on the legal/occupational context (requiring qualifications and professional membership to practice) and partly on finding a law firm prepared to cooperate in such a study. An alternative may be to observe by shadowing; McDonald (2005) does see such shadowing as somewhat different from participant observation as it tends to focus on a single observed person. It could also be argued that it is in the shadower's interest to avoid participating in the observer's activities to avoid contaminating the setting. However, it seems that a certain level of participation is inevitable, no matter how unobtrusive the fieldworker strives to be. Even this divide is not always straightforward. For example, when discussing his own study of hotel general managers, Jauncey (1999, p. 194) described a certain fluidity of fieldwork that "involves a constant and often unintended movement between" different types of participant observation; his plan was to undertake "indirect participant observation" by shadowing his managers, but as much of this occurred in public areas of their hotels, he found himself being approached by guests who assumed he was a member of staff and on occasion he found himself switching "to direct involvement in the work of the operation."

Another option could be to incorporate more than one approach in order to provide an alternative perspective. For example, while researching cashiers' emotions at work Rafaeli (1989) conducted fieldwork in supermarkets, initially observing unobtrusively while acting as a customer and without the cashiers' explicit consent. Later in the research, the observation became more participatory when she actually trained and worked as a cashier for the same company, potentially balancing Peberdy's (1993) opposing requirements of involvement and detachment. Martin (2014) also conducted both participant and nonparticipant observations in her study of "hidden labor" among migrant women in the United States; she "helped with administrative work, made phone calls, helped to organize a health fair and researched grant and funding sources" and pointed out the following:

> The volunteer strategy [i.e. the participation as a volunteer] was beneficial in terms of my research goals, as it allowed me to see activities conducted by staff members that are not part of official programs or events. The informal, day-to-day interactions of staff and clients held a great deal of interest for me; in these "ordinary" encounters of clients and staff, the mission of the organization is negotiated and mediated. (Martin, 2014, p. 19)

Thus, although active participation may not always be possible due to practical concerns, it is likely that if such participation is possible, in Martin's case as a volunteer and in Rafaeli's case as a trainee cashier, aspects of the organization, occupation, and stakeholder experience were likely to be more discernible partly through personal experience (happening to the observer) and partly through a greater level of access to the researched setting and participants.

When considering the type and level of participation, it can also be useful to assess your relative "nativeness"; Narayan's (1993) analysis drew attention to the value and dangers of conducting fieldwork in an environment that the fieldworker is familiar with (i.e., native to). Certainly, there are advantages and disadvantages in holding preconceived ideas about and bias toward the research setting; familiarity may ease access and help overcome initial barriers to entry; for example, as suggested earlier, it is likely to be very difficult for a nonlawyer to gain access to observe in a law firm, while overfamiliarity with a setting may well "breed contempt," however unintentionally. Native fieldworkers are probably more likely to struggle to attain the openness to experience, or contextual naivety, that is so important for effective observation—possibly missing mundane (to them) phenomena, due to prior socialization into the environment and perhaps even lack the legitimacy of the researcher with other fieldworkers (if other participants perceive the fieldworker more as a colleague than a researcher they may be less responsive to informal interviewing during fieldwork). In my own ethnography of public houses (pubs) I explored this:

> Certainly, with considerable prior experience in pub work the fieldworker should be considered as...a native ethnographer with some existing knowledge of this type of environment. Quite apart from any such bias or research error, the influence of the participant observer on the individuals and

> culture studied is also an issue in the study of people. Although ethnographers should seek to minimise any such influence or impact, it seems unreasonable to expect that such participation can avoid at least some such "reactivity." (Hammersley 1992, p. 163)

Care must also be taken by researchers conducting participant observation, especially when defining the fieldworker's role in the society studied. Reinharz (1997, p. 5) identified a number of researcher selves, each of whom had a particular type of influence when in the field. These selves were categorized in three areas: "research based selves"—relating specifically to the research role (e.g., being an observer); "brought selves"—which are more personal and provide a sense of individuality; and "situationally created selves," which may or may not be related to the research project (e.g., being a temporary member of the studied group). When reading the field notes it was often possible to identify when specific selves had dominance over others. There were times when the situationally created self as a member of bar staff was predominant, especially when dealing with either difficult or "good" customers (or colleagues) or at busy times when work demands could sometimes take temporary precedence over observation:

> Such dangers of participant observation are well documented, and require consideration by fieldworkers. Questions of fieldworker role identification are relevant here. For example, is the predominant role observation or participation (observer-as-participant or participant-as-observer)? It may be rather presumptuous for an ethnographer to claim to take only one or the other role type throughout the fieldwork experience, much as it is difficult to clearly delineate which "selves" are dominant at any one time. This is where a reflexive approach to writing ethnography can help both writer and reader. (Sandiford, 2004, p. 99)

The idea of reflexivity is introduced in the excerpt as a possible tool to explore the roles and selves of the participant observer. Such an idea is widely recognized as a key factor in doing and reporting qualitative research in general. Hammersley and Atkinson (1995, p. 16) explain that reflexivity "implies that the orientations of researchers will be shaped by their socio-historical locations, including the values and interests that these locations confer on them" and that, inevitably, "the particular biography of the researcher" will influence their data collection, analysis, interpretation, and conclusions. Although this is probably so for all social researchers, whatever their philosophical orientation, it is perhaps especially so for participant-observers, due to the intentional participation in the research context and the idea of self-as-instrument, raised earlier, that clearly accentuates the reflexive nature of the research. Thus, it is of considerable importance that fieldworkers should recognize and explore the reflexive nature of their position in the field and in relation to other participants. However, any resultant categorization of role/self is rarely simple. For example, Rafaeli's (1989) "unstructured" observation, when posing as a customer, could indeed be perceived as "unobtrusive" by seeking to avoid attracting attention. However, her presence in the research setting is indeed likely to have some impact on the participants, however minor. Even using video technology would be obtrusive to some extent unless the equipment is hidden and covert, although this has been included in the continuum to identify extremes along the continuum. Similarly, "total" immersion in the field is unlikely to ever be absolutely total, if only because the role of researcher will impinge on the fieldworker's behavior, otherwise the exercise becomes participation with no focused observation. As Spradley (1980, p. 51) asserts "the ethnographer [or researcher conducting participant observation] can hardly ever become a complete participant in a social situation," as the necessity of seeing observation as data collection with a purpose (to answer research questions) will always require some distance from the observed group/phenomenon. However, he does suggest that just such a complete participant could develop into or later become a participant-observer if s/he chooses to conduct research into the organization or occupation that they participate in; for example Spradley and Mann's (1975) research in a cocktail bar developed from Mann's existing employment there, Pierce's (1995) work on paralegals was inspired by her earlier experience working as a paralegal; and my own research into pubs (Sandiford, 2004) was facilitated by a lifetime as customer and employee in licensed premises.

Doing the observation

As with any form of research, the best place to start with any participant observation investigation is the literature. Many books, articles, theses, and other publications are available, making the first challenge literature selection—no one can hope to read everything. Because of this, there is a danger of being too focused in your reading; if you are planning to conduct a study of a fast food restaurant do not just read hospitality studies. However different the research context may seem, the key challenges and issues are quite similar in many ways. The literature can be usefully divided into two key types:

First the methodological literature that explores participant observation can provide an invaluable introduction to the philosophies, techniques, and critical arguments associated with the method. This can include critical philosophical and methodological discussions (Hammersley & Atkinson, 1995) and more "practical" explanations and guides to conducting fieldwork (Spradley, 1980). Always try to focus on specialist sources rather than the broad student textbooks that provide a general introduction to research methods.

Second, the empirical literature often includes useful insights into and suggestions about the conduct of participant observation. This is not always the case as journals often work to very strict word limits and writing up this sort of research is always demanding within such requirements, often leading to accounts of fieldwork practice being trimmed in favor of data analysis and theoretical discussion. It can be a challenging exercise to find much helpful guidance in such articles, but it is certainly worth exploring such articles for invaluable, often hidden, fieldwork "hints and tips" (and readers should not feel limited to methodology/research design sections for these). For example, O'Connell Davidson (2008) gave considerable attention to the issue of informed consent as this was of particular significance to her work exploring the particularly sensitive area of sex work and, as will be discussed later in the chapter, Korczynski's (2007) paper on factory workers and music in the workplace gives some attention to establishing participant trust as that was seen as particularly significant given the context of his study.

There are numerous examples of book-length accounts of ethnographic work that give detailed and insightful accounts of participant observation. Classic studies such as Foote-Whyte's (1955) can be worthy of attention. His discussion of fieldwork in an American urban "slum" offers personal insights into the challenges and value of this sort of fieldwork in different kinds of community. Of more obvious relevance to organizational research are books such as Cavendish's (1982) introduction to her fascinating, if impressionistic, account of her experiences participating with and observing the position of women employed in twentieth-century factories. This is a useful example of Spradley's (1980) category of complete participation, as Cavendish's research started not so much as participant observation, but as a personal decision to seek and experience the life of a factory worker, and much of her work was based on her reflections about the experience afterward. Such monographs may lack some of the scholarly precision and succinctness required by journal editors and reviewers, but they often provide the novice participant-observer with insights regarding the conduct of fieldwork that can be lacking in word-limited scholarly articles.

Often the two types of literature do overlap. For example, in his entertaining account of his own research in the Cameroon, anthropologist Nigel Barley (1983) gives a "warts and all" description of the challenges of conducting fieldwork in a very different environment to his own. Early in his book he points out that he plans to give a detailed account of some of the more practical challenges facing researchers conducting this sort of fieldwork in challenging and often alien environments; he explained that he will

> dwell precisely on those aspects that the normal ethnographic monograph punctuates out as "not anthropology", "irrelevant", "unimportant"...this book may, then, serve to redress the balance and show students and, it is hoped, non-anthropologists, how the finished monograph relates to the

"bleeding chunks" of raw reality on which it is based, and convey something of the feel of fieldwork to those who have not had that experience. (Barley, 1983, p. 10)

The aspects of anthropological fieldwork (participant observation) that he draws attention to are the day-to-day practicalities and challenges of living and working in an unfamiliar setting for research purposes. He discusses the difficulties of dealing with alien bureaucracies, negotiating access, climate, food and, particularly graphically, diseases. Although few researchers in the field of business and management can expect the same actual experiences as in Nigel Barley's "mud hut," the insights of doing participant observation and his interactions with his research participants have a methodological relevance that can rarely (if ever) be found in precisely worded scholarly work subject to strict word limits, evaluation criteria, and academically rigorous reviewers.

In addition to playing the role of the basic level of participant, discussed earlier, the fieldworkers' role(s) are of considerable importance here: Will the participation be as some sort of employee or customer or maybe something in between the two? For example, Bowen's (2009, p. 1516) study of a group of tourists seems to leave this question open somewhat when he describes the tour group that he participated in as "9 tourist participants plus the tour group leader and the author." From this, does the reader see Bowen as a tourist (customer) or something else? This also raises the question of how he was perceived by the other group members. In my own research into English pubs, in my first study (Sandiford 2004), I lived with three relatively clear, if not always separable, roles as employee (being a paid member of staff, granted access by senior and unit management), researcher conducting an overt study, and, to some at least, student (on one occasion during a rather heated in-service encounter with a chef, he made it clear that students were not his favorite type of human being). However, during most of the fieldwork, it was clear that the employee role was most recognized by other participants given the nature of our interactions. The second study (Sandiford & Divers, 2011) was actually rather more difficult from a personal perspective; taking the role of customer in my local village pubs, I needed to renegotiate (with employers, customers, my cofieldworker, and myself) my position in those places as we both took on our additional role of fieldworker. This was more uncomfortable and challenging than I had expected as an experienced participant-observer, mainly because I was beginning to observe professionally individuals and places that I was at least partly familiar with before the research began.

Getting started

One of the key skills of the participant-observer is to identify and analyze both the mundane and the extraordinary in a given social setting. It may be tempting to focus on and emphasize unusual behaviors, especially when observing relatively familiar settings, such as work organizations in one's own native land, if only because of a sort of tacit familiarity with the cultural environment; this contrasts with research into very different cultures where the most mundane of activities may seem striking and fascinating to a fieldworker. It could actually be argued that, paradoxically, mundanity may be more significant to people (and researchers investigating their culture/way of life), if only because it is likely to be more representative of the way they live their lives on a day-to-day basis. In order to draw out, analyze, and make sense of behavior, whether mundane or not, while actually observing and participating, it is important for fieldworkers to adopt a level of openness to social phenomena whenever possible, striving to avoid making assumptions about phenomena based on preconceived ideas. One tool that can help in this process is the keeping of field notes or a field diary/journal. Quite apart from providing a detailed record of the participant observation based on "relatively concrete descriptions of social process and their contexts" (Hammersley & Atkinson, 1995, p. 175) the writing (and rereading) of field notes can help to uncover and reflect on what has been observed and experienced, revisiting the day's (and previous days') events. Indeed, Okely (1992, p. 16) suggests that participant-observers learn "through the verbal, the transcript [and] through the senses" striving to develop a "total knowledge." She goes on to point out that field notes contribute to this as an additional data source, as they may "be no more than a trigger for bodily and hitherto subconscious memories" implying that thorough field notes can when analyzed serve as more than a record of observations, also potentially triggering deeper memories of an experience, acting as a sort of catalyst for insight. An example of this is given below, where revisiting more descriptive field notes contributed to conceptual development after the event, even to the extent that I incorporated literature that I was familiar with from my proposal development and fieldwork preparation (the following is quoted verbatim from the field notes):

...the following was written after a rather busy evening

> For some reason I was on a real high all evening—something I hadn't experienced here yet (although I'm usually happy enough) perhaps because I got a real buzz from being busily active. It was quite demanding to keep up at times, with a number of demands at the same time. You don't get much chance to chat with anyone, but most of the customers acknowledge that you've got other demands on your time. Even so there are opportunities to pass a few comments with some of the customers, locals or residents, and the atmosphere is more fun and energetic. I do enjoy the occasional quiet talk with a small group of drinkers or diners, but there is less feeling of doing something, it's more like "professional socialising." When you're

> busy with colleagues running around like headless chickens it always seems more fun, like a party. (Sandiford, 2004, p. 203)

This was written early in the second period of fieldwork, and the weekly reflections returned to the issue, considering why this sort of experience is pleasurable:

> Rereading about Wednesday's "buzz" made me think a bit. It reminds me of the pleasure and satisfaction of holding a dinner party for friends. I'd insist on doing all the cooking and it'd all have to be "just so." This'd mean that I'd generally miss out on lots of the conversation, running about cooking, but I'd still be able to snatch some chat along the way, joining in for a couple of minutes, dashing off and then catching up later on. The technical side is good—getting everything organised; the social side is good—catching up with friends; the sense of achievement is good—making my friends happy. In a sense what happened on Wednesday was a temporary intensification of or "speeding-up" of service work with elements of emotion work—the idea that quantitatively intensifying professional socialising requires a different type of emotion management or emotional labour to the more common pub relationship. It can be great in small doses, but I wouldn't want to keep that level of effort up for too long!
>
> Work satisfaction is often more apparent at such times, despite the impracticality of offering levels of service and attention to individual customers that were also referred to in interviews as being important sources of what Tolich (1993, p. 368) would probably call "stressful satisfaction." This does seem somewhat at odds with a considerable portion of the literature that sees the quantity of emotion management or emotional labour as more stressful and likely to result in more chance of emotional exhaustion. Perhaps this is because such busy periods were not excessive and staff would be unlikely to be constantly "buzzing." Morris and Feldman (1996) did point out that interactive work that was especially emotionally intense and of longer duration are more likely to have adverse effects, while in the pub environment emotional intensity was often less possible when very busy. Even if a single customer was being difficult. (Sandiford, 2004, p. 206)

Asking other participants for explanations is another key part of the process, rather than attributing observed behaviors with the fieldworker's own cultural mores. However, this is not without its practical issues, especially as follows:

> Other participants may occasionally be bemused by the apparently naïf questioning of an ethnographer, especially... [if the fieldworker is known to have] prior work experience in the type of work that they are engaged in. (Sandiford, 2004, p. 100)

As suggested earlier, in many ways the practice of participant observation in work organizations can be similar to that of a new employee, apprentice, or student intern gaining work experience, in that both fieldworker and apprentice/intern are likely to be experiencing a particular context for the first time (even if they are familiar with the actual place, the context of work experience or fieldwork adds a new dimension), both are (ideally) seeking to learn about that context whether from a fieldwork or employment context and both have a level of what Lave and Wenger (1991) call "legitimate peripheral participation," at least an overt fieldworker with negotiated access does. This concept seems particularly pertinent to the participant-observer on many levels; we could see the legitimacy of both as being related to being formally accepted by other participants as members, whether temporary or permanent. However, the idea of legitimacy can go further in that both are recognized as learners/researchers (i.e., novices with an intention to learn for a particular purpose—interns seeking work experience, apprentices learning occupational expertise, and fieldworkers seeking to answer specific research questions)—this is particularly important to enable them to ask the often naïve-sounding questions necessary to learn about how things are done and why they are the way they are. The peripheral nature emphasizes the different types of membership that both have within the social group—both "belong" as a special type of member, but both are inevitably peripheral to the core, group of full members; and of course, both necessarily participate in at least some aspects of the everyday life of the social group. This sort of legitimized peripheral participation is quite common in the participant observation/ethnographic literature on organizations. For example Korczynski (2007, p. 259) explained how this takes place:

> "Because I was not a normal worker (and also because I was not being paid for my labor by the firm [peripheral]), I had some latitude [legitimization] to walk around the shop floor and talk with people [participate and observe] beyond the immediate milieu of my worktable" [annotations added].

This also highlights the challenge of achieving access to an organization for the participant-observer. Korczynski's participant role was that of overt, unpaid worker, negotiated with management and legitimized with his colleagues by his academic position. However, as suggested earlier, other researchers are likely to find it more challenging to gain access to work-participant roles due to barriers to entry into particular occupations. Thus, to take up a work role in an occupation (or organization) with higher barriers to entry, some level of qualification or professional status may be required in addition to negotiated organizational access. For example, Pierce's (1995) study of paralegals was, at least, partly facilitated by her experience as a paralegal earlier in her own career, while without the required legal qualifications and professional membership it is unlikely that she would have been able to conduct participant observation as a lawyer. Pierce's study is particularly interesting methodologically as she highlights how participant observation was conducted almost as a methodological compromise. She explains how she originally planned to conduct more unobtrusive observation with minimal, if any, participation. However, she found it impossible to gain access to any law firms as a researcher, and it was clear that potential gatekeepers were concerned with the implications of her study for a number of reasons. As a result, she decided to take a more participatory approach and become "a covert fieldworker" (Pierce, 1995, p. 19), gaining formal employment as a paralegal herself and keeping her fieldwork secret from her employer—in this case the level of deception is rather blurred as she was open with her role of research student and her research topic (paralegals' occupational stress) and she did conduct overt interviews; it was only the participant observation that was covert. She does discuss the ethics of this approach, essentially concluding that "there was more to be gained than lost from a study of this kind" (1995, p. 19).

It is also important to recognize that participant observation is "a strategy for both listening to people and watching them in natural settings" (Spradley, 1979, p. 32). Ethnographers are particularly focused on the need to collect data in such natural settings rather than conducting experiments in artificial environments that inevitably lack context of socially complex settings or surveying (by interview or questionnaire) research subjects away from the context/place of interest to the researcher. This is based on a need to "achieve access to the native's point of view" (Narayan, 1993, p. 672) and this can be obscured if the fieldworker cannot move beyond her/his own cultural lens. So there will inevitably be a certain tension between trying to find the native's way of understanding the world and interpreting this from a scholarly, theoretical perspective.

Watson and Watson (2012) suggest an additional aspect of fieldwork that adds an additional nuance to the models of participation/observation presented earlier. During their research into pubs, they recognized that other types of participation affected their investigation and provided additional sources of insight. They explained that, although their formal fieldwork took place in and around the pubs themselves, they were aware that these pubs need "to be understood as part of the society of which they are a part" and that

> This has meant treating our own daily lives in our home society as part of the research territory over which we have ranged. It has been done by our acting as "everyday" participant observers in our own society, recognizing that public houses and the narratives relating to them are part of the mundane, day-to-day functioning of our society. (Watson & Watson, 2012, p. 686)

They link this idea of being "everyday participant observers" with "everyday ethnography" rather than purely "organizational ethnographers," leading them to another approach:

> Take note of every occasion in their daily life when such matters come to their attention, so we have taken note of how friends, neighbours, strangers on trains, newspaper writers, people in public houses, characters in television programmes, and so on, speak about pubs. (2012, p. 686)

Thus, they draw from any relevant sources of data and evidence about their research area, drawing on the ethnographic principle of immersion within the society/culture being researched. So, as traditional ethnographers engaging in participant observation overseas would observe and participate in many different aspects of "native" life whatever their focus, organizational fieldworkers would benefit from this everyday participant observation rather than separating the formal field from the rest of their life when it takes place in the societal context of the organization being studied. This is essentially similar to the idea that an ethnographic fieldworker researching religion in a distant culture would not only participate and observe in and around the local temple, but would seek data relevant to the religious life of the society in other parts of the community's daily life. This is likely to be a challenging position to take in a fieldworker's own natural environment; whereas a fieldworker living and researching in an unusual place may be more attuned to everyday mundanity if only because of a general contextual strangeness (Watson, 2006).

What to observe; How to observe; What am I looking for?

As with any other type of research, participant observation needs to be guided by clear research questions and objectives. However, unlike more positivist approaches to research, such questions can evolve during the fieldwork, emerging from observational data over time. Hammersley and Atkinson (1995, p. 29) point out that "the aim of the pre-fieldwork phase (planning) and in the early stages of data collection is to turn the foreshadowed problems into a set of questions to which an answer can be given." The implication here is that the actual practice of participant observation contributes to the honing and focusing of research questions; they go on to suggest that sometimes "the original problems are transformed or even completely abandoned in favour of others" (1995, p. 29). The following excerpt illustrates how revisiting descriptive notes can inspire reflective analysis, insight, and further questions relating to the research topic. In this case, the topic of emotions in the workplace was developed in relation to a particular encounter with a customer (especially in relation to humor and anger) while raising the issue of forms of address that could then be explored more fully. Again, blue text indicates field note material.

...this is the record of the first time the fieldworker served a regular customer referred to as 'the General' who was obviously becoming a little senile:

> I did have one interesting customer—an old guy who had been in each day. Later I found out that all the others know him and he's the "General" and who could be a miserable sod (I could have worked that out for myself!) Our first conversation:
>
> "Are you going to fill this? [indicates empty ½ pint jug on bar]"
>
> "Certainly sir. [he looked like a 'sir'] What did you have in it?"
>
> "Speak up, I can't hear you!"
>
> "What would you like?"
>
> "Don't be so bloody stupid. What does everyone drink in England?"
>
> "But what type of beer would you like?"
>
> "I don't bloody know! Anything!"
>
> "Would Directors be OK?"
>
> "Yes, anything."
>
> (Service)
>
> "£1.13 please."
>
> "Help yourself. [cash on bar] Why is it more than last time?"
>
> "Our beers have different prices and I didn't know what you had last time."
>
> "[disgruntled Cough]"
>
> It's very difficult to get angry with such bad customers as they are so ridiculous and funny. After he'd left the customers on either side of him breathed big sighs of relief with amazed comments like, "Misery guts has finally gone!"

In a relatively short entry the content and flavour of the interaction was captured and available for fuller reflection, analysis and "re-experience" when time allowed. This excerpt contains a variety of ideas that were discussed in earlier findings' chapters in the thesis. Especially noticeable is the coping mechanism (hardly a planned strategy) of being amused by customers and situations that may otherwise inspire anger or frustration. It is perhaps significant that "in the heat of the moment" when recording the encounter the idea that "it's very difficult" to lose your temper. This does not suggest that the fieldworker was trying to be angry, but it seems to be a rhetorical device written to "self" to stress the idea that anger was the last thing on his mind at the time. But the very act of mentioning the concept could be seen as "protesting" too much?

Another personal observation alluded to during the passage is the form of address—the minor aside "he looked like a sir" has implications for the study. How does an employee judge which approach each customer expects? In the individualistic pub environment many such customer analyses are carried out by staff. The concept of using honorifics to depersonalize encounters was referred to earlier in the thesis as a coping strategy, and the fieldworker did find himself using "sir" and "madam" more than in previous working environments. He was often more cautious with "mate" and other informal terms as forms of address, partly because of the nature of the Coaching Inn Company, and partly as a response to the habits of colleagues (being socialised by imitation). However, the value of the technique was obvious in some situations with difficult or unpleasant customers (Sandiford, 2004, pp. 240–241).

This emergence/development of research questions during data collection and analysis ties in with the big questions about any form of observation, especially "what am I actually looking for?" As observational data are collected overtime, this sort of study rarely seeks the sort of snapshot provided in cross-section research; rather it builds up a rich database that can be seen as developmental and growing in focus (Spradley, 1980). This may not be longitudinal in intention (i.e., not seeking to identify trends, changes, etc. over time), though it will often be so in effect. Fieldworkers often describe long periods of data collection; anthropologists can spend many years living in a studied community or return to it many times for further data collection. However, most organizational studies are rather shorter in length, with examples measured in days rather than months or years (e.g., Bowen's 2008 study involved participant observation of a 14-day tour). Despite this, it is clear that intensive, participatory research, also referred to as compressed ethnography (Jeffrey & Troman, 2004), will potentially provide a large number of phenomena to observe and make sense of. This is not to suggest that shorter studies are inferior to longer ones, especially when they, as with Bowen's work, focus on a necessarily time-delimited phenomenon such as an escorted tour or a specific organizational event. Indeed, this sort of investigation can often provide a particularly rich and deep data set if the intensity of the event/phenomenon is reflected adequately in the field record; because of this, such work does not necessarily fall into Gold's (1958) observer as participant category discussed earlier, as the intensity of participation does not really fit with the superficiality implied by his definition of the type of one-visit fieldwork he describes.

Perhaps one useful way of conceptualizing phenomena from a participant-observer's perspective is through the mundane-extraordinary divide introduced earlier. It is likely that much of what is and can be observed will be (or become) relatively mundane or ordinary, which may encourage the fieldworker to ignore this and seek out extraordinary (interesting, striking) phenomena to focus on. However, this may well be rather misguided, especially in a familiar setting (e.g., in the case of a native fieldworker or someone who has been collecting data for a long period of time). Paradoxically, it is likely that research questions seeking to understand organizational (or community) behaviors, morals, values, etc. would be better answered by focusing on the mundane, everyday, taken-for-granted aspects of that organization. So, an investigation into an organization's culture would need to explore and analyze day-to-day routines as much as the more highly visible periodic rituals. Schaffer (2000, p. 1) presents us with another paradox here, suggesting that mundane behavior can help us "recapture the extraordinary essence of our everyday lives." He suggests that focusing on the extraordinary can be hugely distorting. He uses the example of a hypothetical Martian anthropologist researching Humanity and basing its conclusions wholly on extreme behavior, especially that depicted by the popular and news media, and who would be likely to "leave this planet thinking that we're a bunch of freaks" (Schaffer, 2000, p. 2). Although this assertion could seem to lack a certain scholarly balance, notably the comment about freaks, the point is important; after all, initially the Martian anthropologist would not know which behavior is mundane and which is extraordinary and the two types would both require investigation in order to be able to categorize them as such. The problem with a human or already socialized being would be that the mundane is more likely to be taken for granted and even left out of the analytic processes.

As suggested in the previous section, an integral part of the data collection is the recording of actual observations; a participant observer's field notes are not wholly descriptive of observations made, but are likely to include reflective and reflexive commentary in order to maximize the participation:

> The primary type of data for the participant observation was a reflexive field diary recording specific observations and the experiences, thoughts and reflections of the fieldworker. Certainly at the end of the fieldwork this document (or five documents—one for each unit investigated) made up the bulk of the data, despite the numerous interview transcripts. Due to the nature of participating as a full time member of staff it was difficult to write notes during work shifts, thus most of the diary entries were made after each work period. These daily records were largely descriptive, documenting specific observations and thoughts. When more time was available, such as on days off, the writing took a more reflective approach. At such times the fieldworker would reread previous notes and think more deeply about the various issues raised. This exercise helped revisit and clarify various data, as well as planning subsequent data collection (especially relating to more focused observation and interviewing) and analysis.
>
> Certainly in this project the field diary was often written in a personal style of shorthand that would be little help for other individuals...Some notes were originally written with word-processing software, while others were wholly or partially written manually with informal annotations and reflections in the margin. As well as recording events and thoughts, and guiding the project's development, these notes provide a useful reflexive

> resource. The combination of the descriptive and more reflective types of record enabled the fieldworker to recall various aspects of the fieldwork during analysis, including specific observations, personal feelings and thought processes from the time. (Sandiford, 2004, pp. 101–102)

Challenges and issues: negotiating access, informed consent, and establishing rapport

Academic audiences tend to require researchers to discuss the problems or limitations of their work when writing up their research. It is all too easy to focus on what can be seen as inherent weaknesses (limitations) of a research method or a particular study. However, it is probably more academically healthy to show how a project has addressed research issues rather than assume an inevitable limitation. The three issues listed above are often seen as just difficulties or limitations associated with participant observation; however, these often seem to be exaggerated and, perhaps, can unnecessarily discourage researchers from this sort of research.

Due to the immersive and interactive nature of participant observation, a number of practical and potentially ethical issues face fieldworkers, not least of which is achieving access. Whether overtly negotiated or covertly sought, the fieldworker needs to gain some level of access to the setting. If conducting insider research, either as an employee or supernumerary, the fieldworker will require access and cooperation at a number of levels, including senior management (head office) middle management (e.g., branch management, team leadership/supervision), and colleague (employee) level. When discussing research ideas with colleagues (and supervisors in particular), it is likely that this will be one of the early concerns; students and novice researchers are often warned that achieving access for participant research can be particularly challenging, especially if researching sensitive issues within a work organization; imagine, for example, how you would feel if a stranger came up to you at work and calmly explained s/he is researching the unethical behavior of employees in your organization and would very much like to observe you in your natural setting for the study! Effective access is often a challenge whatever the research method used—colleagues have often discussed the difficulty they had in finding sufficient interviewees (in interview studies) and very few questionnaire surveys seem to attract sufficient responses to make the relevance of the sample's original randomness sound convincing.

With participant observation it is clear that participation must be possible in some form, so access must be either negotiated as a fieldworker or (probably in fewer cases now than before) or achieved through some form of subterfuge, perhaps with total nondisclosure of purpose (e.g., simply applying for a job or acting as a customer) or by somehow obscuring the real purpose (in the example above, the fieldworker would be advised to avoid the explicit and threatening word "unethical" in the request for access), not least, as any covert approach to fieldwork has considerable ethical implications. Although it may be reasonable or even necessary to take such an approach in some cases, it would be essential to ensure scrupulous ethical standards of research practice, a point that is now widely recognized by university ethics committees and academic publishers. Access can often be arranged by prospective fieldworkers if key gatekeepers (Hammersley & Atkinson, 1995), who can facilitate (or not) entry into a research context, are approached sensitively, and potential fieldworkers should not be discouraged from seeking it. Indeed, there is a certain paradox that it can sometimes be easier to obtain formal access in very different and sensitive contexts; for example, Punch (1993, p. 183) suggested that being a foreigner was "doubtless an advantage in gaining entry" in his study of Dutch police. He also found that as "a visiting academic, seemingly a bird of passage, whose intention was to publish in English" probably contributed to his ease of access. So, his study participants felt little threat from him. In addition to this, it is likely that his overt role of academic would facilitate a certain legitimization as an observant and enquiring researcher, in the same way that Korczynski (2007, p. 259) overcame suspicion that he could be a "management spy," when conducting his participant observation by showing his university webpage to participants. This also demonstrates a blurred line between negotiating access and developing rapport and trust; Korczynski certainly had organizational access to the setting and the other participants do not seem to have excluded him from their interactions despite some suspicion, but when that suspicion was allayed, access to their activities and conversations seems to have been enhanced, demonstrating increasing rapport. During my own fieldwork I once faced a similar situation; during the final period of fieldwork with different pubs from a single organization developing rapport and trust with one management couple (Damien & Janine) was particularly challenging. The excerpt below also draws attention to the potential value of longer-term fieldwork in building relationships with participants over time, especially when a simple view of the fieldworker's university webpage may not be enough, as described below.

The researcher was very open about this study and its aims with the staff and customers of the pubs sampled, and generally received favorable and enthusiastic assistance. There was, however, one notable exception to this—the pub manager who was referred to earlier. He was initially convinced that the fieldworker was working as a spy for head office, which raised immediate questions as to whether the fieldwork at his unit should continue, in case he was harmed by such concerns. However, after discussing the matter with him, his partner, and the fieldworker's supervisor, it was decided to continue. The manager himself explained that he wasn't worried by the possibility of being spied on as he had nothing to hide. He protested that he was happy for the fieldworker to continue, if only as a source of cheap labor. Thus it was decided to carry on with the research there and monitor progress. By the middle of the fieldwork the manager's doubts seemed to have been allayed, and his earlier suspicions were treated as a joke by all concerned, making it possible to interview him along with a number of his staff. The change in his attitude toward the researcher and the study can be illustrated by the following excerpt from the field notes from the third week of this phase of fieldwork:

> I finally seem to be feeling like a part of the team. I am getting on much better with Damien (and Janine for that matter) and they seem to be trusting me more. Janine got me to do lock up tonight and didn't even go round after me checking up as she always did before (the others [colleagues] all have to put up with the same). Things certainly seem to be looking up. (Sandiford 2004, pp. 121–122; all names of research participants have been kept anonymous)

This showed the advantage of carrying out participant observation over a few weeks, as the relationship that develops between fieldworker and colleagues gives the opportunity to allay any negative feelings about the research and help advance a feeling of trust prior to any formal interviews. It was also reassuring to observe that the couple's often erratic and untrusting behavior was equally aimed at other members of staff who had worked with them for much longer than the fieldworker.

This also demonstrates the complexity of negotiating access and trust at different levels; senior management at head office were enthusiastic about supporting the research, colleagues at unit level were also supportive and happy to engage with the fieldworker, but, although allowing access, the unit managers were openly suspicious for the first part of the fieldwork, often making their suspicions clear through a sort of joking repartee involving colleagues and customers. It also highlights the challenge of balancing professional and personal ethics with practicality. Although informed consent was obtained, as a researcher, I was responsible to ensure my work did not cause any harm to any participants, including, but not limited to, Janine and Damien. In my professional opinion this did not seem to be the case, nor did their expressed attitude necessarily damage the research project at the time. As the fieldwork continued the situation did improve and both did consent to be interviewed and participated (apparently) happily and cooperatively before the research ended.

Kaul (2004, p. 4) presents another aspect of rapport building that is probably not possible in most nonparticipant observation research when he describes the long-term nature of his own fieldwork in a small Irish village. After working (in a local pub) and conducting his fieldwork through the busy tourist season, he observed that at the end of the season, "after we didn't leave, we noticed that people started opening up to us and taking us a bit more seriously"; he attributes this to the

> nature of the tourists, and the semi-transient nature of working-tourists, that sometimes they no longer invest intense emotional energy in people unless they stay for longer periods. (Kaul, 2004, p. 4)

Kaul (2004) also explored the advantages and disadvantages of taking up paid employment during (and as part of) his fieldwork, and although he argues that this is not unethical in itself, he recognizes that anthropologists are often uncomfortable doing so. This is only one of the challenging ethical issues relating to this sort of fieldwork. Researchers more used to conducting questionnaire surveys or stand-alone interviews can sometimes be rather wary of formal observation studies, not least because they are guided by the common requirement of ensuring the informed consent of all participants and, as Jauncey (1999, p. 194) pointed out, in some settings (especially those involving public space) "without wearing a sandwich board declaring the research interests, it would not have been possible or practical to inform everyone of what was intended." They are especially perturbed to hear of studies where participant-observers conduct intentionally covert research (i.e., keep their research secret from other participants). Studies such as Mars and Nicod's (1984) covert work about waiters in hotels have become somewhat notorious with university ethics committees. However, it is worth pointing out that there are many "shades of gray" between complete secrecy and fully informed consent. For example, clinical trials utilizing control groups and placebos require some limits of information provided in advance and the right to withdraw from a study cannot be exercised after publication of the results. The British Sociological Association (2002) statement on ethical practice asserts that,

> As far as possible participation in sociological research should be based on the freely given informed consent of those studied. This implies a responsibility on the sociologist to explain in appropriate detail, and in terms meaningful to participants, what the research is about, who is undertaking and financing it, why it is being undertaken, and how it is to be disseminated and used.

Key ideas here are "as far as possible" recognizing that the practicalities and nature of the research may impact on this (e.g., observing in a public place where it is not possible to inform and receive consent in advance—see O'Connell Davidson, 2008) and "appropriate detail" that suggests that full and detailed disclosure may be a problem (e.g., using research- or discipline-specific jargon to introduce a project may well confuse rather than enlighten a prospective participant. In addition to this, the actual meaning of covert research is of some significance; research that is covert, "disguised or concealed" (*Collins English Dictionary*, 1993), may be very different from fieldwork that is not intentionally disguised or concealed from everybody, but is simply not explicitly explained to everyone present—as in the case where key participants (employees and regular customers) are informed but occasional customers are not necessarily told about the research, but with no intention to deceive anyone. Similarly, Pierce's (1995) covert approach to her fieldwork, discussed earlier, could be seen as blurred somewhat as she did not keep the subject of her research secret, but did not disclose the full nature of her fieldwork strategy. Such cases will inevitably present researchers with personal and professional ethical dilemmas, a challenge made increasingly difficult by ever-more demanding ethical oversight by university managers; gaining approval for research involving any sort of deception or lack of openness with study participants and subjects requires researchers to present ever-more convincing arguments for their research. However, it would be very unfortunate if researchers were discouraged from conducting this sort of research because of managerial concerns and worries, as it is certainly personally rewarding and provides great opportunities for valuable contributions in many areas of business and management research. As such, it is probably best for aspiring participant-observers to seek opportunities for overt fieldwork whenever possible, certainly when starting out on a research career as graduate students.

Analyzing the data and disseminating participant observation research

This section cannot realistically—and does not seek—to provide a how-to-do-it guide for the analysis of participant observation data. This is partly because the subject of data analysis is not straightforward, especially as the number of traditions and techniques of data analysis make it unreasonable to select one particular approach as suitable for all studies. I have been particularly influenced by Spradley's (1970; 1980) guides to data analysis following a structured process of data analysis. However, one of the challenges facing novice participant-observers in business and management research is a relative lack of discussion of data analysis and interpretation within this field (Sandiford & Seymour, 2007). As suggested earlier, this seems to be partly because of a focus on journals with particularly demanding word limits that often seem to ignore the need for qualitative research in general to deliver the word-rich messages of this sort of investigation. As editors and reviewers are often and understandably focused on ensuring their journals provide their readers with cutting-edge theoretical and empirical contributions to knowledge, it is understandable that detailed and user-friendly accounts of qualitative data analysis techniques are relatively rare in the business and management literature. For example, the highly rated *Human Relations* (nd) journal specifies in its guide for submissions that "authors should ensure that their methods section is not too long, avoiding overly long explanations of why particular norms and standards have been chosen." Similarly, many student textbooks on research methods follow the trend of trying to include as many methodologies and techniques as possible given the wide and varied research traditions within business and management. However, despite this, there is a rich tradition of methodological writing in the anthropological and sociological literature that is accessible to business and management researchers, with a number of helpful texts focusing on qualitative data analysis in general (e.g., Miles & Huberman, 1994) and participant observation in particular (e.g., Spradley, 1980). The main limitation of this literature, from a business and management perspective, is that it can focus more on broader community-based participant observation, commonly with ethnographic emphasis, but there is often less attention given to organizationally based research, although organizational ethnographies are relatively easy to find in the empirical literature.

Another challenge for the prospective participant-observer, as hinted earlier, is the relative interchangeability of ethnography and participant observation in the wider literature; it is not always clear whether discussion of participant observation data analysis is based on ethnographic methodological assumptions and ideology. However, this can perhaps be overemphasized. After all, ethnographers probably have more experience of dealing with participant observation data collection and analysis than most other researchers and they have much to offer the novice fieldworker whatever her/his academic discipline is. In his book *Participant observation*, Spradley (1980, p. 33) constantly refers to "ethnographic data" synonymously with participant observation data. He asserts that data analysis "cannot wait until you have collected a large amount of data. In ethnographic inquiry, analysis is a process of question discovery," rather than simply answering predesigned questions. Here, he clearly delimits his discussion to ethnography. However, it is hard to imagine any participant observation that this point does not apply to; it seems almost inevitable that any researcher actively engaged in this sort of fieldwork could ignore phenomena that would suggest alternative directions of investigation—simply keeping to an original research question would seem particularly foolish if the data are opening up an apparently more appropriate line of inquiry. Thus, the ethnographic ideal of concurrent or interactive data collection and analysis (Sandiford & Seymour, 2007, p. 727) seems equally to relate to any form of participant observation.

This also fits with Spradley's (1980) increasingly focused approach to fieldwork that requires an ongoing approach to data analysis rather than seeing analysis as a discrete stage and activity in the research process. This ideal seems particularly clear in ongoing participant observation, although it can apply to other sorts of research, especially involving more qualitative methods. In line with Hammersley and Atkinson's (1995) discussion of developing and emerging research questions during the fieldwork, Spradley (1980, p. 34) sees fieldwork as taking three phases: (1) descriptive observations, which continue throughout the project, providing broad, relatively unfocused observations of the field and helps identify phenomena requiring (2) more focused observations. In turn, this increasing focus gradually enables the fieldworker to seek increasingly (3) selective observations whereby close attention is given to particular behaviors, routines, rituals, etc. that have been identified as central to answering the research questions. However, despite such increasing focus, he does point out that these three stages are not mutually exclusive (i.e., descriptive observations do continue concurrently with focused and selective observations while focused observations continue with selective observations).

From a personal perspective, given the need to maximize the message(s) possible within journal word limits, it may be appropriate to focus on particular methodological issues/challenges faced in a study rather than try to give a full account of the whole methodological story. For example, Sandiford and Seymour's (2013) methodological account is necessarily concise, giving an overview of the approach with supporting references; notably, the data analysis approach is briefly introduced, referring readers to a key methodological source that provides more depth. In this particular study the focus was on participant observation as a public house employee; the paper explored employees' attitudes toward and consumption of alcohol in and around their workplace. Because of this, a key methodological issue was the fieldworker's own position in relation to alcohol during the data collection, so this was explored in rather more depth than other challenges faced during the study as shown in the following excerpt:

> Observing and participating in a number of the after-work drinking sessions helped to better understand the behaviours and interactions of colleagues, although it was often more difficult to separate observer and participant roles when drinking with colleagues after work. An example of this sort of participant research was presented by Gough and Edwards (1998) who analysed audio-recorded dialogue during a drinking session in which Edwards took part. As in the current study, they did consider whether the fieldworker should have more of an observer role, "abstaining from alcohol with a view to taking field notes as the session progressed" but decided against this as it would seem "artificial and unrealistic" (Gough & Edwards 1998, p. 413).

> This does present ethnographers with a further challenge: participation calls for shared consumption (of drink) while observation is likely to be impaired with intoxication. As much as anything, the reflective nature of the field notes helps an ethnographer keep in touch with the researcher self/role in reminding him/her of the research purpose as participation develops over time. (Sandiford & Seymour, 2013, p. 126)

This also highlights the importance of openness and reflexivity when reporting observational studies; it is crucial to discuss the nature, type, level, and implications of the participation if readers are to be able to evaluate the quality of reported research. This excerpt raises at least one potential distraction for the fieldworker (alcohol consumption during data collection)—should I join in and risk losing observational acuity or should I stand back from the drinking and risk losing participatory inclusion as an outsider? A similar issue was highlighted by Graham et al. (1980), albeit from a different perspective. Their study of "Skid Row" bars was based on observation of patrons' behavior, with observers taking an unobtrusive approach, with pairs of observers engaging in minimal participation (though they did purchase a drink and act as customers). Despite this they found themselves to be conspicuous through their behavior—when they "lingered over a single drink for 2 or 21/2 hr" (Graham, 1980, p. 280) and appearance—ethnicity, social class, clothing, etc. This draws attention to another possible paradox, with an unobtrusive strategy, whether as complete observer (Gold, 1958) or engaging in passive participation (Spradley, 1980) actually seeming to draw more attention to the fieldworker because their behavior is likely to be seen as incongruous to the other participants. In the final excerpt below, I reflect on the pilot study of my first public house research.

> Although the research conducted in this project was not covert, and he [I] was open with all the staff about his activities, there was little evidence of the fieldworker being seen as an outsider intruding in their workplace, which was encouraging. Most of the staff, however, did express an interest in the project and were enthusiastic about taking part in the study, sharing and discussing relevant experiences. It is not easy to demonstrate that trust was developed, however, there was a variety of evidence to suggest that a sound level of rapport existed between fieldworker and most of the other study participants. This took two forms, work based and leisure based. There were few examples of tension in the workplace during the pilot study beyond what appeared to be everyday issues of working in public houses, and the fieldworker regularly engaged in out-of-work-hours socializing with a number of his colleagues.
>
> Although there is no guarantee that participants in the study did not act differently than they would normally for the benefit of the researcher, working and, in some cases, living together would make it rather difficult to maintain

such behaviur indefinitely. At work the researcher was involved in joking, arguments, moaning about customers, management, or colleagues, feuding, and other aspects of pub life in the same way as any other colleague in the unit. None of the other service workers had been working there for long, and few were local, so there was no question of the fieldworker being excluded as an outsider. Field-diary excerpts relate to relationships with employees at work and leisure. For example, the following was written about a late night encounter after closing:

> After the customers left, [I] sat down with James [manager] and Kevin [part time barman] for a beer—the subject of relationships among staff came up. Kevin talked about a couple who used to have big public arguments, James said it is "unethical" to argue in public, and went on to condemn as "unprofessional" to publicly yell at a member of staff—he "always" takes them aside (off stage) for that. (Sandiford, 2004, pp. 127–128)

The sort of encounter reported above could be seen as simply a friendly conversation, although as Spradley (1979, p. 58) pointed out "skilled ethnographers often gather most of their data through participant observation and many casual, friendly conversations while introducing a few ethnographic questions." Thus the opportunity to talk to colleagues over drinks after work was important in both developing rapport and gathering data.

Conclusion

The world of research often seems filled with paradoxes, contradictions, philosophical and ethical dilemmas within contextual complexity and ambiguity. It could perhaps be argued that it is somewhat paradoxical to see participant observation as rather less subjective (at an individual level) than nonparticipant forms of observation. For example, the participant can possibly avoid the limitations of perceptual error and/or projection by consulting with other participants when interpreting observed phenomena. This is not to say that such consultation/cooperation would necessarily be objective in itself, rather that, if seeking to find social/cultural sense in phenomena, it would normally be preferable to draw from insiders' sociocultural knowledge rather than distorting this with the outsiders' (observer's) sociocultural knowledge; thus, the reported knowledge would be more intersubjective in nature, based on some level of shared knowledge and experience.

Participant observation presents the researcher with many challenges, not least of which is managing multiple roles within the field. Given that one of these roles is to be the research "instrument" itself, it is important to recognize that personal biases cannot always be cast off, which is one of the justifications for taking a reflexive approach to data collection, analysis, and research dissemination. There is no single right or wrong mix of, or approach to, such roles. Rather, fieldworkers are advised to reflect on their roles as they develop and change over time through a reflexive approach to note keeping and data analysis.

Carrying out participant observation may seem daunting to investigators beginning a research career, but the experience of engaging with fieldwork provides a unique, exciting, and rewarding opportunity to engage with research problems and interact with the research context and other participants first-hand and in real time. This chapter cannot hope to do more than briefly introduce this research approach from a largely personal perspective. In doing this, it does perhaps highlight some particular advantages of participant observation for researchers in organizations while also drawing attention to some of the issues and challenges facing fieldworkers observing as participants There are inevitably various other aspects of participant observation that have either been glossed over or not discussed here at all. For example, issues cover a wide variety of topics including, but certainly not limited to, the practice of online fieldwork (e.g., Garcia et al., 2009; Kulavuz-Onal & Vásquez, 2013), where researchers participate in and observe web-based activities of various types; personal danger risk when conducting fieldwork (e.g., Palmer & Thompson, 2010); the often-linked challenges of insider research and possible data contamination by fieldworkers (Mercer, 2007); and the practicality and ethics of using recording devices in the field (e.g., Speer & Hutchby, 2003).

References

Barley, N. (1983). *The innocent anthropologist: Notes from a mud hut.* London: British Museum Publications.

Bordieu, P. (2003). Participant objectification. *Journal of the Royal Anthropological Institutes, 9*(1), 281–294.

British Sociological Association. (BSA). (2002). *Statement of Ethical Practice for the British Sociological Association* (March) (accessed January 31, 2014). http://www.britsoc.co.uk /about/equality/statement-of-ethical-practice.aspx.

Cavendish, R. (1982). *Women on the line.* London: Routledge & Kogan Page.

Collins English Dictionary. (1993). Glasgow: Harper-Collins.

Eddington, A. (1958). *The philosophy of physical science.* Ann Arbor: The University of Michigan Press.

Foote-Whyte, W. (1955). *Street corner society* (2nd ed.). Chicago: University of Chicago Press.

Gold, R. L. (1958). Roles in sociological fieldwork. *Social Forces, 36*(3), 217–223.

Gough, B., & Edwards, G. (1998). The beer talking: Four lads, a carry out and the reproduction of masculinities. *The Sociological Review, 46*(3), 409–435.

Graham K., La Rocque L., Yetman R., Ross T. J. & Guistra, E. (1980). Aggression and barroom environments. *Journal of Studies on Alcohol, 41*(3), 277–292.

Hammersley, M. (1992). *What's wrong with ethnography? Methodological explorations.* London: Routledge.

Hammersley, M., & Atkinson, P. (1995). *Ethnography: Principles in practice* (2nd ed.). London: Routledge.

Human Relations (nd). *Guidance for Contributors*, accessed March 23, 2014 from http://www.tavinstitute.org/humanrelations/submit_paper/guidance.html.

Jauncey, S. (1999). Observational research. In Bob Brotherton (Ed.). *The handbook of contemporary hospitality management Research* (pp. 191–205). New York: John Wiley & Sons.

Jeffrey, B., & Troman, G. (2004). Time for ethnography. *British Educational Research Journal, 30*(4), 535–548.

Junker, B. (1960). *Fieldwork: An introduction to the social sciences.* Chicago: University of Chicago Press.

Kaul, A. R. (2004). At work in the field: Problems and opportunities associated with employment during fieldwork. *Anthropology Matters Journal, 6*(2) (accessed April 16, 2008) http://www.antrhorpologymatters.com.

Korczynski, M. (2007). Music and meaning on the factory floor. *Work and Occupations, 34*(3), 253–289.

Lave, J., & Wenger, E. (1991). *Situated learning: Legitimate peripheral participation.* Cambridge: Cambridge University Press

Mars, G., & Nicod, M. (1984). *The world of waiters.* London: George Allen and Unwin.

Martin, N. (2014). Spaces of hidden labor: Migrant women and work in nonprofit organizations. *Gender, Place and Culture: A Journal of Feminist Geography, 21*(1), 17–34.

McDonald, S. (2005). Studying actions in context: A qualitative shadowing method for organizational research. *Qualitative research, 5*(4), 455–473.

Mercer, J. (2007). The challenges of insider research in educational institutions: Wielding a double-edged sword and resolving delicate dilemmas. *Oxford Review of Education, 33*(1), 1–17.

Miles, M. B., & Huberman, A. M. (1994). *Qualitative data analysis* (2nd ed.). London: Sage.

Morris, J. A., & Feldman, D. C. (1996). The dimensions, antecedents, and consequences of emotional labour. *Academy of Management Review, 21*(4), 986–1010.

Narayan, K. (1993). How native is a native anthropologist? *American Anthropologist, 95*(3), 671–686.

O'Connell-Davidson, J. (2008). If no means no, does yes mean yes? *History of the Social Sciences, 21*(4), 49–67.

Okely, J. (1992). Anthropology and autobiography: Participatory experience and embodied knowledge. In J. Okely & H. Callaway (Eds.) *Anthropology and autobiography* (pp. 1–128). London: Routledge.

Palmer, C., & Thompson, K. (2010). Everyday risks and professional dilemmas: Fieldwork with alcohol-based (sporting) subcultures. *Qualitative research, 10*(4), 421–440.

Peberdy, A. (1993). Observing. In P. Shakespeare, D. Atkinson, & S. French (Eds.). *Reflecting on research practice: Issues in health and social welfare* (pp. 47–57). Buckingham: Open University Press.

Pierce, J. L. (1995). *Gender trials: Emotional lives in contemporary law firms.* Berkeley: University of California Press.

Punch, M. (1993). Observation and the police: The research experience. In M. Hammersley (Ed.). *Social research: Philosophy, politics and practice* (pp. 181–99) London: Sage.

Rafaeli, A. (1989). When cashiers meet customers: An analysis of the role of supermarket cashiers. *Academy of Management Journal, 32*(2), 245–273.

Reinharz, S. (1997). Who am I? The need for a variety of selves in the field. In H. Rosanna (Ed.). *Reflexivity & voice* (pp. 3–29). London: Sage.

Sandiford, P. J. (2004). *Emotion in organisations: Working in British pubs.* Unpublished PhD Thesis, Oxford Brookes University.

Sandiford, P. J., & Divers, P. (2011 May). The public house as a 21st century community institution. Paper presented at *CHME 20th Annual Research Conference:* 20–20 Back to the Future, Carnegie Pavilion, Headingley Carnegie Stadium, Leeds.

Sandiford, P. J., &. Seymour, D. (2007). A discussion of qualitative data analysis in hospitality research with examples from an ethnography of English public houses. *International Journal of Hospitality Management, 26*(3), 724–742.

Sandiford, P. J. & Seymour, D. (2013). Serving and consuming: Alcohol, work and leisure. *Public Houses, Work, Employment and Society, 27*(1), 122–137.

Schaffer, S. (2000). Introduction: To mundanity and beyond. *Journal of Mundane Behavior, 1*(1), 1–6.

Speer, S. A., & Hutchby, I. (2003). From ethics to analytics: Aspects of participants' orientations to the presence and relevance of recording devices. *Sociology, 37*(2), 315–337.

Spradley, J. P. (1979). *The ethnographic interview.* New York: Holt, Rinehart and Winston.

Spradley, J. P. (1980). *Participant observation.* New York: Holt, Rinehart and Winston.

Spradley, J. P. & Mann, B. J. (1975). *The cocktail waitress: Woman's work in a man's world.* London: John Wiley & Sons.

Tolich, M. B. (1993). Alienating and liberating emotions at work: Supermarket clerks' performance of customer service. *Journal of Contemporary Ethnography, 22*(3), 331–381.

von Koskull, C., & Strandvik, T. (2014). Discovering the unfolding of service innovations. *Journal of Business & Industrial Marketing, 29*(2), 6–16.

Watson, T. J. (2006). *Organising and managing work.* (2nd Ed.). London: Pearson.

Watson, T. J., & Watson, D. H. (2012). Narratives in society, organizations and individual identities: An ethnographic study of pubs, identity work and the pursuit of "the real." *Human Relations, 65*(6), 683–704.

Part IV

Constructivist Applications

23

Constructivist Grounded Theory Applied to a Culture Study

Narasimha Rao Vajjhala

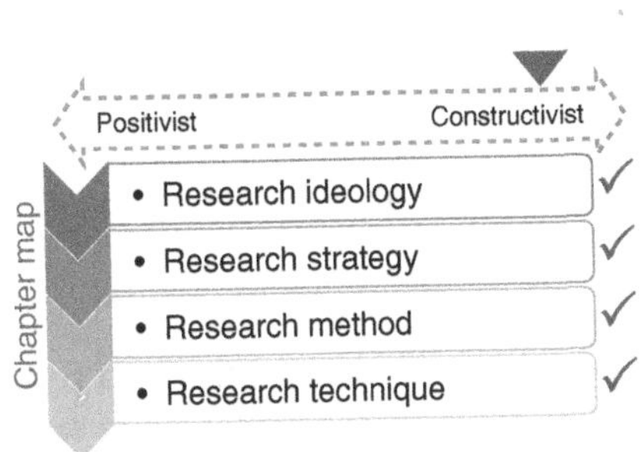

Introduction

Problem statement

Constructivist grounded theories, similar to phenomenology, are an empirical form of inquiry grounded in experiences (Charmaz, 2006; Charmaz & McMullen, 2011; Mills, Bonner & Francis, 2006; Shank, 2006). The difference between phenomenology and constructivist grounded theory is that phenomenologists analyze the contextual dimensions of experience that can be seen and shown by the researcher while constructivist grounded theorists believe that researchers may miss the hidden implications of social locations (Charmaz & McMullen, 2011). According to Mills et al. (2006), constructivist grounded theory reshapes the interaction between the researcher and the participants in the research process and highlights the role of the researcher as the author. Several authors have explained why constructivist grounded theories and phenomenology are useful, but few studies have dealt on how phenomenological studies are carried out using software such as NVivo. Gibbs (2002) uses NVivo to explain various qualitative data analysis methods but without focusing on constructivist grounded theory in particular. Researchers and students need applied examples using computer-assisted qualitative data analysis software (CAQDAS) such as NVivo to assist in the analysis of qualitative data. CAQDAS can assist a researcher in providing a comprehensive picture of data as well as in allowing the researcher to document the audit of the data analysis process (Welsh, 2002). Research practitioners would benefit from the explanation of the various steps involved in the data analysis in a constructivist grounded theory using CAQDAS software. The CAQDAS software used in this study, NVivo, is a dedicated qualitative data analysis software that can also enhance the validity of a qualitative study (Kikooma, 2010).

Purpose

The purpose of this chapter is to help researchers and students working on constructivist grounded theories understand how to use the power and possibilities of CAQDAS software, such as NVivo, for analyzing qualitative data. Consequently, this chapter explores the various stages in a constructivist grounded theory applied to a culture study using NVivo.

Approach

The data used in this chapter are based on the data collected in my doctoral study, a qualitative, multisite, exploratory case study examining the influence of cultural factors on knowledge-sharing activities in medium-sized enterprises in transition economies (Vajjhala, 2013). The data included observations from audio-recorded, in-depth personal interviews with 20 managers working in different departments in 10 different medium-sized companies in Albania. The 10 medium-sized companies included two companies each from five key economic sectors: information and communication technology (ICT), food processing, banking and insurance, construction, and tourism. The interview instrument used in this study was pilot tested and changes were made to the instrument before being used in the study. The central research question driving the study is the following: How do cultural factors influence employees' perceptions of knowledge-sharing initiatives in medium-sized enterprises in transition economies? Three more research questions were created to structure this study:

1. How do cultural factors, especially national culture, influence knowledge-sharing initiatives in SMEs in Albania?
2. How do factors such as employee attitudes, morale, and perceptions affect knowledge-sharing initiatives in SMEs in Albania?
3. What changes, if any, do managers working in medium-sized enterprises observe in the cultural behavior of employees in the last two decades toward knowledge sharing in SMEs in Albania?

The approach used in this chapter is an applied approach with concepts explained in a practical way so that readers can have an understanding of how to approach data analysis in constructivist grounded theory using CAQDAS tools such as NVivo.

Theoretical background

Grounded theory overview

Grounded theory is defined as the discovery of theory from data systematically obtained from social research with the aim of generating or discovering a theory (Glaser, 1978, 1992; Glaser & Strauss, 1967). According to Creswell (2008, p. 183), "Grounded theory design is a systematic, qualitative procedure used to generate a theory that explains, at a broad conceptual level, a process, an action, or an interaction about a substantive topic." Qualitative studies, such as those examined via grounded theory, are conducted when there is either a lack of a theory or an insufficient existing theory (Merriam, 2009). Grounded theory is appropriate in situations where researchers try to understand the process by which actors construct meaning out of intersubjective experience (Suddaby, 2006). Grounded theory is best suited when the research question or problem indicates a need to develop a sound theoretical foundation and such a foundation does not currently exist. Another difference between phenomenological and grounded research design is that researchers using grounded theory concentrate less on the subjective experiences of individuals than in phenomenology. Rather, the focus in grounded theory is on how these subjective experiences could be grouped into causal relationships between the actors (Suddaby, 2006).

Creswell (2008) categorized grounded theory designs into three categories: the systematic design, emerging design, and the constructivist design. Figure 23.1 presents an overview of the categories and processes of grounded theory design. The emphasis in systematic grounded theory design is on the use of data analysis steps of open, axial, and selective coding as well as on the development of a visual picture of the generated theory (Creswell, 2008; Strauss & Corbin, 2006). Grounded theory aims at building theories; for instance, in the culture study referred to in this chapter, a grounded study is used to study the role of cultural and social factors in knowledge sharing in medium-sized enterprises in transition economies.

Theoretical sampling, often the sampling technique of choice in grounded theory research, is critical to the development of conceptually dense and complex theory (Charmaz, 2006; Draucker, Martsolf, Ross & Rusk, 2007). In theoretical sampling, the study sample is not decided before the start of data collection; rather, the participants are selected purposefully based on their ability to provide data contributing to the emergence of the theory (Kennedy &

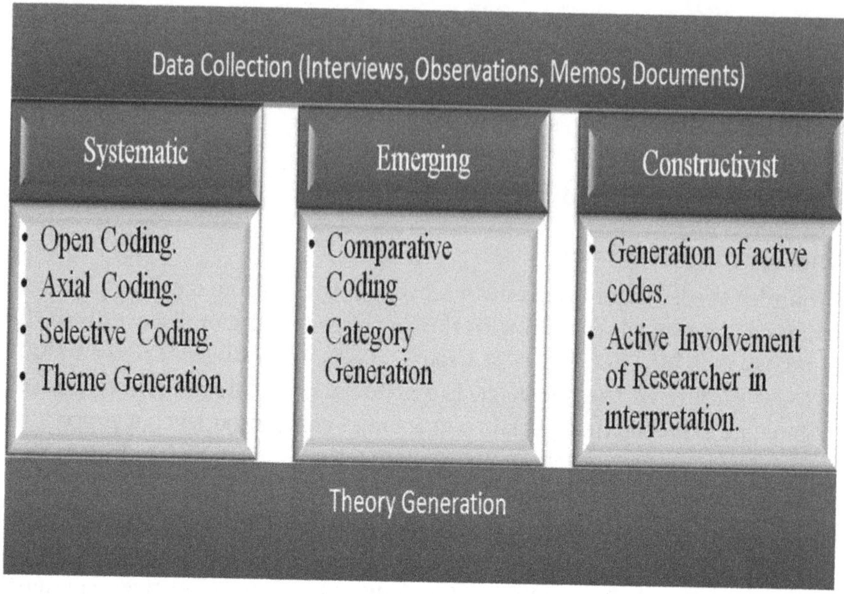

Figure 23.1 Overview of the grounded theory design categories and process.

Lingard, 2006). Theoretical sampling is in contrast to selective sampling where the identification of population is made before data collection commences. Sampling in grounded theory is often sequential, starting with selective sampling and moving gradually to theoretical sampling as guided by emerging theory (Draucker et al., 2007).

The primary tools of data collection in grounded theory are unstructured interviews and observations. The core component of data analysis in grounded theory research approach is the process of coding, which can be categorized into three types: open coding, axial coding, and selective coding (Creswell, 2008; Strauss & Corbin, 2006). In the open coding phase, the initial categories of information are prepared based on the data collected from interviews, observations, and memos written by the researcher. Open coding is the initial phase in which the researcher performs a close, line-by-line examination of the data with the intention of developing provisional concepts and, through a process of constant comparison, collapses the concepts to categories (Draucker et al., 2007). In this phase, the researcher labels and categorizes through comparison and categorization. In vivo codes, often used during open coding, are labels for the themes or categories but are phrased exactly as the participants had stated them. Researchers can also use keywords of their choice to categorize themes rather than use in vivo codes (Creswell, 2008). NVivo facilitates open coding by allowing importing and sorting of data as well as simplifying the process of creating codes. The process of open coding using NVivo with an applied example is explained later in this chapter.

Axial coding is the second phase in grounded theory design in which the researcher selects an open coding category and relates other categories to this category (Creswell, 2008). NVivo facilitates axial coding through the creation of trees apart from allowing the users to link similar words together. The process of axial coding using NVivo is also explained later in this chapter through the same example. In the selective coding procedure, the researcher writes a theory based on the relationship among the categories formed in the axial coding phase. In selective coding, the core category around which other subcategories can be grouped is identified (Strauss & Corbin, 1998). Selective coding involves the examination of the data with the intention of extracting the core category and achieving the integration of the theoretical framework (Draucker et al., 2007). NVivo facilitates selective coding through several tools that allow managing nodes and case nodes.

The emerging grounded theory design mentioned by Creswell (2008) and Glaser (1992) is based on the premise that a theory is grounded in the data and cannot be forced into categories. This is in contrast to the systematic grounded design where axial coding is used to categorize data. Creswell (2008) further adds that emerging grounded theory should be modifiable based on changes that come up in the data as well as meet three key criteria: fitting to the context, work, and relevance to the reality. Researchers need to decide whether a grounded theory research approach is best suited to address a problem before adopting this approach. Research problems that have been dealt with significant amounts of research, for instance, leadership which already has significant amount of literature available, might not be ideal for grounded theory. The most important reason for using grounded theory research design is to generate new theories from the data.

Researchers should also be wary of some of the mistakes associated with research in grounded theory research design. Researchers working with grounded theory research often make mistakes, including forcing analysis in early stages, generating a level of analysis based on fragmentation, and failing to ensure that the analysis moves beyond narrative description and starts generating theoretical concepts (Elliott & Jordan, 2010). Glaser (1978) advocates that researchers avoid being contaminated by preconceived notions. However, such a recommendation of the proponents of the grounded theory approach for the researcher collecting and analyzing theory-free data to avoid preconceptions and bias is often criticized by scientific philosophers (Thornberg, 2012). The constructivist grounded theory approach advocated initially by Charmaz takes a constructivist approach toward grounded theory.

Constructivist grounded theory overview

Constructivist grounded theory approach retains most of the key components of the Strauss and Corbin approach with an emphasis on the role of the researcher in the development of codes and categories. Charmaz (2006), the proponent of constructivist grounded theory approach, included issues of reflexivity, personal schemas, and existing research base affecting the process described by Schreiber and Asner-Self (2011). Constructivist grounded theory recognizes the role of the researcher as part of the research process rather than as just a distant objective observer as in classical grounded theory research (Mills et al., 2006). Grounded theory can be considered an objectivist approach to generating theories while constructivist grounded theory is interpretivist in nature with the notion of shared reality interpreted by the researcher (Gardner, McCutcheon & Fedoruk, 2013). The grounded theory approach is objectivist in nature while the constructivist grounded theory is constructivist in approach (Shank, 2006).

The constructivist approach to grounded theory design sees the data and analysis created from shared experiences with the participants, the researcher, and other sources of data (Ghezeljeh & Emami, 2009). The researchers are actively involved in the construction of the theory and no longer have an objective role. A constructivist grounded theory has its inherent limitations because of factors such as researcher bias and limitations on generalizability. Researcher bias is quite relevant in the constructivist grounded study approach because of the significant involvement of the researcher in the generation of the theory.

Data analysis using NVivo

The first step in analyzing the data in a constructivist grounded theory approach is creating a new project in NVivo. As we proceed in this chapter, we will be exploring different options in the interface. A new project can be created by clicking on the File menu item and selecting a new project. The user has the option of adding a title and description, or selecting a file name if there is an existing NVivo project. As this is the first NVivo project, the user can enter the title and description for the project.

The Sources tab on the left hand side of the screen allows the users to import interviews and other data sources. A folder can be created wherein all the interview transcripts can be stored. However, the interviews need to be transcribed before they can be imported. In the example of the culture study, twenty interviews were conducted, transcribed, and imported into NVivo. To import the interview, click on the External Data tab in the main menu. This tab provides the users with the option of importing the data from multiple sources. Multiple interviews can be imported at the same time. NVivo imports the documents with their default names, although users have the option of renaming the

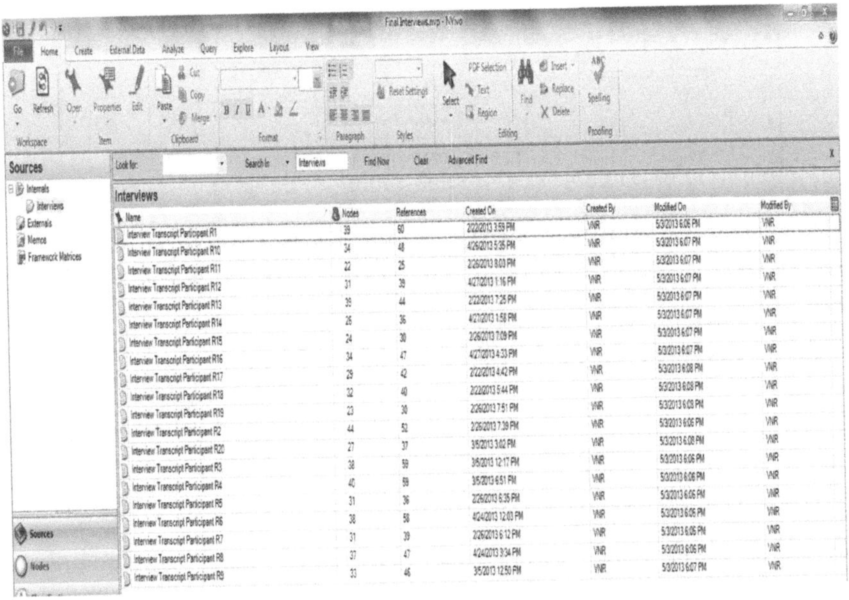

Figure 23.2 NVivo interface.

documents. Figure 23.2 shows the screenshot of NVivo visual interface after the interviews are imported.

When coding with NVivo, we will start with creating nodes. Nodes are labels for managing related information in different data sources. As they help in grouping and arranging together information by giving names to logically related data in the data sources, nodes facilitate gathering of information from the sources in the project by helping to create and manipulate codes from the sources of data. NVivo supports storing of data sources as well as the creation and manipulation of code in the form of nodes (Gibbs, 2002). NVivo has two interfaces: the document explorer and the node explorer. The document explorer helps to maintain information about documents while the node explorer is used to manage nodes. Using the document properties tab in the document explorer, users can store metadata about the document, including the document name, description of the document, the date on which the document was created, modified, and any other information. Figure 23.3 shows the information document properties window for the first interview transcript.

Nodes help in organizing ideas as the data sources are read. Nodes can be created either before or after the documents are imported. If the nodes are created before, it might help the researchers in organizing information easily and, as the researcher comes across new information or ideas, new nodes can be added (Gibbs, 2002). There are three types of nodes: free nodes, tree nodes,

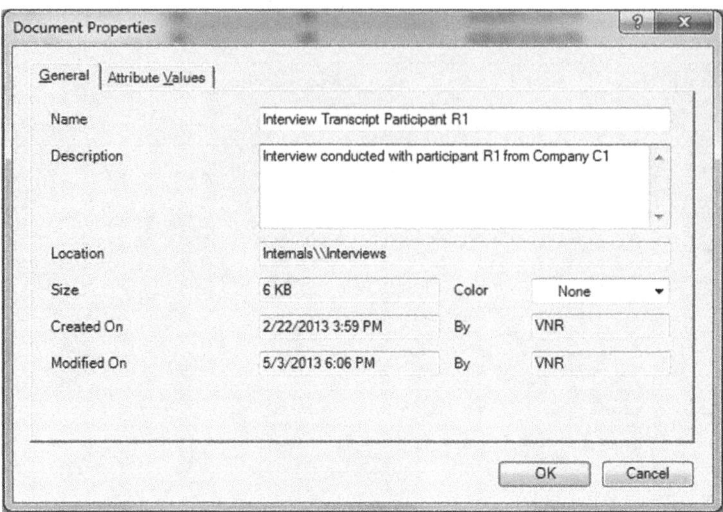

Figure 23.3 Manipulating document properties.

and case nodes. Free nodes appear as normal codes, and can be organized into tree nodes indicating a hierarchy among the nodes. Case nodes are used for organizing coding about cases.

The simplest form of creating nodes in NVivo is the use of "in vivo" codes. In vivo codes refer to the use of words taken directly from the data sources to name the nodes. For instance, "ability to adapt" and "Albanian culture" are two in vivo codes that were created in the culture study referred to in this chapter. In vivo codes can be created by selecting text from the document and adding the code in the "code at" text box as shown in Figure 23.4. In this figure, the in vivo code "Albanian Culture" is created and labeled for the sentence, indicating that the selected block of data has information related to Albanian culture. Similarly, when similar information about the same code is encountered in other data sources, the same label or node can be used to group the information together.

An alternative mechanism of creating nodes, especially when the documents have not been browsed, is through the node explorer. This method is quite useful for creating totally new nodes as well as for adding additional information about nodes, such as the node description. The node description option allows the researchers to modify the information about the node as the researcher comes across new data. In Figure 23.5, the screenshot demonstrates how a new node can be created without associating it with any data. After the node is created, the data can be associated via the same method as shown for the creation of in vivo codes. In a constructivist grounded theory, such as the culture study explored in this chapter, in vivo codes are quite useful as theory generation is based completely on the data, and codes are created as concepts emerge from the coding initiatives of knowledge sharing.

Q27: **What are the national cultural characteristics typical to Albanian culture that might facilitate or hinder knowledge sharing?**

As typical to Albania culture peoples are afraid to express openly their opinion, as a consequence of communism system. We can say that for people who lived in that period and perhaps now in their mid- or last-stages before retirements. Nowadays, having a very young average age of population our society is changing. Young people are more open- minded, flexible, open to changes etc. It is two decades now since the fall of communism so we still have some more time for the new generation to take over. The new generation should not carry the legacy of the culture that has been severely constrained and influenced by communism.

Figure 23.4 Creating nodes—in vivo codes.

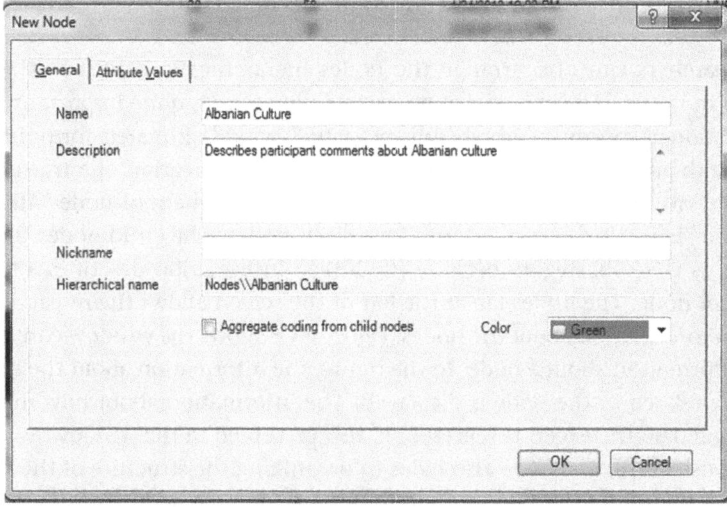

Figure 23.5 Creating nodes—node explorer.

process. Nodes help in connecting a theoretical concept or idea with text in the data sources. Creation of nodes is the foremost step in the formation of a concept or idea based on the data collected. NVivo stores a wide range of information about nodes, including the name of the researcher, date of coding, analytical

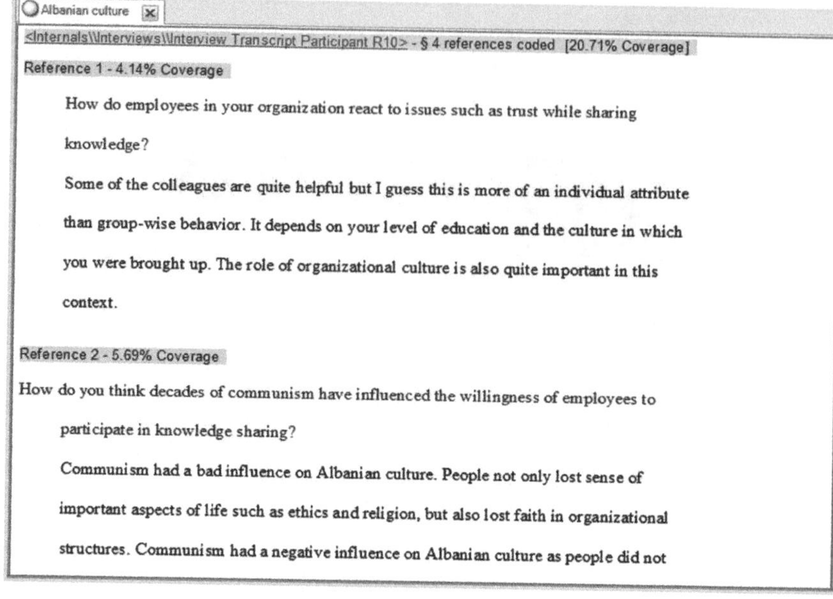
Albanian culture

<Internals\\Interviews\\Interview Transcript Participant R10> - § 4 references coded [20.71% Coverage]

Reference 1 - 4.14% Coverage

How do employees in your organization react to issues such as trust while sharing knowledge?

Some of the colleagues are quite helpful but I guess this is more of an individual attribute than group-wise behavior. It depends on your level of education and the culture in which you were brought up. The role of organizational culture is also quite important in this context.

Reference 2 - 5.69% Coverage

How do you think decades of communism have influenced the willingness of employees to participate in knowledge sharing?

Communism had a bad influence on Albanian culture. People not only lost sense of important aspects of life such as ethics and religion, but also lost faith in organizational structures. Communism had a negative influence on Albanian culture as people did not

Figure 23.6 Node detail view.

description of the node, and the link to the document from where the text was found.

Researchers can also arrange the nodes hierarchically, referred to as tree nodes in NVivo. The creation of nodes in a hierarchy is quite important in the generation of concepts and subconcepts, which would ultimately form the basis for the themes and subthemes. A simple example of creation of a tree node is a node with one level of hierarchy. In this example, the root node "Albanian Culture" is further expanded into four child nodes. The child nodes indicate that this is a subcategory because the linked information describes a part of the root node. The nodes tab at the left of the screen allows the researchers to obtain information about the nodes. Figure 23.6 shows the window containing the information about a node. In the figure, the information about the sources of data related to the node is displayed. The information about how much of the total data the excerpts represent is also presented in the window.

The use of the tree node also helps in organizing the structure of the nodes. Most of the nodes initially created by the user are free nodes, and as the process of coding proceeds these free nodes can be organized into tree nodes. The creation of tree nodes also reduces the overall number of nodes, reducing the possibility of duplicating nodes (Gibbs, 2002). Case nodes are another type of nodes, the purpose of which is to organize the text belonging to a case. The case node is different from free and tree nodes as the case node cannot have children.

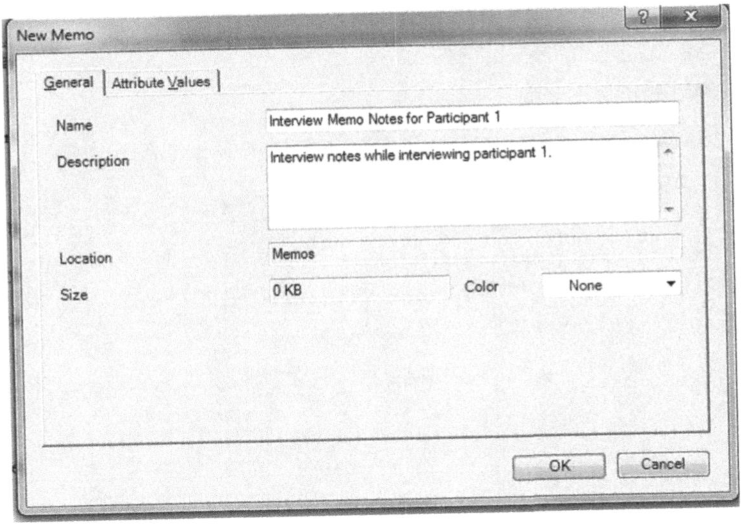

Figure 23.7 Creating a new memo.

NVivo also allows the researcher to create memos, helping the researcher to maintain notes before, during, or after the interview. Researchers can also use memos during the coding process as they gain new insights from the processed data. To create a new memo, the user has to select the Create tab from the main menu and click on Memo. As shown in Figure 23.7, a dialog box will open and the name of the memo can be given. NVivo creates a blank document in which the researcher can type his or her thoughts. One way of linking the interview with the memo is by using the Memo link. For this, click on the Analyze tab, and click on Memo link, the researcher has two options: click on New Memo or select an existing memo. When a previously created memo is created, it is locked for editing; however, the user can easily remove the locking mode. The researcher may consider merging nodes if the memos have similar content. The contents of the new menu could include discussion among researchers, reflective remarks from the researcher, or general comments from the researcher during the interview process.

NVivo has two key types of text-based queries: the word frequency query and the text search query. The results of the word frequency query will help identify the words most often used in the data sources. This query provides ways to visualize these results. To perform the word frequency query, click on the Query tab and select Word Frequency from the ribbon. A dialog box will appear and the criteria for the query can be selected. Figure 23.8 shows the word frequency query dialog box. The dialog box gives the researcher several options including a sliding scale through which the user can select

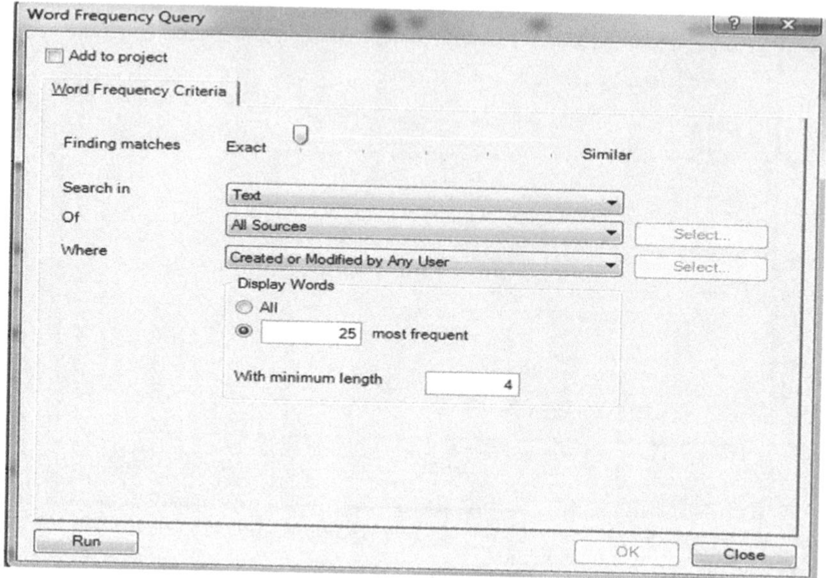

Figure 23.8 Word frequency query.

the matching criteria, the sources where the search needs to be made and the number of frequently used words that the researcher is looking for.

NVivo has a stop list of words, such as "a," "an," "the," and several other such words. These stop list of words are not counted by NVivo while looking for frequency of words. In addition, the researcher has the option of adding or removing words to the stop list. The results of the query are shown in the summary tab by default. The researcher has three other types of views through which the results can be interpreted, including word cloud, tree map, and cluster analysis. The word cloud presents a visual representation of up to the top 100 words where the size of the word represents its relative frequency. There are a number of available options of how to present the word cloud. Figure 23.9 shows a word cloud for the frequency of the 25 words that were queried. While the word cloud could be a good visual representation of the dominant words in the documents, the tree map is the geometric representation of the relative frequency of the words. When we use multiple sources in the query, the fourth tab, cluster analysis, will provide a representation of which words appear more frequently in the same document.

Researchers also have an option for exporting the output of the queries into images and other formats for presentation in reports. A text search query is another text-based query. To run a text-based query, select the Text Query option from the query option in the ribbon. In figure 23.10, the text-based

Figure 23.9 Word cloud map.

Text Search Query
Add to project
Text Search Criteria | Query Options
Search for culture
Special
Finding matches Exact Similar
Search in Text
Of All Sources Select...
Where Created or Modified by Any User Select...
Run OK Close

Figure 23.10 Text-based criteria dialog box.

criteria dialog box is given. The results of a text-based query are best viewed in a word tree. A sample word tree based on the search for word "culture" is shown in figure 23.11. Using the text search, the researcher is given five different options for finding matches: exact, stemmed words, synonyms, specializations, and generalizations. For instance, if the option synonym is

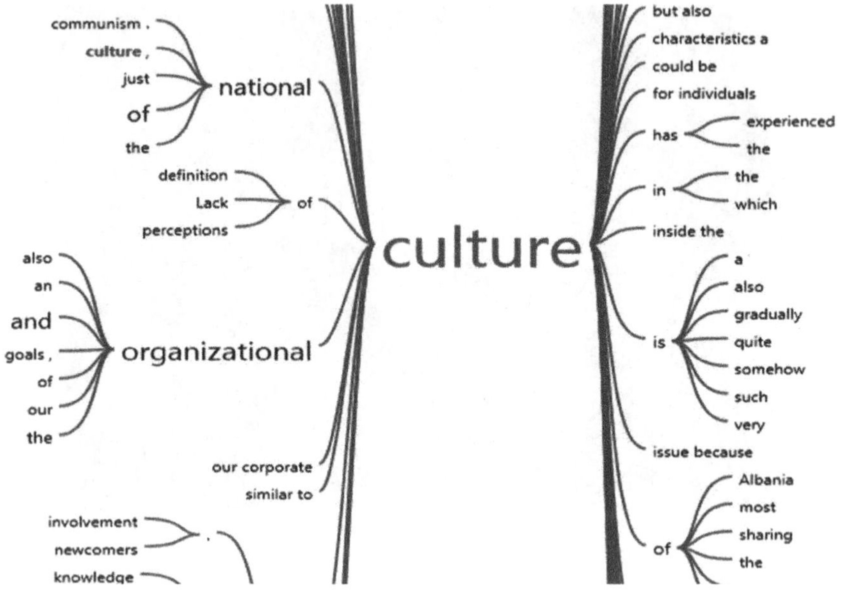

Figure 23.11 A sample word tree.

included, then the word "culture" along with its synonyms is included in the search.

In the case of the culture study, the transcription did not use NVivo, but NVivo does provide options for importing transcriptions. Although the transcription is still manual, the user-friendly transcription is convenient when integrating with NVivo. The media tab in NVivo software provides several options for transcription of both audio and video data. The researcher can use a combination of keys to start and pause listening to the audio stream and key in the transcription with great ease using the options presented in the media tab. Once the transcription is complete, the entire transcript can be exported to different formats or used within NVivo.

NVivo also allows the creation of models while analyzing data. Models present researchers with the option of visually exploring or presenting the data in the project. Models allow researchers to identify theories and also review concepts already identified during coding. Models created in NVivo are of two types: static and dynamic. All the models created in NVivo are dynamic by default. Researchers have the option of storing a static model, which is nothing but the snapshot of a dynamic model at a point of time. Dynamic models allow the researchers to modify the model by adding shapes and project items.

NVivo provides several tools for summarizing large amounts of qualitative data available to researchers. One of the popular approaches to summarizing data is through the use of framework matrices, as they provide a tabular view of data with the case nodes in rows and themes segregated vertically. Moreover, framework matrices allow the researchers to look at the themes in columns and the relationship with each case node in rows, enabling researchers to observe how different themes are related to each other by comparing the results across different case nodes. Apart from the tree maps, word clouds, and cluster analysis, NVivo provides several visualization options, including charts and graphs.

Culture study analysis using NVivo

Based on the nature of the study and the focus of the research, a general data analysis strategy was identified. Content analysis was used in this study because content analysis serves to reveal the content in a source of communication (Neuman, 2006). The use of software for analyzing data was essential because of the large number of interview transcripts to be analyzed. The manual analysis of the 20 interview transcripts, apart from the field notes, would have been time consuming; the use of software facilitated the task of data analysis.

Two NVivo (Version 9.0) projects were established, one for the pilot study and the other for the final study. The audio-recorded interviews were transcribed in a Word document, and these documents were imported as sources. The transcribed recording resulted in 148 pages of text. The pilot study had five transcripts, and the final study had 20 transcripts. The participants in the pilot study are referred to in this study as Participant 1 (P1), Participant 2 (P2), and so on. The respondents in the final study are referred to as R1, R2, and so on. All the participants were shown copies of their transcripts within 48 hours of completion of their interviews and were given the opportunity to identify errors or omissions. Because none of the participants opted to make any changes in the transcripts, inter-rater analysis was not required.

The open coding process was used to divide the text into segments, label the segments with codes, examine the codes for redundancy, and collapse the codes into broad themes. First, the transcripts were transcribed verbatim from the audio-recorded interviews. The key phrases from the transcripts were then recorded and a list of code words collected; redundant codes were either removed or merged. The process of reduction continued until six main themes along with some subthemes were identified. Member checking was conducted by showing the findings and interpretations to the participants to improve the reliability of the findings.

After the data were imported to NVivo and coding completed, text-based queries were used for reducing the codes into categories, and six themes were generated. The text-based tools, word frequency search and text search were used for narrowing down the number of themes. Text search was used and tree

Table 23.1 Influence of national culture on employee behavior

Respondent	Excerpts of participant statements
R1	Years of communism have taught people to keep quiet about what they know and not to share information.
R3	The fear of knowledge of sharing is a national cultural problem because people did not share information as they did not trust each other.
R7	Albanian culture is quite open and inclusive.
R8	Albanian people are quite friendly and are quite inquisitive. [incomplete.] inquisitive
R10	Albanians were quite social toward foreigners, but there is still some hostility and lack of trust among Albanians themselves.
R12	Albanians are a bit hesitant to trust people who are not part of an inner circle or among close friends.
R13	Albania is a small and patriarchal society, and knowledge sharing is more open between family and friends but limited with outsiders.
R14	The communist regime thrived on insecurity and lack of trust and did not create an atmosphere where people could trust each other.
R15	Albanians are open-minded.
R17	Albanians do not trust that easily.

maps were used to identify subthemes within the six main themes. Initially, most of the nodes generated in NVivo were free nodes; gradually, tree nodes were introduced to structure the generation of themes. Text-based search using NVivo also helped to identify the sources for the most frequently used sources; a sample of the participant excerpts is included in table 23.1.

The final study generated six themes with some of the themes containing several subthemes. The six themes and the subthemes are as follows:

1. Influence of national culture on employee behavior
   a. Cultural diversity and sensitivities
   b. Influence of communism on Albanian national culture
   c. Fear of sharing knowledge
   d. Lack of trust
   e. Cultural openness
   f. Voluntary participatory behavior
2. Role of organizational culture in knowledge sharing
   a. Organizational environment
   b. Knowledge-sharing culture
   c. Culture of willingness
   d. Top management initiative and support
   e. Organizational regulations

3. Factors influencing active employee participation in knowledge-sharing activities.
   a. Incentives for knowledge sharing
   b. Training and workshops
   c. Awareness of benefits of knowledge sharing
4. Perceived risks of knowledge sharing.
   a. Clustering among employees
   b. Fear of loss of position at workplace
   c. Lack of information about knowledge sharing
   d. Risk of losing confidential information
5. Knowledge as an organizational property.
6. Using information systems for knowledge sharing.

Conclusions

NVivo simplifies the data analysis involved in a constructivist grounded theory approach. The process of theory generation in constructivist grounded theory involves significant amounts of data generated from interviews, observations, memos, and documents. Using software such as NVivo simplifies and assists the researcher by providing efficient tools for the researcher. The applied example of the culture study demonstrates to the readers the steps involved in constructivist grounded theory approach.

References

Charmaz, K. (2006). *Constructing grounded theory: A practical guide* (2nd ed.). London: Sage.

Charmaz, K., & McMullen, L. M. (2011). *Five ways of doing qualitative analysis: Phenomenological psychology, grounded theory, discourse analysis, narrative research, and intuitive inquiry.* New York: Guilford Publishers.

Creswell, J. W. (2008). *Educational research: Planning, conducting, and evaluating quantitative and qualitative research.* Upper Saddle River, NJ: Prentice Hall.

Draucker, C. B., Martsolf, D. S., Ross, R., & Rusk, T. B. (2007). Theoretical sampling and category development in grounded theory. *Qualitative Health Research, 17*(8), 1137–1148. doi: 10.1177/1049732307308450.

Elliott, N., & Jordan, J. (2010). Practical strategies to avoid the pitfalls in grounded theory research. *Nurse Researcher, 17*(4), 29–40.

Gardner, A., McCutcheon, H., & Fedoruk, M. (2013). Discovering constructivist grounded theory's fit and relevance to researching contemporary mental health nursing practice. *Australian Journal of Advanced Nursing (Online), 30*(2), 66–74.

Ghezeljeh, T. N., & Emami, A. (2009). Grounded theory: Methodology and philosophical perspective. *Nurse Researcher, 17*(1), 15–23.

Gibbs, G. R. (2002). *Qualitative data analysis: Explorations with NVivo.* New York: McGraw-Hill Company.

Glaser, B. (1978). *Theoretical sensitivity: Advances in the methodology of grounded theory.* Mill Valley, CA: Sociology Press.

Glaser, B. (1992). *Basics of grounded theory analysis: Emergence vs. forcing*. Mill Valley, CA: Sociology Press.

Glaser, B., & Strauss, A. (1967). *The discovery of grounded theory: Strategies for qualitative research*. Chicago, IL: Aldine.

Kennedy, T. J. T., & Lingard, L. A. (2006). Making sense of grounded theory in medical education. *Medical Education, 40*(2), 101–108.

Kikooma, J. F. (2010). Using qualitative data analysis software in a social constructionist study of entrepreneurship. *Qualitative Research Journal, 10*(1), 40–51. doi: 10.3316/qrj1001040.

Merriam, S. B. (2009). *Qualitative research: A guide to design and implementation. Revised and expanded from qualitative research and case study applications in education*. New York: Wiley.

Mills, J., Bonner, A., & Francis, K. (2006). The development of constructivist grounded theory. *International Journal of Qualitative Methods, 5*(1), 1–10.

Neuman, W. L. (2006). *Social research methods: Qualitative and quantitative approaches* (6th ed.). New York: Allyn & Bacon.

Schreiber, J. B., & Asner-Self, K. (2011). *Educational research: The interrelationship of questions, sampling, design, and analysis*. New York: Wiley.

Shank, G. D. (2006). *Qualitative research: A personal skills approach* (2nd ed.). Upper Saddle River, NJ: Prentice Hall.

Strauss, A., & Corbin, J. (1998). *Basics of qualitative research: Techniques and procedures for developing grounded theory* (2nd ed.). Thousand Oaks, CA: Sage.

Strauss, A., & Corbin, J. (2006). *Basics of qualitative research:Grounded theory procedures and techniques*. Newbury Park, CA: Sage Publications.

Suddaby, R. (2006). From the editors: What grounded theory is not, Editorial, *Academy of Management Journal*, pp. 633–642. Retrieved from http://search.ebscohost.com/login.aspx?direct=true&db=bth&AN=22083020&site=ehost-live.

Thornberg, R. (2012). Informed grounded theory. *Scandinavian Journal of Educational Research, 56*(3), 243–259. doi: 10.1080/00313831.2011.581686.

Vajjhala, N. R. (2013). *Cultural factors and knowledge sharing in medium-sized enterprises in Albania: A qualitative, multisite case study*. Doctoral dissertation, University of Phoenix.

Welsh, E. (2002). Dealing with data: Using NVivo in the qualitative data analysis process. *Forum Qualitative Sozialforschung / Forum: Qualitative Social Research, 3*(2), 26–28.

24

Phenomenology Variations from Traditional Approaches to Eidetic and Hermeneutic Applications

Jillian McCarthy

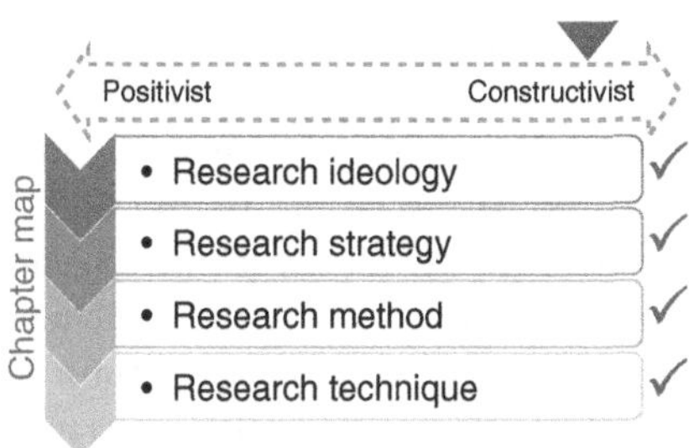

Chapter overview

McCarthy discusses a constructivist research ideology using two phenomenology method variations: eidetic phenomenology and hermeneutic phenomenology. The unit of analysis when using the phenomenology method is usually the "lived experience" of a human participant and the level of analysis is individual within-group. As she explains, eidetic phenomenology is interpretative, which means the research is at the left of a constructivist ideology, having some researcher bias, by comparison to hermeneutic phenomenology where only the participants create the meaning of the data.

Introduction

This chapter examines phenomenology both as a philosophical concept and a qualitative research method. It contextualizes the subject by scrutinizing the origins of the philosophy, noting how this has changed over time from being a purely philosophical concept to now being applied as a research paradigm that is growing in popularity with many disciplines, including business and management. The chapter describes phenomenology in all its variances, noting similarities or differences and then discussing these using examples where possible. It is important for researchers to glean an understanding of the early concepts of this philosophy in order to provide a strong underpinning of knowledge from which to apply the more modern interpretations of phenomenology to research studies. It is intended that this chapter will give a broad overview of the philosophy for the researcher, and it is suggested that it is read in conjunction with the following chapter (which proposes how phenomenology can be applied to research studies concerned with business and management).

Contextualizing the concept

Phenomenology is both a philosophy and a research methodology (Morse & Field, 1995). It can be traced back to Immanuel Kant (1724–1804) in the eighteenth century and later to Georg Hegel (1770–1831) in his work *Phenomenology of spirit* published in 1807 (Moran, 2000). However, it is most often credited with originating in Germany from the work of Edmund Husserl (1859–1938), at the beginning of the twentieth century, who developed the philosophy as an investigation of consciousness as experienced by the individual (Baker et al., 1992). Husserl took the term phenomenology from his tutor Brentano (1838–1917) at the University of Vienna, who provided the inspiration for Husserl's development of the philosophy (Moran, 2000). In 1901, Husserl published *Logical investigations* and later revised his philosophy and in 1939 published *Experience and judgement* (Keller, 1999).

The philosophy was later adapted by Martin Heidegger (1889–1976); Maurice Merleau-Ponty (1908–1961); Paul Ricoeur (1913–2005); Jean-Paul Sartre (1905–1980); and Alfred Schultz (1899–1956), to name just some of the philosophers credited with expanding Husserl's ideas (Groenewald, 2004). Heidegger's work on phenomenology is debatably as well respected as Husserl's, although Husserl himself came to regard it as a faulty departure from, and misunderstanding of, his own teachings (Sheehan, 2007). Various approaches to phenomenology flourish; Caelli (2000) discussed how at a conference in America, 18 different types of phenomenology were presented for discussion, although this number can by no means be regarded as an exhaustive list. Already, it can be seen that notions of "pure" phenomenology or the "classic approach" (Crotty, 1996) are saturated by numerous variations of the method that are ambiguous.

Phenomenology as a research methodology was developed from philosophy (Moustakas, 1994), although this version is not without its critics either. Several authors have published work that discussed the difficulties of translating philosophy into practice (e.g., Bell, 1990; Dreyfus, 1993; Lapointe, 1980; Smith &

Smith, 1989; Ströker, 1993; Zahavi, 2003). Primarily, phenomenology is concerned with the "lived experience" of a phenomenon, in order to obtain universal knowledge through suspension of subjectivity. Thus the phenomenon under scrutiny is researched through inquiry into those who have experienced it. It is not their subjective view that is sought, but their objective experience prior to forming opinions of the experience.

Davis (1991) discussed how phenomenology requires an objective view to investigate the participant's presubjective experience of a phenomenon, but, how this is not actually possible. To illustrate, the participant is subjective as the research is post experience and opinions have been formed; the researcher is also subjective, because the writing is by nature subjective, and then on top of this comes the reader's subjectivity. Here is the problem. A participant attempts to form an objective view of a presubjective phenomenon, and this is captured through a data collection approach (e.g., interviewing), which when articulated by the participant becomes subjective to some degree. Then the researcher reads or listens to this, trying to maintain an objective view, but the researcher's brain may alter the meaning as part of the cognitive process that is necessary to document the meaning of the phenomenon. Put simply, Davis believed that the purity of philosophy does not translate well into practice (see figures 24.1 and 24.2 for conceptual models of this dilemma).

Phenomenology as a philosophy has grown, developed, splintered, and evolved (Kaelin & Schrag, 1990; Stewart & Mickunas, 1990). It is regarded as a philosophical movement, which indicates that its original ideas are still growing (Lopez & Willis, 2004). The seminal concepts have been considered

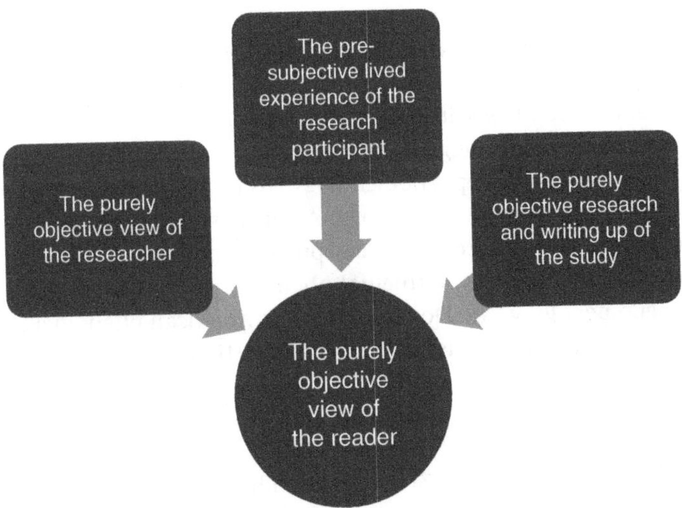

Figure 24.1 Objectivity versus subjectivity in phenomenology—ideologically.

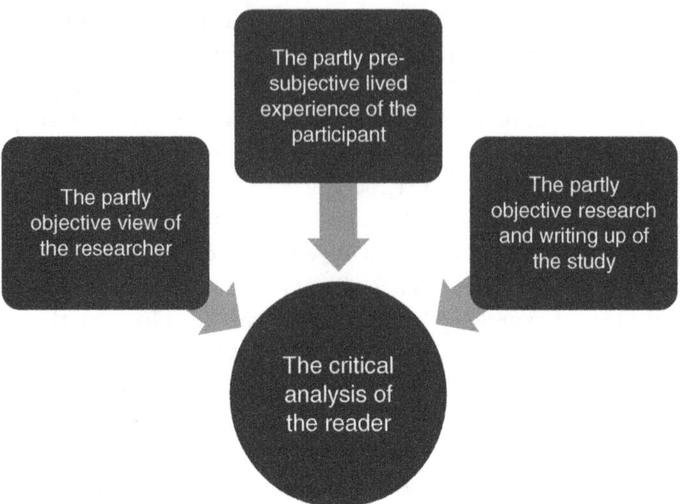

Figure 24.2 Objectivity versus subjectivity in phenomenology—realistically.

by philosophers and academics in more detail, from various angles, and then modified and polished. Moreover, as time has progressed and societies have changed, modern ideas have been incorporated into philosophy in order to update it and make it applicable to the society concerned. It is gaining in popularity with researchers, and many disciplines have adapted phenomenology from its original European design to better suit research into various fields (Lavesque-Lopman, 1988). Claims by purists that phenomenological approaches do not adhere to the roots of philosophy may be correct, but this should not be regarded as a flaw. These meanderings can be seen as an indication that the movement is continuing to advance in order to maintain relevance in changing times within changing specialities.

The research design ideology literature is confusing with respect to the epistemology used to describe phenomenology. To illustrate, the hybrid methods of phenomenology originating in North America, which are popularly applied to research, are often referred to as new phenomenology. However, Silverman (1987) referred to these as Continental phenomenology, Giorgi, (1997) as scientific phenomenology, and Dowling (1997) as American phenomenology. For the purpose of clarity, throughout this chapter they are referred to as modern phenomenology. Likewise, original European phenomenology, which was intended purely as a philosophical concept, was referred to by Crotty (1996) as traditional phenomenology, whereas it was referred to as European phenomenology by Silverman (1987) and philosophical phenomenology by Giorgi (1994,1997). Again, for the purpose of clarity, throughout this chapter it is referred to as traditional phenomenology (see figure 24.3).

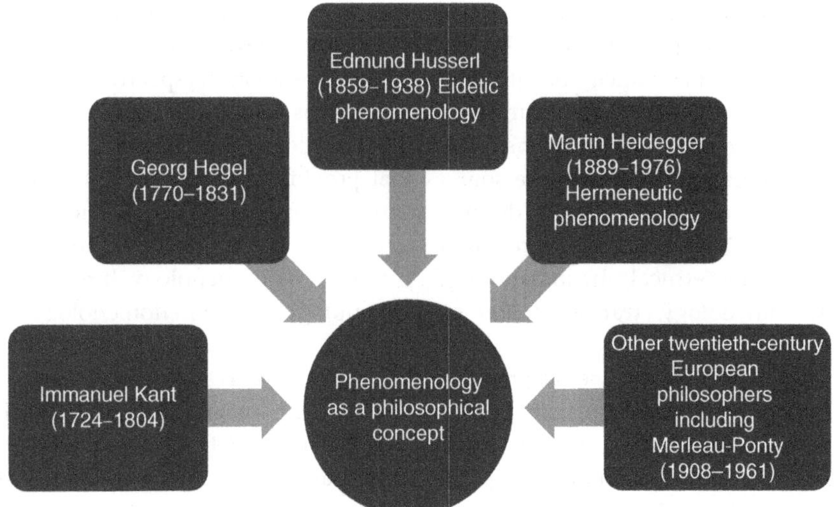

Figure 24.3 Traditional phenomenology.

Figure 24.3 highlights that phenomenology is often confusing and contradictory when reviewed in the research design literature. Many texts on qualitative research discuss a simplified generic form of phenomenology, which gives the impression that this is a straightforward methodology concerned simply with obtaining an objective view of the lived experience, which we have previously claimed is not possible. Although many of these texts discuss the main features of phenomenology and its application; such as bracketing, essences, reflexivity, rich descriptive data, and thematic analysis, the complexity of the concept is not fully explored nor applied in those sources. This topic is tackled in the next chapter where an example of a research topic is used to illustrate how the phenomenology method and the related techniques can be successfully applied when designing research studies in business and management from the perspective of constructivist or pragmativist ideologies.

Students learn about phenomenology through various layers of literature; apart from the research books just discussed, there are the works of the traditional European philosophers, which have been translated from the original texts. Then there is a body of literature that discusses and critiques the work of European philosophers. There are the works of the new phenomenologists, and finally, there are studies carried out by researchers who are using phenomenology to inform their research. In addition, every author has his or her own interpretation of phenomenology, and discrepancies and contradictions within the literature abound. To add to this ambiguity and confusion, there are epistemological differences between Husserlian and Heideggerian phenomenologies, which are described as eidetic (or descriptive) phenomenology and hermeneutical (or interpretive) phenomenology, respectively (Lopez and Willis, 2004). In addition, phenomenology is sometimes combined with other theories such as deconstruction to form deconstructive phenomenology. There are several online sources that provide access to articles, monographs, and other materials, discussing and exemplifying phenomenological research. Many of these sources delve into rare applications of phenomenology such as ethical phenomenology, existential phenomenology, linguistical phenomenology, transcendental phenomenology, and phenomenology of practice.

It is not uncommon to see phenomenology described as analytical, constructionist, constructivist, existentialist, hermeneutical, imaginative, intentionalist, interpretive, interpretivist, intuitionist, intuitivist, objectivist, positivist, post-positivist, reductionist, subjectivist, and transformationalist, to name just some of the positions from the pragmativist to the constructivist ideology in the research design typology. It would take a very experienced philosopher or researcher to make sense of this minefield of terminology. To add to this confusion, it is worth noting that none of the original European philosophers actually developed research methods from their philosophies—these have all arisen from interpretations of the original works.

Dreyfus (1994) observed that much qualitative research is concerned with practical concepts such as meanings, skilled know-how, lifeworld, and everyday skilled ethical comportment. Contrast this with the classical phenomenologists who studied such ethereal subjects as consciousness (Husserl, 1931, 1970), being (Heidegger, 1927/1962), and perception (Merleau-Ponty, 1945/1962). It can be seen why this philosophy has been adapted and adjusted to better suit the needs of research. Across disciplines, phenomenology is being modified to fit the peculiarities of the specialism concerned. In the introduction to their book, *American phenomenology: Origins and developments*, Kaelin, and Schrag (1990) noted:

> American phenomenologists have devised new directions for its application to the American experience in such disciplines as philosophy, literature, the human sciences, education, rhetoric and communication. This very interdisciplinary spread serves to give notice of the range and breadth of the impact of phenomenology on American thought in our own lifetime. (p. 2)

Van Manen (2002) discussed a phenomenological orientation he referred to as phenomenology of practice, which he stated could also be termed experiential phenomenology, lifeworld phenomenology, or applied phenomenology. He believed that professional researchers are less interested in the philosophical foundations of phenomenology than they are in its practical application and that this distinction should be made when reading research reports:

> For example, a philosopher may investigate the possibility of the phenomenological constitution of the transcendental ego, or the relation between transcendental phenomenology in Husserl and ontological phenomenology in Heidegger. In contrast, professional practitioners tend to work within the applied domains of the human sciences such as education, clinical psychology, nursing, medicine, and specializations such as psychiatry or midwifery. (van Manen, 2002, p.1)

Scholars of business, management, and leadership can also be added to this list.

Van Manen's view reinforced the practical side of research and the need for pragmatic answers to work-based issues. Phenomenology is evolving and modern phenomenology is part of this evolution. Phenomenology is a movement, and it is advancing to fit the needs of the disciplines it supports. This is not to say that modern phenomenology is a diluted version of the original philosophy, simply that it has evolved to suit the endeavors of its age. Traditional phenomenology is a product of its time; it had to evolve to maintain relevance and credibility in the postmodern world we now inhabit. Interestingly, Husserl (1931), the founding father of phenomenology, did not regard his own philosophy as perfect and stated:

> The ideal of the philosopher, to work out systematically a completed logic, ethics, and metaphysics which he could justify to himself and others for all time on the basis of an absolutely compelling insight—is an ideal the author has had to renounce early on and to this day. (p. 159)

The move from traditional to modern phenomenology

As the number of research studies inquiring into aspects of business and management has grown, so has an interest in designing a phenomenological approach to research these areas (e.g., Anosike et al., 2012; Bombala, 2012; Ehrich, 2005). It has become a popular method of inquiry as it reinforces the view that "individuals need to be understood as a whole person within a particular situation, not separated from the environments in which they function" (Kelly, 1996, p. 238). The main criticism presented against phenomenological research, in all its applications, is that it is often applied without truly understanding the original European philosophies from which it stems. It is believed that modern phenomenology bears little resemblance to the traditional phenomenologist approach originating from the works of Husserl. This is because researchers do not adhere to the constructionist epistemological position regarded as essential to Husserl's phenomenology, which has resulted in a less critical approach.

Initially, in order to examine this criticism, it is logical to explore what is meant by the term constructionist epistemological position as the research design ideology. Spiegelberg (1982) succinctly defined the traditional approach to phenomenology as centering on a search for an objective reality of a phenomenon. It is this objective reality that constructs knowledge of the phenomenon. Husserl's famous phrase "Zu den Sachen" means both "to the things themselves" and "let's get down to what matters!" (van Manen, 2001, p. 2). The things themselves and what matters according to Husserl were the objective view. Husserl believed that the key to phenomenology lay in intentionality, which is the peculiarity of consciousness to be conscious of something (Føllesdal, 1969). However, problems arise in the philosophy when the thing towards which the consciousness is directed does not exist, for example, a dream. Husserl's notion of noema is the basis to his theory of intentionality. Husserl resolves this dilemma by claiming that every act of consciousness is directed, even when there is no object to direct it to (Føllesdal, 1969).

The differences between traditional and modern phenomenology pivot on intentionality. The traditional phenomenologists believed that intentionality involves the individual's objective primordial consciousness of the phenomenon, that is, the thoughts prior to the application of logic and reasoning (Husserl, 1931). Husserl defined phenomenology as a descriptive analysis of pure consciousness. He explained that phenomenology is a theory of pure phenomena, and that it is not a theory of actual experiences. Although he believed that experience, as perceived by the human mind, should be scientifically studied in order to understand motivation. To achieve scientific rigor, researchers must bracket, or put aside, all prior notions, experiences, and bias in regard to the phenomenon under scrutiny (Natanson, 1973). The ability to suspend preconceived ideas is in keeping with notions of scientific objectivity, and it was Husserl's claim that phenomenology would stand up to scientific scrutiny (Le Vasseur, 2003).

Therefore, when applying traditional phenomenology, it seems logical that descriptions should be taken from research participants without a discussion of the concept under scrutiny, so that they are not aware of the focus of the study and will not discuss their "views" or reflections. A phenomenon should be researched prior to a research participant reflecting upon it to ensure that the primordial consciousness, not a subjective view, is described. This immediately raises ethical implications regarding conducting research without informed consent. Also, it would seem that this may be in conflict with business research, which could seek to discover the lived experiences of participants following an event on which reflection would take place, for example, a takeover bid. In addition, it would not be appropriate with traditional phenomenology to reinterview participants to elicit more information when conducting descriptive phenomenological research, as this would allow for an opportunity to reflect upon the concept prior to the second interview (Caelli, 2000). Thus, when applying traditional phenomenology, the first interview should take place without participants knowing what is the topic they are being interviewed for, and second interviews would only be conducted in order to confirm meanings given in first accounts. This may also conflict with business and management research, which often seeks to research experiences over time, for example, the lived experiences of participants prior to and following the event of a takeover bid. From this it can be seen why modern phenomenologists have altered the philosophy somewhat to make it fit with current research design requirements (Ahern, 1999).

Husserl furthered the concept of intentionality with what he termed phenomenological reduction or epistemological reduction (Husserl, 1907/1999). His notion of eidos or experienced essence is to be arrived at through reductionism, which is not to be confused with scientific reductionism. Husserl suggested that the essence or crux of a phenomenon could be arrived at by studying similarities in experiences of phenomena and by the researcher maintaining an open, objective mind. These eidetic structures (essences) are the common features of any lived experience, which are universal to everyone. According to Husserl, for lived experiences to be regarded as science, the commonalities must be identified and described. Reality is considered objective and independent of whatever context it is viewed from, including time (Lopez and Willis, 2004). Epoche is the word Husserl used, when discussing reductionism, to describe the continual endeavor of the researcher to suspend or bracket previous assumptions or understandings. Epoche "bars me from using any judgement that concerns spatio-temperal existence" (Husserl, 1913, p.111). This is not so much to suspend bias as to look at the world through fresh eyes, to see objectively without the encumbrance of preconceived notions (Lopez & Willis, 2004). The researcher must not attempt to interpret the phenomena, but, should be open to the phenomena revealing itself. This openness on the part of the researcher should continue throughout the research process.

Reductionism and epoche may be clear and rational when discussed as a philosophy; however, difficulties arise when this is applied to practice. How can somebody suppress their knowledge of the world? How does the researcher view previously known and considered experiences as though through the eyes of a child? Husserl's abstract, theoretical reductionism is precise and does not dovetail with most phenomena of everyday human life, which tend to emphasize the chaotic and disorderly nature of human experience. Bracketing, or putting away preconceived notions, when trying to logically apply theory is not always practical or achievable in real terms (Lopez & Willis, 2004). Furthermore, the problem is that Husserl does not describe in any practical way how this is to be achieved.

Therefore, practitioner-scholars have developed their own variations of the phenomenology method and techniques to fit into either pragmativist or constructivist research ideology designs, according to the unit of analysis in the research strategy. It is common for researchers to adapt methodologies and methods to suit when unexpected events occur that are not discussed in the literature. Some texts recommend that the phenomenologist does not conduct a literature review prior to undertaking the study, nor have a research question in mind apart from an inquiry into the lived experience of the phenomenon. This is in order to achieve the Husserlian notion of transcendental subjectivity. For the pragmatic world of many researchers, these views are neither desirable nor practical. Business and management research often addresses real-life dilemmas or concerns in the workplace, which means that it is essential that the literature is reviewed prior to undertaking a study and that a research question or hypothesis is posed. Johnson et al., (2001) suggested that researchers adapt phenomenological methods to better suit the uniqueness of the world they are researching. Bracketing throughout the research process may be attempted in research, but, it could be argued, it would not be helpful for the majority of studies as it would not allow for a literature search and review for example, as the researcher would or could form ideas from prior reading that may taint objectivity.

With reference to bracketing, it is often regarded by many researchers that bracketing is the main feature of the phenomenological tradition, albeit it could be argued that the main features are the philosophical underpinnings of phenomenology. Dowling (2007) pointed out that in research, bracketing usually refers to the researcher examining their biases and views and does not involve the research participants. Again, this illustrates the practicalities of much modern research, if it were to involve both participants and researcher then it would become a philosophical endeavor as opposed to research. Writers disagree as to when bracketing should occur within a study, one school of thought stating that bracketing will alienate the researcher from the research participants to some degree (which is undesirable as research participants are more open to disclosure when a relationship has built) and so bracketing should only occur during data analysis. However, as discussed, Husserlian phenomenologists believe that epoche (maintaining objectivity) should take place throughout the data generation, collection, and analysis phases.

Other theorists do not regard bracketing as possible at all, believing it impossible to separate preconceived notions from one's thoughts. Van Manen (1997) stated, "If we simply try to forget or ignore what we already 'know,' we might find that the presupposition persistently creep [sic] back into our reflections" (p. 47). This may be likened to being told not to think about pink elephants; the image immediately springs to mind.

Eidetic (descriptive) phenomenology seeks to distinguish between views learned through socialization and acculturation, which are often stale and predictable and underlying personal understanding of concepts that are more authentic and meaningful. It questions the sociocultural beliefs and practices handed down by society, by penetrating the mundane versions of human experience to arrive at something more authentic (Goodwin & Strang, 2012). Husserl (1931) believed that the difference between immanent (existing within something) and transcendent perception corresponds to the difference between "Being as Experience" and "Being as Thing" (p. 133). Reality is considered objective and independent of time and context. Therefore, notions of culture, society, and politics are superfluous to Husserl's philosophy of transcendental subjectivity.

It can be seen that traditional phenomenology would be an interesting concept to apply to many studies in business and management, to really delve below the surface of constructed beliefs to find the authentic experience. Imagine a research study that explored absenteeism from work by exploring the actual experience of an absentee. It may discover that the real essence of absenteeism is not workloads, stress, illness, hangovers, or childcare as often thought, but a fleeting need for freedom on waking up on that particular day. This could alter the way absenteeism is dealt with and may lead to policies that allow for the instant booking of a one-day holiday. Despite the perceived efficacy of traditional phenomenology, problems lie in its application, as discussed, and thus modern phenomenology has emerged to deal with these.

Traditional phenomenology intends that the world should be seen as it is first encountered, not as constructed by society or people, in other words, not through acculturation (Husserl, 1931). Husserl (1999) stated that lifeworld (*lebenswell*) is the pre-reflective state, the lived experience prior to contemplation. In order to achieve this, phenomenology seeks to look beyond traditional, cultural, and societal understanding of phenomena to the raw thoughts that are uncontaminated by influences. Business is a multicultural endeavor and much emphasis in business education is placed on global issues and respect for diversity. It is hard to imagine how personal tradition and culture can be bracketed when we are so steeped in it that we are often unaware of it. Much business research crosses countries and involves inquiry into cultural issues in order to further inform and illuminate these areas (Goodwin & Strang, 2012). Indeed, phenomenology is a popular methodology for conducting research into these areas, which, again, illustrates the shift away from the traditional form of inquiry.

Many researchers apply modern interpretations of phenomenology to their research, but, acknowledge Husserl, oft regarded as the founding father of phenomenology, as the influence for their study. Heidegger, likewise, is often acknowledged in studies as an influence upon a design that may have leanings toward hermeneutic phenomenology, in that the realities of the researcher and research participants is intertwined. Giorgi (2000a; 2000b) discussed the distinction between influence and inspiration and stated that, "Often, to be inspired means that one is attracted by someone's thought, even though one is aware that he or she has to modify what was said in order to make it meaningful in the context where the one inspired wants to use it." This seems an acceptable compromise and a rationale that may explain the attraction of modern phenomenology.

It could be asserted that the move away from reductionism (or bracketing) places modern phenomenology in a different epistemological position; it is no longer constructionist but now supports subjectivist views of knowledge generation. Constructivism (or constructionism) is the theory that knowledge is created out of human engagement with objects that are already present in the world, as opposed to subjectivism, which espouses that meaning is discovered or created by every individual independently. There are opposing views to this opinion, and it can be also reasoned that if the epistemological position was of a subjectivist nature, then it could be assumed that much research would be discovering new ways of looking at the world. A lot of research, however, does not really challenge established views of concepts, even though it may be concerned with the lived experience of participants.

As previously discussed, it is impossible to attain truly objective research as there are layers of subjectivity to cut through (Davis, 1991). Perhaps, no research can be regarded as truly objective and that constructivism achieves little more objectivity than subjectivism? Husserl's philosophy has received a great deal of criticism from modern philosophers (e.g., Bell 1990; Lapointe, 1980; Smith & Smith, 1989; Ströker, 1993; Zahavi, 2003) much of this directed at problems inherent in its structure and application. Bell (1990) discussed how Husserl himself, toward the end of his life, dismissed his own philosophy as a failure (pp. 232–233). Caelli, (2000) commented how the changes in new phenomenology are apparent because the approach is now applied through research and not merely philosophical meditations as advocated by Husserl and Heidegger.

Phenomenological reduction applied

Transcendental subjectivity is a Husserlian notion attained by constantly assessing the impact of the researcher on the study. Achieving transcendental subjectivity through reductionism, or bracketing (of pre-conceived ideas), is not without its critics (Bell, 1990; Lapointe, 1980; Smith & Smith, 1989; Stroker 1993, Zahavi, 2003), who believe it is either not desirable or not possible. The criticism that it is not possible focuses on the argument that to enact transcendental subjectivity would render the researcher incapable of functioning in the social world, as interaction is based upon preconceived ideas. To illustrate, if the researcher were to transcend preconceived ideas, how could they conduct a research interview with a participant? They would be incapable of forming questions as their preconceived ideas of questions would be bracketed and, therefore, temporarily void. Many researchers regard the concept of reduction, as described by Husserl (1931), as untenable; however, Kern (1997) believed that reduction is a necessary step and that there are several other practical ways to accomplish this state. While this view edges away from ideas of pure eidetic phenomenology, it still maintains the essential concept of the philosophy. Thus, research that uses methods to obtain objectivity preserves the intrinsic character of methodological openness by searching, probing, and describing, rather than declaring, which is still within the spirit of Husserlian phenomenology (Barua, 2003).

To illustrate how this can be achieved in modern research studies; it is common for a reflexive account to be weaved throughout, in order to place the researcher in context within the study. This allows the reader to be aware of the researcher's preconceptions and it serves to remind the researcher of these also. For example, if a part-time researcher in a hypothetical study of leadership styles was to declare him/herself as working in a leadership position in the introduction to the study, it becomes clear that he/she will have their own ideas regarding the attributes and behaviors of a leader and how this is adopted by followers. The researcher may also chose to reflexively explore his/her style of leadership and why it is considered effective, to expose possible bias and suppositions. In addition to this method of exposing subjectivity, reflexive journals can be kept throughout the research process. With this tool, the researcher records preconceptions about the subject of the research, plus other relevant ideas, emotions, and feelings, which can all support notions of objectivity by later scrutinizing and coding this data into categories (Allan, 2006). Thus researcher bias is noted and used as research data within the study, for review by both the researcher and readers of the study. Ahern (1999) discussed how such journals assist researchers with bracketing preconceived ideas and suggested that researchers make notes of interests that may be taken for granted, but which may disclose areas of subjectivity. In this way, an ongoing record of subjectivity is maintained in order to expose predispositions while gathering and analyzing data.

Notes from research journals can be discussed in research reports in order to maintain credibility and transparency. Also, to provide further attempts at objectivity when conducting interviews, all preliminary analyses of interview data should be checked for accuracy of interpretations with the participants concerned. While these actions may not merge with Husserl's philosophical notion of phenomenological reduction, and, as such are subject to purist criticisms, they are a practical means of achieving a degree of presubjective consciousness, which is what eidetic phenomenology espouses (Giorgi, 2000a). Gadamer (1975) believed that there was no method to apply phenomenology to research as there is a practical/theoretical dichotomy between the two. However, with slight adjustments workable solutions are possible (Giorgi, 2000b).

On describing reductionism, Husserl (1931) stated that empirical or individual intuition could be transformed into essential intuition from which the essence is obtained. He further described the technique of free variation whereby the researcher adds essences or subtracts them from the phenomenon to see if it still holds as a concept, enabling identification of what is and isn't an essential component (Husserl, 1931). To illustrate, consider a research study that seeks to identify the qualities of a business leader; interview data with business leaders was thematically analyzed and reduced to four essences: humanistic qualities; professionalism; proficiency in leadership skills; and knowledgeable in regards to the organization. If the concept of humanistic qualities is subtracted from the concepts of professional, proficiency in leadership skills, and knowledgeable in regards to the organization, would these three essences still be the essential components of a leader? In other words, are humanistic qualities essential essences of a business leaders' identity? Or if the component dedicated to business is added to the equation, would this be essential to describe the essence of business leaders' identity?

The technique of free variation has also been the subject of literary criticism. As can be seen from the previous example, it is not always a straightforward, logical, or objective procedure. Husserl describes how intuitively the researcher becomes aware of the universal description (Husserl, 1931). Bell (1990) highlighted that this is an imaginative procedure and not an empirical one. In research studies the description of essences is often composed of accounts of participants, whereas Husserl's notion of description has to be that of the researcher's objective consciousness, which would have no reference to the external world. This would not be desirable in the majority of business and management studies as findings need to be relevant to the external world of business. On this subject, Giorgi (2000b) stated that if "the nature of the experience depends on the manner in which it was experienced, how can one avoid obtaining descriptions from subjects?" (p. 14).

This point appears to be contradictory in Husserls' work as the hub of his philosophy focused on investigating the nature of phenomena as an essentially human experience (van Manen, 1997) and yet he opposes subjective experiences. So, in practice, it becomes necessary for researchers to move away from pure philosophical notions and apply practical solutions by describing the essence of the phenomenon through participants' dialogue. Many phenomenological researchers, therefore, are of the opinion that phenomenological designs should be flexible and adapted to suit the research investigation

(Crotty, 1998; Giorgi, 1994, 1997; Pollio et al., 1997; Valle & King, 1978; van Manen, 1997).

Phenomenology in business and management

Phenomenology is usually applied within an interpretive-constructivist research ideology, which holds that reality is constructed in the human mind as opposed to independently of people (Neuman, 2003). There are a variety of genres within the interpretive paradigm as highlighted within this book. A research paradigm may be considered a combination of philosophical, epistemological, and ontological positions as well as the methodology that underpins these (Denzin & Lincoln, 1994).

Many researchers in business and management design their studies with influences from a pragmativist philosophy, as a variation of eidetic phenomenology as proposed by Husserl (1931, 1970, 1971/1927, 1999/1907), or from a hermeneutic phenomenology as proposed by Heidegger (1962/1927). Experiences that are based on everyday life are regarded as being the most suitable for the phenomenological approach, which should be recognizable to those who have had the experience and provide an insight for those who are new to the phenomenon. Recognition of the description of essences is lightheartedly referred to in the literature as the phenomenological nod (Bollnow as discussed in van Manen, 1997), as when reading about the essence, a person experienced with the phenomena in question will nod in recognition of this universal concept.

Essences common to all shared experiences and concepts is a principal feature of eidetic phenomenology; Husserl (1931) referred to these essences as eidetic structures or universal essences. It is the aim of eidetic phenomenological research to discover the shared essences of the phenomenon under study and describe these (Portney & Watkins, 2000); hence it is also known as descriptive phenomenology. So, to illustrate, a phenomenological research study into effective leadership in business may consist of interviewing effective leaders within business. Rich, detailed descriptions of their leadership styles and how these came about would be rendered down through thematic analysis into the essence of these concepts. Although participants' accounts would be individual, when the data are reduced and further reduced until just the essences remain, commonalities appear.

A popular research methodology for business and management is interpretive (or hermeneutic) phenomenology as proposed by Heidegger (1962), which places emphasis on individual, subjective accounts. It differs from eidetic phenomenology in both how findings are created and how they are used to expand professional knowledge. In Heidegger's philosophy, hermeneutic phenomenology seeks to look further than core concepts to the meanings that are embedded in common practices (Conroy, 2003). To illustrate, in the example study previously discussed, leaders may be asked to describe their leadership style and how they achieved this identity. With hermeneutic phenomenology, however, they may be asked about their lifeworld, perhaps by describing a typical business day, which would provide further detailed insights into their style of leadership and characteristics. The focus in hermeneutic phenomenology is on human experience rather than knowledge (Barua, 2003).

Heidegger's philosophy does not support the notion of bracketing preconceived ideas, as he believed that humans are inextricably linked with their environment and the socialization processes that occur (Conroy, 2003). Thus it may be regarded as subjectivist and pragmatistic in nature as opposed to Husserl's philosophy, which places emphasis on an objective view gained through the notion of bracketing and reductionism. In addition, hermeneutic phenomenology is more concerned with individual experiences than general findings and does not lend itself to studies concerned with comparing data across sample groups. This may diminish the generalization of the research results. Thus, the hermeneutic phenomenology method could be used in research design strategies with questions that refer to between-groups in the unit of analysis focus.

The hermeneutic phenomenologist will seek to interpret the participants' narratives as opposed to the eidetic phenomenologist who concentrates on seeking and describing the shared essences. Co-constitutionality is Heidegger's concept for intersubjectivity attained by blending the meanings produced by researcher and participant (Heidegger, 1962). Prior knowledge is regarded as useful for interpreting data in the hermeneutic tradition in order to attain fused horizons (Gadamer, 1976). Thus, in hermeneutical phenomenology, the research does not seek to establish the one true meaning but rather, the goal is to ensure the meanings reflect the realities of all participants and, moreover, they must be logical and plausible within the framework of the study. Thus, eidetic phenomenology would better inform research studies that seek to find shared essences within research data (Barua, 2003), from which to make recommendations for practice (van Manen, 1997). Figure 24.4 is a conceptual comparison between the ideologies underpinning eidetic and hermeneutic phenomenology methods in business and management research designs.

For Husserl, the aim of phenomenology was the rigorous and unbiased study of phenomena as they appeared, in order to arrive at an essential understanding of human consciousness and experience (Valle et al., 1989). Both Husserl and Heidegger were critical of the consequences that culture and tradition could have on the examination of pure phenomena (Caelli, 2000). Husserl held that phenomenological reduction does not negate the world, but demonstrates the possibility for a belief in the world as it exists prior to any theoretical positing. However, this view opposes business philosophy, which often emphasizes the importance of culture, tradition, and individuality. To ignore cultural

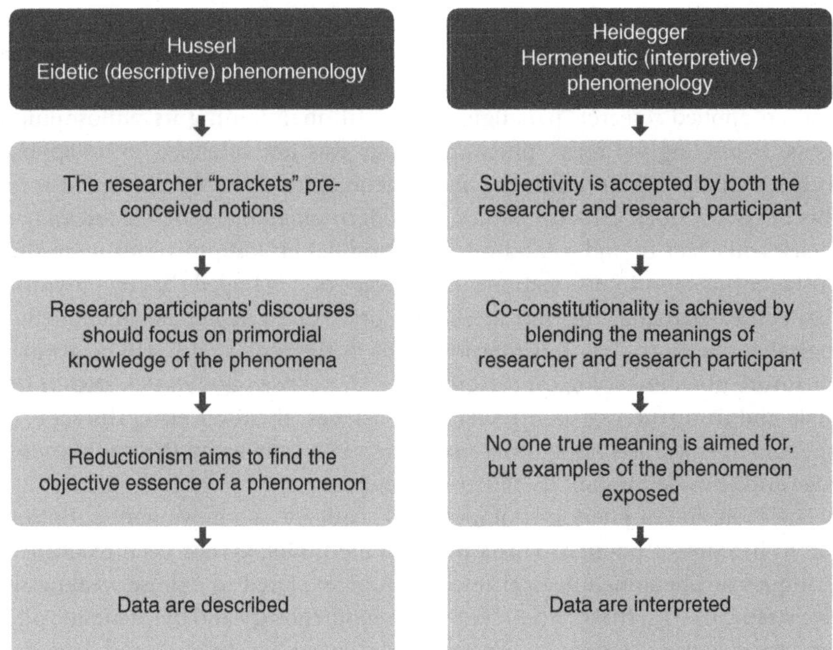

Figure 24.4 Comparison between eidetic and hermeneutic phenomenology (here).

references in a participant's dialogue is tantamount to presenting an ethical dilemma for a researcher. Once again researchers have to lean away from purity toward pragmatism by adjusting the methodology and, as reinforced throughout the chapter, many researchers use phenomenological research methods to explore cultural issues.

Husserl (1931) also purported that the primordial consciousness required to study phenomena strips the concept of all cultural and societal influences, including time and place. On first consideration, this might also seem problematic in research, as it is difficult to demonstrate how, for example, the concept of a manager would be the same today as it was in, for example, the 1920s, since business has undergone such radical changes. However, when considered in depth, the essences that may appear, such as management skills and knowledge of the organization, are universal phenomena devoid of time constrictions. It is only the adverbs used to illustrate the essences, for example, technically proficient, that may carry a modern ring to them.

Chapter summary

This chapter has explored phenomenology from its roots as a pure philosophical notion to modern-day interpretations of this as a research paradigm useful in business and management studies. It was intended that the chapter would clearly contextualize the concept for the readers affording them an understanding of how the philosophy has effectively evolved over the centuries into an applied research paradigm, while still maintaining its philosophical roots. In its original form, phenomenology was not intended to be applied to research studies, and modern phenomenologists have since adapted it for this purpose. Much criticism aimed at modern phenomenological researchers focuses on a lack of understanding of the original philosophy resulting in simplistic or incorrect interpretations in application. It is hoped that by providing this contextualizing, theoretical chapter prior to a chapter on phenomenological application, such misinterpretations of the philosophy will be avoided for future phenomenological researchers, or for those purely interested in the topic and in furthering their research knowledge. By discovering the roots of phenomenology, it is hoped that researchers can now apply this with knowledge and consideration of its earlier intentions.

The evolution of phenomenology and its concept as a movement culminating in its current popularity as a research methodology has been examined. Critiques of phenomenological research were explored to expose weaknesses and strengths with this concept. Eidetic phenomenology and hermeneutic phenomenology were compared, contrasted, discussed, scrutinized, and defended where applicable. Also included was a discussion and comparison of various authors and theorists who were influential in the formulation and application of this philosophy.

Much research into the fields of business and management is born out of a perceived problem, issue, or question within these areas or within particular organizations. The very nature of much of this research is, therefore, practical with the intention of future application of recommendations discovered through research results. It is carried out with the intention of improving the situation under scrutiny, or discovering theories that can be then applied to situations, such as effective management theories. A supporting research design is required to guide and underpin these studies, and modern phenomenology can offer such a framework, provided it concurs with the worldview of the researchers concerned. This design must clearly identify where on the research ideology continuum the researcher is approaching from. It must contain research questions that identify the unit of analysis as within or between groups, when more than a single participant is sampled. If the techniques are varied from the fundamental phenomenology methods discussed earlier (hermeneutic or eidetic), this must be articulated with the rationale, otherwise other practitioner-scholars could consider the research design itself was fatally flawed, and the inductive findings from the study become less credible.

Phenomenology in all its forms is primarily concerned with the "lived experience" of the phenomena under scrutiny and, therefore, its favored (but not exclusive) data collection tool is the in-depth interview with participants who have firsthand experience of the phenomena under scrutiny. It is a popular research paradigm in business and management studies for these reasons; for example, it is currently in vogue to examine business successes and failures from the perspective of the managing directors or chief executives concerned.

The following chapter builds upon the foundations of this contextualizing chapter by applying phenomenology to business and management research studies in order to examine the various nuances in its application and to explore possible benefits and drawbacks in these. The two chapters combined aim to afford readers a detailed and practical understanding of applied phenomenology in management and business, in order that they may confidently adopt this paradigm for their own application in future research studies.

References

Ahern, K. J. (1999). Pearls, pith and provocation: Ten tips for reflexive bracketing. *Qualitative Health Research, 9*(3), 407–411.

Allan, H. T. (2006). Using participant observation to immerse oneself in the field. *Journal of Research in Nursing, 11*(5), 397–407.

Anosike, P.; Ehrich, L. C., & Ahmed, P. (2012). Phenomenology as a method for exploring management practice. *International Journal of Management Practice* (IJMP), *5*(3), 205–224.

Baker, C., Wuest, J., & Stern, P. N. (1992). Method slurring: The grounded theory/ phenomenology example. *Journal of Advanced Nursing, 17*(13), 55–60.

Barua, A. (2003). Husserl, Heidegger and the intentionality question. *Minerva—An Internet Journal of Philosophy, 7*(1), 44–59.

Bell, D. A. (1990). *Husserl*. London: Routledge.

Bombala, B. (2012). Phenomenology of management—didactic aspects. *Management and Business Administration, 3*(116), 50–59.

Caelli, K. (2000). The changing face of phenomenological research: Traditional and American phenomenology in nursing. *Qualitative Health Research, 10*(3), 366.

Callister, L. C., Semenic, S., & Foster, J. C. (1999). Cultural and spiritual meanings in childbirth: Orthodox Jewish and Mormon women. *Journal of Holistic Nursing, 17*(3), 280–295.

Conroy, S. A. (2003). A pathway for interpretive phenomenology. *International Journal of Qualitative Methods, 2*(3), Article 4.

Crotty, M. (1996) *Phenomenology and nursing research*. Oxford: Churchill Livingstone.

Crotty, M. (1998). *The foundations of social research*. Sydney: Allen and Unwin,

Davis, K. (1991). The phenomenology of research: The construction of meaning in data analysis. Conference Paper. *Conference on College Composition and Communication*. (42nd, Boston, MA, March 21–23).

Denzin, N. K., & Lincoln, Y. S. (1994). *Handbook of qualitative research*. London: Sage.

Dowling, M. (2007). From Husserl to van Manen: A review of different phenomenological approaches. *International Journal of Nursing Studies, 44*(1), 131–142.

Dreyfus, H. (1994). Preface in P. Benner (Ed.). *Interpretive phenomenology: Embodiment, caring and ethics and health and illness*. Thousand Oaks, CA: Sage.

Ehrich, L. (2005). Revisiting phenomenology: Its potential for management research. In *Proceedings challenges or organisations in global markets, British Academy of Management Conference*, pp. 1–13, Said Business School, Oxford University.

Føllesdal, D. (1969). Husserl's notion of noema. *The Journal of Philosophy, 66*(20), 680–687.

Gadamer, H. G. (1976) *Philosophical hermeneutics*. Berkeley: University of California Press.

Giorgi, A. (1994). A phenomenological perspective on certain qualitative research methods. *Journal of Phenomenological Psychology, 25*(1), 190–220.

Giorgi, A. (1997). The theory, practice, and evaluation of the phenomenological method as a qualitative research procedure. *Journal of Phenomenological Psychology, 28*(1), 236–260.

Giorgi, A. (2000a). The status of Husserlian phenomenology in caring research. *Scandinavian Journal of Caring Science, 14*(1), 3–10.

Giorgi, A. (2000b). Concerning the application of phenomenology to caring research. *Scandinavian Journal of Caring Science, 14*(1), 11–15.

Goodwin, Y., & Strang, K. D. (2012). Socio-cultural and multi-disciplinary perceptions of risk. *International Journal of Risk and Contingency Management, 1*(1), 1–11.

Groenewald, T. (2004). A phenomenological research design illustrated. *International Journal of Qualitative Methods, 3*(1), 14–19.

Heidegger, M. (1962). *Being and time* (7th ed.). (J. Macquarrie and E.Robinson. Trans.). Oxford: Basil Blackwell (Original work published 1927).

Husserl, E. (1931). *Ideas: General introduction to pure phenomenology.* (Boyce Gibson W.R. Trans.). London: Allen and Unwin (Originally written in 1913).

Husserl, E. (1970). *Logical investigations* (Vol. 1). Englewood Cliffs, NJ: Humanities Press.

Husserl, E. (1971). Phenomenology. (Palmer, R. E. Trans.). *Journal of the British Society for Phenomenology, 2*(1), 77–90 (Originally published in 1927).

Husserl, E. (1999). *The idea of phenomenology* (L. Hardy, Trans.). Guildford: Springer (Originally published in 1907).

Johnson, M., Long, T., & White, A. (2001). Arguments for "British Pluralism" in qualitative health research. *Journal of Advanced Nursing, 33*(2), 243–249.

Kaelin, E. F., & Schrag, C. O. (1990). *American phenomenology: Origins and developments*. Dordrecht: Reidel Publishing Company.

Keller, P. (1999). *Husserl and Heidegger on human experience*. Cambridge: Cambridge University Press.

Kelly, G. (1996). Understanding occupational therapy: A hermeneutic approach. *British Journal of Occupational Therapy, 59*(1), 237–242.

Kern, I. (1977). The three ways to the transcendental phenomenological reduction in the philosophy of Edmund Husserl. In F. Elliston & P. McCormick (Eds). *Husserl Espositions and Appraisals*. Notre Dame, IN: University of Notre Dame Press.

Lapointe, F. (1980). *Edmund Husserl and his Critics. An international bibliography, 1894–1979: Preceded by a bibliography of Husserl's writings*. Bowling Green, OH: Bowling Green State University Press.

Lavesque-Lopman, L. (1988). *Claiming reality: Phenomenology and women's experience*. Lanham, MD: Rowman and Littlefield.

Le Vasseur, J. J. (2003). The problem of bracketing in phenomenology. *Qualitative Health Research, 13*(1), 408–420.

Lopez, K. A., & Willis, D. G. (2004). Descriptive versus interpretive phenomenology. *Qualitative Health Research, 14*(5), 726–735.

Moustakas, C. (1994). *Phenomenological research methods*. London: Sage.

Moran, D. (2000). *Introduction to phenomenology*. London: Routledge.

Morse, J. M., & Field, P. A. (1995). *Qualitative research methods for health professionals*. (2nd ed.). London: Sage.

Natanson, M. (1973). *Edmund Husserl: Philosophy of infinite tasks*. Evanston, IL: Northwestern University Press.

Neuman, W. L. (2000). *Social research methods: Qualitative and quantitative approaches.* 4th ed. Boston, MA: Allyn and Bacon.
Pollio, H. R., Henley, T. B., & Thompson, C. J. (1997). *The phenomenology of everyday life.* Cambridge: Cambridge University Press.
Portney, L. G., & Watkins, M. P. (2000). *Foundations of clinical research:Applications in practice* (2nd ed.). Upper Saddle, NJ: Prentice Hall Health.
Sheehan, T. (2007). Husserl and Heidegger: The making and unmaking of a relationship. Stanford: Stanford University Press, Education Department.
Silverman, H. (1987). *Inscriptions: Between phenomenology and structuralism.* New York: Routledge Kegan Paul.
Smith, B., & Smith, D. B. (eds.). (1995). *The Cambridge companion to Husserl.* Cambridge: Cambridge University Press.
Spiegelberg, H. (1982). The phenomenological movement: A historical introduction. (3rd ed.). The Hague: Martinus Hijhoff.
Stewart, D. & Mickunas, A. (1990). *Exploring phenomenology. A guide to the field and its literature.* Athens: Ohio University Press.
Ströker, E. (1993). Husserl's transcendental phenomenology. Stanford, CA: Stanford University Press.
Valle, R. S., King, M., & Halling, S. (1989). An introduction to existential-phenomenological thought in psychology. In R. S. Valle & S. Halling (Eds). *Existential-phenomenological perspectives in psychology: Exploring the breadth of human experience.* New York: Plenum Press.
van Manen, M. (1997). *Researching lived experience: Human science for an action sensitive pedagogy.* New York: State University Press.
van Manen, M. (2002). Inquiry: phenomenology of practice. *Phenomenology On-line.* http://www.phenomenologyonline.com. (accessed September 12, 2012).
Zahavi, D. (2003). *Husserl's phenomenology.* Stanford, CA: Stanford University Press.

25
Hermeneutic and Eidetic Phenomenology Applied to a Clinical Health-Care Study

Jillian McCarthy

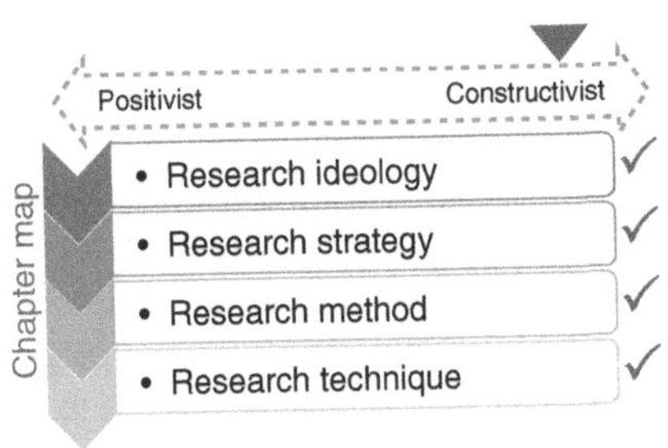

Chapter overview

As an extension to her theoretical chapter, McCarthy goes through two examples from a constructivist research ideology perspective using two phenomenology method variations. She illustrates two positions on this continuum, an interpretive one with the eidetic phenomenology and the hermeneutic descriptive method. The unit of analysis in the research strategy for the first study was "the lived experience of telephone follow-up appointments for physicians and patients," and "the lived experience of health care managers" for the second, both having an inductive within-group focus. The level of analysis was individual and the generalization target was to scholars in the health-care discipline (as an inductive model).

Introduction

This chapter continues from the previous chapter, which contextualized phenomenology from its early roots as a philosophical concept to its present-day application as a research paradigm. In this chapter, two of the common and most popular styles of phenomenology, hermeneutic (interpretive) and eidetic (descriptive) phenomenology, are applied to case studies in order to afford a practical demonstration and in-depth overview of how these concepts can provide a successful framework for research studies within the fields of business and management.

As discussed in the previous chapter, there is not one definitive model of phenomenology, as this has splintered and evolved over the years from its original philosophical underpinnings. It seems a pragmatic solution to suggest that if a strong rationale is provided for the style of phenomenology applied to the particular study, and as long as this adheres to the key pointers of the original underpinning philosophy, this would appear to be an acceptable compromise in terms of academic practice and academic publishing. This view is not without its purist critics but, nonetheless, it appears to be acceptable practice in research studies for reasons of practicality, realism, and progression.

Paradigms and methodologies

This chapter will apply two of the most common styles of phenomenology to case studies in order to examine in detail the nuances and variances in these differing styles, affording the reader a clear example of how these paradigms may be applied. Eidetic and hermeneutic phenomenology are popular for their application in the areas of business and management (e.g., Anosike et al., 2012; Bombala, 2012; Ehrich, 2005). Phenomenology is a popular research method for qualitative research studies in these areas, as it concentrates on a particular phenomenon as experienced by those who have lived through this; hence these studies often have in their title the term "the lived experience of..." (see: Buchanan & Badham, 1999; Dobscha, 1998; Samra-Fredericks, 2003). Much of the research within the fields of business and management is focused on practical, real-life issues in order to improve, emulate, or explore these areas in more detail, and thus phenomenology provides a supportive framework for investigating such topics.

Phenomenology is applied to research studies as a research paradigm that incorporates a whole methodology, as opposed to simply a research method. Denzin and Lincoln, (1994) define a research paradigm as a combination of philosophical, epistemological, and ontological positions and the methodology that underpins these. Kuhn (1986) defines a paradigm as dictating

- what is studied and researched,
- the type of questions that are asked,
- the exact structure and nature of the questions, and
- how the results of any research are interpreted.

It can be reasoned that a paradigm should match the researcher's worldview and provide a framework that governs the research study, whereas a methodology consists of the combination of a paradigm, the research questions, suitable research methods stemming from these, and a suitable style of data analysis that is fitting for the research methods and paradigm concerned. The term methodology is often used erroneously in research studies, simply replacing the term methods; however, as can be read, it is actually more encompassing than this.

As stated, a paradigm is an overarching concept or framework, which means that the phenomenological researcher should have faith that the answers to a research problem or issue lie in studying the views of people who have experience of this phenomenon. It is little use in having a firm belief in the absolute certainty of scientific empirical research and then conducting a study that applies a qualitative interpretive paradigm; this is neither authentic nor practical. Qualitative research relies on the honesty and integrity of the researcher, and this is often exposed within the study through reflexive accounts that uncover the researcher's ideas and ideologies, thus allowing the reader to judge the validity and authenticity of the study. It is, therefore, essential that the researcher has belief in the methodology or paradigm that is being applied. In practical terms, this means that the phenomenological paradigm must be chosen prior to the study commencing, as it must be compatible with the researcher's worldview; the research methods used in the study will then be led by the paradigm. Thorough literature search, reading and comprehension of research paradigms is, therefore, required prior to the study commencing, in order that a compatible paradigm and methodology is chosen. See figure 25.1 for an illustration of a research methodology.

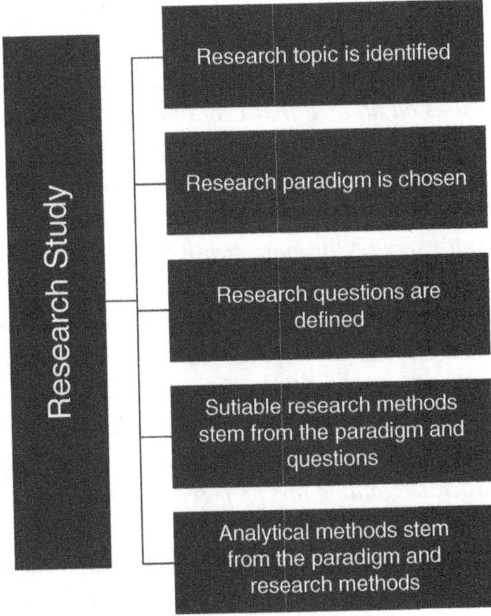

Figure 25.1 Research methodology.

Applying eidetic phenomenology

This section of the chapter will apply a style of eidetic (often referred to as descriptive) phenomenology to a research study within the field of business and management. It should be remembered that there is no one definitive style of eidetic phenomenology as this was originally devised as a purely philosophical concept by Edmund Husserl, and has since been amended and adjusted by academics to be applied to research studies (as discussed in the previous chapter). This section will discuss the research study in question, from the viewpoint of the researcher, in order to afford readers a practical example of how they may adopt this paradigm within their own research studies. The discussion is written in the form of researcher field notes that document the research process and are written in italics to differentiate from other writings within this chapter.

* * *

I am a middle manager working in the health sector in the newly formed Clinical Commissioning Group (CCG) within the United Kingdom. I am responsible for the commissioning of acute services within the CCG area, for a diverse population of approximately 200,000 patients. I manage a team of 8 staff and I report directly to the commissioning officer of the CCG. I am presently studying part-time for an MBA (funded by my organization) and I am about to commence a piece of work-based research for my final dissertation project of 25,000 words.

I am keen that my research is pertinent to my organization as this was part of the remit when being funded to undertake this degree. I will be disseminating the results back into my organization through a presentation to the governing body, and through a research report forwarded to all CCG staff (approximately 50 staff). I am also keen that my research focuses on an area that is of interest to me personally, as I wish to sustain my interest throughout the 9 months of the study, and have been advised to choose an area that will do so. The Acute Commissioning Team (which I manage) has been directed to consider methods of lessening the burden on the local hospitals by utilizing community services in more creative and innovative ways. One of the solutions we are considering is the choice of telephone follow-up appointments with consultants following surgery, as opposed to out-patient appointments, as a way to lessen the footfall at the Out Patient Departments (OPD). As I am being asked to head this project, it seemed pertinent and logical to research the efficacy of this proposal, to examine other organizations that have implemented similar initiatives, research the best methods for introducing this innovation, and to gather the opinions of staff, stakeholders, and patients regarding this proposed scheme.

First, I discussed the initiative with my research supervisor at the university. We discussed what it was that I wanted to research, why I wanted to research this topic, and how I thought I would go about this. Together we bounced ideas back and forth and I discovered that from a vague notion of "this area would be interesting and useful for me to research," I left his office with a clearer direction and an action plan. I also found that by talking my ideas through, I was clearer in my thinking regarding the research topic. I was keen to use a qualitative design as I placed faith in the opinions of people who had lived the experience under review, and I wished to engage with research that examined people's opinions through interviews or focus groups. I was not as keen on surveys as I felt that this did not allow for points to be fully explored. My supervisor suggested that I devise an overall question or statement that summarized what I wanted to research. She then suggested that stemming from this question or statement, I devise three or four further questions, using which I could devise data research methods that can answer these questions. She also suggested that I make a strong case for why I wanted to research this area, as this would not only be useful in my dissertation in the introductory chapter, but also when presenting it back to my organization.

She also recommended that I read about the various styles of qualitative research and discover which appealed to me and fitted my particular worldview. It was clear that I felt the answer to the question of how best to introduce new systems of outpatients' appointments lay in examining the experiences of people who had been involved in this process and then to emulate their successes and learn from their mistakes. We discussed using an ethnographical approach that would involve fieldwork observation—I could observe the process of phone follow-up appointments and make field notes from this. I could also consider grounded theory in which I would first collect my data with no specific prior knowledge of the subject and through my data analysis I would discover a theory of introducing telephone follow-up appointments, which I would then link to the current evidence base on this topic. Last, I could explore a phenomenological approach in which the lived experience of people who had gone through the process of telephone follow-up appointments and their views could be recorded. This framework or paradigm appealed to me as it made sense to my way of viewing the world, more so than the other two paradigms, as I would be able to elicit the views of both staff and patients who had been involved in this new style of appointment. I agreed, however, to research and read about all three paradigms, to ensure that I chose the correct paradigm for my study and also to answer the questions that my research posed.

I left my supervisor's office with a plan to:

- *conduct a preliminary literature search and review on my subject to discover what studies had already been conducted on this topic and what was already known about this,*
- *devise my research questions and working title, which could be refined later,*
- *research and read up on the three qualitative paradigms or frameworks we had discussed: ethnography, grounded theory, and phenomenology,*
- *devise an action plan and timetable for my research journey, and*
- *email all of these to my supervisor to review by the end of the week.*

My supervisor explained that it may be helpful to split the research journey into two distinct phases each of which contained its own set of tasks.

* * *

This is represented in figures 25.2 and 25.3.

As can be read from the researchers' field notes, it became clear early in the conception of this study that the research lends itself to qualitative methods of inquiry. It was considered that the research questions could be best answered by listening to the individual perspectives of both surgeons and patients who were involved with this particular phenomenon. Lincoln and Guba (1985) stated that qualitative research assumes a different ontological position than traditional quantitative research, claiming that it is characterized by the researcher constructing a reality as he or she discovers it. Alongside this is the

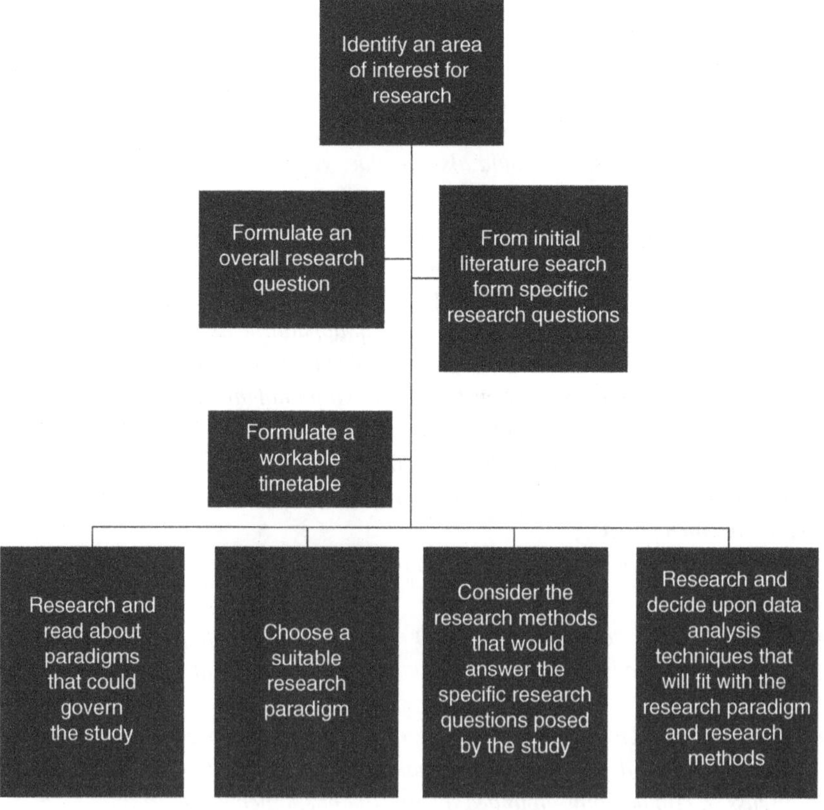

Figure 25.2 The first part of the research journey.

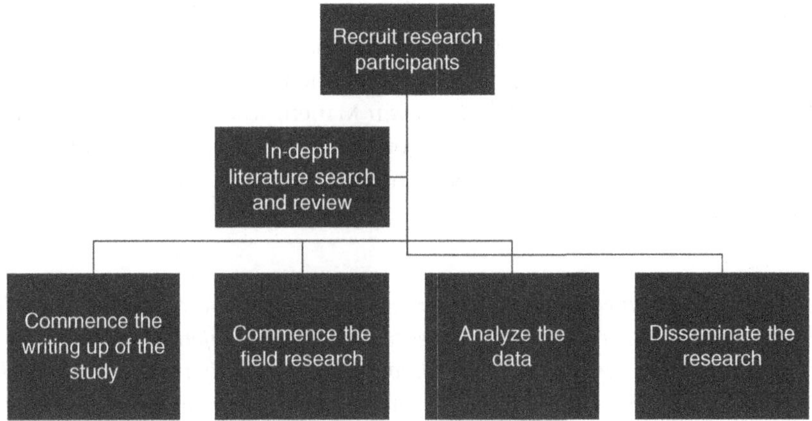

Figure 25.3 The second part of the research journey.

idea that participants also construct their individual reality. Epistemological foundations of qualitative research are based on values and value judgments, not facts; the researcher's values guide and shape the conclusions of the study because the researcher constructs the reality of the inquiry (Lincoln & Guba, ibid.). However, the researcher needs to demonstrate sensitivity to the "truths" of others, and the consequent differences and possibly conflicting values, therefore, it would seem that all findings in a qualitative study are socially negotiated.

For this particular researcher, a true constructivist research ideology was held. The unit of analysis was the essence of the experience between groups—the surgeons and patients. Descriptive phenomenology was regarded as being the most suitable method with telephone interviewing as the data collection technique. Descriptive phenomenology focuses on the meaning of specific phenomenon from the viewpoint of those who have experienced it and supports exploring data in order to discover the essence of the experience under scrutiny, thus allowing for comparisons to be made between groups of participants—the surgeons and the patients. This study may be regarded as hybrid in its phenomenological design as it is tailored to fit the research, in accordance with much modern phenomenology. Many phenomenological researchers believe that method designs should be flexible and adapted to the phenomena being researched (e.g., Crotty, 1996; Giorgi, 1997; Pollio et al., 1997; Valle & Mohs, 1998; van Manen, 1997). Giorgi (2000b) believed that researchers should be inspired by theorists, not by applying their ideas, but by being attracted to these ideas and then modifying and adapting them to suit particular needs. Overall, the design is in keeping with eidetic (descriptive) phenomenology as opposed to hermeneutic (interpretive) phenomenology. Although originally conceived by Husserl (1999/1907), many modern researchers choose this style of phenomenology as they are influenced by the works of modern descriptive phenomenologists such as Giorgi and van Manen, who focus on phenomena as they appear through experience or consciousness and provide rich textured descriptions of participants' stories in their writings.

* * *

Following on from my first meeting I conducted a literature search and review prior to writing the research questions, in order to discover what information was already known in regard to the specific topic. Although this is a fairly new initiative in the United Kingdom, there was already research in this area from the United States and Australia, and I also discovered two recently printed articles from the United Kingdom. I also reviewed qualitative research methods and frameworks and decided upon descriptive or eidetic phenomenology as this placed emphasis on examining a phenomenon through the lived experience, in other words, exploring the viewpoint of those who been through this experience. Popular research methods for this style of research were in-depth semistructured interviews and in-depth, semistructured focus groups, both of which allowed for in-depth questioning and exploration. I set about devising my working title and research question and objectives:

Working title: The Lived Experience of Telephone Follow-up Appointments Post-Surgery

Overall research question: Do telephone follow-up appointments provide satisfactory standards of assessment of post-operative patients as compared to face-to-face appointments?

Research objectives: To discover

1. if telephone follow-up appointments provide satisfactory standards of assessment for the post-operative patients concerned?
2. if telephone follow-up appointments provide satisfactory standards of assessment for the surgeons concerned?
3. if telephone follow-up appointments are as satisfactory as face-to-face outpatient appointments for both the patient and surgeon concerned? and
4. what are the best ways to introduce and conduct phone-call follow-up appointments for post-operative patients?

I carefully considered each question and the best method of answering these research objectives and decided upon the following data collection methods.

Research objectives and corresponding data collection methods:

1. Do phone-call follow-up appointments provide satisfactory standards of assessment for the post-operative patients concerned?

Data collection method:

- in-depth interviews with patients who have experienced phone-call follow-up appointments and
- from a review of the literature on this topic.

2. Do phone-call follow-up appointments provide satisfactory standards of assessment for the surgeons concerned?

Data collection method:

- in-depth interviews with surgeons who conduct phone-call follow-up appointments and
- from a review of the literature on this topic.

3. Are telephone follow-up appointments as satisfactory as face-to-face outpatient appointments for both the patient and surgeon concerned?

Data collection method:

- in-depth interviews with patients and surgeons who have experience of telephone follow-up appointments,
- review of the hospital data for patients who are readmitted to hospital with complications following the first appointment—a comparison of telephone and face-to-face appointments, and
- from a review of the literature on this topic

4. What are the best ways to introduce and conduct telephone follow-up appointments for post-operative patients?

Data collection method:

- from a review of the literature on this topic and
- also with two sets of focus groups,

- surgical patients who have experienced telephone follow-up appointments from a nearby hospital trust and
- surgeons from a nearby hospital trust who have introduced telephone follow-up appointments.

These research methods fitted in with phenomenological research as I would be examining the lived experience of clinicians and patients who have been involved in post-surgical phone-call follow-up appointments.

Reading about phenomenological research made me aware of several issues that needed to be addressed within my research. These are particularly relevant to phenomenological research and especially to eidetic phenomenology. It appears from the literature that the researcher is required to be objective throughout the research study in order that preconceived notions do not taint the research process and bring bias to the study. Bracketing of preconceived ideas is essential when interviewing or conducting focus groups and the literature indicated that there were several ways in this objectivity could be obtained.

* * *

Figure 25.4 Achieving objectivity within the eidetic phenomenological paradigm.

See figure 25.4 for an illustration of research objectivity within the eidetic phenomenological paradigm,

I discussed eidetic phenomenological approaches with my supervisor and decided that I would still conduct the literature search and review prior to the data collection stage of the research; I was aware that this contravened "pure" phenomenological research in the eidetic style, but the rationale behind this decision was that my research was time limited and it would cause delay to carry out the whole of a lengthy literature search and review post data collection. In addition, I had already conducted a preliminary literature search, so that I had already read articles around the topic and would, therefore, already have preformed opinions on these. It was also decided to inform research participants of the overall topic of the research, but not to inform them of the actual research question, in this way ethical issues were not contravened, but unintentional influence was kept to a minimum, as it is known that participants will often try to give the answers that they think researchers may want to hear.

I was keen on the idea of keeping a journal not only to record my research journey, but also to record thoughts and ideas that I could later scrutinize for possible bias or preformed ideas on my topic. I had already commenced a research journal that contained my notes pertaining to the research, so to this I would add any thoughts or bias that I noted within my ideas or work. I realized that this was particularly important during the data collection, analysis, and writing up stages of the research. I also liked the idea of a research buddy who could act as an additional support and "devil's advocate" questioning my work, ideas, thoughts, methods, etc. I was in touch with others from my MBA group and thought that I would approach one of my peers and ask them if they would offer this service in return for it being reciprocated by me for their study.

I felt it was important to expose my opinions with regard to post-operative follow-up appointments by telephone with the inclusion of an in-depth reflexive account that displayed openly and honestly my opinions on this topic and why these might be so. I talked this through at length with my supervisor who explored this with me by the use of open questioning and I decided to also discuss this with my research buddy. I realized through discussion that I had reservations about the efficacy of this style of follow-up appointment compared to traditional outpatient appointments, as I considered it a cost-cutting exercise. I also discovered that I felt resentment to cost cutting within the health service as my grandfather had recently died through post-operative complications when in a busy hospital, which I felt was due, in some part, to shortage of staff. I made notes in my research journal to be aware that I did not subjectively lean toward these explanations in my data analysis or literature review.

I decided that post interviews and focus groups, I would ask participants to check the thematic analysis, to ensure that I had analyzed their conversations correctly and themed these under headings that the participants agreed with. Likewise I would request that my research buddy also check my thematic analysis for uniformity and parity across interviews and focus groups.

Some of the steps that this researcher suggests contravene traditional phenomenological methods of inquiry; however like many modern phenomenologists his study can be seen to be influenced by phenomenology. Literature searching and reviewing prior to the study and, indeed, having a research question in mind are not in keeping with a constructivist epistemology that seeks objectivity through reductionism (Crotty, 1996). Participants in the interviews and focus groups are to be primed that the study is investigating post-operative telephone follow-up appointments and, although they will not be made aware of the actual research aim, this still removes the objectivity from their descriptions to some degree. It would, however, be unethical not to inform them what the research is in regard to and, also, it would be obvious from the focus of the questioning. Like other researchers who have adapted phenomenology to suit their investigations, without these modifications and fine-tunings the researcher would not have been able to fully answer the research inquiry. Perhaps it is time to redefine phenomenological research and to declare the common ground in all approaches to this methodology. Giorgi (2000b) discussed the distinction between influence and inspiration and stated that "often, to be inspired means that one is attracted by someone's thought, even though one is aware that he or she has to modify what was said in order to make it meaningful in the context where the one inspired wants to use it" (p.10).

It would not be appropriate for this researcher to conduct the study without making clear his preconceptions and beliefs about post-operative telephone follow-up appointments. Flaming (2005) discussed the importance, from a research perspective, of the researcher situating him/herself "explicitly or implicitly within a variety of frameworks when studying phenomena" (p.95). This allows for a more robust study as the reader is given an overview of the researcher's viewpoints. The researcher in this study obviously has many ideas, experiences, and beliefs that have influenced his construct of this topic. She intends to include self-reflections within the study because, as Lincoln and Guba (1985) point out, we cannot escape theoretical presuppositions, but we can try to make our approach as explicit as possible. In this study the author intends to include a reflexive account in order to place herself contextually within the study (Parahoo, 2006). This allows for readers to be aware of the researcher's preconceptions and serves to remind the researcher of these too. For example, by declaring that she believes there are financial implications to this initiative, it becomes clear that she may subconsciously be regarding this style of follow-up appointment as inferior.

Throughout the study the researcher intends to keep a reflexive journal in which she can record any preconceptions she may discovered about herself in regard to the subject under scrutiny, plus other relevant ideas, emotions, and feelings that can later be scrutinized by coding the data into categories (Allan, 2006). This is a common technique in qualitative studies, and Richmond (2007) stated that during her study, "I made comprehensive field notes regarding my feelings" (p.61) in order to examine how these changed over the study period. Ahern (1999) discussed how such journals assist researchers with bracketing preconceived ideas; for example, Ahern suggested that the researcher makes notes of interest, which could be taken for granted. In this way, an ongoing record of subjectivity is maintained in order to clarify ideas and to avoid influencing the study, as far as possible, while gathering and analyzing data (Bradbury-Jones, 2007). Relevant notes from the research journal can be discussed within the study, perhaps alongside participant discourses, in order to achieve credibility and transparency. Koch (1994) discussed how field journals assisted her, among other things, to acknowledge prejudice within her role as researcher and within the research process. Thoughts and emotions can be recorded prior to and following interviews and during focus groups to later reflect upon these entries in order to observe for bias, which could affect the authenticity of the research findings.

In addition, to provide further attempts at objectivity, the researcher is intending that all preliminary analyses of interview data are to be checked for accuracy of interpretations with the participants concerned. While all of these actions may not merge perfectly with Husserl's philosophical notion of phenomenological reduction, they are a practical means of achieving a degree of presubjective consciousness, which is what eidetic phenomenology espouses (Giorgi, 2000a). Gadamer (1976) believed that there was no method to apply phenomenology to research as there is a practical/theoretical dichotomy between the two; however, Giorgi (2000b) believed that with slight adjustments, such as these discussed, workable solutions are possible. Giorgi (2000b) stated that the phenomenological method of data analysis has four principal characteristics:

1. *It is descriptive.* In brief, description refers to the idea that the researcher must analyze the data as the participant intended it and not interpret meanings or give explanations from the researcher's standpoint.
2. *It uses reduction.* Reduction refers to the meaning of any concept as it appears in the consciousness, "Whatever presents itself to consciousness should be taken precisely with the meaning with which it presented itself, and one should refrain from affirming that it is what it presents itself to be" (Giorgi, 1985, p. 50). This involves a radical transformation in approach whereby the researcher must strive to suspend presuppositions and go beyond assumed understanding. "No work can be consider[ed] to be phenomenological if some sense of the reduction is not articulated and utilized" (Giorgi, 1997, p. 240).
3. *It searches for essences.* The search for essences is looking for the unchangeable characteristics of the particular phenomenon under study; for example in this study, the search is for the essences of nurse identity in traditional

and e-learning students and also the search for the essences of how this identity is constructed and adopted.

4. *It is focused on intentionality.* Finally, Giorgi's last characteristic refers to the intentional act of a human mind to be aware of their world. Intentiality is within human consciousness, and it means that humans are constantly consciously aware of something.

It is recommended with phenomenology that researchers submerge themselves into the data in order to become familiar with it. Giorgi calls this familiarization, the purpose of which is to comprehend the participant's experience (Giorgi, 1985). To accomplish this the researcher can listen to the interview and focus group recordings on several occasions. She can then transcribe the recordings, which involves continually playing and replaying them while transcribing what was spoken. Once transcribed, the researcher will need to examine each participant's data systematically line by line, examining the data and creating new questions to ask participants at the follow-up interview in order to clarify issues and comprehend the discourse from the participant's experience. Once an initial impression of the participant's experiences is gained from the data, descriptions can be divided into what Giorgi (1997) termed "meaning units," which are sentences or phrases that possess a self-contained meaning. Although meaning units are self-contained, it is important to understand them in terms of the overall meaning of the discourse, so that assumptions are not assigned to the meaning units that the participant did not intend.

The next step is to transform the meaning units by allocating a word or phrase that neatly summarizes their meaning. Giorgi (1997) commented that the units are divided by searching for different key terms, aspects, attitudes, or values of the participant. For example, when discussing telephone follow-up appointments in this study, a patient may have stated that he or she felt more distant from the doctor and thus less able to talk freely than in face-to-face appointments in which they met the surgeon. The meaning unit could be allocated the phrase "less personal" to summarize the participant's meaning. Following the stage of transforming the meaning units, the researcher will need to read and re-read the text in an attempt to ensure, as far as was possible, that she is not interpreting this to suit hi or her own assumptions, but, to reflect the experience of the research participant. Giorgi stressed at this point in the data analysis that the researcher should not transform the data into expressions that suit the research, but should maintain the situated context of the participant.

The third step is imaginative variation, which involves considering the meaning units and imagining all the possible meanings these could have, while striving to attain the essential and unchangeable meaning. To illustrate using the same example in the previous paragraph; the participant may have stated: "I feel distant from the doctor as I can't see them and I'm less able to chat freely about my condition." When it comes to applying imaginative variation to this meaning unit, the researcher should consider that the participant could have meant "distant" in several ways and not necessarily meaning geographically apart from the physician, which it may be taken to mean at first glance. For example, the participant could have meant distant as in less relaxed, distant as in the relationship was not as friendly, or distant as in the voice on the phone sounded a long way off. All of these interpretations can bring a differing perspective to this conversation and the meaning should be checked with the participant at a follow-up interview. However, on considering the meaning unit within the whole of the discussion, and by the researcher imagining him/herself in the participants' position, he/she may reach the correct conclusion for the meaning in this discourse without checking with the participant. This follows Husserl's recommendation that phenomenologists imagine the other's viewpoint. "I not only empathize with his [*sic*] thinking, his feeling, and his action, but I must also follow him in them" (Husserl, cited in Davidson, 2003, p.121).

Finally, the last stage in data analysis takes place by integrating the transformed meaning units into one coherent and consistent description; in order to assist with this process, the transformed meaning units are gathered into clusters within the essence under scrutiny, in order to disclose what the descriptions have in common.

This first section of the chapter examined the field notes of a researcher about to embark on a research journey using eidetic or descriptive phenomenology as the framework for her study. Extracts from the researcher's field notes have been provided to add clarity and detail and to explore theories and concepts that underpin these notes. Practical examples of how descriptive phenomenology may be undertaken have been provided, but as noted in the introduction to this chapter, there are many variances in phenomenology, and modern researchers may alter the framework to suit their particular studies while maintaining the main structures of this paradigm.

Applying hermeneutic phenomenology

In this section of the chapter, we will explore the field notes of a researcher about to embark on a similar journey as the previous researcher, with a similar style of research question in mind; however, this researcher is drawn to hermeneutic phenomenology as the framework for the particular research study. Again, the researcher's field notes will be written in italic script, in order that it stand out and, again, further explanations of these notes will be provided in order to explore underpinning theories and concepts and add detail and clarity to the notes.

I am an assistant nurse director at a general hospital within the United Kingdom (UK). I am undertaking a PhD, part-time, in the area of Health-Care Management at my local university and am about to embark on writing a thesis, which is a work-based research project. I am interested in what makes an effective leader in health care, in order that we can replicate these qualities within my organization and further afield, also, on a personal level, that I may replicate these factors in my own role. I am interested in discussing this topic with well-known effective leaders within the health-care arena in the United Kingdom, in order to discover their views on the topic and to learn from their experiences.

Prior to the first meeting with my supervisor, he had directed me to choose a topic to research on and to undertake some preliminary research and reading on this topic to further inform my ideas. He also directed me to consider a framework for my study and to come to our first supervision meeting ready to discuss these ideas. My research has informed me that there are numerous articles and research on what makes a good leader in health care and that these have changed focus over the years. I have also discovered that I am interested in phenomenology as the framework for my study, and that I am leaning toward modern interpretations of hermeneutic or interpretive phenomenology, as I am finding it difficult to come to terms with the researcher objectivity that is required with eidetic or descriptive phenomenology. This is because I have my own opinions on what makes for good leadership in health care and I am more drawn toward interpretive phenomenology, which acknowledges the notions of the researcher within the research.

At the first meeting with my supervisor I discussed my ideas for the research project and how I was drawn toward hermeneutic phenomenology. My supervisor discussed how phenomenology may be regarded as hermeneutical when its method is taken to be interpretive rather than purely descriptive as in eidetic/descriptive/transcendental phenomenology. He discussed how hermeneutics is about the art of understanding and the theory of interpretation and that there is a tension between these two meanings. My supervisor explained how the etymology of the word derives from the messenger god Hermes, whose job it was to understand messages from the gods and to interpret these for mortals. We further discussed how hermeneutic phenomenology emanated from the work of Martin Heidegger who believed that description cannot be objective and must always be based on an interpretation. Heidegger argued that every form of human awareness is interpretive and in his later works he introduced poetry and art as expressive ways of interpreting the nature of being, which included language, thinking, truth, and dwelling. I found that I could align with these ideas, as I too could not see how describing somebody else's experiences could be free from subjectivity. I left my supervisor's office with a plan to focus my research into an overarching research question and to explore hermeneutic phenomenology further and to formulate an outline of how I could conduct my research using this framework.

* * *

The word "hermeneutic" was first used by Aristotle to describe how the logical structure of language is used to describe the nature of phenomena in the world. Heidegger, who was originally Husserl's pupil at the university in Vienna, embraced phenomenology but adapted it from Husserl's original emphases on ideas, thoughts, and mental processes to a sole emphasis on "being." His interest in existentialism led to the belief that a human being is the embodiment of "being," and it was his interest in what humans do that was the focus of his interpretation of phenomenology. Some of the key philosophers in regard to hermeneutic phenomenology are Martin Heidegger, Hans-Georg Gadamer, and Paul Ricoeur (Thompson, 1981). Gadamer, a student of Heidegger, explored the role of language in hermeneutic phenomenology including conversation, particularly the notion of questioning and the significance of prejudice, history, and tradition in human understanding. Many modern writers also discuss how understanding language and texts is an essential component of hermeneutic phenomenology and how intuition is required for providing a rich and detailed account of the phenomena under scrutiny. Van Manen (1990) a modern-day phenomenologist suggested that in hermeneutic research the researcher must describe the essence of the phenomenon so that the lived experience is revealed in such a way that the reader can easily grasp the nature of this experience. Wilsonnand Hutchinson (1991) discuss how hermeneutic phenomenology is concerned with lived experience or lifeworld as it is happening and that understanding and explanations must be given to the small, often unnoticed details of experience. The researcher must bring sense and understanding to these experiences through the medium of eloquent language and analogies. There are often unspoken and unnoticed nuances that through idiomatic expression and rich language can represent emotions and intentions not available through ordinary language and everyday dialogue. It is just as important in hermeneutic phenomenology as in descriptive phenomenology that the researcher is aware of his or her own underlying assumptions and that these be weaved into the study and thus exposed. This is often achieved by a rich descriptive interweaving of experiences, assumptions, and stories of both the researcher and participants.

There is no one way to conduct hermeneutic phenomenology in research, nor is there a set of specific steps to follow for the researcher. Like eidetic phenomenology, there are many possible interpretations of this. Merleau-Ponty (1962) identified four characteristics that are considered as "celebrated themes" common to the various schools of phenomenology. These qualities he discussed as

1. description—the researcher describes the phenomenon under scrutiny,
2. reduction—the researcher reduces the data to the essences of the phenomenon under scrutiny,

3. essences—the data are reduced and reduced until all that remains is the very essence of the phenomenon, and
4. intentionality—the notion that the mind is always conscious of something; it cannot be empty. In phenomenology it is the striving to understand the consciousness of the phenomenom under scrutiny.

Kafle (2011), when discussing how there is no one specific way to conduct hermeneutic phenomenology, explains that, however, there should be a "dynamic interplay" between six principles, which he defines as:

1. commitment to an abiding concern,
2. oriented stance toward the research question,
3. investigating the experience as it is lived,
4. describing the phenomenon through writing
5. rewriting and refining this, and
6. considering the parts of the phenomenon and the whole.

In this example, the researcher will be holding an interpretative-constructivistic ideology. The research strategy will be inductive in nature and the unit of analysis will be the meaning of the knowledge generated and constructed through the lived experience of leaders within health care, a within-group focus. In the hermeneutic phenomenology method, unstructured interviews are often the research technique of choice because this enables the researcher to openly explore the narratives or stories of lived experiences and these also provide a vehicle in which to develop conversations in regard to the meaning

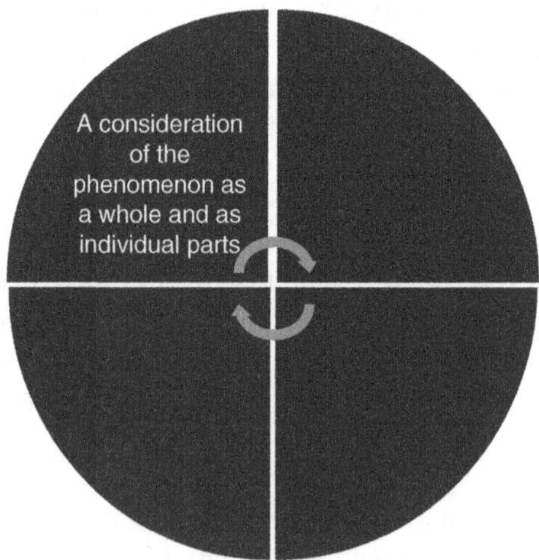

Figure 25.5 Principles for hermeneutic phenomenology.

of those experiences with participants through reflective and thoughtful dialogue (van Manen, 1997). See figure 25.5 for the main principles of hermeneutic phenomenology.

I was concerned that I would not be able to write in the manner required for this style of research and discussed this at the second meeting with my tutor. My tutor suggested that I begin to write and then hone and refine this until the writing is rich and reflective and summarizes the essences of the interviews and focus groups that I am conducting. He reassured me that with time and practice this skill would emerge and he also assured me that analogies used to explain concepts would also emerge as I became submersed in the research and the research data.

In addition we discussed notions of validity and reliability within the research study and he explained that these concepts are more common to scientific research studies and that in qualitative research these notions have been replaced by the concepts of rigor, honesty, and transparency obtained through several means:

- *triangulation of data,*
- *critical friend or research buddy,*
- *reflective account weaved throughout the work,*
- *research diaries or field notebooks,*
- *discussions of data analysis with research buddy and interview participants,*
- *fusion of consciousness—the thoughts and experiences of the research participants and the researcher,*
- *focus on the lifeworld of the participants and how they live with the phenomenon under question*
- *in-depth interviews and re-interviews to really understand the meanings of participants' answers,*
- *bracketing (achieving objectivity) throughout the data collection and analysis phases, and*
- *reduction of data and rich description of the essences of the phenomenon.*

In this study, the emphasis is on knowledge generated and constructed through the lived experience of leaders within health care. The scientific ideal of objectivity has been rejected in favor of a holistic approach that incorporates the diverse perspectives, values, agendas, and interpretations of the participants involved. However, as Dick (1992, 1999), Guba and Lincoln (1989), and Thomas (2000) suggest, rigor need not be lost in this approach. Mayoux and Chambers (2005) argue that when used well, "participatory methods generate not only qualitative insights but also quantitative data which are generally more accurate than those from conventional survey approaches and methods" (p. 272). Guba and Lincoln (1989) propose that the criteria of trustworthiness, which parallel the conventional criteria of internal and external validity, reliability, and objectivity, are: "credibility, transferability, dependability and confirmability" (p. 236).

The credibility criterion in hermeneutic research involves establishing that the results are credible or believable from the perspective of the participants and the researcher within the study. Since from this perspective, the purpose is to describe or understand the phenomena of interest from the participant's and researcher's view; both the participants and researcher are the only ones who can legitimately judge the credibility of the results. If the phenomenon is known to others, however, they should also recognize the essences described. Issues of credibility may be incorporated into this researcher's work by "prolonged engagement with research participants" (Sandelowski, 1998, p.467) through in-depth interview and re-interviewing and by checking all data analysis with participants in order to address any assumptions and ensure correct interpretation of statements and, also, correct reduction of data into essences.

Transferability refers to the degree to which the results of qualitative research can be generalized or transferred to other contexts or settings. In this study, describing the research context and the assumptions that are central to the research may enhance transferability. In addition, the leadership participants in this study are restricted to successful leaders and this must be judged against a yardstick within the health-care arena, such as staff turnover, key performance targets, successful patient outcomes, and the like; and this will ensure that the data from this study will be transferable to other health-care situations and may be informative for leadership in many organizations.

The notion of dependability stresses the need for the researcher to account for the ever-changing context within which research occurs and to ensure that results are as unbiased as possible. In this study, a mixed methods approach to collecting data could achieve this—analysis of health-care organizational data to ensure these are credible and successful leaders; in-depth interviews and re-interviews with such leaders, and research journals that note the researchers ideas could ensure that results are as consistent as possible. A critical friend or research buddy could cross-check interview data analysis in order to lessen the likelihood of researcher influence or bias.

Hermeneutic phenomenology assumes that each researcher brings a unique perspective to the study. Confirmability refers to the degree to which results can be confirmed or corroborated by others. In this study, it may be achieved by deep immersion in the data and profound commitment to purpose (Sandelowski, 1998); in addition the data gathering and data analysis procedures used within the study will need to be richly detailed for the readers. Also, the researcher's personal reflections and experience of the phenomenon of successful leadership will be woven throughout the study in a "fusion of horizons" (Heidegger) in order that results may be viewed with openness and transparency.

In addition, the researcher should attempt to develop an atmosphere of mutual trust and open communication with the participants of this study by actively listening in an empathic way, facilitating discussions, and gathering feedback that can be used to improve the data analysis and therefore the results of the study. The development of such relationships are vital to achieving high-quality outcomes and more trustworthy and richer data, as well as leading to better feedback in terms of re-interviewing and interpretation of the data. However, as Koch (1994) pointed out, "previous experiences no doubt influenced the way in which I interpreted and participated in making the data" (p. 984). This is corroborated by Mavundla (2000), who also noted how the results of qualitative research are not value free. Although Koch (1994) acknowledged that this is inevitable with qualitative research, she also explained why it is important to expose researcher bias by providing honesty and transparency for the reader, which this researcher should attempt in this study by discussing weak spots within the research process and discussing his or her experiences and lifeworld in regard to successful health-care leadership. This may be executed by displaying excerpts from researcher journals. Sandelowski (1998) stated that researchers should move away from a preoccupation with validation of findings toward issues of craftsmanship and accountability within their research, which is essential in hermeneutic phenomenology. This degree of craftsmanship within this study can be achieved through researchers honing their writing style, especially within the chapters which discuss the data findings. Accountability can also be achieved through honesty, transparency, bracketing, attention to detail, and thoroughness while gathering, analyzing, and displaying the data throughout the study.

Although mixed methods, or triangulation, are not always a feature of hermeneutic phenomenology, which favors the in-depth interview method, in this particular study they may bring additional credibility by ensuring that participants are indeed "successful" leaders in health care (a subjective notion at best). When designing the methodology, the researcher may reflect that analysis of health-care data from which the leader participants are employed will provide additional information on how the term "successful" is being judged in this study. This type of triangulation is referred to as within-method triangulation, which is where a mixture of methods is utilized; for example in this study, in-depth interviews, health-care organization data, and researcher journals may be utilized. Within-method triangulation is used to increase confidence in the research data in addition to providing a clearer understanding of the problem (Thurmond, 2001), as data are gathered from a variety of sources offering different perspectives in answering the research question. For example, although during interviews the leaders may discuss their particular methods of leadership, the health-care data analyzed prior to choosing a leader to interview will reinforce that these are indeed successful methods of leadership according to the criteria defined in the study.

Data analysis

Data from the interviews will need to be analyzed in order to discover the essences of good leadership. Giorgi (2000a) believed that meaning can be found within data by using comparative methods and that comparisons are best approached by harnessing significant types and amounts of data. In this study, data may be compared across the leaders and researcher and gathered by two different research methods: in-depth interview and re-interview, and researcher journals. Data from the interviews may be reduced using thematic analysis and this may also be used to reduce the researcher journal data. Instead of just applying the analysis to interviews, it may also be applied to field notes taken from researcher journals. Phenomenological methods are systematic in approach and individual phenomena can best be understood not as isolated snapshots, but as belonging to a complex system of experiences all of which are related together (Giorgi, 2000a).

There are numerous methods of thematic analysis, for example, Giorgi (1997) suggests a stepwise method that has been discussed in part in the first case study, and Struebert (1991) suggets a sequential method. Streubert recommends that researchers submerge themselves into the interview data and review the transcripts to uncover essences in order to capture essential relationships. However, Giorgi's (1997) method gives specific details as to how to thematically analyze data. These methods are clear and detailed, and provide a step-by-step guide to thematically analyzing data, which may be data from interviews or researcher notes. For example, Giorgi (1997) provides clear details in regard to transcribing interviews and thematically analyzing such data; in addition, he details a constant comparative approach to determine similarities and differences across data, which may be relevant to this study. Streubert's method may assist initially in the data-generation stages, as it holds a generic stance toward phenomenological research; however, at a later stage within data analysis, the researcher may prefer a more detailed approach. It is advisable that researchers new to hermeneutic phenomenology be influenced by the work of experienced researchers more familiar with this style of inquiry, data analysis, and fusion of horizons. Through reading such works the novice researcher may become familiar and thus apply these methods to their own studies.

Chapter summary

Like most research in business and management, the example studies in this chapter are born out of perceived problems or issues in practice (the two case study examples were applicable to the business of health care and detailed the need to lessen the footfall in surgical out-patient departments, and the need for optimum leadership in health care). These are real-world problems and the findings from these research studies can offer effective solutions to enhance health care and patient experience, while minimizing financial expenditure—a win-win situation for all concerned. In both examples, the issues in question fed directly into the research questions, which in turn were answered by the methods of data collection and analysis. The studies focused on eidetic or descriptive phenomenology and hermeneutic phenomenology, and by including extracts from the researchers' field notes, working, practical examples of research issues and concerns could be explored. The studies do not adhere to "classic" or "pure" application of eidetic or hermeneutic phenomenology, as these are more in keeping with philosophical concepts and not practical lifeworld issues. The case studies in this chapter are in keeping with modern phenomenology in which research frameworks are designed by molding, adapting, and tweaking them to suit the research in question. Issues of rigor are extremely important in all research studies, and this chapter has focused in detail and with practical examples of how such rigor may be maintained.

References

Ahern, K. J. (1999). Pearls, pith and provocation: Ten tips for reflexive bracketing. *Qualitative Health Research, 9*(3), 407–411.

Allan, H.T. (2006). Using participant observation to immerse oneself in the field. *Journal of Research in Nursing, 11*(5), 397–407.

Anosike, P., Ehrich, L. C.. & Ahmed, P. (2012). Phenomenology as a method for exploring management practice. *International Journal of Management Practice* (IJMP), *5*(3), 205–224.

Bradbury-Jones, C. (2007). Exploring research supervision through Peshkins's I's: The yellow brick road. *Journal of Advanced Nursing, 60*(2), 220–228.

Buchanan, D., & Badham, R. (1999). Politics and organizational change: The lived experience. *Human Relations, 52*(5), 609–629.

Bombala, B. (2012). Phenomenology of management—didactic aspects. *Management and Business Administration, 116*(1), 50–59.

Cohen, A. (2001). Review of literature: Responses to "empirical and hermeneutic approaches to phenomenological research in psychology, a comparison." *Gestalt, 5*(2). Retrieved from http://www.g-gej.org/5-2/reviewlit.html.

Crotty, M. (1996). *Phenomenology and nursing research*. Melbourne: Churchill Livingstone.

Davidson, L. (2003). *Living outside mental illness: Qualitative studies of recovery in schizophrenia*. New York: New York University Press.

Denzin, N. K., & Lincoln, Y. S. (1994). *Handbook of qualitative research*. London: Sage.

Dick, B. (1992). Qualitative action research: Improving the rigour and economy. *Proceedings of the Second World Congress on Action Learning* (pp. 432–435). Brisbane: University of Queensland.

Dick, B. (1999). Sources of rigour in action research: Addressing the issues of trustworthiness and credibility. Paper presented at the *Association for Qualitative Research Conference*. Melbourne, Victoria. 6–10 July (accessed June 06, 2012). http://www.latrobe.edu.au/www/aqr/offer/papers/BDick.htm.

Dobscha, S. (1998). The lived experience of consumer rebellion against marketing. *Advances in Consumer Research, 25*(1), 91–97.

Ehrich, L. (2005). Revisiting phenomenology: Its potential for management research. In Proceedings challenges or organisations in global markets, *British Academy of Management Conference* (pp. 1–13). Said Business School, Oxford University.

Evans, R. (1999). *The pedagogic principal.* Edmonton, AB: Qualitative Institute Press.

Flaming, D. (2005). Becoming a nurse: "It's just who I am." *Journal of Medical Ethics; Medical Humanities, 31*(1), 95–100.

Gadamer, H. G. (1976). *Philosophical hermeneutics.* Berkeley: University of California Press.

Giorgi, A. (1985). Sketch of a psychological phenomenological method. In Giorgi, A. (Ed.). *Phenomenological and psychological research.* Pittsburg, PA: Duquesne University Press.

Giorgi, A. (1997). The theory, practice, and evaluation of the phenomenological method as a qualitative research procedure. *Journal of Phenomenological Psychology, 28*(1), 236–260.

Giorgi, A. (2000a). The status of Husserlian phenomenology in caring research. *Scandinavian Journal of Caring Science, 14*(1), 3–10.

Giorgi, A. (2000b). Concerning the application of phenomenology to caring research. *Scandinavian Journal of Caring Science,* 14(1), 11–15.

Guba, E., & Lincoln, Y. (1989). *Fourth generation evaluation.* Thousand Oaks, CA: Sage.

Husserl, E. (1999). *The idea of phenomenology* (L. Hardy, Trans.). Guildford: Springer (Originally published in 1907).

Kafle, N. P. (2011). Hermeneutic phenomenological research method simplified. *Bodhi: An Interdisciplinary Journal, 5*(1), 2091–0479.

Koch, T. (1994). Establishing rigour in qualitative research: The decision trail. *Journal of Advanced Nursing, 19*(1), 976–986.

Kuhn, T. S. (1962). *The structure of scientific revolutions.* Chicago: University of Chicago Press, 1962.

Lincoln Y. S., & Guba, E. G. (1985). *Naturalistic inquiry.* London: Sage Publications.

Mavundla, T. R. (2000). Professional nurses' perception of nursing mentally ill people in a general hospital setting. *Journal of Advanced Nursing, 32*(6), 1569–1578.

Mayoux, L., & Chambers, R. (2005). Reversing the paradigm: Quantification, participatory methods and pro-poor impact assessment. *Journal of International Development, 17*(1), 271–298.

Merleau-Ponty, M. (1962). *Phenomenology of perception.* (C. Smith, Trans.). London: Routledge (Original work published 1945).

Parahoo, K. (2006). *Nursing research principles: Process and issues.* (2nd ed.). Hampshire: Palgrave Macmillan.

Pollio, H. R., Henley, T. B., & Thompson, C. J. (1997). *The phenomenology of everyday life.* Cambridge: Cambridge University Press.

Richmond, J. (2007). *Being pregnant and living with Type 1 diabetes: Women's accounts.* Unpublished PhD thesis, Manchester Metropolitan University, United Kingdom.

Samra-Fredericks, D. (2003). Strategizing as lived experience and strategists' everyday efforts to shape strategic direction. *Journal of Management Studies, 40*(1), 141–176.

Sandelowski, M. (1998). Focus on qualitative methods: The call to experts in qualitative research. *Research in Nursing and Health, 21,* 467–471.

Streubert, H. J. (1991). Phenomenologic research as a theoretic initiative in community health nursing. *Public Health Nursing, 8*(2), 119–123.

Thomas, L. (2000). Bums on seats; or "listening to voices": Evaluating widening participation initiatives using participatory action research. *Studies in Continuing Education, 22*(1), 95–113.

Thompson, J. (1981). *Critical hermeneutics: A study in the thought of Paul Ricoeur and Jürgen Habermas.* Cambridge: Cambridge University Press.

Thurmond, V. A. (2001). The point of triangulation. *Journal of Nursing Scholarship, 33*(3), 253–258.

Valle, R., & Mohs, M. (1998). Transpersonal awareness in phenomenological research: Philosophy, reflections, and recent research. In W. Braude & R. Anserson (eds.). *Transpersonal research methods for the social sciencs: Honoring human experience*, Thousand Oaks, CA: Sage.

van Manen, M. (1990). *Researching lived experience.* Suny series, The Philosophy of Education. Edmonton, AB: Suny Press.

van Manen, M. (1997). *Researching lived experience: Human science for an action sensitive pedagogy.* New York: State University Press.

Wilson, H., & Hutchinson, S. (1991). Triangulation of qualitative methods: Heideggerian hermeneutics and grounded theory. *Qualitative Health Research, 1*(1), 263–276.

26
Structure of a Dissertation for a Participatory Phenomenology Design

Judith Hahn

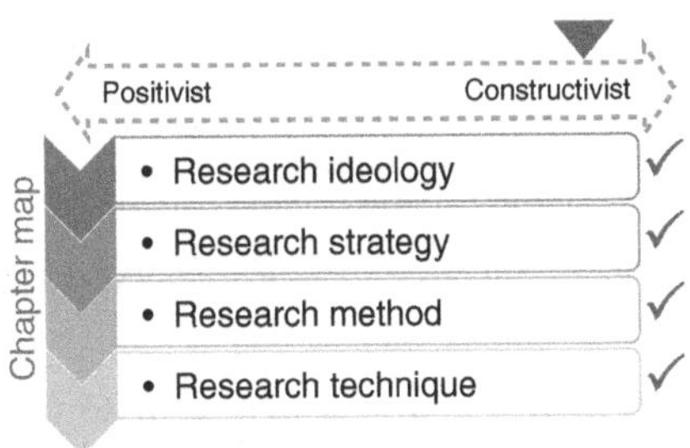

Chapter overview

Hahn clearly follows the constructivist research ideology. The interesting aspect of this chapter is that she integrates action research as a technique to become the participatory-phenomenology method. Compare this to the definition and application by Lim and Seok-Chai when using the pragmatist ideology (previous section). Furthermore, consider the interpretative eidetic versus descriptive hermeneutic phenomenology method variations discussed in the previous chapters by McCarthy. This is why action research is both a technique and a method that can be used in interpretative or constructivist ideologies, but phenomenology as a method is generally positioned under the constructivistic ideology. In this chapter, Hahn discusses how a researcher with a constructivist ideology would articulate and then apply the participatory-phenomenology method on a health-care nurse's experience as an inductive within-group unit of analysis with a group level of analysis (the nurses at a particular hospital).

Introduction

Qualitative phenomenological participatory action research is a self-reflective, systematic, and critical approach to an inquiry. The unit of analysis in the

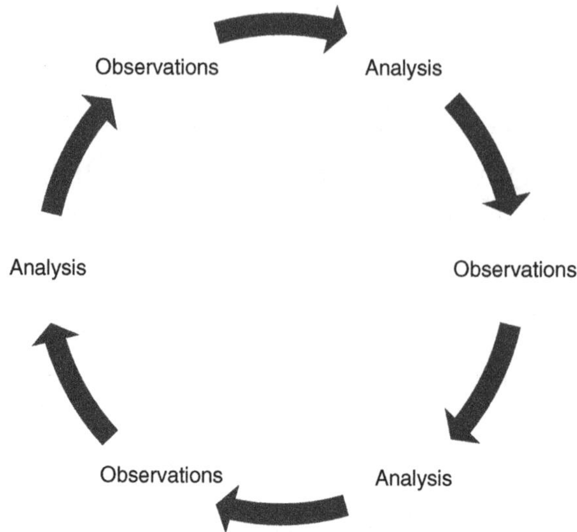

Figure 26.1 Participatory phenomenology methodology conceptual model.

research strategy is to identify a problematic situation or issue considered to be worthy of study, to bring about critically informed changes in practices (Burns,1999). There are two objectives to qualitative phenomenological participatory action research. The first is to produce knowledge and action directly useful to a group of people through research, adult education, and sociopolitical action. The second is to empower people through the process of constructing their own knowledge (Reason, 1998).

Qualitative research is much more subjective than quantitative research and uses very different methods of collecting information, mainly individual, in-depth interviews, and focus groups. Figure 26.1 is a conceptual model of the participatory phenomenology methodology. The nature of this type of research is exploratory and open-ended. Small numbers of people are interviewed in-depth and/or a relatively small number of focus groups are conducted.

Participants are asked to respond to general questions and the interviewer or group moderator probes and explores their responses to identify and define people's perceptions, opinions, and feelings about the topic or idea being discussed and to determine the degree of agreement that exists in the group. The quality of the finding from qualitative research is directly dependent upon the skills, experience, and sensitivity of the interviewer or group moderator.

This type of research is often less costly than surveys and is extremely effective in acquiring information about people's communications needs and their responses to and views about specific communications.

Quantitative research objective; Qualitative research subjective

Quantitative research seeks explanatory laws; qualitative research aims at in-depth description. Qualitative research measures what it assumes to be a static reality in hopes of developing universal laws. Qualitative research is an exploration of what is assumed to be a dynamic reality. It does not claim that what is discovered in the process is universal and, thus, replicable.

In general, qualitative research generates rich, detailed, and valid (process) data that contribute to in-depth understanding of the context. Quantitative research generates reliable population-based and generalizable data and is well suited to establishing cause-and-effect relationships. The decision of whether to choose a quantitative or a qualitative design is a philosophical question. This is driven by the positivist ideology, looking for quantitative evidence or inferential statistical proof, versus the other extreme, seeking meaning of qualitative data that cannot be analyzed with inferential statistics.

The method chosen will depend on the nature of the project, the type of information needed, the context of the study, and the availability of resources (time, money, and human). It is important to keep in mind that these are two different philosophies, not necessarily polar opposites. In fact, elements of both designs can be used together in mixed-methods studies.

Combining of qualitative and quantitative research is becoming more and more common. Every method is a different line of sight directed toward the same point, observing social and symbolic reality. The use of multiple lines of sight is called triangulation. It is a combination of two types of research. It is also called pluralistic research.

Advantages of combining both types of research include: research development (one approach is used to inform the other, such as using qualitative research to develop an instrument to be used in quantitative research), increased validity (confirmation of results by means of different data sources), complementarities (adding information, that is, words to numbers and vice-versa), and creating new lines of thinking by the emergence of fresh perspectives and contradictions. Barriers to integration include philosophical differences, cost, inadequate training, and publication bias.

Qualitative data analysis

Qualitative analysis involves a continual interplay between theory and analysis. In analyzing qualitative data, we seek to discover patterns such as changes over time or possible causal links between variables.

What is qualitative research?

Qualitative research is aimed at gaining a deep understanding of a specific organization or event, rather a than surface description of a large sample of a population; it aims to provide an explicit rendering of the structure, order, and broad patterns found among a group of participants. It is also called ethnomethodology or field research, and it generates data about human groups in social settings and does not introduce treatments or manipulate variables, or impose the researcher's operational definitions of variables on the participants. Rather, the meaning emerges from the participants and is more flexible in that it can adjust to the setting, and the concepts, data collection tools, and data collection methods can be adjusted as the research progresses.

Qualitative research enables a researcher to get a better understanding through firsthand experience, truthful reporting, and quotations of actual conversations. It can help a researcher gain insight and understanding into how the participants derive meaning from their surroundings and how their meaning influences their behavior.

Qualitative research uses observation as the data collection method. Observation is the selection and recording of behaviors of people in their environment, and it is useful for generating in-depth descriptions of organizations or events, for obtaining information that is otherwise inaccessible, and for conducting research when other methods are inadequate.

Observation is used extensively in studies by psychologists, anthropologists, sociologists, and program evaluators. Direct observation reduces distortion, between the observer and what is observed, that can be produced by an instrument (i.e., questionnaires). It occurs in a natural setting, not in a laboratory or as a controlled experiment. The context or background of behavior is included in observations of both people and their environment and is useful with inarticulate subjects, such as children or others unwilling to express themselves.

Topic and background

The researcher tentatively identifies the problem or phenomenon of interest, and tries to discern what will yield the greatest understanding of that problem or phenomenon. The researcher then identifies preliminary concepts and what data will be gathered as indicators of those concepts.

This work is fun and this is where you can start looking at the topics of interest that you want to research. The literature review should start as soon as the topic of interest is either assigned or stirs within you. The literature review should start with the earliest known date of reach on the subject and followed through to the current date, given a historical reference on the subject, for example: The Hundred Days WWI (18 July-11 November 1918) (Rickard, 2007), questioning older and current veterans about their understanding and experiences about serving in the military until 2014 would be one aspect of a historical review, and what does the current research have to say about the topics relating to your inquiry?

The topic can be anything that is going to make a difference to what you want to do if it is not been assigned by your instructor, which is the best part of this research project. The whole focus of selecting your topic is to make sure that you are going to be interested through the whole dissertation process because it is a commitment, and you do not want to spend hours looking for information and find out that you are totally bored with the subject and have to start all over again. You should know within the first the week of reviewing the literature that your topic is not going to hold your interest, or that there are too many avenues of discussion to hone in on one area for the topic, or that something else has caught your interest. Talk to your advisor or whoever assigned the project, and keep them abreast of the situation that you would like to change the subject so that they are onboard with you, and let them know that your progress is still on target.

The purpose of the background section is to provide information on how the problem evolved, what has been researched in previous studies, and what dimension of the problem (conceptual/theoretical framework) will be focused on the research. The most salient references that support the problem should be found in your introduction as opposed to the literature review section. A discussion reflects why the research problem is of important social concern or theoretical interest.

Health-care study example

Purpose

The purpose of this qualitative phenomenological study is to describe the lived experiences of ______. In any research there is always a purpose, there is a purpose when you get on the Internet to look for a computer, a video game, or a car, you want to know something about the item. Research is no different, except now you want to know about people and what makes them think, act, and feel; qualitative research gives you that opportunity. You gain insight into the lived experiences of people's lives that otherwise you would not have, and it is not every day you can walk up to a total stranger and say, "Tell me why do you do the things you do?" without being told to mind your own business. The significance section establishes a global reason for doing a worthwhile study.

Research lets you dig and probe until there is data saturation and no new answers come forth from any of the participants in your sample group, and the timeline does not matter if it takes one hour or four weeks, as long as your sample group keeps giving you information that is on your questionnaire, and the information is new, and different from one volunteer, and saturation is not complete. That is your purpose, to gather all the data necessary to gain insight into the lived experiences of your sample population no matter what your subject matter.

Research questions

There are two benefits to using the exploratory phase of designing your survey: (1) you can create your own survey and (2) your survey will be more focused on your research. In qualitative research you will be asking open-ended questions, the sample size will be smaller, and this will allow the respondents to give a greater insight into the lived experiences of the population you are either observing or questioning.

The research aim is to gain insight into how individuals perceive, conceptualize, and understand a common experience; as Moustakas (1994) suggested, a person relies on perceptions and experiences when making decisions.

Theoretical framework

A theoretical framework sets limits or boundaries to studies, supports studies looking for relationships among variables, and attempts to bring ideas, facts, and theories into meaning or thoughts (Salkind, 1985).What do other researchers have to say about your study? What is the correlation? For example: a study by______, or the results of a study by______.?

Definitions

Include definitions in your paper; no matter how insignificant you think it may be to you, the person reading your paper might not understand the acronym for ROFLOL. So you will have to spell it out for them, and reference the definitions, do not quote here either, paraphrase.

ROFLOL rolling on floor laughing out loud.

Nature of study

The purpose of this qualitative research is to gain insight into the lived experiences of the______. This is the area where you justify why you are using the design of the study versus quantitative or Delphi, etc.

Use references to support your claim, and do not quote anything in your paper. Paraphrase and reference everything. The last thing you want to do is plagiarize an author. Give credit where credit is due.

Argument against design

The idea behind this is why are you using one type of research design versus another and explain your reasoning. For example: The focus of this proposed qualitative phenomenological participative action research study is the sharing of the lived experiences and history of the participants of a research project. Quantitative research pertains to the statistical analysis, trends, or methods of a research project and focuses on the variable outcomes (Neuman 2003). Quantitative research measures statistics, numbers, emotions, portions, and numbers (Shields &Twycross, 2003).

Sample

According to Moustakas (1994), in-depth face-to-face interviews can provide valuable data in the form of the lived experience and knowledge of the person, and through interviewing feedback and insight into the decision-making process of health care choices. In a study by Oliver (2006), 15–20 participants is adequate in a purposive sample.

Data collection

The process of gathering information through in-depth interviews, discussion pertaining to the viewpoint from a person's lived experiences, and how they made their own health-care choices throughout their lives may lead to a fuller understanding on how the elderly decide to follow their medication regimen (Moustakas, 1994). The proposed study will involve a qualitative phenomenological design. The study will involve 15–20 participants' responses to the questions using the open-ended questionnaire and a four-hour face-to-face recorded interview session for the purpose of discovery and to meet the aims and objectives of the study. When the data no longer produces new information or sheds no new light on the information pertaining to the study, the interviewing process will end, and that becomes the point of saturation (Glaser & Strauss, 1967, as cited in Mason, 2010), and the start of the analysis process using the software program for data analysis.

Significance of the study

The focus of this proposed qualitative phenomenological study will be to gain insights into the lived experiences of the______. Who is the beneficiary upon completion of the study? What makes your study unique? How will this affect leadership after completion?

Limitations

Limitations identify the potential weaknesses of a study and those that are uncontrollable. Some limitations of the proposed study are as follows:

1. The study will only include:
2. The study will only include:
3. The focus of the study will be the participants'______.

Delimitations

The proposed study will only include the______. A thorough explanation will have to be provided for what or who will not be part of the study. Is it because of a lack of resources, or lack of participants who decided to withdraw from the study at the last minute; whatever the situation, there is always going to be something that arises when dealing with human subjects.

Summary

Always provide a summary of the section or chapter such as "_______ is an overview of the of the problem of_______."

Conclusion

Always provide an overall conclusion such as "The proposed qualitative phenomenological study regarding _____."

Review of literature

The literature review consists of research findings relating to the phenomenological qualitative study regarding the related topics using ProQuest and EBSCOhost databases. Title searches provide the most relevant information, including keywords. The use of Internet search engines (e.g.,: World Wide Web and Google) for online journals and related websites affiliated with government agencies and nonprofit organizations yield relevant perspectives and resources.

The identification and description of key areas of the literature review serve as a foundation from which to identify and build themes to describe the elderly's perspective of medication adherence and provided adequate information on medication noncompliance. The literature review consists of peer-reviewed journals, articles, reports, and research studies from the Center of Disease Control and Prevention (CDC), US Census Bureau (USCB), National Council on Patient Information and Education (NCPIE), and World Health Organization (WHO).

Historical overview

This chapter contains results from searches of related literature and discussions pertaining to areas that contribute to an understanding of the phenomenon under investigation, notably related issues.

Current findings

For example: Heart diseases, stroke, diabetes, are the leading cause of death and disability (CDC, 2009a). In the United States, four out of five older Americans have at least one chronic condition, an average of 48% of Medicare beneficiaries age 65 or older have three or more chronic conditions, and 21% have five or more (Norris et al., 2008). By 2030, approximately 70 million Americans will reach age 65 or older, increasing the need for health-care services (Traynor, 2008 as cited in Tricoche, 2012; US Census Bureau, 2008).

Alternative viewpoints

The effort to improve the quality of health literacy accomplishes strong health informational skills and the ability to function adequately in a health care environment (*Healthy People*, 2010).

Discussion on the research variables

The study titled Diabetes, Attitudes, Wishes, and Needs (DAWN) (Delamater, 2006) has indicated that diabetics have problems regarding adhering to a medication regimen because of poor psychological well-being. The DAWN study indicated that the identification of psychological problems by many healthcare providers makes them uncomfortable because of a lack of inexperience (Scheppers, van Dongen, Dekker, Geertzen, & Dekker, 2006).

Summary

Again provide a summary, "in this section, a discussion of the historical and current research discoveries with respect to______." Summarize it.

Conclusion

Provide a conclusion and a look toward what to expect in the next section such as method, research questions, nature of study, population, sample, data collection, data analysis, etc.

Method

Reiterate the importance of your choice, and it is just a matter of cut and paste from earlier sections.

Research questions

There are two benefits to using the exploratory phase of designing your survey:

1. Creating your own survey.
2. Your survey will be more focused on your research. In qualitative research you will be asking open-ended questions, the sample size will be smaller, and your observing and questioning will allow the respondents to give a greater insight into their lived experiences.

Nature of study

The purpose of this qualitative research is to gain an insight into the lived experiences of ______. This is the area where you justify why you are using the design of the study versus quantitative or Delphi, etc.

Use references to support your claim, and do not quote anything in your paper. Paraphrase and reference everything. The last thing you want to do is plagiarize an author. Give credit where credit is due.

Argument against design

This is where you mention why are you using one type of research design versus another and explain your reasoning. For example: The focus of this proposed qualitative phenomenological participative action research study is the sharing of the lived experiences and history of the participants of a research project. Quantitative research pertains to the statistical analysis, trends, or methods of a research project and focuses on the variable outcomes (Neuman 2003). Quantitative research measures statistics, numbers, emotions, portions, and numbers (Shields &Twycross, 2003).

Sample

According to Moustakas (1994), in-depth face-to-face interviews can provide valuable data in the form of the lived experience and knowledge of the person, and thorough interviewing can provide feedback and insight into the decision-making process of health-care choices. In a study by Oliver (2006), 15–20 participants is adequate in a purposive sample.

Data collection

In qualitative studies, research methods are set up, which suggest the type of methods of observation used and the type of data collected. Analysis begins as soon as data are collected. Analysis and data collection proceed in a cyclical fashion, where preliminary analysis informs subsequent data collection and interviews are done until data saturation occurs.

Challenges with qualitative studies include that it is more time consuming, difficult to code data, enormous amount of data to transcribe, not applicable to all social settings, difficult to quantify, and difficult to control the researcher's bias. Methods of obtaining research information can be gathered through telephone or email surveys, in-person face-to face interviews, and participant observations. In each of these techniques there have positive and negative sides, and depending on the time frame for your research project the options and costs of each method should be a consideration prior to starting your research.

Validity and reliability

This refers to the methods of communicating and demonstrating that research findings are trustworthy and accurate and are consistent, valid, and reliable (Roberts, Priest & Traynor, 2006). Establishing the truthfulness and credibility of research findings is the goal of social researchers. Honest and fair viewpoints from the participants lived experiences is validity and implies authenticity of the findings of the study. The consistency of the questionnaires and interviewing techniques to record the observations is the reliability of the study (Neuman, 2003). Precautions will be taken to prevent potential threats to internal validity; for example: researchers' own opinions will not be interjected during the interviewing process.

Internal validity

Internal validity refers to the accuracy of data obtained and its link to reality (Bartlett & Toms, 2004). The accuracy of obtaining the data and linking the data to reality refers to internal validity (Bartlett & Toms, 2004).

Reliability

Studying qualitative data content analysis is a reliable method of coding because determinations can be confirmed by revising previous coded data (Priest, Roberts & Woods, 2002). Evaluating the participants' original responses and confirming interpretations of narrations by providing updates and clarifications of original data enable the researcher to obtain a validation for the process (Bartlett & Toms, 2004).

Significance of the study

The focus of this proposed qualitative phenomenological study will be to gain insight into the lived experiences of the______. Who is the beneficiary upon completion of the study? What makes your study unique? How will this affect leadership after completion?

Geographic Location

Once you decide on a topic you can start looking at locations where you want to gather your subjects, and the group of people who will be your subjects and what is the commonality or the inidicators you are looking for in them. Are the volunteers going to all have brown hair, brown eyes; are all the subjects going to be the same height; are they all going to have mole on the left cheek? These are just far-fetched examples; the idea is that they all have the same thing in common, which could be some kind of indicator, and this concept is where you will find cycling to be useful; in a group counseling setting, as an observer, you are going to be a participant-observer and you need to have a clear focus of where you are going with this prior to walking up to someone and saying, Will you take my survey questions?

Population

The number of participants used for your study, and in a study by Oliver (2006), 15–20 participants is adequate in a purposive sample.

Sampling

Nonprobability sampling is usually used in qualitative research. According to Moustakas (1994), in-depth face-to-face interviews can provide valuable data in the form of the lived experience and knowledge of the person and thorough interviewing can provide feedback and insight into the decision-making process of health-care choices.

Informed consent and confidentiality

The consent letter will (1) describe the purpose of the study, (2) outline the interview process, (3) the geographic location, (4) inform participants of who will view the data collected, (5) identify any risks associated with the study, (6) inform of the time commitment, and (7) remind each that participating in the study would be voluntary, and withdrawing from the study at any time will not have any negative consequences. After informing the volunteers of their rights and any other further information regarding the research project, participants shall read the consent form before signing.

Confidentiality

Participant confidentiality denotes that any personal and identifying information, such as names or other distinguishable characteristics pertaining to the identity, will not be on the research project. Privacy will also be ensured by coding the participants' responses. A locked filing cabinet will be used to store data, files, and it will be in the sole custody of the researcher; the data will be shredded and incinerated after three years according to HIPPA 1996 regulations.

Summary

Again provide a summary. Here I will provide a more authentic example from one of my manuscripts:

> In Chapter 3, the research method for the qualitative phenomenological study was presented, and a detailed discussion of the research method and design included. A discussion of the volunteer population, method, and description of the data collection, research instruments. Details also included using the qualitative data analytical capabilities of the qualitative data analytical program, the geographical location, and the process for the recording of the proposed study.

Also remember to close with a conclusion to summarize the section or chapter and preview what is coming up next.

Findings, Discussion, and Conclusions

I will not elaborate on these sections since they do not impact the research design. Nonetheless, they will be provided in any scholarly paper or doctoral dissertation.

Conclusion

This chapter demonstrated how to design and execute a constructivist research design ideology using the participatory-phenomenology method (which integrates action research as a technique). This chapter illustrated the topical framework for the first three sections (or chapters) in a doctoral dissertation. The scholarly journal manuscript follows a similar although more abbreviated format. In my example, I explored the lived experiences of health-care nurses going through their learning curve (at the group level of analysis) as the unit of analysis. This was inductive and it was a constructivist ideology.

References

Burns, A., (1999). *Collaborative action research for English language teachers*. Cambridge: Cambridge University Press.

Center for Disease Control and Prevention. (2009). *Heart disease and stroke*. Retrieved from http://www.cdc.gov/phlp/publications/topic/heart.html.

Mason, M. (2010). *Sample size and saturation in PhD studies using qualitative interviews [63 paragraphs]. 11*(3). Retrieved from http://www.qualitative-research.net/index.php/fqs/article/view/1428/3027.

Moustakas, C., (1994). The I and thou of evidence: A fusion of opposites. *The Humanistic Psychologist, 22*(1), 238–240. Retrieved from http://www.mispp.edu/downloads/library/clark_moustakas_publications.pdf.

Neuman, W. L. (2003). *Social research methods: Qualitative and quantitative approaches* (5th ed.). Boston: Pearson Education.

Reason, P. (1998). Three approaches to participative inquiry. In N. K. Denzin & Y.S. Lincoln (Eds.). *Strategies of qualitative research* (p. 271). London: Sage.

Rickard, J. (2007, September 13). *The hundred days, 18 July-11 November 1918*. Retrieved from http://www.historyofwar.org/articles/wars_hundred_days.html.

Shields, L., & Twycross, A. (2003). *The difference between quantitative and qualitative research, 15*(9). Retrieved from http://www.rcn.org.uk/__data/assets/pdf_file/0016/9214/Quantitative_qualitative.pdf.

27
Emancipatory Phenomenology Applied to a Child Sex Offender Study

Rodney Alexander

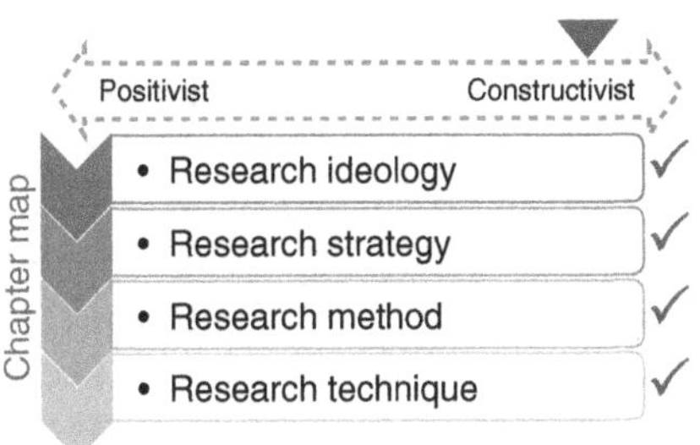

Chapter overview

Alexander demonstrates how to apply the emancipatory-phenomenology method with the Van Kaam technique using a constructivist research ideology. As discussed in chapter 4 (research method) the emancipatory research method has been titled advocacy, social advocacy, or participant advocacy, and it is similar to action research except that the focus is purely on less advantaged individuals (as a group). This topic could present additional challenges for doctoral students and organizational researchers because the participants are often drawn from protected groups. The unit of analysis when using this variation of the phenomenology method is usually the "socially advocated problem" or the "extent of social advocacy for the problem." This generalizes to other people in the community (generally practitioners) although it could also be generalized to researchers so as to motivate them to continue to investigate the phenomenon. The level of analysis is usually a group or community (within-group), although it could also be an individual (such as exploring the perceptions of rape victims so as to improve social policies). With the emancipatory or social advocacy method in a constructivist ideology, the researcher draws the meaning of the data or phenomenon from the community.

Introduction

Phenomenology as a method has many variations, as explained in other chapters of this handbook. One variation could be described as traditional or emancipatory phenomenology. This chapter discusses how such a variation of phenomenology was applied to a study focused on a very socially advocated topic: Protecting children against sex offenders on the Internet.

In keeping with the constructivistic ideology, I will write this chapter as though I were actually writing the scholarly paper, except that I will leave out certain sections, such as the details of the "lived experiences" reported by the children and the enforcement officers (for obvious reasons). Nonetheless, I want to warn the reader that some passages in this paper may be harsh to read for some people. In fact I will show this chapter as a doctoral student ought to write a dissertation proposal (except that would need to be in future tense) or a dissertation (and again the participant statement details would be needed).

Van Kaam phenomenology method

The methodology used in this study was the modified Van Kaam method of phenomenological analysis described by Moustakas (1994). It is intended to capture the essence of the participants' experience. Because the modified Van Kaam method was applied, data analysis software was not be used. Each interview transcript was reviewed using a modified Van Kaam method.

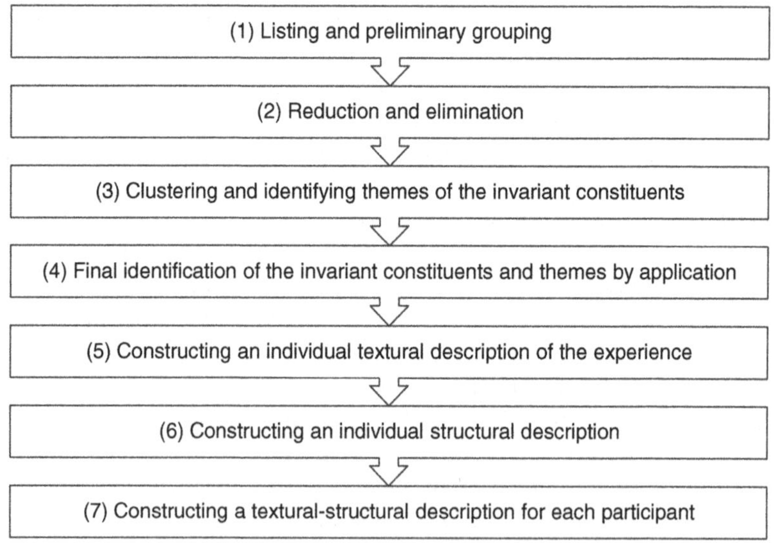

Figure 27.1 Van Kaam phenomenology method overview.

First, the literature is reviewed to identify a priori concepts to serve as a lens in guiding the study. Generally though, the literature review is intended to serve the reader more than the researcher with this type of study, since the goal is to capture the meaning of the data from the view of the participant (not interpretation by the researcher).

This modified Van Kaam method, described by Moustakas (1994), has seven steps to use for each participant interview, as outlined in figure 27.1. The steps in this modified Van Kaam method are: (1) listing and preliminary grouping; (2) reduction and elimination; (3) clustering and thematizing the invariant constituents; (4) final identification of the invariant constituents and themes by application; (5) constructing an individual textural description of the experience; (6) constructing an individual structural description; and (7) constructing a textural-structural description for each participant.

Phenomenology applied to a child sex offender study

In the applied example below, I will illustrate how to establish a theoretical lens for a phenomenology study when using the emancipatory variation of the method. This starts with showing the problem as significant and then reviewing the factors that have been raised as problems by any previous researchers concerning the unit of analysis.

Problem and rationale

The Internet has become very important in society; it is present in the majority of households in America, but it is also becoming a new venue for sexual predators. According to van Manen (2010) sharing personal information (online) can be unexpectedly risky—in part because sexual predators and pedophiles prey on unsuspecting social network users. Places such as chat rooms are becoming places where child predators meet 13-to-17-year-olds in order to solicit them for sex. According to Wolak, David, Mitchell, and Ybarra (2008), the Internet is becoming an increasingly dangerous place for children.

Social networking websites such as Facebook®, MySpace™, Twitter©, and instant messaging can open the door for teen exploitation on the Internet. For example, according to anonymous (2011) the federal authorities are seeking access to multiple email and Facebook® accounts, including some bearing the name of slain North Carolina teen Phylicia Barnes, as part of a child pornography and sexual exploitation of children investigation. This qualitative, phenomenological study was intended to increase knowledge in the law enforcement, educator, mental health professionals, and the parental community on how to reduce this relatively new threat to children.

An exhaustive review of the literature helped to determine that the current research did not provide adequate information to educators, parents, mental health professionals, and law enforcement. It was also inadequate when educating 13-to-17-year-olds on how to avoid predators on the Internet. The qualitative, phenomenological study consisted of interviews with teachers/counselors who had worked with teen victims of sexual assault from someone whom they met on the Internet.

Significance of the problem

Chat rooms and social networking websites such as Facebook®, MySpace™, and Twitter© are places where Internet predators often go to solicit teens for sex. According to Bower (2008) most of online sex offenders are adults who contact vulnerable 13-to-17-year-olds and seduce them into sexual relationships. Adult predators use social websites such as Facebook®, MySpace™, and Twitter© to entice teens into sexual activity. According to Dylan and Fuller (2010) the Facebook® management repeatedly failed to reveal the activity of an international child pornography syndicate operating on their site.

Teens inadvertently posted personal information on these sites that predators often use to entice them into a sexual relationship. According to Shao (2009) individuals participated [on the Internet] through interacting with the content as well as with other users for enhancing social connections and virtual communities; and they produced their own contents for self-expression and self-actualization. Teenagers were often seeking gratification via the Internet and these adults take advantage of those who are seeking relationships on the Internet.

User-generated media (UGM) like YouTube, MySpace, and Wikipedia have become tremendously popular over the last few years (Shao, 2009). Social websites such as Facebook®, MySpace™, and Twitter© serve as teen social gathering places to share photos and exchange gossip. According to Peter, Valkenburg, Schouten, and Alexander (2005) the Internet [is seen] as a new social environment in which universal adolescent issues such as identity, sexuality, and a sense of self-worth are played out in a virtual world. An influential tradition in media research, U&G presents media use in terms of the gratification of psychological needs of the individual (Shao, 2009).

This new social environment is growing not only in the United States, but globally as well. It has become woven into the everyday activity of most teens. According to Shannon (2008), a recent study of Swedish children's media habits found that 95% of 12-to-16-year-olds used the Internet and that 28% and 54%, respectively, use the Internet every day.

The increased number of teens using the Internet increases the probability that they are likely to meet a predator. Online sexual assault among juveniles seems to be prevalent among teenagers and less so among younger children. Children coming into contact with Internet predators become increasingly common as children approach and enter their teenage years (Shannon, 2008).

Nissley (2008) reported that the Internet is increasingly becoming the method in which predators meet teen victims, stating that between 2000 and 2001 most predators used the Internet to develop relationships with children to meet them for sex. About 5% of offenders pretended to be teens while developing relationships with teens online and often enter chat rooms to meet them. This study was intended to help to develop different approaches for combating teen sexual assault on the Internet. Strategies that target 13-to-17-year-olds directly acknowledge that normal adolescent interests in romance and sex are needed (Wolak et al., 2008).

Age-driven educational strategies are necessary for teens to help them avoid online predators. According to Johnson, McGue, and Jacono (2009), individual characteristics involving school performance and ultimately educational attainment that transcend generations may slot individuals into social categories that restrict their opportunities and reinforce the antisocial characteristics that slotted them into the restrictive social categories in the first place. These educational strategies can directly target this new teen Internet sexual assault phenomenon.

Preventing school failure can act to reduce exposure to other environmental influences contributing to antisocial behavior and to reduce expression of both genetic and nonshared environmental influences on antisocial behavior (Johnson et al., 2009). Parents, teachers, mental health professionals, and law enforcement also need additional data to have a better understanding of this growing form of assault against teenagers. Teen Internet sexual assault is a growing problem for society, one that requires understanding of the type of gratification that teens gain from using the Internet and how to prevent the seeking of that gratification from leading to sexual assault.

Very low age 17 GPA encouraged expression of genetically influenced antisocial behavior and that something about high GPA minimized expression of these genetic and environmental influences on antisocial behavior (Johnson et al., 2009). New approaches are needed to help prevent the increasing sexual assaults against teens on the Internet. Prevention approaches take into consideration the nuances of the Internet such as personal information protection and the control of personal relationships on the Internet.

Theoretical interest

Teenagers use the Internet more than adults. According to van den Eijnden, Spijkerman, Vermulst, van Rooij, and Engels (2010), adolescents aged 14 and older regard Internet use as a more important leisure time activity than watching television. Not only do teens use the Internet more, they also use Internet tools such as social websites and chat rooms more than adults.

The rising popularity of the Internet and the ever-increasing amount of time adolescents spend online pose challenges to parents who want to protect their teenage children from excessive Internet use (van den Eijnden et al., 2010). The Internet plays an important role in the social lives of teens. These new forms of communications offer greater opportunity for predators to meet and engage teenagers on the Internet. Adolescents may develop an uncontrollable urge to use the Internet, often accompanied by a loss of control, a preoccupation with Internet use, and continued use despite negative consequences (van den Eijnden et al., 2010). Social networking sites such as Facebook®, MySpace™, and Twitter© also offer anonymity for both the teenager and the predator. This anonymity may decrease inhibition for both the teenager and a potential predator. Further research is needed on the role of anonymity and reduced cues in the teen Internet sexual assault phenomenon.

Currently, there are two theories that address why teenagers seek relationships on the Internet. Scholars have put forward two opposing hypotheses on the relationship between introversion/extraversion and online friendship formation (Peter et al., 2005). Both introverted and extroverted teens could fall victim to sexual predators on the Internet. The two opposing hypotheses are the rich-get-richer and the social compensation hypothesis.

According to the rich-get-richer hypothesis, because contact can be made more easily online, extroverted teens use their enhanced social skills to develop friendships in chat rooms and on social networking sites (Peter et al., 2005). The rich-get-richer hypothesis states that the Internet will primarily benefit extroverted individuals (Peter et al., 2005). Using the Internet, extroverted teens may practice meeting people, consequently enhancing their ability to make friends. According to the rich-get-richer theory, extroverted teens are more likely than introverts to establish relationships online.

A teen's ability to establish relationships online may lead to teens establishing relationships with Internet predators. Extroverted teens may feel an increase in self-esteem when they successfully meet someone online. Lee (2009) stated that extroverted teens felt better when they used the Internet; they felt more confident and felt less isolated. Extroverted teens felt as though they were part of a social group, and felt better about themselves when they used the Internet.

The social compensation hypothesis is the second. The social compensation hypothesis according to Desjarlais and Willoughby (2010) suggests that some socially anxious individuals report that compensating for their social anxiety is a reason they use computers with friends, particularly online communication. Under this hypothesis teenagers attempt to compensate for weak social skills by seeking attention on the Internet where fewer social skills are required. In contrast to extroverts, introverts showed declines in well-being associated with these same variables. The theory implies that the Internet satisfies emotional needs, more so for extroverted teens than for introverted teens.

Because of reduced auditory and visual cues and anonymity, introverted teens may compensate for their shyness by using the Internet (Peter et al., 2005). Introverted teens may be unable to respond effectively to cues such as body language or facial expressions and find it easier to communicate online where these cues play a lesser role (Peter et al., 2005). Introverted teens using the Internet may communicate better without having to respond to actual conversation and meeting individuals face to face (Peter et al., 2005). The Internet may support and enhance the weak social skills of introverted teens.

Based on the social compensation hypothesis introverted individuals may easily self-disclose personal information online that may facilitate the formation of online friendships (Lee, 2009). The Internet may serve as a substitute for lack of a social network offline because socially anxious people may feel more at an advantage in developing intimate relationships online (Lee, 2009). Introverted teens who feel uncomfortable with establishing relationships in person may feel more comfortable with establishing relationships online (Lee, 2009). Internet predators can take advantage of introverted teens who are more willing to post personal information on social websites such as Facebook®, MySpace™, and Twitter©.

Problem statement

General problem. "Some news reports have suggested that law enforcement is facing an epidemic of these [child molestation] sex crimes perpetrated through a new medium [the Internet] by a new type of criminal," (Wolak et al., 2008, p. 2). The rise of the Internet has led to a new wave of child molestation, caused by a new type of criminal, the Internet predator. Given adequate information, law enforcement may be able to prevent this epidemic from deepening.

Specific problem. Youth in Tucson, Arizona, are establishing dangerous relationships online with people whom they have never met. According to News 4 Tucson, KVOA.com (2012), a Massachusetts youth volunteer has been arraigned after a Tucson boy told local authorities that he was enticed into sexual acts by the man as they chatted over an Internet web cam. Chat rooms and online social websites are places where in a recent survey, 25% of youth in the United States reported that they established online friendships with strangers (Peter et al., 2005). A group of Tucson, Arizona, area teachers and counselors were asked open-ended qualitative questions to help discover causes and possible solutions to this phenomenon.

Purpose

The purpose of this phenomenological qualitative study was to explore the perceptions that teachers/counselors have of the issues involving 13-to-17-year-old teenagers falling victim to child predators on the Internet, and it was designed to obtain knowledge by allowing teachers/counselors to answer open-ended interview questions about their opinions on the lived Internet sexual assault experiences of teenagers. Its purpose was also to find ways that may help reduce the number of sex offenses against teenagers by someone whom he or she met on the Internet. The study involved the interviewing of 25 Tucson, Arizona, area teachers/counselors who have worked with teenaged Internet sexual assault victims about their opinion on teen Internet sexual assault causes and possible solutions. This research explored the social needs, which teenagers are fulfilling on the Internet, and how those needs could be met without exposing the teenagers to Internet predators.

The study may add to the amount of information available to educators, parents, mental health professionals, and law enforcement about the Internet teen rape phenomenon in the Tucson, Arizona, area. Tucson has a population of 1 million; there are 25 middle and high schools in the area and 1000 teachers/counselors residing within the Tucson area. Using qualitative research methods including open-ended interview questions was an appropriate research method for uncovering the participants' opinions about some of the causes of Internet sexual offenses among teenagers. This study was intended to provide insight to educators, parents, mental health professionals, and law enforcement to help teenagers avoid encountering child predators on the Internet. These teachers/counselors have opinions that could possibly lead to insight into how teenagers fall victim to Internet predators and how to prevent the assault.

Significance

General importance. University of New Hampshire researchers have shown that in one year, one fifth of the people using chat rooms and social networking sites were asked to engage in sexual activity (Grenada, 2008). These solicitations, if accepted by teens, could lead to sexual exploitation or rape. The importance of this study was that it was intended to provide educators, parents, mental health professionals, and law enforcement information on the teen online sexual offense phenomenon, on which to develop laws, to build curriculum, and to develop parenting strategies. Unlike previous studies of teenage online sexual assault this study focused on teen needs and behavior on the Internet, and how those needs and behaviors increase the likelihood of encounters with predators. Previous studies like the McCarthy (2010) study explored the Internet sexual activity of two groups of adult male child pornography offenders; this study sought to identify potential risk factors associated with those offenders who also sexually abused minors. Also the Bagwell (2009) study, which is titled "Trends in Arrests of 'Online Predators,'" found that arrests of Internet predators stalking children rose by 400% between 2000 and 2006. These studies do not address the role that teen behavior plays in the teen Internet sexual assault phenomenon.

Leadership importance. Leaders of law enforcement organizations and secondary education institutions are able to use the data collected in this research to establish or improve upon Internet rape prevention curriculum. Because they are likely to see the results in increased teen drug use, alcoholism, or in decreased academic performance, mental health practitioners need an accurate assessment of the nature and prevalence of this new teen Internet sexual assault phenomenon (Wolak et al., 2008). Mental health professionals can then also assist parents in educating their teens. Finally, this study can be significant because it provides parents with information that they can use to discuss with their teenager—how to prevent online sexual assault.

Nature of the Study

This qualitative, phenomenological study evaluated the interview responses of 25 Tucson area teachers/counselors who had worked with teens that have experienced a sexual relationship with someone whom they met on the Internet. The purpose of the interviews was to ask open-ended questions concerning the causes of teen Internet sexual assault among 13-to-17-year-olds. The study evaluated the responses to the question of which type of student he or she believes would most likely be rape victims following initial contact on the Internet. Finally the interviewees were asked their opinion on potential solutions to the teen Internet sexual assault problem.

A qualitative research method that uses open-ended research questions to collect data about the teen Internet sexual assault phenomenon is more appropriate than the quantitative or mixed research methods. The qualitative method provides for the collection of a variety of opinions from adults who interact with teenagers daily. The qualitative research method used in this study also provided for the ranking of responses to interview questions, and in the determination of which teen needs or behavior would most likely result in contact with Internet predators. Finally, using the qualitative research method would help to determine which solutions to teen Internet sexual assault are most useful in the opinion of the interviewees.

The qualitative, open-ended questions given to the interviewees helped to form a picture of the teenager's motivation for seeking companionship on the Internet. The questions helped to provide insight into the question of which teens are likely to fall victim to predators. Finally, the qualitative method uncovered techniques that may result in the prevention of teenage Internet assault.

Research questions

The primary research question was: What are the perceptions of teachers/counselors concerning the causes of the teen Internet sexual assault phenomenon? The following questions were secondary research questions. What are the perceptions of teachers/counselors concerning the following questions? What role does teen needs play in the teen Internet sexual assault phenomenon, needs such as identity, companionship, and sex? Are social networking websites relevant in teen Internet sexual assault? What measures could possibly reduce the phenomenon; for example, education, parenting, and law enforcement? The teachers/counselors participating in the study were asked a set of interview questions. To determine which type of teenager is most likely to fall victim to an Internet predator, they were asked the following questions:

1. Please share with me your opinion on what circumstances most likely lead to teenage sexual encounters with someone whom they meet on the Internet?
2. Please share with me your opinion on how teenagers will most likely meet people on the Internet, for example, in a chat room, on MySpace™, on Facebook®, or something totally different?
3. What role do you feel a teen's personality (e.g., introverted, extraverted, or something totally different) plays in whether they will meet a predator on the Internet?
   a. Do you feel that an introverted teen is more likely to attract a predator?
   b. Do you feel that an extroverted teen is more likely to attract a predator?
4. Please share with me your opinion on the role that teen gratification, for example, sex, companionship, self-esteem, or something else plays in whether a teen will meet an Internet predator?
5. Demographic data
   a. sex (male or female),
   b. number of children, and
   c. ethnicity.

Finally, to seek possible solutions to the problem, the interviewees were asked to please share with their opinion on what support would most likely help, for example, more parental supervision, better law enforcement, better high school curriculum or other, to prevent teen's contact with an Internet predator, and would it be okay to contact them if there are follow-on questions?

Conceptual framework

At this point I will skip to the analysis of the data collected rather than focus on how to collect data (other chapters have covered that). In the following sections I will try to make sense of the data collected, through literature reviews and interviews with informants at an organization that has experienced this terrible phenomenon.

Broad theoretical area. The broad theoretical area that this research dealt with was social change or a paradigm shift among teenagers caused by the Internet revolution. The Internet is creating a new global social paradigm. According to Greenfield and Zheng (2006), teen values such as whom they identify with, how they deal with sexual needs, and how they increase their self-esteem are played out in chat rooms and on Facebook®, MySpace™, and Twitter©.

In the past, teens may have established their identity by cruising down Main Street on a Friday night, but currently they establish their identity in Internet social networking websites such as Facebook®, MySpace™, and Twitter©. Adult parents who use the Internet less than teens need to understand the risk of sexual exploitation that teens face on the Internet. Teens also use more Internet-based tools than adults such as chat rooms and instant messaging, which could subject them to more contact with Internet predators. The frequency of teen Internet use and the type of tools used could be factors that influence teen Internet sexual assault. Table 27.1 list the generic child sex offender terms emerging from the literature to serve as a theoretical lens in analyzing the transcripts of the interviews.

Table 27.1 Terms from the literature review

Introverted. A person's tendency to prefer his or her own company to large social events and quiet reflection to social interaction (Peter et al., 2005).
Extroverted. A person's inclination to seek company and social interaction (Peter et al., 2005).
Rich-Get-Richer Hypothesis. The Internet will primarily benefit extroverted individuals. Because contact can be made more easily online, the greater social skills of extroverted individuals can develop fully and will facilitate the formation of online friendships (Peter et al., 2005).
Social Compensation Hypothesis. Because of reduced auditory and visual cues and anonymity, the Internet may enable introverted people to compensate for their weaker social skills (Peter et al., 2005).
Sexual Solicitations and Approaches. Includes requests to engage in sexual activities or sexual talk or give personal sexual information unwanted or whether wanted or not, made by an adult (Taylor, Caeti, Loper, Fritsch & Liederbach, 2006).
Aggressive Sexual Solicitation. Includes sexual solicitations involving offline contact with the perpetrator through regular mail, by telephone, or in person or attempts for requests for offline contact (Taylor et al., 2006).
Harassment. The threat or other offensive behavior (not sexual solicitation) sent online to the youth or posted online about the youth for others to. Not all such incidents were distressing to the youth who experienced them (Taylor et al., 2006).
Distressing Incidents. Episodes that youth rated themselves as very or extremely upsetting andbecoming afraid as a result of the incident (Taylor et al., 2006).
Cyber abuse. A term that encompasses a wide range of aggressive online activities, including bullying, stalking, sexual solicitation and pornography (Mishna, McLuckie & Saini, 2009).
Child sex tourism. The United Nations (UN) defines child sex tourism (CST) as organized tourism (the nature of which encompasses many activities) that facilitates the commercial sexual exploitation of anyone under 18 years of age (Patterson, 2007).

Theoretical gap. No study was found that examined specifically the role of teenage developmental behavior in Internet rape cases. The role that introverted or extroverted personality plays in the teen Internet assault phenomenon has not been fully explored. Interest in whether a teen is more likely or less likely to encounter a predator on the Internet based on introversion/extroversion is growing.

Assumptions

Burns and Grove (2001) stated that recognizing and stating the assumptions of the study is necessary because assumptions present a potential for bias and misunderstanding; they also influence the logic of the study. An assumption was that participants would understand how the confidentiality and anonymity of their responses will be maintained; in turn it was also assumed that they would answer interview questions honestly when sharing their opinion on lived experiences. Additional assumptions included that the participants knew victims of teen Internet sexual assault as defined in the study and were representative of the teacher/counselor population.

A further assumption was that participants have some understanding of teen gratification and needs. According to Benner (1994), in qualitative, phenomenological design studies assumptions are important because these studies engage participants in contrast to the disengaged, participant-object approach used in quantitative research. It was assumed that the participants would understand and interpret interview questions as written. Understanding is threefold: (a) a familiarity one has with the world, (b) a point of view one has from their background, and, last, (c) an expectation about the interpretation (Benner, 1994). According to Shank (2002), while recognizing that there are many realities, phenomenological studies must be designed to take into consideration "personal" assumptions regarding reality (p. 95).

Finally, I assumed that the participants understood what social networking websites and chat rooms were. I also assumed that the participants understood basic needs such as the need for attention, companionship, and sex. An assumption was also made that the participants could recognize teenage introverted and extroverted personality.

Scope

The scope of the study is intended to add to a growing body of literature about the teen Internet sexual assault and ways to help prevent the phenomenon. The sample focused on teachers/counselors who have worked with teenagers who were sexually assaulted by someone whom they met on the Internet. The body of knowledge on teen Internet assault risk factors and the importance of parental, educational, and law enforcement support in preventing this phenomenon forms the scope of this research. A phenomenological exploration of teen personality types that are more likely to lead to encounters with predators on the Internet and the type of measures that are likely to prevent these encounters will add insight about ways to help protect teens while they use the Internet.

Limitations

Study participants were not selected randomly, which was a limitation. Phenomenology seeks only individuals who are willing to describe their experiences about the phenomenon being studied (Burns & Grove, 2001). A further limitation was that only teachers/counselors who were willing to volunteer their opinion on teen Internet sexual assault causes were contacted about the study; those unwilling to participate will not be contacted. Gilgun (2005) noted that problems associated with qualitative research include "generalizability, subjectivity and language" (p. 40); those difficulties could have occurred in this phenomenological study and were recognized. The geographic area in which the study was conducted constrains the outcomes because of the unique law enforcement, mental health, and educational programs available in the Tucson, Arizona, area that may not be available in other locations. Participants could stop the interview at any time, in which case the participant's information would not be included with the study. Subjectivity was minimized during the interview by remaining objective with participant information and following the modified Van Kaam method. Using the modified Van Kaam method and remaining objective with participant information will help reduce subjectivity limitations. Finally, a male researcher interviewed both male and female participants.

Delimitations

According to Critchlow (2005), delimitations narrow the study's scope by listing what is not included or intended in the study. A delimitation of the study was that information about specific social support persons, services, or agencies was not intended to be evaluative or accurate reflections of programs; rather the information was shared as a descriptive, personal report of the participants' view. A second delimitation was that the study did not claim to provide exhaustive or quantitative data about characteristics of teenagers or social needs, particularly of teenaged Internet sexual assault victims.

Findings and discussion

Teenage Internet rape is a negative outgrowth of the Internet revolution. Yet, there is very little research regarding the effects of teenage development in this phenomenon. This research is used to examine the role that teenage development plays in Internet teenage rape cases. Research findings may be important for school leaders and law enforcement leaders for developing curriculum that will assist in the prevention of teenage Internet rape.

Table 27.2 Themes emerging from the interviews

Interview Questions	Themes
Circumstances that might lead to encounters with predators	1. Lack of parental support
	2. Anonymity
	3. Loneliness
	4. Additional circumstances
How teens meet predators	5. Social networking websites and chat rooms
Role teenage personality	6. Introverts and extroverts
	7. Teenage rebellion
Role teenage needs/gratification	8. Need for a relationship
	9. Instant gratification
	10. Low self-esteem
Support for the teen	11. Improved parental support
	12. Improved education
	13. Improved law enforcement

The research included interviews with 25 Tucson area teachers/counselors who have worked with teens that experienced a sexual relationship with someone who they met on the Internet. The interviews consisted of open-ended questions involving potential causes of the phenomenon, most likely victims and potential ways to reduce the problem of teenage Internet rape. A later topic in this chapter will review recent literature covering teen Internet sexual assault. The review will further cover literature on (a) the role of teen behavior, (b) role of the ages of the teen and the predator, (c) social networking sites, and (d) the teen Internet sex phenomenon knowledge gap. The following themes emerged from the analysis, as outlined in table 27.2; note that the details of the thematic analysis were not included in this chapter due to copyright and sensitivity issues.

Conclusion

In this chapter I demonstrated how to articulate a scholarly constructivist research ideology using the Van Kaam technique with the emancipatory-phenomenology method. This method is also known as social advocacy when combined with phenomenology. I also discussed how the Van Kaam technique should be applied. In keeping with the constructivist ideology, I wrote this chapter as a scholarly paper, except that I left out certain graphic (inappropriate) sections (notably the "lived experiences" reported by children and teachers during the interviews). The reason I used the Van Kaam technique was to capture the essence of the participants' experience. A notable implication of using the Van Kaam technique is that the participants help the researcher to understand the meaning of the transcripts; therefore, during data analysis, software was not be used.

References

Anonymous. (2005). Internet predator jailed for grooming 2 victims: 10 years for chat-room fiend. *Evening Times* (Glasgow).

Bagwell, K. (2009). Study finds increase in arrests of online child predators. *Education Daily, 42*(97), 3.

Benner, P. (1994). *Interpretive phenomenology: Embodiment caring, and ethics in health and illness*. Thousand Oaks, CA: Sage Publications Inc.

Bower, B. (2008). Internet seduction, *Science News,* Washington: *173*(8), 1.

Burns, N., & Grove, S. (2001). *The practice of nursing research: Conduct, critique and utilization* (4th ed.). Philadelphia, PA: W. B. Saunders.

Critchlow, K. A. (2005). *A phenomenological study of the career accession of African American females into community college presidencies*. Dissertation, UMI#3202464. Retrieved from ebscohost.

Desjarlais, M., & Willoughby, T. (2010). A longitudinal study of the relation between adolescent boys and girls' computer use with friends and friendship quality: Support for the social compensation or the rich-get-richer hypothesis? *Computers in Human Behavior, 26*(5), 896–905, ISSN 0747-5632, 10.1016/j.chb.2010.02.004.

Dylan, W., & Fuller, B. (2010, August). Facebook "failed to act" on child pornography group. *Illawarra Mercury*, p. 3.

Gilgun, J. F. (2005). Qualitative research and family psychology. *Journal of Family Psychology, 19*(1), 40–50, Retrieved from EBSCOhost.

Greenfield, P., & Zheng, Y. (2006). Children, adolescents, and the Internet: A new field of inquiry in developmental psychology. *Developmental Psychology, 42*(3), 391–394. doi:10.1037/0012-1649.42.3.391.

Johnson, W., McGue, M., & Iacono, W. G. (2009). School performance and genetic and environmental variance in antisocial behavior at the transition from adolescence to adulthood. *Developmental Psychology, 45*(4), 973–987. doi:10.1037/a0016225.

Lee, S. (2009). Online communication and adolescent social ties: Who benefits more from Internet use? *Journal of Computer-Mediated Communication, 14*(3), 509–531. doi:10.1111/j.1083-6101.2009.01451.x.

McCarthy, J. A. (2010). Internet sexual activity: A comparison between contact and non-contact child pornography offenders. *Journal of Sexual Aggression, 16*(2), 181–195. doi:10.1080/13552601003760006.

Mishna, F., McLuckie, A., & Saini, M. (2009). Real-world dangers in an online reality: A qualitative study examining online relationships and cyber abuse. *Social Work Research, 33*(2), 107–118. Retrieved from Academic Search Complete database.

Moustakas, C. (1994). *Phenomenological research methods.* Thousand Oaks, CA: Sage Publications, Inc. doi: http://dx.doi.org.ezproxy.apollolibrary.com/10.4135/9781412995658.

News 4 Tucson, KVOA. (2012). *Tucson teen says Mass. man enticed sex acts over webcam.* Retrieved from http://www.kvoa.com.

Nissley, E. (2008, March). Study shows Internet child predators not necessarily posing as teenagers. *Citizens' Voice.* Wilkes-Barre, Pa. p. T.26.

Patterson, T. (2007). Child sex tourism. *FBI Law Enforcement Bulletin, 76*(1), 16–21. Retrieved from http://search.proquest.com/docview/204187369?accountid=27965.

Peter, J,. Valkenburg, P., Schouten, A., & Alexander P. (2005). Developing a model of adolescent friendship formation on the Internet. *CyberPsychology & Behavior, 8*(5), 423–430. doi:10.1089/cpb.2005.8.423.

Shao, G. (2009). Understanding the appeal of user-generated media: A uses and gratification perspective. *Internet Research, 19*(1), 7–25. doi:10.1108/10662240910927795.

Shannon, D. (2008). Online sexual grooming in Sweden: Online and offline sex offenses against children as described in Swedish police data. *Journal of Scandinavian Studies in Criminology & Crime Prevention, 9*(2), 160–180. doi:10.1080/14043850802450120.

Taylor, R., Caeti, T., Loper, D., Fritsch, E., & Liederbach, J. (2006). *Digital crime and digital terrorism.* Upper Saddle River, NJ: Pearson Education, Inc.

van den Eijnden, R., Spijkerman, R., Vermulst, A., van Rooij, T., & Engels, R. (2010). Compulsive internet use among adolescents: Bidirectional parent-child relationships. *Journal of Abnormal Child Psychology, 38*(1), 77–89.

van Manen, M. (2010). The pedagogy of Momus technologies: Facebook, privacy, and online intimacy. *Qualitative Health Research, 20*(8), 1023–1032. ISSN 1049–7323, 08/2010.

Wolak, J., David, F., Mitchell, K., & Ybarra, M. (2008). Online "predators" and their victims: Myths, realities, and implications for prevention treatment. *American Psychologist, 63*(2), 111–128. doi:10.1037/0003–066X.63.2.111.

Part V

Final Generalizations and Descriptive Characteristics

28
Gaps to Address in Future Research Design Practices

Kenneth D. Strang, Linda Brennan, Narasimha Rao Vajjhala, and Judith Hahn

Controversies in contemporary research design practices

In keeping with the unique visual exciting style of the handbook, we wanted to finish with a thinking-outside-the-box implication for future research design practices to question the status quo rather than summarize what is already articulated in the preface and introductory chapters. Four contributing authors volunteered to collaborate on this final concluding chapter. Each author brings a distinct sociocultural and ideological perspective to the table based on his or her contribution being in different sections of this book and his or her research experience being grounded in diverse epistemological disciplinary roots. In other words, each of us works in a different discipline, and we have different dominant research ideologies and ontological approaches to research.

Ideology in the research design typology is relative to the conscious perspective of the researchers. Based on this, we propose a Socratic question: Would a researcher applying the phenomenology method hold a positivist ideology or might a statistician conducting distributional analysis hold a constructivist ideology? Some writers have suggested that variations of ideology are not necessarily welded to the method. This is the premise of this handbook. First, we will briefly look at the theoretical and philosophical practice gaps. Then we will go through a short empirical example to illustrate why more guidelines are needed for research design in business and management.

Relativity of research ideology

An old saying is "beauty is in the eye of the beholder," which means that people see and understand the same thing differently. As discussed in the first section of this handbook, researchers' ideologies are composed on their disciplinary epistemology (knowledge terminology of their industry) along with their axiology (socio-ultural value system) and their ontology perspective (what they consider is real or imaginary, conscious vs. subconscious, observable or invisible, known or unknowable).

Pernecky and Jamal (2010) made an interesting and unusual statement in the research methods literature while working on an empirical tourism study, which is worth quoting verbatim for authenticity. "Husserl's phenomenology corresponds to a positivistic approach, Merleau-Ponty to post-positivist, Heidegger, and Gadamer to interpretivist orientations" (p. 1066).

What they mean by this is that the thought leaders whose ideologies underlie today's phenomenology method variations (Husserl, Heidegger, van Kaam, Colaizzi, Giorgi, and others) span the research ideology in our typology from positivist to social constructivist. This is an interesting proposition that we did not explore in our handbook but one that may be relevant to investigate to inform future research design practices in business and management.

In their paper, Pernecky and Jamal (2010) discussed how thought leader phenomenologists such as van Kaam (1966) and Giorgi (2000) have adopted a positivist ideology in developing and applying descriptive phenomenology methods. Recall that McCarthy provided a variation of this with the eidetic phenomenology (researcher interprets the data meaning), which we placed as an interpretative rather than positivist ideology but at the far left in the constructivist continuum, as compared to hermeneutic phenomenology where only the participants provide the meaning of the data. The reason for this placement on the research design continuum ideology was due to her axiology, ontology, and epistemology—she clearly held an interpretative ideology rather than a fixed positivist, post-positivist, or pragmativist one.

Going back to the Pernecky and Jamal (2010) paper, they contrasted the positivists with contemporary phenomenologists such as Heidegger and Gadamer who take an interpretivist or constructivist ideology, to develop and apply hermeneutic phenomenology method variations. The key differentiator for hermeneutic and other constructivist ideology orientations is that the meaning of the data is provided, influenced, or articulated by the participants. The more the researcher is involved as a participant, the more accurate and authentic the data meaning becomes because the participants achieve a shared understanding—at least theoretically. Practically, this must be difficult for studies where the researcher has a diverse grounding in one or more of the ideological components (axiology, epistemology, or ontology). Reconciling concurrent but obverse philosophical stances can be problematic for the researcher. Seeking to contribute to the body of knowledge requires an acceptance that tacit knowledge can be articulated to the extent that it is explicit and therefore independent from the participant.

Furthermore, underpinning this is an assumption that tacit meaning can actually be explicitly conveyed (Borsboom, 2005). This raises an issue to address in future research design practices: examining applied practices of studies where the researcher is grounded in different sociocultural axiologies, disciplinary epistemologies, and/or knowledge ontology experiences. Thus, more research design applications need to be illustrated with combinations of one or more researchers having ideological differences from one another as compared to the sampled participants. In stating this, we assume the participant is human, so this may exclude general analytical methods but leave room for applying inferential statistical methods (e.g., surveys) and qualitative approaches (e.g., grounded theory, ethnography, phenomenology, action research, and so on).

The methods predominately employed by researchers holding interpretative and constructivist ideologies are considered newer than those practiced by positivists and post-positivists. Phenomenology (as an example of a method commonly used with a constructivist ideology) was developed in the middle of the nineteenth century but inferential statistics predates that by centuries. The first description of a normal distribution was by De Moivre in 1733. The theory of normal distribution is based on probability. The basic concept of statistics is that human and nonhuman behavior is in some way predictable, so by collecting sample data (instead of a census), the future can be predicted with a level of confidence. Prediction could refer to being able to state that things (people, events, observations, or other data types) are either similar or different. The *central limit theorem* (*CLT*) is based on normal distribution and posits that we can (by sampling) predict how likely a sample average would represent the population mean. According to *CLT*, in 95 out of 100 samples from a population, 68% of the sample distribution means should lie within ±3 standard deviations of the population mean. This is called making an inference—a prediction that another sample would have a similar mean as compared to the population mean, based on parameters such as the size and homogeneity of the data.

Parametric statistical techniques were developed to allow researchers to test hypotheses based on the normal distribution and the *CLT*. Nonparametric statistical techniques were developed based on similar inferential probability concepts but using different distributions (namely the *chi square*, *uniform*, *binomial*, or *Poisson*) or in some cases no distribution (e.g., by using sorting and rank comparison tests). Most of the techniques employed by researchers holding positivistic ideologies involve inferential statistics. Often the belief is that variables are related in a linear manner to one another (e.g., a straight line can be fitted to represent the data or residual pattern), which can be tested using correlation and regression techniques. Our purpose here is not to write a statistics chapter but merely to reintroduce the basics before discussing an applied example.

Applied example of a research design ideological dilemma

In this example, the research team is exploring data collected from a recent sample in New York, United States. We will keep the exact nature of the data secret until the end so we ask the reader to follow along to obtain maximum understanding of the ideological dilemma's that can unfold even for experienced scholar-practitioners. The research team first takes on a post-positivist ideology, looking for facts. Note that this does not mean quantitative because qualitative data may be just as factual (e.g., a picture or a recording are very factual). Our research question dealt with a recognizable predictive pattern that exists in the data archives at this particular case study institution in New York. We are using the company business unit level of analysis. The unit of analysis is the predictive trend relationship between samples taken at different points in time (i.e., sample 1 through 12) for the business unit. The independent factor is be the sample point in time or sample period while the dependent variable is the value of the data point (intensity or economic value). The hypothesis statement is:

- H0: there is no linear relationship (trend) between the data points and the sample period.
- H1: there is a linear relationship (trend) between the data points and the sample period.

Figure 28.1 and table 28.1 represent two views of the same sample data. The drawing depicts a qualitative perspective of the data, except that more data

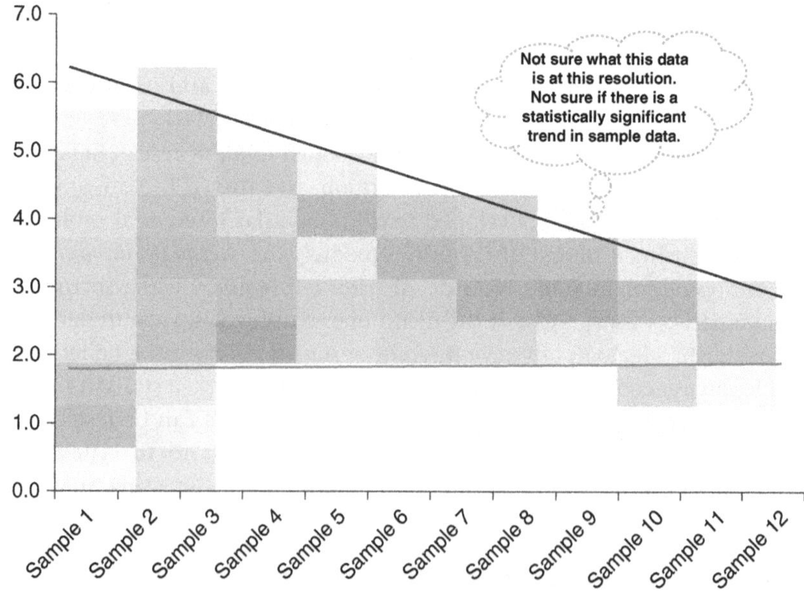

Figure 28.1 Qualitative sample data at 5% resolution with quantitative analysis framework.

Table 28.1 Quantitative sample data at 68% resolution using averages

Sample#	Label	High	Low	Mean
1	Sample 1	6.0	0.5	3.3
2	Sample 2	6.5	0.1	3.3
3	Sample 3	6.6	2.0	4.3
4	Sample 4	5.0	2.0	3.5
5	Sample 5	4.9	2.0	3.5
6	Sample 6	4.8	2.0	3.4
7	Sample 7	4.7	2.0	3.4
8	Sample 8	4.5	2.2	3.4
9	Sample 9	4.2	2.2	3.2
10	Sample 10	3.9	2.3	3.1
11	Sample 11	3.5	2.3	2.9
12	Sample12	3.0	1.7	2.4

points are being shown as compared to the table. The drawing was reduced to 5% resolution from the source to illustrate the concept of positivistic researchers sampling only 5% of the population. The obvious limitation with figure 28.1 is that the sample size is too small to obtain any useful information from the data.

Being positivistic, we attempted to suggest there might be a pattern in the data, by superimposing a quantitative framework using a scale from 0 to 7 on the y-axis with the sample numbers being on the x-axis. However, we were not sure at this resolution what the data represented and we could not identify any statistically significant trend in the sample data.

Table 28.1 presents a quantitative list of the average sampled values from an object at a 5% resolution, which encompassed only the high and low data points that the research team investigated. There were 12 samples, so the numbers represent averages. One series of data refers to a "high" value group while the other a low value, with the third being a trend between the two (the average, or statistical mean). These data points may be considered measures of intensity or economic values, on the y-axis, with sample number on the x-axis. Note that table 28.1 represents the same sample size as figure 28.1, so beware of drawing premature conclusions. Nonetheless, we will try to do that anyway.

We took on a pragmatic ideology by combining perspectives. One researcher wanted to sample more of the qualitative data to understand the meaning. We sampled 68% of the data, which is shown as a background image at 68% resolution in figure 28.2, but we retained the quantitative data points (averages of high and low with overall means across the 12 samples). On the other hand, other team members held a positivistic ideology—they were certain this was

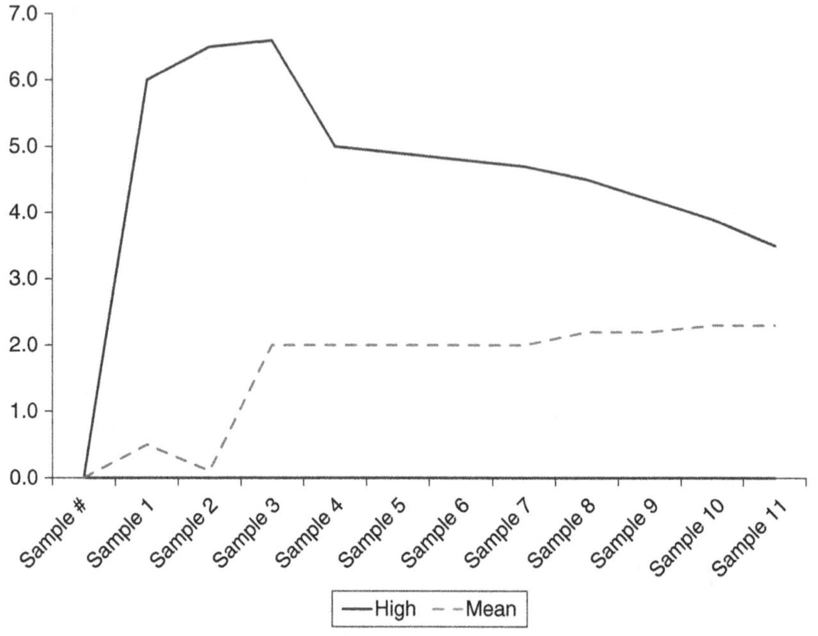

Figure 28.2 Data at 68% resolution with quantitative analysis framework.

data about the company stock prices from the New York Stock Exchange. If this were true, and if we could predict a pattern in the stock price data over time, we could make a lot of money.

We performed preliminary analysis to screen and clean data prior and then verify that it conformed to the normal distribution. In this process, we identified some data points in figure 28.2 that appeared to be outliers, so we chose to ignore them when applying inferential statistical techniques. Recall that when applying inferential statistics, a positivistic researcher will choose a level of confidence and if the hypothesis test is supported, they will be 99.99% certain (0.001 significance), 95% certain (0.05 significance), or 90% certain (0.10 significance) in making predictions or implications. We chose the 95% confidence level here. Note that this is a two-tailed test, so results will be +/– 2.5% at each end of the normal distribution curve.

We would like to identify a pattern in these data and make predictions for the future, using inferential statistics, namely *t*-tests, ANOVA, and regression. Although figure 28.1 (5% of the population) was too vague to identify, we have chosen to be positivistic and rely on the quantitative sample data in table 28.1, which are the averages of the high, low, and average values. Figure 28.2 is a line chart we have drawn to represent the trend pattern of the data. We feel that there is a significant pattern here, so we will apply a *t*-test to determine

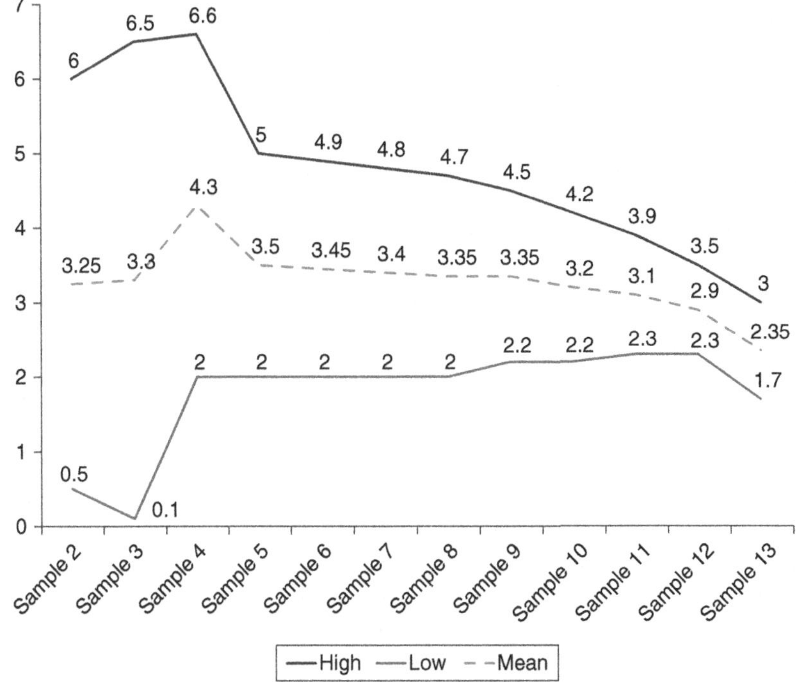

Figure 28.3 Data sample in quantitative line series chart.

if the high and low values are related. If they are related significantly (at the 95% level of confidence) then we will apply simple regression to measure the strength of the predictive relationship between sample time and the value on the y-axis.

We performed the *t*-test on the data, comparing the high and low data values. Indeed, the results indicated that the high and low mean values varied similarly across the 12 samples. The *t*-test (19) = 7.886054598, *p*-value = 2.07258E-07 (two-tailed). Thus, the *t*-test "proved" that the high and low values were similar, to a statistically significant level. Next, we performed two ANOVAs to test if the mean variances were similar across the two sampling groups of high versus low. We then produced a better quality line series chart as depicted in figure 28.3, with the data value points printed above the trend lines, but without the qualitative background image. The positivist researchers felt this was ideal and, obviously, they had solved this complex problem. Now all that remains is to test the hypothesis and then determine what implications would flow from those results.

The estimates for the high value test are listed at the top of table 28.2 showing the ANOVA results. Table 28.2 indicates that the correlation between

Table 28.2 Inferential statistical estimates (ANOVA and Regression) on high value trend

Regression statistics: High values					
Multiple *R*	0.94702197				
R Square	0.89685062				
Adjusted *R* Square	0.88653568				
Standard error	0.37756118				
Observations	12				
ANOVA	*Df*	*SS*	*MS*	*F-test*	*p-value*
Regression	1	12.39448	12.39448	86.94677459	3.01E-06
Residual	10	1.425524	0.142552		
Total	11	13.82			
	Coefficients	*Standard Error*	*t-test*	*p-value*	*Lower 95%*
Intercept	6.71363636	0.232373	28.89166	5.75003E-11	6.195877
Sample#	−0.29440559	0.031573	−9.32453	3.00602E-06	−0.36476

sample# and high value was 94% (*Pearson Product Moment R* = 0.947, *p-value* < *0.001*). The coefficient of partial determination was moderate, at $r^2 = 0.897$ meaning that 90% of the variation in the high values were explained from period to period in the sample data. We completed the analysis with an *F-test* (1, 10) = 86.94677459, *p-value* < 0.001 that indicated there was a statistically significant linear relationship between sample# period and the high value. We then performed a *t*-test on the linear equation to estimate the predictor. The *alpha* coefficient (intercept) for the linear equation was +6.71363636, *t-test* (11) =28.89166, *p-value*=5.75003E-11, which was significant. The *beta* coefficient for Sample# was −0.29440559, *t-test* (11) = −9.32453, *p-value* = 3.00602E-06, which was also statistically significant. This was great news for the positivist ideology.

Next, we performed the same set of procedures on the low values to determine if we could also predict the value from the period if we knew the low value. The summarizing of the inferential statistical estimates in table 28.3 proved all were significant.

According to table 28.3, the correlation between sample# and low value was 65% (*Pearson Product Moment R* = 0.648, *p-value* < 0.05). The coefficient of partial determination was moderate, at $r^2 = 0.42$ meaning that 42% of the variation in the low values were explained from period to period in the sample data. We completed the analysis with an *F-test* (1, 10) = 7.250153412, *p-value*=0.022598 that indicated there was a statistically significant linear relationship between sample# period and the low value. We then performed a *t*-test on the linear equation to estimate the predictor. The *alpha* coefficient (intercept) for the

Table 28.3 Inferential statistical estimates (ANOVA and Regression) on low value trend

Regression statistic: Low values					
Multiple *R*	0.64830164				
R Square	0.42029501				
Adjusted *R* Square	0.36232451				
Standard error	0.56989448				
Observations	12				
ANOVA	*df*	*SS*	*MS*	*F-test*	*p-value*
Regression	1	2.354703	2.354703	7.250153412	0.022598
Residual	10	3.247797	0.32478		
Total	11	5.6025			
	Coefficients	*Standard error*	*t-test*	*p-value*	
Intercept	0.94090909	0.350746	2.682595	0.022990068	
Sample#	0.12832168	0.047657	2.692611	0.022598191	

linear equation was +0.94090909, *t-test* (11) = 2.682595, *p-value* = 0.022990068, which was significant. The *beta* coefficient for Sample# was +0.12832168, *t-test* (11) = 2.692611, *p-value* = 0.022598191, which was also statistically significant. This was more good news for the researchers holding the positivist ideology.

Based on the above results, we accepted our hypothesis that there was a predictive linear relationship between the value in the sample data and the sampled period. The result of the above ANOVA, *F*-tests, and *t*-tests allowed us to create two predictive linear equations that could predict the value for any given period. The two equations were:

- Predicted high value = 6.713636364 + (–0.294405594 * NewPeriod);
- Predicted low value = 0.940909091 + (0.128321678 * NewPeriod).

The pragmatists and positivists among us were very excited now. Given that we had concluded the sample data we had found for the case study organization were stock prices for this company, we felt we could make some money on the stock market. For example, if we wanted to predict the high trading stock price for period 12 (even though it was already in the data), the formula would be 6.713636364 + (–0.294405594 * 12) = 3.180769236 or rounded to $3.18 (USD assumed). In similar fashion, we could predict the low stock price for period 12 using this equation: 0.940909091 + (0.128321678 * 12) = 2.480769227 rounded to $2.48 USD.

The positivists among us knew we could leverage this to make a lot of money on the stock market. Just to illustrate, if we could predict the high, average, and low stock prices for a given period, we could issue a buy or sell option and then benefit from this, for example, if we decided to risk 1,000,000 worth of shares, which at the average trading price for period 10 would be $2.996853147 * 1,000,000 = $2,996,853.18 (a lot of money at stake). We will pretend for illustrative purposes we were in period 10 and did not know any data for period 11. The actual sample data for period 10 was (remember we want to predict period 11, as we do not know it):

- Actual sample data for high value period *n*–1 (10) = 3.9;
- Actual sample data for low value period *n*–1 (10) = 2.3;
- Shares to be traded or optioned = 1,000,000.

One of the positivists had some stock market experience. That researcher suggested creating a leveraged option listed at the 95% likely low value for the next period (11) and then exercising the option (selling it) at the assumed 95% likely high value for that next period (11). The 95% confidence interval requires knowing the standardized *CLT z*-score value of 1.96, which is used to create the intervals. The 95% confidence intervals for the entire sample data were as follows:

- High value confidence intervals (2.23, 4.72);
- Average values of both high and low n–1 (10) = (2.42, 3.41);
- Low value confidence intervals (1.56, 3.14).

Thus, to take a pessimistic estimate of the lower 95% confidence interval for the average of high and low values, the 2.42 could be used, while 3.41 may be used for the high value estimate. Let us assume we designed the stock option where we would effectively buy the stock when it reaches $2.42 and hold it, then exercise the option to sell when it reaches $3.41 (again these are estimates based on *CLT* and inferential statistical probabilities). The actual period 11 data are:

- Actual sample data for high value period *n* (11) = 3.5;
- Actual sample data for low value period *n* (11) = 2.3.

Thus, our stock options strategy would have worked in this sample data. The actual low of $2.3 was below our predicted mean of $2.42 (therefore investors would have been interested), and the actual high of $3.5 was above the predicted average of $3.41 so we would have been able to exercise the option at our advantage, as long as we patiently watched the ticker. *If we had exercised this option as designed, the profit would have been $990,000.00 which was calculated as ((3.41–2.42)*1,000,000).*

Wow. This was quick a potential profit. The pragmatists and positivists among us were very proud. Unfortunately, we were myopic. No surprise, according to our researchers with the interpretivistic and constructivist ideology, we had missed the picture, pun intended.

The researchers on the team with an interpretivist ideology took another look at the original sample data at the 68% resolution, and then darkened in the data points to ignore the details, in order to see the big picture. Then an idea struck one researcher, looking at this modified interpretation. Using sense making (since the case study company was not available for interviewing or surveying), they thought that the data was an image not a data set from the New York Stock Exchange. They cross checked this insight using the principles of triangulation and found that this was indeed an image of a hat. Furthermore, if the image were rotated 90% counter clockwise (following the format of the Saratoga Race Track Philosophy) it looked like either a bird or a hat. Both interpretations are illustrated in figure 28.4 (darkened on left and rotated on right).

This new perspective of a bird or hat seemed interesting even to the researchers holding a positivist or pragmativist ideology. Of course, the researcher with the interpretivistic ideology was convinced that this was some sort of organization cultural symbol—an artifact—for their annual festival. However, there was another researcher with a constructivist ideology, proposing that they look more deeply into the sample data and triangulate with other samples. Eventually the constructivist-oriented researcher was able to find more data in the sample along with some textual documentation. This researcher conducted some preliminary textual analysis and came up with the following

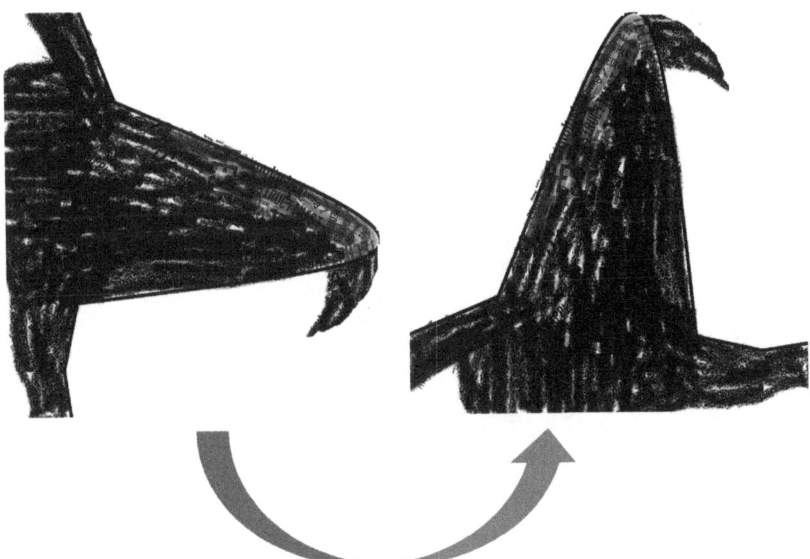

Figure 28.4 Qualitative data sample using interpretative sense making.

thematic diagram, which apparently supported the hat idea but refuted all other hypotheses.

All researchers in the team, even those with different ideologies, brainstormed and reflected on what this could mean. As a team, they finally uncovered the true meaning of this interesting data that had emerged from a vague blob in figure 28.1 into the theoretical model of figure 28.5. It was a thematic cloud of keywords from research design epistemology. The size of the word in the figure 28.5 that indicated the frequency of the term used in the abstracts for this handbook. A threshold was established so that infrequently used keywords did not appear in this diagram. The implications were that the larger the word, the more important it was in the handbook.

However, this was not the end of the analysis. An interview with the case study company informant (the handbook editor) revealed that their constructed interpretations were correct and almost complete. The final missing piece was why and in particular why this shape? The answer for the hat thematic design shape came from interviewing doctoral students when writing

Figure 28.5 Keyword cloud.

the handbook introductory chapters. Apparently, the editor wanted to use a crown as a cross-cultural symbol of high knowledge but it was too small to hold all the keywords. The dissertation style cap was also too small to hold the words. The editor then looked at other symbols, particularly a magician hat as a symbol of special powers (supposedly from reading the handbook). The editor nostalgically reminisced about positive memories from wearing a straw hat in Australia and decided to try this as a catchy shape to use for the thematic word cloud diagram. Apparently, it was just the right size to hold all the keywords although there was one small gap in the lower left corner of the brim. We hope you enjoyed our humorous anecdote to illustrate the pitfalls of tunnel-vision in the research ideology. Just to make sure there was no misunderstanding—this was a fictitious research project.

Finally, the researchers (coauthors of this chapter) reflected on their experience of collaborating. In this way, they would identify their strengths and areas for improvement, as experiences learned. Each author brings unique experiences and insights to the conduct of research from designing to communicating outcomes to others. The combination of diverse strengths provides opportunities for examining big issues in new and innovative ways. Diversity and interdisciplinary studies collaboration are difficult terrain for researchers seeking certainty. However, such differences lead to an appreciation of the big picture *and* identification of the salient details that will allow for prediction, should that be the goal.

Improving research designs

Given these paradoxical oversights that researchers may make, due to groupthink or simply from being encompassed within an extreme ideology, we recommend to select for diversity in the composition of the research team. Furthermore, as seen with the example, more than one method should be used on any type of data (qualitative, quantitative, or mixed) before rushing to any premature conclusions. This is intended to be over and above validity and reliability.

To accomplish this, in business and management, triangulation is an epistemological term that has various meanings. As discussed in chapter 5, triangulation requires at least three sources of confirmation. The point of triangulation is to "see" the research object from more than one perspective. This means checking facts from at least three different standpoints before assuming that they are "true." Triangulation can be done with method (e.g., survey, interviews, focus groups), data sources (e.g., newspapers, websites, and transcripts), participants (e.g., parole officers, prisoners, family members), or other forms of approach such as interview comments, personnel files, and observations of employee behaviors.

Triangulation can be used to validate findings or to test for the level of reliability. The idea is that a finding will remain relatively stable within the object "space" from each of the perspectives from which the object is viewed. For example, the interview data, the employee records, and the observations will describe substantively similar phenomena (validation). The research process can be repeated and the results will follow the same patterns in different groups or with the same group over time (reliability).

Triangulation of research is important regardless of ideological stance. Grounded theorists seek to ensure that their descriptions are accurate even if they are difficult to repeat. For example, in disaster research, you cannot repeat the event, although you can ensure that there are multiple perspectives brought to bear on the problems that flow from a natural disaster such as an earthquake. Positivists often attempt to ensure that their results are reliable through repetition of previously validated scales and survey data. Both of these perspectives work toward ensuring the veracity of the findings for the use of others in their research. While this seems to complicate research design by insisting that there are multiple sources of "everything" from data to participants, it ensures that when the outcome of research is communicated to others it is useful and fit for purpose.

Improving the future research design handbook

A significant limitation in the handbook was that we simply did not have enough researchers to address all possible combinations of ideologies, strategies, and methods-techniques. In the positivistic section, we did not address ANOVA or other types of regression. We had one chapter focused on logistic regression, but there are many variations of correlational designs that use other regression methods, such as multiple, multivariate, etc. We did not address other variations of factor analysis, in the Structural Equation Modeling chapter, such as principal component analysis. Multiple Correspondence Analysis was examined but the simple and more popular variation was not addressed. Only a small example of operations research techniques was examined, namely queuing/waiting line theory and simulation, leaving over 200 variations untouched. We should have more applied examples using widely available spreadsheet software such as in this last chapter and in Kadry's simulation chapter. Several esoteric techniques that are popular in positivistic ideologies were also overlooked, such as Analytical Hierarchy Procedure and its variations for making decisions.

Constructivist grounded theory was applied in the context of a case study on cultural-driven knowledge sharing. In that example the NVivo 10 software was used in one example, along with how to code the collected data, work with nodes, summarize codes, identify main themes as well as subthemes, querying data, creating reports, and developing visual models. The main source of data used in the culture case study was transcripts stored in a Word document. NVivo allows importing data from several sources, including PDFs, spreadsheets, and audio as well as video files. Future editions of this handbook ought to examine importing and exporting other data types (besides Word). Furthermore, future editions of the handbook should explore multiple case studies that would facilitate demonstration of the key capabilities of NVivo so that readers would have an applied view of the key topics associated with constructivist grounded theory. Finally, future editions of the handbook should cover examples and cases from different functional areas and across more industries so that students and scholar-practitioners can understand the applicability of constructivist grounded theory in different situations. Also, different software besides NVIVO should be examined using applied examples.

The constructivist/interpretative section of this handbook covers several important topics, including grounded theory, phenomenology, ethnography, hermeneutics, and action research. Future editions of the handbook will include some of the other topics related to the constructivist paradigm, including sections on applied naturalistic studies as well as topics, such as, symbolic interaction, and participatory action research. Some of the topics included in the constructivist/interpretative section of the handbook, such as grounded theory, could also be categorized as post-positivist approaches. Future editions of the book will explore different research designs from different research paradigm perspectives. Most of the chapters in this section use qualitative data analysis methods; future editions of this book would explore the use of mixed data analysis methods. Future editions should also consider the use of cloud computing to foster collaboration with other researchers across the globe as well as for data collection (if applicable to the study).

One thing we realized when writing this handbook is that we were too close to the work to realize what was missing. For this reason we intend to ask readers for their opinions about what needs to be improved upon. We would like to have feedback from students and scholar-practitioners who purchased the book. This will be done by asking readers to complete the online survey (anonymous of course).

We invite you the reader to complete this brief online survey to allow us to improve future handbooks based on your constructive feedback (the survey is very brief – it will take only a few minutes). Please use this URL address http://unitydiversity.multinations.org/handbooksurvey.php. If you optionally provide your name and email address we will thank you in future editions and we may invite you to participate in upcoming projects.

We are also asking our publisher to provide a limited amount of discounted handbooks to dissertation chairs at selected public universities that have a doctoral program, so that we can ensure that the knowledge is shared with those most in need (the doctoral students). If you are a dissertation supervisor or university faculty coordinating a dissertation program, please provide your request via the above survey (there will be a comment file at the end for this) and feel free to contact the corresponding chapter author at kenneth.strang@gmail.com

Handbooks such as this can also assist those in developing countries design and develop rigorous research; however, they are often unobtainable simply due to prevailing publishing pricing structures. We are asking people to consider buying books for their colleagues in developing countries to use: meeting the publishers halfway on helping those in need of knowledge such as that provided in this handbook.

References

Borsboom, D. (2005). *Measuring the mind: Conceptual issues in contemporary psychometrics.* New York: Cambridge University Press.

Giorgi, A. (2000). Concerning the application of phenomenology to caring research. *Scandinavian Journal of Caring Science, 14*(1), 11–15.

Pernecky, T., & Jamal, T. (2010). Hermeneutic phenomenology in tourism studies. *Annals of Tourism Research, 37*(4), 1055–1075.

van Kaam, A. (1966). Application of the phenomenological method. In A. van Kaam (Ed.). *Existential foundations of psychology.* Lanham, MD: University Press of America.

Index

Printed in the United States
By Bookmasters